Equality and Discrimination:
The New Law

Equality and Discrimination: The New Law

Dr Brian Doyle
Regional Employment Judge

Catherine Casserley
Barrister, Cloisters

Simon Cheetham
Barrister, Ely Place Chambers

Vivienne Gay
Regional Employment Judge

Oliver Hyams
Barrister, Devereux Chambers

JORDANS

Published by
Jordan Publishing Limited
21 St Thomas Street
Bristol BS1 6JS

British Library Cataloguing-in-Publication Data

A catalogue record for this book is available from the British Library.

ISBN 978 1 84661 201 5

Loughborough
COLLEGE est 1909

Typeset by Letterpart Ltd, Reigate, Surrey

Printed in Great Britain by CPI Antony Rowe, Chippenham, Wiltshire

PREFACE

The Equality Act 2010 has two main purposes – to harmonise discrimination law and to strengthen the law to support progress on equality. It is the most significant development in equality and discrimination law in a generation. Domestic discrimination law was previously found in five separate Acts and four sets of principal regulations, reflecting six main EU Directives. The 2010 Act is part consolidation and part codification of the existing law, bringing all the relevant legislation into one source and reaffirming important case-law principles. At the same time the Act corrects inconsistencies between the different protected characteristics and addresses the boundaries between the different forms of prohibited conduct. Overall the Equality Act attempts to restate the law in simpler terms (although with varying degrees of success). The Act will also reform the law in a number of important areas.

At the institutional level it introduces a new public sector duty regarding socio-economic inequalities; extends the public sector equality duty to other protected characteristics; enlarges the permitted use of positive action to all the protected characteristics, and to recruitment and promotion; and broadens the power of employment tribunals to make recommendations affecting the workforce beyond the individual claimant.

Ministers are empowered to add caste to the definition of race, while the definitions of disability and gender reassignment are simplified, and a new definition of sex is introduced. New and uniform definitions of direct and indirect discrimination are worthy of remark. The Act also prohibits discrimination arising from disability; extends indirect discrimination to disability; formulates a consistent and less complex definition of the duty of reasonable adjustments; confirms the irrelevance of an alleged discriminator's characteristics; simplifies victimisation as a form of prohibited conduct; introduces the concept of combined discrimination based on dual characteristics; and limits enquiries about disability and health. A general thrust of the Act, with some exceptions, is to extend protection from discrimination, victimisation and harassment to all the protected characteristics and across a wider field of activity beyond employment.

Major changes are made in the field of equal pay law. The Act defines the relevant types of work to which an equality clause or equality rule apply; recognises an employer's long term objective of reducing pay inequality as being a legitimate part of the material factor defence; enables claims of direct sex discrimination or dual discrimination in relation to contractual pay in the absence of a comparator doing equal work; ensures that there can be greater transparency and dialogue within workplaces about pay; and empowers the minister to make regulations which require private and voluntary sector employers of 250+ employees to publish information about gender-based pay differences.

A flavour of the many other noteworthy changes to discrimination and equality law is reflected in the measures harmonising the provisions on services; dealing with reasonable adjustments to common parts of premises; allowing political parties to take proportionate action in selection arrangements to address under-representation in elected bodies; requiring political parties to publish anonymised information on the diversity of candidate selections; ensuring licensing authorities cannot refuse licences to wheelchair accessible vehicles on the grounds of controlling taxi numbers; excepting charities benefiting only people of the same age group or with the same disability; allowing exceptions from age discrimination in the provision of services and the exercise of public functions; reforming the law on family property and civil partnerships; ensuring the future harmonisation of the areas of the Act covered by EU law and those that are domestic in origin; and making new provisions affecting information society services.

It is expected that the Act will be brought into force in October 2010 (although the implementation of some provisions will be postponed). From that date the legacy legislation will cease to have effect, although it will continue to apply to causes of action arising before the Equality Act 2010 was implemented. Thus for some years yet the courts and tribunals will be working with both legal regimes. Therefore, the large body of pre-existing case-law will continue to exert its influence and to be developed.

This raises the interesting question of how relevant the legacy case-law will remain in interpreting the Equality Act 2010 itself. The authors of this book have drawn heavily upon that body of cases where relevant and appropriate. However, considerable care will need to be taken if using the pre-existing case-law as a guide to how the new Act might be interpreted judicially. Where the principles of the prior legislation have been imported into the 2010 legislation they are likely to have been redrafted in simpler language and set in a modified context. Thus it cannot safely be assumed that established interpretation or existing precedent will continue to apply. Reliance upon earlier judicial interpretation will become even less confident where provisions have been harmonised or reformed. We can thus expect courts, tribunals and judges to approach the Act without preconception and with a fresh start to the interpretative task, although in many places the Government believes that no change to existing law has been made or is intended.

This book seeks to provide the reader with a restatement and first analysis of the new law. Our intention is to provide a user-friendly and readable description of the law – so that the reader does not need to find his or her way around the statute – with the relevant parts pulled together in each part of the book. Each chapter examines a particular theme of the Act, placing it in the context of the legislation it replaces and drawing upon the various sources which informed the legislative process. Brian Doyle acted as general editor in the project and authored Chapters 1, 3 (with Oliver Hyams), 5–7, 11 and 14. Catherine Casserley was responsible for Chapter 4. Simon Cheetham wrote Chapters 2, 10 and 12. Vivienne Gay contributed Chapter 8. Oliver Hyams was the author of Chapters 3 (with Brian Doyle), 9 and 13. We have attempted to state the law as we understood it as the book went to press in May 2010.

BD

CC

SC

VG

OH

May 2010

CONTENTS

Chapter 4
Services and Functions

TABLE OF CASES

References are to paragraph numbers.

TABLE OF STATUTES

References are to paragraph numbers.

TABLE OF STATUTORY INSTRUMENTS

References are to paragraph numbers.

TABLE OF ABBREVIATIONS

ACAS	Advisory, Conciliation & Arbitration Service
BERR	Department for Business, Enterprise and Regulatory Reform
CA	Court of Appeal
CA 1989	Children Act 1989
Council Directive 75/117/EEC	On the approximation of the laws of the Member States relating to the application of the principle of equal pay for men and women
Council Directive 76/207/EEC	On the implementation of the principle of equal treatment for men and women as regards access to employment, vocational training and promotion, and working conditions, as amended by the European Parliament and Council Directive 2002/73/EC
Council Directive 2000/43/EC	Implementing the principle of equal treatment between persons irrespective of racial or ethnic origin
Council Directive 2000/78/EC	Establishing a general framework for equal treatment in employment and occupation
Council Directive 2004/113/EC	Implementing the principle of equal treatment between men and women in the access to and supply of goods and services
Council Directive 2006/54/EC	On the implementation of the principle of equal opportunities and equal treatment of men and women in matters of employment and occupation
Cm	Command Paper
DCSF	Department for Children, Schools and Families
DDA 1995	Disability Discrimination Act 1995
DfT	Department for Transport
DIUS	Department for Innovation, Universities & Schools
DLR	Discrimination Law Review
DPTAC	Disabled Persons Transport Advisory Committee
DRC	Disability Rights Commission
DWP	Department for Work & Pensions
EA 1996	Education Act 1996
EAT	Employment Appeal Tribunal
EC	European Communities (or European Community)
ECHR	European Convention on Human Rights
ECJ	European Court of Justice
EEA	European Economic Area
EEC	European Economic Community
EE(A)R 2006	Employment Equality (Age) Regulations 2006

EE(RoB)R 2003	Employment Equality (Religion or Belief) Regulations 2003
EE(SO)R	Employment Equality (Sexual Orientation) Regulations 2003
EFTA Court	European Free Trade Association Court
EHRC	Equality and Human Rights Commission
EIA	Equality Impact Assessment
EJ	Employment Judge
EN	Explanatory notes (to the Equality Bill)
EOC	Equal Opportunities Commission
EQA 2006	Equality Act 2006
EQA 2010	Equality Act 2010
EqPA 1970	Equal Pay Act 1970
EqA(SO)R 2007	Equality Act (Sexual Orientation) Regulations 2007
ERA 1996	Employment Rights Act 1996
ET	Employment Tribunal
EU	European Union
E&W	England & Wales
GB	Great Britain
GCSE	General Certificate of Secondary Education
GEO	Government Equalities Office
GP	General practitioner
HC	House of Commons
HC Deb	House of Commons Debates (Hansard)
HL	House of Lords
HL Deb	House of Lords Debates (Hansard)
HRA 1998	Human Rights Act 1998
IAA 1999	Immigration and Asylum Act 1999
LLP	limited liability partnership
NEP	National Equality Panel
NHS	National Health Service
NHSA 2006	National Health Service Act 2006
NI	Northern Ireland
NICA	Northern Ireland Court of Appeal
NIQB	Northern Ireland High Court Queen's Bench
ODI	Office for Disability Issues
PSV	public service vehicle
RIA	Regulatory Impact Assessment
RNIB	Royal National Institute for the Blind
RRA 1976	Race Relations Act 1976
SCDEA	Scottish Crime and Drugs Enforcement Agency
SDA 1975	Sex Discrimination Act 1975
SD(EC)A 2002	Sex Discrimination (Election Candidates) Act 2002
SOCA	Serious Organised Crime Agency
SPSA	Scottish Police Services Authority
SSFA 1998	School Standards and Framework Act 1998

TFEU	Treaty on the Functioning of the European Union
UK	United Kingdom
WI	Women's Institute

BIBLIOGRAPHY

Butcher, Louise. 2009a. *Transport: Access for Disabled People*. Standard Note SN/BT/601. London: House of Commons Library.

Butcher, Louise. 2009b. *Taxis and Private Hire Vehicles*. Standard Note SN/BT/2005. London: House of Commons Library.

Cabinet Office. 2009. *New Opportunities: Fair Opportunities for the Future*. Cm 7533. London: The Stationery Office.

Cheetham, Simon. 2006. *Age Discrimination: The New Law*. Bristol: Jordan Publishing Ltd.

Commission for Social Justice. 1994. *Social Justice: Strategies for National Renewal*. London: Vintage.

Department for Communities and Local Government. 2007. *A Framework for Fairness: Proposals for a Single Equality Bill for Great Britain*. London: The Department.

Department for Transport. 2009. *Consultation on Improvising Access to Taxis*. London: Department for Transport.

Doyle, Brian. 2008. *Disability Discrimination: Law and Practice*. 6th ed. Bristol: Jordan Publishing Ltd.

Duggan, Michael. 2009. *Equal Pay: Law and Practice*. Bristol: Jordan Publishing Ltd.

Equality and Human Rights Commission. 2010a. *Employment Statutory Code of Practice: Draft for Consultation*.

Equality and Human Rights Commission. 2010b. *Equal Pay Statutory Code of Practice: Draft for Consultation*.

Equality and Human Rights Commission. 2010c. *Services, Public Functions and Associations Statutory Code of Practice: Draft for Consultation*.

Government Equalities Office. 2008a. *Framework for a Fairer Future – the Equality Bill*. Cm 7431. London: The Stationery Office.

Government Equalities Office. 2008b. *The Equality Bill – Government Response to the Consultation*. Cm 7454. London: The Stationery Office.

Government Equalities Office. 2009a. *A Fairer Future: The Equality Bill and Other Action to Make Equality a Reality*. London: Government Equalities Office.

Government Equalities Office. 2009b. *The Equality Bill: Making It Work: Policy Proposals for Specific Duties: A Consultation*. London: Government Equalities Office.

Government Equalities Office. 2009c. *The Equality Bill: Making It Work: Ending Age Discrimination in Services and Public Functions: A Consultation*. London: Government Equalities Office.

Government Equalities Office. 2009d. *The Equality Bill: Assessing the Impact of a Multiple Discrimination Provision: A Consultation*. London: Government Equalities Office.

Government Equalities Office. 2009e. *Equality Bill: Memorandum for the Joint Committee on Human Rights*. London: Government Equalities Office.

Government Equalities Office. 2009f. *Myth-busting: the Equality Bill and Religion*. London: Government Equalities Office.

Government Equalities Office. 2010. *The Equality Bill: Duty to Reduce Socio-economic Inequalities: A Guide*. London: Government Equalities Office.

Government Equalities Office. 2010a. *Working Towards Equality: A Framework for Action*. London: Government Equalities Office.

Hepple, Bob, et al. 2000. *Equality: A New Framework: Report of the Independent Review of the Enforcement of UK Anti-Discrimination Legislation*. Oxford: Hart Publishing Ltd.

House of Commons Procedure Committee. 2009. *Interleaving of Bills and Explanatory Notes: First Report of Session 2008–2009*. HC Paper 377. London: The Stationary Office.

House of Commons Work and Pensions Committee. 2009a. *The Equality Bill: How Disability Equality Fits Within a Single Equality Act: Third Report from the Committee, 2008–09*. HC Paper 158. London: The Stationery Office.

House of Commons Work and Pensions Committee. 2009b. *The Equality Bill: How Disability Equality Fits Within a Single Equality Act: Government Response to the Third Report from the Committee, 2008–09: Third Special Report of Session 2008–09*. HC Paper 836. London: The Stationery Office.

House of Lords Delegated Powers and Regulatory Reform Committee. 2010. *Second Report of Session 2009–10*. HL Paper 24. London: The Stationery Office.

Joint Committee on Human Rights. 2009. *Legislative Scrutiny: Equality Bill. 26th Report of Session 200–809*. HL Paper 169 and HC Paper 736. London: Stationery Office.

Keter, Vincent. 2009a. *Equality Bill. Research Paper 09/42*. London: House of Commons Library.

Keter, Vincent. 2009b. *Equality Bill Committee Stage Report*. Research Paper 09/83. London: House of Commons Library.

Office for Disability Issues. 2008. *Consultation on Improving Protection from Disability Discrimination*. London: Office for Disability Issues.

Office for Disability Issues. 2009. *Consultation on Improving Protection from Disability Discrimination: Government Response*. London: Office for Disability Issues.

Oxera Consulting Ltd. 2009. *The Use of Aged-Based Practices in Financial Services*. Prepared for the Government Equalities Office. Oxford: Oxera Consulting Ltd.

National Equality Panel. 2010. *An Anatomy of Economic Inequality in the UK: Report of the National Equality Panel*. London: Government Equalities Office.

Rubenstein, Michael. 2007a. 'Discrimination Law Review: EOR Guide'. *Equal Opportunities Law Review* Issue 167.

Rubenstein, Michael. 2007b. 'Responses to the Discrimination Law Review'. *Equal Opportunities Law Review* Issue 171.

Rubenstein, Michael. 2008a. 'More detail on the Equality Bill'. *Equal Opportunities Law Review* Issue 179.

Rubenstein, Michael. 2008b. 'Equality Bill: Government response to the consultation'. *Equal Opportunities Law Review* Issue 180.

Rubenstein, Michael. 2010. 'Equality Bill: Commons Report Stage'. *Equal Opportunities Law Review* Issue 197.

Rubenstein, Michael. 2010a. 'Intolerance does not need to be tolerated'. *Equal Opportunities Law Review* Issue 199.

Rubenstein, 2010b. *Discrimination: A Guide to the Relevant Case Law*. 23rd edition. Michael Rubenstein Publishing.

Schneider-Ross. 2009. *Equality Duties: Assessing the Cost and Cost Effectiveness of the Specific Race, Disability and Gender Equality Duties*. Prepared for the Government Equalities Office. Andover: Schneider-Ross.

The Equalities Review. 2006. *The Equalities Review: Interim Report for Consultation*. London: Cabinet Office.

The Equalities Review. 2007a. *The Consultation Process*. London: Cabinet Office.

The Equalities Review. 2007b. *Fairness and Freedom: The Final Report of the Equalities Review*. London: Cabinet Office.

Webster, S. 2010. 'Misconceptions about the nature of religious belief'. *Equal Opportunities Law Review* Issue 199.

Women and Work Commission. 2006. *Shaping a Fairer Future*. London: Department of Trade and Industry.

Chapter 1

INTRODUCTION

INTRODUCTION

1.1 The development of anti-discrimination legislation in the United Kingdom has been incremental and piecemeal. Prior to the enactment of the Equality Act 2010, the different strands of discrimination law were to be found spread across numerous statutes and statutory instruments.[1] Separate and additional provisions are found in Northern Ireland, which is not subject to the Equality Act 2010.

1.2 Before the Equality Act 2010, the main sources of the relevant law in Great Britain were the:

- Equal Pay Act 1970

- Sex Discrimination Act 1975

- Race Relations Act 1976

- Sex Discrimination Act 1986

- Disability Discrimination Act 1995

- Employment Equality (Religion or Belief) Regulations 2003[2]

- Employment Equality (Sexual Orientation) Regulations 2003[3]

- Employment Equality (Age) Regulations 2006[4]

- Equality Act 2006

- Equality Act (Sexual Orientation) Regulations 2007[5]

---

[1]   A useful survey of the background to the introduction of an Equality Bill is to be found in Keter, 2009a and in the Explanatory Notes (EN) to the Equality Act 2010: EN paras 3–9.
[2]   SI 2003/1660.
[3]   SI 2003/1661.
[4]   SI 2006/1031.
[5]   SI 2007/1263.

- Sex Discrimination (Amendment of Legislation) Regulations 2008.[6]

There was also a raft of supporting secondary legislation. In turn, those sources incorporated important amendments made by other legislation, while important anti-discrimination provisions were to be founded in other statutory measures.[7] Of course, much of the UK's recent reforms of anti-discrimination law have been as a result of the need to implement European legal obligations.[8]

PROPOSED SINGLE EQUALITY ACT

Commission on Social Justice

1.3   The idea of a Single Equality Act was first mooted in the early 1990s. The Commission on Social Justice was set up by the Labour Party under the auspices of the Institute for Public Policy Research. It published its ground-breaking report *Social Justice: Strategies for National Renewal* in 1994.[9] The Commission anticipated the problems that would inevitably arise from a piecemeal approach to anti-discrimination and equality legislation. Such an approach was promoted by fragmented policy-making and incremental law-making via European directives. The Commission advocated an omnibus discrimination statute addressing unjustified discrimination across the board and in all fields of human activity.

The Independent Review

1.4   It would be another 6 years, however, before the concept of a Single Equality Act would be fleshed out and given its intellectual and empirical underpinning by Professor Bob Hepple and his colleagues as part of the Independent Review of the Enforcement of UK Anti-Discrimination Legislation. The Independent Review published its influential report in 2000.[10]

---

6   SI 2008/963.
7   See, for example: Local Government Act 1988; Employment Act 1989; Social Security Act 1989; Pensions Act 1995; Occupational Pension Schemes (Equal Treatment) Regulations 1995, SI 1995/3183; Greater London Authority Act 1999; Sex Discrimination (Election Candidates) Act 2002; Disability Discrimination Act 1995 (Pensions) Regulations 2003, SI 2003/2770; Occupational Pension Schemes (Equal Treatment) (Amendment) Regulations 2005, SI 2005/1923.
8   These include: Council Directive 75/117/EEC (on equal pay for men and women); Council Directive 76/207/EEC (on equal treatment for men and women in respect of employment, as amended by the European Parliament and Council Directive 2002/73/EC); Council Directive 2000/43/EC (on equal treatment between persons irrespective of racial or ethnic origin); Council Directive 2000/78/EC (establishing a general framework for equal treatment in employment and occupation); Council Directive 2004/113/EC (on equal treatment between men and women in the access to and supply of goods and services); and European Parliament and Council Directive 2006/54/EC (on equal opportunities and equal treatment of men and women in matters of employment and occupation). Also relevant in this context is Article 141 of the EC Treaty (on equal pay for men and women).
9   Commission on Social Justice, 1994.
10   Hepple et al, 2000.

The recommendation of a Single Equality Act was the centrepiece of the Independent Review's proposals for a root and branch reform of UK discrimination and equality law.[11]

1.5   The Hepple report did not lead to government-sponsored legislation designed to give effect to its agenda for change. Instead, a private members' Equality Bill was introduced in the House of Lords in 2003 by Lord Lester of Herne Hill QC. Its long title hints at the ambitious scope of the proposed measure:

> 'A Bill to make provision making it unlawful to discriminate on the grounds of age, gender reassignment, religion or belief or sexual orientation; to make new provision with respect to discrimination on the grounds of disability, race or sex; to make provision making it unlawful to harass or victimise another person on any of those grounds; to make provision facilitating progress towards the achievement of equality as between persons of certain descriptions; to establish and provide for the functions of the Equality Commission for Great Britain; and for connected purposes.'

Yet this was to be achieved in only 94 clauses and 3 Schedules. In the event, the Bill did not progress.

Equality Act 2006

1.6   One element of these early efforts at achieving a Single Equality Act did eventually emerge by separate effort. A Single Equality Commission was brought into existence in the shape of the Equality and Human Rights Commission through the Equality Act 2006. That Act also prohibited unlawful discrimination on the grounds of religion or belief in the provision of goods, facilities and services, education, the use and disposal of premises, and the exercise of public functions. Moreover, it enabled provision to be made for discrimination on the grounds of sexual orientation in the provision of goods, facilities and services, education, the use and disposal of premises and the exercise of public functions. Furthermore, the Equality Act 2006 created a duty on public authorities to promote equality of opportunity between women and men, and prohibited sex discrimination and harassment in the exercise of public functions. Nevertheless, it did not address the problems created by the volume of anti-discrimination legislation and its internal inconsistencies.

1.7   In 2000 the Independent Review had expressed its dissatisfaction with the then four separate anti-discrimination regimes in the UK covering sex, race, disability and (in Northern Ireland) fair employment. The law was seen as outdated, fragmented and inconsistent. The existing legislation was in need of being made user-friendly and accessible. At the same time pressure had built to extend the grounds of unlawful discrimination beyond sex, race and disability.

---

[11]   Keter, 2009a.

By the time of the Equality Act 2006 separate regulations had been introduced in order to give effect to European law in relation to age, sexual orientation and religion or belief.

The Equalities Review

1.8   In 2005 the Labour Party promised to introduce a Single Equality Act to modernise and simplify equality legislation.[12] On 25 February 2005 the Department for Trade and Industry and the Cabinet Office jointly announced a review of discrimination legislation. This took the form of an Equalities Review and a Discrimination Law Review. The Equalities Review was largely concerned with the social, economic and cultural causes and effects of discrimination. Yet its work was also to inform the modernisation of equality legislation (by working towards a Single Equality Act) and the development of the new Commission for Equality and Human Rights. The Equalities Review reported in 2006 and 2007.[13]

Discrimination Law Review

1.9   Working in parallel with the Equalities Review was the Discrimination Law Review. Its task was the development of a simpler and fairer legal framework and the assessment of how anti-discrimination legislation could be modernised. The dilemma for the Discrimination Law Review was to consider approaches that would be effective in eradicating discrimination, while avoiding the imposition of unnecessary, bureaucratic burdens on business and public services. It was asked to address inconsistencies in the current anti-discrimination legislative framework. In doing so, it was to reconsider the fundamental principles and underlying concepts of the legislation, and to create a clearer and more streamlined equality legislation framework, so as to produce better outcomes for those who experience disadvantage. It was briefed to investigate new ways of enforcing the law and to suggest new models for encouraging and incentivising compliance with it. A key priority was seen to be to achieve greater consistency in the protection afforded to different groups, while taking into account evidence that different legal approaches may be appropriate for different groups.

Green Paper

1.10   In June 2007 the Government published for consultation a Green Paper resulting from the Discrimination Law Review.[14] The Green Paper mooted a Single Equality Act in which discrimination law would be simplified. It rejected a model based simply upon a consolidating statute. Instead, it proposed a Single Equality Act that would review the existing law with a view to making it fit for the new century. However, the proposals were not seen as being radical.

---

12   Keter, 2009a: 100.
13   The Equalities Review, 2006; 2007a; 2007b.
14   Department for Communities and Local Government, 2007.

Instead the Green Paper opted for the status quo on many issues.[15] For example, the then statutory commissions had urged that a Single Equality Act should contain a purpose clause setting out the goals and underlying principles of the law. The Green Paper was at best lukewarm on this suggestion.

1.11 The Green Paper mooted the retention of a comparator in direct discrimination; it rejected the idea of extending indirect discrimination to disability cases; and it floated the idea of a single test of objective justification for disability discrimination. The Green Paper supported a further simplification of the definition of disability through the removal of the lists of capacities in relation to normal day-to-day activities. It suggested that there should be an equivalent to the genuine occupational requirement test in employment cases that service providers could use to justify direct discrimination in services cases.

1.12 The Government found that the evidence did not support legislation mandating equal pay reviews. It continued to prefer to distinguish between contractual and non-contractual pay matters. Nevertheless, the Green Paper suggested that it would be possible to codify settled principles of equal pay law. It was not persuaded that hypothetical comparators should be permitted in equal pay claims as in other discrimination complaints.

1.13 In discrimination law generally, while positive discrimination would remain unlawful, voluntary positive action ('balancing measures') would be permitted but not required. The Green Paper proposed that the race, disability and gender equality duties should be replaced with a single duty on public authorities to promote race, disability and gender equality. However, it also suggested that public authorities might be permitted to prioritise within and between their equality duties. Furthermore, it was proposed that public authorities might be relieved of specific duties, such as that of monitoring their workforce. Nevertheless, the consultation also questioned whether a single public sector equality duty should be extended to cover age, sexual orientation and/or religion or belief.

1.14 The Green Paper did not advance the case for employment tribunals to be empowered to make expanded and enforceable action recommendations. It also did not favour broadening the jurisdiction of employment tribunals so as to deal with non-employment discrimination cases. The arguments for permitting representative actions in discrimination litigation did not meet favour with the Government. The Green Paper did not advance the case for extending age discrimination into the non-employment field. It did set out the Government's intention to implement the principle of equal treatment between men and women in the access to and the supply of goods and services contained in the EU Gender Directive.[16]

---

[15] See Rubenstein, 2007a.
[16] Now implemented via the Sex Discrimination (Amendment of Legislation) Regulations 2008.

White Paper

1.15 In June 2008 the Government published its White Paper in response to the earlier Green Paper based upon the Discrimination Law Review.[17] Shortly afterwards, it also published its response to the Discrimination Law Review consultation.[18] Disappointingly, the White Paper did not contain a draft Single Equality Bill by which the Government's intentions could be judged. However, it did promise the consolidation of nine major pieces of discrimination legislation and the associated statutory instruments in a Bill to be written in plain English. Despite its status as a White Paper, it was apparent from this document that the Government had not yet made up its mind on a number of important issues, including multiple discrimination and representative actions.

1.16 The foreword to the White Paper established the purpose of the proposed Bill and its accompanying package of measures as being 'to strengthen protection, advance equality and declutter the law'. It promised to introduce a new equality duty on the public sector; to end age discrimination; to require transparency; to extend the scope of positive action; and to strengthen enforcement. Curiously, however, much of the detail of the Government's position was to be found not in the White Paper but in the Government's response to the Discrimination Law Review consultation.[19]

Response to Discrimination Law Review consultation

1.17 Read together, the White Paper and the Government's response to the Discrimination Law Review consultation promised to place a new single equality duty on public bodies and to extend it to gender reassignment, age, sexual orientation, and religion or belief. The proposed Single Equality Bill would contain powers to outlaw unjustifiable age discrimination in the provision of goods, facilities and services and in the carrying out of public functions. A key feature of the proposed Bill would be the requirement of transparency. Public bodies would be expected to report on inequalities in gender pay, ethnic minority employment and disability employment. The equality duty would expect public bodies to use their purchasing power to tackle discrimination and to promote equality. It was announced that pay secrecy clauses would be banned.

1.18 A controversial feature of the Government's response to the Discrimination Law Review consultation was the intention to extend positive action. This would enable employers to take into account the under-representation of disadvantaged groups when selecting between two equally qualified candidates. It was also intended to extend the permission to use women-only shortlists in selecting parliamentary candidates to 2030.

---

[17] Government Equalities Office, 2008a. See also Rubenstein, 2008a.
[18] Government Equalities Office, 2008b. See also Rubenstein, 2007b (summarising the major contributions to the consultation exercise) and Rubenstein, 2008b.
[19] Government Equalities Office, 2008b.

1.19 The Government undertook to strengthen the enforcement of the new law by allowing tribunals to make wider recommendations in discrimination cases. It promised to explore further the question of discrimination on multiple grounds. It undertook to consult on representative actions as part of the wider civil justice reforms. However, it did not suggest that non-employment discrimination cases would be heard by a cadre of specialist judges or tribunals. It favoured instead appropriate training for judges hearing non-employment discrimination cases, supported by specialist assessors.

1.20 The White Paper and the Government's response to the Discrimination Law Review consultation focused upon simplifying the law. They also championed standardising the definition of discrimination across the existing protected characteristics, and between the employment and non-employment spheres. They foreshadowed a model for exceptions which would include a genuine occupational requirement for all grounds of discrimination at work, except for disability. However, the Government rejected introducing a genuine service requirement for discrimination outside work. The law would be streamlined and strengthened in particular areas, especially affecting transsexual people; pregnant women and new mothers; disabled people; members of private clubs; and in relation to harassment.

1.21 The Government stated that it did not intend to include a purpose clause in a Single Equality Bill. It also rejected introducing particular protection against discrimination for carers (other than addressing the concept of associative discrimination). Moreover, there would be no opportunity taken in the Bill to introduce statutory protection against discrimination on grounds of genetic predisposition. Nor would the Bill introduce specific protection against caste discrimination or discrimination for Welsh speakers.

Other developments

1.22 In January 2009, the Government published its New Opportunities White Paper.[20] This committed the Government to considering legislation to address disadvantage associated with socio-economic inequality. During the course of 2009, the Government Equalities Office also published various documents, assessing the impact of a multiple discrimination provision; making policy proposals for specific duties; and considering ending age discrimination in services and public functions.[21]

EQUALITY BILL 2008–09 AND 2009–10

1.23 The Equality Bill received its First Reading in the House of Commons on 24 April 2009 in the 2008–09 parliamentary session. It was published on 27

---

[20] Cabinet Office, 2009.
[21] Government Equalities Office, 2009a; 2009b; 2009c; 2009d.

April 2009.[22] It was sponsored by Harriet Harman QC, Leader of the House of Commons and Lord Privy Seal, in her capacity as Minister of State in the Government Equalities Office. The Solicitor General, Vera Baird QC, was primarily responsible for steering the Bill through the House of Commons. The Bill was published in an experimental format in that the Explanatory Notes (EN) on each clause were printed opposite that clause. The aim was to make the explanatory material easier to use (although that experiment was not continued in later versions of the Bill). Considerable assistance was also to be had from the research paper published by the House of Commons Library in support of the Bill.[23]

1.24 The Bill received its Second Reading debate in the House of Commons on 11 May 2009.[24] The Bill was then committed to a Public Bill Committee. Power was also taken to allow the Bill to be carried over from one parliamentary session to the next if proceedings on the Bill had not been completed.

1.25 The Bill was considered in Committee in the Commons over a total of 20 sittings between 2 June 2009 and 7 July 2009.[25] During its first four sessions the Committee considered witness evidence on the Bill. A number of technical amendments were made to correct drafting errors or omissions. However, new clauses dealing with combined discrimination (dual characteristics) and with trustees and managers of occupational schemes were also introduced.[26] The Government also undertook to give further consideration to the list of bodies to be covered by the socio-economic duty; to make clearer the distinct nature of protection against disability discrimination (including the fact that treating disabled people more favourably is not discrimination against people who are not disabled); to provide greater clarity in respect of discrimination arising from disability; to limit the use of pre-employment questionnaires in relation to disability-related enquiries prior to an offer of employment; and to consider the possible introduction of representative actions.

1.26 The summer recess 2009 and then the conclusion of the 2008–09 parliamentary session of Parliament intervened. The Bill made no progress before the new 2009–10 session commenced on 18 November 2009. The Bill was referred to in the Queen's Speech. Consideration of it resumed in accordance with the power to do so previously taken. The Bill received a formal First and Second Reading without debate in the House of Commons on 19 November 2009.[27] The Bill was reprinted.[28] Having already completed its Committee stage, the Bill navigated the Report stage and its Third Reading

---

[22] HC Bill 85 (2008–09).
[23] Keter, 2009a (upon which this chapter draws).
[24] HC Deb vol 492 col 553–655 (11 May 2009).
[25] HC PBC Deb (Equality Bill) 2008–09.
[26] Keter, 2009b. See HC Bill 131 (2008-09).
[27] HC Deb vol 501 col 142 (19 November 2009).
[28] HC Bill 5 (2009–10).

debate in the House of Commons on 2 December 2009.[29] The lack of time for debate on the floor of the House of Commons attracted much criticism and was to inform its progress in the House of Lords.

1.27 The Bill proceeded to the House of Lords, where it received a formal First Reading on 3 December 2009.[30] The Bill was reprinted, incorporating amendments made in the House of Commons at Report stage.[31] A new edition of the Explanatory Notes to the Bill was also published.[32] In the House of Lords the Bill was sponsored and led by Baroness Royall of Blaisdon, Leader of the House of Lords and Chancellor of the Duchy of Lancaster.

1.28 The Bill received its Second Reading in the House of Lords on 15 December 2009 and was committed to a Committee of the Whole House.[33] The Bill was considered in Committee over 6 days between 11 January 2010 and 9 February 2010.[34] Before Report the Bill was reprinted as amended.[35] The Report stage in the House of Lords took place on 2 March 2010.[36] The Bill as amended on Report was reprinted.[37] The Third Reading debate occurred on 23 March 2010 and the Bill was returned to the House of Commons.[38] The Lords amendments were reprinted with separate Explanatory Notes.[39]

1.29 On the day the Lords amendments were due to be considered in the Commons – 6 April 2010 – Prime Minister Gordon Brown announced a General Election on 6 May 2010. No doubt to avoid a 'ping pong' between the House of Commons and House of Lords over the amendments, or to ensure that the Bill was not the subject of negotiation in the 'wash up' of remaining Bills, the Government accepted all the Lords amendments and in a short debate the Bill was finally approved.[40] The Bill received Royal Assent on 8 April 2010.[41]

---

[29] HC Deb vol 501 col 1111–1233 (2 December 2009).
[30] HL Deb vol 715 col 842 (3 December 2009).
[31] HL Bill 20 (2009–10).
[32] HL Bill 20 EN (2009–10).
[33] HL Deb vol 715 cols 1404–1418 and 1432–1516 (15 December 2009).
[34] HL Deb vol 716 cols 298–351 and 367–392 (11 January 2010); cols 518–566 and 574–600 (13 January 2010); cols 878–949 and 964–986 (19 January 2010); cols 1197–1266 and 1278–1290 (25 January 2010); cols 1415–1472 and 1487–1512 (27 January 2010); and HL Deb Vol 717 cols 634–660 and 689–724 (9 February 2010).
[35] HL Bill 35 (2009–10).
[36] HL Deb vol 717 cols 1326–1408 and 1414–1442 (2 March 2010).
[37] HL Bill 39 (2009–10).
[38] HL Deb vol 718 cols 851–873 (23 March 2010).
[39] HC Bill 96 (2009–10) and HC Bill 96 EN (2009–10).
[40] HC Deb vol 508 cols 927–942.
[41] Equality Act 2010 c.15. The Act was published shortly afterwards and the final version of the Explanatory Notes (EN) followed.

EQUALITY ACT 2010

Short title and purpose

1.30   The long title of the Act makes clear its purpose to:

> 'Make provision to require Ministers of the Crown and others when making
> strategic decisions about the exercise of their functions to have regard to the
> desirability of reducing socio-economic inequalities; to reform and harmonise
> equality law and restate the greater part of the enactments relating to
> discrimination and harassment related to certain personal characteristics; to
> enable certain employers to be required to publish information about the
> differences in pay between male and female employees; to prohibit victimisation in
> certain circumstances; to require the exercise of certain functions to be with regard
> to the need to eliminate discrimination and other prohibited conduct; to enable
> duties to be imposed in relation to the exercise of public procurement functions; to
> increase equality of opportunity; to amend the law relating to rights and
> responsibilities in family relationships; and for connected purposes.'

The Act may be cited as the Equality Act 2010 (EQA 2010).[42]

1.31   The Act does not contain a purpose clause (as had been urged upon the
Government in the pre-history of the Act). The Joint Committee on Human
Rights had accepted that the objectives of a constitutional guarantee to
equality and a purpose clause are not identical. However, it had urged the
Government to use the Equality Bill to enshrine a freestanding constitutional
right to equality. It considered that problems of interpretation could be
alleviated by the inclusion of a constitutional guarantee or purpose clause.[43] In
the event, the Government resisted attempts to include a purpose clause on the
face of the Act itself.

Interpretation

1.32   Provision is made for aids to interpretation of words, terms and phrases
used throughout the Act.[44] They are supplemented helpfully by a list of the
places where expressions used in the Act are defined or otherwise explained.[45]
Appropriate references to these aids to interpretation are made throughout the
substantive chapters below.

Money

1.33   The Act provides that there is to be paid out of money provided by
Parliament any increase attributable to the Act in the expenses of a Minister of
the Crown.[46]

---

42   EQA 2010, s 218.
43   Joint Committee on Human Rights, 2009: para 25.
44   EQA 2010, ss 212–214.
45   EQA 2010, Sch 28. See EN paras 667–670.
46   EQA 2010, s 215.

Commencement

1.34 Section 216 provides that s 186(2)[47] and Part 16 (general and miscellaneous provisions) – except ss 202 (civil partnerships on religious premises), 206 (information society services) and 211 (amendments, repeals and revocations) – come into force on the day on which the Act is passed. The other provisions of the Act come into force on such day as a Minister of the Crown may by order appoint.[48]

1.35 When introducing the Equality Bill the Labour Government always intended that the legislation would come into force in October 2010. However, the provisions on caste discrimination will need to be implemented by secondary legislation following a report into the issue due to be published in August 2010.[49] The provisions in s 14 on combined discrimination (dual characteristics) are likely to be postponed until April 2011. The power to make regulations in s 78 (on gender pay gap information) is not likely to be acted upon before April 2013 so as to allow voluntary arrangements time to work. As a result of the Conservative Government-Liberal Democrat coalition resulting from the General Election on 6 May 2010, in which the Conservatives are the majority partner, it is likely that the more controversial parts of the Act will not be implemented (in particular, the duties on socio-economic inequalities, the positive action provisions and the measures on equal pay audits).[50]

Territorial extent and application

1.36 The Act forms part of the law of England and Wales.[51] With two exceptions,[52] it also forms part of the law of Scotland.[53] It does not apply generally to Northern Ireland.[54] In relation to Part 5 (work), the Act delegates to the employment tribunals the task of determining whether the law applies in the particular circumstances of the connection between the employment relationship and Great Britain.[55] The Act is also silent as to territorial extent in relation to the non-work provisions of the Act. The courts will determine whether the law applies on the particular facts of each case.[56]

---

[47] EQA 2010, s 186 is concerned with rail vehicle accessibility (compliance). Schedule 20 (rail vehicle accessibility: compliance) is to have effect. However, s 186(2) provides that s 186 and Sch 20 are repealed at the end of 2010 if the Schedule is not brought into force (either fully or to any extent) before the end of that year.

[48] EQA 2010, s 216(2).

[49] HC Deb vol 508 cols 927–928 (Solicitor-General).

[50] HC Deb vol 508 col 932 (Mr Mark Harper).

[51] EQA 2010, s 217(1).

[52] EQA 2010, s 190 (improvements to let dwelling houses) and Part 15 (family property).

[53] EQA 2010, s 217(2).

[54] EQA 2010, s 217(3), except in relation to s 82 (offshore work), s 105(3)–(4) (expiry of Sex Discrimination (Election Candidates) Act 2002) and s 199 (abolition of presumption of advancement).

[55] EN para 15. This reflects the approach taken in the Employment Rights Act 1996 (as amended). However, note EQA 2010, ss 81–82 in relation to ships and hovercraft, and offshore work.

[56] However, note that express provision is made for particular provisions of the Act to apply (or

Devolution

1.37 The EQA 2010 replicates existing provisions whereby the Scottish Ministers can impose specific equality duties on Scottish public bodies and on the devolved functions of cross-border bodies.[57] It contains a number of provisions conferring additional powers on the Scottish Ministers to make secondary legislation.[58] Equal opportunities and discrimination are not devolved matters in relation to Wales. However, the EQA 2010 contains a limited number of express powers to enable the Welsh Ministers to make provisions in relation to particular parts of the Act.[59] In Northern Ireland, equal opportunities and discrimination are transferred matters under the Northern Ireland Act 1998. As such, with a few exceptions, the Act does not form part of the law of Northern Ireland.[60]

Human rights

1.38   In introducing the Bill that became the Equality Act 2010 ministers made the conventional declaration that its provisions were compatible with the rights contained in the European Convention on Human Rights (ECHR).[61] The Government considers that the main articles of the ECHR that are engaged by the EQA 2010 are Art 8 (right to respect for private and family life); Art 9 (right to freedom of thought, conscience and religion); Art 10 (right to freedom of expression); Art 11 (right to freedom of association); Art 14 (prohibiting discrimination in the field of enjoyment of rights guaranteed by the Convention); and Art 1 of Protocol 1 (right to peaceful enjoyment of property).[62] It sees the Act as 'a rights-enhancing piece of legislation the majority of which is required to implement the UK's obligations under EU law'.[63]

1.39   As the Explanatory Notes acknowledge,[64] the most significant issues arising under the ECHR are the exceptions in the Act to the prohibition on

---

potentially apply) outside the UK. See EQA 2010, s 29(9) (in respect of immigration and entry clearance) and s 30 (in respect of the territorial application of the services provisions of Part 3 in relation to ships and hovercraft).

[57]   EN paras 16–17. See EQA 2010, ss 151 and 153, and Part 3 of Sch 19.

[58]   See, for example, EQA 2010, ss 2, 96 and 162; Sch 11, para 4; Sch 14, para 2; Sch 17, para 10.

[59]   EN para 18. See EQA 2010, ss 2, 151 and 153; Part 2 of Sch 19.

[60]   EN paras 19–20. The DDA 1995 remains in force in Northern Ireland as its repeal by the EQA 2010 only applies in England, Wales and Scotland. The exceptional cases where the Act does apply in Northern Ireland are to be found in EQA 2010, ss 82 (offshore work), 105 (expiry of Sex Discrimination (Election Candidates) Act 2002) and 199 (abolition of presumption of advancement).

[61]   As is required by the Human Rights Act 1998, s 19(1)(a). See EN para 33 (HL Bill 20) (in footnotes 61–63 the references are to the version of the EN that accompanied HL Bill 20 and which do not appear in the final version of the EN). See also the Human Rights Memorandum submitted by the Government Equalities Office to the Joint Committee on Human Rights on 5 May 2009: Joint Committee on Human Rights, 2009: Ev 22–58.

[62]   EN para 34 (HL Bill 20).

[63]   EN para 34 (HL Bill 20).

[64]   EN paras 34–35 (HL Bill 20).

discrimination and those cases where the rights to non-discrimination conflict with each other. In the Government's view, wherever the EQA 2010 provides for exceptions to the non-discrimination principle it has considered the impact upon individual human rights. It has concluded that the exceptions are pursuing a legitimate aim in a proportionate manner and that the exceptions have been drafted narrowly to ensure that end.[65]

1.40 The Joint Committee on Human Rights considered that there was a number of significant human rights issues that arose in the context of the Act. In its view it also contained a number of measures which potentially enhanced human rights.[66] Both categories of issues are referred to in the text below where appropriate.

Explanatory Notes

1.41 As is now usual, the Government published various editions of Explanatory Notes as the Equality Bill navigated the parliamentary process. The Explanatory Notes were prepared by the various contributory government departments. As they explain:

> 'Their purpose is to assist the reader of the [Act] and to help inform debate on it. They do not form part of the [Act] and have not been endorsed by Parliament. The notes need to be read in conjunction with the [Act]. They are not, and are not meant to be, a comprehensive description of the [Act].'[67]

They record that the Equality Act 2010 has two main purposes: to harmonise discrimination law and to strengthen the law to support progress on equality.[68] To that end, the Act brings together and re-states all the major enactments already referred to above, together with a number of other related provisions. Its intention is to harmonise existing provisions to give a single approach where appropriate, repealing most of the existing legislation (except the Equality Act 2006).[69]

---

[65] In EN paras 36–37 (HL Bill 20), the Government offers as an example of such consideration the exceptions provided in EQA 2010, Sch 23 to permit religious organisations to discriminate because of religion or belief or on grounds of sexual orientation, which are said to apply only in certain limited circumstances (but see the discussion in Chapter 7 below). See also EN para 38 (HL Bill 20) citing the further examples of the balancing exercise said to have been conducted in EQA 2010, s 101 and Sch 16 in relation to single characteristic clubs. Note also EN para 39 (HL Bill 20) (on the broader definition of harassment applied to religion or belief, sexual orientation and gender reassignment, discussed in Chapter 3) and EN para 40 (HL Bill 20) (on the special procedure in discrimination cases in the civil courts where national security interests rise: EQA 2010, s 117).

[66] Joint Committee on Human Rights, 2009: para 26.

[67] EN paras 1–2.

[68] EN para 10.

[69] EN para 11.

1.42   The Explanatory Notes declare that the Act will strengthen the law in a number of areas. They set out the major points of the Act as follows. The Act will:[70]

- place a new duty on certain public bodies to consider socio-economic disadvantage when making strategic decisions about how to exercise their functions;

- extend the circumstances in which a person is protected against discrimination, harassment or victimisation because of a protected characteristic;

- extend the circumstances in which a person is protected against discrimination by allowing people to make a claim if they are directly discriminated against because of a combination of two relevant protected characteristics;

- create a duty on listed public bodies when carrying out their functions and on other persons when carrying out public functions to have due regard when carrying out their functions to:
  - the need to eliminate conduct which the Act prohibits;
  - the need to advance equality of opportunity between persons who share a relevant protected characteristic and those who do not; and
  - the need to foster good relations between people who share a relevant protected characteristic and people who do not;[71]

- allow an employer or service provider or other organisation to take positive action so as to enable existing or potential employees or customers to overcome or minimise a disadvantage arising from a protected characteristic;

- extend the permission for political parties to use women-only shortlists for election candidates to 2030; and

- enable an employment tribunal to make a recommendation to a respondent who has lost a discrimination claim to take certain steps to remedy matters not just for the benefit of the individual claimant (who may have already left the organisation concerned) but also the wider workforce;

- amend family property law to remove discriminatory provisions and provide additional statutory property rights for civil partners in England and Wales;

---

[70]   EN para 12.
[71]   The practical effect is that listed public bodies will have to consider how their policies, programmes and service delivery will affect people with the protected characteristics.

- amend the Civil Partnership Act 2004 to remove the prohibition on civil partnerships being registered in religious premises.

1.43 In its evidence to the Joint Committee on Human Rights the Government also set out the main purposes of the Act as being:

- to harmonise and simplify the law on discrimination;

- to extend coverage of the public sector duty across all the protected characteristics and unify them into one single equality duty;

- to permit more measures which are designed to redress under-representation and disadvantage amongst those with protected characteristics (that is, more positive action);

- to reinstate protection along the lines of disability-related discrimination and extend indirect discrimination to disability;

- to extend protection from discrimination against a person associated with someone who has a protected characteristic or against a person who is perceived to have a protected characteristic;

- to prohibit unjustifiable age discrimination in the provision of goods, facilities and services for people aged 18 or over;

- to impose a new duty on certain public authorities to consider socio-economic disadvantage in their strategic decision-making;

- to increase the protection on grounds of gender reassignment so that it is on a par with other protected characteristics;

- to provide consistent protection for all protected characteristics against harassment of an employee by a third party;

- to prohibit discrimination and harassment in private clubs and associations.[72]

Impact assessments

1.44 The Equality Bill was accompanied by a Regulatory Impact Assessment and Equality Impact Assessment. These are not considered further here.[73]

---

[72] Joint Committee on Human Rights, 2009: Ev 22 para 4.
[73] See the summary in EN paras 14–25 (HL Bill 20) (which includes a summary of the carbon impact of the Act). See *Equality Bill: Equality Impact Assessment* (House of Lords) (December 2009), London: Stationery Office; *Equality Bill: Impact Assessment* (Version 4: House of Lords Introduction) (December 2009), London: Stationery Office.

Delegated powers

1.45 The Act contains a number of delegated legislative powers. These have been subject to the scrutiny of the House of Lords Delegated Powers and Regulatory Reform Committee.[74] The Government originally stated that there are 89 delegated powers, of which 20 are new powers. There are 23 powers subject to the affirmative procedure and 13 Henry VIII powers permitting amendment of primary legislation.[75] The Bill was amended in a number of places in the House of Lords to meet concerns on delegated powers. Nevertheless, the final version of the Act contains at least 18 sections in which there is a power to make an order and at least 24 sections where there is a power to make regulations.[76]

Codes of practice

1.46 On 12 January 2010 the Equality and Human Rights Commission opened its consultation on draft Codes of Practice for employment, equal pay, and services, public functions and associations.[77] Consultation remained open until 2 April 2010.

---

[74] See its report at House of Lords Delegated Powers and Regulatory Reform Committee, 2010.
[75] See House of Lords Delegated Powers and Regulatory Reform Committee, 2010: Appendix 2.
[76] Further such powers are found in various Schedules to the Act.
[77] See EHRC, 2010a; 2010b; 2010c. The draft codes are issued under EQA 2006, ss 14–15 (as amended by EQA 2010, s 211 and Sch 26, para 10).

Chapter 2

PROTECTED CHARACTERISTICS

INTRODUCTION

2.1 A key aim of the Equality Act 2010 (EQA 2010) is to harmonise the different strands of discrimination law. They are brought together as characteristics that are protected by the subsequent provisions of the Act. There are nine protected characteristics and they are listed in alphabetical order:[1]

(i)   age;

(ii)   disability;

(iii) gender reassignment;

(iv) marriage and civil partnership;

(v)   pregnancy and maternity;

(vi) race;

(vii) religion or belief;

(viii) sex;

(ix) sexual orientation.

2.2 Each characteristic is then defined,[2] except for pregnancy and maternity, which are further defined in the sections dealing with the prohibited conduct on that ground.[3]

AGE

2.3 There is no intrinsic factor that defines age as a characteristic, compared with race, sex or any of the other protected characteristics. A 60-year-old

---

[1]   EQA 2010, s 4.
[2]   EQA 2010, Part 2, Chapter 1, ss 5–12.
[3]   EQA 2010, ss 17 and 18. See Chapter 3.

person might be considered old within one set of circumstances and young within another. Different ages are also likely to attract different types of discrimination. As Fredman says:

> 'While young people will necessarily grow out of the group, and may therefore shake free of any discrimination attaching to their youth, older people cannot escape their age and the attached stigma and stereotyping, material disadvantage, and social exclusion'.[4]

2.4 The protected characteristic of age is defined by a reference to a person of a particular age group, such as 'over 65'. A reference to persons who share the protected characteristic is a reference to persons of the same age group, such as '18 to 21 year olds'.[5] An age group is defined by reference to a particular age or to a range of ages.[6] This is the same definition as in the previous legislation, save that a reference to age no longer includes an explicit reference to a person's apparent age.[7] However, age groups could be linked to physical appearance as well as other strictly non-chronological terms, such as 'grey-haired' or 'youthful'.[8]

2.5 The flexibility of the definition of 'age group' depending on the circumstances is shown by this example. A person aged 21 does not share the same characteristic of age with the age group of 'people in their 40s'. However, a person aged 21 and people in their 40s can share the characteristic of the age group of those 'under 50'. The Draft Employment Code of Practice gives the example of a man of 86, who could be said to share the protected characteristic of age with: '86 year olds', 'over 80s', 'over 65s', 'pensioners', 'senior citizens', 'older people' and 'the elderly'.[9]

DISABILITY

2.6 The definition of disability and the guidance on determining whether a claimant is disabled largely reflect the previous legislation.[10] The definition is that a person (P) has a disability if P has a physical or mental impairment and the impairment has a substantial and long-term adverse effect on P's ability to carry out normal day-to-day activities.[11] A reference to persons who share a protected characteristic is a reference to persons who have the same disability, for example, deafness.[12] The provision applies to a person who has had a

---

4   Sandra Fredman, 2002. *Discrimination Law*. (Oxford: Oxford University Press).
5   EQA 2010, s 5(1).
6   EQA 2010, s 5(2).
7   Employment Equality (Age) Regulations 2006, SI 2006/1031, reg 3.
8   Draft Employment Code of Practice, para 2.3.
9   Draft Employment Code of Practice, para 2.4.
10   DDA 1995, s 1 and Sch 1.
11   EQA 2010, s 6(1).
12   EQA 2010, s 6(3)(b).

disability as it applies to a person who has a disability, save in respect of Part 12 (disabled persons: transport) and s 190 (improvements to let dwelling houses).[13]

2.7   Schedule 1 to the EQA 2010 provides the tests for determining whether a person has a disability and reflects similar provisions in the Disability Discrimination Act 1995 (DDA 1995). Provision is made for regulations to provide further definition, since the previous regulations will be replaced, and also for new guidance. This is mostly familiar from previous legislation and guidance. Most of the amendments discussed during the progress of the EQA 2010 through Parliament, such as the removal of 'substantial' and 'long-term' from the definition of disability, have not been implemented.

2.8   However, the EQA 2010 introduces one significant change by removing the requirement that the tribunal or court considers a list of eight specific capacities (such as mobility, speech, hearing or eyesight) when considering the ability of a person to carry out normal day-to-day activities.

2.9   It is suggested in the Explanatory Notes that this change will make it easier for some people to demonstrate that they meet the definition of a disabled person and that it will assist those who currently find it difficult to show that their impairment adversely affects their ability to carry out a normal day-to-day activity which involves one of these capacities.[14] The example given is of a man with depression who finds even the simplest of tasks or decisions difficult: for example, getting up in the morning and getting washed and dressed. He is also forgetful and cannot plan ahead.

2.10   The component parts of the definition of 'normal day-to-day activities' must still be met. It has been said that '[w]hat is a day-to-day activity is best left unspecified: easily recognised, but defined with difficulty'.[15] What is 'normal' is anything that is neither abnormal nor unusual; it is given its ordinary everyday meaning.

2.11   The first paragraph of Sch 1 to the EQA 2010 establishes the pattern by stating that regulations may make provision for a condition of a prescribed description to be, or not to be, an impairment.[16] The previous Regulations excluded addiction to alcohol, nicotine or any other substance, as well as, for example, tendencies to set fires or steal.[17] It is likely that, both in respect of this paragraph and throughout the Schedule, the new regulations will reflect the old.

2.12   The effect of an impairment is long-term if (a) it has lasted for at least 12 months, (b) it is likely to last for at least 12 months or (c) it is likely to last for the rest of the life of the person affected. If its effect is likely to recur, then it is

---

[13]   EQA 2010, s 6(4).
[14]   EN para 682.
[15]   *Goodwin v Patent Office* [1999] IRLR 4, per Morison J.
[16]   EQA 2010, Sch 1, para 1.
[17]   Disability Discrimination (Meaning of Disability) Regulations 1996, SI 1996/1455.

to be treated as continuing even though its effect has ceased. Regulations may further determine the definition of 'long-term effects'.[18]

2.13　An impairment which consists of a severe disfigurement is to be treated as having a substantial adverse effect, subject to regulations providing when that might not be the case and dealing with deliberately acquired disfigurement.[19] The previous Regulations excluded tattoos and body piercing.[20] Similarly, regulations may make provision for an effect of a prescribed condition on the ability of a person to carry out normal day-to-day activities to be treated as being or not being a substantial adverse effect.[21] 'Substantial' has previously been defined as an effect that is more than 'minor' or 'trivial'.[22]

2.14　An impairment is to be treated as having a substantial adverse effect on the ability of the person concerned to carry out normal day-to-day activities if it would be likely to have that effect, but measures are being taken to treat or correct it. The term 'measures' includes, in particular, medical treatment and the use of a prosthesis or other aid. This does not apply in relation to the impairment of a person's sight, to the extent that the impairment is correctable by wearing glasses or contact lenses. There is provision to allow other impairments to be prescribed.[23] The wording of this provision has changed slightly from the equivalent provision in the DDA 1995,[24] although the guidance in *SCA Packaging Ltd v Boyle*[25] – that the correct test was whether the adverse effect of the impairment 'could well happen' unless the measures were taken – remains relevant.

2.15　There are certain medical conditions which are deemed as disabilities, namely cancer, HIV infection and multiple sclerosis. HIV infection is defined as infection by a virus capable of causing the Acquired Immune Deficiency Syndrome. Regulations may further define who has or does not have a deemed disability.[26] Persons who were certified as blind or partially sighted were deemed disabled under the previous Regulations.[27]

2.16　Progressive conditions are likely to change and develop over time. Where a person has a progressive condition which causes an impairment which has (or had) some effect on that person's ability to carry out normal day-to-day activities, he or she is to be taken as having an impairment which has a substantial adverse effect, so long as the condition is likely to result in such an

---

[18]　EQA 2010, Sch 1, para 2.
[19]　EQA 2010, Sch 1, para 3.
[20]　Disability Discrimination (Meaning of Disability) Regulations 1996, SI 1996/1455.
[21]　EQA 2010, Sch 1, para 4.
[22]　DRC Code of Practice: Employment & Occupation (2004).
[23]　EQA 2010, Sch 1, para 5.
[24]　DDA 1995, Sch 1, para 6(1).
[25]　[2009] UKHL 37, [2009] IRLR 746.
[26]　EQA 2010, Sch 1, paras 5 and 6.
[27]　Disability Discrimination (Blind and Partially Sighted Persons) Regulations 2003, SI 2003/712.

impairment. Regulations may make provision for a particular condition to be treated as being, or as not being, progressive.[28]

2.17 A question as to whether a person had a disability at a particular time is to be determined as if the provisions of the EQA 2010 were in force when the discriminatory act complained of was done.[29]

2.18 The statutory mechanism to allow guidance on the protected characteristic of disability to be issued is also set out in Sch 1 to the EQA 2010.[30] An 'adjudicating body' must take account of such guidance as it thinks is relevant. An adjudicating body is a court, a tribunal or a person deciding a claim relating to Part 6 (education).[31] This will replace the previous Guidance.[32]

2.19 The Explanatory Notes provide two examples of persons who would be disabled within the statutory definition, as follows. First, a man works in a warehouse, loading and unloading heavy stock. He develops a long-term heart condition and no longer has the ability to lift or move heavy items of stock at work. Lifting and moving such heavy items is not a normal day-to-day activity. However, he is also unable to lift, carry or move moderately heavy everyday objects such as chairs, at work or around the home. This is an adverse effect on a normal day-to-day activity. He is likely to be considered a disabled person.[33]

2.20 Secondly, a young woman has developed colitis, an inflammatory bowel disease. The condition is a chronic one which is subject to periods of remissions and flare-ups. During a flare-up, she experiences symptoms that make it very difficult for her to travel or go to work. This has a substantial adverse effect on her ability to carry out normal day-to-day activities. She is also likely to be considered a disabled person.

GENDER REASSIGNMENT

2.21 The definition of the protected characteristic of gender reassignment replaces similar provisions in the SDA 1975,[34] but changes the definition by no longer requiring a person to be under medical supervision. This is because gender reassignment is a personal process, rather than a medicalised process.[35] The definition is that a person has the protected characteristic of gender reassignment if the person is proposing to undergo, is undergoing, or has

---

[28]   EQA 2010, Sch 1, para 8.
[29]   EQA 2010, Sch 1, para 9.
[30]   EQA 2010, s 6(5) and Sch 1, Pt 2.
[31]   EQA 2010, s 6(5) and Sch 1, Pt 2, para 12.
[32]   Guidance on the Definition of Disability issued by Secretary of State for Work and Pensions (2006).
[33]   EN para 40.
[34]   SDA 1975, ss 2A and 82(1).
[35]   Draft Employment Code of Practice, para 2.19.

undergone a process (or part of a process) for the purpose of reassigning the person's sex by changing physiological or other attributes of sex.[36]

2.22 A reference to people who have or share the common characteristic of gender reassignment is a reference to all transsexual people.[37] Therefore, a woman making the transition to being a man and a man making the transition to being a woman both share the characteristic of gender reassignment, as does a person who has only just started out on the process of changing his or her sex and a person who has completed the process.[38]

2.23 The Explanatory Notes provide two examples. First, a person who was born physically male decides to spend the rest of his life living as a woman. He declares his intention to his manager at work, who makes appropriate arrangements, and she then starts life at work and home as a woman. After discussion with her doctor and a Gender Identity Clinic, she starts hormone treatment and after several years she goes through gender reassignment surgery. She would be undergoing gender reassignment for the purposes of this provision.[39]

2.24 Secondly, an unemployed person who was born physically female decides to spend the rest of her life as a man. He starts and continues to live as a man. He decides not to seek medical advice as he successfully 'passes' as a man without the need for any medical intervention. He would also be undergoing gender reassignment.[40]

2.25 A further example in the Draft Employment Code of Practice makes the point that a person who has started a gender reassignment process, but then withdrawn from it, still has the protected characteristic because they have undergone part of a process of gender reassignment. So, a woman born physically male may start the process and decide to go no further, but she retains the protected characteristic.[41]

MARRIAGE AND CIVIL PARTNERSHIP

2.26 A person has the protected characteristic of marriage and civil partnership if the person is married or is a civil partner.[42] Therefore, someone who is engaged to be married or who is divorced or whose civil partnership has been dissolved does not have this protected characteristic and neither does an

---

[36] EQA 2010, s 7(1).
[37] EQA 2010, s 7(3).
[38] EN para 42.
[39] EN para 43.
[40] EN para 43.
[41] Draft Employment Code of Practice, para 2.25.
[42] EQA 2010, s 8(1).

unmarried couple or those sharing a same sex relationship that is not a civil partnership.[43] This provision replaces similar provisions in the SDA 1975.[44]

2.27 Marriage is not defined, but would cover any formal union of a man and woman that is legally recognised in the UK as a marriage. A civil partnership refers to a registered civil partnership,[45] including those registered outside the UK.[46]

RACE

2.28 The protected characteristic of race includes colour, nationality and ethnic or national origins.[47] This replaces similar provisions in the Race Relations Act 1976.[48]

2.29 Colour includes being black or white.[49] Nationality includes citizenship, so would include, for example, being a British, Australian or Swiss citizen.[50] Being of a particular ethnic origin will depend on whether a person belongs to an ethnic group, which is one that regards itself or is regarded by others as a distinct and separate community by virtue of certain distinguishing characteristics. An ethnic group must have two essential characteristics: a long shared history and a cultural tradition of its own. Other characteristics may include a common language, religion or geographical origin. Recognised examples would be Sikhs, Jews, Romany Gypsies and Irish Travellers.[51]

2.30 A national group giving rise to national origin must have identifiable historic and geographic elements indicating – at least at some point – the existence or previous existence of a nation. Examples would include the English and the Basques. National origin is distinct from nationality, although these will often be the same, so that, for example, people of Chinese national origin may be citizens of China, but equally could be citizens of the UK.[52]

2.31 Interestingly – and perhaps unexpectedly – the provision also allows for an amendment to provide for caste to be an aspect of race.[53] This was an addition at the Report stage in the House of Lords, following debate during the Committee stage.

2.32 The Explanatory Notes provide the following definition of 'caste':

---

[43]   EN para 47.
[44]   SDA 1975, s 3(2).
[45]   Under the Civil Partnership Act 2004.
[46]   Draft Employment Code of Practice, para 2.28.
[47]   EQA 2010, s 9(1).
[48]   RRA 1976, s 3(1).
[49]   EN para 50.
[50]   Draft Employment Code of Practice, para 2.33; EN para 50.
[51]   Draft Employment Code of Practice, paras 2.34–2.37.
[52]   Draft Employment Code of Practice, paras 2.38–2.39.
[53]   EQA 2010, s 9(5).

'The term "caste" denotes a hereditary, endogamous (marrying within the group) community associated with a traditional occupation and ranked accordingly on a perceived scale of ritual purity. It is generally (but not exclusively) associated with South Asia, particularly India, and its diaspora. It can encompass the four classes (varnas) of Hindu tradition (the Brahmin, Kshatriya, Vaishya and Shudra communities); the thousands of regional Hindu, Sikh, Christian, Muslim or other religious groups known as jatis; and groups amongst South Asian Muslims called biradaris. Some jatis regarded as below the varna hierarchy (once termed "untouchable") are known as Dalit.'[54]

2.33 The Government's initial position was that the inclusion of caste was unnecessary, because the existing definition of race was sufficiently extensive to include caste within the term 'ethnic or national origins'. Although still not persuaded, it commissioned the National Institute of Economic and Social Research to conduct in-depth research to explore the nature, extent and severity of caste prejudice and discrimination in Britain, and its associated implications for future government policy.[55]

2.34 An amendment to include caste could also provide for an exception to a provision of the EQA 2010 to apply (or not apply) to caste or to apply to caste in specified circumstances, for example in respect of single-characteristic associations.[56]

2.35 In relation to race, a reference to a person who has a particular protected characteristic is a reference to a person of a particular 'racial group', which is a group of persons defined by reference to race (for example, Afro-Caribbean).[57] However, the fact that a racial group comprises two or more distinct racial groups does not prevent it from constituting a particular racial group.[58] For example, a racial group could be 'black Britons', which would encompass those people who are both black and who are British citizens. Another racial group could be 'Asian', which could include Indians, Pakistanis, Bangladeshis and Sri Lankans.[59]

RELIGION OR BELIEF

2.36 'Religion' means any religion, and a reference to religion includes a reference to a lack of religion.[60] 'Belief' means any religious or philosophical belief, and a reference to belief includes a reference to a lack of belief.[61] This reflects the previous definition of religion and belief, which itself had been amended to remove the word 'similar' from the original definition that a belief

---

54 EN para 49.
55 HL Deb vol 717 col 1349 (2 March 2010) (Baroness Thornton).
56 EQA 2010, s 9(5)(b).
57 EQA 2010, s 9(2).
58 EQA 2010, s 9(4).
59 Draft Employment Code of Practice, para 2.43.
60 EQA 2010, s 10(1).
61 EQA 2010, s 10(2).

means 'any religious or similar philosophical belief'.[62] A person has the protected characteristic of religion or belief if he or she has the particular religion or belief (or lack of it) or shares it with others of the same religion or belief (or lack of it).[63]

2.37 The definition is broad and consistent with Article 9 of the ECHR – which guarantees freedom of thought, conscience and religion – as well as the European case law that defines its parameters.[64]

2.38 The examples of religions provided in the Explanatory Notes accompanying the EQA 2010 are: the Baha'i faith, Buddhism, Christianity, Hinduism, Islam, Jainism, Judaism, Rastafarianism, Sikhism and Zoroastrianism. This could extend to those sharing a particular form of (for example) Christianity, such as Catholics or Protestants.[65] These examples of religions all have mainstream status and cogency, but a religion need not be mainstream to fall within the protected characteristic, as long as it is identifiable and has a clear structure and belief system.[66]

2.39 Atheists will fall within the statutory definition because of their lack of religious belief.

2.40 The scope of the term 'philosophical belief' has been considered by the EAT in *Grainger v Nicholson*,[67] in which a belief in man-made climate change, and the alleged resulting moral imperatives, was held to be capable of being a philosophical belief if genuinely held. Drawing on the case law relating to the ECHR, the EAT applied the following limitations to the term 'philosophical belief': (i) the belief must be genuinely held; (ii) it must be a belief and not an opinion or viewpoint based on the present state of information available; (iii) it must be a belief as to a weighty and substantial aspect of human life and behaviour; (iv) it must attain a certain level of cogency, seriousness, cohesion and importance; and (v) it must be worthy of respect in a democratic society, be not incompatible with human dignity and not conflict with the fundamental rights of others.

2.41 The philosophical belief must have a similar status or cogency to a religious belief to be protected. This is despite the absence of the word 'similar' from the definition that belief means any religious or philosophical belief. However – as with religious beliefs – it is not a bar if the belief is not shared by others or is a 'one-off belief', namely one that does not govern the entirety of a person's life. Examples given in *Grainger* of one-off beliefs that could be

---

[62] Employment Equality (Religion or Belief) Regulations 2003, SI 2003/1660, reg 2(1), as amended by the EQA 2006, s 77(1).

[63] EQA 2010, s 10(3).

[64] For example: *Campbell & Cosans v UK* (1982) 4 EHRR 293, ECHR; *Kokkinakis v Greece* (1994) 17 EHRR 397.

[65] EN paras 52 and 53.

[66] Draft Employment Code of Practice, para 2.48.

[67] [2010] IRLR 5.

philosophical beliefs are pacifism and vegetarianism. The philosophical belief does not need to constitute or allude to a fully-fledged system of thought, nor does it need to be an '-ism'.

2.42 While support of a political party might not meet the description of a philosophical belief, a belief in Marxism or free-market capitalism might qualify. However, a racist political philosophy (for example) would not qualify because it would not be worthy of respect in a democratic society and would be incompatible with human dignity.

2.43 The judgment in *Grainger* also considered the lack of a philosophical belief. If the belief in man-made climate change amounts to a philosophical belief, that does not necessarily mean that the absence of such a belief would also amount to a philosophical belief. It may be possible for someone to establish such a philosophical belief, but the existence of a positive philosophical belief does not depend upon the existence of a negative philosophical belief to the contrary.

2.44 Whether a particular religion or belief meets the definition of a protected characteristic is a question for the court or tribunal. Applying these guidelines, belief in a football team, however devoted and consuming, would not be sufficient,[68] nor could membership of the International Church of Jediism, given that the Jedi is an entirely fictitious film creation.[69]

SEX

2.45 In respect of the particular protected characteristic of sex, a reference to a person who has the protected characteristic is a reference to a man or to a woman. A 'man' or 'woman' means a male or female of any age.[70] A reference to persons who share a protected characteristic is a reference to persons of the same sex.[71] This is a new provision and is unlikely to be contentious.

SEXUAL ORIENTATION

2.46 The protected characteristic of sexual orientation means a person's sexual orientation towards: (a) persons of the same sex as him or her (in other words the person is a gay man or a lesbian), (b) persons of the opposite sex to him or her (the person is heterosexual), or (c) persons of either sex (the person

---

[68]   EN para 53.
[69]   'Jedi discrimination case highlights trend for "bizarre" claims', *Personnel Today*, 18 March 2010.
[70]   EQA 2010, s 212(1).
[71]   EQA 2010, s 11.

is bisexual). A reference to persons sharing the protected characteristic of sexual orientation means the same sexual orientation, so, for example, gay men.[72]

2.47 The Explanatory Notes provide three explanatory examples. First, a man who experiences sexual attraction towards both men and women is 'bisexual' in terms of sexual orientation even if he has only had relationships with women. Secondly, a man and a woman who are both attracted only to people of the opposite sex from them share a sexual orientation. Thirdly, a man who is attracted only to other men is a gay man. A woman who is attracted only to other women is a lesbian. So a gay man and a lesbian share a sexual orientation.[73]

---

[72] EQA 2010, s 12(1), (2).
[73] EN para 57.

Chapter 3

PROHIBITED CONDUCT

INTRODUCTION

3.1 Sections 13–27 of the Equality Act 2010 (EQA 2010) are devoted to one of the key concepts of equality, namely, what amounts to prohibited conduct?[1] Prohibited conduct falls naturally into four divisions: discrimination;[2] failure to comply with a duty to make adjustments for disabled persons;[3] harassment;[4] and victimisation.[5] In turn, the concept of discrimination may be further sub-divided into: direct discrimination;[6] indirect discrimination;[7] combined (dual characteristics) discrimination;[8] discrimination arising from disability;[9] gender reassignment discrimination (cases of absence from work);[10] and pregnancy and maternity discrimination (work and non-work cases).[11] Supplementary provision in relation to discrimination is made so as to require comparison by reference to similar circumstances; by making irrelevant an alleged discriminator's characteristics; and by explaining references to particular strands of discrimination.[12]

3.2 As noted in the Preface to this book, it remains to be seen how relevant the legacy case-law will remain to the recast provisions on employment discrimination in the EQA 2010. It is arguable that the new provisions will have to be approached afresh and that pre-existing case-law can be no more than illustrative. Nevertheless, the relevant legacy case-law has been footnoted in this chapter.[13]

3.3 In addition, it is necessary whenever interpreting statutory provisions which implement European Union (EU) law to take into account any relevant case-law emanating from the European Court of Justice (ECJ). Accordingly,

---

[1]   EQA 2010, Chapter 2 of Part 2.
[2]   EQA 2010, ss 13–19.
[3]   EQA 2010, ss 20–22.
[4]   EQA 2010, s 26.
[5]   EQA 2010, s 27.
[6]   EQA 2010, s 13.
[7]   EQA 2010, s 19.
[8]   EQA 2010, s 14.
[9]   EQA 2010, s 15.
[10]   EQA 2010, s 16.
[11]   EQA 2010, ss 17–18.
[12]   EQA 2010, ss 23–25.
[13]   Drawing strongly upon Rubenstein, 2010b and *Harvey on Industrial Relations and Employment Law* (Butterworths Lexis-Nexis).

when applying the EQA 2010 reference may need to be made to that case-law as well as to the legacy case-law arising from disputes litigated in the UK.

DIRECT DISCRIMINATION

Introduction

3.4   Direct discrimination is a concept which used to be stated in slightly different ways in different parts of the legislation which preceded the EQA 2010. It was usually stated to be less favourable treatment 'on the ground of' or 'on grounds of' what would now be called a protected characteristic. It was not infrequent that the term 'ground' would be used in the plural when the singular would have been more accurate, which was perhaps a reflection of the infrequency in everyday language of the use of the words 'on the ground of' or 'on grounds of'. The new word used is 'because', which the Government was sure would make no change to the prior law,[14] and which the Explanatory Notes assert will effect no change to the prior law.[15] The purpose of the change of wording is to make the language of the statute more accessible to the lay person.[16]

3.5   Thus, direct discrimination occurs where the reason for the action complained about is a protected characteristic. Even if the protected characteristic is only a minor cause of the action, the action will be unlawful, since '[only] "no discrimination whatsoever" is compatible with the Burden of Proof Directive'.[17]

Definition of direct discrimination

3.6   The definition of direct discrimination is in EQA 2010, s 13. The key words are these: 'A person (A) discriminates against another (B) if, because of a protected characteristic, A treats B less favourably than A treats or would treat others.'[18] The Explanatory Notes helpfully state that this definition:

> 'is broad enough to cover cases where the less favourable treatment is because of the victim's association with someone who has that characteristic (for example, is disabled), or because the victim is wrongly thought to have it (for example, a particular religious belief).'[19]

---

[14]   See for example: HL Deb vol 716 col 526 (Baroness Thornton, Parliamentary Under-Secretary of State, Department of Health, speaking on behalf of the Government).

[15]   EN para 61.

[16]   HL Deb vol 716 col 527 (Baroness Thornton); EN para 61.

[17]   *Igen Ltd v Wong* [2005] ICR 931 CA, at 957. See further Chapter 12 (**12.61** onwards) below concerning EQA 2010, s 136, which implements the Burden of Proof Directive. See also **3.143** where a helpful passage from the speech of Lord Nicholls in *Nagarajan v London Regional Transport* [1999] ICR 877 is set out.

[18]   EQA 2010, s 13(1).

[19]   EN para 59.

The Explanatory Notes continue:[20]

> 'However, a different approach applies where the reason for the treatment is marriage or civil partnership, in which case only less favourable treatment because of the victim's status amounts to discrimination. It must be the victim, rather than anybody else, who is married or a civil partner.'

Exceptions to prohibition of direct discrimination

3.7 There is no scope for justifying direct discrimination because of the protected characteristics apart from in the following exceptional circumstances which are provided for by EQA 2010, s 13 and which in some cases mirror the previous law.

Age and justified treatment

3.8 Age discrimination may be justified. If the protected characteristic is age, then there will be no discrimination by the treatment of one person of another person if the first person can show that the treatment was 'a proportionate means of achieving a legitimate aim'.[21] This concept of 'a proportionate means of achieving a legitimate aim' applies also to treatment which might be indirect discrimination.[22] Ultimately the words mean 'justified'. Both words involve some sort of valuation. After all, the word 'legitimate' is meaningless in a vacuum. This is because, interpreted literally, it depends on a law which has already been made to give it meaning. Similarly, the word 'justified' assumes that which has yet to be proved. The word 'proportionate' adds something, but not much, to the equation.

3.9 The interpretation of the 'proportionate means of achieving a legitimate aim' exception should be in accordance with any relevant ECJ case law.[23] There is no scope for applying the 'range of reasonable responses of a reasonable employer' test in this context.[24] One helpful statement of the applicable test, which has stood the test of time, is that of Balcombe LJ in *Hampson v Department of Education and Science*:[25]

> 'In my judgment "justifiable" requires an objective balance between the discriminatory effect of the condition and the reasonable needs of the party who applies the condition.'

---

[20] EN para 60.

[21] EQA 2010, s 13(2).

[22] See further **3.83**.

[23] If authority for this proposition is needed, it can be found in *Clymo v Wandsworth London Borough Council* [1989] ICR 250, EAT. However, the EAT concluded (at 271) that the principles to be derived from the ECJ case law did not differ fundamentally from those which fell to be derived from the relevant UK case law. The case contains a useful exposition of the case law as it stood at that time.

[24] *Hardy & Hansons plc v Lax* [2005] ICR 1565, CA.

[25] [1989] ICR 179 at 191.

3.10 In *Allonby v Accrington and Rossendale College*,[26] Sedley LJ, with whose judgment Gage J expressly agreed, said this in relation to a claim of indirect discrimination on the ground of sex:

'Once a finding of a condition having a disparate and adverse impact on women had been made, what was required was at the minimum a critical evaluation of whether the college's reasons demonstrated a real need to dismiss the applicant; if there was such a need, consideration of the seriousness of the disparate impact of the dismissal on women including the applicant; and an evaluation of whether the former were sufficient to outweigh the latter.'

3.11 However, the litmus test here is surely still that of the ECJ in *Bilka-Kaufhaus GmbH v Weber von Hartz*:[27]

'If the national court finds that the measures chosen by Bilka correspond to *a real need on the part of the undertaking, are appropriate with a view to achieving the objectives pursued and are necessary to that end*, the fact that the measures affect a far greater number of women than men is not sufficient to show that they constitute an infringement of article 119.' (Emphasis added).

Positive discrimination and disabled persons

3.12 If a claimant is not disabled, but claims that he or she has been discriminated against because of the protected characteristic of disability, then there will be no direct discrimination for that reason if the only basis for claiming that there has been such discrimination is that the alleged discriminator has treated (or does treat or would treat) disabled persons more favourably than the alleged discriminator treats the claimant.[28] This was already reasonably clear as a result of the decision of the House of Lords in *Archibald v Fife Council*.[29]

Special treatment in connection with pregnancy or childbirth

3.13 There will be no unlawful discrimination against a man purely because of special treatment afforded to a woman in connection with pregnancy or childbirth.[30] As the Explanatory Notes put it, 'men cannot claim privileges for women connected with pregnancy or childbirth'.[31]

---

[26]   [2001] ICR 1189 at 1201.
[27]   [1987] ICR 110 at 126 (para 7).
[28]   EQA 2010, s 13(3).
[29]   [2004] ICR 954.
[30]   EQA 2010, s 13(6)(b).
[31]   EN para 62.

Clarification of definition of direct discrimination

Breastfeeding

3.14 If the protected characteristic in issue is sex, then, for the purposes of cases other than those concerning work, it will constitute direct discrimination against a woman because of her sex if she is treated less favourably than others are or would be treated 'because she is breastfeeding' a baby who is more than 6 months old.[32]

Segregation of persons of different races

3.15 Racial segregation will always be discriminatory.[33]

Discrimination because of marriage or civil partnership

3.16 A claim of discrimination against a person because of marriage or civil partnership in respect of work can succeed only if the claimant has the protected characteristic of being married or in a civil partnership.[34]

Changes made by the new definition of discrimination

3.17 The Explanatory Notes contain this statement of the effect of the new definition of direct discrimination:

> '[Section 13 of the EQA 2010] replaces the definitions of direct discrimination in previous legislation and is designed to provide a more uniform approach by removing the former specific requirement for the victim of the discrimination to have one of the protected characteristics of age, disability, gender reassignment and sex. Accordingly, it brings the position in relation to these protected characteristics into line with that for race, sexual orientation and religion or belief in the previous legislation.'

Clarification in the prior case law

3.18 Unreasonable behaviour against a person who has a protected characteristic will not necessarily be discriminatory.[35] Strictly speaking, the fact that the employer has acted unreasonably is irrelevant.[36]

3.19 The question of whether or not there has been unlawful discrimination is objective in the sense that the motive of the alleged discriminator is irrelevant.[37]

---

[32]   EQA 2010, ss 13(6)(a), 13(7), 13(8) and 17.
[33]   EQA 2010, s 13(5); EN para 62.
[34]   EQA 2010, s 13(4).
[35]   *Glasgow City Council v Zafar* [1998] ICR 120, HL.
[36]   Ibid.
[37]   *R (E) v Governing Body of JFS* [2009] UKSC 15, [2010] 2 WLR 153.

Direct discrimination because of a protected characteristic can never be justified unless there is a specific provision to that effect in the EQA 2010.[38]

COMBINED DISCRIMINATION: DUAL CHARACTERISTICS

Introduction

3.20 In the Government's view:

'It is increasingly recognised that some people can experience particular disadvantage because of a combination of protected characteristics. For example, black women, or men of a particular religion, can face discrimination and disadvantage because of stereotyped attitudes or prejudice relating to particular combinations of protected characteristics. This type of discrimination is known as *multiple discrimination*.'[39]

The Bill as originally published did not contain any provision providing protection from 'multiple discrimination' – what the Government described as 'intersectional multiple discrimination based on a combination of two protected characteristics'.[40] The concept of combined discrimination was introduced into the Bill in the House of Commons at the Committee stage following public consultation.[41] It underwent further amendments upon Report.

3.21 The pre-existing law required a claimant to bring separate claims: for example, under the race, sex or religious discrimination provisions.[42] Such claims entail problems of proof or in establishing the reality of multiple discrimination. For example, a black woman denied promotion because she is a black woman would have to bring separate claims of race and sex discrimination. She could not simply compare herself with the actual or hypothetical treatment of a white man. She would have to compare her treatment as a woman with a comparable man and then compare her treatment as a black person with that of a comparable white person. She might not succeed in either claim if her employer could show that black men and white women were not discriminated against. Her treatment would not be because of race or sex alone.[43]

---

38 *Amnesty International v Ahmed* [2009] ICR 1450, EAT.
39 Government Equalities Office, 2009d: para 2.2.
40 Government Equalities Office, 2009d.
41 See House of Commons Public Bill Committee on the Equality Bill, Session 2008–09, cols 682–686 (2 July 2009). See also: Keter, 2009a: 21–23.
42 *Bahl v The Law Society* [2003] IRLR 640, EAT; [2004] IRLR 799, CA.
43 Government Equalities Office, 2009d: para 2.4.

Multiple discrimination

3.22 The Government described 'multiple discrimination' as occurring when a person is treated less favourably because of more than one of the protected characteristics.[44] Multiple discrimination can arise in a number of ways. First, a person might be treated less favourably because of more than one protected characteristic, but where each form of discrimination occurs separately. Secondly, a person might be treated less favourably on the same occasion because of more than one protected characteristic, but where the two forms of discrimination are not related to each other. The Government described this as 'additive discrimination', as where a lesbian person experiences both homophobia and sexist bullying from her employer during the same incident. In both cases, the pre-existing law provided a remedy.

3.23 However, the discrimination complained of might involve more than one protected characteristic where it is the unique and completely inseparable combination of the characteristics that results in the discrimination. The Government provided the following examples:

> 'An older woman applies for a job as a driving instructor. She is unsuccessful in her application and when she asks for feedback she is told that she was not appointed to the job because it is not considered a suitable job for an older woman. The driving school advises her that they don't think she would have the strength and agility needed to grab the steering wheel or be able to brake quickly. She is told that she would have been appointed had she been an older man or a younger woman.'[45]

> 'A bus driver does not allow a Muslim man onto her bus, claiming that he could be a "terrorist". While it might not be possible for the man to demonstrate less favourable treatment because of either of the protected characteristics of religion or belief or sex if considered separately, a multiple discrimination claim will allow him to show that the reason for his treatment was the specific combination of being a man and a Muslim, which resulted in him being stereotyped as a potential terrorist.'[46]

The Government termed this 'intersectional multiple discrimination'. Whether the pre-existing law provided a remedy in these situations is more problematic.

Section 14

3.24 The problem of combined discrimination is now dealt with by EQA 2010, s 14.[47] A person (A) discriminates against another (B) if, because of a combination of two relevant protected characteristics, A treats B less favourably than A treats or would treat a person who does not share either of

---

44   Government Equalities Office, 2009d: para 3.4.
45   Government Equalities Office, 2009d: para 3.6.
46   Government Equalities Office, 2009d: para 3.12; EN para 68.
47   As to how s 14 will work in practice, see Government Equalities Office, 2009d: chapter 5.

those characteristics.[48] The relevant protected characteristics are age; disability; gender reassignment; race; religion or belief; sex; and sexual orientation.[49]

3.25 The Explanatory Notes suggest that s 14 provides for the discrimination prohibited by the Act to include direct discrimination because of a combination of two protected characteristics.[50] The protected characteristics of marriage and civil partnership, or pregnancy and maternity, cannot be used in combination with another protected characteristic to establish combined discrimination. The Government explains that claims involving pregnancy and maternity do not require a comparator. In its view it is difficult to see how pregnancy and maternity could be included in a multiple discrimination claim in combination with another characteristic which does require a comparator.[51] Equally, it considered that there was no evidence that pregnancy and maternity, or marriage and civil partnership, when combined with any other characteristic, caused problems in practice that could not be addressed as a single strand discrimination claim.[52]

The limits of section 14

3.26 This new form of combined discrimination based upon dual characteristics can arise only in a case of direct discrimination.[53] It does not extend to indirect discrimination, to harassment or to victimisation. The claimant must also be able to demonstrate that the less favourable treatment occurred because of the combination of characteristics alleged.[54] It is also clear that this is a 'combined discrimination' measure – involving no more that two protected characteristics intersecting – rather than a 'multiple discrimination' provision. The Government did not consider that the case was made out for combining three of more protected characteristics in a multiple discrimination claim.[55]

Section 14 comparators

3.27 Direct discrimination based upon dual characteristics will continue to require the identification of an actual or hypothetical comparator who does not share the protected characteristics of the claimant, but whose circumstances are not materially different from those of the claimant.[56] The Government suggests that the comparator would be someone who does not have either of the protected characteristics relied upon in combination. For example, if a 50-year-old man claims he was discriminated against because he is an older

---

48   EQA 2010, s 14(1).
49   EQA 2010, s 14(2).
50   EN para 64.
51   Government Equalities Office, 2009d: para 4.3.
52   Government Equalities Office, 2009d: para 4.3.
53   Government Equalities Office, 2009d: paras 4.1 and 4.5–4.6.
54   Government Equalities Office, 2009d: para 4.7.
55   Government Equalities Office, 2009d: paras 4.9–4.10.
56   Government Equalities Office, 2009d: paras 4.14–4.15.

disabled person, the comparator would be an actual or hypothetical non-disabled younger person in comparable circumstances.[57]

3.28 That this will often work tolerably well in practice is illustrated by a further example:

> 'A black woman is passed over for promotion to work on reception because her employer thinks black women do not perform well in customer service roles. Because the employer can point to a white woman and a black man who have equivalent qualifications and experience and who have been appointed to the role in question, the woman needs to be able to compare her treatment on grounds of race and sex combined to demonstrate that she has been subjected to less favourable treatment because of her employer's prejudice against black women.'[58]

Nevertheless, in many cases of combined discrimination it may be difficult to find an actual comparator whose circumstances are comparable but who does not possess either of the protected characteristics being relied upon. In such cases, tribunals and courts will need to construct a hypothetical comparator.[59]

Section 14 and single strand discrimination

3.29 In order to establish a contravention of the Act,[60] B need not show that A's treatment of B is direct discrimination[61] because of each of the characteristics in the combination (taken separately).[62] Thus, in order to bring a successful claim, the claimant must show that the direct discrimination (less favourable treatment) was because of the combination alleged. The comparison is with how a person who does not share either of the characteristics in the combination is or would be treated.[63] The claimant does not have to show that a claim of direct discrimination in respect of each protected characteristic would have been successful if brought separately.[64]

3.30 It is thus not implied that a claim in relation to each characteristic included in the combination would be successful if brought separately. The Government explains that, for example:

> 'if a person claims that they were discriminated against because of a combination of disability and sex, the allegedly less favourable treatment they received would have to be prohibited in respect of each of the protected characteristics of disability and sex. The claimant must be able to demonstrate that the reason for the treatment was the combination of the protected characteristic of disability and

---

57   Government Equalities Office, 2009d: paras 4.16.
58   Government Equalities Office, 2009d: 19; EN para 68.
59   Government Equalities Office, 2009d: para 4.17.
60   By virtue of EQA 2010, s 14(1).
61   That is, by virtue of EQA 2010, s 13 (see s 14(7)).
62   EQA 2010, s 14(3).
63   EN para 65.
64   EN para 66.

sex together, but need not be able to succeed if the claims were brought as disability and sex discrimination separately.'[65]

3.31 Equally, a claimant can bring separate direct discrimination claims based upon individual protected characteristics and based upon dual discrimination simultaneously (including more than one dual discrimination claim). Section 14 does not prevent single strand claims being brought alongside multiple discrimination claims.[66] If an individual wishes to bring a claim of multiple discrimination, he or she would not be prevented from also bringing separate claims for each of the protected characteristics included in the combined claim. The Government concluded that to prevent claimants from bringing single strand claims alongside multiple discrimination claims would be neither compatible with EU law nor appropriate in policy terms.

3.32 Thus, a claimant who believes that they have experienced age and gender reassignment discrimination – but is unsure whether it is a matter of multiple discrimination or single strand discrimination – would be able to bring claims for age discrimination, gender reassignment discrimination and combined discrimination in tandem. This is likely to lead to an increase in the number of claims, although not necessarily more than a marginal increase in hearing times.[67] It is estimated that 7.5 per cent of existing discrimination cases would now include a claim for multiple discrimination, while there might be an increase of 10 per cent in new cases.[68] At the same time, given the uncertainty surrounding the new provision, the propensity for settlement of combined discrimination cases might be 20 per cent higher.[69]

Section 14 and exceptions or justifications

3.33 However, B cannot establish a contravention of the Act[70] if, in reliance on another provision of the Act or any other enactment, A shows that A's treatment of B is not direct discrimination[71] because of either or both of the characteristics in the combination.[72] Therefore, a claim of dual discrimination will not succeed where an exception or justification applies to the treatment in respect of either of the relevant protected characteristics. For example, in the context of work, an occupational requirement might render any otherwise direct discrimination lawful.[73]

3.34 What this means is that the treatment the person experienced must be prohibited for each protected characteristic individually. If another provision of the EQA 2010 has the effect that the less favourable treatment contended for is

---

65   Government Equalities Office, 2009d: para 4.7.
66   Government Equalities Office, 2009d: paras 4.11–4.13.
67   Government Equalities Office, 2009d: paras 4.13, 5.6–5.7 and Annex C (Impact Assessment).
68   Government Equalities Office, 2009d: paras 5.17–5.18.
69   Government Equalities Office, 2009d: para 5.20.
70   By virtue of EQA 2010, s 14(1).
71   That is, by virtue of EQA 2010, s 13 (see s 14(7)).
72   EQA 2010, s 14(4).
73   EN para 65. See EQA 2010, Sch 9.

actually lawful in relation to either of the characteristics in the combination, then the less favourable treatment would not be unlawful under the multiple discrimination provision.[74] For example, an exception or justification might apply. The Government illustrates the point in this way:

'if a man who is denied a job in a domestic violence refuge alleges this denial is because he is a disabled man, but in fact it is because being a woman is an occupational requirement for the post, a multiple discrimination claim combining sex and disability would not succeed.'

On these facts, there would be no disability discrimination and the sex discrimination would not be unlawful. Therefore, there could be no unlawful combined discrimination.

3.35 A further example arises in this way:

'A black woman is charged £100 for insurance. As white men are only charged £50 for the same insurance, she alleges this is multiple discrimination because of the combination of sex and race. By pointing to a white woman who also pays £100, or a black man who pays £50, the insurance company is able to demonstrate that the difference in premium is entirely due to sex, not race. Insurance companies can lawfully set different premiums for women and men.'

Thus, provided the exception applies in this case, the claim of multiple discrimination cannot succeed. The less favourable treatment is because of sex and an exception makes the sex discrimination lawful.[75]

3.36 Also excluded from the scope of s 14 are circumstances involving disability discrimination in schools. The section does not apply to a combination of characteristics that includes disability in circumstances where, if a claim of direct discrimination[76] because of disability were to be brought, it would come within the provisions of the Act that relate to education cases.[77] Disability discrimination claims in education in England are the exclusive preserve of the Health, Education and Social Care Chamber of the First Tier Tribunal (previously the Special Educational Needs and Disability Tribunal).[78] Such claims rely upon the protected characteristic of disability only. They could not also rely upon dual characteristics in combined discrimination (for example, race and disability in combination).[79]

---

[74] Government Equalities Office, 2009d: para 4.8.
[75] Government Equalities Office, 2009d: para 4.8; EN para 68.
[76] That is, by virtue of EQA 2010, s 13 (see s 14(7)).
[77] EQA 2010, ss 14(5) and 116.
[78] In Wales, the Special Educational Needs and Disability Tribunal for Wales; in Scotland, an Additional Support Needs Tribunal for Scotland. The exclusion will also apply to the appeal arrangements for admissions or exclusions decisions. See EQA 2010, s 116 and Sch 17.
[79] See House of Commons Public Bill Committee on the Equality Bill, Session 2008–09, cols 682–686 (2 July 2009), Solicitor-General.

Power to amend section 14

3.37   A Minister of the Crown is empowered to amend s 14 by order so as to make further provision about circumstances in which B can, or in which B cannot, establish a contravention of the Act by virtue of the section. The section might also be amended by these means so as to specify other circumstances in which the section does not apply.[80]

Other considerations

3.38   For the purpose of establishing a contravention of the Act by virtue of s 14 (combined discrimination: dual characteristics), it does not matter whether A has one of the protected characteristics in the combination; or whether A has both.[81] It is no defence to a claim of dual discrimination that the alleged discriminator shares one or both of the protected characteristics with the victim.[82]

3.39   Note that s 23 of the Act provides that on a comparison of cases for the purpose of s 14 (combined discrimination: dual characteristics) there must be no material difference between the circumstances relating to each case.[83] The circumstances relating to a case include a person's abilities if, on a comparison for the purposes of s 14 (combined discrimination: dual characteristics), one of the protected characteristics in the combination is disability.[84]

3.40   The Government believes that the new provision is not unduly complex and will not place an undue burden on business. Nevertheless, it would appear that the Government intends that s 14 will be brought into force in or after April 2011 in order to allow businesses time to prepare for it.[85]

Does section 14 go far enough?

3.41   The Joint Committee on Human Rights welcomed the extension of protection to a combination of two grounds. However, it recorded a view that multiple discrimination should not be limited to two grounds alone, but should relate to an unlimited number of grounds; and that protection should be extended to encompass indirect discrimination and harassment as well as direct discrimination.[86] It expressed its concern that combined discrimination would apply only to direct discrimination and not to other forms of discrimination, such as indirect discrimination and harassment. It also noted with disappointment that maternity, pregnancy, marriage and civil partnership are excluded from the scope of s 14.[87]

---

[80]   EQA 2010, s 14(6).
[81]   EQA 2010, s 24(2).
[82]   EN para 94.
[83]   EQA 2010, s 23(1).
[84]   EQA 2010, s 23(2)(b).
[85]   Government Equalities Office, 2009d: paras 2.6, 5.12–5.14.
[86]   Joint Committee on Human Rights, 2009: para 95.
[87]   Joint Committee on Human Rights, 2009: para 99.

DISCRIMINATION ARISING FROM DISABILITY

Introduction

3.42 In a disability-specific provision, s 15 of the 2010 Act states that a person (A) discriminates against a disabled person (B) if A treats B unfavourably because of something arising in consequence of B's disability, and A cannot show that the treatment is a proportionate means of achieving a legitimate aim.[88] Discrimination arising from disability does not apply if A shows that A did not know, and could not reasonably have been expected to know, that B had the disability.[89]

3.43 The Explanatory Notes suggest that s 15 provides that it is discrimination to treat a disabled person unfavourably not because of the person's disability itself but because of something arising from, or in consequence of, his or her disability, such as the need to take a period of disability-related absence.[90] However, such treatment may be justified if it is a proportionate means of achieving a legitimate aim. Nevertheless, in order to establish discrimination arising from disability, the alleged discriminator must know (or reasonably be expected to know) that the disabled person has a disability.

Disability-related discrimination

3.44 Section 15 is a wholly new provision. It is not to be found in the DDA 1995 (as amended). It is designed to replace the concept of 'disability-related discrimination' found in the earlier Act.

3.45 In the employment provisions of the DDA 1995,[91] a person discriminated against a disabled person if, for a reason which related to the disabled person's disability, the person treated the disabled person less favourably than the person treated (or would treat) others to whom that reason did not (or would not) apply and the person cannot show that the treatment in question was justified.[92] Treatment was justified for this purpose if, but only if, the reason for it was both material to the circumstances of the particular case

---

88 EQA 20101, s 15(1).
89 EQA 2010, s 15(2) disapplying s 15(1) in these circumstances.
90 EN para 69.
91 See Doyle, 2008: section 3.2 (upon which this account draws).
92 See, in the employment context, DDA 1995, s 3A(1). See: *Clark v TDG Ltd t/a Novacold* [1999] IRLR 318, CA; *H J Heinz Co Ltd v Kenrick* [2000] IRLR 144, EAT; *Hammersmith LBC v Farnsworth* [2000] IRLR 691, EAT; *Jones v Post Office* [2001] IRLR 384, CA; *Callagan v Glasgow City Council* [2001] IRLR 724, EAT; *Surrey Police v Marshall* [2002] IRLR 843, EAT; *Murray v Newham CAB Ltd* [2003] IRLR 340, EAT; *Williams v J Walter Thompson Group Ltd* [2005] IRLR 376, CA; *Rothwell v Pelikan Hardcopy Scotland Ltd* [2006] IRLR 24, EAT; *Royal Liverpool Children's NHS Trust v Dunsby* [2006] IRLR 351, EAT; *Taylor v OCS Group Ltd* [2006] IRLR 613, CA; *O'Hanlon v Commissioners for HM Revenue & Customs* [2006] IRLR 840, EAT; *Abbey National plc v Fairbrother* [2007] IRLR 320, EAT; *HM Prison Service v Johnson* [2007] IRLR 951, EAT; *London Borough of Lewisham v Malcolm* [2008] IRLR 700, HL; *Child Support Agency (Dudley) v Truman* [2009] IRLR 277, EAT.

and substantial.[93] However, treatment of a disabled person could not be justified in this way if it amounted to direct discrimination.[94] Moreover, if a person was under a duty to make reasonable adjustments in relation to the disabled person, but failed to comply with that duty, the treatment of the disabled person could not be justified unless it would have been justified even if that duty had been complied with.[95]

3.46   The question which arose under the DDA 1995 was whether the basis of the comparison required by the concept of 'disability-related discrimination' was to be drawn widely or narrowly? This depended upon the interpretation to be placed upon the phrase 'that reason'.[96] Take, for example, a disabled employee who was dismissed for absenteeism, including disability-related absences. With whom should the employee be compared for the purpose of establishing less favourable treatment? One possibility was to compare how the disabled employee had been treated relative to an employee who had been absent from work for the same length of time, but for a reason which was not related to disability. This would reflect the usual expectation in discrimination cases that like should be compared with like. However, under the DDA 1995, disability-related discrimination did not require the comparison to be based upon a consideration of the comparators in relevant circumstances which were the same or not materially different.

Clark v Novacold

3.47   Thus, a second possibility was to compare how the disabled employee (who is unable to perform the functions of his or her job) had been treated in comparison with other employees who were not absent from work at all (that is, who were performing the main functions of their jobs). This focused upon the reason for the treatment (that is, the reason for the dismissal) and not the reason for the absence which led to the dismissal. The disabled employee had been dismissed for absenteeism. Some of those absences were related to his or her disability. Thus the dismissal was for a reason (absenteeism) which related to the disabled person's disability. For the purposes of establishing less favourable treatment, the comparison would then be with others to whom that reason (absenteeism) did not (or would not) apply. Attention would then switch to the employer's justification defence.[97] That was the approach favoured by the Court of Appeal in *Clark v TDG Ltd t/a Novacold* and was the authoritative one in the employment field (and elsewhere in the DDA 1995) over the last decade.[98]

---

93   DDA 1995, s 3A(3).
94   DDA 1995, s 3A(4).
95   DDA 1995, s 3A(6).
96   DDA 1995, s 3A(1)(a).
97   DDA 1995, s 3A(1)(b), subject to the duty to make reasonable adjustments.
98   [1999] IRLR 318, CA. See also DDA 1995, s 20(1) (goods and services); s 21D(1) (public authorities); s 21G(1) (associations); s 24(1) (premises); s 28B(1) (schools); s 28S(1) (further and higher education).

London Borough of Lewisham v Malcolm

3.48 However, in 2008, the House of Lords held that *Novacold* had been wrongly decided. The housing case of *London Borough of Lewisham v Malcolm* concerned a disabled tenant of a local authority.[99] The assumed basis of the case is that the tenant was in breach of his tenancy agreement for a reason that might be said to be related to his disability. The local authority sought to take possession of the rented property. Could the tenant rely upon the concept of disability-related discrimination to defeat the possession proceedings (especially where the justification defence in housing cases was more narrowly defined)? Relying upon *Novacold* he argued that his treatment should be compared with a tenant who was not in breach of the tenancy agreement and who would thus not be the subject of possession proceedings.

3.49 The House of Lords overruled *Novacold*. It held that the correct basis of comparison would be to compare how an actual or hypothetical non-disabled tenant in breach of the tenancy agreement has been (or would be) treated in comparison with the disabled tenant (also in breach). It is widely accepted that the result of *Malcolm* was to render the concept of disability-related discrimination largely ineffective.

Proposals for reform

3.50 At first, the Government proposed to deal with *Malcolm* by replacing the concept of disability-related discrimination via the inclusion of disability as a protected characteristic to which the concept of indirect discrimination would be made available for the first time.[100] This approach would require persons subject to any duty to make reasonable adjustments to discharge that duty before seeking to justify indirect disability discrimination. In the event, while the extension of indirect discrimination to disability cases was widely welcomed, it was not seen as the solution to the problems created by *Malcolm* for disability-related discrimination.[101] There was strong support for returning the law to its pre-*Malcolm* state by abolishing the need for a comparator at all in disability-related discrimination.[102]

3.51 The Government was persuaded by this case.[103] The new s 15 recognises that the concept of disability-related discrimination no longer provides the degree of protection from disability-related discrimination that was intended for disabled people when the DDA 1995 was first enacted. It is aimed at re-establishing 'an appropriate balance between enabling a disabled person to

---

[99] [2008] UKHL 43; [2008] IRLR 700.
[100] Office for Disability Issues, 2008.
[101] See Keter, 2009a: 26–34.
[102] See House of Commons Work and Pensions Committee. 2009a: paras 22–34.
[103] Office for Disability Issues, 2009.

make out a case of experiencing a detriment which arises because of his or her disability, and providing an opportunity for an employer or other person to defend the treatment.'[104]

Section 15 in practice

3.52   Section 15 is not a re-working of the DDA 1995 concept of unjustified disability-related discrimination. It is a considerably simpler test of discrimination. Most notably, it does not require a comparator in order to establish discrimination arising from disability. It focuses upon (1) the way in which the disabled person has been treated, (2) why he or she has been so treated, (3) whether that treatment is unfavourable treatment and (4) whether the treatment is a proportionate means of achieving a legitimate aim. In practice, a disabled person should find it comparatively easier to establish the first three ingredients. Many cases will depend upon whether the respondent to the claim can objectively justify the treatment via the fourth ingredient.

3.53   As originally drafted, the clause that led to s 15 employed the formula 'because of B's disability, the treatment amounts to a detriment'. The intention appeared to be that a disabled person should be enabled to demonstrate 'that they have been subjected to detrimental treatment because of something connected with their disability'.[105] The final wording of s 15 – which focuses upon unfavourable treatment 'because of something arising in consequence of B's disability' – seems more sure-footed in achieving the Government's intention.[106]

3.54   The Explanatory Notes give the following examples of how the new concept of 'discrimination arising from disability' might work in practice:

- An employee with a visual impairment is dismissed because he cannot do as much work as a non-disabled colleague. If the employer sought to justify the dismissal, he would need to show that it was a proportionate means of achieving a legitimate aim.

- The licensee of a pub refuses to serve a person who has cerebral palsy because she believes that he is drunk as he has slurred speech. However, the slurred speech is a consequence of his impairment. If the licensee is able to show that she did not know, and could not reasonably have been expected to know, that the customer was disabled, she has not subjected him to discrimination arising from his disability.

- However, in the example above, if a reasonable person would have known that the behaviour was due to a disability, the licensee would have

---

[104]   EN para 70.

[105]   See House of Commons Public Bill Committee on the Equality Bill, Session 2008–09, col 275 (17 June 2009), Solicitor-General.

[106]   It appears to meet the concerns of the Joint Committee on Human Rights, 2009: paras 120–124.

subjected the customer to discrimination arising from his disability, unless she could show that ejecting him was a proportionate means of achieving a legitimate aim.[107]

Knowledge

3.55 Somewhat controversially, what the alleged discriminator knew at the time of the alleged discrimination will be a key feature of this discrimination concept. Knowledge had not been relevant in disability-related discrimination. Discrimination arising from disability does not apply if the alleged discriminator shows that it did not know, and could not reasonably have been expected to know, that the disabled person had the disability.

3.56 The Government's stated aim here 'is to achieve a balance between the right of the disabled person to keep their disability confidential, and the right of the duty holder not to be held liable for discrimination on the basis of a disability of which the duty holder was not aware and had no reason to be aware.'[108] It specifically rejected the notion that the question of knowledge might be considered as part of the justification defence. Instead, the question of knowledge has to be considered as part of establishing whether there has been unfavourable treatment of the disabled person because of something arising from the person's disability.[109]

3.57 During debate, the minister stated that:

'As a matter of principle, the [Act] does not place an onus on a disabled person to make a declaration about their [disability], and neither does it place an onus on those with duties under the [Act] to make inquiries of a disabled person, because we think that it is for the disabled person to decide whether or not to declare the [disability]. Similarly, we think it inappropriate to require a person to make inquiries to determine whether somebody is disabled, because it would place undue burdens on those with duties under the [Act].'[110]

3.58 However, the Joint Committee on Human Rights considered that the knowledge requirement should be deemed to be satisfied when an employer or service provider failed to ask a claimant whether they had a disability when it was reasonable to do so. This would ensure that employers and service providers could not rely upon deliberate ignorance or a policy of not asking appropriate questions.[111] Nevertheless, there is no such deeming provision on the face of the Act.

---

[107] EN para 70.
[108] Office for Disability Issues, 2009: 17–18.
[109] Office for Disability Issues, 2009: 17–18.
[110] See House of Commons Public Bill Committee on the Equality Bill, Session 2008–09, col 276 (16 June 2009), Solicitor-General.
[111] Joint Committee on Human Rights, 2009: paras 132–135.

GENDER REASSIGNMENT DISCRIMINATION: ABSENCE FROM WORK

3.59 Section 16 of the Act applies to gender reassignment discrimination in cases of absence from work. The section has effect for the purposes of the application of Part 5 of the Act (work) to the protected characteristic of gender reassignment.[112]

3.60 A person (A) discriminates against a transsexual person (B) if, in relation to an absence of B's that is because of gender reassignment, A treats B less favourably than A would treat B if B's absence was because of sickness or injury, or B's absence was for some other reason and it is not reasonable for B to be treated less favourably.[113] A person's absence is because of gender reassignment if it is because the person is proposing to undergo, is undergoing or has undergone a process (or part of a process) for the purpose of reassigning the person's sex by changing physiological or other attributes of sex.[114]

3.61 The Explanatory Notes explain that s 16 provides for discrimination against transsexual people where they are treated less favourably for being absent from work because they propose to undergo (are undergoing or have undergone) gender reassignment than they would be treated if they were absent because they were ill or injured. Transsexual people are also discriminated against in relation to absences relating to their gender reassignment if they are treated less favourably than they would be treated for absence for reasons other than sickness or injury and it is unreasonable to treat them less favourably.[115]

3.62 The section is designed to replicate the effect of a similar provision in the Sex Discrimination Act 1975,[116] although with less complex drafting. For example, if a female to male transsexual person takes time off work to receive hormone treatment as part of his gender reassignment, his employer cannot discriminate against him because of his absence from work for this purpose.[117] However, as before, the protection afforded to transsexual people relies upon a comparative test of less favourable treatment: how has the transsexual person been treated relative to others? The provision does not afford absolute protection to transsexual people from absence-related discrimination.

---

[112] EQA 2010, s 16(1). The pre-existing case law of importance is: *Croft v Royal Mail Group plc* [2003] IRLR 592, CA; *A v Chief Constable of West Yorkshire Police* [2004] IRLR 573, HL.

[113] EQA 2010, s 16(2).

[114] EQA 2010, ss 7(1) and 16(3).

[115] EN para 71.

[116] Sex Discrimination Act 1975, s 2A inserted by the Sex Discrimination (Gender Reassignment) Regulations 1999, SI 1999/1102, from 1 May 1999 as a result of *P v S and Cornwall County Council* [1996] IRLR 347 (ECJ) ruling that transsexual discrimination was covered by the Equal Treatment Directive. See also *Chessington World of Adventures Ltd v Reed* [1997] IRLR 556, EAT and *Croft v Royal Mail Group plc* [2003] IRLR 592, CA.

[117] EN para 72.

PREGNANCY AND MATERNITY DISCRIMINATION

Non-work cases

3.63 Section 17 has effect for the purposes of the application to the protected characteristic of pregnancy and maternity of (a) Part 3 (services and public functions); (b) Part 4 (premises); (c) Part 6 (education); and (d) Part 7 (associations).[118] The section defines what it means to discriminate because of a woman's pregnancy or maternity, as distinct from her gender, in specified situations in a non-work-related context.[119] It is designed to replace and to extend the provisions in s 3B of the Sex Discrimination Act 1975 (discrimination on the ground of pregnancy or maternity leave in relation to goods, facilities, services or premises).[120]

3.64 In this context, a person (A) discriminates against a woman if A treats her unfavourably because of a pregnancy of hers.[121] A person (A) also discriminates against a woman if, in the period of 26 weeks beginning with the day on which she gives birth,[122] A treats her unfavourably because she has given birth.[123] The reference to treating a woman unfavourably because she has given birth includes, in particular, a reference to treating her unfavourably because she is breastfeeding.[124]

3.65 The provisions on direct sex discrimination[125] do not apply to anything done in relation to a woman insofar as it is for the reason of her pregnancy[126] or it is done in the 26 weeks following the birth of her child and because she has given birth.[127]

3.66 As the Explanatory Notes explain, s 17 defines what it means to discriminate because of a woman's pregnancy or maternity, as distinct from her sex, in specified situations outside work.[128] The section protects a woman from discrimination because of her current or a previous pregnancy, and it also protects her from maternity discrimination. This includes treating her less

---

[118] EQA 2010, s 17(1). As originally drafted, what is now s 17(1)(c) provided an exemption in schools. That was removed at Committee stage in the House of Lords.

[119] See Keter, 2009a: 34.

[120] Inserted by SI 2008/963 with effect from April 2008 in order to implement Council Directive 2004/113/EC which implements the principle of equal treatment between men and women in the access to, and supply of, goods and services. See Keter, 2009a: 36.

[121] EQA 2010, s 17(2).

[122] The day on which a woman gives birth is the day on which (a) she gives birth to a living child, or (b) she gives birth to a dead child (more than 24 weeks of the pregnancy having passed): EQA 2010, s 17(5). Note the contrast with the protected period of 52 weeks under EQA 2010, s 18 below; although after the 26 weeks the woman should be able to rely upon direct and/or indirect sex discrimination rather than pregnancy and maternity discrimination.

[123] EQA 2010, s 17(3).

[124] EQA 2010, s 17(4).

[125] EQA 2010, s 13 as it applies to the protected characteristic of sex.

[126] The reason mentioned in EQA 2010, s 17(2).

[127] That is, in the period and for the reason mentioned in EQA 2010, s 17(3). See EQA 2010, ss 13(8) and 17(6).

[128] EN para 73.

favourably because she is breastfeeding, for 26 weeks after giving birth. For example, a café owner must not ask a woman to leave his café because she is breastfeeding her baby; a shopkeeper must not refuse to sell cigarettes to a woman because she is pregnant.[129] Section 17 provides that pregnancy or maternity discrimination as defined cannot be treated as sex discrimination.

3.67 The provision is designed to replicate the effect of similar provisions in the Sex Discrimination Act 1975 and to extend the protection to cover discrimination in relation to public functions, further and higher education, and to associations, where no such protection previously existed.[130] For example, this might concern the way a pregnant woman is treated when remanded in custody at a police station.[131] The section also extends explicit protection against pregnancy discrimination to further and higher education and to associations. Previously these were areas where there may have been only implicit protection provided by the Sex Discrimination Act 1975.[132] It also extends the same protection to school pupils. For the first time the rights of breastfeeding mothers in non-work situations is directly addressed.

Work cases

3.68 Section 18 has effect for the purposes of the application of Part 5 (work) to the protected characteristic of pregnancy and maternity.[133] The section defines what it means to discriminate in the workplace because of a woman's pregnancy or pregnancy-related illness, or because she takes or tries to take maternity leave.[134] Protection from discrimination in this context extends for the period of the pregnancy and any statutory maternity leave to which the women is entitled. During this period, the woman cannot rely upon sex discrimination.

3.69 A person (A) discriminates against a woman if, in the protected period in relation to a pregnancy of hers, A treats her unfavourably (a) because of the pregnancy, or (b) because of illness suffered by her as a result of it.[135] For this purpose, if the treatment of a woman is in implementation of a decision taken in the protected period, the treatment is to be regarded as occurring in that period (even if the implementation is not until after the end of that period).[136] In relation to a woman's pregnancy, the protected period begins when the pregnancy begins. It ends at the end of the additional maternity leave period[137] or (if earlier) when she returns to work after the pregnancy (if she has the right

---

[129] EN para 74.
[130] EN para 74.
[131] See Keter, 2009a: 34.
[132] See Keter, 2009a: 34.
[133] EQA 2010, s 18(1).
[134] EN para 75. The reference to maternity leave means compulsory maternity leave or ordinary maternity leave or additional maternity leave: EQA 2010, s 213(2).
[135] EQA 20101, s 18(2).
[136] EQA 2010, s 18(5).
[137] That is, in exercise of the right to additional maternity leave (of 26 weeks in addition to ordinary maternity leave) conferred by Employment Rights Act 1996, s 73(1) and (2): EQA

to ordinary and additional maternity leave).[138] If she does not have that right, it ends at the end of the period of 2 weeks beginning with the end of the pregnancy.[139]

3.70 A person (A) also discriminates against a woman if A treats her unfavourably because she is on compulsory maternity leave.[140] A person (A) further discriminates against a woman if A treats her unfavourably because she is exercising or seeking to exercise (or has exercised or sought to exercise) the right to ordinary maternity leave or additional maternity leave.[141]

3.71 For example, an employer must not demote or dismiss an employee, or deny her training or promotion opportunities, because she is pregnant or on maternity leave. An employer must not take into account an employee's period of absence due to pregnancy-related illness when making a decision about her employment.[142]

3.72 Section 13 in respect of direct discrimination, so far as relating to sex discrimination, does not apply to treatment of a woman insofar as it is in the protected period in relation to her and is (a) because of the pregnancy, or (b) because of illness suffered by her as a result of it.[143] Section 13 will also not apply in this way if the treatment is because the woman is on compulsory maternity leave or because she is exercising or seeking to exercise (or has exercised or sought to exercise) the right to ordinary or additional maternity leave.[144]

3.73 These provisions are designed to replicate the effect of similar provisions in the Sex Discrimination Act 1975.[145] Discrimination on the grounds of pregnancy has long been recognised as a species of sex discrimination. This was

---

2010, s 213(6)–(8). See generally Maternity and Parental Leave etc Regulations 1999, SI 1999/3312; Maternity and Parental Leave (Amendment) Regulations 2002, SI 2002/2789.

[138] EQA 2010, s 18(6)(a).

[139] EQA 2010, s 18(6)(b).

[140] EQA 2010, s 18(3). The reference to compulsory maternity leave means that the woman is absent from work (for the compulsory period of two weeks) because she satisfied the conditions prescribed for the purposes of Employment Rights Act 1996, s 72(1): EQA 2010, s 213(3). See generally Maternity and Parental Leave etc Regulations 1999, SI 1999/3312; Maternity and Parental Leave (Amendment) Regulations 2002, SI 2002/2789.

[141] EQA 2010, s 18(4). The reference to ordinary maternity leave is a reference to the right to 26 weeks leave conferred by Employment Rights Act 1996, s 71(1): EQA 2010, s 213(4)–(5). The reference to additional maternity leave is a reference to the right conferred by Employment Rights Act 1996, s 73(1) and (2): EQA 2010, s 213(6)–(8). See generally Maternity and Parental Leave etc Regulations 1999, SI 1999/3312; Maternity and Parental Leave (Amendment) Regulations 2002, SI 2002/2789.

[142] EN para 76.

[143] EQA 2010, ss 13(8) and 18(7)(a).

[144] EQA 2010, ss 13(8) and 18(7)(b).

[145] EN para 76. See: *Webb v EMO Air Cargo (UK) Ltd* [1993] IRLR 27, HL and [1995] IRLR 645, HL; *O'Neill v Governors of St Thomas More Roman Catholic Voluntary Aided Upper School* [1996] IRLR 372, EAT; *British Telecommunications plc v Roberts* [1996] IRLR 601, EAT; *Iske v P & O European Ferries (Dover) Ltd* [1997] IRLR 401, EAT; *Day v T Pickles Farms Ltd* [1999] IRLR 217, EAT; *Abbey National plc v Formoso* [1999] IRLR 222, EAT; *GUS*

explicitly recognised by amendments to the Sex Discrimination Act 1975 in 2005 so as to implement the EU Equal Treatment Directive 2002/73.[146] The need for any form of comparator was removed in 2008.[147] During the protected period, less favourable treatment on the ground of a woman's pregnancy (or on the ground that the woman exercises or has exercised a statutory right to maternity leave) is unlawful discrimination. The duration of the protected period relates to the period of maternity leave taken. All female employees are now entitled to 52 weeks maternity leave regardless of service. During this period the woman must rely upon pregnancy and maternity discrimination rather than sex discrimination.[148]

INDIRECT DISCRIMINATION

Introduction

3.74 The term 'indirect discrimination' is defined by s 19 of the EQA 2010. The wording of that section is in one sense beguilingly simple. It explains the concept in plain language. However, the concepts behind the language used can be difficult to apply in practice. Certainly some of the words need to be considered particularly carefully.

3.75 The definition in s 19(1) is this: 'A person (A) discriminates against another (B) if A applies to B a provision, criterion or practice which is discriminatory in relation to a relevant protected characteristic of B's'.

3.76 The words 'provision, criterion or practice' are used because they appear in the EU Directives which are implemented by the EQA 2010. For example, Directive 2006/54/EC (which concerns sex discrimination) contains this definition of indirect discrimination. It occurs:

> 'where an apparently neutral *provision, criterion or practice* would put persons of one sex at a particular disadvantage compared with persons of the other sex, unless that provision, criterion or practice is objectively justified by a legitimate aim, and the means of achieving that aim are appropriate and necessary'.[149]

3.77 The latter part of the definition is implemented in the UK by s 19(2) of the EQA 2010, which must be read with s 19(3). Those subsections provide:

> '(2) For the purposes of subsection (1), a provision, criterion or practice is discriminatory in relation to a relevant protected characteristic of B's if -

Home Shopping Ltd v Green [2001] IRLR 75, EAT; *Hardman v Mallon* [2002] IRLR 516, EAT; *Hoyland v Asda Stores Ltd* [2005] IRLR 438, EAT; *Fletcher v Blackpool Fylde & Wyre Hospitals NHS Trust* [2005] IRLR 689, EAT.

146 Sex Discrimination Act 1975, s 3A added by SI 2005/2467 from 1 October 2005.

147 As a result of the challenge in *EOC v Secretary of State for Trade and Industry* [2007] EWHC 483 (Admin), [2007] IRLR 327, QBD. See SI 2008/656 (from 6 April 2008).

148 See Keter, 2009a: 35–36.

149 Directive 2006/54/EC, Art 2(1)(b) (emphasis added).

      (a)   A applies, or would apply, it to persons with whom B does not share the characteristic,

      (b)   it puts, or would put, persons with whom B shares the characteristic at a particular disadvantage when compared with persons with whom B does not share it,

      (c)   it puts, or would put, B at that disadvantage, and

      (d)   A cannot show it to be a proportionate means of achieving a legitimate aim.

  (3)   The relevant protected characteristics are –

age;

disability;

gender reassignment;

marriage and civil partnership;

race;

religion or belief;

sex;

sexual orientation.'

What is a provision, criterion or practice?

3.78 The words 'provision, criterion or practice' are not defined by the EQA 2010. A 'provision' must mean a requirement or condition,[150] which is the wording which was originally used in the legislation which prohibited discrimination in the UK.[151] A provision need not be applied to others, and the application of a provision may even be an isolated event.[152] A condition or requirement that a person be, for example, white-skinned is direct rather than indirect discrimination.[153]

3.79 The word 'criterion' is defined by the Oxford English Dictionary as 'a test, principle, rule, canon or standard, by which anything is judged or estimated'.[154] It is accordingly something less than a 'requirement or condition'. Equally, a 'practice' is not a requirement or condition. The words 'provision, criterion or practice' are used in the alternative and not cumulatively.[155]

How is a 'particular disadvantage' proved?

3.80 It will usually be helpful to have some statistical evidence of the disproportionate impact of a provision, criterion or practice on the group of persons with whom the claimant shares the characteristic in question. Under the original provisions (such as s 1(1)(b) of the SDA 1975) there was a need to prove that the proportion of persons in the group of which the claimant formed a part, which could in practice comply with a requirement or condition,

---

[150] *British Airways plc v Starmer* [2005] IRLR 862, EAT, para 17.1.
[151] See for example SDA 1975, s 1(1)(b).
[152] *British Airways plc v Starmer* [2005] IRLR 862, EAT, para 18.
[153] *Cf James v Eastleigh Borough Council* [1990] ICR 554.
[154] Oxford English Dictionary, 2nd ed, 1989, meaning b.
[155] *British Airways plc v Starmer* [2005] IRLR 862, EAT, para 17.1.

was 'considerably smaller' than the proportion of persons in a group which was chosen for comparison purposes (in that case, it was men). Statistical evidence was usually necessary. However, statistical evidence is not now strictly necessary following the EQA 2010.

3.81 Nevertheless, it will be necessary to choose a group for comparison purposes when considering whether there is a 'particular disadvantage' within the meaning of EQA 2010, s 19(2)(b). A good illustration of the application of this process in practice is the case of *Price v Civil Service Commission*,[156] which concerned the practice of requiring all job applicants for a particular post to be at least 17-and-a-half years old, but below the age of 28. The claimant was aged 35 and argued that the requirement was indirectly discriminatory. She contended that the proportion of women who could comply with it was considerably smaller than the proportion of men who could comply with it. This was because many women were having and bringing up children between those ages. In addition, the requirement was not objectively justified. The employer argued that the comparison should be between all men and women, so that (of course) the requirement was not indirectly discriminatory against women. The EAT rejected this argument. It ruled that there was a 'good deal in the present case for saying that the appropriate "pool" is that of qualified men and qualified women as the case may be'.[157]

3.82 In any event, there is no need to take into account only statistical evidence when such evidence is put before the court or tribunal.[158] On the other hand, such evidence as is put before the court or tribunal should not itself be tainted by discrimination.[159]

What is a proportionate means of achieving a legitimate aim?

3.83 A party defending a claim of indirect discrimination within the meaning of s 19 of the EQA 2010 would do so successfully in the event of satisfying the court or tribunal that the application of the provision, criterion or practice in question constituted a proportionate means of achieving a legitimate aim. The question of whether direct age discrimination is justified is determined by applying the same test. Thus, the factors and case law to which reference is made above in that context will be relevant when deciding whether there was unlawful indirect discrimination.[160]

---

[156] [1978] ICR 27, EAT.
[157] *Ibid*, 32. The matter was remitted to a freshly-constituted industrial tribunal, and that issue was subsequently conceded by the employer: see [1978] IRLR 3.
[158] *British Airways plc v Starmer* [2005] IRLR 862, para 27.
[159] *R v Secretary of State for Education ex parte Schaffter* [1987] IRLR 53, DC.
[160] See **3.8–3.11** for a short discussion about the matter and some of the applicable case-law.

Explanatory Notes examples

3.84 Two helpful examples of what would constitute indirect discrimination are given in the Explanatory Notes:[161]

> 'A woman is forced to leave her job because her employer operates a practice that staff must work in a shift pattern which she is unable to comply with because she needs to look after her children at particular times of day, and no allowances are made because of those needs. This would put women (who are shown to be more likely to be responsible for childcare) at a disadvantage, and the employer will have indirectly discriminated against the woman unless the practice can be justified.
>
> An observant Jewish engineer who is seeking an advanced diploma decides (even though he is sufficiently qualified to do so) not to apply to a specialist training company because it invariably undertakes the selection exercises for the relevant course on Saturdays. The company will have indirectly discriminated against the engineer unless the practice can be justified.'

ADJUSTMENTS FOR DISABLED PERSONS

3.85 A central feature of the Disability Discrimination Act 1995 was to impose a duty upon employers, service providers and others to make reasonable adjustments for disabled persons. A failure to comply with such a duty was a form of discrimination.[162]

3.86 The Equality Act 2010 continues that approach. However, it amends the pre-existing duty so as to provide consistency across the reasonable adjustment provisions. Thus there is now only one threshold for the reasonable adjustment duty (that is, substantial disadvantage) where previously there were two thresholds. It also applies the duty to provide an auxiliary aid explicitly to employment. There will no longer be a justification defence in goods and services cases. Finally, it consistently refers to a provision, criterion or practice rather than a practice, policy or procedure used in some provisions in the 1995 Act.[163]

---

[161] EN para 81.

[162] See, in the employment context, DDA 1995, ss 3A(2) and (6), 4A and 18B. See: *Kenny v Hampshire Constabulary* [1999] IRLR 76, EAT; *Morse v Wiltshire County Council* [1999] IRLR 352, EAT; *Ridout v TC Group* [1999] IRLR 628, EAT; *British Gas Services Ltd v McCaull* [2001] IRLR 60, EAT; *Beart v HM Prison Service* [2003] IRLR 238, CA; *Paul v National Probation Service* [2004] IRLR 190, EAT; *Archibald v Fife Council* [2004] IRLR 651, HL; *Nottinghamshire County Council v Meikle* [2004] IRLR 703, CA; *Smith v Churchill Stairlifts plc* [2006] IRLR 41, CS; *Tarbuck v Sainsbury's Supermarkets Ltd* [2006] IRLR 664, EAT; *O'Hanlon v Commissioners for HM Customs & Revenue* [2006] IRLR 840, EAT; *Latif v Project Management Institute* [2007] IRLR 579, EAT; *HM Prison Service v Johnson* [2007] IRLR 951, EAT; *Environment Agency v Rowan* [2008] IRLR 20, EAT; *Matuszowicz v Kingston-upon-Hull City Council* [2009] IRLR 288, CA; *Eastern & Coastal Kent PCT v Grey* [2009] IRLR 429, EAT; *Fareham College Corporation v Walters* [2009] IRLR 991, EAT; *Da'Bell v NSPCC* [2010] IRLR 19, EAT; *Secretary of State for Work & Pensions v Alam* [2010] IRLR 283, EAT.

[163] EN paras 82–86 and examples. See Keter, 2009a: 37–38.

3.87   As the duty to make a reasonable adjustment for a disabled person might be viewed as a form of positive action or preferential treatment, it is necessary to note how the duty interacts with the prohibited conduct of direct discrimination in s 13. A person (A) discriminates against another (B) if, because of a protected characteristic, A treats B less favourably than A treats or would treat others.[164] However, if the protected characteristic is disability, and B is not a disabled person, A does not discriminate against B only because A treats or would treat disabled persons more favourably than A treats B.[165] This reflects the asymmetrical nature of disability discrimination law.[166] It is not unlawful discrimination to treat a disabled person more favourably than a non-disabled person.

3.88   Where the Equality Act 2010 imposes a duty to make reasonable adjustments on a person, ss 20–22 and the applicable Schedule apply. For those purposes, a person on whom the duty is imposed is referred to as A.[167]

Duty to make adjustments

3.89   The duty to make adjustments comprises three requirements.[168] A reference in ss 21 or 22 or an applicable Schedule to the first, second or third requirement is to be construed in accordance with s 20.[169] The applicable Schedule means, in relation to Part 3 (services and public functions), Schs 2 and 21; in relation to Part 4 (premises), Schs 4 and 21; in relation to Part 5 (work), Schs 8 and 21; in relation to Part 6 (education), Schs 13 and 21; and in relation to Part 7 (associations), Schs 15 and 21.[170]

3.90   The first requirement arises where a provision, criterion or practice of A's puts a disabled person at a substantial (that is, more than minor or trivial)[171] disadvantage in relation to a relevant matter in comparison with persons who are not disabled. A is required to take such steps as it is reasonable to have to take to avoid the disadvantage.[172] Where the first requirement relates to the provision of information, the steps which it is reasonable for A to have to take include steps for ensuring that in the circumstances concerned the information is provided in an accessible format.[173]

---

[164]   EQA 2010, s 13(1).
[165]   EQA 2010, s 13(3). The inclusion of the word 'only' appears to be unnecessary, but perhaps has been included as a precaution to ensure that this provision is not used as a cover for discrimination on the basis of some other protected characteristic in tandem with disability.
[166]   See Joint Committee on Human Rights, 2009: paras 126–127.
[167]   EQA 2010, s 20(1).
[168]   EQA 2010, s 20(2).
[169]   EQA 2010, s 20(8).
[170]   EQA 2010, s 20(13).
[171]   EQA 2010, s 212(1).
[172]   EQA 2010, s 20(3).
[173]   EQA 2010, s 20(6).

3.91 The second requirement arises where a physical feature puts a disabled person at a substantial (that is, more than minor or trivial)[174] disadvantage in relation to a relevant matter in comparison with persons who are not disabled. A is required to take such steps as it is reasonable to have to take to avoid the disadvantage.[175] A reference to avoiding a substantial disadvantage includes a reference to (a) removing the physical feature in question or (b) altering it or (c) providing a reasonable means of avoiding it.[176] A reference to a physical feature is a reference to (a) a feature arising from the design or construction of a building; (b) a feature of an approach to, exit from or access to a building; (c) a fixture or fitting, or furniture, furnishings, materials, equipment or other chattels, in or on premises; (d) any other physical element or quality.[177]

3.92 The third requirement arises where a disabled person would, but for the provision of an auxiliary aid, be put at a substantial (that is, more than minor or trivial)[178] disadvantage in relation to a relevant matter in comparison with persons who are not disabled. A is required to take such steps as it is reasonable to have to take to provide the auxiliary aid.[179] A reference to an auxiliary aid includes a reference to an auxiliary service.[180] Where the third requirement relates to the provision of information, the steps which it is reasonable for A to have to take include steps for ensuring that in the circumstances concerned the information is provided in an accessible format.[181]

3.93 Subject to express provision to the contrary, a person (A) (who is subject to a duty to make reasonable adjustments) is not entitled to require a disabled person (in relation to whom A is required to comply with the duty) to pay to any extent A's costs of complying with the duty.[182]

3.94 As the Explanatory Notes explain, s 20 defines what is meant by the duty to make reasonable adjustments for the Equality Act 2010. It lists the Parts of the Act which impose the duty and the related Schedules which stipulate how the duty will apply in relation to each Part.[183] The first requirement covers changing the way things are done (such as changing a practice), the second covers making changes to the built environment (such as providing access to a building), and the third covers providing auxiliary aids and services (such as providing special computer software or providing a different service).[184]

---

[174] EQA 2010, s 212(1).
[175] EQA 2010, s 20(4).
[176] EQA 2010, s 20(9).
[177] EQA 2010, s 20(10). A reference to chattels is to be read, in relation to Scotland, as a reference to moveable property: s 20(12).
[178] EQA 2010, s 212(1).
[179] EQA 2010, s 20(5).
[180] EQA 2010, s 20(11).
[181] EQA 2010, s 20(6).
[182] EQA 2010, s 20(7).
[183] EN para 82.
[184] EN para 82.

Failure to comply with duty

3.95 A failure to comply with the first, second or third requirement is a failure to comply with a duty to make reasonable adjustments.[185] A discriminates against a disabled person if A fails to comply with that duty in relation to that person.[186] However, a provision of an applicable Schedule which imposes a duty to comply with the first, second or third requirement applies only for the purpose of establishing whether A has contravened the Act by discriminating. A failure to comply is not actionable by virtue of another provision of the Act or otherwise.[187]

Regulations

3.96 Section 22 makes provision for regulations to be made in support of the duty to make adjustments for disabled persons. Such regulations may prescribe (a) matters to be taken into account in deciding whether it is reasonable for A to take a step for the purposes of a prescribed provision of an applicable Schedule; and (b) descriptions of persons to whom the first, second or third requirement does not apply.[188] Such regulations may also make provision as to (a) circumstances in which it is, or in which it is not, reasonable for a person of a prescribed description to have to take steps of a prescribed description; (b) what is, or what is not, a provision, criterion or practice; (c) things which are, or which are not, to be treated as physical features; (d) things which are, or which are not, to be treated as alterations of physical features; (e) things which are, or which are not, to be treated as auxiliary aids.[189]

3.97 Provision made by virtue of s 22 may amend an applicable Schedule.[190]

Reasonable adjustments: supplementary provisions

3.98 The supplementary provisions in Sch 21 take effect in relation to the duty to make reasonable adjustments.[191] These supplementary provisions apply for the purposes of Sch 2 (services and public functions: reasonable adjustments), Sch 4 (premises: reasonable adjustments), Sch 8 (work: reasonable adjustments), Sch 13 (education: reasonable adjustments) and Sch 15 (associations: reasonable adjustments).[192] They are conveniently dealt with in detail here, as follows.

3.99 Put simply, the supplementary provisions on reasonable adjustments set out in Sch 21 apply to the fields of services, premises, work, education, and associations where a person providing a service (or delivering functions, or an

---

[185]   EQA 2010, s 21(1).
[186]   EQA 2010, s 21(2).
[187]   EQA 2010, s 21(3).
[188]   EQA 2010, s 22(1).
[189]   EQA 2010, s 22(2).
[190]   EQA 2010, s 22(3).
[191]   EQA 2010, s 189.
[192]   EQA 2010, Sch 21, para 1.

employer, or an education provider, or an association – as the case may be) is required to consider reasonable adjustments to premises which it rents and would require the landlord's consent to proceed.[193] Schedule 21 replaces similar provisions in the DDA 1995.[194] It also applies in relation to the new duty to make alterations to the physical features of common parts of let and commonhold residential premises in England and Wales and tenements in Scotland.[195]

3.100 Schedule 21 sets out what steps it is reasonable for a person to take in discharging a duty to make reasonable adjustments in a case where a binding agreement requires that consent must be obtained from a third party before that person may proceed to make the adjustment to let premises or the common parts of let premises. Where a person wishes to make an adjustment in order to fulfil a duty to make reasonable adjustments but is unable to do so, Sch 21 enables the adjustment to be made by deeming the tenancy to include certain provisions. Where a landlord has refused consent to an alteration or gives consent subject to a condition, the person requesting the consent (or a disabled person who has an interest in the alteration being made) can refer the refusal (or the conditional consent) to a county or sheriff court. Schedule 21 also provides for a landlord to be joined as a party to proceedings before an employment tribunal, county or sheriff court where a disabled person is bringing an action under the reasonable adjustment duty.[196]

Binding obligations, etc

3.101 There are three situations where a binding obligation may affect the duty to make reasonable adjustments. A binding obligation is a legally binding obligation in relation to premises, however arising.[197] First, a binding obligation might require A to obtain the consent of another person to an alteration of premises which A occupies.[198] Secondly, where A is a controller of let premises, a binding obligation might require A to obtain the consent of another person to a variation of a term of the tenancy.[199] Thirdly, where A is a

---

[193] EN para 981.
[194] DDA 1995, ss 18A, 27 and Sch 4; Disability Discrimination (Providers of Services) (Adjustment of Premises) Regulations 2001, SI 2001/3253; Disability Discrimination (Employment Field) (Leasehold Premises) Regulations 2004, SI 2004/153; Disability Discrimination (Service Providers and Public Authorities Carrying Out Functions) Regulations 2005, SI 2005/2901; Disability Discrimination (Educational Institutions) (Alteration of Leasehold Premises) Regulations 2005, SI 2005/1070. See Doyle, 2008: 205–217.
[195] EN para 986.
[196] This paragraph draws directly on EN paras 981–986.
[197] EQA 2010, Sch 21, para 2(3).
[198] EQA 2010, Sch 21, para 2(1)(a). Here the reference to a binding obligation does not include a reference to an obligation imposed by a tenancy: para 2(3).
[199] EQA 2010, Sch 21, para 2(1)(b).

responsible person in relation to common parts, a binding obligation might require A to obtain the consent of another person to an alteration of the common parts.[200]

3.102   For the purpose of discharging a duty to make reasonable adjustments, it is always reasonable for A to have to take steps to obtain the consent in question.[201] However, it is never reasonable for A to have to make the alteration before the consent is obtained.[202]

Landlord's consent

3.103   The need for a landlord's consent might affect the duty to make reasonable adjustments. Provision is made for that circumstance. It will apply if:

- A occupies premises under a tenancy; and

- A is proposing to make an alteration to the premises so as to comply with a duty to make reasonable adjustments; and

- but for this provision, A would not be entitled to make the alteration.[203]

3.104   It will also apply if:

- A is a responsible person in relation to common parts; and

- A is proposing to make an alteration to the common parts so as to comply with a duty to make reasonable adjustments; and

- A is the tenant of property which includes the common parts; and

- but for this provision, A would not be entitled to make the alteration.[204]

For both these purposes, A must be treated as not entitled to make the alteration if the tenancy (a) imposes conditions which are to apply if A makes an alteration, or (b) entitles the landlord to attach conditions to a consent to the alteration.[205]

---

[200]   EQA 2010, Sch 21, para 2(1)(c). Here the reference to a binding obligation does not include a reference to an obligation imposed by a tenancy: para 2(3).
[201]   EQA 2010, Sch 21, para 2(2)(a), (4) The steps referred to do not include applying to a court or tribunal: para 2(4).
[202]   EQA 2010, Sch 21, para 2(2)(b).
[203]   EQA 2010, Sch 21, para 3(1).
[204]   EQA 2010, Sch 21, para 3(2).
[205]   EQA 2010, Sch 21, para 3(5).

3.105 In those circumstances, the tenancy has effect as if it provided:

- for A to be entitled to make the alteration with the written consent of the landlord; and

- for A to have to make a written application for that consent; and

- for the landlord not to withhold the consent unreasonably; and

- for the landlord to be able to give the consent subject to reasonable conditions.[206]

Then if a question arises as to whether A has made the alteration (and, accordingly, complied with a duty to make reasonable adjustments), any constraint attributable to the tenancy must be ignored unless A has applied to the landlord in writing for consent to the alteration.[207]

Proceedings before county court or sheriff

3.106 Provision is made where, in a case within Part 3 (services and public functions), Part 4 (premises), Part 6 (education) or Part 7 (associations) of the 2010 Act, A has applied in writing to the landlord for consent to the alteration, and the landlord has refused to give consent or has given consent subject to a condition.[208] A (or a disabled person with an interest in the alteration being made) may refer the matter to a county court (in Scotland, the sheriff).[209]

3.107 The county court or sheriff must determine whether the refusal or condition is unreasonable.[210] If the county court or sheriff finds that the refusal or condition is unreasonable, the county court or sheriff may make such declaration as it thinks appropriate.[211] The county court or sheriff may also make an order authorising A to make the alteration specified in the order (and requiring A to comply with such conditions as are so specified).[212]

Joining a landlord as a party to proceedings

3.108 Provision is made for joining a landlord to any proceedings relating to a contravention of the 2010 Act by virtue of s 20 (duty to make adjustments).[213] A party to the proceedings may request the employment tribunal, county court or sheriff ('the judicial authority') to direct that the landlord is joined (in

---

[206] EQA 2010, Sch 21, para 3(3).
[207] EQA 2010, Sch 21, para 3(4).
[208] EQA 2010, Sch 21, para 4(1).
[209] EQA 2010, Sch 21, para 4(2).
[210] EQA 2010, Sch 21, para 4(3).
[211] EQA 2010, Sch 21, para 4(4)(a).
[212] EQA 2010, Sch 21, para 4(4)(b).
[213] EQA 2010, Sch 21, para 5(1).

Scotland, sisted) as a party to the proceedings.[214] The judicial authority must grant the request if it is made before the hearing of the complaint or claim begins.[215] It may refuse the request if it is made after the hearing begins.[216] It must refuse the request if it is made after the complaint or claim has been determined.[217]

3.109 If the landlord is joined (in Scotland, sisted) as a party to the proceedings, the judicial authority may determine whether (a) the landlord has refused to consent to the alteration; or (b) the landlord has consented subject to a condition; or (c) the refusal or condition was unreasonable.[218] If the judicial authority finds that the refusal or condition was unreasonable, it (a) may make such declaration as it thinks appropriate; (b) may make an order authorising A to make the alteration specified in the order (and requiring A to comply with such conditions as are so specified); or (c) may order the landlord to pay compensation to the complainant or claimant.[219] In particular, in employment proceedings, an employment tribunal may order the landlord to pay compensation to the complainant or claimant under this provision instead of, or in addition to, acting in reliance on its power to award compensation against the respondent.[220] If a county court or the sheriff orders the landlord to pay compensation, it may not order A to do so.[221]

Regulations

3.110 Regulations may make provision as to circumstances in which a landlord is taken for these purposes to have (a) withheld consent; (b) withheld consent reasonably; or (c) withheld consent unreasonably.[222] Regulations may also make provision as to circumstances in which a condition subject to which a landlord gives consent is taken (a) to be reasonable or (b) to be unreasonable.[223] Regulations may further make provision supplementing or modifying Sch 21 in relation to a case where A's tenancy is a sub-tenancy.[224] Such regulations may also amend the provisions of the Schedule.[225]

---

[214] EQA 2010, Sch 21, para 5(2).
[215] EQA 2010, Sch 21, para 5(3)(a).
[216] EQA 2010, Sch 21, para 5(3)(b).
[217] EQA 2010, Sch 21, para 5(3)(c).
[218] EQA 2010, Sch 21, para 5(4).
[219] EQA 2010, Sch 21, para 5(5).
[220] EQA 2010, Sch 21, para 5(6) cross-referring to s 124(2). If the employment tribunal orders the landlord to pay compensation it must not do so in reliance on s 124(2).
[221] EQA 2010, Sch 21, para 5(7).
[222] EQA 2010, Sch 21, para 6(1).
[223] EQA 2010, Sch 21, para 6(2).
[224] EQA 2010, Sch 21, para 6(3).
[225] EQA 2010, Sch 21, para 6(4).

Examples

3.111 The Explanatory Notes give two examples of Sch 21 in practice:

- An insurance company works from a rented two storey building and has plans to install a stair lift to make the building more accessible to employees with mobility impairments. The terms of the lease preclude alterations to the staircase. The company writes to the landlord for permission to make the alteration. The landlord consults the superior landlord who agrees to waive this condition of the lease thereby allowing the installation of the chair lift to proceed. However, as a condition of consent, the landlord requires that the chair lift is removed on surrender of the lease.

- A disabled tenant asks to have automated doors put in at the entrance of her block of flats. Her landlord would like to agree but is unable to do so as he is a tenant of a superior landlord who does not agree to the alteration. The tenant's remedy is to bring an action against her landlord in the county court where she can ask that the superior landlord is brought in as an additional party to the case. The court can order the alteration to be made and order the superior landlord to pay compensation if it finds he has acted unreasonably in refusing his consent.[226]

DISCRIMINATION: SUPPLEMENTARY

Comparison by reference to circumstances

3.112 Section 23 of the Act provides that on a comparison of cases for the purposes of s 13 (direct discrimination), s 14 (combined discrimination: dual characteristics) or s 19 (indirect discrimination) there must be no material difference between the circumstances relating to each case.[227] The circumstances relating to a case include a person's abilities if, on a comparison for the purposes of s 13 (direct discrimination), the protected characteristic is disability.[228] The circumstances relating to a case include a person's abilities if, on a comparison for the purposes of s 14 (combined discrimination: dual characteristics), one of the protected characteristics in the combination is disability.[229] If the protected characteristic is sexual orientation, the fact that one person (whether or not the person referred to as B) is a civil partner while another is married is not a material difference between the circumstances relating to each case.[230]

---

[226] EN para 986.
[227] EQA 2010, s 23(1). This provision was redrafted during the passage of the Bill and now appears to meet the concerns of the Joint Committee on Human Rights, 2009: paras 128–131.
[228] EQA 2010, s 23(2)(a).
[229] EQA 2010, s 23(2)(b).
[230] EQA 2010, s 23(3).

3.113 The section works in the following way.[231] It provides that like must be compared with like in cases of direct discrimination, combined discrimination (dual characteristics) or indirect discrimination. The treatment of the claimant must be compared with that of an actual or a hypothetical comparator. The comparator is a person who does not share the same protected characteristic as the claimant. In the case of dual discrimination, the comparator is a person who does not share either of the protected characteristics in the combination. In order to be a valid comparator, the person is someone who is (or who is assumed to be) in not materially different circumstances from the claimant. In cases of direct or dual discrimination, those circumstances can include their respective abilities where the claimant is a disabled person.[232]

3.114 Section 23 replicates similar provisions in pre-existing legislation, but it extends the principle to the new concept of combined discrimination (dual characteristics).[233] The section also enables a civil partner who is treated less favourably than a married person in similar circumstances to bring a claim for sexual orientation discrimination.[234]

3.115 The Explanatory Notes provide the following examples:[235]

> 'A blind woman claims she was not short listed for a job involving computers because the employer wrongly assumed that blind people cannot use them. An appropriate comparator is a person who is not blind — it could be a non-disabled person or someone with a different disability — but who has the same ability to do the job as the claimant.
>
> A Muslim employee is put at a disadvantage by his employer's practice of not allowing requests for time off work on Fridays. The comparison that must be made is in terms of the impact of that practice on non-Muslim employees in similar circumstances to whom it is (or might be) applied.'

Irrelevance of alleged discriminator's characteristics

3.116 Section 24 provides that, for the purpose of establishing a contravention of the Act by virtue of direct discrimination,[236] it does not matter whether A has the protected characteristic.[237] For the purpose of establishing a contravention of the Act by virtue of combined discrimination (dual characteristics),[238] it does not matter whether A has one of the protected characteristics in the combination or whether A has both.[239]

---

[231]   EN para 91.
[232]   EN para 91.
[233]   EN para 93.
[234]   EN para 92.
[235]   EN para 93.
[236]   EQA 2010, s 13(1).
[237]   EQA 2010, s 24(1).
[238]   EQA 2010, s 14(1).
[239]   EQA 2010, s 24(2).

3.117 These provisions were introduced at Report stage in the House of Commons. The effect is that it is no defence to a claim of direct discrimination that the alleged discriminator shares the protected characteristic with the victim. It is equally no defence to a claim of dual discrimination that the alleged discriminator shares one or both of the protected characteristics with the victim.[240] It is believed that the wording of s 24 is broad enough to cover cases of discrimination based on association or perception. It applies to all the protected characteristics a principle that previously only applied in relation to the same religion or belief as the victim. So an employer cannot argue that because he is a gay man he is not liable for unlawful discrimination for rejecting a job application from another gay man because of the applicant's sexual orientation.[241]

References to particular strands of discrimination

3.118 Section 25 sets out what is meant by references to the types of discrimination referred to in the Act.[242] The section speaks for itself and is not analysed further here.

HARASSMENT

Introduction

3.119 Section 26 of the Equality Act 2010 addresses harassment. The Act:

> 'preserves existing legislative provisions on harassment. Harassment as it has come to be defined in legislation will probably always be directly discriminatory, but represents a different and more aggravated form of discrimination. In bringing a unified provision for harassment within a single enactment, the [Act] will effectively extend free standing harassment provisions to other strands not currently protected by specific harassment provisions.'[243]

Harassment takes three possible forms. For this purpose, the relevant protected characteristics are age; disability; gender reassignment; race; religion or belief; sex; and sexual orientation.[244] Notably, pregnancy and maternity, and marriage and civil partnership, are not protected characteristics in relation to harassment.

---

[240] EN para 94.
[241] EN para 95.
[242] EN paras 96–97.
[243] Keter, 2009a: 39. See generally: *Snowball v Gardner Merchant Ltd* [1987] IRLR 397, EAT; *Wileman v Minilec Engineering Ltd* [1988] IRLR 144, EAT; *Insitu Cleaning Co Ltd v Heads* [1995] IRLR 4, EAT; *British Telecommunications plc v Williams* [1997] IRLR 668, EAT; *Reed & Bull Information Systems Ltd v Stedman* [1999] IRLR 299, EAT; *Driskel v Peninsula Business Services Ltd* [2000] IRLR 151, EAT; *Moonsar v Fiveways Express Transport Ltd* [2005] IRLR 9, EAT; *Saini v All Saints Haque Centre* [2009] IRLR 74, EAT; *English v Thomas Sanderson Blinds Ltd* [2009] IRLR 206, CA; *Richmond Pharmacology Ltd v Dhaliwal* [2009] IRLR 336, EAT; *EBR Attridge Law LLP v Coleman* [2010] IRLR 10, EAT.
[244] EQA 2010, s 26(5).

Unwanted conduct harassment

3.120   The first form of harassment applies in general to unwanted conduct that has the purpose or effect of creating an intimidating, hostile, degrading, humiliating or offensive environment for the complainant or violating the complainant's dignity.[245] Thus a person (A) harasses another (B) if (a) A engages in unwanted conduct related to a relevant protected characteristic, and (b) the conduct has the purpose or effect of (i) violating B's dignity, or (ii) creating an intimidating, hostile, degrading, humiliating or offensive environment for B.[246] In deciding whether conduct has that effect, each of the following must be taken into account, namely, (a) the perception of B; (b) the other circumstances of the case; and (c) whether it is reasonable for the conduct to have that effect.[247]

Sexual harassment

3.121   The second form of harassment is sexual harassment or unwanted conduct of a sexual nature where this has the same purpose or effect as the first type of harassment.[248] Thus, A also harasses B if (a) A engages in unwanted conduct of a sexual nature, and (b) the conduct has the purpose or effect of (i) violating B's dignity, or (ii) creating an intimidating, hostile, degrading, humiliating or offensive environment for B.[249] In deciding whether conduct has that effect, each of the following must be taken into account, namely, (a) the perception of B; (b) the other circumstances of the case; and (c) whether it is reasonable for the conduct to have that effect.[250]

Non-submission harassment

3.122   The third form of harassment is treating someone less favourably than another because they have either submitted or failed to submit to sexual harassment, or harassment related to sex or gender reassignment.[251] Thus, harassment also arises where A or another person engages in unwanted conduct of a sexual nature or that is related to gender reassignment or sex. The conduct in question must have the purpose or effect of (i) violating B's dignity, or (ii) creating an intimidating, hostile, degrading, humiliating or offensive environment for B. If so, the cause of action is complete if A has treated B less favourably than A would treat B if B had not rejected or submitted to the conduct because of B's rejection of or submission to the conduct.[252]

---

[245]   EN para 98.
[246]   EQA 2010, s 26(1).
[247]   EQA 2010, s 26(4).
[248]   EN para 98.
[249]   EQA 2010, s 26(2).
[250]   EQA 2010, s 26(4).
[251]   EN para 98.
[252]   EQA 2010, s 26(3).

Uniformity of approach

3.123 The Explanatory Notes suggest that, while current legislation provides freestanding protection against harassment, that protection is not uniform for the different protected characteristics. Thus s 26 is said to be intended to achieve uniformity of approach across all protected characteristics and in all fields where the first type of harassment described above is prohibited.[253] The Explanatory Notes venture that courts and tribunals will continue to balance competing rights on the particular facts of each case, including freedom of expression and academic freedom.

3.124 The Explanatory Notes offer three examples of how the new definition of harassment might work:

- A white worker who sees a black colleague being subjected to racially abusive language could have a case of harassment if the language also causes an offensive environment for her.

- An employer who displayed any material of a sexual nature, such as a topless calendar, may be harassing her employees where this makes the workplace an offensive place to work for any employee, female or male.

- A shopkeeper propositions one of his shop assistants, she rejects his advances and then is turned down for promotion which she believes she would have got if she had accepted her boss's advances. The shop assistant would have a claim of harassment.[254]

3.125 It is apparent that the Government intended that prohibition of associative and perceptive discrimination would apply equally to harassment and across all the strands and areas where this did not previously currently apply.[255] The Equality Act prohibits harassment based on association and perception in respect of race, sex, gender reassignment, disability, sexual orientation, religion or belief and age in relation to both employment and non-employment areas. It goes beyond what is required by EU law.[256]

Exclusions

3.126 It is important to note that, as previously mentioned, the unwanted conduct harassment provision[257] does not apply to pregnancy and maternity, and marriage and civil partnership, at all. In addition, somewhat controversially, the protected characteristics of sexual orientation and religion

---

[253] EN para 99.

[254] EN para 100.

[255] House of Commons Work and Pensions Committee. 2009a: para 52; House of Commons Work and Pensions Committee. 2009b: 3.

[256] *Attridge Law v Coleman* [2007] IRLR 88 (EAT); *Coleman v Attridge Law* (C-303/06) [2008] IRLR 722 (ECJ); *EBR Attridge Law LLP v Coleman* [2010] IRLR 10 (EAT).

[257] EQA 2010, s 26(1). The remaining forms of harassment are linked to any particular protected characteristic, as it is the nature of the harassment in these cases that matters.

or belief do not apply in relation to harassment outside the workplace or further and higher education (where European legal obligations apply). However, this does not pre-empt the future extension of European law on harassment beyond work and education.[258]

Human rights

3.127　The Joint Committee on Human Rights has expressed the view that the definition of harassment in s 26 'clarifies and extends existing protection against harassment while striking an appropriate balance between protecting the right to freedom of expression . . . and the right to equality . . .'[259] It urged courts and tribunals to apply the new definition of harassment in the light of the relevant case law under the European Convention on Human Rights (Art 10 on the right to freedom of expression). It acknowledged that a more restrictive definition of harassment on the basis of sexual orientation may be appropriate in the context of service provision and the performance of public functions.

3.128　Strong arguments were said to exist for prohibiting harassment on the grounds of being married or in a civil partnership, and harassment on the grounds of pregnancy or maternity, so as to ensure comprehensive protection against forms of discrimination on the basis of marital status, pregnancy or maternity. In the Joint Committee's opinion, this would also eliminate confusing distinctions between the different characteristics, thereby improving the clarity of the legislation. It wished to make it easier to challenge harassment based on the characteristics of marital status, pregnancy or maternity rather than having to rely indirectly on the characteristics of sex or sexual orientation.[260]

3.129　The Joint Committee considered that the absence of an explicit prohibition on harassment related to sexual orientation in the areas of service provision; the performance of public functions; and the disposal, management and occupation of premises represented 'a significant gap in the protection against discrimination offered by the [Act].'[261] In its view this left individuals 'without clear protection against demeaning and degrading harassment in important areas of their life.' The Joint Committee was concerned that this gave rise to issues in respect of the prohibition of discrimination in Art 14 of the ECHR read in conjunction with the right to respect for private and family life (Art 8), to freedom of thought, conscience and religion (Art 9) or the prohibition on inhuman or degrading treatment (Art 3).[262] It acknowledged that the Act may offer some protection against harassment in these areas as a result of the general prohibition against direct and indirect discrimination on

---

[258]　Keter, 2009a: 39. See EQA 2010, s 29(8) excluding harassment because of religion or belief or sexual orientation in relation to the provision of services or when exercising a public function.

[259]　Joint Committee on Human Rights, 2009: para 105.

[260]　Joint Committee on Human Rights, 2009: para 108.

[261]　Joint Committee on Human Rights, 2009: para 114.

[262]　Joint Committee on Human Rights, 2009: para 114.

the grounds of sexual orientation.[263] However, it opined that the absence of explicit provisions on harassment relating to sexual orientation in service provision or the performance of public functions 'leaves the legal position unclear and ambiguous, to the benefit of neither service users nor service providers'.[264]

3.130 The Government has noted some concerns that the application of a broader domestic definition of harassment (compared with the narrower definition required by European law) to the characteristics of religion or belief, sexual orientation and gender reassignment might infringe Art 9 and Art 10 ECHR rights.[265] It concluded that such protection is compatible with ECHR rights because the Art 9(2) and 10 rights are qualified rights. They may be restricted to protect the rights of others. In addition, the relevant provisions of the Act need to be read compatibly with those rights.[266] The fact that protection from harassment outside the workplace is not extended to all the protected characteristics is also considered to be compliant with Art 14. The Government contends that giving different levels of protection in some circumstances to different protected groups does not amount to discrimination on grounds of a protected characteristic for the purposes of Art 14.[267]

Detriment and harassment

3.131 Throughout the Act, the term 'detriment' does not include conduct which amounts to 'harassment'.[268] However, where the Act disapplies a prohibition on harassment in relation to a specified protected characteristic, that disapplication does not prevent conduct relating to that characteristic from amounting to a detriment for the purposes of direct discrimination[269] because of that characteristic.[270]

VICTIMISATION

Introduction

3.132 There is a more simply-worded definition of victimisation in s 27 of the EQA 2010 than the definition of the term which was in the legislation which the EQA 2010 replaced. Victimisation means subjecting a person to a detriment

---

[263] Joint Committee on Human Rights, 2009: para 115.
[264] Joint Committee on Human Rights, 2009: para 115. The Joint Committee drew comfort from the way in which, in Northern Ireland, the Equality Act (Sexual Orientation) Regulations (NI) 2006, SR 2006/439 prohibit harassment on the grounds of sexual orientation in service provision and the performance of public functions, and yet could be read compatibly with ECHR Arts 9 and 10: paras 116–117. See *Christian Institute and ors, Re Judicial Review* [2007] NIQB 66 (Weatherup J).
[265] EN para 39 (HL Bill 20).
[266] HRA 1998, s 23.
[267] EN para 39 (HL Bill 20).
[268] EQA 2010, s 212(1).
[269] EQA 2010, s 13.
[270] EQA 2010, s 212(5).

because that person does 'a protected act', or because the person who is alleged to have victimised the other believes that the other has done or may do a protected act.[271]

What is a 'protected act'?

3.133 A 'protected act' is defined for this purpose as:

> '(a)   bringing proceedings under this Act;
> (b)   giving evidence or information in connection with proceedings under this Act;
> (c)   doing any other thing for the purposes of or in connection with this Act;
> (d)   making an allegation (whether or not express) that A or another person has contravened this Act.'[272]

It is expressly provided that a reference to a contravention of the EQA 2010 'includes a reference to committing a breach of an equality clause or rule'.[273]

No protection where the protected act is committed in bad faith

3.134 However, giving 'false evidence or information' – that is to say, evidence or information which is determined by a court or tribunal to have been untrue – or 'making a false allegation' will not constitute a 'protected act' if the evidence or information is given (or the allegation is made) 'in bad faith'.[274]

No need for a comparator

3.135 Unlike under the provisions which s 27 of the EQA 2010 replaces, there is no need for a person who claims that he or she has been victimised to show that he or she has been treated less favourably than a person who had not committed the protected act in question was (or would have been) treated.

Difficulties of application

3.136 Nevertheless, there will be occasions when it will be difficult to apply the concept of victimisation. The most difficult will be where the protected act was acknowledged by the alleged victimiser to have been the cause of the treatment which is alleged to have contravened EQA 2010, s 27.

Khan

3.137 The problem arose in an acute form in *Chief Constable of West Yorkshire v Khan*,[275] where the claimant was a sergeant in the West Yorkshire

---

[271]   EQA 2010, s 27(1). A claim may be made under s 27 only by an individual: s 27(4).
[272]   EQA 2010, s 27(2).
[273]   EQA 2010, s 27(5).
[274]   EQA 2010, s 27(3).
[275]   [2001] ICR 1065, HL.

Police. He presented a complaint to an industrial tribunal (as it was at the time) alleging racial discrimination in connection with the failure of two applications for promotion to the post of inspector. While that claim was pending he applied for a post as an inspector in the Norfolk police. The Norfolk police asked for, in effect, a reference. The Chief Constable, on legal advice, declined to provide one for fear of prejudicing his own case before the tribunal. The claimant amended his claim to complain of that refusal as an act of victimisation. The amended claim was upheld in the industrial tribunal, and appeals to the EAT and the Court of Appeal were dismissed. The House of Lords allowed the respondent's appeal on the basis that the Chief Constable's refusal of a reference could not properly be described as having been 'by reason that' the applicant had brought his discrimination claim. The House of Lords stated that the applicable test was whether or not an honest and reasonable employer would have done the same thing.

Derbyshire

3.138 The appropriateness of that test was the subject of consideration by the House of Lords in *Derbyshire v St Helens Metropolitan Borough Council*,[276] where the claimants had been sent letters by their employer during the course of equal pay proceedings. The claimants were female catering staff engaged in the provision of school meals. The letters stated that a successful equal pay claim would be likely to lead to the cost of school meals rising to such an extent that the employer would have to consider ceasing to provide them, except to those entitled to receive them by law, with a consequent reduction in the school meals service for which only a very small proportion of the existing workforce would be required.

3.139 Lord Neuberger's speech in *Derbyshire* was agreed with by three of the other members of the Judicial Committee in that case. Lord Neuberger doubted some of the reasoning in *Khan*, but nevertheless thought that the question whether or not the actions of the employer were 'honest and reasonable' could assist.[277] He focused, however, on 'detriment' as an alternative test.[278]

Chaudhary

3.140 In *British Medical Association v Chaudhary*,[279] the Court of Appeal commented that while:

> 'the House of Lords did not support Lord Nicholls' formulation of the test as whether the employer had acted honestly and reasonably . . . it reaffirmed the essential statement of law that a person does not discriminate if he takes the impugned decision in order to protect himself in litigation.'

---

[276] [2007] ICR 841.
[277] See paras 65–69 of his speech.
[278] See para 68 of his speech.
[279] [2007] IRLR 800.

Bullimore

3.141 In *Bullimore v Pothecary Witham Weld*,[280] an employment tribunal had upheld a claim of victimisation in relation to a reference. A prospective new employer had asked the respondent, one of the claimant's former employers, a number of questions, including the reason why the claimant had left her employment with the respondent. The respondent had then written that the claimant had resigned and made a claim to an employment tribunal. She had in fact resigned and claimed unfair 'constructive' dismissal, in part because of, she claimed, discrimination on the ground of her sex. She had then compromised that claim.

3.142 The reference given by the respondent did not state that the claimant had made a claim of discrimination on the ground of sex, and the respondent's reason for referring to the fact of the claim was, he said, that merely saying that the claimant had resigned would not give the prospective new employer the reason why the claimant had left her employment with the respondent. The employment tribunal, in determining the claim, relied on a mixture of statements made by the House of Lords in *Khan* and *Derbyshire*. The respondent former employer appealed to the EAT. The EAT dismissed the appeal, and in the course of doing so gave the following helpful guidance in relation to the application of *Khan* and *Derbyshire*:

> '18. *Overview* We have felt it necessary to set out the reasoning in *Khan* and *Derbyshire* in some detail because the Tribunal in this case clearly regarded those decisions as affording the principal source of guidance on the issues which it had to resolve. But we are bound to say that we regard them as something of a red herring. As Ms Monaghan [counsel for the Equality and Human Rights Commission, which intervened] persuasively submitted, it is crucial to appreciate that both are cases of a very particular type, namely cases where the employer has taken action in order to protect his position in current litigation; and that the particular problems discussed in them are peculiar to that type of situation. We accept Ms Monaghan's submission that in most cases the familiar approach of (a) deciding whether the Claimant has suffered "less favourable treatment" (which in practice answers also whether he or she has suffered a detriment) and (b) asking whether the protected act was, or was part of, the reason why he suffered that detriment, following the guidance in *Nagarajan*, will suffice; and the complexities addressed in *Khan* and *Derbyshire* simply do not arise. The present case is not of the *Khan/Derbyshire* type. There was no litigation between the Claimant and the Appellants at the time that [the Respondent] gave the reference complained of or conducted the grievance meeting. (For the avoidance of doubt, however, we should make clear that we are not to be taken as saying that the often-quoted observations in para. 29 of Lord Nicholls' speech in *Khan* are no longer relevant on the general question of the correct approach to the "reason why" question.)
>
> 19. In these circumstances we need not attempt any elaborate analysis of how the law stands post-*Derbyshire* in the kinds of case with which it is concerned. Since, however, we heard some useful submissions on the question it may be helpful in

---

[280] UKEAT/0158/09/JOJ; judgment handed down on 29 March 2010.

other cases if we briefly summarise the position as we understand it, while repeating that in most cases this analysis is unnecessary:

(1) It remains necessary formally to ask all three questions which arise from the statutory wording - namely (a) whether the claimant has suffered "less favourable treatment"; (b) whether, if so, that is "by reason that" he or she did the protected act; and (c) whether he or she has suffered a detriment (although, as noted above, questions (a) and (c) substantially overlap). That follows inevitably from the statutory language but it is in any event made clear by Lady Hale: see para. 36 of her speech in *Derbyshire* (p. 854 D-F).

(2) In the case of an act done by an employer to protect himself in litigation involving a discrimination claim, the act should be treated straightforwardly as done by reason of the protected act, i.e. the bringing/continuance of the claim; and the subtle distinctions advanced in *Khan* as to the different capacities of employer and party to litigation should be eschewed.

(3) In considering whether the act complained of constituted a detriment the starting-point is how it would have been perceived by a reasonable litigant; but such a litigant could not properly regard as a detriment conduct by the employer which constituted no more than reasonable conduct in defence of his position in the litigation.

(4) There is no "honest and reasonable" defence as such; but the exercise required under (3) will in all or most cases lead to the same result as if there were.'

Nagarajan

3.143 This, then, leads to a passage in the speech of Lord Nicholls in *Nagarajan v London Regional Transport*,[281] which remains a helpful guide in deciding whether or not there has been victimisation, although it should be read in the light of the case law concerning what is now s 136 of the EQA 2010, concerning the burden of proof in claims of a contravention of that Act.[282] The passage is in these terms:[283]

'Although victimisation has a ring of conscious targeting, this is an insufficient basis for excluding cases of unrecognised prejudice from the scope of section 2. Such an exclusion would partially undermine the protection section 2 seeks to give those who have sought to rely on the Act or been involved in the operation of the Act in other ways.

Decisions are frequently reached for more than one reason. Discrimination may be on racial grounds even though it is not the sole ground for the decision. A variety of phrases, with different shades of meaning, have been used to explain how the legislation applies in such cases: discrimination requires that racial grounds were a cause, the activating cause, a substantial and effective cause, a substantial reason, an important factor. No one phrase is obviously preferable to all others, although in the application of this legislation legalistic phrases, as well as subtle distinctions, are better avoided so far as possible. If racial grounds or protected acts had a significant influence on the outcome, discrimination is made out.'

---

[281] [1999] ICR 877.
[282] See **12.62** concerning s 136.
[283] [1999] ICR 877, 886.

3.144　The application of EQA 2010, s 136 will mean that the final sentence of that extract is no longer applicable. Thus, if the claimant is able to satisfy the court or tribunal that 'there are facts from which the court [or tribunal] could decide, in the absence of any other explanation, that [the defendant/respondent] contravened [s 27 of the EQA 2010], the court must hold that the contravention occurred' unless '[the defendant/respondent] shows that [he, she or it] did not contravene [s 27]'. However, subject to that qualification, the passage from *Nagarajan* set out immediately above is a good guide to courts and tribunals when applying s 27 of the EQA 2010.

ANCILLARY PROVISIONS

3.145　Part 8 of the Equality Act 2010 deals with several provisions that are ancillary to the account of prohibited conduct contained in Part 2, Chapter 2, and discussed in this chapter above. Here are to be found familiar rules regarding (1) relationships that have ended, (2) liability of employers and principals, (3) liability of employees and agents, (4) instructing, causing or inducing discrimination, and (5) aiding contraventions.

Relationships that have ended

3.146　Section 108 of the 2010 Act makes it unlawful to discriminate against or harass someone after a relationship covered by the Act. It extends to any former relationship in which the Act prohibits one person from discriminating against or harassing another (for example, in employment or in the provision of services). The intention is to ensure that unlawful treatment proximate to the former relationship remains unlawful after that relationship has ended. The section replaces similar provisions in pre-existing legislation, but goes further. It extends to discrimination outside the workplace because of age, religion or belief, and sexual orientation.[284]

3.147　The Explanatory Notes provide the following examples:

- A school or employer refuses to give a reference to an ex-pupil or ex-employee because of their religion or belief. This would be direct discrimination.

- A builder or plumber addresses abusive and hostile remarks to a previous customer because of her gender after their business relationship has ended. This would be harassment. It would not be harassment, however, where the reason for the treatment was not the customer's gender but, for example, a dispute over payment.

- A disabled former employee's benefits include life-time use of the company's in-house gym facilities. The employer or owner of the premises

---

[284]　EN paras 357–362.

must make reasonable adjustments to enable the former employee to continue using the facilities even after she has retired.[285]

These examples illustrate how s 108 works in practice. The detail of this section is as follows.

3.148 A person (A) must not discriminate against another (B) if (a) the discrimination arises out of and is closely connected to a relationship which used to exist between them, and (b) conduct of a description constituting the discrimination would, if it occurred during the relationship, contravene the Act.[286] Equally a person (A) must not harass another (B) if (a) the harassment arises out of and is closely connected to a relationship which used to exist between them, and (b) conduct of a description constituting the harassment would, if it occurred during the relationship, contravene the Act.[287] It does not matter whether the relationship ended before or after the commencement of s 108.[288]

3.149 Section 108 works in relation to the duty to make reasonable adjustments in the following way. A duty to make reasonable adjustments applies to A insofar as B continues to be placed at a substantial (that is, more than minor or trivial)[289] disadvantage (as required by the s 20 duty to make adjustments).[290] For this purpose, ss 20–22 (adjustments for disabled persons) and Schs 2, 4, 8, 13, 15 and 21 (which deal with the detail of the duty to make adjustments in services and public functions, premises, work, education and associations respectively) are to be construed as if the relationship had not ended.[291]

3.150 For the purposes of Part 9 (enforcement), a contravention of s 108 (relationships that have ended) relates to the Part of the 2010 Act that would have been contravened if the relationship had not ended.[292] However, conduct is not a contravention of s 108 insofar as it also amounts to victimisation of B by A.[293] In that case, the conduct will be dealt with under the victimisation provisions of the Act.[294]

Liability of employers and principals

3.151 Section 109 contains the familiar provision whereby employers and principals are made liable for acts of discrimination, harassment and victimisation carried out by their employees in the course of employment or by

---

[285] EN para 362.
[286] EQA 2010, s 108(1).
[287] EQA 2010, s 108(2).
[288] EQA 2010, s 108(3).
[289] EQA 2010, s 212(1).
[290] EQA 2010, s 108(4).
[291] EQA 2010, s 108(5).
[292] EQA 2010, s 108(6).
[293] EQA 2010, s 108(7).
[294] EQA 2010, s 27.

their agents acting under their authority. Knowledge or approval of such acts is not required to establish liability. However, employers might be able to show that they took all reasonable steps to prevent their employees from acting unlawfully and thereby escape liability. The section replaces similar provisions in pre-existing legislation.[295]

3.152 The Explanatory Notes offer the following examples:[296]

- A landlord (the principal) instructs an agent to collect rent at a property. The agent harasses an Asian couple, who bring a claim in which the agent is held to have acted unlawfully. The principal may be held liable for breaching the harassment provisions even if unaware of the agent's actions.

- A shop owner becomes aware that her employee is refusing to serve disabled customers. The employer tells the employee to treat disabled customers in the same way as other customers and sends the employee on a diversity training course. However, the employee continues to treat disabled customers less favourably. One such customer brings a claim against both the employee and the employer. The employer may avoid liability by arguing that she took all reasonable steps to stop the employee from acting in a discriminatory way.

The section applies in the following way.

3.153 Anything done by a person (A) in the course of A's employment must be treated as also done by the employer.[297] In like manner, anything done by an agent for a principal, with the authority of the principal, must be treated as also done by the principal.[298] It does not matter whether the thing is done with the employer's or principal's knowledge or approval.[299] The effect is that both the employer and employee (and principal and agent, as the case may be) are jointly liable for the unlawful act.[300]

---

[295] EN paras 363–366. SDA 1975, s 41; RRA, s 32; DDA 1995, s 58. See: *Kingston v BRB* [1982] IRLR 274, EAT; *Balgobin v Tower Hamlets LBC* [1987] IRLR 401, EAT; *Nagarajan v Agnew* [1994] IRLR 61, EAT; *Jones v Tower Boot Co Ltd* [1997] IRLR 168, CA; *Waters v Commissioner of Police of the Metropolis* [1997] IRLR 589, CA; *Chief Constable of Lincolnshire Police v Stubbs* [1999] IRLR 81, EAT; *Canniffe v East Riding of Yorkshire Council* [2000] IRLR 555, EAT; *Lana v Positive Action Training in Housing (London) Ltd* [2001] IRLR 501, EAT; *Liversidge v Chief Constable of Bedfordshire Police* [2002] IRLR 651, CA; *Croft v Royal Mail Group plc* [2003] IRLR 592, CA.

[296] EN para 366.

[297] EQA 2010, s 109(1). The common law rules on 'in the course of employment' in the context of vicarious liability will not apply: *Bracebridge Engineering Ltd v Darby* [1990] IRLR 3, EAT; *Jones v Tower Boot Co Ltd* [1997] IRLR 168, CA; *Chief Constable of Lincolnshire Police v Stubbs* [1999] IRLR 81, EAT.

[298] EQA 2010, s 109(2).

[299] EQA 2010, s 109(3).

[300] This is the effect of the interaction of EQA 2010, ss 109 and 110: *Enterprise Glass Co Ltd v Miles* [1990] ICR 787, EAT; *AM v WC and SPV* [1999] IRLR 410, EAT.

3.154 In proceedings against A's employer (B) in respect of anything alleged to have been done by A in the course of A's employment it is a defence for B to show that B took all reasonable steps to prevent A (a) from doing the thing, or (b) from doing anything of that description.[301] Section 109 does not apply to criminal offences under the Act, with the exception of offences under Part 12 (disabled persons: transport).[302]

Liability of employees and agents

3.155 Section 110 provides that an employee is personally liable for unlawful acts committed in the course of employment where, because of s 109 discussed immediately above, the employer is also liable (or would be but for the defence of having taken all reasonable steps to prevent the employee from doing the relevant thing). An agent would also be personally liable under s 110 for any unlawful acts committed under a principal's authority. However, an employee or agent will not be liable if he or she has been told by the employer or principal that the act is lawful and he or she reasonably believes this to be true.[303]

3.156 Section 110 does not replicate exactly the provisions in existing legislation that address the aiding of unlawful acts.[304] It is said to take 'a more direct approach' and, unlike the law which it replaces, it is not necessary to show that the employee or agent knew that the act was unlawful.[305]

3.157 The Explanatory Notes illustrate how s 110 is intended to work:

- A factory worker racially harasses her colleague. The factory owner would be liable for the worker's actions, but is able to show that he took all reasonable steps to stop the harassment. The colleague can still bring a claim against the factory worker in an employment tribunal.

- A principal instructs an agent to sell products on her behalf. The agent discriminates against a disabled customer. Both the principal and the agent are liable, but the courts are able to determine that evidence provided by the principal indicate the authority given to the agent did not extend to carrying out an authorised act in a discriminatory manner. The disabled customer can still bring a claim against the agent.

The detailed provisions of s 110 appear as follows.

---

[301] EQA 2010, s 109(4). See *Balgobin and Francis v London Borough of Tower Hamlets* [1987] IRLR 401, EAT; *Canniffe v East Riding of Yorkshire Council* [2000] IRLR 555, EAT.
[302] EQA 2010, s 109(5).
[303] EN paras 367–370.
[304] SDA 1975, s 42; RRA 1976, s 33; DDA 1995, s 57.
[305] EN para 370.

3.158 A person (A) contravenes s 110 if the following conditions are met.[306] First, A is an employee or agent. Secondly, A does a thing which, by virtue of s 109(1) or (2), is treated as having been done by A's employer or principal (as the case may be). Anything done by a person (A) in the course of A's employment is treated as also done by the employer, while anything done by an agent for a principal, with the authority of the principal, is treated as also done by the principal. Thirdly, the doing of the thing by A amounts to a contravention of the Act by the employer or principal (as the case may be).

3.159 It does not matter whether, in any proceedings, the employer is found not to have contravened the Act by virtue of s 109(4).[307] As we have seen, ordinarily s 109(4) provides that in proceedings against A's employer (B) in respect of anything alleged to have been done by A in the course of A's employment it is a defence for B to show that B took all reasonable steps to prevent A (a) from doing the thing, or (b) from doing anything of that description.

3.160 A does not contravene s 110 if:

(a) A relies on a statement by the employer or principal that doing the thing is not a contravention of the Act, and

(b) it is reasonable for A to do so.[308] However, a person (B) commits an offence if B knowingly or recklessly makes such a statement which is false or misleading in a material respect.[309] A person guilty of such an offence is liable on summary conviction to a fine not exceeding level 5 on the standard scale (£5,000).[310]

3.161 Part 9 of the Act (on enforcement) applies to a contravention of s 110 by A as if it were a contravention of the Act by the employer or principal (as the case may be).[311] The reference to a contravention of the Act does not include a reference to disability discrimination in contravention of Chapter 1 of Part 6 (schools).[312]

Instructing, causing or inducing discrimination

3.162 Section 111 addresses instructing, causing or inducing discrimination. A person (A) must not instruct another (B) to do in relation to a third person (C) anything which contravenes Part 3 (service and public functions), Part 4 (premises), Part 5 (work), Part 6 (education) or Part 7 (associations) of the

---

[306] EQA 2010, s 110(1).
[307] EQA 2010, s 110(2).
[308] EQA 2010, s 110(3).
[309] EQA 2010, s 110(4).
[310] EQA 2010, s 110(5).
[311] EQA 2010, s 110(6).
[312] EQA 2010, s 110(7).

Act.[313] A must not instruct B to do in relation to C anything which contravenes s 108(1) or s 108(2) (discrimination or harassment in relation to a relationship which has ended).[314]

3.163 A must not instruct B to do in relation to C anything which contravenes s 112(1) (aiding contraventions: a basic contravention).[315] A must not cause B to do in relation to C anything which is a basic contravention.[316] A must not induce B to do in relation to C anything which is a basic contravention.[317] For this last purpose, inducement may be direct or indirect.[318]

3.164 Proceedings for a contravention of s 111 may be brought (a) by B, if B is subjected to a detriment as a result of A's conduct; or (b) by C, if C is subjected to a detriment as a result of A's conduct; or (c) by the Equality and Human Rights Commission.[319] For these purposes, it does not matter whether the basic contravention occurs or whether any other proceedings are (or may be) brought in relation to A's conduct.[320]

3.165 Section 111 does not apply unless the relationship between A and B is such that A is in a position to commit a basic contravention in relation to B.[321] A reference in s 111 to causing or inducing a person to do a thing includes a reference to attempting to cause or induce the person to do the thing.[322] For the purposes of Part 9 (enforcement), a contravention of s 111 is to be treated as relating, in a case within s 111(5)(a), to the Part of the Act which, because of the relationship between A and B, A is in a position to contravene in relation to B.[323] A contravention of s 111 is to be treated as relating, in a case within s 111(5)(b), to the Part of the Act which, because of the relationship between B and C, B is in a position to contravene in relation to C.[324]

3.166 These are undoubtedly difficult provisions. The Explanatory Notes start by making the obvious point that s 111 makes it unlawful for a person to instruct, cause or induce someone to discriminate against, harass or victimise another person, or to attempt to do so. The section provides a remedy for both the recipient of the instruction and the intended victim. This is so whether or not the instruction is carried out, provided the recipient or intended victim suffers a detriment as a result. However, the section only applies where the

---

[313] EQA 2010, s 111(1).
[314] EQA 2010, s 111(1).
[315] EQA 2010, s 111(1).
[316] EQA 2010, s 111(2).
[317] EQA 2010, s 111(3).
[318] EQA 2010, s 111(4).
[319] EQA 2010, s 111(5).
[320] EQA 2010, s 111(6).
[321] EQA 2010, s 111(7).
[322] EQA 2010, s 111(8).
[323] EQA 2010, s 111(9)(a).
[324] EQA 2010, s 111(9)(b).

person giving the instruction is in a relationship with the recipient of the instruction in which discrimination, harassment or victimisation is prohibited.[325]

3.167 The Equality and Human Rights Commission can enforce s 111 using its statutory powers under the Equality Act 2006. Both the recipient of the instruction and the intended victim can also bring individual claims for its breach against the person giving the instructions where they have suffered a detriment as a result. A claim brought by the recipient of the instruction will be dealt with in the same tribunal or court as a direct claim for discrimination, harassment or victimisation against the person giving the instruction would be brought. A claim brought by the intended victim against the person giving the instruction will be dealt with in the same tribunal or court as a claim for discrimination, harassment or victimisation against the person carrying out the instruction would be brought.[326]

3.168 Section 111 replaces the uneven coverage of similar provisions in parts of the existing legislation.[327] However, it extends protection to all protected characteristics in all areas covered by the 2010 Act. It also empowers the Equality and Human Rights Commission to bring enforcement proceedings in a uniform way in relation to any action in breach of the section. Largely new provision is made to allow persons instructed to bring proceedings as a statutory right.[328] The provision allowing the intended victim to bring proceedings, even where the instruction is not carried out, is also new.[329]

3.169 The Explanatory Notes offer the following illustration of s 111 in action. A GP instructs his receptionist not to register anyone with an Asian name. The receptionist would have a claim against the GP if subjected to a detriment for not doing so. A potential patient would also have a claim against the GP if she discovered the instruction had been given and was put off applying to register. The receptionist's claim against the GP would be brought before the employment tribunal as it relates to employment, while the potential patient's claim would be brought in the county court as it relates to services.[330]

3.170 An unpublished, but widely leaked, reasoned opinion was sent to the UK Government on 26 November 2009 by the European Commission. In part, the reasoned opinion questioned whether UK legislation (pre-Equality Act 2010) dealt adequately with instructions to discriminate.[331] This appears to have been addressed by the Equality Act 2010.

---

[325] EN paras 371–373.
[326] EN para 374.
[327] SDA 1975, ss 39–40; RRA, ss 30–31; DDA 1995, s 16C. See *CRE v Imperial Society of Teachers of Dancing* [1983] IRLR 315, EAT.
[328] See *Weathersfield v Sargent* [1999] IRLR 94.
[329] EN para 375.
[330] EN para 375.
[331] The challenge is to the compatibility of Employment Equality (Sexual Orientation) Regulations 2003, SI 2003/1661, reg 7(3) with Art 4 of the EU Equal Treatment Framework Directive. See Rubenstein, 2010.

Aiding contraventions

3.171 Section 112(1) is concerned with the unlawfulness of aiding contraventions. A person (A) must not knowingly help another (B) to do anything which contravenes Part 3, 4, 5, 6 or 7 or ss 108(1) or (2) or 111 (a basic contravention).[332]

3.172 It is not a contravention of s 112(1) if (a) A relies on a statement by B that the act for which the help is given does not contravene the Act, and (b) it is reasonable for A to do so.[333] However, B commits an offence if B knowingly or recklessly makes such a statement which is false or misleading in a material respect.[334] A person guilty of this offence is liable on summary conviction to a fine not exceeding level 5 on the standard scale (£5,000).[335]

3.173 For the purposes of the enforcement provisions in Part 9 of the Act (enforcement), a contravention of s 112 (aiding contraventions) is to be treated as relating to the provision of the Act to which the basic contravention relates.[336] The reference in s 112(1) to a basic contravention does not include a reference to disability discrimination in contravention of Chapter 1 of Part 6 of the Act (schools).[337]

3.174 The Explanatory Notes offer the following explanation.[338] Section 112 makes it unlawful for a person to help someone carry out an act which he or she knows is unlawful under the Act. However, it is not unlawful if the person giving assistance has been told that the act is lawful, provided he or she reasonably believes this to be true. Breaches of the prohibition on aiding contraventions are dealt with under the same procedures in the Act as the contraventions themselves.

3.175 Section 112 is designed to replicate the effect of similar provisions in the legacy legislation.[339] It ensures that a person who helps another to do something which they know to be prohibited by the Act is liable in their own right. Taken together with ss 109–111 it should ensure that both the person carrying out an unlawful act and any person on whose behalf or with whose help they were acting can be held to account where appropriate.[340] The Explanatory Notes furnish this example. On finding out that a new tenant is

---

[332] EQA 2010, s 112(1).
[333] EQA 2010, s 112(2).
[334] EQA 2010, s 112(3).
[335] EQA 2010, s 112(4).
[336] EQA 2010, s 112(5).
[337] EQA 2010, s 112(6).
[338] EN paras 376–378.
[339] SDA 1975, s 42; RRA 1976, s 33; DDA 1995, s 57. See: *Anyanwu v South Bank Student Union* [2001] IRLR 305, HL; *Hallam v Avery* [2001] IRLR 312, HL; *Yeboah v Crofton* [2002] IRLR 634, CA; *Sinclair Roche & Temperley v Heard* [2004] IRLR 763, EAT; *Shepherd v North Yorkshire County Council* [2006] IRLR 190, EAT; *Gilbank v Miles* [2006] EWCA Civ 543, [2006] IRLR 538, CA; *Allaway v Reilly* [2007] IRLR 864, EAT; *Bird v Sylvester* [2008] IRLR 232, CA.
[340] EN para 379.

gay, a landlord discriminates against him by refusing him access to certain facilities, claiming that they are not part of the tenancy agreement. Another tenant knows this to be false but joins in with the landlord in refusing the new tenant access to the facilities in question. The new tenant can bring a discrimination claim against both the landlord and the tenant who helped him.[341]

---

[341] EN para 379.

Chapter 4

SERVICES AND FUNCTIONS

INTRODUCTION

Scope

4.1   The Equality Act 2010 (EQA 2010) Part 3 covers the provision of services and public functions.[1] Broadly it reflects the scope of pre-existing legislation which addresses discrimination in relation to services and functions in respect of all the protected characteristics except age, marriage and civil partnership.[2] However, the protection of the pre-existing legislation is not uniform for the different protected characteristics. For example, there is no protection from discrimination in the exercise of public functions because of pregnancy and maternity or because a person is intending to undergo, is undergoing or has undergone gender reassignment. In addition, there is no protection for discrimination because of age, either in the provision of services or in the exercise of public functions.[3] These provisions aim to address this.

4.2   Section 28 begins by dealing with the application of Part 3 of the Act.

Age, marriage and civil partnership

4.3   Part 3, on services and public functions, does not apply to the protected characteristic of age, so far as relating to persons who have not yet attained the age of 18, nor to the protected characteristics of marriage and civil partnership.[4] Thus the Act does not make it unlawful to discriminate against or harass people in relation to the provision of services or the exercise of public functions because they are married or in a civil partnership or because of their age if under 18.

4.4   The government's approach to implementation of the age discrimination services provisions was set out in the evidence given to the Joint Committee on Human Rights (JCHR) Legislative Scrutiny of the Equality Bill and contained

---

1   EQA 2010, ss 28–31 and Sch 3.
2   The pre-existing provisions are the Sex Discrimination Act 1975 (SDA 1975), ss 21A and 29; Race Relations Act 1976 (RRA 1976), ss 19B and 20(1); Disability Discrimination Act 1995 (DDA 1995), ss 19 and 21B; Equality Act 2006, ss 46(1) and 52(1); Equality Act (Sexual Orientation) Regulations 2007, SI 2007/1263, regs 4 and 8.
3   EN para 115.
4   EQA 2010, s 28(1).

in their report.[5] This stated that the ban on age discrimination together with any orders providing for exceptions to this ban are intended to be implemented by 2012.[6]

4.5   The Joint Committee on Human Rights in its report on the Equality Bill (Joint Committee on Human Rights, 2009) was critical of the government's approach to age discrimination and services and functions, stating that:[7]

> 'The total absence of protection against age discrimination for those under 18 in service provision and the limited protection in relation to the performance of public functions means that children who are subject to unjustified discrimination are left with little or no legal protection. This may prevent children enjoying full protection of their rights as set out in the UN Convention on the Rights of the Child (UNCRC).'[8]

The Joint Committee further recommended that the prohibition of discrimination against married persons or persons in a civil partnership should be extended to cover harassment and discrimination in the provision of goods and services.[9]

Premises, work and education

4.6   Part 3 on services and functions does not apply to discrimination, harassment or victimisation that is prohibited by Part 4 (premises), Part 5 (work) or Part 6 (education) or anything that would be so prohibited but for an express exception.[10] Thus if an act of discrimination, harassment or victimisation is made unlawful by other Parts of the Act covering premises, work or education, then those provisions, rather than the provisions covering services and public functions, apply.[11]

Equality clauses and non-discrimination rules

4.7   Part 3 on services and public functions does not apply to a breach of an equality clause or rule.[12] It also does not apply to anything that would be a breach of an equality clause or rule but for s 69 (defence of material factor) or Part 2 of Sch 7 (occupational pension schemes).[13] Additionally, Part 3 does not apply to a breach of a non-discrimination rule.[14]

---

[5]   Joint Committee on Human Rights, 2009.
[6]   Joint Committee on Human Rights, 2009: para 38, and Ev 67 at Q24. See also Government Equalities Office, 2009c.
[7]   Joint Committee on Human Rights, 2009.
[8]   Joint Committee on Human Rights, 2009: para 44.
[9]   Joint Committee on Human Rights, 2009, para 68.
[10] EQA 2010, s 28(2).
[11] EN para 108.
[12] EQA 2010, s 28(3)(a).
[13] EQA 2010, s 28(3)(b).
[14] EQA 2010, s 28(3)(c).

SERVICES

Service provider

4.8 Section 29 of the Act sets out what is prohibited under the services provisions.

4.9 A service provider is a person who is concerned with the provision of a service to the public or a section of the public, for payment or not.[15] The provision of a service includes the provision of goods or facilities.[16] There is no list of examples of service provision as there was in pre-existing legislation. However, the draft Code of Practice[17] (the Draft Code) sets out a lengthy non-exhaustive list of what services might be covered, including those services, such as access to a place which members of the public are permitted to enter, which were previously listed in the legislation.[18]

4.10 There is no territorial limitation to these provisions, other than in relation to information society services (the Internet)[19] – more detail is given in relation to this in Chapter 14.

4.11 Where an employer arranges for another person to provide a service only to the employer's employees, the employer is not to be regarded as the service provider, but the employees are to be regarded as a section of the public.[20] This means that employees who are subjected to discrimination in the provision of such a service can bring a claim under the services provisions. This is not the case, however, in relation to a relevant financial service arranged by an employer[21] – more detail is given below under exceptions.

4.12 In relation to the provision of a service by either House of Parliament, the service provider is the Corporate Officer of the House concerned; and if the service involves access to, or use of, a place in the Palace of Westminster which members of the public are allowed to enter, both Corporate Officers are jointly the service provider.[22]

---

[15] EQA 2010, s 29(1).
[16] EQA 2010, s 31(2).
[17] Services Public Functions and Associations: Statutory Code of Practice, Draft for Consultation, December 2009 ('Draft Code'). See Equality and Human Rights Commission, 2010c.
[18] See Draft Code para 11.3.
[19] EQA 2010, s 206 and Sch 25.
[20] EQA 2010, s 31(5).
[21] EQA 2010, Sch 3, para 20.
[22] EQA 2010, s 31(8).

Services discrimination

4.13 A service provider must not discriminate against a person requiring the service by not providing the person with the service.[23] 'Requiring a service' includes a reference to a person who is seeking to obtain or use the service.[24]

4.14 Not providing a service includes not providing a service of the quality that the service provider usually provides to the public (or the section of it which includes the person); or the service provider not providing the service in the manner in which or on the terms on which the service provider usually provides the service to the public (or the section of it which includes the person).[25]

4.15 In addition, a service provider (A) must not, in providing the service, discriminate against a person (B): (a) as to the terms on which A provides the service to B; (b) by terminating the provision of the service to B; or (c) by subjecting B to any other detriment.[26] Subjecting to a detriment was not, in any of the pre-existing legislation, a type of prohibited conduct for the purposes of the services provisions. Including 'detriment' brings these provisions into line with those relating to education and to premises and enables conduct which does not easily fit within the other types of unlawful conduct to be covered.

4.16 The Explanatory Notes include some basic examples of discrimination in services:[27]

- A man and two female friends plan a night out at a local night club. At the entrance the man is charged £10 entry; the two women are charged £5 each. The owner explains the night club is trying to attract more women and has decided to charge them half the entrance fee. This would be direct sex discrimination.

- A company which organises outdoor activity breaks requires protective headwear to be worn for certain activities, such as white water rafting and rock climbing. This requirement could be indirectly discriminatory against Sikhs unless it can be justified, for example on health and safety grounds.

Harassment

4.17 In addition, a service provider must not, in relation to the provision of the service, harass a person requiring the service, or a person to whom the service provider provides the service.[28]

---

[23] EQA 2010, s 29(1).
[24] EQA 2010, s 31(6).
[25] EQA 2010, s 31(7)(a) and (b).
[26] EQA 2010, s 29(2).
[27] EN para 116.
[28] EQA 2010, s 29(3).

4.18 The Explanatory Notes provides the following example of how this might operate. A black man goes into a bar to watch a football match. He is served a pint of beer and takes a seat at an empty table. Whilst watching the football match the bartender and a number of customers make racist remarks about some of the footballers on the pitch. When the man complains he is then called a number of derogatory names. This would be harassment because of race.[29]

4.19 Harassment as a form of prohibited conduct is defined in s 26 of the Act and has been discussed in Chapter 3 above. However, in the application of s 26 (harassment) in the context of s 29(3) (harassment in relation to the provision of a service), religion or belief and sexual orientation are not relevant protected characteristics.[30]

4.20 The Joint Committee expressed its concern about the exclusion of sexual orientation from the harassment provisions. It considered that the absence of an explicit prohibition on harassment related to sexual orientation in the areas of service provision and the performance of public functions 'represents a significant gap in the protection against discrimination offered by the Bill'.[31]

4.21 Claims for harassment based on sexual orientation and/or religion and belief may still be possible if the treatment amounts to direct discrimination. The Act specifically provides[32] that where the Act disapplies a prohibition on harassment in relation to a specified protected characteristic, the disapplication does not prevent conduct relating to that characteristic from amounting to a detriment for the purposes of discrimination within s 13 because of that characteristic.

Victimisation

4.22 A service provider must not victimise a person requiring the service by not providing them with the service.[33] In addition, a service provider (A) must not, in providing the service, victimise a person (B) (a) as to the terms on which A provides the service to B; (b) by terminating the provision of the service to B; or (c) by subjecting B to any other detriment.[34]

---

29   EN para 116.
30   EQA 2010, s 29(8).
31   Joint Committee on Human Rights, 2009: para 114.
32   EQA 2010, s 212(5).
33   EQA 2010, s 29(4).
34   EQA 2010, s 29(5).

REASONABLE ADJUSTMENTS: SERVICES

Overview

4.23 Disabled people enjoy the same rights in respect of the provision of services as apply to persons with other protected characteristics. However, they also benefit from the duty to make reasonable adjustments, which does not apply to other protected characteristics. Broadly, the duty is similar to the duty which applied under the Disability Discrimination Act 1995 (DDA 1995).[35] Services providers must make anticipatory adjustments to the way in which their services are provided to ensure that disabled people can use them.

4.24 A duty to make reasonable adjustments applies to a service provider.[36] Schedule 2 sets out the specifics of the duty. The basic components of the duty to make reasonable adjustments are set out in s 20, and this has been explained in Chapter 3.

The duty

4.25 A services provider (A) must comply with the first, second and third requirements (provision, criterion or practice; auxiliary aids and services; physical features).[37] The Schedule specifically states that for the purposes of these duties the reference in ss 20(3), 20(4) or 20(5) to a disabled person is to disabled persons generally.[38]

4.26 It is this application to disabled people as a whole which is intended to make the duty 'anticipatory' and thereby different from the duty applied in the employment and the premises context. It is explained in the Explanatory Notes as follows: 'As the duty is owed to disabled persons generally, it is an anticipatory duty which means service providers and people exercising public functions must anticipate the needs of disabled people and make appropriate reasonable adjustments.'[39]

Physical features

4.27 There are specific provisions relating to the definition of physical features in the context of services and functions, and the nature of the reasonable adjustment duty relating to them.

---

[35] See DDA 1995, ss 19(1)(b) and 21. Cases determined under these provisions will undoubtedly be of assistance in any reasonable adjustment cases under these services provisions. See, for example, *Ross v Ryanair and Stansted Airport* [2004] EWCA Civ 1751; and *Royal Bank of Scotland v David Allen* [2009] EWCA Civ 1213.

[36] EQA 2010, s 29(7)(a).

[37] EQA 2010, Sch 2, para 2(1).

[38] EQA 2010, Sch 2, para 2(2).

[39] EN para 684. See also *Roads v Central Trains Ltd* [2004] EWCA Civ 1541 for a discussion of the anticipatory nature of the duty to make reasonable adjustments under DDA 1995, s 21.

4.28 Physical features are defined as including a physical feature brought by or on behalf of A (in the course of providing the service) onto premises other than those that A occupies (as well as including a physical feature in or on premises that A occupies).[40]

4.29 In addition, the second requirement – in relation to physical features – is to be read as though for avoiding the disadvantage there were substituted (a) to avoid the disadvantage, or (b) to adopt a reasonable alternative method of providing the service.[41]

4.30 As the reference to 'substantial disadvantage' includes a reference to removing, altering or providing a reasonable means of avoiding the feature,[42] the wording of the duty in relation to services reflects the wording of the duty relating to physical features in the DDA 1995. This provided that reasonable steps should be taken to remove a feature; to alter a feature; to provide a reasonable means of avoiding a feature; or to provide a reasonable alternative method of providing the service.[43]

4.31 Thus services providers are subject to the following obligations:

- where a provision, criterion or practice puts disabled people at a substantial disadvantage in relation to the provision of the service in comparison with persons who are not disabled, the service provider must take such steps as it is reasonable to have to take to avoid the disadvantage;

- where a physical feature puts disabled people at a substantial disadvantage in relation to the provision of the service in comparison with persons who are not disabled, the service provider must take such steps as it is reasonable to have to take to avoid the disadvantage (including removing the feature; altering it, or providing a reasonable means of avoiding it)[44] or to adopt a reasonable alternative method of providing the service;

- where disabled people would, but for the provision of an auxiliary aid, be put at a substantial disadvantage in relation to the provision of the service in comparison with persons who are not disabled, the service provider must take such steps as it is reasonable to have to take to provide the auxiliary aid.

---

[40] EQA 2010, Sch 2, para 2(6).

[41] EQA 2010, Sch 2, para 2(3).

[42] EQA 2010, s 20(9). This was inserted as a result of a relatively late amendment – see Hansard, 23 March 2010, col 859.

[43] DDA 1995, s 21(2).

[44] Although there is no explicit hierarchy to these adjustments, the Minister, when introducing this amendment, referred in effect to an implicit hierarchy, stating: 'It makes clear that an association should consider a reasonable alternative method of affording access to a benefit facility or service, et cetera, where the substantial disadvantage caused by a physical feature cannot be reasonably avoided' Hansard, 23 March 2010, col 858.

4.32　An example of how the duties might operate is given in the Explanatory Notes.[45] 'The manager of a large shop in a national chain installs a ramp, automatic entry doors, hearing induction loops and waives the 'no dogs policy' in respect of assistance dogs, to comply with the duty to make reasonable adjustments.'

Limitations

4.33　There is a limitation on the duty in relation to service provision, in that nothing requires a service provider (A) to take steps which would fundamentally alter (a) the nature of the service; or (b) the nature of A's trade or profession.[46] This limitation appeared in the equivalent DDA 1995 provisions.[47] Although there is no detail in the Draft Code about this provision, the Code of Practice: Rights of Access; Services to the Public, Public Authority Functions and Private Clubs[48] indicates a relatively narrow meaning, stating, at para 10.39, that this means that a service provider does not have to comply with a duty to make reasonable adjustments in a way that would so alter the nature of its business that the service provider would effectively be providing a completely different kind of service.

PUBLIC FUNCTIONS

4.34　It is unlawful to do anything that constitutes discrimination, harassment or victimisation in the exercise of a public function which does not involve the provision of a service.[49]

A public function

4.35　A public function is a function that is a function of a public nature for the purposes of the Human Rights Act 1998.[50] The Explanatory Notes provide examples of public functions not involving the provision of a service, which include licensing functions; Government and local authority public consultation exercises; the provision of public highways; planning permission decisions; and core functions of the prison service and the probation service[51]. As Part 3 does not apply to discrimination harassment or victimisation that is prohibited by other parts of the Act,[52] the public function provisions are to some extent 'residual', applying where other provisions do not.

---

[45]　EN para 686.
[46]　EQA 2010, Sch 2, para 2(7).
[47]　DDA 1995, s 21(6).
[48]　Disability Rights Commission, 2006. Although this Code will be revoked once the Draft Code is finalised and so it will have no legal force, it will nevertheless provide useful illustrations of some of the disability specific concepts in the services and function provisions.
[49]　EQA 2010, s 29(6).
[50]　EQA 2010, s 31(4).
[51]　EN para 125.
[52]　EQA 2010, s 28(2) and see **4.6**.

4.36 The need for explicit coverage of public functions arose primarily from case-law under the Race Relations Act 1976 (RRA 1976) which determined that the carrying out of certain activities did not fall within the services provisions of the RRA 1976 but were functions, and, as there were no provisions covering functions, were therefore excluded from the scope of the RRA 1976. The distinction became irrelevant, bar in the context of the DDA 1995,[53] once the pre-existing legislation introduced provisions to cover functions.

4.37 The provisions in the Act are in effect the same for services as for functions, including in relation to disability discrimination.

4.38 Whilst all the anti-discrimination provisions prior to the Equality Act contained provisions prohibiting discrimination in the exercise of public functions, the definition of public function was never explicitly tied to the Human Rights Act 1998. The Joint Committee was critical of the Equality Act's approach to the definition. Its view was that the development of the case-law concerning the interpretation of s 6 of the HRA 1998 'has left real gaps and inadequacies in human rights protection in the UK. The use of the HRA definition in this Bill to define the scope of public functions ensures that these gaps are carried across into the definition of public functions'.[54] The Committee went on to state, however, that the impact in the context of public functions (as opposed to under the equality duties) would be less of a problem as the prohibition on discrimination extends to services and is not limited to public functions.

4.39 There is no further elaboration in the Act of the particular situations in which it is unlawful to discriminate – it is simply in the exercise of public functions. This reflects the approach in pre-existing legislation. The Draft Code explains the provisions as including:

> 'refusing to allow someone to benefit from the exercise of a function (for example, being refused a discretionary welfare benefit such as the social fund); and/or treating a person in a worse manner in the exercise of a function (for example, being dismissive of an application to adopt).'[55]

Harassment

4.40 Harassment as a form of prohibited conduct is defined in s 26 of the Act and has been discussed in Chapter 3 above. In the application of s 26 (harassment) in the context of s 29(3), religion or belief and sexual orientation are not relevant protected characteristics. The Joint Committee on Human Rights made the same comments regarding the limitations of harassment in relation to public functions as it did in relation to services, and as set out above.

---

[53] The DDA 1995 provisions on functions provided additional justifications to those found in the services provisions – DDA 1995, s 21D(4).
[54] Joint Committee on Human Rights, 2009: 143.
[55] Draft Code of Practice, para 12.20.

As with the services provisions, claims for harassment based on sexual orientation and/or religion and belief may still be possible if the treatment amounts to direct discrimination. The Act specifically provides[56] that where the Act disapplies a prohibition on harassment in relation to a specified protected characteristic, the disapplication does not prevent conduct relating to that characteristic from amounting to a detriment for the purposes of discrimination within s 13 because of that characteristic.

REASONABLE ADJUSTMENTS: PUBLIC FUNCTIONS

Overview

4.41 Disabled persons enjoy the same rights in respect of the exercise of a public function as apply to persons with other protected characteristics. However, they also benefit from the duty to make reasonable adjustments, which does not apply to other protected characteristics.

4.42 A duty to make reasonable adjustments applies to a person who exercises a public function that is not the provision of a service to the public or a section of the public.[57] Schedule 2 sets out the specifics of the duty. The basic components of the duty to make reasonable adjustments are set out in s 20, and this has been explained in Chapter 3.

The duty

4.43 As with the duty to make reasonable adjustments in relation to the provision of a service, a person exercising a public function must comply with the first, second and third requirements.[58] The duty, as with that imposed upon services providers, is anticipatory – the Schedule specifically states that for the purposes of these duties the reference in s 20(3), 20(4) or 20(5) to a disabled person is to disabled persons generally.[59]

4.44 Similarly, the definition of physical features applies to those exercising public functions as it does to services providers. A physical feature includes a physical feature brought by or on behalf of the person exercising a public function (in the course of exercising the function) on to premises other than those occupied by them (as well as including a physical feature in or on premises that they occupy).[60]

---

56 EQA 2010, s 212(5).
57 EQA 2010, s 29(7)(b).
58 EQA 2010, Sch 2, para 2(1).
59 EQA 2010, Sch 2, para 2.
60 EQA 2010, Sch 2, para 2(6).

4.45 The second requirement – in relation to physical features – is to be read as though for avoiding the disadvantage there were substituted: (a) to avoid the disadvantage, or (b) to adopt a reasonable alternative method of exercising the function.[61]

4.46 As set out above, as the reference to 'substantial disadvantage' includes a reference to removing, altering or providing a reasonable means of avoiding the feature,[62] the wording of the duty in relation to functions reflects the wording of the duty relating to physical features in the DDA 1995. This provided that reasonable steps should be taken to remove a feature; to alter a feature; to provide a reasonable means of avoiding a feature; or to provide a reasonable alternative method of providing the function.[63]

4.47 Being placed at a substantial disadvantage in relation to the exercise of a function means:

(a) if a benefit is or may be conferred in the exercise of the function, being placed at a substantial disadvantage in relation to the conferment of the benefit; or

(b) if a person is or may be subjected to a detriment in the exercise of the function, suffering an unreasonably adverse experience when being subjected to the detriment.[64]

4.48 This wording is taken broadly from the wording in the DDA 1995.[65] The wording, as set out in the draft Code of Practice, is intended to reflect the different way in which the exercise of functions impacts upon people. For example, being awarded a state benefit will be in effect the conferment of a benefit. Being arrested will be a detriment. The aim of the duty is to ensure that disabled people are not worse off than others in such situations.[66]

4.49 Thus those exercising public functions are subject to the following obligations:

• where a provision criterion or practice puts disabled people at a substantial disadvantage in relation to the exercise of the function in comparison with persons who are not disabled, the person exercising public functions must take such steps as it is reasonable to have to take to avoid the disadvantage;

---

[61] EQA 2010, Sch 2, para 2(3).
[62] EQA 2010, s 20(9). This was inserted as a result of a relatively late amendment – see Hansard, 23 March 2010: col 859.
[63] DDA 1995, s 21E(4).
[64] EQA 2010, Sch 2, para 2(5).
[65] DDA 1995, s 21E.
[66] See Draft Code of Practice, 12.26.

- where a physical feature puts disabled people at a substantial disadvantage in relation to the exercise of the function in comparison with persons who are not disabled, the person exercising the public function must take such steps as it is reasonable to have to take to avoid the disadvantage (including removing the feature, altering it, or providing a reasonable means of avoiding the feature) or to adopt a reasonable alternative method of providing the function;

- where disabled people would, but for the provision of an auxiliary aid, be put at a substantial disadvantage in relation to the exercise of the function in comparison with persons who are not disabled, the person exercising public functions must take such steps as it is reasonable to have to take to provide the auxiliary aid.

Limitations of the duty

4.50 There is a limitation placed upon the duty in relation to public functions in that there is no requirement to take a step which a person exercising a public function has no power to take.[67]

EXCEPTIONS

4.51 There are a number of exceptions to the services and function provisions. These exceptions are contained in Sch 3 to the Act. Many of these are based on pre-existing legislation. There are in addition general exceptions to which service providers and those exercising public functions are subject. These are contained in Part 14 of the Act and are dealt with in Chapter 14 of this book.

4.52 The exceptions in Sch 3 which are specific to service providers and those exercising public functions are detailed below.

Parliament

4.53 Section 29 does not apply to the exercise of (a) a function of Parliament; or (b) a function exercisable in connection with proceedings in Parliament.[68] This exception is qualified, however, in that it does not permit anything to be done in contravention of that section or in relation to an individual unless it is done by or in pursuance of a resolution or other deliberation of either House or of a Committee of either House.[69]

---

[67] EQA 2010, Sch 2, para 2(8).
[68] EQA 2010, Sch 3, para 1(1).
[69] EQA 2010, Sch 3, para 1(2).

Legislation

4.54 Section 29 does not apply to any steps within the legislative process in Parliament, the Scottish Parliament or the National Assembly for Wales. This includes:

- preparing, making or considering an Act or a Bill for an Act;

- preparing, making, confirming, approving or considering an instrument made under an Act by a Minister of the Crown, the Scottish Minister or a member of the Scottish Executive, the Welsh Ministers, the First Minister for Wales or the Counsel General to the Welsh Assembly Government; or

- preparing, making, confirming, approving or considering an instrument by the General Synod, Her Majesty in Council or the Privy Council.[70]

This provision means that activity related to the preparation and making of primary legislation would be excepted from the prohibition on discrimination. However, activity related to the making of a bye-law by a local authority would not be within these exceptions.[71]

4.55 In addition, s 29 does not apply to anything done in connection with the imposition of a requirement or condition which comes within Sch 22[72] (which sets out circumstances in which it will not be a contravention of the Act in relation to certain protected characteristics to do anything pursuant to a requirement of an enactment).

Judicial functions

4.56 Section 29 does not apply to:

- a judicial function and anything done on behalf of or on the instructions of a person exercising a judicial function;

- a decision not to commence or continue criminal proceedings, and anything done for the purpose of reaching, or in pursuance of, that decision.[73]

A 'judicial function' includes judicial functions exercised by a person other than a court or tribunal.[74]

---

[70]   EQA 2010, Sch 3, para 2(1)–(5).
[71]   EN para 691.
[72]   EQA 2010, Sch 3, para 2(6).
[73]   EQA 2010, Sch 3, para 3(1).
[74]   EQA 2010, Sch 3, para 3(2).

4.57 An example of how this exception would work in practice is given in the Explanatory Notes.[75] Section 29 would not apply to a decision of a judge on the merits of a case. An administrative decision of court staff (for example, about which contractor to use to carry out maintenance jobs or which supplier to use when ordering stationery) would be covered by the provisions.

Armed forces

4.58 The public function provisions in s 29(6) – in relation to age, disability, gender reassignment and sex discrimination – do not apply to anything done for the purpose of ensuring the combat effectiveness of the armed forces.[76]

Security services etc

4.59 Section 29 does not apply to the Security Service; the Secret Intelligence Service; the Government Communication Headquarters; or a part of the armed forces which is, in accordance with a requirement of the Secretary of State, assisting the Government Communications Headquarters.[77]

Education

4.60 Part 2 of Sch 3 contains a number of exceptions relating to education. In particular, the exceptions are concerned with the role of public authorities in the provision of schools, and in ancillary matters, such as school transport; as well as exceptions to mirror those applicable to individual schools under the education provisions.

Provision of schools: age and religion or belief

4.61 Section 29 does not apply to a local authority in England and Wales, so far as relating to age or religious or belief-related discrimination, in the exercise of its functions under s 14 of the Education Act 1996 (functions in the provision of primary and secondary schools in a given catchment area); and the exercise of its functions under s 13 of that Act (general responsibility for education) insofar as it relates to a function of its under s 14 of that Act.[78]

4.62 Section 29 similarly does not apply to an education authority in Scotland, so far as relating to age or religious or belief-related discrimination, in:

- the exercise of the authority's functions under s 17 of the Education (Scotland) Act 1980 (provision of schools);

---

75 EN para 691.
76 EQA 2010, Sch 3, para 4.
77 EQA 2010, Sch 3, para 5.
78 EQA 2010, Sch 3, para 6.

- the exercise of its functions under s 1 of that Act, s 2 of the Standards in Scotland's Schools etc Act 2000 or s 4 or 5 of the Education (Additional Support for Learning) (Scotland) Act 2004 (general responsibility for education) insofar as it relates to a matter specified in the preceding bullet point;

- the exercise of its functions under s 50(1) of the Education (Scotland) Act 1980 (education of pupils in exceptional circumstances) insofar as it consists of making arrangements of the description referred to in subs (2) of that section.[79]

4.63 The Explanatory Notes state that the reason for these exceptions is to prevent a local authority being bound to provide schools for pupils of different faiths, or no faith, or for particular age groups, in every catchment area.[80] Examples of how the exceptions will apply are given in the Explanatory Notes:[81]

- Catholic parents will not be able to claim that their local authority is discriminating unlawfully if there is no Catholic school in their catchment area, or if there are fewer places in Catholic schools than in Church of England schools.

- Parents of secondary age children will not be able to claim that it is age discrimination if their children have to travel further than younger ones to reach their school.

Provision of schools: sex

4.64 Section 29 does not apply to a local authority in England or Wales (or an education authority in Scotland), so far as relating to sex discrimination, in the exercise of the authority's functions in relation to the establishment of a school.[82] This means that an authority will be able to establish a single sex school. However, this is not to be taken as disapplying the provisions in relation to the exercise of the authority's functions under s 14 of the Education Act 1996 or s 17 of the Education (Scotland) Act 1982,[83] whereby authorities must secure that sufficient schools for providing primary and secondary education in their area are available.

Age

4.65 Section 29 does not apply, so far as relating to age discrimination, in relation to anything done in connection with:

---

[79] EQA 2010, Sch 3. para 7.
[80] EN para 694.
[81] EN para 694.
[82] EQA 2010, Sch 3, para 8(1).
[83] EQA 2010, Sch 3, para 8(2).

- the curriculum of a school;

- admission to a school;

- transport to or from a school; or

- the establishment, alteration or closure of schools.[84]

These exceptions are stated by the Explanatory Notes[85] to be intended to ensure that policies and practices which relate to things that schools are allowed to do under the Act, such as basing schools admissions policies on ages of prospective pupils, do not become unlawful when carried out by public authorities.

Disability: reasonable adjustments

4.66 A local authority in England or Wales exercising functions under the Education Acts (or an education authority in Scotland exercising relevant functions) is not required under s 29, so far as relating to disability discrimination, to remove or alter a physical feature.[86]

4.67 Relevant functions are functions under:

- the Education (Scotland) Act 1980;

- the Education (Scotland) Act 1996;

- the Standards in Scotland's Schools etc Act 2000; or

- the Education (Additional Support for Learning) (Scotland) Act 2004.

These Acts relate to the provision of school education, including the meeting of additional support needs for pupils where they have a learning difficulty.

4.68 The Explanatory Notes[87] state that these exceptions are designed to replicate the effect of provisions in the DDA 1995 and ensure that local authorities, when carrying out their education functions, do not have to take account of altering physical features since such things will fall within the requirements on them to produce accessibility strategies as set out in Sch 12.

Faith and non-faith institutions

4.69 Section 29 does not apply, so far as relating to religious or belief-related discrimination, in relation to anything done in connection with:

---

[84] EQA 2010, Sch 3, para 9.
[85] EN para 699.
[86] EQA 2010, Sch 3, para 10.
[87] EN para 701.

- the curriculum of a school;

- admission to a school which has a religious ethos;

- acts of worship or other religious observance organised by or on behalf of a school (whether or not forming part of the curriculum);

- the responsible body of a school which has a religious ethos;

- transport to or from a school; or

- the establishment, alteration or closure of schools.[88]

4.70 Examples of how this exception will apply are contained in the Explanatory Notes as follows.[89] A public authority will not be open to claims of religious discrimination as a result of its decision to establish, alter or close a faith school. A local authority can select a person of a particular religion or belief to be a governor of a school with a religious ethos.

Health and care

4.71 There are a number of exceptions relating to blood services, health and safety, and care within the family.

Blood services

4.72 A person operating a blood service does not contravene s 29 only by refusing to accept a donation of an individual's blood if specified conditions are met. Those conditions are that: (a) the refusal is because of an assessment of the risk to the public, or to the individual, based on clinical, epidemiological or other data obtained from a source on which it is reasonable to rely, and (b) the refusal is reasonable.[90]

4.73 A blood service is defined as being a service for the collection and distribution of human blood (which includes blood components) for the purposes of medical services.[91]

4.74 This provision is designed to replicate the effect of the Equality Act (Sexual Orientation) Regulations 2007,[92] and to extend the exception to the other protected characteristics.[93]

---

[88] EQA 2010, Sch 3, para 11.
[89] EN para 703.
[90] EQA 2010, Sch 3, para 13(1).
[91] EQA 2010, Sch 3, para 13(2) and (3).
[92] SI 2007/1263; reg 28.
[93] EN para 707.

4.75 Examples of how this provision might operate are given in the Explanatory Notes:[94]

- If there is evidence that people who have been sexually active in a particular country are more likely to be infected with HIV, the operator of the blood service can refuse to accept donations of blood or blood components from people who have been sexually active there, even if that disproportionately affects members of a particular nationality and so might otherwise be unlawful indirect discrimination because of race.

- If there is evidence that women who have recently given birth are likely to suffer detrimental effects from giving blood or blood components, then a blood service can refuse to accept donations from them. This would not be unlawful direct discrimination because of maternity.

Health and safety

4.76 Provisions making it unlawful for a person to discriminate against a pregnant woman in the provision of services were introduced into the SDA 1975 by the Sex Discrimination Act 1975 (Amendment) Regulations 2008.[95] Those provisions contain an exception on health and safety grounds,[96] which is reproduced in the EQA 2010.

4.77 Where a service-provider (A) refuses to provide a service to a pregnant woman (B), A will not be acting in contravention of s 29 because B is pregnant provided that specific conditions are met.[97] These conditions are that:

(a) A reasonably believes that providing B with the service would create a risk to B's health or safety because B is pregnant;

(b) A refuses to provide the service to persons with other physical conditions; and

(c) the reason for that refusal is that A reasonably believes that providing the service to such persons would create a risk to their health or safety.

4.78 In addition, where a service-provider (A) who provides (or offers to provide) the service to a pregnant woman (B) imposes conditions on her, A does not discriminate against B in contravention of s 29 because B is pregnant provided that the conditions conform to certain requirements.[98] These requirements are that:

---

[94] EN para 707.
[95] SI 2008/656.
[96] SDA 1975, s 3B(2).
[97] EQA 2010, Sch 3, para 14(1).
[98] EQA 2010, Sch 3, para 14(2).

(a) the conditions are intended to remove or reduce a risk to B's health or safety;

(b) A reasonably believes that the provision of the service without the conditions would create a risk to B's health or safety;

(c) A imposes conditions on the provision of the service to persons with other physical conditions; and

(d) the reason for the imposition of those conditions is that A reasonably believes that the provision of the service to such persons without those conditions would create a risk to their health or safety.

4.79 Examples given in the Explanatory Notes[99] of how this exception will apply are as follows:

- a leisure centre could refuse to allow a pregnant woman to use certain gym equipment (for example, a rowing machine) after a certain point in her pregnancy if it reasonably believed that allowing her to use the equipment would create a risk to her health and safety and it would also refuse, for example, to allow a man with a serious heart condition to use the equipment;

- an airline could refuse to allow a pregnant woman to travel beyond her 35th week of pregnancy if it reasonably believed that allowing her to travel would create a risk to her health and safety, and it would also refuse to allow people with other physical conditions to travel.

Care within the family

4.80 Where a person (A) takes into their home, and treats as members of their family, persons requiring particular care and attention, A will not be contravening s 29.[100] This exception is designed to ensure that people who provide foster care, or other similar forms of care, in their own home are not subject to the prohibitions on discriminating against, harassing or victimising a person in the provision of services while providing that care.[101] Similar provisions are present in pre-existing legislation for race, religion or belief, and sexual orientation.[102] This provision extends the exception to all of the protected characteristics.

4.81 Examples of how the exception would work are given in the Explanatory Notes:[103]

---

[99] EN para 709.
[100] EQA 2010, Sch 3, para 15.
[101] EN para 710.
[102] See RRA 1976, s 23(2); Equality Act 2006, s 62; and Equality Act (Sexual Orientation) Regulations 2007, SI 2007/1263, reg 6(1).
[103] EN para 712.

- A Muslim family could choose to foster only a Muslim child. This would not constitute discrimination against a non-Muslim child.

- A woman who is the main carer for her mother decides to provide care for another person too, and decides to restrict any offer of care to another woman. This would not constitute discrimination against a man who needed similar care.

Immigration

4.82 There are a number of exceptions relating to immigration functions. These have been subject to criticism from the Joint Committee of Human Rights – further detail of which is given below.

4.83 A reference in the exceptions to entry clearance, leave to enter or remain, or immigration rules is to be construed in accordance with the Immigration Act 1971.[104]

Disability

4.84 Section 29 does not apply, in relation to disability discrimination, to a decision (whether or not taken in accordance with immigration rules), or anything done for the purposes of or in pursuance of such a decision:

(a) to refuse entry clearance;

(b) to refuse leave to enter or remain in the UK;

(c) to cancel leave to enter or remain in the UK;

(d) to vary leave to enter or remain in the UK;

(e) to refuse an application to vary leave to enter or remain in the UK.

This exception only applies, however, where the decision is taken on the ground that doing so is necessary for the public good.[105]

4.85 In addition, s 29 does not apply in relation to disability discrimination to:

(a) a decision taken, or guidance given, by the Secretary of State in connection with a decision under the above categories; or

---

[104] EQA 2010, Sch 3, para 19.
[105] EQA 2010, Sch 3, para 16(2) and (3).

(b)   a decision taken in accordance with guidance given by the Secretary of State in connection with a decision above.[106]

4.86 This exception is new to disability discrimination provisions. The Explanatory Notes state that an express exception was not previously needed.[107] The DDA 1995 did not prohibit direct discrimination in the provision of services or the exercise of a public function. Disability-related discrimination – which did apply to the provision of services or the exercise of a public function, including immigration functions – could be justified if it was necessary for a number of reasons, including not to endanger the health or safety of any person.

4.87 The Joint Committee expressed the view that this provision is inconsistent with the object and purpose of the UN Convention on the Rights of Persons with Disabilities.[108] It went on to state that this exception could permit treatment of disabled persons which could violate their right to equal treatment. Potentially it also threatens other rights, such as the right to life (protected under ECHR, Art 2) and the right to freedom from inhuman and degrading treatment (Art 3). This threat could arise if disabled persons with serious illnesses are denied entry to (or leave to remain in) the UK, and are deported back to countries where they may be subject to life-threatening conditions, in the absence of a reason to do so under immigration law. Further, the Joint Committee stated that the scope of this exception is excessively wide, in particular, in how it exempts all acts done 'if necessary for the public good'.[109] There is no explicit requirement that any discriminatory acts must be done for a legitimate aim and be objectively justified.

Nationality and ethnic or national origins

4.88 Section 29 does not apply in relation to race discrimination – on the basis of nationality or ethnic or national origins – to anything done by a relevant person in the exercise of functions exercisable by virtue of a relevant enactment.[110]

4.89 A relevant person is defined as a Minister of the Crown acting personally, or a person acting in accordance with a relevant authorisation.[111] A relevant authorisation is a requirement imposed or express authorisation given (a) with respect to a particular case or class of case, by a Minister of the Crown acting personally; or (b) with respect to a particular class of case, by a relevant enactment or by an instrument made under or by virtue of a relevant enactment.[112] The relevant enactments are:[113]

---

[106]   EQA 2010, Sch 3, para 16(4).

[107]   EN para 715.

[108]   Joint Committee on Human Rights, 2009: 147.

[109]   Joint Committee on Human Rights, 2009: 148.

[110]   EQA 2010, Sch 3, para 17(1) and (2).

[111]   EQA 2010, Sch 3, para 17(3).

[112]   EQA 2010, Sch 3, para 17(4).

(a)   the Immigration Acts;[114]

(b)   the Special Immigration Appeals Commission Act 1997;

(c)   a provision made under s 2(2) of the European Communities Act 1972 which relates to immigration or asylum; and

(d)   a provision of Community law which relates to immigration or asylum.

4.90 Examples of how these provisions would apply are set out in the Explanatory Notes:[115]

•   Different visa requirements for nationals of different countries, which arise for a variety of historical and political reasons, do not constitute unlawful race discrimination.

•   Granting asylum to members of a minority ethnic group being targeted by the majority ethnic group in a country would similarly not be unlawful discrimination.

4.91 The Joint Committee also expressed its concern regarding the scope of this exception.[116] Its view was that the Government had not established a case for retaining the ethnicity and nationality immigration exception in its current form. It stated that, whilst discrimination on the basis of nationality is an unavoidable feature of immigration control, the case-law of the European Court of Human Rights, the House of Lords and other courts has established that pressing justification must be shown for the use of distinctions based on race, ethnicity or associated concepts (such as national origin). The provisions of the UN Convention on the Elimination of Racial Discrimination also require states to take steps to avoid the use of race-based distinctions. In the Committee's view, the Government had not established the existence of a pressing justification for the continuation in force of this exception insofar as it extends to distinctions based on ethnicity and national origin.

Religion or belief

4.92 Section 29 does not apply, in relation to religious or belief-related discrimination, to a decision (or anything done for the purposes of or in pursuance of a decision) taken in accordance with immigration rules:

---

[113]   EQA 2010, Sch 3 para 17(5).
[114]   Although not including a reference to ss 28A–28K of the Immigration Act 1971 (powers of arrest, entry and search, etc) or s 14 of the Asylum and Immigration (Treatment of Claimants, etc.) Act 2004 (power of arrest).
[115]   EN para 717.
[116]   Joint Committee on Human Rights, 2009: 152.

(a)   to refuse entry clearance or leave to enter the UK, or to cancel leave to enter or remain in the UK, on the grounds that the exclusion of the person from the UK is conducive to the public good; or

(b)   to vary leave to enter or remain in the UK, or to refuse an application to vary leave to enter or remain in the UK, on the grounds that it is undesirable to permit the person to remain in the UK.[117]

4.93   In addition, s 29 does not apply to a decision (or anything done for the purposes of or in pursuance of a decision), whether or not taken in accordance with immigration rules, in connection with an application for entry clearance or for leave to enter or remain in the UK if the decision is taken on specified grounds. Those grounds are that:

(a)   a person holds an office or post in connection with a religion or belief, or provides a service in connection with a religion or belief;

(b)   a religion or belief is not to be treated in the same way as certain other religions or beliefs; or

(c)   the exclusion from the UK of a person to whom paragraph (a) applies is conducive to the public good.[118]

Section 29 also does not apply to (a) a decision taken, or guidance given, by the Secretary of State in connection with a decision referred to above; or (b) a decision taken in accordance with guidance given by the Secretary of State in connection with any such decision.

4.94   Examples of how these provisions would apply are set out in the Explanatory Notes:[119]

* the immigration services may differentiate between certain religious groups in order to allow a person, such as a Minister of Religion, to enter the UK to provide essential pastoral services, without being challenged by groups which could operate against the public interest, but which might also claim to represent a religion.

* a decision to prevent a person who holds extreme religious views from entering or remaining in the country if their presence is not conducive to the public good – for example, preachers who use the pulpit to incite violence – would not constitute unlawful discrimination because of religion or belief.

4.95   The Joint Committee also expressed its concerns relating to this exception. Whilst it recognised the basis for this exception, it emphasised that

---

[117]   EQA 2010, Sch 3, para 18(1)–(3).
[118]   EQA 2010, Sch 3, para 18(4)–(6).
[119]   EN para 720.

the exception should not affect the duty of public authorities exercising immigration functions to comply with the duty of non-discrimination under ECHR, Art 14, where these functions engage the right to manifest religion under Art 9, or rights to respect for private or family life under Art 8. It also considered that the wide scope of the existing power to exclude persons whose presence in the UK would not be conducive to the public good rendered the exception unnecessary.[120]

Insurance

4.96   Part 5 of Sch 3 sets out specific provisions relating to insurance provided as part of employment. In addition, there are specific provisions to deal with situations where a person is disabled, or of a particular sex, and this is used as a factor in deciding whether to provide insurance services to that person and, if so, on what terms. Equally gender reassignment, maternity or pregnancy can be treated as relevant considerations in relation to insurance.

Services arranged by employer

4.97   Section 29 does not apply to certain financial services where they are provided as part of arrangements made by an employer for the service-provider to provide the service to the employer's employees (and others) as a consequence of their employment.[121] The relevant financial services are insurance or a related financial service or a service relating to membership of (or benefits under) a personal pensions scheme.[122]

4.98   The Explanatory Notes[123] provide the following example of how this exception might work. An employer enters into a contract with an insurer for the provision of health insurance to employees. As the health insurance is part of the package of benefits provided by the employer to the employee, the employer must ensure that the provision complies with Part 5. So, if benefits under the health insurance policy differ between men and women, the employer may have to justify the difference by reference to para 20 of Sch 9 (insurance contracts etc).

Disability

4.99   It is not a contravention of s 29, in relation to disability discrimination, to do anything in connection with insurance business if certain conditions are met.[124] Those conditions are that:

---

[120]   Joint Committee on Human Rights, 2009: 152.
[121]   EQA 2010, Sch 3, para 20(1).
[122]   EQA 2010, Sch 3, para 20(2). A personal pension scheme is one within the meaning of s 1 of the Pension Schemes Act 1993.
[123]   EN para 722.
[124]   EQA 2010, Sch 3, para 21(1).

(a) the thing is done by reference to information that is both relevant to the assessment of the risk to be insured and from a source on which it is reasonable to rely; and

(b) it is reasonable to do the thing.[125]

'Insurance business' is defined as business which consists of effecting or carrying out contracts of insurance.[126]

4.100 The provisions replicate those contained in regulations made under the DDA 1995.[127] Examples given in the Explanatory Notes[128] of how these provisions might apply are as follows:

• A disabled person with cancer applies for a life insurance policy. The insurance company refuses to provide life insurance cover based on a medical report from the person's doctor which provides a prognosis on the person's condition.

• An insurer charges higher premiums for travel insurance for a person with a particular disability because actuarial evidence suggests that people with this disability are at increased risk of having a heart attack.

Sex, gender reassignment, pregnancy and maternity

4.101 It is not a contravention of s 29 – so far as relating to gender reassignment, pregnancy and maternity and sex discrimination – to do anything in relation to an annuity, life insurance policy, accident insurance policy or similar matter involving the assessment of risk if certain conditions are met.[129] Those conditions are that: (a) the thing is done by reference to actuarial or other data from a source on which it is reasonable to rely, and (b) it is reasonable to do the thing.[130]

4.102 Where a contract of insurance, or a contract for related financial services, was entered into before 6 April 2008, this exception applies only in relation to differences in premiums and benefits that are applicable to a person under the contract.[131]

[125] EQA 2010, Sch 3, para 21(1)(a) and (b).
[126] EQA 2010, Sch 3, para 21(2), and that definition is to be read with – (a) s 22 of the Financial Services and Markets Act 2000, (b) any relevant order under that Act, and (c) Sch 2 to that Act.
[127] See the Disability Discrimination (Service Providers and Public Authorities Carrying out Functions) Regulations, SI 2005/2901.
[128] EN para 724.
[129] EQA 2010, Sch 3, para 22(1).
[130] EQA 2010, Sch 3, para 21(1)(a), (b).
[131] EQA 2010, Sch 3, para 22(2).

4.103 Where a contract of insurance or a contract for a related financial service has been entered into on or after 6 April 2008, the exception will only apply if:

(a) the use of sex as a factor in the assessment of risk is based on relevant and accurate actuarial and statistical data;

(b) the data are compiled, published (whether in full or in summary form) and regularly updated in accordance with guidance issued by the Treasury;

(c) the differences are proportionate having regard to the data; and

(d) the differences do not result from costs related to pregnancy or to a woman's having given birth in the period of 26 weeks ending on the day on which the thing in question is done (other than in relation to a contract entered into before 22 December 2008).[132]

4.104 Examples of how these exceptions might apply are set out in the Explanatory Notes.[133] An insurer can lawfully quote higher motor insurance premiums for young men if this is based on actuarial and statistical up-to-date data that is published so that customers can see the information that justifies proportionate differences in male and female premiums and benefits.

Existing insurance policies

4.105 It is not a contravention of s 29, so far as relating to any of the protected characteristics to which the services and function provisions apply, to do anything in connection with insurance business in relation to an existing insurance policy.[134] 'Insurance business' is a business which consists of effecting or carrying out contracts of insurance.[135] An 'existing insurance policy' is defined as a policy of insurance entered into before the date on which this provision of the Act comes into force.[136]

4.106 This exception does not apply, however, where an existing insurance policy was renewed on or after the date on which this provision of the Act comes into force; or where the terms of such a policy were reviewed (other than where it was reviewed as part of or incidental to a general reassessment by the service provider of the pricing structure for a group of policies).[137]

---

[132] EQA 2010, Sch 3, para 22(3) and (6).
[133] EN para 729.
[134] EQA 2010, Sch 3, para 23(1) and (2).
[135] EQA 2010, Sch 3, para 23(6) applying para 21(2).
[136] EQA 2010, Sch 3, para 23(3).
[137] EQA 2010, Sch 3, para 23(4) and (5).

4.107 Examples of how these exemptions might work are set out in the Explanatory Notes:[138]

- An existing life insurance policy which was taken out in 1989, and has not been subsequently renewed or reviewed, continues to be lawful and does not have to be altered to comply with current relevant discrimination law.

- A company has a death in service benefit insurance policy for its employees which has been in place for many years and whose terms have not been reviewed. It benefits from the exception unless and until the policy is reviewed or renewed.

4.108 The Joint Committee on Human Rights expressed its concern about this exemption – in particular that it is very widely framed and that it raised concerns as to the principle of non-regression not being respected.[139]

Marriage

4.109 Whilst a person with a full Gender Recognition Certificate acquired under the Gender Recognition Act 2004 is able to marry someone of the opposite gender to his or her acquired gender, s 5B of the Marriage Act 1949 contains an exception where the clergyman or clerk reasonably believes one of the party's gender is acquired under the Gender Recognition Act. The Act therefore contains exceptions to the services and function provisions relating to marriage and gender reassignment. The explanation for the introduction of these provisions in the Explanatory Notes is that there was previously no prohibition on discriminating against people because of gender reassignment in the exercise of public functions, and hence there was no exception necessary in relation to the solemnizing of marriages.[140]

4.110 The Act says that a person does not contravene s 29 so far as relating to gender reassignment discrimination, only because of anything done in relation to s 5B of the Marriage Act 1949. Similar provisions are made in the section in relation to a clerk in holy orders of the Church in Wales.

4.111 In addition, similar exceptions are made for a person whose consent to the solemnisation of a person's marriage is required under s 444(1) of the Marriage Act 1949 (relating to solemnisation in a registered building); for a person who solemnises marriages according to a form, rite or ceremony of a body of persons who meet for religious worship;[141] and in relation to Scotland and the Marriage (Scotland) Act 1977.[142]

---

[138] EN para 732.
[139] Joint Committee on Human Rights, 2009: 159.
[140] EN para 734.
[141] EQA 2010, Sch 3, para 24(1)–(4).
[142] EQA 2010, Sch 3 para 25.

Separate and single services

4.112   There are a variety of situations in which it is lawful to provide services only for particular groups, based on a shared protected characteristic. Part 6 of Sch 3 sets out those situations.

Separate services for the sexes

4.113   Separate services for people of each sex can be provided without acting in contravention of s 29, so far as relating to sex discrimination, provided that certain conditions are met.[143] These conditions are that: (a) a joint service for persons of both sexes would be less effective, and (b) the limited provision is a proportionate means of achieving a legitimate aim.[144]

4.114   In addition, the Act states that it is not a contravention of s 29, so far as relating to sex discrimination, to provide separate services differently for persons of each sex provided that certain conditions are met. These are that:

(a)   a joint service for persons of both sexes would be less effective;

(b)   the extent to which the service is required by one sex makes it not reasonably practicable to provide the service otherwise than as a separate service provided differently for each sex; and

(c)   the limited provision is a proportionate means of achieving a legitimate aim.[145]

This exception applies to a person exercising a public function in relation to the provision of a service as it applies to the person providing the service.[146]

4.115   As the Explanatory Notes state,[147] this paragraph replaces similar provisions in the SDA 1975 that only cover public functions.[148] The exceptions have been extended to cover all services, whether privately or publicly provided.

4.116   The example given in the Explanatory Notes[149] as to how this would apply in practice is that it would not be unlawful for a charity to set up separate hostels, one for homeless men and one for homeless women, where the hostels provide the same level of service to men and women because the level of need is the same but a unisex hostel would not be as effective.

---

[143]   EQA 2010, Sch 3, para 26(1).
[144]   EQA 2010, Sch 3, para 26(1)(a) and (b).
[145]   EQA 2010, Sch 3, para 26(2).
[146]   EQA 2010, Sch 3, para 26(3).
[147]   EN para 741.
[148]   SDA 1975, s 21A(4)–(10).
[149]   EN para 741.

Single-sex services

4.117 A service can be provided only to people of one sex without contravening s 29, so far as relating to sex discrimination, if one of the specified conditions is met, and if the limited provision is a proportionate means of achieving a legitimate aim.[150]

4.118 The conditions are as follows:

- only persons of that sex have need of the service;[151]

- the service is also provided jointly for persons of both sexes, and the service would be insufficiently effective were it only to be provided jointly;[152]

- a joint service for persons of both sexes would be less effective, and the extent to which the service is required by persons of each sex makes it not reasonably practicable to provide separate services;[153]

- the service is provided at a hospital, or a place which is part of a hospital, or another establishment for persons requiring special care, supervision or attention;[154]

- the service is provided for, or is likely to be used by, two or more persons at the same time, and the circumstances are such that a person of one sex might reasonably object to the presence of a person of the opposite sex;[155]

- there is likely to be physical contact between a person (A) to whom the service is provided and another person (B), and B might reasonably object if A were not of the same sex as B.[156]

This exception applies to a person exercising a public function in relation to the provision of a service as it applies to the person providing the service.[157]

4.119 The Explanatory Notes state[158] that this exception replaces some similar provisions that only covered public functions and some that applied to services in the SDA 1975.[159] These exceptions have been extended to cover both services and public functions.

---

[150] EQA 2010, Sch 3, para 27(1)(a) and (b).
[151] EQA 2010, Sch 3, para 27(2).
[152] EQA 2010, Sch 3, para 27(3).
[153] EQA 2010, Sch 3, para 27(4).
[154] EQA 2010, Sch 3, para 27(5).
[155] EQA 2010, Sch 3, para 27(6).
[156] EQA 2010, Sch 3, para 27(7).
[157] EQA 2010, Sch 3, para 27(8).
[158] EN para 746.
[159] See SDA 1975, ss 21A(4) and 35.

4.120 Examples given in the Explanatory Notes of what these exceptions might allow are as follows:[160]

- a cervical cancer screening service to be provided to women only, as only women need the service;

- a fathers' support group to be set up by a private nursery as there is insufficient attendance by men at the parents' group;

- a domestic violence support unit to be set up by a local authority for women only but there is no men-only unit because of insufficient demand;

- separate male and female wards to be provided in a hospital;

- separate male and female changing rooms to be provided in a department store;

- a massage service to be provided to women only by a female massage therapist with her own business operating in her clients' homes because she would feel uncomfortable massaging men in that environment.

Gender reassignment

4.121 Section 29 will not be contravened, so far as relating to gender reassignment discrimination, by doing anything in relation to one of the following:

- the provision of separate services for persons of each sex;

- the provision of separate services differently for persons of each sex;

- the provision of a service only to persons of one sex.[161]

This exception will only apply, however, if the conduct in question is a proportionate means of achieving a legitimate aim.

4.122 The example given in the Explanatory Notes[162] of how this might operate is that of a group counselling session which is provided for female victims of sexual assault. The organisers do not allow transsexual people to attend as they judge that the clients who attend the group session are unlikely to do so if a male-to-female transsexual person was also there. This would be lawful.

---

[160] EN para 747.
[161] EQA 2010, Sch 3, para 28(1) and (2).
[162] EN para 749.

Services relating to religion

4.123 A minister can provide a service only to persons of one sex, or separate services for persons of each sex, without acting in contravention of s 29 in relation to sex discrimination if certain conditions are met.[163] Those conditions are that:

(a)   the service is provided for the purposes of an organised religion;

(b)   it is provided at a place which is (permanently or for the time being) occupied or used for those purposes; and

(c)   the limited provision of the service is necessary in order to comply with the doctrines of the religion or is for the purpose of avoiding conflict with the strongly held religious convictions of a significant number of the religion's followers.[164]

4.124 A minister is a minister of religion, or other person, who (a) performs functions in connection with the religion, and (b) holds an office or appointment in, or is accredited, approved or recognised for purposes of, a relevant organisation in relation to the religion.[165] A relevant organisation in relation to the religion is an organisation whose sole or main purpose is not commercial[166] and whose purpose is to practise the religion, advance it, teach its practices or principles of the religion; to enable persons of the religion to receive benefits, or to engage in activities, within the framework of that religion, or to foster or maintain good relations between persons of different religions.[167]

4.125 An example of the application of this exemption given in the Explanatory Notes is that of a synagogue having separate seating for men and women at a reception following a religious service.[168]

Services generally provided only for persons who share a protected characteristic

4.126 A service provider, who generally provides a service only for persons who share a protected characteristic, will not be acting in contravention of s 29(1) or (2) by insisting on providing the service in the way that they normally provide it, or, if the service provider reasonably thinks it is impracticable to provide the service to persons who do not share that characteristic, by refusing to provide the service.[169]

---

[163]   EQA 2010, Sch 3, para 29(1).
[164]   EQA 2010, Sch 3, para 29(1)(a), (b) and (c).
[165]   EQA 2010, Sch 3, para 29(2).
[166]   EQA 2010, Sch 3, para 29(4).
[167]   EQA 2010, Sch 3, para 29(3).
[168]   EN para 752.
[169]   EQA 2010, Sch 3, para 30.

4.127 The Explanatory Notes[170] state that this is designed to replicate the effect of provisions currently contained in the SDA 1975,[171] and the Equality Act 2006,[172] and extends the clarification they provide across all other protected characteristics for the first time.

4.128 The examples given in the Explanatory Notes[173] are:

- A hairdresser who provides Afro-Caribbean hairdressing services would not be required to provide European hair dressing services as well. However, if a white English person wanted his hair braided, and there was no technical difficulty to prevent that, it would be unlawful for the hairdresser to refuse to provide her services to him.

- A butcher who sells halal meat is not required also to sell non-halal meat or kosher meat. However, if a non-Muslim customer wanted to purchase the meat that was on offer, he could not refuse to sell it to her.

Television, radio and on-line broadcasting and distribution

4.129 Section 29 does not apply to the provision of a content service, within the meaning of s 32(7) of the Communications Act 2003.[174] This exception does not apply, however, to the provision of an electronic communications network, electronic communications service or associated facility (within the meaning ascribed in the Communications Act 2003).[175] This means that the broadcasters will not be subject to a challenge under the Act relating to the content, but the means by which the content is delivered may be subject to challenge.

4.130 This is a new provision, which is said by the Explanatory Notes to be intended to 'safeguard the editorial independence of broadcasters when broadcasting or distributing content, whether on television, radio or on-line'.[176]

---

[170] EN para 754.
[171] SDA 1975, s 21A(9).
[172] EQA 2006, s 57.
[173] EN para 754.
[174] EQA 2010, Sch 3, para 31(1). Section 32(7) of the Communications Act 2003 provides that a content service is so much of any service as consists in one or both of the following: (a) the provision of material with a view to its being comprised in signals conveyed by means of an electronic communications network; (b) the exercise of editorial control over the contents of signals conveyed by means of a such a network.
[175] EQA 2010, Sch 3, para 31(2).
[176] EN para 757.

Chapter 5

PREMISES

INTRODUCTION

5.1 The Equality Act 2010 (EQA 2010) Part 4 deals with the disposal, management and occupation of premises.[1] In broad terms, it reflects the position in current legislation, which addresses discrimination in relation to premises in respect of all the protected characteristics, except age, marriage and civil partnership.[2] Section 32 begins by dealing with the application of Part 4 of the Act.

Age and marriage and civil partnership

5.2 Part 4 on premises does not apply to the protected characteristics of age, marriage and civil partnership.[3] Thus the EQA 2010 does not make it unlawful to discriminate against or harass people in relation to the disposal, management and occupation of premises because they are married or in a civil partnership or because of age.[4]

5.3 The Joint Committee on Human Rights, in its scrutiny of the Equality Bill before becoming law, received little written evidence on this exclusion of age discrimination in the context of premises.[5] However, the Joint Committee recommended that the prohibition of discrimination against married persons or persons in a civil partnership should be extended to harassment and discrimination in the provision of premises.[6]

Work and education

5.4 Part 4 on premises does not apply to discrimination, harassment or victimisation that is prohibited by Part 5 (work) or Part 6 (education), or would be so prohibited but for an express exception.[7] This means that if an act of

---

1   EQA 2010, ss 32–38 and Schs 4–5.
2   Explanatory Notes (EN): EN paras 126–128. See, in particular, SDA 1975, ss 3B, 30–32 (as amended); RRA 1976, ss 21–24 (as amended); DDA 1995, ss 18A, 22–24M; Equality Act 2006, ss 47–48; Equality Act (Sexual Orientation) Regulations 2007, regs 5–6.
3   EQA 2010, s 32(1).
4   EN para 126.
5   Joint Committee on Human Rights, 2009: para 160.
6   Joint Committee on Human Rights, 2009: paras 68 and 108.
7   EQA 2010, s 32(2).

discrimination, harassment or victimisation is made unlawful by other Parts of the Act covering work or education, then those provisions, rather than the provisions covering premises, apply.[8]

Short stay accommodation, etc

5.5   Part 4 on premises does not apply to the provision of accommodation if the provision is generally for the purpose of short stays by individuals who live elsewhere, or for the purpose only of exercising a public function or providing a service to the public or a section of the public.[9] The references to the exercise of a public function and to the provision of a service are to be construed in accordance with Part 3 of the Act (services and public functions).[10] The effect of this is that if accommodation is provided either as a short-term let or as part of a service or public function Part 3 of the Act (services and public functions) applies instead of Part 4 (premises).[11]

Equality clauses and non-discrimination rules

5.6   Part 4 on premises does not apply to a breach of an equality clause or an equality rule.[12] It also does not apply to anything that would be a breach of an equality clause or an equality rule but for s 69 (defence of material factor) or Part 2 of Sch 7 (occupational pension schemes).[13] Furthermore, Part 4 on premises does not apply to a breach of a non-discrimination rule (in an occupational pension scheme).[14]

5.7   This is explained as signifying that if the act in question results in a breach of an equality clause in a person's terms of work or a non-discrimination rule in an occupational pension scheme then the present provisions will not apply.[15] The person affected must look to any remedy available for breach of the equality clause or the non-discrimination rule.

Interpretation

5.8   A reference to premises in Part 4 of the Act is a reference to the whole or part of the premises.[16] A reference to disposing of premises includes, in the case of premises subject to a tenancy, a reference to assigning the premises, or sub-letting them, or parting with possession of them.[17] A reference to disposing

---

8   EN para 127.
9   EQA 2010, s 32(3).
10   EQA 2010, s 32(4).
11   EN para 127. See Chapter 4.
12   EQA 2010, s 32(5)(a): that is, a sex equality clause or rule under ss 66 or 67 or a maternity
     equality clause or rule under ss 73 or 75: EQA 2010, s 212(1). See Chapter 7.
13   EQA 2010, s 32(5)(b).
14   EQA 2010, ss 32(5)(c) and 61.
15   EN para 127. See Chapter 4.
16   EQA 2010, s 38(2).
17   EQA 2010, s 38(3).

of premises also includes a reference to granting a right to occupy them.[18] A reference to disposing of an interest in a commonhold unit includes a reference to creating an interest in a commonhold unit.[19]

5.9 A reference to a tenancy is to a tenancy created (whether before or after the passing of the Act) by a lease or sub-lease, or by an agreement for a lease or sub-lease, or by a tenancy agreement, or in pursuance of an enactment. A reference to a tenant is to be construed accordingly.[20] A reference to commonhold land, a commonhold association, a commonhold community statement, a commonhold unit or a unit-holder is to be construed in accordance with the Commonhold and Leasehold Reform Act 2002.[21] Schedule 4 (reasonable adjustments) and Sch 5 (exceptions) have effect.[22]

5.10 The interpretation provisions in s 38 replace similar provisions in pre-existing legislation.[23] In particular s 38 sets out the kinds of property transactions meant by 'disposing of premises' in the case of premises which are subject to a tenancy. It also defines what is meant by 'tenancy'. The details of how the reasonable adjustments duty applies in relation to 'let premises', 'premises to let', 'commonhold land' and 'common parts' of let premises or commonhold premises are contained in Sch 4, discussed below. The exceptions which apply to this part of the Act are contained in Sch 5, also discussed below.

DISPOSAL AND MANAGEMENT

Disposals, etc

5.11 Section 33 replaces similar provisions in current legislation. It is concerned with a person who has the authority to dispose of premises (for example, by selling, letting or subletting a property). The section makes it unlawful for a person who has the authority to dispose of premises to discriminate against or victimise someone else in a number of ways. This includes offering the premises to them on less favourable terms; not letting or selling the premises to them; or treating them less favourably (for example, in relation to a council house waiting list). Section 33 also makes it unlawful for a person with authority to dispose of premises to harass someone who occupies or applies for them. However, it is not made unlawful to harass someone because of sexual orientation, or religion or belief when disposing of premises.[24]

5.12 First, a person (A) who has the right to dispose of premises must not discriminate against another (B) as to the terms on which A offers to dispose of

---

18   EQA 2010, s 38(4).
19   EQA 2010, s 38(5).
20   EQA 2010, s 38(6).
21   EQA 2010, s 38(7).
22   EQA 2010, s 38(8) and (9).
23   EN paras 142–145.
24   EN paras 129–130.

the premises to B; or by not disposing of the premises to B; or in A's treatment of B with respect to things done in relation to persons seeking premises.[25]

5.13 Secondly, where an interest in a commonhold unit cannot be disposed of unless a particular person is a party to the disposal, that person must not discriminate against a person by not being a party to the disposal.[26] Where an interest in a commonhold unit cannot be disposed of unless a particular person is a party to the disposal that person must not victimise a person by not being a party to the disposal.[27]

5.14 Thirdly, a person who has the right to dispose of premises must not, in connection with anything done in relation to their occupation or disposal, harass (a) a person who occupies them; or (b) a person who applies for them.[28] Harassment as a form of prohibited conduct is defined in s 26 of the Act and has been discussed in chapter 3 above. In the application of s 26 (harassment) in the present context,[29] religion or belief and sexual orientation are not relevant protected characteristics.[30]

5.15 Fourthly, a person (A) who has the right to dispose of premises must not victimise another (B) as to the terms on which A offers to dispose of the premises to B; or by not disposing of the premises to B; or in A's treatment of B with respect to things done in relation to persons seeking premises.[31]

5.16 The Explanatory Notes offer two examples of s 33 in operation.[32] First, if a landlord refuses to let a property to a prospective tenant because of her race this is said to be direct discrimination when disposing of premises. Secondly, where a vendor offers her property to a prospective buyer who is disabled at a higher sale price than she would to a non-disabled person because of the person's disability this is direct discrimination when disposing of premises.

5.17 The Joint Committee on Human Rights considered that the absence of an explicit prohibition on harassment related to sexual orientation in respect of the disposal, management and occupation of premises represented a significant gap in the protection against discrimination offered by the Act.[33] It suggested that this might give rise to issues under the European Convention on Human Rights (ECHR) Art 14 (prohibition of discrimination) when read with Art 3 (prohibition on inhuman and degrading treatment), Art 8 (right to respect for

---

[25]   EQA 2010, s 33(1). In relation to a private disposal of premises by an owner-occupier, s 33(1) applies only insofar as it relates to race: EQA 2010, Sch 5, para 1(3). Where the small premises exception applies, s 33(1) applies only insofar as it relates to race: EQA 2010, Sch 5, para 3(1).

[26]   EQA 2010, s 33(2).

[27]   EQA 2010, s 33(5).

[28]   EQA 2010, s 33(3).

[29]   EQA 2010, s 33(3).

[30]   EQA 2010, s 33(6).

[31]   EQA 2010, s 33(4).

[32]   EN para 131.

[33]   Joint Committee on Human Rights, 2009: para 114.

private and family life) and Art 9 (freedom of thought, conscience and religion). Nevertheless, the general prohibition against direct and indirect discrimination might offer some protection against harassment related to sexual orientation in the premises field.[34]

Permission for disposal

5.18 Section 34 replaces similar provisions in current legislation.[35] It makes it unlawful for a person whose permission is needed to dispose of premises to discriminate against or victimise someone else by withholding that permission. For example, this provision would apply to a person whose permission is needed to sell, manage, let or sublet a property. It also makes it unlawful for such a person to harass someone who seeks that permission or someone to whom the property would be sold or let if the permission were given. However, it is not made unlawful to harass someone because of sexual orientation or religion or belief by withholding permission to dispose of premises. Section 34 also does not apply where permission to dispose of premises is refused by a court in the context of legal proceedings.

5.19 First, a person whose permission is required for the disposal of premises must not discriminate against another by not giving permission for the disposal of the premises to the other.[36]

5.20 Secondly, a person whose permission is required for the disposal of premises must not, in relation to an application for permission to dispose of the premises, harass a person who applies for permission to dispose of the premises or to whom the disposal would be made if permission were given.[37] Harassment as a form of prohibited conduct is defined in s 26 of the Act and has been discussed in chapter 3 above. In the application of s 26 (harassment) in the present context,[38] religion or belief or sexual orientation are not relevant protected characteristics.[39]

5.21 Thirdly, a person whose permission is required for the disposal of premises must not victimise another by not giving permission for the disposal of the premises to the other.[40]

5.22 Section 34 does not apply to anything done in the exercise of a judicial function.[41]

---

[34] Joint Committee on Human Rights, 2009: para 115.

[35] This paragraph draws directly upon EN paras 132–134.

[36] EQA 2010, s 34(1). In relation to a private disposal of premises by an owner-occupier, s 34(1) does not apply insofar as it relates to religion or belief, or sexual orientation: EQA 2010, Sch 5, para 1(4). Where the small premises exception applies, s 34(1) applies only insofar as it relates to race: EQA 2010, Sch 5, para 3(1).

[37] EQA 2010, s 34(2).

[38] EQA 2010, s 34(2).

[39] EQA 2010, s 34(4).

[40] EQA 2010, s 34(3).

[41] EQA 2010, s 34(5).

5.23   The Explanatory Notes give the following example.[42] A disabled tenant seeks permission from his landlord to sublet a room within his flat to help him pay his rent. The landlord tells him that he cannot because he is disabled. This is said to be direct discrimination in permission for disposing of premises.

Management

5.24   Section 35 replaces similar provisions in current legislation. The section makes it unlawful for a person who manages premises to discriminate against or victimise someone who occupies the property in the way he or she allows the person to use a benefit or facility associated with the property; or by evicting the person; or by otherwise treating the person unfavourably. It also makes it unlawful for a person who manages a property to harass a person who occupies or applies to occupy the property. It is not made unlawful to harass someone because of sexual orientation or religion or belief in the management of premises.[43]

5.25   First, a person (A) who manages premises must not discriminate against a person (B) who occupies the premises in the way in which A allows B (or by not allowing B) to make use of a benefit or facility; or by evicting B (or taking steps for the purpose of securing B's eviction); or by subjecting B to any other detriment.[44]

5.26   Secondly, a person who manages premises must not, in relation to their management, harass a person who occupies them or who applies for them.[45] Harassment as a form of prohibited conduct is defined in s 26 of the Act and has been discussed in Chapter 3 above. In the application of s 26 (harassment) in the present context,[46] religion or belief and sexual orientation are not relevant protected characteristics.[47]

5.27   Thirdly, a person (A) who manages premises must not victimise a person (B) who occupies the premises in the way in which A allows B (or by not allowing B) to make use of a benefit or facility; or by evicting B (or taking steps for the purpose of securing B's eviction); or by subjecting B to any other detriment.[48]

5.28   The Explanatory Notes give three examples of how s 35 will work in practice:[49]

---

[42]   EN para 134.
[43]   This paragraph draws directly upon EN paras 135–136.
[44]   EQA 2010, s 35(1). Where the small premises exception applies, s 35(1) applies only insofar as it relates to race: EQA 2010, Sch 5, para 3(1).
[45]   EQA 2010, s 35(2).
[46]   EQA 2010, s 35(2).
[47]   EQA 2010, s 35(4).
[48]   EQA 2010, s 35(3).
[49]   EN para 136.

- A manager of a property restricts a tenant's use of a communal garden by setting fixed times when she can use the garden because she is undergoing gender reassignment, while allowing other tenants unrestricted access to the garden. This would be direct discrimination in the management of premises.

- A manager of a property refuses to allow a lesbian tenant to use facilities which are available to other tenants, or deliberately neglects to inform her about facilities which are available for the use of other tenants, because she had previously made a claim of discrimination against the manager. This would be victimisation.

- A manager of a property responds to requests for maintenance issues more slowly or less favourably for one tenant than similar requests from other tenants, because the tenant has a learning disability. This would be direct discrimination in the management of premises.

Premises and disabled tenants

5.29 Disabled persons enjoy the same rights in respect of the disposal and management of premises as apply to persons with other protected characteristics. However, they also have the advantage of the duty to make reasonable adjustments. Before addressing that duty as it applies in the area of housing and premises, this is an appropriate place to say how the Equality Act 2010 resolves the problems created for disabled persons in the housing field by the House of Lords judgment in *London Borough of Lewisham v Malcolm* (discussed in chapter 3 above).[50]

5.30 The House of Commons Work and Pensions Committee considered that *Malcolm* had its most direct effect in limiting disabled tenants' rights of redress in the face of discrimination.[51] It recognised that the duty to make adjustments was more restrictive in relation to housing and premises. That duty could not be used easily to mitigate the effects of *Malcolm* in relation to premises (in contrast with, for example, employment). The Committee recommended that the Equality Bill should reverse the effects of *Malcolm*. It also proposed that the premises duties to make reasonable adjustments should be anticipatory in nature. The new concept of disability-related discrimination in s 15 of the Act (discussed in chapter 3 above) addresses the legacy of *Malcolm*. However, in the context of premises, the Government has not accepted the case for making the duty to make reasonable adjustments anticipatory in nature.[52] We now turn to the duty to make reasonable adjustments in relation to premises.

---

[50] [2008] UKHL 43; [2008] IRLR 700, HL.
[51] House of Commons Work and Pensions Committee, 2009a: paras 290–292.
[52] House of Commons Work and Pensions Committee, 2009b: paras 98–99.

REASONABLE ADJUSTMENTS

Overview[53]

5.31 Section 36 places the duty to make reasonable adjustments (contained in s 20) on those who let premises, commonhold associations and those who are responsible for the common parts of let or commonhold premises. The section also defines common parts and who is responsible for them. It includes a power to prescribe premises to which the requirements do not apply. Section 36 replaces similar provisions in the DDA 1995 relating to let premises and premises to let.[54] However, the provisions relating to common parts are new. In addition, the particular applications of the duty to make adjustments contained in Sch 4 to the Act (and the exceptions in Sch 5) apply.[55]

5.32 Schedule 4 explains how the duty to make reasonable adjustments in s 20 applies. The duty affects a controller of let premises or of premises to let, as well as a commonhold association. It arises where a disabled person is a tenant (or prospective tenant) or is a unit-holder in commonhold land or is legally occupying the property. The duty is triggered where such a disabled person is placed at a substantial (that is, more than minor or trivial)[56] disadvantage. The intention is that by the discharge of the duty the disabled person can enjoy the premises or make use of them. However, the duty does not require the removal or alteration of a physical feature. What are and what are not physical features for these purposes is clarified by the Act. The duty only applies if a request for an adjustment is made by or on behalf of a disabled person.

5.33 Schedule 4 also explains how the duty to make reasonable adjustments in s 20 applies in relation to the common parts of premises (for example, an entrance hall in a block of flats). These provisions relate specifically to physical features. The Schedule sets out the process that must be followed by the person responsible for the common parts (for example, a landlord or a commonhold association) if a disabled tenant requests an adjustment. This includes a consultation process with affected persons. That consultation must be carried out within a reasonable period of the request being made. The responsible person then decides whether to make an adjustment to avoid the disadvantage to the disabled person. If so, a written agreement must be entered into between them setting out their rights and responsibilities. Schedule 4 also makes it unlawful for a controller or responsible person to victimise a disabled tenant because costs have been incurred in making a reasonable adjustment.

5.34 Schedule 4 partly replaces similar provisions in the DDA 1995. However, the EQA 2010 introduces a new requirement for disability-related alterations to

---

[53] This overview draws directly upon EN paras 137–138 and 770–773.

[54] DDA 1995, ss 24A–24M; the Disability Discrimination (Premises) Regulations 2006, SI 2006/887; the Rights of Access Code of Practice 2006, chapter 15. See also Doyle, 2008 chapter 6.

[55] EQA 2010, s 38(8) and (9).

[56] EQA 2010, s 212(1).

the physical features of the common parts of let residential premises or premises owned on a commonhold basis.[57]

The duty

5.35 The duty to make reasonable adjustments applies to a controller of let premises; a controller of premises to let; a commonhold association; and a responsible person in relation to common parts.[58] A reference to letting includes a reference to subletting.[59] In relation to a controller of let premises or a controller of premises to let, a reference to let premises includes premises subject to a right to occupy.[60] The reference above to a commonhold association is a reference to the association in its capacity as the person who manages a commonhold unit.[61]

5.36 A controller of let premises is a person by whom premises are let or a person who manages them.[62] A controller of premises to let is a person who has premises to let or a person who manages them.[63]

5.37 In relation to identifying a responsible person in relation to common parts, the commonhold association will be the responsible person in relation to common parts where the premises to which the common parts relate are part of commonhold land.[64] Where the premises to which the common parts relate are let – and are not part of commonhold land or of a tenement in Scotland – the person by whom the premises are let will be the responsible person in relation to common parts.[65]

5.38 In this context, common parts are as follows. The first situation is in relation to let premises which are not part of commonhold land or of a tenement in Scotland. Here the common parts are the structure and exterior of the building or part of a building which includes the premises. This includes any common facilities within or used in connection with the building or part of a building which includes the premises.[66] The second situation is in relation to commonhold land. In that context the common parts are every part of the

---

[57] For the background to the problem this new provision addresses, see Keter, 2009a: 49–53; House of Commons Work and Pensions Committee, 2009b: 291.

[58] EQA 2010, s 36(1). There is a small premises exception of general application in relation to s 36(1): EQA 2010, Sch 5, para 4. Note also the owner-occupier (only or principal home) exception that applies to a controller of let premises or premises to let: EQA 2010, Sch 5, para 2.

[59] EQA 2010, s 36(7).

[60] EQA 2010, s 36(7).

[61] EQA 2010, s 36(4).

[62] EQA 2010, s 36(2).

[63] EQA 2010, s 36(3).

[64] EQA 2010, s 36(5)(a).

[65] EQA 2010, s 36(5)(b).

[66] EQA 2010, s 36(6)(a).

commonhold which is not for the time being a commonhold unit in accordance with the commonhold community statement.[67]

5.39 Section 36 will not apply to premises of such description as may be prescribed by regulations yet to be made.[68]

5.40 The Explanatory Notes illustrate these provisions as follows. An agency used by a landlord to let and manage leasehold premises is a controller of premises under this provision. The agency is under the duty to make reasonable adjustments for disabled people, such as making information about the property available in accessible formats.[69]

Adjustments to common parts in Scotland

5.41 Section 37 is a new provision. It deals with adjustments to common parts in Scotland. The 'common parts' in relation to premises are the structure and exterior of the building or part of a building which includes the premises. Common parts include any common facilities within or used in connection with the building or part of a building which includes the premises. In both cases, this is only insofar as the structure, exterior and common facilities are not solely owned by the owner of the premises.[70]

5.42 The Scottish Ministers may by regulations provide that a disabled person is entitled to make 'relevant adjustments' to common parts in relation to premises in Scotland.[71] The reference here to a disabled person is a reference to a disabled person who is a tenant of the premises; or is an owner of the premises, or is otherwise entitled to occupy the premises, and who uses or intends to use the premises as the person's only or main home.[72] The term 'relevant adjustments' here means, in relation to a disabled person, alterations or additions which are likely to avoid a substantial (that is, more than minor or trivial)[73] disadvantage to which the disabled person is put in using the common parts in comparison with persons who are not disabled.[74]

5.43 Regulations made by the Scottish Ministers[75] may, in particular:

- prescribe things which are, or which are not, to be treated as relevant adjustments;

- prescribe circumstances in which the consent of an owner of the common parts is required before a disabled person may make an adjustment;

---

[67]   EQA 2010, s 36(6)(b).
[68]   EQA 2010, s 36(8).
[69]   EN para 138.
[70]   EQA 2010, s 37(5).
[71]   EQA 2010, s 37(1).
[72]   EQA 2010, s 37(2).
[73]   EQA 2010, s 212(1).
[74]   EQA 2010, s 37(5).
[75]   EQA 2010, s 37(1).

- provide that the consent to adjustments is not to be withheld unreasonably;

- prescribe matters to be taken into account, or to be disregarded, in deciding whether it is reasonable to consent to adjustments;

- prescribe circumstances in which consent to adjustments is to be taken to be withheld;

- make provision about the imposition of conditions on consent to adjustments;

- make provision as to circumstances in which the sheriff may make an order authorising a disabled person to carry out adjustments;

- make provision about the responsibility for costs arising (directly or indirectly) from an adjustment;

- make provision about the reinstatement of the common parts to the condition they were in before an adjustment was made;

- make provision about the giving of notice to the owners of the common parts and other persons;

- make provision about agreements between a disabled person and an owner of the common parts;

- make provision about the registration of information in the Land Register of Scotland or the recording of documents in the Register of Sasines relating to an entitlement of a disabled person or an obligation on an owner of the common parts;

- make provision about the effect of such registration or recording;

- make provision about who is to be treated as being (or as not being) a person entitled to occupy premises otherwise than as tenant or owner.[76]

Before making any such regulations the Scottish Ministers must consult a Minister of the Crown.[77]

5.44 The Explanatory Notes explain these provisions as follows.[78] Section 37 confers a power on the Scottish Ministers to make regulations entitling disabled people to make disability-related alterations to the common parts of some residential property in Scotland. This new provision is intended to facilitate disability-related alterations to the common parts of residential premises in

---

[76] EQA 2010, s 37(4).
[77] EQA 2010, s 37(3).
[78] EN paras 139–141.

Scotland where the premises are the disabled person's only or main home. Provision for disabled people in tenanted property in Scotland was made in the Housing (Scotland) Act 2006. However, in relation to common parts the 2006 Act only covers the consent required from the person's landlord. It was not concerned with the consent required from other common owners. The process for obtaining consent from common owners needs to fit into and to operate within the devolved areas of property and housing, land registration and civil justice in Scotland. Thus it was considered appropriate to confer a power on the Scottish Ministers in the Equality Act 2010 so as to permit them to make the necessary provision via regulations yet to be made.

The duty in relation to let premises

5.45 Schedule 4 applies where a duty to make reasonable adjustments is imposed on a person (A) by Part 4 of the 2010 Act (on premises).[79] What of the position where A is a controller of let premises?[80]

5.46 A controller of let premises (A) must comply with the first and third requirements of the duty of reasonable adjustments.[81] So, where a provision, criterion or practice of A's (including a term of the letting[82]) puts a disabled person at a substantial (that is, more than minor or trivial)[83] disadvantage in relation to a relevant matter in comparison with persons who are not disabled, A is required to take such steps as it is reasonable to have to take to avoid the disadvantage.[84] Where a disabled person would, but for the provision of an auxiliary aid, be put at a substantial (that is, more than minor or trivial)[85] disadvantage in relation to a relevant matter in comparison with persons who are not disabled, A is required to take such steps as it is reasonable to have to take to provide the auxiliary aid.[86]

5.47 The duty in both its aspects applies to a disabled person who is a tenant of the premises or who is otherwise entitled to occupy them.[87] In respect of the first and third requirements as they apply to premises, the relevant matters are the enjoyment of the premises and the use of a benefit or facility, entitlement to which arises as a result of the letting.[88]

5.48 A controller of let premises (A) need only comply with the first and third requirements of the duty if the following conditions are satisfied. First, A receives a request from or on behalf of the tenant or a person entitled to

---

[79] EQA 2010, s 38(8) and Sch 4 para 1.
[80] EQA 2010, Sch 4, para 2(1).
[81] EQA 2010, Sch 4, para 2(2). See chapter 3.
[82] EQA 2010, Sch 4, para 2(3). The terms of a letting include the terms of an agreement relating to it: Sch 4, para 2(10).
[83] EQA 2010, s 212(1).
[84] EQA 2010, s 20(3).
[85] EQA 2010, s 212(1).
[86] EQA 2010, s 20(5).
[87] EQA 2010, Sch 4, para 2(4).
[88] EQA 2010, Sch 4, para 2(5).

occupy the premises. Secondly, that is a request to take steps to avoid the disadvantage or to provide the auxiliary aid.[89] If a term of the letting that prohibits the tenant from making alterations puts the disabled person at the disadvantage referred to in the first requirement, A is required to change the term only so far as is necessary to enable the tenant to make alterations to the let premises so as to avoid the disadvantage.[90]

5.49 It is never reasonable for the controller of let premises (A) to have to take a step which would involve the removal or alteration of a physical feature.[91] However, none of the following is an alteration of a physical feature: the replacement or provision of a sign or notice; the replacement of a tap or door handle; the replacement, provision or adaptation of a door bell or door entry system; or changes to the colour of a wall, door or any other surface.[92] In this context, physical features do not include furniture, furnishings, materials, equipment or other chattels in or on the premises.[93]

The duty in relation to premises to let

5.50 Schedule 4 applies where a duty to make reasonable adjustments is imposed on a person (A) by Part 4 of the 2010 Act (on premises).[94] What is the position where A is a controller of premises to let?[95]

5.51 The controller of premises to let (A) must comply with the first and third requirements of the duty to make reasonable adjustments.[96] So, where a provision, criterion or practice of A's puts a disabled person (who is considering taking a letting of the premises) at a substantial (that is, more than minor or trivial)[97] disadvantage in relation to a relevant matter (that is, becoming a tenant of the premises) in comparison with persons who are not disabled, A is required to take such steps as it is reasonable to have to take to avoid the disadvantage.[98] Where a disabled person (who is considering taking a letting of the premises) would, but for the provision of an auxiliary aid, be put at a substantial (that is, more than minor or trivial)[99] disadvantage in relation to a relevant matter (that is, becoming a tenant of the premises) in comparison with persons who are not disabled, A is required to take such steps as it is reasonable to have to take to provide the auxiliary aid.[100]

---

[89] EQA 2010, Sch 4, para 2(6).
[90] EQA 2010, Sch 4, para 2(7). The terms of a letting include the terms of an agreement relating to it: Sch 4, para 2(10).
[91] EQA 2010, Sch 4, para 2(8).
[92] EQA 2010, Sch 4, para 2(9).
[93] EQA 2010, Sch 4, para 2(9).
[94] EQA 2010, s 38(8) and Sch 4, para 1.
[95] EQA 2010, Sch 4, para 3(1).
[96] EQA 2010, Sch 4, para 3(2).
[97] EQA 2010, s 212(1).
[98] EQA 2010, s 20(3) and Sch 4, para 3(3) and (4).
[99] EQA 2010, s 212(1).
[100] EQA 2010, s 20(5) and Sch 4, para 3(3) and (4).

5.52 The duty applies only if A receives a request by or on behalf of a disabled person (who is considering taking a letting of the premises) for A to take steps to avoid the disadvantage or provide the auxiliary aid.[101] It does not require A to take a step which would involve the removal or alteration of a physical feature (as previously defined above).[102]

The duty in relation to commonhold units

5.53 Schedule 4 applies where a duty to make reasonable adjustments is imposed on a person (A) by Part 4 of the 2010 Act (on premises).[103] What is the position where A is a commonhold association?[104] The reference here to a commonhold association is a reference to the association in its capacity as the person who manages a commonhold unit.[105]

5.54 The commonhold association (A) must comply with the first and third requirements of the duty to make reasonable adjustments.[106] So, where a provision, criterion or practice of A's puts a disabled person at a substantial (that is, more than minor or trivial)[107] disadvantage in relation to a relevant matter in comparison with persons who are not disabled, A is required to take such steps as it is reasonable to have to take to avoid the disadvantage.[108] Where a disabled person would, but for the provision of an auxiliary aid, be put at a substantial (that is, more than minor or trivial)[109] disadvantage in relation to a relevant matter in comparison with persons who are not disabled, A is required to take such steps as it is reasonable to have to take to provide the auxiliary aid.[110]

5.55 In this context, the reference to a provision, criterion or practice of A's includes a reference to a term of the commonhold community statement or any other term applicable by virtue of the transfer of the unit to the unit-holder.[111] The reference to a disabled person is a reference to a disabled person who is the unit-holder or who is otherwise entitled to occupy the unit.[112] In relation to each requirement of the duty, the relevant matters are (a) the enjoyment of the unit and (b) the use of a benefit or facility, entitlement to which arises as a result of a term of the commonhold community statement or any other term applicable by virtue of the transfer of the unit to the unit-holder.[113] However, the duty only applies if A receives a request from or on behalf of the

---

[101] EQA 2010, Sch 4, para 3(5).
[102] EQA 2010, Sch 4, para 3(6) and (7). See Sch 4, para 2(9).
[103] EQA 2010, s 38(8) and Sch 4 para 1.
[104] EQA 2010, Sch 4, para 4(1).
[105] EQA 2010, Sch 4, para 4(1).
[106] EQA 2010, Sch 4, para 4(2).
[107] EQA 2010, s 212(1).
[108] EQA 2010, s 20(3).
[109] EQA 2010, s 212(1).
[110] EQA 2010, s 20(5).
[111] EQA 2010, Sch 4, para 4(3).
[112] EQA 2010, Sch 4, para 4(4).
[113] EQA 2010, Sch 4, para 4(5).

unit-holder or a person entitled to occupy the unit to take steps to avoid the disadvantage or provide the auxiliary aid.[114]

5.56 If a term of the commonhold community statement (or any other term applicable by virtue of the transfer of the unit to the unit-holder) that prohibits the unit-holder from making alterations puts the disabled person at the disadvantage referred to in the first requirement,[115] A is required to change the term only so far as is necessary to enable the unit-holder to make alterations to the unit so as to avoid the disadvantage.[116] However, it is never reasonable for A to have to take a step which would involve the removal or alteration of a physical feature (as previously defined above).[117]

The duty in relation to common parts

5.57 Schedule 4 applies where a duty to make reasonable adjustments is imposed on a person (A) by Part 4 of the 2010 Act (on premises).[118] What is the position where A is a responsible person in relation to common parts?[119]

5.58 A responsible person in relation to common parts (A) must comply with the second requirement.[120] Thus, where a physical feature puts a disabled person at a substantial (that is, more than minor or trivial)[121] disadvantage in relation to a relevant matter in comparison with persons who are not disabled, the requirement is to take such steps as it is reasonable to have to take to avoid the disadvantage.[122] In this context, the reference to a physical feature is a reference to a physical feature of the common parts.[123] The reference here to a disabled person is a reference to a disabled person who is a tenant of the premises, or who is a unit-holder, or who is otherwise entitled to occupy the premises. The disabled person must be a person who uses or intends to use the premises as the person's only or main home.[124] In relation to the second requirement of the duty, the relevant matter is the use of the common parts.[125]

5.59 The duty of a responsible person in relation to the common parts to comply with the second requirement applies only as follows.[126] A must receive a request by or on behalf of the disabled person in question. The disabled person

---

[114] EQA 2010, Sch 4, para 4(6).
[115] That is, where a provision, criterion or practice of A's puts a disabled person at a substantial (more than minor or trivial) disadvantage in relation to a relevant matter in comparison with persons who are not disabled, A is required to take such steps as it is reasonable to have to take to avoid the disadvantage.
[116] EQA 2010, Sch 4, para 4(7).
[117] EQA 2010, Sch 4, para 4(8). See Sch 4, para 9(2).
[118] EQA 2010, s 38(8) and Sch 4, para 1.
[119] EQA 2010, Sch 4, para 5(1).
[120] EQA 2010, Sch 4, para 5(2).
[121] EQA 2010, s 212(1).
[122] EQA 2010, s 20(4).
[123] EQA 2010, Sch 4, para 5(3).
[124] EQA 2010, Sch 4, para 5(4).
[125] EQA 2010, Sch 4, para 5(5).
[126] EQA 2010, Sch 4, para 5(6).

must be a person who is a tenant of the premises, or who is a unit-holder, or who is otherwise entitled to occupy the premises. That person must use or intend to use the premises as the person's only or main home. The request must be for A to take steps to avoid the disadvantage. The steps requested must be likely to avoid or reduce the disadvantage.

Consultation on adjustments relating to common parts

5.60 In deciding whether it is reasonable to take a step for the purposes of the duty in relation to common parts, A (the responsible person in relation to common parts) must consult all persons A thinks would be affected by the step.[127] The consultation must be carried out within a reasonable period of the request being made.[128] However, the responsible person in relation to common parts (A) is not required to have regard to a view expressed against taking a step insofar as A reasonably believes that the view is expressed because of the disabled person's disability.[129]

5.61 Nothing in this particular provision affects anything a commonhold association is required to do pursuant to Part 1 of the Commonhold and Leasehold Reform Act 2002.[130] Among other things, the 2002 Act established a scheme that combined the security of freehold ownership with the management potential of positive covenants that could be made to apply to each owner of an interdependent property. This scheme is commonhold. In particular, Part 1 of the 2002 Act defines the common parts of a commonhold development and regulates their use, maintenance and transactions (such as charging).

Agreement on adjustments relating to common parts

5.62 If the responsible person in relation to common parts (A) decides that it is reasonable to take a step for the purposes of the duty to make an adjustment, A and the disabled person must in writing agree the rights and responsibilities of each of them in relation to the step.[131] If such a written agreement is made, A's obligations under the agreement become part of A's interest in the common parts and they pass on subsequent disposals accordingly.[132]

5.63 Such an agreement must, in particular, make provision as to the responsibilities of the parties in relation to the costs of any work to be undertaken; other costs arising from the work; and the restoration of the common parts to their former condition if the relevant disabled person stops living in the premises.[133] It is always reasonable before the agreement is made for A to insist that the agreement should require the disabled person to pay the

---

127   EQA 2010, Sch 4, para 6(1).
128   EQA 2010, Sch 4, para 6(2).
129   EQA 2010, Sch 4, para 6(3).
130   EQA 2010, Sch 4, para 6(4).
131   EQA 2010, Sch 4, para 7(1).
132   EQA 2010, Sch 4, para 7(4).
133   EQA 2010, Sch 4, para 7(2).

costs of any work to be undertaken or other costs arising from the work.[134] Moreover, it is always reasonable before the agreement is made for A to insist that the agreement should require the disabled person to pay the costs of the restoration of the common parts to their former condition if the relevant disabled person stops living in the premises.[135]

5.64 Regulations may require a party to such an agreement to provide in prescribed circumstances prescribed information about the agreement to persons of a prescribed description.[136] Those regulations may require the information to be provided in a prescribed form.[137] They may make provision as to circumstances in which such an agreement is to cease to have effect, insofar as the agreement does not itself make provision for termination.[138] There are no regulations made at the time of writing.

Victimisation

5.65 A prohibition upon victimisation arises where a relevant disabled person is otherwise entitled to occupy premises. A must not subject a tenant of the premises or the unit-holder to a detriment because of costs incurred in connection with taking steps to comply with a duty to make reasonable adjustments.[139]

Regulations

5.66 For the purposes of s 36 (reasonable adjustments: leasehold and commonhold premises and common parts) and Sch 4 (premises: reasonable adjustments) there is a general regulation-making power.[140] Regulations may make provision as to:[141]

- circumstances in which premises are to be treated as let, or as not let, to a person;

- circumstances in which premises are to be treated as being, or as not being, to let;

- who is to be treated as being, or as not being, a person entitled to occupy premises otherwise than as tenant or unit-holder;

- who is to be treated as being, or as not being, a person by whom premises are let;

---

[134] EQA 2010, Sch 4, para 7(3)(a).
[135] EQA 2010, Sch 4, para 7(3)(b).
[136] EQA 2010, Sch 4, para 7(5).
[137] EQA 2010, Sch 4, para 7(6).
[138] EQA 2010, Sch 4, para 7(7).
[139] EQA 2010, Sch 4, para 8.
[140] EQA 2010, Sch 4, para 9(1).
[141] EQA 2010, Sch 4, para 9(2).

- who is to be treated as having, or as not having, premises to let;

- who is to be treated as being, or as not being, a manager of premises.

Provision may be made by regulations to amend Sch 4.[142] There are no regulations made at the time of writing.

Examples

5.67 The Explanatory Notes offer the following additional examples of the duty in practice:[143]

- A landlord has a normal practice of notifying all tenants of any rent arrears in writing with a follow-up visit if the arrears are not reduced. A disabled person explains to the landlord that he cannot read standard English so would not be aware that he was in arrears. He asks to be notified of any arrears in person or by telephone. The landlord arranges to visit or telephone the learning disabled person to explain when he has any arrears of rent. This personal contact may be a reasonable adjustment for the landlord to make.

- A landlord is asked by a disabled tenant to install a ramp to give her easier access to the communal entrance door. The landlord must consult all people he thinks would be affected by the ramp. If he believes that it is reasonable to provide it, he must enter into a written agreement with the disabled person. This must set out matters such as responsibility for payment for the ramp. The landlord can insist the tenant pays for the cost of making the alteration.

IMPROVEMENTS TO LET DWELLING HOUSES

5.68 Section 190 applies in relation to a lease of a dwelling house if each of the following conditions applies:[144]

---

[142] EQA 2010, Sch 4, para 9(3).
[143] EN para 773.
[144] EQA 2010, s 190(1).

- the tenancy is not a protected tenancy,[145] a statutory tenancy[146] or a secure tenancy;[147]

- the tenant or another person occupying or intending to occupy the premises is a disabled person (D);[148]

- D occupies or intends to occupy the premises as D's only or main home;

- the tenant is entitled, with the consent of the landlord, to make improvements to the premises;

- the tenant applies to the landlord for consent to make a relevant improvement.

The term 'lease' in this context includes a sub-lease or other tenancy. The terms 'landlord' and 'tenant' are to be construed accordingly.[149]

5.69 An 'improvement' means an alteration in or addition to the premises. It includes (a) an addition to or alteration in the landlord's fittings and fixtures; (b) an addition or alteration connected with the provision of services to the premises; (c) the erection of a wireless or television aerial; or (d) carrying out external decoration.[150] An improvement to premises is a relevant improvement if, having regard to D's disability, it is likely to facilitate D's enjoyment of the premises.[151]

5.70 If the landlord refuses to give consent where the tenant has applied in writing for the consent, the landlord must give the tenant a written statement of the reason why the consent was withheld.[152] If the landlord neither gives nor refuses to give consent within a reasonable time, consent must be taken to have been unreasonably withheld.[153] If the landlord gives consent subject to a

---

[145] The term 'protected tenancy' has the same meaning as in Rent Act 1977, s 1: EQA 2010, s 190(9). A tenancy under which a dwelling-house (which may be a house or part of a house) is let as a separate dwelling is a protected tenancy for the purposes of the Rent Act 1977 (and any reference to a protected tenant shall be construed accordingly).

[146] The term 'statutory tenancy" is to be construed in accordance with Rent Act 1977, s 2: EQA 2010, s 190(9). After the termination of a protected tenancy of a dwelling-house the person who, immediately before that termination, was the protected tenant of the dwelling-house shall, if and so long as he occupies the dwelling-house as his residence, be the statutory tenant of it.

[147] The term 'secure tenancy' has the same meaning as in Housing Act 1985, s 79: EQA 2010, s 190(9). A tenancy under which a dwelling-house is let as a separate dwelling is a secure tenancy at any time when the conditions described in Housing Act 1985, ss 80–81 as the landlord condition and the tenant condition are satisfied.

[148] EQA 2010, s 190 only applies to a person who has a present disability. It does not apply to a person who has had a past disability: EQA 2010, s 6(4).

[149] EQA 2010, s 190(9).

[150] EQA 2010, s 190(9).

[151] EQA 2010, s 190(7).

[152] EQA 2010, s 190(2)(a).

[153] EQA 2010, s 190(2)(b).

condition which is unreasonable, the consent must be taken to have been unreasonably withheld.[154] If the landlord's consent is unreasonably withheld, it must be taken to have been given.[155] On any question as to whether consent was unreasonably withheld or a condition imposed was unreasonable, it is for the landlord to show that it was not.[156] If the tenant fails to comply with a reasonable condition imposed by the landlord on the making of a relevant improvement, the failure is to be treated as a breach by the tenant of an obligation of the tenancy.[157]

5.71   The above provisions apply only in so far as provision of a like nature is not made by the lease.[158] They apply in England and Wales only.[159]

5.72   The Explanatory Notes explain that s 190 provides a procedure for a disabled tenant or a disabled occupier of rented residential premises to seek consent to make a disability-related improvement to the premises. This arises where the lease allows a tenant to make an improvement only with the consent of the landlord.[160] In that case, the landlord may not unreasonably withhold consent. However, the landlord may place reasonable conditions on the consent. A landlord who refuses consent must give reasons for that refusal. In deciding whether a refusal or condition is unreasonable, the onus is on the landlord to show that it is not.

5.73   Because similar rights already apply under the Housing Acts 1980 and 1985, s 190 of the Equality Act 2010 applies to all leases of residential property used as the occupier's or tenant's only or main residence, other than a protected tenancy, a statutory tenancy or a secure tenancy.[161] Section 190 replaces similar provisions in the DDA 1995.[162]

5.74   The Explanatory Notes provide the following examples of s 190 in action:[163]

- A disabled tenant who has mobility problems asks her landlord to consent to the installation of a walk-in shower and a grab rail to help her use the lavatory. Her landlord refuses consent. It would be for the landlord to give reasons for the refusal, and to show that it was not unreasonable.

- The landlord consents to the fitting of the grab rail and shower, on condition that their colour matches the other bathroom fittings, and that

---

[154]   EQA 2010, s 190(3).
[155]   EQA 2010, s 190(4).
[156]   EQA 2010, s 190(5).
[157]   EQA 2010, s 190(6).
[158]   EQA 2010, s 190(8).
[159]   EQA 2010, s 217(2); EN para 611.
[160]   EN para 610.
[161]   EN para 610.
[162]   DDA 1995, s 49G. See EN para 612 and Doyle, 2008: 217–218.
[163]   EN para 612.

they must be removed if the disabled person moves out of the property. These might be reasonable conditions, but it is for the landlord to show that they are.

EXCEPTIONS

Overview[164]

5.75 Schedule 5 (premises: exceptions) to the EQA 2010 contains various exceptions that apply to the premises provisions of Part 4.[165] The Explanatory Notes observe that these are limited exceptions to the prohibitions on discrimination and harassment contained in the premises provisions. The Schedule replaces similar provisions in current legislation. The Joint Committee on Human Rights, in its scrutiny of the Equality Bill before becoming law, considered that the exceptions struck an appropriate balance between protecting the right to equality and the rights of privacy and freedom of association.[166]

5.76 An exception applies where a person who owns and lives in a property sells or lets it privately without using the services of an estate agent or publishing an advertisement. This exception does not apply to race discrimination in disposing of premises. That remains unlawful. In relation to discrimination in respect of permission to dispose of premises, the exception only applies where the discrimination is based on religion or belief or sexual orientation.

5.77 A further exception also exempts a controller of leasehold premises from the duty to make reasonable adjustments in the following circumstances. The premises must have been let. They must be (or have been) the controller's main or only home. He or she must not have used the services of a manager since letting the premises. Where the premises are to let, the exception applies where the premises are the controller's main or only home and he or she has not used the service of an estate agent for letting purposes.

5.78 There is also a small premises exception. This applies to the disposal, management or occupation of part of small premises. The exception arises where the alleged discriminator (or his or her relative) lives in another part of the premises and the premises include facilities shared with other people who are not part of the alleged discriminator's household. However, this exception is not engaged in respect of race discrimination when disposing of (or giving permission for the disposal of) premises or in the management of premises.

5.79 A further small premises exception also exempts a controller of premises (or a person responsible in relation to common parts) from the duty to make

---

[164] EN paras 774–782.
[165] EQA 2010, s 38(9).
[166] Joint Committee on Human Rights, 2009: para 161.

reasonable adjustments in relation to small premises. This arises where that person (or a relative) lives in one part of the premises and residents who are not members of that person's household live in another part of the premises.

5.80　These provisions are now considered in detail.

Private disposal by owner-occupier exception

5.81　This exception relates to the private disposal of premises by an owner-occupier.[167] An 'owner-occupier' is a person who both owns an estate or an interest in premises and occupies the whole of them.[168] A disposal is a private disposal only if the owner-occupier does not (a) use the services of an estate agent for the purpose of disposing of the premises or (b) publish (or cause to be published) an advertisement in connection with their disposal.[169] The term 'estate agent' means a person who, by way of profession or trade, provides services for the purpose of finding premises for persons seeking them or assisting in the disposal of premises.[170]

5.82　In relation to a private disposal of premises by an owner-occupier, s 33(1) applies only insofar as it relates to race.[171] Section 33(1) provides that a person (A) who has the right to dispose of premises must not discriminate against another (B) as to the terms on which A offers to dispose of the premises to B or by not disposing of the premises to B or in A's treatment of B with respect to things done in relation to persons seeking premises.[172]

5.83　In relation to a private disposal of premises by an owner-occupier, s 34(1) does not apply in so far as it relates to religion or belief, or sexual orientation.[173] Section 34(1) provides that a person whose permission is required for the disposal of premises must not discriminate against another by not giving permission for the disposal of the premises to the other.

Only or principal home exception

5.84　In relation to leasehold and commonhold premises and common parts, a controller of let premises has a duty to make reasonable adjustments.[174] However, exceptionally, that particular duty (as it applies to a controller of let premises) does not apply if the premises are (or have been) the only home (or principal home) of a person by whom they are let and, since entering into the letting, neither that person (nor any other by whom they are let) has used a

---

[167]　EQA 2010, Sch 5, para 1(1).
[168]　EQA 2010, Sch 5, para 1(5).
[169]　EQA 2010, Sch 5, para 1(2).
[170]　EQA 2010, Sch 5, para 1(5).
[171]　EQA 2010, Sch 5, para 1(3).
[172]　EQA 2010, s 33(1).
[173]　EQA 2010, Sch 5, para 1(4).
[174]　EQA 2010, s 36(1)(a).

manager for managing the premises.[175] A manager is a person who by profession or trade manages let premises.[176]

5.85 In relation to leasehold and commonhold premises and common parts, a controller of premises to let has a duty to make reasonable adjustments.[177] However, exceptionally, that particular duty (as it applies to a controller of premises to let) does not apply if the premises are (or have been) the only home (or principal home) of a person who has them to let and neither that person nor any other who has the premises to let uses the services of an estate agent for letting the premises.[178] An estate agent is a person who by way of profession or trade provides services for the purpose of finding premises for persons seeking them or assisting in the disposal of premises.[179]

Small premises exceptions

5.86 An exception relates to small premises. Where the small premises exception applies, ss 33(1), 34(1) and 35(1) apply only insofar as they relate to race.[180]

5.87 Section 33(1) provides that a person (A) who has the right to dispose of premises must not discriminate against another (B) (a) as to the terms on which A offers to dispose of the premises to B; (b) by not disposing of the premises to B; or (c) in A's treatment of B with respect to things done in relation to persons seeking premises. Section 34(1) provides that a person whose permission is required for the disposal of premises must not discriminate against another by not giving permission for the disposal of the premises to the other. Section 35(1) provides that a person (A) who manages premises must not discriminate against a person (B) who occupies the premises (a) in the way in which A allows B (or by not allowing B) to make use of a benefit or facility; (b) by evicting B (or taking steps for the purpose of securing B's eviction); or (c) by subjecting B to any other detriment.

5.88 The exception applies to anything done by a person in relation to the disposal, occupation or management of part of small premises. It arises if the person (or a relative[181] of that person) resides, and intends to continue to

---

175 EQA 2010, Sch 5, para 2(1).
176 EQA 2010, Sch 5, para 2(2).
177 EQA 2010, s 36(1)(b).
178 EQA 2010, Sch 5, para 2(3).
179 EQA 2010, Sch 5, paras 1(5) and 2(4).
180 EQA 2010, Sch 5, para 3(1).
181 The term 'relative' means a spouse or civil partner, an unmarried partner, a parent or grandparent, a child or grandchild (whether or not legitimate), the spouse, civil partner or unmarried partner of a child or grandchild, or a brother or sister (whether of full blood or half-blood). It also includes a parent or grandparent, a child or grandchild (whether or not legitimate), the spouse, civil partner or unmarried partner of a child or grandchild, or a brother or sister (whether of full blood or half-blood), in all cases whose relationship arises as a result of marriage or civil partnership. A reference to an unmarried partner is a reference to the other member of a couple consisting of (a) a man and a woman who are not married to

reside, in another part of the premises. The premises in question must include parts (other than storage areas and means of access) shared with residents of the premises who are not members of the same household as the said resident.[182]

5.89   Premises are small premises if:

* the only other persons occupying the accommodation occupied by the said resident are members of the same household; and

* the premises also include accommodation for at least one other household; and

* the accommodation for each of those other households is let, or available for letting, on a separate tenancy or similar agreement; and

* the premises are not normally sufficient to accommodate more than two other households.[183]

Premises are also small premises if they are not normally sufficient to provide residential accommodation for more than six persons (in addition to the said resident and members of the same household).[184]

5.90   An additional exception applies to s 36(1). That is the provision that, in relation to leasehold and commonhold premises and common parts, places a duty to make reasonable adjustments upon a controller of let premises, a controller of premises to let, a commonhold association and a responsible person in relation to common parts. Section 36(1) does not apply if:

* the premises in question are small premises;

* the relevant person or a relative of that person resides, and intends to continue to reside, in another part of the premises; and

* the premises include parts (other than storage areas and means of access) shared with residents of the premises who are not members of the same household as the said resident.[185]

The relevant person is the person who, for the purposes of s 36(1), is the controller of the premises or the responsible person in relation to the common

---

each other but are living together as husband and wife, or (b) two people of the same sex who are not civil partners of each other but are living together as if they were. See EQA 2010, Sch 5, para 3(5) and (6).
[182]   EQA 2010, Sch 5, para 3(2).
[183]   EQA 2010, Sch 5, para 3(3).
[184]   EQA 2010, Sch 5, para 3(4).
[185]   EQA 2010, Sch 5, para 4(1).

parts to which the premises relate.[186] The terms 'small premises' and 'relative' have the same meaning as discussed above.[187]

5.91 A Minister of the Crown may by order amend Sch 5, para 3 or 4.[188]

Examples

5.92 The Explanatory Notes offer the following examples of the exceptions in practice:[189]

- A homeowner makes it known that she is preparing to sell her flat privately. A work colleague expresses an interest in buying it but she refuses to sell it to him because he is black. That refusal would not be covered by an exception and so would be unlawful.

- A homeowner makes it known socially that he wants to sell his house privately. Various prospective buyers come forward and the homeowner opts to sell it to a fellow Christian. The other prospective buyers cannot claim that they were discriminated against because the homeowner's actions are covered by an exception.

- A single woman owns a large house in London and lives on the top floor, although the bathroom and toilet facilities are on the first floor. The ground floor is unoccupied and she decides to take in a lodger, sharing the bathroom and toilet facilities. Various prospective tenants apply but she chooses only to let the ground floor to another woman. This would be permissible and excepted.

- A Jewish family own a large house but only live in part of it. They decide to let out an unoccupied floor but any new tenant will have to share kitchen and cooking facilities. The family choose only to let the unoccupied floor to practising Jews as they are concerned that otherwise their facilities for keeping their food kosher may be compromised. This would be permissible as an exception.

---

[186] EQA 2010, Sch 5, para 4(2).
[187] EQA 2010, Sch 5, para 4(3).
[188] EQA 2010, Sch 5, para 5.
[189] EN para 782.

Chapter 6

WORK: GENERAL PRINCIPLES

INTRODUCTION

6.1   This first of two chapters on work and equality considers Part 5 (Chapter 1) of the Equality Act 2010 (EQA 2010) (employment, etc). Sections 39 to 59 set out the acts or omissions that are capable of giving rise to a claim in the employment tribunal where, by reference to a protected characteristic, a person (A) discriminates against another person (B), or harasses or victimises that other. These sections are concerned with work and employment in the broadest sense. They cover employees and applicants for employment, police officers, partners, barristers and advocates, office-holders, qualifications bodies, providers of employment services, trade organisations, and members of local authorities.[1] These provisions are supported by the Draft Employment Code of Practice (2010).[2]

6.2   The prohibited conduct of discrimination, harassment and victimisation – together with what would amount to a failure to make a reasonable adjustment – is defined in Part 2 (Chapter 2) of the Act. This has been discussed in Chapter 3 above.

6.3   In relation to direct discrimination,[3] it is worth noting some exceptional or differential treatment that arises in the context of work. If the protected characteristic is marriage and civil partnership, the prohibited conduct of direct discrimination applies to a contravention of Part 5 (work) only if the treatment is because it is B who is married or a civil partner.[4] If the protected characteristic is sex, less favourable treatment of a woman usually includes less favourable treatment of her because she is breast-feeding.[5] However, this does not apply for the purposes of Part 5 (work).[6]

6.4   Note also that in relation to gender reassignment discrimination and cases of absence from work, special provision is made for the form of

---

1   Although EQA 2010, s 60 (enquiries about disability and health) is strictly part of Chapter 1 of Part 5, that provision is considered in Chapter 7 on work that follows below.
2   Equality and Human Rights Commission, 2010a. The draft code is issued under EQA 2006, ss 14–15 (as amended by EQA 2010).
3   EQA 2010, s 13.
4   EQA 2010, s 13(4).
5   EQA 2010, s 13(6)(a).
6   EQA 2010, s 13(7).

prohibited conduct that arises there in Part 5 (work).[7] Similarly, particular provisions have effect for the purposes of the application of Part 5 (work) to discrimination in relation to the protected characteristic of pregnancy and maternity.[8] See Chapter 3 above.

6.5   As noted in the Preface to this book, it remains to be seen how relevant the legacy case-law will remain to the recast provisions on employment discrimination in the Equality Act 2010. It is arguable that the new provisions will have to be approached afresh and that pre-existing case law can be no more than illustrative. Nevertheless, the relevant legacy case law has been footnoted in this chapter and that which follows.[9]

EMPLOYMENT

Employees and applicants

6.6   Section 39 addresses prohibited conduct in relation to employees and applicants for employment. It embraces those already in work and those seeking to obtain work in the recruitment and selection process. It focuses upon the prohibited conduct of discrimination and victimisation, and upon the duty to make a reasonable adjustment. It applies to all the protected characteristics.

6.7   Section 39 replaces similar provisions in current legislation.[10] The Explanatory Notes confirm that the section makes it unlawful for an employer to discriminate against or victimise employees and people seeking work. It applies where the employer is making arrangements to fill a job. The section also applies in respect of anything done in the course of a person's employment.[11]

6.8   The section begins by dealing with applicants for employment. An employer (A) must not discriminate against a person (B) (a) in the arrangements A makes for deciding to whom to offer employment; or (b) as to the terms on which A offers B employment; or (c) by not offering B employment.[12] An employer (A) must not victimise a person (B) (a) in the

---

[7]   EQA 2010, s 16.

[8]   EQA 2010, s 18.

[9]   Drawing strongly upon Rubenstein, 2010b and *Harvey on Industrial Relations and Employment Law* (Butterworths Lexis-Nexis).

[10]   EN para 147. See: *Saunders v Richmond-upon-Thames Borough Council* [1977] IRLR 362, EAT; *Noble v David Gold & Son (Holdings) Ltd* [1980] IRLR 252, CA; *Hurley v Mustoe* [1981] IRLR 208, EAT; *Horsey v Dyfed County Council* [1982] IRLR 395, EAT; *Brennan v J H Dewhurst Ltd* [1983] IRLR 357, EAT; *Adeyeke v Post Office (No 2)* [1997] IRLR 105, CA; *Nagarajan v London Regional Transport* [1999] IRLR 572, HL; *Anya v University of Oxford* [2001] IRLR 377, CA.

[11]   EN para 146.

[12]   EQA 2010, s 39(1).

arrangements A makes for deciding to whom to offer employment; or (b) as to the terms on which A offers B employment; or (c) by not offering B employment.[13]

6.9 It is noteworthy that an employer (A) must not discriminate against a person (B) as to the terms on which A offers B employment.[14] So far as relating to sex or pregnancy and maternity, this prohibition does not apply to a term that relates to pay unless, were B to accept the offer, an equality clause or rule would have effect in relation to the term.[15] Alternatively, where that condition does not apply, and so far as relating to sex or pregnancy and maternity, this prohibition does not apply to a term that relates to pay except insofar as making an offer on terms including that term amounts to a contravention of this prohibition[16] by virtue of s 13 (direct discrimination), s 14 (combined discrimination: dual characteristics) or s 18 (pregnancy and maternity discrimination: work cases).[17]

6.10 The Explanatory Notes explain that, in respect of discrimination relating to sex or pregnancy and maternity, a term of an offer of employment which relates to pay is treated as discriminatory where, if accepted, it would give rise to an equality clause. If an equality clause does not apply, then in respect of discrimination relating to sex or pregnancy and maternity, a term of an offer of employment which relates to pay is treated as discriminatory where the offer of the term constitutes direct discrimination or dual discrimination (or pregnancy and maternity discrimination at work).[18]

6.11 Section 39 then considers the rights of employees. An employer (A) must not discriminate against an employee of A's (B) (a) as to B's terms of employment; or (b) in the way A affords B access (or by not affording B access) to opportunities for promotion, transfer or training or for receiving any other benefit, facility or service; or (c) by dismissing B; or (d) by subjecting B to any other detriment.[19] An employer (A) must not victimise an employee of A's (B) (a) as to B's terms of employment; or (b) in the way A affords B access, or by not affording B access, to opportunities for promotion, transfer or training or for any other benefit, facility or service; or (c) by dismissing B; or (d) by subjecting B to any other detriment.[20]

---

[13] EQA 2010, s 39(3).
[14] EQA 2010, s 39(1)(b).
[15] EQA 2010, s 39(6)(a).
[16] EQA 2010, s 39(1)(b).
[17] EQA 2010, s 39(6)(b).
[18] EN para 146.
[19] EQA 2010, s 39(2). Detriment does not include conduct which amounts to harassment: EQA 2010, s 212(1). However, where the Act disapplies a prohibition on harassment in relation to a specified protected characteristic, that disapplication does not prevent conduct relating to that characteristic from amounting to a detriment for the purposes of direct discrimination because of that characteristic: EQA 2010, s 212(5).
[20] EQA 2010, s 39(4). Detriment does not include conduct which amounts to harassment: EQA 2010, s 212(1). However, where the Act disapplies a prohibition on harassment in relation to a specified protected characteristic, that disapplication does not prevent conduct relating to that

6.12 Both references to dismissing B in the previous paragraph include a reference to the termination of B's employment by the expiry of a period (including a period expiring by reference to an event or circumstance).[21] However, this does not apply if, immediately after the termination, the employment is renewed on the same terms.[22] Both references to dismissing B in this paragraph also include a reference to the termination of B's employment by an act of B's (including giving notice) in circumstances such that B is entitled, because of A's conduct, to terminate the employment without notice.[23]

6.13 A duty to make reasonable adjustments applies to an employer.[24] Thus, s 39 also imposes the reasonable adjustments duty set out in s 20 on employers in respect of disabled employees and applicants.[25]

6.14 The Explanatory Notes offer the following examples of how s 39 works in practice:[26]

- An employer decides not to shortlist for interview a disabled job applicant because of her epilepsy. This would be direct discrimination.

- An employer offers a woman a job on lower pay than the set rate because she is pregnant when she applies. She cannot bring an equality clause case as there is no comparator. However, she will be able to claim direct discrimination.

- An employer refuses to interview a man applying for promotion, because he previously supported a discrimination case against the employer brought by another employee. This would be victimisation.

- An employer enforces a 'no beards' policy by asking staff to shave. This could be indirect discrimination, because it would have a particular impact on Muslims or Orthodox Jews.

---

characteristic from amounting to a detriment for the purposes of direct discrimination because of that characteristic: EQA 2010, s 212(5). See generally: *Schmidt v Austicks Bookshops Ltd* [1977] IRLR 360, EAT; *Home Office v Holmes* [1984] IRLR 299, EAT; *Burrett v West Birmingham Health Authority* [1994] IRLR 7, EAT. *Smith v Safeway plc* [1996] IRLR 456, CA; *Jiad v Byford* [2003] IRLR 232, CA; *Shamoon v Chief Constable of the Royal Ulster Constabulary* [2003] IRLR 285, HL; *Department for Work and Pensions v Thompson* [2004] IRLR 348, EAT. Other case law examples of detrimental treatment can be found in Rubenstein, 2010b: 45.

21   EQA 2010, s 39(7)(a).
22   EQA 2010, s 39(8).
23   EQA 2010, s 39(7)(b).
24   EQA 2010, s 39(5).
25   EN para 146.
26   EN para 147. See also: *Eke v Commissioners of Customs & Excise* [1981] IRLR 334, EAT. *West Midlands PTE v Singh* [1988] IRLR 186, CA; *Clymo v Wandsworth LBC* [1989] IRLR 241, EAT; *Mecca Leisure Group plc v Chatprachong* [1993] IRLR 531, EAT; *Iske v P & O European Ferries (Dover) Ltd* [1997] IRLR 401, EAT; *Wakeman v Quick Corporation* [1999] IRLR 424, EAT.

Employees and applicants: harassment

6.15 Section 40 is concerned with harassment of employees and applicants for employment in the workplace. An employer (A) must not, in relation to employment by A, harass a person (B) who is an employee of A's or who has applied to A for employment.[27]

6.16 The circumstances in which A is to be treated as harassing B include those where a third party harasses B in the course of B's employment, and A failed to take such steps as would have been reasonably practicable to prevent the third party from doing so.[28] However, that circumstance does not apply unless A knows that B has been harassed in the course of B's employment on at least two other occasions by a third party and it does not matter whether the third party is the same or a different person on each occasion.[29] In this context, a third party is a person other than A or an employee of A's.[30]

6.17 Section 40 is designed to replicate the effect of provisions in pre-existing legislation in respect of harassment by employers. However, it extends the position in relation to employer liability for sex harassment under the Sex Discrimination Act 1975 (SDA 1975) to the other protected characteristics (apart from marriage and civil partnership and pregnancy and maternity).[31] The effect is that it is unlawful for an employer to harass employees and applicants for employment. It also makes the employer liable for harassment of its employees by third parties, such as customers or clients, over whom the employer does not have direct control. However, liability in relation to third party harassment will arise only when (1) harassment has occurred on at least two occasions, (2) the employer is aware that it has taken place, and (3) the employer has not taken reasonable steps to prevent it happening again.[32]

6.18 The Explanatory Notes illustrate the operation of s 40 with the following example. A shop assistant with a strong Nigerian accent tells her manager that she is upset and humiliated by a customer who regularly uses the shop and each time makes derogatory remarks about Africans in her hearing. If her manager does nothing to try to stop it happening again, he would be liable for racial harassment.[33]

---

[27] EQA 2010, s 40(1).

[28] EQA 2010, s 40(2). See: *Chessington World of Adventures Ltd v Reed* [1997] IRLR 556, EAT; *Macdonald v Advocate General for Scotland, Pearce v Governing Body of Mayfield Secondary School* [2003] IRLR 512, HL; *EOC v Secretary of State for Trade and Industry* [2007] IRLR 327, HC.

[29] EQA 2010, s 40(3). The Joint Committee on Human Rights (2009: para 119) considered that the threshold requirement should be reduced to one previous incident or that this requirement should be replaced with a provision that an employer will be liable when they ought reasonably to have been aware of the risk of third party harassment.

[30] EQA 2010, s 40(4).

[31] EN para 149.

[32] EN para 148.

[33] EN para 149.

Contract workers

6.19   Contract workers enjoy separate protection from discrimination by their employer (for example, the agency which employs them) under s 39. However, s 41 also makes it unlawful for a person ('a principal') who makes work available to contract workers to discriminate against, harass or victimise them. Section 41 also imposes a duty on the principal to make reasonable adjustments for disabled contract workers (in addition to the duty on the contract worker's employer).[34]

6.20   The Explanatory Notes suggest that s 41 is designed to replicate the effect of provisions in previous legislation, while codifying case law to make clear that there does not need to be a direct contractual relationship between the employer and the principal for the protection to apply.[35]

6.21   In the context of s 41, a 'principal' is a person who makes work available for an individual who is (a) employed by another person, and (b) supplied by that other person in furtherance of a contract to which the principal is a party (whether or not that other person is a party to it).[36] Then 'contract work' is such work.[37] A 'contract worker' is an individual supplied to a principal in furtherance of a contract such as is mentioned at (b) above.[38]

6.22   A principal must not discriminate against a contract worker (a) as to the terms on which the principal allows the worker to do the work; or (b) by not allowing the worker to do (or to continue to do) the work; or (c) in the way the principal affords the worker access (or by not affording the worker access) to opportunities for receiving a benefit, facility or service; or (d) by subjecting the worker to any other detriment.[39]

6.23   A principal must not, in relation to contract work, harass a contract worker.[40]

6.24   A principal must not victimise a contract worker (a) as to the terms on which the principal allows the worker to do the work; or (b) by not allowing the worker to do (or to continue to do) the work; or (c) in the way the principal

---

[34]   EN para 150.
[35]   EN para 151. See SDA 1975, s 9; RRA 1976, s 7; DDA 1995, s 4B. See further: *BP Chemicals Ltd v Gillick* [1995] IRLR 128, EAT; *Harrods Ltd v Remick* [1997] IRLR 583, CA; *Abbey Life Assurance Co Ltd v Tansell* [2000] IRLR 387, CA; *Patefield v Belfast City Council* [2000] IRLR 664, NICA; *Allonby v Accrington & Rossendale College* [2001] IRLR 364, CA; *Jones v Friends Provident Life Office* [2004] IRLR 783, NICA.
[36]   EQA 2010, s 41(5).
[37]   EQA 2010, s 41(6).
[38]   EQA 2010, s 41(7).
[39]   EQA 2010, s 41(1). Detriment does not include conduct which amounts to harassment: EQA 2010, s 212(1). However, where the Act disapplies a prohibition on harassment in relation to a specified protected characteristic, that disapplication does not prevent conduct relating to that characteristic from amounting to a detriment for the purposes of direct discrimination because of that characteristic: EQA 2010, s 212(5).
[40]   EQA 2010, s 41(2).

affords the worker access (or by not affording the worker access) to opportunities for receiving a benefit, facility or service; or (d) by subjecting the worker to any other detriment.[41]

6.25 A duty to make reasonable adjustments applies to a principal (as well as to the employer of a contract worker).[42]

6.26 The Explanatory Notes offer the following examples:[43]

- A hotel manager refuses to accept a black African contract worker sent to him by an agency because of fears that guests would be put off by his accent. This would be direct discrimination.

- A bank treats a female contract worker less well than her male counterparts, for example by insisting that she makes coffee for all meetings. This would be direct discrimination.

POLICE OFFICERS

Introduction

6.27 Sections 42 and 43 provide that police constables and police cadets are treated as employees for the purposes of Part 5 of the Act (work).[44] They identify the relevant employer as either the chief officer (or, in Scotland, the chief constable)[45] or the responsible authority, depending on who commits the act in question.[46] These sections replicate existing provisions and extend their coverage. They remove the requirement to pay out of police funds compensation and related costs arising from the personal liability of chief officers for acts which are unlawful under the Act. Instead such payments in future fall to be dealt with under the Police Act 1996 and the Police (Scotland) Act 1967.[47]

Chief officers

6.28 For the purposes of Part 5 of the Act (work), s 42 provides that holding the office of constable is to be treated as employment by the chief officer, in respect of any act done by the chief officer in relation to a constable or

---

[41] EQA 2010, s 41(3). Detriment does not include conduct which amounts to harassment: EQA 2010, s 212(1). However, where the Act disapplies a prohibition on harassment in relation to a specified protected characteristic, that disapplication does not prevent conduct relating to that characteristic from amounting to a detriment for the purposes of direct discrimination because of that characteristic: EQA 2010, s 212(5).

[42] EQA 2010, s 41(4).

[43] EN para 151.

[44] EQA 2010, s 43 acts as the interpretation section for s 42: s 43(1). See EN paras 152–158.

[45] EQA 2010, s 43(9).

[46] EN para 152.

[47] EN para 156.

appointment to the office of constable.[48] So, if a chief officer refuses to allocate protective equipment to female constables, the chief officer would be treated as the employer in a direct discrimination claim.[49]

6.29 In relation to an appointment under a relevant Act,[50] the deemed employer will be the chief officer of police for the police force to which the appointment relates.[51] In relation to any other appointment, the chief officer will be the person under whose direction and control the body of constables or other persons to which the appointment relates is to be found.[52] In relation to a constable or other person under the direction and control of a chief officer of police, the deemed employer will be that chief officer of police.[53] In relation to any other constable or any other person, the deemed employer is the person under whose direction and control the constable or other person is to be found.[54] In Scotland, the appropriate reference is to the chief constable rather than to a chief officer.[55]

Responsible authorities

6.30 For the purposes of Part 5 of the Act (work), s 42 also provides that holding the office of constable is to be treated as employment by the responsible authority, in respect of any act done by the authority in relation to a constable or appointment to the office of constable.[56]

6.31 In relation to an appointment under a relevant Act,[57] the 'responsible authority' means the police authority that maintains the police force to which the appointment relates.[58] In relation to any other appointment, it is the person by whom a person would be paid (if appointed).[59] In relation to a constable or other person under the direction and control of a chief officer of police, the 'responsible authority' means the police authority that maintains the police force for which that chief officer is the chief officer of police.[60] In relation to any other constable or any other person, it will be the person by whom the constable or other person is paid.[61]

---

48 EQA 2010, s 42(1)(a).
49 EN para 156.
50 The relevant Acts are the Metropolitan Police Act 1829; the City of London Police Act 1839; the Police (Scotland) Act 1967; the Police Act 1996: EQA 2010, s 43(8).
51 EQA 2010, s 43(2)(a).
52 EQA 2010, s 43(2)(b).
53 EQA 2010, s 43(2)(c).
54 EQA 2010, s 43(2)(d).
55 EQA 2010, s 43(9).
56 EQA 2010, s 42(1)(b).
57 The relevant Acts are the Metropolitan Police Act 1829; the City of London Police Act 1839; the Police (Scotland) Act 1967; the Police Act 1996: EQA 2010, s 43(8).
58 EQA 2010, s 43(3)(a).
59 EQA 2010, s 43(3)(b).
60 EQA 2010, s 43(3)(c).
61 EQA 2010, s 43(3)(d).

Police cadets

6.32 Furthermore, for the purposes of Part 5 of the Act (work), holding an appointment as a police cadet is to be treated as employment by the chief officer, in respect of any act done by the chief officer in relation to a police cadet or appointment as one.[62] Alternatively, it is to be treated as employment by the responsible authority, in respect of any act done by the authority in relation to a police cadet or appointment as one.[63] The terms 'chief officer' and 'responsible authority' having the meanings already explained above. In Scotland, the appropriate reference is to the chief constable rather than to a chief officer.[64] A 'police cadet' means a person appointed to undergo training with a view to becoming a constable.[65]

Exceptions

6.33 The holding of the office of constable is not to be treated as employment by the chief officer or by the responsible authority, as the case might be, in relation to service with the Civil Nuclear Constabulary.[66] Members of the Civil Nuclear Constabulary are employees of the Civil Nuclear Police Authority under the direction and control of its chief constable.[67]

6.34 Moreover, the holding of the office of constable is not to be treated as employment by the chief officer or by the responsible authority, as the case might be, in relation to a constable at the Serious Organised Crime Agency (SOCA), the Scottish Police Services Authority (SPSA) or Scottish Crime and Drugs Enforcement Agency (SCDEA).[68] Instead, a constable at SOCA or SPSA is to be treated as employed by it, in respect of any act done by it in relation to the constable.[69] A constable at SCDEA is to be treated as employed by the Director General of SCDEA, in respect of any act done by the Director General in relation to the constable.[70]

6.35 A reference to a constable at SOCA is a reference to a constable seconded to it to serve as a member of its staff.[71] A reference to a constable at SPSA is a reference to a constable seconded to it to serve as a member of its staff, and not at SCDEA.[72] A reference to a constable at SCDEA is a reference to a constable who is a police member of it.[73]

---

[62] EQA 2010, s 42(2)(a).
[63] EQA 2010, s 42(2)(b).
[64] EQA 2010, s 43(9).
[65] EQA 2010, s 43(4).
[66] EQA 2010, s 42(3).
[67] Energy Act 2004, s 55(2).
[68] EQA 2010, s 42(4).
[69] EQA 2010, s 42(5).
[70] EQA 2010, s 42(6).
[71] EQA 2010, s 43(5).
[72] EQA 2010, s 43(6).
[73] By virtue of Police, Public Order and Criminal Justice (Scotland) Act 2006, Sch 2, para 7(2)(a) or (b) (secondment): EQA 2010, s 43(7).

PARTNERS

6.36   Sections 44 to 46 of the EQA 2010 deal with partners, partnerships and limited liability partnerships.[74]

Partnerships

6.37   Section 44 makes it unlawful for firms (and those intending to set up a firm) to discriminate against, harass or victimise their partners, or people seeking to be partners in the firm.[75] The Explanatory Notes suggest that the activities covered by s 44 could include the offering of partnerships or giving existing partners access to opportunities such as training and/or transfers to other branches of the firm.[76] The section also imposes on firms and people setting up firms a duty to make reasonable adjustments for disabled partners and prospective partners. In the case of limited partnerships, these prohibitions only apply in relation to those partners who are involved with the operation of the firm (general partners).[77]

6.38   The Explanatory Notes set out the background to s 44 in this way. Partners are mainly governed by the partnership deed or agreement. Their relationship is not regulated by an employment contract. Accordingly, separate provisions are needed to provide protection from discrimination, harassment and victimisation for partners in ordinary and limited partnerships.[78] Section 44 replicates existing provisions, but now provides consistent protection in respect of race. For example, if a firm refuses to accept an application for partnership from a black candidate, who is qualified to join, because he is of African origin this would be direct discrimination.[79]

6.39   Section 44 provides that a firm or proposed firm[80] must not discriminate against a person (a) in the arrangements it makes for deciding to whom to offer a position as a partner;[81] or (b) as to the terms on which it offers the person a position as a partner; or (c) by not offering the person a position as a partner.[82] Equally, a firm (A) must not discriminate against a partner (B) (a) as to the terms on which B is a partner; or (b) in the way A affords B access (or by not

---

[74]   EQA 2010, s 46 acts as the interpretation section to ss 44–45: s 46(1).
[75]   The terms 'partnership' and 'firm' have the same meaning as in the Partnership Act 1890: EQA 2010, s 46(2).
[76]   EN para 160.
[77]   EN para 161.
[78]   EN para 162.
[79]   EN para 162.
[80]   The term 'proposed firm' means persons proposing to form themselves into a partnership: EQA 2010, s 46(3).
[81]   In the application of s 44 to a limited partnership within the meaning of the Limited Partnerships Act 1907, the term 'partner' means a general partner within the meaning of that Act: EQA 2010, s 44(8).
[82]   EQA 2010, s 44(1).

affording B access) to opportunities for promotion, transfer or training or for receiving any other benefit, facility or service; or (c) by expelling B; or (d) by subjecting B to any other detriment.[83]

6.40 A reference to the expulsion of a partner of a firm includes a reference to the termination of the person's position as such (a) by the expiry of a period (including a period expiring by reference to an event or circumstance); or (b) by an act of the person (including giving notice) in circumstances such that the person is entitled, because of the conduct of other partners or members, to terminate the position without notice; or (c) as a result of the dissolution of the partnership.[84] However, points (a) or (c) do not apply if, immediately after the termination, the position is renewed on the same terms.[85]

6.41 A firm must not, in relation to a position as a partner, harass a partner or a person who has applied for the position.[86] A proposed firm must not, in relation to a position as a partner, harass a person who has applied for the position.[87]

6.42 A firm or proposed firm must not victimise a person (a) in the arrangements it makes for deciding to whom to offer a position as a partner; or (b) as to the terms on which it offers the person a position as a partner; or (c) by not offering the person a position as a partner.[88] A firm (A) must not victimise a partner (B) (a) as to the terms on which B is a partner; or (b) in the way A affords B access (or by not affording B access) to opportunities for promotion, transfer or training or for receiving any other benefit, facility or service; or (c) by expelling B; or (d) by subjecting B to any other detriment.[89]

6.43 A duty to make reasonable adjustments applies to a firm and to a proposed firm.[90]

---

[83] EQA 2010, s 44(2). Detriment does not include conduct which amounts to harassment: EQA 2010, s 212(1). However, where the Act disapplies a prohibition on harassment in relation to a specified protected characteristic, that disapplication does not prevent conduct relating to that characteristic from amounting to a detriment for the purposes of direct discrimination because of that characteristic: EQA 2010, s 212(5).

[84] EQA 2010, s 46(6).

[85] EQA 2010, s 46(7).

[86] EQA 2010, s 44(3).

[87] EQA 2010, s 44(4).

[88] EQA 2010, s 44(5).

[89] EQA 2010, s 44(6). Detriment does not include conduct which amounts to harassment: EQA 2010, s 212(1). However, where the Act disapplies a prohibition on harassment in relation to a specified protected characteristic, that disapplication does not prevent conduct relating to that characteristic from amounting to a detriment for the purposes of direct discrimination because of that characteristic: EQA 2010, s 212(5).

[90] EQA 2010, s 44(7).

Limited liability partnerships

6.44 Section 45 applies to a limited liability partnership (LLP) within the meaning of the Limited Liability Partnerships Act 2000.[91] An LLP or proposed LLP[92] must not discriminate against a person (a) in the arrangements it makes for deciding to whom to offer a position as a member; or (b) as to the terms on which it offers the person a position as a member; or (c) by not offering the person a position as a member.[93] An LLP (A) must not discriminate against a member (B) (a) as to the terms on which B is a member; or (b) in the way A affords B access (or by not affording B access) to opportunities for promotion, transfer or training or for receiving any other benefit, facility or service; or (c) by expelling B; or (d) by subjecting B to any other detriment.[94]

6.45 A reference to the expulsion of a member of an LLP includes a reference to the termination of the person's position as such (a) by the expiry of a period (including a period expiring by reference to an event or circumstance); or (b) by an act of the person (including giving notice) in circumstances such that the person is entitled, because of the conduct of other partners or members, to terminate the position without notice.[95] However, point (a) does not apply if, immediately after the termination, the position is renewed on the same terms.[96]

6.46 An LLP must not, in relation to a position as a member, harass a member or a person who has applied for the position.[97] A proposed LLP must not, in relation to a position as a member, harass a person who has applied for the position.[98]

6.47 An LLP or proposed LLP must not victimise a person (a) in the arrangements it makes for deciding to whom to offer a position as a member; or (b) as to the terms on which it offers the person a position as a member; or (c) by not offering the person a position as a member.[99] An LLP (A) must not victimise a member (B) (a) as to the terms on which B is a member; or (b) in the way A affords B access (or by not affording B access) to opportunities for promotion, transfer or training or for receiving any other benefit, facility or service; or (c) by expelling B; or (d) by subjecting B to any other detriment.[100]

---

[91] EQA 2010, s 46(4).

[92] That is, persons proposing to incorporate an LLP with themselves as members: EQA 2010, 46(5).

[93] EQA 2010, s 45(1).

[94] EQA 2010, s 45(2). Detriment does not include conduct which amounts to harassment: EQA 2010, s 212(1). However, where the Act disapplies a prohibition on harassment in relation to a specified protected characteristic, that disapplication does not prevent conduct relating to that characteristic from amounting to a detriment for the purposes of direct discrimination because of that characteristic: EQA 2010, s 212(5).

[95] EQA 2010, s 46(6).

[96] EQA 2010, s 46(7).

[97] EQA 2010, s 45(3).

[98] EQA 2010, s 45(4).

[99] EQA 2010, s 45(5).

[100] EQA 2010, s 45(6). Detriment does not include conduct which amounts to harassment: EQA 2010, s 212(1). However, where the Act disapplies a prohibition on harassment in relation to a

6.48 A duty to make reasonable adjustments applies to an LLP and a proposed LLP.[101]

6.49 Should there be any doubt, the Explanatory Notes venture that s 45 makes it unlawful for an LLP (or a group of people setting up an LLP) to discriminate against, harass or victimise a member (or prospective member). The activities covered by this section are said to include offers of membership or access to opportunities that the LLP makes available to its members. Section 45 imposes on an LLP a duty to make reasonable adjustments for disabled members and prospective members.[102] Section 45 is necessary because an LLP is distinct from a general and limited partnership. It replicates pre-existing statutory provisions, but it seeks to achieve the same consistency in respect of race as in s 44.[103]

6.50 The Explanatory Notes supply the following examples:

- An LLP refuses a member access to use of a company car because he has supported a discrimination or harassment claim against the LLP. This would be victimisation.

- An LLP refuses a Muslim member access to its child care scheme because all the other children who attend the scheme have Christian parents. This would be direct discrimination.

- A gay partner in a firm, who, because of constant homophobic banter, feels compelled to leave his position as a partner, can claim to have been expelled from the partnership because of his sexual orientation. Should an Employment Tribunal agree with him, the firm could be found to be in breach of these provisions in a similar way to how the Employment Tribunal would find for an employee who wins a claim for constructive dismissal.[104]

THE BAR

6.51 Sections 47 and 48 of the Equality Act 2010 are concerned with equality and discrimination among barristers and advocates.

---

specified protected characteristic, that disapplication does not prevent conduct relating to that characteristic from amounting to a detriment for the purposes of direct discrimination because of that characteristic: EQA 2010, s 212(5).
[101] EQA 2010, s 45(7).
[102] EN para 163.
[103] EN para 164.
[104] EN paras 164 and 165.

Barristers

6.52 Section 47 makes it unlawful for a barrister or a barrister's clerk to discriminate against, harass or victimise a pupil barrister or tenant in the barristers' chambers, in relation to the professional relationship between them. It also makes it unlawful for a barrister or a barrister's clerk to discriminate against, harass or victimise people seeking to be a pupil or tenant, in relation to the professional relationship between them. Furthermore, it imposes on barristers a duty to make reasonable adjustments for disabled pupils and tenants. Moreover, it makes it unlawful for a person instructing a barrister to discriminate against, harass or victimise a barrister in relation to the giving of instructions.[105]

6.53 So, by way of example, if a barrister treats a female pupil less favourably than his male pupils by allowing her to be involved in a narrower range of cases, this would be direct discrimination. Where a barrister's clerk gives instructions to a Christian barrister in his chambers in preference to a Hindu barrister, because he fears that the barrister's religion would prevent him representing a Christian client properly, this would be direct discrimination.[106]

6.54 Section 47 replaces pre-existing provisions providing similar protection for barristers, pupils, tenants (and prospective pupils or tenants) in barristers' chambers. However, it no longer protects clients and clerks from discrimination by barristers. They must seek redress under Part 3 of the Act (services) or under s 39 (employees and applicants) or s 41 (contract workers) above.[107]

6.55 These provisions in detail may be set out as follows. A reference to a barrister's clerk below includes a reference to a person who carries out the functions of a barrister's clerk.[108] A reference to a tenant includes a reference to a barrister who is permitted to work in chambers (including as a squatter or door tenant) and a reference to a tenancy is to be construed accordingly.[109]

6.56 A barrister (or a barrister's clerk) (A) must not discriminate against a person (B) (a) in the arrangements A makes for deciding to whom to offer a pupillage or tenancy; or (b) as to the terms on which A offers B a pupillage or tenancy; or (c) by not offering B a pupillage or tenancy.[110]

6.57 A barrister (or a barrister's clerk) (A) must not discriminate against a person (B) who is a pupil or tenant (a) as to the terms on which B is a pupil or tenant; or (b) in the way A affords B access (or by not affording B access) to opportunities for training or gaining experience or for receiving any other

---

[105] EN paras 166 and 167.
[106] EN para 168.
[107] EN para 168.
[108] EQA 2010, s 47(8).
[109] EQA 2010, s 47(9).
[110] EQA 2010, s 47(1) and (8).

benefit, facility or service; or (c) by terminating the pupillage; or (d) by subjecting B to pressure to leave chambers; or (e) by subjecting B to any other detriment.[111]

6.58 A barrister (or a barrister's clerk) must not, in relation to a pupillage or tenancy, harass the pupil or tenant or a person who has applied for the pupillage or tenancy.[112]

6.59 A barrister (or a barrister's clerk) (A) must not victimise a person (B) (a) in the arrangements A makes for deciding to whom to offer a pupillage or tenancy; or (b) as to the terms on which A offers B a pupillage or tenancy; or (c) by not offering B a pupillage or tenancy.[113] A barrister (or a barrister's clerk) (A) must not victimise a person (B) who is a pupil or tenant (a) as to the terms on which B is a pupil or tenant; or (b) in the way A affords B access (or by not affording B access) to opportunities for training or gaining experience or for receiving any other benefit, facility or service; or (c) by terminating the pupillage; or (d) by subjecting B to pressure to leave chambers; or (e) by subjecting B to any other detriment.[114]

6.60 A person must not, in relation to instructing a barrister (a) discriminate against a barrister by subjecting the barrister to a detriment; or (b) harass the barrister; or (c) victimise the barrister.[115]

6.61 A duty to make reasonable adjustments applies to a barrister and to a barrister's clerk.[116]

Advocates

6.62 Section 48 recognises that the legal profession of an advocate in Scotland is organised differently from that of a barrister in England and Wales. The section makes it unlawful for practising advocates and their clerks to

---

[111] EQA 2010, s 47(2) and (8). Detriment does not include conduct which amounts to harassment: EQA 2010, s 212(1). However, where the Act disapplies a prohibition on harassment in relation to a specified protected characteristic, that disapplication does not prevent conduct relating to that characteristic from amounting to a detriment for the purposes of direct discrimination because of that characteristic: EQA 2010, s 212(5).

[112] EQA 2010, s 47(3) and (8).

[113] EQA 2010, s 47(4) and (8).

[114] EQA 2010, s 47(5) and (8). Detriment does not include conduct which amounts to harassment: EQA 2010, s 212(1). However, where the Act disapplies a prohibition on harassment in relation to a specified protected characteristic, that disapplication does not prevent conduct relating to that characteristic from amounting to a detriment for the purposes of direct discrimination because of that characteristic: EQA 2010, s 212(5).

[115] EQA 2010, s 47(6). This provision does not apply to a barrister's clerk, as might be otherwise obvious from its context: s 47(8). Detriment does not include conduct which amounts to harassment: EQA 2010, s 212(1). However, where the Act disapplies a prohibition on harassment in relation to a specified protected characteristic, that disapplication does not prevent conduct relating to that characteristic from amounting to a detriment for the purposes of direct discrimination because of that characteristic: EQA 2010, s 212(5).

[116] EQA 2010, s 47(7) and (8).

discriminate against, harass or victimise trainee advocates or members of the stable (a group of advocates working in shared premises) or people seeking to be a devil or member, in respect of the professional relationship between them. It imposes on advocates a duty to make reasonable adjustments for disabled devils and stable members.[117] It also makes it unlawful for a person instructing an advocate to discriminate against, harass or victimise an advocate in relation to the giving of instructions.[118]

6.63 Like s 47, s 48 replaces similar provisions in the pre-existing legislation. In like fashion, it no longer protects clients and clerks from discrimination by advocates. They must look for protection under the services provisions or as employees and applicants for employment.[119]

6.64 Before looking at how s 48 works in detail, it is worth noting the examples provided by the Explanatory Notes:[120]

- An advocate treats one devil less favourably than another by refusing to allow him to be involved in a particular case because he fears the devil's sexual orientation may affect his involvement in the case. This would be direct discrimination.

- An advocate puts pressure on a stable member to leave because the member is disabled and the advocate does not want to make reasonable adjustments. This would be direct discrimination.

6.65 An advocate (A) must not discriminate against a person (B) (a) in the arrangements A makes for deciding who to take as A's devil or to whom to offer membership of a stable; or (b) as to the terms on which A offers to take B as A's devil or offers B membership of a stable; or (c) by not offering to take B as A's devil or not offering B membership of a stable.[121]

6.66 In this context, an 'advocate' means a practising member of the Faculty of Advocates.[122] The terms 'devil' and 'stable' are not defined in the statute. A devil is a trainee advocate, while a stable is a group of advocates working in shared premises.[123]

6.67 An advocate (A) must not discriminate against a person (B) who is a devil or a member of a stable (a) as to the terms on which B is a devil or a member of the stable; or (b) in the way A affords B access (or by not affording B access) to opportunities for training or gaining experience or for receiving any other benefit, facility or service; or (c) by terminating A's relationship with

---

[117] EN para 169.
[118] EN para 170.
[119] EN para 171.
[120] EN para 171.
[121] EQA 2010, s 48(1).
[122] EQA 2010, s 48(9).
[123] EN para 169.

B (where B is a devil); or (d) by subjecting B to pressure to leave the stable; or (e) by subjecting B to any other detriment.[124]

6.68 An advocate must not, in relation to a relationship with a devil or membership of a stable, harass a devil or member or a person who has applied to be taken as the advocate's devil or to become a member of the stable.[125]

6.69 An advocate (A) must not victimise a person (B) (a) in the arrangements A makes for deciding who to take as A's devil or to whom to offer membership of a stable; or (b) as to the terms on which A offers to take B as A's devil or offers B membership of a stable; or (c) by not offering to take B as A's devil or not offering B membership of a stable.[126] An advocate (A) must not victimise a person (B) who is a devil or a member of a stable (a) as to the terms on which B is a devil or a member of the stable; or (b) in the way A affords B access (or by not affording B access) to opportunities for training or gaining experience or for receiving any other benefit, facility or service; or (c) by terminating A's relationship with B (where B is a devil); or (d) by subjecting B to pressure to leave the stable; or (e) by subjecting B to any other detriment.[127]

6.70 A person must not, in relation to instructing an advocate (a) discriminate against the advocate by subjecting the advocate to a detriment; or (b) harass the advocate; or (c) victimise the advocate.[128]

6.71 A duty to make reasonable adjustments applies to an advocate.[129]

6.72 As in s 47, s 48 applies in relation to an advocate's clerk as it applies in relation to an advocate.[130] The reference to an advocate's clerk includes a reference to a person who carries out the functions of an advocate's clerk.

---

[124] EQA 2010, s 48(2). Detriment does not include conduct which amounts to harassment: EQA 2010, s 212(1). However, where the Act disapplies a prohibition on harassment in relation to a specified protected characteristic, that disapplication does not prevent conduct relating to that characteristic from amounting to a detriment for the purposes of direct discrimination because of that characteristic: EQA 2010, s 212(5).

[125] EQA 2010, s 48(3).

[126] EQA 2010, s 48(4).

[127] EQA 2010, s 48(5). Detriment does not include conduct which amounts to harassment: EQA 2010, s 212(1). However, where the Act disapplies a prohibition on harassment in relation to a specified protected characteristic, that disapplication does not prevent conduct relating to that characteristic from amounting to a detriment for the purposes of direct discrimination because of that characteristic: EQA 2010, s 212(5).

[128] EQA 2010, s 48(6). Detriment does not include conduct which amounts to harassment: EQA 2010, s 212(1). However, where the Act disapplies a prohibition on harassment in relation to a specified protected characteristic, that disapplication does not prevent conduct relating to that characteristic from amounting to a detriment for the purposes of direct discrimination because of that characteristic: EQA 2010, s 212(5).

[129] EQA 2010, s 48(7).

[130] EQA 2010, s 48(8), with the exception of s 48(6).

OFFICE-HOLDERS

Introduction

6.73 Sections 49–51 are concerned with discrimination and equality in relation to office-holders. Section 52 supplies interpretations and exceptions regarding ss 49–51.[131] Before looking at the detail of these provisions, it might be helpful to take an overview of them by drawing directly from the Explanatory Notes.

6.74 Section 49 makes it unlawful to discriminate against, harass or victimise people who are or who wish to become personal office-holders.[132] These provisions apply insofar as other work provisions do not. Where office-holders are also employees, they will be protected by the provisions dealing with employment in respect of their employment relationship. Personal office-holders are people who perform a function personally at a time and place specified by another person. In return they are entitled to payment (other than expenses or compensation for lost income). However, where a personal office is a public office at the same time, it is to be treated as a public office only.[133]

6.75 In practice, an office-holder is often appointed by one person and then an entirely different person becomes responsible for providing facilities for the office-holder to perform his or her functions. Recognising this, s 49 prohibits both the person who makes the appointment and any other relevant person from discriminating against, victimising or harassing the office holder. The relevant person is the person who is responsible for the act complained of in each case.[134]

6.76 Section 49 places a duty to make reasonable adjustments on a person who makes the appointment and any relevant person in relation to the needs of disabled people who seek or hold personal offices.[135]

6.77 Section 49 replicates the effect of provisions in previous legislation.[136] How it works is illustrated by the following examples. A company board refuses to appoint a candidate as director because she is black. This would be direct discrimination. A company terminates the appointment of a director because it is discovered that she is pregnant. This would be direct discrimination.

6.78 Section 50 makes it unlawful to discriminate against, harass or victimise people who are or wish to become public office-holders.[137] For example, if a Government Minister with the power to appoint the non-executive board members of a non-departmental public body failed to appoint a candidate

---

131 EQA 2010, s 52(1). See EN paras 172–186.
132 EN para 172.
133 EN para 173.
134 EN para 174.
135 EN para 175.
136 EN para 176.
137 EN para 177.

because he is gay this would be direct discrimination.[138] Section 50 applies insofar as other work provisions do not. Where public office-holders are also employees, they will be protected by the provisions dealing with employment in respect of their employment relationship.[139]

6.79 Public office-holders are people appointed by or on the recommendation of or with the approval of a member of the executive branch of Government (such as a Government Minister). They also include people who are appointed on the recommendation or subject to the approval of either of the Houses of Parliament, the National Assembly for Wales, or the Scottish Parliament.[140] Section 50 recognises that a public office holder can be appointed by one person and then an entirely different person can be responsible for providing facilities for the office-holder to perform his or her functions. Accordingly, s 50 prohibits both the person with the power to make the appointment and any relevant person from discriminating against, victimising or harassing the office holder. The relevant person is the person who is responsible for the act complained of in each case.[141]

6.80 Section 50 also places on the person who has the power to make an appointment and any relevant person a duty to make reasonable adjustments for disabled people seeking or holding public offices.[142]

6.81 Section 50 is not new law. However, it extends protection from discrimination, harassment and victimisation to those appointed on the recommendation or approval of law-making bodies such as the Scottish Parliament and the Welsh Assembly.[143]

6.82 Section 51 makes it unlawful for a person with power to make recommendations about or to approve appointments to public offices to discriminate against, harass or victimise people seeking or being considered as public office-holders in respect of the recommendation or approval process. It also imposes a duty on the person with the power to make a recommendation or to approve an appointment to make reasonable adjustments for disabled people who seek or are being considered for appointment to public offices.[144] Section 51 only applies to those public offices to which the appointment is made on the recommendation or approval of a member of the executive or where the appointment is made by a member of the executive on the recommendation or approval of a relevant body (for example, a non-departmental public body).[145]

---

138 EN para 181.
139 EN para 177.
140 EN para 178.
141 EN para 179.
142 EN para 180.
143 EN para 181.
144 EN para 182.
145 EN para 183.

6.83 For example, it would be direct discrimination for the Government Minister responsible for approving the appointment of members of the BBC Trust to refuse to approve the appointment of a person because he has a hearing impairment.[146]

6.84 Section 51 broadly reflects existing statutory provision. However, it extends protection from discrimination, harassment and victimisation to those appointed by a member of the executive on the recommendation or with the approval of a non-departmental public body (in respect of that appointment or recommendation).[147]

Personal offices: appointments, etc

6.85 Section 49 applies in relation to personal offices.[148] A personal office is an office or post (a) to which a person is appointed[149] to discharge a function personally under the direction of another person, and (b) in respect of which an appointed person is entitled to remuneration.[150]

6.86 For this purpose, a person is to be regarded as discharging functions personally under the direction of another person if that other person is entitled to direct the person as to when and where to discharge the functions.[151] In this context, a person is not to be regarded as entitled to remuneration merely because the person is entitled to payments in respect of expenses incurred by the person in discharging the functions of the office or post.[152] Moreover, a person is not to be regarded as entitled to remuneration merely because the person is entitled to payments by way of compensation for the loss of income or benefits the person would or might have received had the person not been discharging the functions of the office or post.[153]

6.87 A person (A) who has the power to make an appointment to a personal office must not discriminate against a person (B) (a) in the arrangements A makes for deciding to whom to offer the appointment; or (b) as to the terms on which A offers B the appointment; or (c) by not offering B the appointment.[154]

6.88 In respect of the terms on which A offers B an appointment,[155] so far as relating to sex or pregnancy and maternity, the prohibition on discrimination does not apply to a term that relates to pay unless, were B to accept the offer, an

---

[146] EN para 184.
[147] EN para 184.
[148] EQA 2010, ss 49(1) and 52(2). An office or post which is both a personal office and a public office is to be treated as being a public office only: s 52(4).
[149] Appointment to an office does not include election to it: EQA 2010, s 52(5).
[150] EQA 2010, s 49(2).
[151] EQA 2010, s 49(10).
[152] EQA 2010, s 49(11)(a).
[153] EQA 2010, s 49(11)(b).
[154] EQA 2010, s 49(3).
[155] EQA 2010, s 49(3)(b).

equality clause or rule would have effect in relation to the term.[156] Furthermore, in the same context,[157] so far as relating to sex or pregnancy and maternity, the prohibition does not apply to a term that relates to pay where an equality clause or rule does not have effect, except insofar as making an offer on terms including that term amounts to a contravention of the prohibition on discrimination as to the terms on which A offers B the appointment[158] by virtue of s 13 (direct discrimination), s 14 (combined discrimination: dual characteristics) or s 18 (pregnancy and maternity discrimination: work cases).[159] What this means is that, in respect of sex or pregnancy and maternity discrimination, a term of an offer of an appointment to office which relates to pay is treated as discriminatory where, if accepted, it would give rise to an equality clause or, if that is not the case, where the offer of the term constitutes direct or dual discrimination (or pregnancy and maternity discrimination at work).[160]

6.89 A person who has the power to make an appointment to a personal office must not, in relation to the office, harass a person seeking (or being considered for) the appointment.[161]

6.90 A person (A) who has the power to make an appointment to a personal office must not victimise a person (B) (a) in the arrangements A makes for deciding to whom to offer the appointment; or (b) as to the terms on which A offers B the appointment; or (c) by not offering B the appointment.[162]

6.91 A person (A) who is a 'relevant person' in relation to a personal office must not discriminate against a person (B) appointed to the office (a) as to the terms of B's appointment; or (b) in the way A affords B access (or by not affording B access) to opportunities for promotion, transfer or training or for receiving any other benefit, facility or service; or (c) by terminating B's appointment; or (d) by subjecting B to any other detriment.[163]

6.92 A 'relevant person', in relation to an office, means the person who, in relation to a matter specified in the first column of the Table below, is specified in the second column.[164]

---

[156] EQA 2010, s 49(12)(a).
[157] EQA 2010, s 49(3)(b).
[158] EQA 2010, s 49(3)(b).
[159] EQA 2010, s 49(12)(b).
[160] EN para 172.
[161] EQA 2010, s 49(4).
[162] EQA 2010, s 49(5).
[163] EQA 2010, s 49(6). Detriment does not include conduct which amounts to harassment: EQA 2010, s 212(1). However, where the Act disapplies a prohibition on harassment in relation to a specified protected characteristic, that disapplication does not prevent conduct relating to that characteristic from amounting to a detriment for the purposes of direct discrimination because of that characteristic: EQA 2010, s 212(5).
[164] EQA 2010, s 52(6) (but a reference to a relevant person does not in any case include the House of Commons, the House of Lords, the National Assembly for Wales or the Scottish Parliament).

Matter	*Relevant person*
A term of appointment	The person who has the power to set the term.
Access to an opportunity	The person who has the power to afford access to the opportunity (or, if there is no such person, the person who has the power to make the appointment).
Terminating an appointment	The person who has the power to terminate the appointment.
Subjecting an appointee to any other detriment	The person who has the power in relation to the matter to which the conduct in question relates (or, if there is no such person, the person who has the power to make the appointment).
Harassing an appointee	The person who has the power in relation to the matter to which the conduct in question relates.

A relevant person in relation to a personal office must not, in relation to that office, harass a person appointed to it.[165]

6.93 A person (A) who is a relevant person in relation to a personal office must not victimise a person (B) appointed to the office (a) as to the terms of B's appointment; or (b) in the way A affords B access (or by not affording B access) to opportunities for promotion, transfer or training or for receiving any other benefit, facility or service; or (c) by terminating B's appointment; or (d) by subjecting B to any other detriment.[166]

6.94 A duty to make reasonable adjustments applies to a person who has the power to make an appointment to a personal office and to a relevant person in relation to a personal office.[167]

6.95 A reference throughout s 49 above to termination of a person's appointment includes a reference to termination by the expiry of a period (including a period expiring by reference to an event or circumstance) unless immediately after the termination, the appointment is renewed on the same terms.[168] A reference throughout s 49 above to termination of a person's

---

[165] EQA 2010, s 49(7).

[166] EQA 2010, s 49(8). Detriment does not include conduct which amounts to harassment: EQA 2010, s 212(1). However, where the Act disapplies a prohibition on harassment in relation to a specified protected characteristic, that disapplication does not prevent conduct relating to that characteristic from amounting to a detriment for the purposes of direct discrimination because of that characteristic: EQA 2010, s 212(5).

[167] EQA 2010, s 49(9).

[168] EQA 2010, s 52(7)(a) and (8).

appointment also includes a reference to termination by an act of the person (including giving notice) in circumstances such that the person is entitled, because of the relevant person's conduct, to terminate the appointment without notice.[169]

Public offices: appointments, etc

6.96 Sections 50 and 51 apply in relation to public offices.[170] A public office is (a) an office or post, appointment to which is made by a member of the executive; or (b) an office or post, appointment to which is made on the recommendation of, or subject to the approval of, a member of the executive; or (c) an office or post, appointment to which is made on the recommendation of, or subject to the approval of, the House of Commons, the House of Lords, the National Assembly for Wales or the Scottish Parliament.[171]

6.97 Provision is made in relation to a person (A) who has the power to make an appointment to a public office which is (a) an office or post, appointment to which is made by a member of the executive; or (b) an office or post, appointment to which is made on the recommendation of, or subject to the approval of, a member of the executive. In those particular circumstances, A must not discriminate against a person (B) (a) in the arrangements A makes for deciding to whom to offer the appointment; or (b) as to the terms on which A offers B the appointment; or (c) by not offering B the appointment.[172]

6.98 In relation to the terms on which A offers B the appointment, so far as relating to sex or pregnancy and maternity, this provision does not apply to a term that relates to pay unless, were B to accept the offer, an equality clause or rule would have effect in relation to the term.[173] If that were not applicable, the provision would not apply except insofar as making an offer on terms including that term amounts to a contravention of the prohibition on discrimination as to the terms on which A offers B the appointment[174] by virtue of s 13 (direct discrimination), s 14 (combined discrimination: dual characteristics) or s 18 (pregnancy and maternity discrimination: work cases).[175] This means that, in respect of sex or pregnancy and maternity discrimination, a term of an offer of an appointment to office which relates to pay is treated as discriminatory where, if accepted, it would give rise to an equality clause or, if that is not the case, where the offer of the term constitutes direct or dual discrimination (or pregnancy and maternity discrimination at work).[176]

---

[169] EQA 2010, s 52(7)(b).
[170] EQA 2010, s 50(1).
[171] EQA 2010, s 50(2).
[172] EQA 2010, s 50(3).
[173] EQA 2010, s 50(12)(a).
[174] EQA 2010, s 50(3)(b).
[175] EQA 2010, s 50(12)(b).
[176] EN para 177.

6.99 Provision is made in relation to a person (A) who has the power to make an appointment to a public office which is (a) an office or post, appointment to which is made by a member of the executive; or (b) an office or post, appointment to which is made on the recommendation of, or subject to the approval of, a member of the executive. In those particular circumstances, that person must not, in relation to the office, harass a person seeking, or being considered for, the appointment.[177]

6.100 Provision is also made in relation to a person (A) who has the power to make an appointment to a public office which is (a) an office or post, appointment to which is made by a member of the executive; or (b) an office or post, appointment to which is made on the recommendation of, or subject to the approval of, a member of the executive. In those particular circumstances, A must not victimise a person (B) (a) in the arrangements A makes for deciding to whom to offer the appointment; or (b) as to the terms on which A offers B the appointment; or (c) by not offering B the appointment.[178]

6.101 Provision is further made in relation to a person (A) who is a relevant person in relation to a public office which is (a) an office or post, appointment to which is made by a member of the executive; or (b) an office or post, appointment to which is made on the recommendation of, or subject to the approval of, a member of the executive. In those particular circumstances, A must not discriminate against a person (B) appointed to the office (a) as to B's terms of appointment; or (b) in the way A affords B access (or by not affording B access) to opportunities for promotion, transfer or training or for receiving any other benefit, facility or service; or (c) by terminating the appointment; or (d) by subjecting B to any other detriment.[179]

6.102 Moreover, provision is made in relation to a person (A) who is a relevant person in relation to a public office which is an office or post, appointment to which is made on the recommendation of, or subject to the approval of, the House of Commons, the House of Lords, the National Assembly for Wales or the Scottish Parliament. In those circumstances, A must not discriminate against a person (B) appointed to the office (a) as to B's terms of appointment; or (b) in the way A affords B access (or by not affording B access) to opportunities for promotion, transfer or training or for receiving any other benefit, facility or service; or (c) by subjecting B to any other detriment (other than by terminating the appointment).[180]

---

[177] EQA 2010, s 50(4).

[178] EQA 2010, s 50(5).

[179] EQA 2010, s 50(6). Detriment does not include conduct which amounts to harassment: EQA 2010, s 212(1). However, where the Act disapplies a prohibition on harassment in relation to a specified protected characteristic, that disapplication does not prevent conduct relating to that characteristic from amounting to a detriment for the purposes of direct discrimination because of that characteristic: EQA 2010, s 212(5).

[180] EQA 2010, s 50(7). Detriment does not include conduct which amounts to harassment: EQA 2010, s 212(1). However, where the Act disapplies a prohibition on harassment in relation to a

6.103 A relevant person in relation to a public office must not, in relation to that office, harass a person appointed to it.[181]

6.104 Further provision is made in respect of a person (A) who is a relevant person in relation to a public office which is (a) an office or post, appointment to which is made by a member of the executive; or (b) an office or post, appointment to which is made on the recommendation of, or subject to the approval of, a member of the executive. In those particular circumstances, A must not victimise a person (B) appointed to the office (a) as to B's terms of appointment; or (b) in the way A affords B access (or by not affording B access) to opportunities for promotion, transfer or training or for receiving any other benefit, facility or service; or (c) by terminating the appointment; or (d) by subjecting B to any other detriment.[182]

6.105 Particular circumstances apply to a person (A) who is a relevant person in relation to a public office which is an office or post, appointment to which is made on the recommendation of, or subject to the approval of, the House of Commons, the House of Lords, the National Assembly for Wales or the Scottish Parliament. In those circumstances, A must not victimise a person (B) appointed to the office (a) as to B's terms of appointment; or (b) in the way A affords B access (or by not affording B access) to opportunities for promotion, transfer or training or for receiving any other benefit, facility or service; or (c) by subjecting B to any other detriment (other than by terminating the appointment).[183]

6.106 A duty to make reasonable adjustments applies to a relevant person in relation to a public office.[184] A duty to make reasonable adjustments also applies to a person who has the power to make an appointment to a public office which is (a) an office or post, appointment to which is made by a member of the executive; or (b) an office or post, appointment to which is made on the recommendation of, or subject to the approval of, a member of the executive.[185]

---

specified protected characteristic, that disapplication does not prevent conduct relating to that characteristic from amounting to a detriment for the purposes of direct discrimination because of that characteristic: EQA 2010, s 212(5).

[181] EQA 2010, s 50(8).

[182] EQA 2010, s 50(9). Detriment does not include conduct which amounts to harassment: EQA 2010, s 212(1). However, where the Act disapplies a prohibition on harassment in relation to a specified protected characteristic, that disapplication does not prevent conduct relating to that characteristic from amounting to a detriment for the purposes of direct discrimination because of that characteristic: EQA 2010, s 212(5).

[183] EQA 2010, s 50(10). Detriment does not include conduct which amounts to harassment: EQA 2010, s 212(1). However, where the Act disapplies a prohibition on harassment in relation to a specified protected characteristic, that disapplication does not prevent conduct relating to that characteristic from amounting to a detriment for the purposes of direct discrimination because of that characteristic: EQA 2010, s 212(5).

[184] EQA 2010, s 50(11)(a).

[185] EQA 2010, s 50(11)(b).

Public offices: recommendations for appointments, etc

6.107 Provision is made for a person (A) who has the power to make a recommendation for or give approval to an appointment to a public office which is (a) an office or post, appointment to which is made by a member of the executive;[186] or (b) an office or post, appointment to which is made on the recommendation of, or subject to the approval of, a member of the executive. In those particular circumstances, A must not discriminate against a person (B) (a) in the arrangements A makes for deciding who to recommend for appointment or to whose appointment to give approval; or (b) by not recommending B for appointment to the office; or (c) by making a negative recommendation of B for appointment to the office; or (d) by not giving approval to the appointment of B to the office.[187]

6.108 Such a person must not, in relation to the office, harass a person seeking or being considered for the recommendation or approval.[188] In addition, such a person must not victimise a person (B) (a) in the arrangements A makes for deciding who to recommend for appointment or to whose appointment to give approval; or (b) by not recommending B for appointment to the office; or (c) by making a negative recommendation of B for appointment to the office; or (d) by not giving approval to the appointment of B to the office.[189] A duty to make reasonable adjustments also applies to such a person.[190]

Excluded offices

6.109 For the purposes of ss 49 to 52 (office-holders), Sch 6 (excluded offices) has effect.[191]

6.110 The first group of offices excluded from the application of the provisions on office-holders concerns work to which other provisions apply. An office or post is not a personal or public office insofar as one or more of the following provisions applies in relation to the office or post, or would apply in relation to the office or post but for the operation of some other provision of the 2010 Act.[192] Those provisions are s 39 (employment); s 41 (contract work); s 44 (partnerships); s 45 (limited liability partnerships); (e) s 47 (barristers); s 48

---

[186] The reference here is a reference only to a relevant body which has that power. For that purpose it means a body established by or in pursuance of an enactment, or by a member of the executive: EQA 2010, s 51(5).

[187] EQA 2010, s 51(1).

[188] EQA 2010, s 51(2).

[189] EQA 2010, s 51(3).

[190] EQA 2010, s 51(4).

[191] EQA 2010, s 52(10).

[192] EQA 2010, Sch 6, para 1(1).

(advocates); and s 55 (employment services).[193] The excluded office-holder or post-holder must rely upon those other provisions.

6.111 The second group of offices excluded from the application of the provisions on office-holders concerns political offices. An office or post is not a personal or public office if it is a political office.[194] A political office is an office or post set out in the second column of the following Table.[195]

Political setting	*Office or post*
Houses of Parliament	An office of the House of Commons held by a member of that House
	An office of the House of Lords held by a member of that House
	A Ministerial office within the meaning of s 2 of the House of Commons Disqualification Act 1975
	The office of the Leader of the Opposition within the meaning of the Ministerial and other Salaries Act 1975
	The office of the Chief Opposition Whip, or of an Assistant Opposition Whip, within the meaning of that Act
Scottish Parliament	An office of the Scottish Parliament held by a member of the Parliament
	The office of a member of the Scottish Executive
	The office of a junior Scottish Minister
National Assembly for Wales	An office of the National Assembly for Wales held by a member of the Assembly
	The office of a member of the Welsh Assembly Government

---

[193] EQA 2010, Sch 6, para 1(2). The exclusion of employment services covered by s 55 extends so far as applying to the provision of work experience within s 56(2)(a) or arrangements within s 56(2)(c) for such provision.

[194] EQA 2010, Sch 6, para 2(1).

[195] EQA 2010, Sch 6, para 2(2).

Local government in England (outside London)	An office of a county council, district council or parish council in England held by a member of the council
	An office of the Council of the Isles of Scilly held by a member of the Council
Local government in London	An office of the Greater London Authority held by the Mayor of London or a member of the London Assembly
	An office of a London borough council held by a member of the council
	An office of the Common Council of the City of London held by a member of the Council
Local government in Wales	An office of a county council, county borough council or community council in Wales held by a member of the council
Local government in Scotland	An office of a council constituted under s 2 of the Local Government etc (Scotland) Act 1994 held by a member of the council
	An office of a council constituted under s 51 of the Local Government (Scotland) Act 1973 held by a member of the council
Political parties	An office of a registered political party

In this Table, the reference to a registered political party is a reference to a party registered in the Great Britain register under Part 2 of the Political Parties, Elections and Referendums Act 2000.[196]

6.112 The third group of offices excluded from the application of the provisions on office-holders concerns honours etc. A life peerage (within the meaning of the Life Peerages Act 1958) or any other dignity or honour conferred by the Crown is not a personal or public office.[197]

6.113 The Explanatory Notes explain that Sch 6 provides that an office or post is not treated as a personal or public office in circumstances where the office-holder is protected by one of the other forms of protection given in

---

[196] EQA 2010, Sch 6, para 2(3).
[197] EQA 2010, Sch 6, para 3.

Part 5 of the Act.[198] So, where an office-holder is provided with protection from discrimination, etc under the provisions relating to employment, contract work, employment services (as they relate to work experience), partnerships, limited liability partnerships, barristers and advocates, reliance cannot be placed upon the office-holders provisions in ss 49–52. Schedule 6 also provides that political offices, life peerages and any other dignity or honour conferred by the Crown are not personal or public offices for the purposes of the Act.

6.114 Schedule 6 replaces similar provisions in the legacy legislation. However, the conferral of honours and dignities is treated as a public office for the purposes of the Act. The specific provisions previously located in the Race Relations Act 1976 alone are not replicated.[199] The Explanatory Notes suggest that a person appointed as a commissioner of a public body may be both an employee and an office-holder. Such a person will be protected under the employment provisions in s 39 as against his or her employer, and under the office-holder provisions in ss 49 or 50 and 51 as against the person who appointed him or her and/or any relevant person.[200] However, the commissioner must rely upon s 39 in these circumstances.

QUALIFICATIONS

Introduction

6.115 Section 53 makes it unlawful for a qualifications body to discriminate against, harass or victimise a person when conferring relevant qualifications. It also provides that applying a competence standard to a disabled person is not disability discrimination, provided the application of the standard is justified. It also imposes a duty on qualifications bodies to make reasonable adjustments for disabled people.[201] Except to the extent that it extends the protection to cover discrimination in the arrangements made for determining upon whom a relevant qualification should be conferred, it simply replaces similar provisions in the legacy legislation.[202]

6.116 The Explanatory Notes supply the following working illustrations:

• A body which confers diplomas certifying that people are qualified electricians refuses to confer the qualification on a man simply because he is gay. This would be direct discrimination.

---

[198] EN para 783.
[199] EN para 784. See RRA 1976, s 76ZA.
[200] EN para 784.
[201] EN para 187.
[202] EN para 188.

- An organisation which maintains a register of professional trades people refuses to include a person's details on the register because her name does not sound English. This would be direct discrimination.[203]

Qualifications and qualifications bodies

6.117 Section 53 is concerned with discrimination, etc by qualifications bodies.[204] A qualifications body is an authority or body which can confer a relevant qualification.[205] A relevant qualification is an authorisation, qualification, recognition, registration, enrolment, approval or certification which is needed for, or facilitates engagement in, a particular trade or profession.[206] A reference to conferring a relevant qualification includes a reference to renewing or extending the conferment of a relevant qualification.[207]

6.118 An authority or body is not a qualifications body insofar as:[208]

- it can confer a qualification to which s 96 applies (general qualifications bodies);

- it is the responsible body of a school to which s 85 applies (admission and treatment of school pupils);

- it is the governing body of an institution to which s 91 applies (admission and treatment of students in further and higher education);

- it exercises functions under the Education Acts; or

- it exercises functions under the Education (Scotland) Act 1980.

These exceptions are designed to make it clear that bodies such as schools, institutions of further and higher education, and education authorities which confer qualifications such as A Levels and GCSEs are not qualifications bodies for the purposes of s 53.[209] See Chapter 8 (Education) below.

6.119 The upshot is that a qualifications body is a body which can confer any academic, medical, technical or other standard which is required to carry out a particular trade or profession, or which better enables a person to do so by, for example, determining whether the person has a particular level of competence or ability.[210] The Explanatory Notes suggest that examples of qualifications

---

[203] EN para 188.
[204] EQA 2010, s 54 is the interpretation section for s 53: s 54(1).
[205] EQA 2010, s 54(2).
[206] EQA 2010, s 54(3).
[207] EQA 2010, s 54(5).
[208] EQA 2010, s 54(4).
[209] EN para 190.
[210] EN para 189.

bodies are the Public Carriage Office (which licenses cab drivers in London), the British Horseracing Authority and the General Medical Council. They also suggest that these provisions include any body which confers a diploma on people pursuing a particular trade (for example, plumbers), even if the diploma is not strictly necessary to pursue a career in that trade but shows that the person has reached a certain standard.[211]

Discrimination etc by qualifications bodies

6.120 Section 53 provides that a qualifications body (A) must not discriminate against a person (B) (a) in the arrangements A makes for deciding upon whom to confer a relevant qualification; or (b) as to the terms on which it is prepared to confer a relevant qualification on B; or (c) by not conferring a relevant qualification on B.[212] Moreover, a qualifications body (A) must not discriminate against a person (B) upon whom A has conferred a relevant qualification (a) by withdrawing the qualification from B; or (b) by varying the terms on which B holds the qualification; or (c) by subjecting B to any other detriment.[213]

6.121 A qualifications body must not, in relation to conferment by it of a relevant qualification, harass a person who holds the qualification, or a person who applies for it.[214]

6.122 A qualifications body (A) must not victimise a person (B) (a) in the arrangements A makes for deciding upon whom to confer a relevant qualification; or (b) as to the terms on which it is prepared to confer a relevant qualification on B; or (c) by not conferring a relevant qualification on B.[215] A qualifications body (A) must not victimise a person (B) upon whom A has conferred a relevant qualification (a) by withdrawing the qualification from B; or (b) by varying the terms on which B holds the qualification; or (c) by subjecting B to any other detriment.[216]

6.123 A duty to make reasonable adjustments applies to a qualifications body.[217] However, the application by a qualifications body of a competence standard to a disabled person is not disability discrimination unless it is

---

[211] EN para 191.
[212] EQA 2010, s 53(1).
[213] EQA 2010, s 53(2). Detriment does not include conduct which amounts to harassment: EQA 2010, s 212(1). However, where the Act disapplies a prohibition on harassment in relation to a specified protected characteristic, that disapplication does not prevent conduct relating to that characteristic from amounting to a detriment for the purposes of direct discrimination because of that characteristic: EQA 2010, s 212(5).
[214] EQA 2010, s 53(3).
[215] EQA 2010, s 53(4).
[216] EQA 2010, s 53(5). Detriment does not include conduct which amounts to harassment: EQA 2010, s 212(1). However, where the Act disapplies a prohibition on harassment in relation to a specified protected characteristic, that disapplication does not prevent conduct relating to that characteristic from amounting to a detriment for the purposes of direct discrimination because of that characteristic: EQA 2010, s 212(5).
[217] EQA 2010, s 53(6).

discrimination by virtue of s 19 (indirect discrimination).[218] A competence standard is an academic, medical or other standard applied for the purpose of determining whether or not a person has a particular level of competence or ability.[219]

6.124   These provisions draw upon pre-existing legislation.[220]

EMPLOYMENT SERVICES

Introduction

6.125   As the Explanatory Notes set out, s 55 makes it unlawful to discriminate against, harass or victimise a person when providing an employment service. It also places a duty on providers of employment services to make reasonable adjustments for disabled people. Of particular note is the legislature's view that the duty is an anticipatory duty (except for providers of a vocational service).[221] Section 55 replaces the separate pre-existing provisions for vocational training and employment agencies and provisions for assisting persons to obtain employment. There is now a single provision covering all these aspects.[222]

6.126   The following examples in the Explanatory Notes serve as a helpful point of entry to the detailed consideration of s 55 that follows:

- A company which provides courses to train people to be plumbers refuses to enrol women. This would be direct discrimination.

- An agency which finds employment opportunities for teachers in schools offers placements only to white teachers. This would be direct discrimination.

- An agency advertises job vacancies on its website. It will need to have the website checked for accessibility and make reasonable changes to enable disabled people using a variety of access software to use it.[223]

Examples of the types of activities covered by s 55 include providing CV writing classes, English or Maths classes to help adults into work; training in IT/keyboard skills; or providing work placements.[224]

---

[218]   EQA 2010, s 53(7).
[219]   EQA 2010, s 54(6).
[220]   SDA 1975, s 13; RRA 1976, s 12. See further: *British Judo Association v Petty* [1981] 484, EAT; *Tattari v Private Patients Plan* [1997] IRLR 586, CA; *Treisman v Ali* [2002] IRLR 489, CA; *Patterson v Legal Services Commission* [2004] IRLR 153, CA; *Ahsan v Watt* [2008] IRLR 243, HL.
[221]   EN para 192.
[222]   EN para 193.
[223]   EN para 193.
[224]   EN para 194.

Employment services

6.127 Section 56 defines the scope of employment services for the purposes of placing duties and liabilities upon employment service-providers under s 55.[225]

6.128 The provision of an employment service includes:[226]

- the provision of vocational training;[227]

- the provision of vocational guidance;

- making arrangements for the provision of vocational training or vocational guidance;

- the provision of a service for finding employment for persons;

- the provision of a service for supplying employers with persons to do work;

- the provision of a service in pursuance of arrangements made under s 2 of the Employment and Training Act 1973 (functions of the Secretary of State relating to employment);

- the provision of a service in pursuance of arrangements made or a direction given under s 10 of the Employment and Training Act 1973 (careers services);

- the exercise of a function in pursuance of arrangements made under s 2(3) of the Enterprise and New Towns (Scotland) Act 1990 (functions of Scottish Enterprise, etc. relating to employment);

- an assessment related to the conferment of a relevant qualification within the meaning of s 53 of the Equality Act 2010 above (except insofar as the assessment is by the qualifications body which confers the qualification).

6.129 Section 56 does not apply in relation to training or guidance in so far as it is training or guidance in relation to which another provision of Part 5 (work) applies.[228] It does not apply in relation to training or guidance for pupils of a school to which s 85 (admission and treatment of school pupils) applies insofar as it is training or guidance to which the responsible body of the school has power to afford access (whether as the responsible body of that school or as the responsible body of any other school at which the training or guidance is

---

[225] EQA 2010, s 56(1).
[226] EQA 2010, s 56(2)(a)–(i).
[227] Vocational training means training for employment, or work experience (including work experience the duration of which is not agreed until after it begins): EQA 2010, s 56(6).
[228] EQA 2010, s 56(3).

provided).[229] Section 56 also does not apply in relation to training or guidance for students of an institution to which s 91 (admission and treatment of students in further and higher education) applies insofar as it is training or guidance to which the governing body of the institution has power to afford access.[230] See Chapter 8 below. A reference to training includes a reference to facilities for training.[231]

Employment service-providers

6.130   Section 55 provides that a person (an employment service-provider) concerned with the provision of an employment service must not discriminate against a person (a) in the arrangements the service-provider makes for selecting persons to whom to provide (or to whom to offer to provide) the service; or (b) as to the terms on which the service-provider offers to provide the service to the person; or (c) by not offering to provide the service to the person.[232] Furthermore, an employment service-provider (A) must not, in relation to the provision of an employment service, discriminate against a person (B) (a) as to the terms on which A provides the service to B; or (b) by not providing the service to B; or (c) by terminating the provision of the service to B; or (d) by subjecting B to any other detriment.[233]

6.131   Section 55 also provides that an employment service-provider must not, in relation to the provision of an employment service, harass (a) a person who asks the service-provider to provide the service; or (b) a person for whom the service-provider provides the service.[234]

6.132   An employment service-provider (A) must not victimise a person (B) (a) in the arrangements A makes for selecting persons to whom to provide (or to whom to offer to provide) the service; or (b) as to the terms on which A offers to provide the service to B; or (c) by not offering to provide the service to B.[235] Moreover, an employment service-provider (A) must not, in relation to the provision of an employment service, victimise a person (B) (a) as to the terms on which A provides the service to B; or (b) by not providing the service to B; or (c) by terminating the provision of the service to B; or (d) by subjecting B to any other detriment.[236]

---

[229]   EQA 2010, s 56(4).
[230]   EQA 2010, s 56(5).
[231]   EQA 2010, s 56(8).
[232]   EQA 2010, s 55(1).
[233]   EQA 2010, s 55(2). Detriment does not include conduct which amounts to harassment: EQA 2010, s 212(1). However, where the Act disapplies a prohibition on harassment in relation to a specified protected characteristic, that disapplication does not prevent conduct relating to that characteristic from amounting to a detriment for the purposes of direct discrimination because of that characteristic: EQA 2010, s 212(5).
[234]   EQA 2010, s 55(3).
[235]   EQA 2010, s 55(4).
[236]   EQA 2010, s 55(5). Detriment does not include conduct which amounts to harassment: EQA 2010, s 212(1). However, where the Act disapplies a prohibition on harassment in relation to a

6.133 A duty to make reasonable adjustments applies to an employment service-provider, except in relation to the provision of a vocational service.[237] Section 29(7)(a) also imposes a duty to make reasonable adjustments upon a service-provider under Part 3 of the Act (services and public functions) (see Chapter 4 above). However, while the duty imposed by s 29(7)(a) applies to a person concerned with the provision of a vocational service, a failure to comply with that duty in relation to the provision of a vocational service is a contravention of Part 5 (work) for the purposes of Part 9 (enforcement) (see Chapter 11 below).[238]

TRADE ORGANISATIONS

6.134 Section 57 is concerned with discrimination by trade organisations. It makes it unlawful for a trade organisation to discriminate against, harass or victimise a person who is (or who is applying to be) a member. It also requires trade organisations to make reasonable adjustments for disabled people.[239] While s 57 replicates the effect of similar provisions in previous legislation, it also extends protection against discrimination in the arrangements made for determining to whom membership should be offered.[240] So, for example, if a trade union restricts its membership to men, this would be direct discrimination. If an organisation of employers varies membership subscriptions or access to conferences because of a person's race, this would be direct discrimination.[241]

6.135 A trade organisation is (a) an organisation of workers, or (b) an organisation of employers, or (c) any other organisation whose members carry on a particular trade or profession for the purposes of which the organisation exists.[242] This will include an organisation of workers (such as a trade union) or employers (such as a Chamber of Commerce). It will also cover an organisation

---

specified protected characteristic, that disapplication does not prevent conduct relating to that characteristic from amounting to a detriment for the purposes of direct discrimination because of that characteristic: EQA 2010, s 212(5).

[237] EQA 2010, s 55(6). A reference to the provision of a vocational service is a reference to the provision of an employment service within s 56(2)(a)–(d) (or an employment service within s 56(2)(f) or (g) insofar as it is also an employment service within s 56(2)(a)–(d)); and for that purpose (a) the references to an employment service within s 56(2)(a) do not include a reference to vocational training within the meaning given by s 56(6)(b), and (b) the references to an employment service within s 56(2)(d) also include a reference to a service for assisting persons to retain employment: EQA 2010, s 56(7).

[238] EQA 2010, s 55(7).

[239] EN para 195.

[240] EN para 197. See SDA 1975, s 12; RRA 1976, s 11. See further: *FTATU v Modgill* [1980] IRLR 142, EAT; *National Federation of Self-Employed and Small Businesses Ltd v Philpott* [1997] IRLR 340, EAT; *Fire Brigades Union v Fraser* [1998] IRLR 697, CS; *Sadek v Medical Protection Society* [2005] IRLR 57, CA.

[241] EN para 197.

[242] EQA 2010, s 57(7).

whose members carry out a particular trade or profession (such as the British Medical Association, the Institute of Civil Engineers and the Law Society).[243]

6.136   A trade organisation (A) must not discriminate against a person (B) (a) in the arrangements A makes for deciding to whom to offer membership of the organisation; or (b) as to the terms on which it is prepared to admit B as a member; or (c) by not accepting B's application for membership.[244]

6.137   A trade organisation (A) must not discriminate against a member (B) (a) in the way it affords B access (or by not affording B access) to opportunities for receiving a benefit, facility or service; or (b) by depriving B of membership; or (c) by varying the terms on which B is a member; or (d) by subjecting B to any other detriment.[245]

6.138   A trade organisation must not, in relation to membership of it, harass (a) a member, or (b) an applicant for membership.[246]

6.139   A trade organisation (A) must not victimise a person (B) (a) in the arrangements A makes for deciding to whom to offer membership of the organisation; or (b) as to the terms on which it is prepared to admit B as a member; or (c) by not accepting B's application for membership.[247] A trade organisation (A) must not victimise a member (B) (a) in the way it affords B access (or by not affording B access) to opportunities for receiving a benefit, facility or service; or (b) by depriving B of membership; or (c) by varying the terms on which B is a member; or (d) by subjecting B to any other detriment.[248]

6.140   A duty to make reasonable adjustments applies to a trade organisation.[249]

---

[243]   EN para 196.

[244]   EQA 2010, s 57(1).

[245]   EQA 2010, s 57(2). Detriment does not include conduct which amounts to harassment: EQA 2010, s 212(1). However, where the Act disapplies a prohibition on harassment in relation to a specified protected characteristic, that disapplication does not prevent conduct relating to that characteristic from amounting to a detriment for the purposes of direct discrimination because of that characteristic: EQA 2010, s 212(5).

[246]   EQA 2010, s 57(3).

[247]   EQA 2010, s 57(4).

[248]   EQA 2010, s 57(5). Detriment does not include conduct which amounts to harassment: EQA 2010, s 212(1). However, where the Act disapplies a prohibition on harassment in relation to a specified protected characteristic, that disapplication does not prevent conduct relating to that characteristic from amounting to a detriment for the purposes of direct discrimination because of that characteristic: EQA 2010, s 212(5).

[249]   EQA 2010, s 57(6).

LOCAL AUTHORITY MEMBERS

Overview

6.141 Section 58 makes it unlawful for local authorities to discriminate against, harass or victimise their members in relation to providing access to facilities (such as training) which relate to the carrying out of their official business. An exception applies to election or appointment to posts within the local authority. The section also imposes a duty on local authorities to make reasonable adjustments for disabled members.[250] It extends protection currently in the DDA 1995 only to all protected characteristics.[251]

6.142 The Explanatory Notes provide the following examples of how the extended provisions of s 58 are designed to work. A local authority does not equip meeting rooms with hearing loops for a member who has a hearing impairment, in order to enable her to take full part in the business for which she has been elected. This would be discrimination if provision of hearing loops were considered to be a reasonable adjustment.[252] A local authority member who is considering an application for planning permission whilst sitting on a council's Planning Committee would be undertaking official business.[253]

Official business of members

6.143 Section 58 provides that a local authority must not discriminate against a member of the authority in relation to the member's carrying out of official business (a) in the way the authority affords the member access (or by not affording the member access) to opportunities for training or for receiving any other facility; or (b) by subjecting the member to any other detriment.[254] A member of a local authority is not subjected to a detriment for this purpose only because the member is (i) not appointed or elected to an office of the authority, or (ii) not appointed or elected to (or to an office of) a committee or subcommittee of the authority, or (iii) not appointed or nominated in exercise of an appointment power of the authority.[255] For the purpose of (iii), an appointment power of a local authority is a power of the authority (or of a group of bodies including the authority) to make appointments to a body; or nominations for appointment to a body.[256]

---

[250] EN para 198.
[251] EN para 199. See DDA 1995, ss 15A–15C.
[252] EN para 199.
[253] EN para 200.
[254] EQA 2010, s 58(1). Detriment does not include conduct which amounts to harassment: EQA 2010, s 212(1). However, where the Act disapplies a prohibition on harassment in relation to a specified protected characteristic, that disapplication does not prevent conduct relating to that characteristic from amounting to a detriment for the purposes of direct discrimination because of that characteristic: EQA 2010, s 212(5).
[255] EQA 2010, s 58(4).
[256] EQA 2010, s 58(5).

6.144 A local authority must not, in relation to a member's carrying-out of official business, harass the member.[257]

6.145 A local authority must not victimise a member of the authority in relation to the member's carrying out of official business (a) in the way the authority affords the member access (or by not affording the member access) to opportunities for training or for receiving any other facility; or (b) by subjecting the member to any other detriment.[258] A member of a local authority is not subjected to a detriment for this purpose only because the member is (i) not appointed or elected to an office of the authority, or (ii) not appointed or elected to (or to an office of) a committee or subcommittee of the authority, or (iii) not appointed or nominated in exercise of an appointment power of the authority.[259] For the purpose of (iii), an appointment power of a local authority is a power of the authority (or of a group of bodies including the authority) to make appointments to a body; or nominations for appointment to a body.[260]

6.146 A duty to make reasonable adjustments applies to a local authority.[261]

Interpretation

6.147 Section 59 (interpretation) applies for the purposes of s 58.[262] In s 59 the term 'local authority' means:

* a county council in England;

* a district council in England;

* the Greater London Authority;

* a London borough council;

* the Common Council of the City of London;

* the Council of the Isles of Scilly;

* a parish council in England;

* a county council in Wales;

---

[257] EQA 2010, s 58(2).
[258] EQA 2010, s 58(3). Detriment does not include conduct which amounts to harassment: EQA 2010, s 212(1). However, where the Act disapplies a prohibition on harassment in relation to a specified protected characteristic, that disapplication does not prevent conduct relating to that characteristic from amounting to a detriment for the purposes of direct discrimination because of that characteristic: EQA 2010, s 212(5).
[259] EQA 2010, s 58(4).
[260] EQA 2010, s 58(5).
[261] EQA 2010, s 58(6).
[262] EQA 2010, s 59(1).

- a community council in Wales;

- a county borough council in Wales;

- a council constituted under s 2 of the Local Government etc. (Scotland) Act 1994;

- a community council in Scotland.[263]

A Minister of the Crown may by order amend s 59 so as to add, vary or omit a reference to a body which exercises functions that have been conferred on a local authority within the list above.[264]

6.148 A reference to the carrying-out of official business by a person who is a member of a local authority is a reference to the doing of anything by the person (a) as a member of the authority, or (b) as a member of a body to which the person is appointed by (or appointed following nomination by) the authority or a group of bodies including the authority, or (c) as a member of any other public body.[265] In relation to the Greater London Authority, the term 'member' means (a) the Mayor of London; or (b) a member of the London Assembly.[266]

---

[263] EQA 2010, s 59(2).
[264] EQA 2010, s 59(3).
[265] EQA 2010, s 59(4).
[266] EQA 2010, s 59(5).

Chapter 7

WORK: EXCEPTIONS, ETC

INTRODUCTION

7.1   This is the second of two chapters on work and equality. It discusses the specific and exceptional provisions affecting work in ss 60–63 and 81–83 of the Equality Act 2010 (EQA 2010), together with Schs 8 and 9 to the Act. These provisions are supported by the Draft Employment Code of Practice (2010).[1]

7.2   The discussion begins with an analysis of the novel stipulations in s 60 on pre-work inquiries about disability and health. The way in which the Act affects occupational pension schemes is next considered (ss 61–63). There then follows a lengthy account and assessment of the recast duty to make reasonable adjustments for disabled persons in the context of work (Sch 8). The occupational requirement exceptions (Sch 9, Part 1); the exceptions relating to age (Sch 9, Part 2); and miscellaneous other exceptions (Sch 9, Part 3) are then addressed. The chapter concludes with a treatment of various supplementary provisions relevant to work (ss 81–83).

INQUIRIES ABOUT DISABILITY AND HEALTH

Background

7.3   The House of Commons Work and Pensions Committee endorsed the Disability Rights Taskforce's recommendation that pre-employment disability-related enquiries should be permitted only in very limited circumstances.[2] The Committee considered that such questions should only be permitted once a conditional or provisional job offer has been made. As originally drafted, the Bill did not address this issue. At first the Government was not convinced of the need to outlaw pre-employment disability-related enquiries. It argued that the information provided was a necessary part of deciding what reasonable adjustments a disabled person might require.[3]

7.4   However, the Government reconsidered the position following the Committee stage of the Bill in the House of Commons.[4] A new clause was

---

[1]   Equality and Human Rights Commission, 2010a. The draft code is issued under EQA 2006, ss 14–15 (as amended by EQA 2010).
[2]   House of Commons Work and Pensions Committee, 2009a: paras 145–156.
[3]   House of Commons Work and Pensions Committee, 2009b: paras 42–43.
[4]   Keter, 2009b: 13.

introduced on Report. This is now s 60 of the Act. At first this section was not as simply or as clearly drafted as it might have been. However, it was extensively redrafted at the Committee Stage in the House of Lords.

Section 60

7.5 A person (A) to whom an application for work is made must not ask about the health of the applicant (B) before offering work to B.[5] Where A is not in a position to offer work to B, A must not ask about the health of B before including B in a pool of applicants from whom A intends (when in a position to do so) to select a person to whom to offer work.[6] Whether or not a person has a disability is to be regarded as an aspect of that person's health.[7]

7.6 In this context, 'work' means employment, contract work, a position as a partner, a position as a member of a limited liability partnership (LLP), a pupillage or tenancy, being taken as a devil, membership of a stable, an appointment to a personal or public office, or the provision of an employment service.[8] References to offering a person work are, in relation to contract work, to be read as references to allowing a person to do the work.[9] A reference to offering work is a reference to making a conditional or unconditional offer of work.[10] In relation to contract work, it is a reference to allowing a person to do the work subject to fulfilment of one or more conditions.[11]

7.7 A contravention of this provision[12] is enforceable as an unlawful act under Part 1 of the Equality Act 2006. Such a contravention is enforceable only by the Equality and Human Rights Commission under that Part.[13]

7.8 A does not contravene a relevant disability provision merely by asking about B's health.[14] So far as relating to direct discrimination because of disability,[15] the following are relevant disability provisions:[16]

- discrimination by an employer in the arrangements made for deciding to whom to offer employment or by not offering employment;

---

[5]   EQA 2010, s 60(1)(a).
[6]   EQA 2010, s 60(1)(b).
[7]   EQA 2010, s 60(13).
[8]   EQA 2010, s 60(9).
[9]   EQA 2010, s 60(9).
[10] EQA 2010, s 60(10).
[11] EQA 2010, s 60(10).
[12] EQA 2010, s 60(1) or a contravention of s 111 (instructing, causing or inducing discrimination) or s 112 (aiding contraventions) that relates to a contravention of s 60(1).
[13] EQA 2006, s 120(8).
[14] EQA 2010, s 60(3).
[15] EQA 2010, s 13.
[16] EQA 2010, s 60(11). See, respectively, ss 39(1)(a), 39(1)(c), 41(1)(b), 44(1)(a), 44(1)(c), 45(1)(a), 45(1)(c), 47(1)(a), 47(1)(c), 48(1)(a), 48(1)(c), 49(3)(a), 49(3)(c), 50(3)(a), 50(3)(c), 51(1), 55(1)(a) or 55(1)(c).

- discrimination by a principal against a contract worker by not allowing the worker to do (continue to do) contract work;

- discrimination by a firm or proposed firm in the arrangements it makes for deciding to whom to offer a position as a partner or by not offering a position as a partner;

- discrimination by an LLP or proposed LLP in the arrangements it makes for deciding to whom to offer a position as a member or by not offering a position as a member;

- discrimination by a barrister in the arrangements made for deciding to whom to offer a pupillage or tenancy or by not offering a pupillage or tenancy;

- discrimination by an advocate in the arrangements made for deciding who to take as a devil or to whom to offer membership of a stable or by not offering to take a devil or by not offering membership of a stable;

- discrimination by a person who has the power to make an appointment to a personal office in the arrangements made for deciding to whom to offer the appointment or by not offering the appointment;

- discrimination by a person who has the power to make an appointment to a relevant public office in the arrangements A made for deciding to whom to offer the appointment or by not offering the appointment;

- discrimination by a person who has the power to make a recommendation for (or give approval to) an appointment to a relevant public office in the arrangements made for deciding who to recommend for appointment or to whose appointment to give approval; by not recommending for appointment to the office; by making a negative recommendation for appointment to the office; or by not giving approval to the appointment to the office;

- discrimination by an employment service-provider concerned with the provision of an employment service in the arrangements the service-provider makes for selecting persons to whom to provide (or to whom to offer to provide) the service or by not offering to provide the service.

However, A's conduct in reliance on information given in response may be a contravention of a relevant disability provision.[17]

7.9 What happens if B brings proceedings before an employment tribunal on a complaint that A's conduct in reliance on information given in response to a

---

[17] EQA 2010, s 60(3).

question about B's health is a contravention of a relevant disability provision?[18] In the application of the statutory provisions on the burden of proof in those proceedings,[19] the particulars of the complaint are to be treated as facts from which the tribunal could decide that A contravened the provision.[20] In other words, A's conduct in relying upon information derived from pre-employment inquiries about B's health are facts from which the tribunal could decide, in the absence of any other explanation, that A contravened the provision concerned and, if so, the tribunal must hold that the contravention occurred.[21] The reversal of the burden of proof is brought about as a result of the pre-employment questions.

7.10 These provisions do not prevent A from asking a question that is necessary for establishing whether B will be able to comply with a requirement to undergo an assessment (that is, an interview or other process designed to give an indication of a person's suitability for the work concerned).[22] A may also ask such a question in order to establish whether a duty to make reasonable adjustments is (or will be) imposed on A in relation to B in connection with a requirement to undergo an assessment.[23] Pre-employment health inquiries are also permitted to establish whether B will be able to carry out a function that is intrinsic to the work concerned.[24] Where A reasonably believes that a duty to make reasonable adjustments would be imposed on A in relation to B in connection with that work, the reference to a function that is intrinsic to the work is to be read as a reference to a function that would be intrinsic to the work once A complied with the duty.[25]

7.11 A ban on pre-employment, disability-related inquiries might hinder monitoring diversity in the range of persons applying to A for work. Such inquiries are allowed.[26] Positive action for disabled persons might also be inhibited. Accordingly, A is not prohibited from asking a question that is necessary for the purpose of taking positive action in relation to disability and disabled persons.[27] If A applies a requirement to have a particular disability in relation to the work in question, pre-employment questions are not prohibited if their purpose is to establish whether B has that disability.[28] This last concession applies only if A shows that, having regard to the nature or context of the work, the requirement is an occupational requirement, and the application of the requirement is a proportionate means of achieving a legitimate aim.[29]

---

18 EQA 2010, s 60(4).
19 EQA 2010, s 136.
20 EQA 2010, ss 60(5) and 136(2).
21 EQA 2010, s 136(2).
22 EQA 2010, s 60(6)(a) and (12).
23 EQA 2010, s 60(6)(a).
24 EQA 2010, s 60(6)(b).
25 EQA 2010, s 60(7).
26 EQA 2010, s 60(6)(c).
27 EQA 2010, ss 60(6)(d) and 158.
28 EQA 2010, s 60(6)(e).
29 EQA 2010, s 60(8).

7.12 Section 60 does not apply to anything done for the purpose of vetting applicants for work for reasons of national security.[30]

7.13 The Explanatory Notes suggest that where EQA 2010, s 60 applies an employer must not ask about a job applicant's health until that person has been either offered a job (conditionally or unconditionally) or has been included in a pool of successful candidates to be offered a job when a suitable position arises. Where an employer makes a health or disability-related enquiry which falls outside the specified exceptions, it would be acting unlawfully under the EQA 2006. The EHRC would be able to conduct an investigation if there was evidence that a large employer was routinely asking prohibited questions in its recruitment. Where the employer asks a prohibited question and rejects the applicant, the applicant may make a claim to an Employment Tribunal for direct disability discrimination. It will then be for the employer to show that it had not discriminated against the candidate.[31]

7.14 The Government believes that s 60 will limit the making of enquiries and help to tackle their disincentive effect on disabled people applying for work.[32] The Explanatory Notes offer the following examples of the section in action. If applicants are asked on an application form whether they have a disability that requires the employer to make a reasonable adjustment to the recruitment process (for example, to allow people with a speech impairment more time for interview) this enquiry would be permitted. Where an applicant applies for a job in a warehouse, which requires the manual lifting and handling of heavy items (a function which is intrinsic to the job) the employer is permitted to ask the applicant questions about his or her health to establish whether he or she is able to do the job (with reasonable adjustments for a disabled applicant, if required). The employer would not be permitted to ask the applicant other health questions until it offered the candidate a job.[33]

OCCUPATIONAL PENSION SCHEMES

Introduction

7.15 Sections 61–63 of the EQA 2010 are concerned with occupational pension schemes.[34] Prior to the Act, occupational pension schemes were already required to have non-discrimination rules in respect of age, disability, religion or belief, and sexual orientation. The 2010 Act extends this requirement to gender reassignment, marriage and civil partnership, and sex.[35]

---

30   EQA 2010, s 60(14).
31   EN paras 201–205.
32   EN para 206.
33   EN para 206.
34   See EN paras 207–220. See Keter, 2009a: 56–57.
35   EN para 214.

Non-discrimination rule

7.16 An occupational pension scheme must be taken to include a non-discrimination rule.[36] A non-discrimination rule is a provision by virtue of which a responsible person (A) must not discriminate against another person (B) in carrying out any of A's functions in relation to the scheme.[37] In addition, A must not, in relation to the scheme, harass B or victimise B.[38] The provisions of an occupational pension scheme have effect subject to the non-discrimination rule.[39] A non-discrimination rule does not apply in relation to a person who is a pension credit member of a scheme.[40]

7.17 A responsible person in relation to an occupational pension scheme and a non-discrimination rule will include the trustees or managers of the scheme or an employer whose employees are (or may be) members of the scheme.[41] Also included is a person exercising an appointing function in relation to an office the holder of which is (or may be) a member of the scheme.[42] An appointing function is the function of appointing a person or terminating a person's appointment or recommending a person for appointment or approving an appointment.[43]

7.18 A breach of a non-discrimination rule is treated as a contravention of Part 5 of the Act (work) for the purposes of Part 9 of the Act (enforcement).[44] The rule does not apply to pension rights built up or benefits payable for periods of service before the commencement of this provision. Periods of service prior to this date will be subject to the previous discrimination legislation.[45]

7.19 It is not a breach of a non-discrimination rule for the employer or the trustees or managers of a scheme to maintain or use in relation to the scheme rules, practices, actions or decisions relating to age which are of a description specified by order by a Minister of the Crown.[46] An order authorising the use of rules, practices, actions or decisions which are not in use before the order comes into force must not be made unless the Minister consults such persons as

---

[36] EQA 2010, s 61(1).
[37] EQA 2010, s 61(2)(a).
[38] EQA 2010, s 61(2)(b) and (c).
[39] EQA 2010, s 61(3).
[40] EQA 2010, s 61(5). Pension credit members are not protected from discrimination because their rights are derived from an order of the court, rather than directly from employment: EN para 211.
[41] EQA 2010, s 61(4)(a) and (b).
[42] EQA 2010, s 61(4)(c).
[43] EQA 2010, s 61(6).
[44] EQA 2010, s 61(7).
[45] EN para 209.
[46] EQA 2010, s 61(8).

the Minister thinks appropriate.[47] Exceptions to the non-discrimination rule in relation to age are currently set out at Sch 2 to the Employment Equality (Age) Regulations 2006.[48]

7.20 A non-discrimination rule does not have effect in relation to an occupational pension scheme in so far as an equality rule has effect in relation to it or would have effect in relation to it but for Part 2 of Sch 7 to the Act.[49] As the Explanatory Notes put it in plain words,[50] Part 2 of Sch 7 to the EQA 2010 replaces similar provisions in s 64 of the Pensions Act 1995. It sets out certain circumstances where a sex equality rule does not have effect in relation to an occupational pension scheme. Payments of different amounts for comparable men and women are allowed in prescribed circumstances if the difference is only because of differences in retirement benefits to which men and women are entitled. Payment of different amounts is permitted where those differences result from the application of prescribed actuarial factors to the calculation of employer's contributions to an occupational pension scheme. Payment of different amounts is also acceptable where actuarial factors are applied to the determination of certain prescribed benefits.[51]

7.21 A duty to make reasonable adjustments applies to a responsible person.[52]

Non-discrimination alterations

7.22 Section 62 applies if the trustees or managers of an occupational pension scheme do not have power to make non-discrimination alterations to the scheme.[53] It also applies if the trustees or managers of an occupational pension scheme have power to make non-discrimination alterations to the scheme, but the procedure for doing so is liable to be unduly complex or protracted or involves obtaining consents which cannot be obtained or which can be obtained only with undue delay or difficulty.[54]

7.23 In either of the above circumstances, s 62 permits the trustees or managers of the occupational pension scheme by resolution to make non-discrimination alterations to the scheme.[55] Such non-discrimination alterations may have effect in relation to a period before the date on which they are made.[56] Non-discrimination alterations to an occupational pension scheme are such alterations to the scheme as may be required for the provisions of the

---

[47] EQA 2010, s 61(9).
[48] SI 2006/1031; EN para 215.
[49] EQA 2010, s 61(10).
[50] EN paras 787–790.
[51] There is also a regulation-making power to vary or add to these circumstances. Such regulations may make provision for past periods, but not for pensionable service before 17 May 1990.
[52] EQA 2010, s 61(11).
[53] EQA 2010, s 62(1).
[54] EQA 2010, s 62(2).
[55] EQA 2010, s 62(3).
[56] EQA 2010, s 62(4).

scheme to have the effect that they have in consequence of s 61(3) – that is, so that the provisions of the occupational pension scheme have effect subject to the non-discrimination rule.[57]

7.24 Section 62 is based on similar provisions which allow trustees and managers to secure conformity with the non-discrimination rules in the Disability Discrimination Act 1995, the Employment Equality (Religion or Belief) Regulations 2003 (EE(RoB)R 2003),[58] the Employment Equality (Sexual Orientation) Regulations 2003 (EE(SO)R 2003),[59] and the Employment Equality (Age) Regulations 2006 (EE(A)R 2006).[60]

Communications

7.25 Section 63 is concerned with communications in the context of an occupational pension scheme and its disabled members. In their application to communications, the following provisions apply in relation to a disabled person who is a pension credit member of an occupational pension scheme as they apply in relation to a disabled person who is a deferred member or pensioner member of the scheme.[61] The provisions are s 61 (occupational pension schemes: non-discrimination rules); s 120 (employment tribunals: jurisdiction); s 126 (remedies: occupational pension schemes); and para 19 (and its associated provisions) of Sch 8 (reasonable adjustments: occupational pensions). Communications include the provision of information and the operation of a dispute resolution procedure.[62]

7.26 Section 63 applies the listed statutory provisions in their application to communications to a disabled person who is entitled to the present payment of dependants' or survivors' benefits under an occupational pension scheme or who is entitled to a pension derived from a divorce settlement (pension credit member).[63] It replaces the provisions previously found in the DDA 1995.[64]

REASONABLE ADJUSTMENTS

Introduction

7.27 As the Explanatory Notes explicate,[65] Sch 8 to the EQA 2010 explains how the duty to make reasonable adjustments in s 20 of the Act applies to an employer or other persons under Part 5 of the Act (work). The Schedule establishes the three requirements of the duty which apply where an interested

---

57 EQA 2010, s 62(5).
58 SI 2003/1660.
59 SI 2003/1661.
60 SI 2006/1031; EN para 218.
61 EQA 2010, s 63(1).
62 EQA 2010, s 63(2).
63 EN paras 219–220.
64 DDA 1995, s 4K.
65 EN paras 791–793.

disabled employee or job applicant is placed at a substantial (that is, more than minor or trivial)[66] disadvantage compared to non-disabled employees or applicants. The duty is not an anticipatory duty. An employer is not required to anticipate the needs of potential disabled employees or job applicants. An employer is also not expected to make reasonable adjustments in advance of being faced with an actual disabled employee or job applicant.[67]

7.28 Although the EQA 2010 goes a considerable way towards simplifying equality and discrimination law generally, it must be observed that the treatment of the duty to make reasonable adjustments is not readily accessible or negotiable. A set of statutory tables relates who is an interested disabled person in relation to different categories of relevant matters and the circumstances in which the duty applies in each case. The tables ascertain how the duty applies in a number of areas related to work.[68] Schedule 8 also makes clear the circumstances in which lack of knowledge of the person's disability, or of the fact that a disabled person may be an applicant for a job, means that the duty to make reasonable adjustments does not apply.[69]

7.29 Schedule 8 replaces similar provisions in the DDA 1995. However, the Government believes that it has clarified that a duty to make reasonable adjustments includes a requirement to provide an auxiliary aid if this would overcome the substantial (more than minor or trivial) disadvantage to the disabled person.[70] The Explanatory Notes furnish two examples. An employer provides specially-adapted furniture for a new employee with restricted movement in his upper limbs. This is likely to be a reasonable adjustment for the employer to make. A large employer is recruiting for posts which routinely attract a high number of applications. He arranges for large print application forms to be available for any visually-impaired people applying for a job. This is likely to be a reasonable adjustment for the employer to make.[71]

The duty

7.30 Schedule 8 applies where a duty to make reasonable adjustments is imposed on A by Part 5 of the EQA 2010 (work).[72] The duty requires A to comply with the first, second and third requirements in s 20 of the Act.[73]

7.31 The first requirement arises where a provision, criterion or practice of A's puts an **interested disabled person** at a substantial (that is, more than minor or trivial)[74] disadvantage in relation to a **relevant matter** in comparison with persons who are not disabled. The first requirement is to take such steps as it is

---

66 EQA 2010, s 212(1).
67 EN para 791.
68 EN para 792.
69 EN para 793.
70 EN para 794.
71 EN para 794.
72 EQA 2010, Sch 8, para 1.
73 EQA 2010, Sch 8, para 2(1).
74 EQA 2010, s 212(1).

reasonable to have to take to avoid the disadvantage.[75] The reference to a provision, criterion or practice is a reference to a provision, criterion or practice applied by or on behalf of A.[76] The reference to a disabled person is to an interested disabled person.[77]

7.32   The second requirement arises where a physical feature puts an **interested disabled person** at a substantial (that is, more than minor or trivial)[78] disadvantage in relation to a **relevant matter** in comparison with persons who are not disabled. The second requirement is to take such steps as it is reasonable to have to take to avoid the disadvantage.[79] The reference to a physical feature is a reference to a physical feature of premises occupied by A.[80] The reference to a disabled person is to an interested disabled person.[81]

7.33   The third requirement arises where a disabled person would, but for the provision of an auxiliary aid, be put at a substantial (that is, more than minor or trivial)[82] disadvantage in relation to a **relevant matter** in comparison with persons who are not disabled. The third requirement is to take such steps as it is reasonable to have to take to provide the auxiliary aid.[83]

Relevant matters

7.34   In relation to the first and third requirements, a relevant matter is any matter specified in the first column of the applicable table in Part 2 of Sch 8 to the Act.[84] In relation to the second requirement, a relevant matter is a matter specified in the second entry of the first column of the applicable table in Part 2 of Sch 8 or, where there is only one entry in a column, a matter specified there.[85] The composite table below, prepared by the present author, might assist the discussion which follows.[86]

Relevant matter	Description of disabled person
Employers (s 39)	
Deciding to whom to offer employment.	A person who is, or who has notified A that the person may be, an applicant for the employment.

75   EQA 2010, s 20(3).
76   EQA 2010, Sch 8, para 2(2)(a).
77   EQA 2010, Sch 8, para 2(2)(c).
78   EQA 2010, s 212(1).
79   EQA 2010, s 20(4).
80   EQA 2010, Sch 8, para 2(2)(b).
81   EQA 2010, Sch 8, para 2(2)(c).
82   EQA 2010, s 212(1).
83   EQA 2010, s 20(5).
84   EQA 2010, Sch 8, para 2(3).
85   EQA 2010, Sch 8, para 2(4).
86   The table is drawn from EQA 2010, Sch 8, Part 2, paras 5–19.

| Employment by A. | An applicant for employment by A. |
| | An employee of A's. |

Principals in contract work (s 41)

| Contract work that A may make available. | A person who is, or who has notified A that the person may be, an applicant to do the work. |
| Contract work that A makes available. | A person who is supplied to do the work. |

Partnerships (s 44)

Deciding to whom to offer a position as a partner.	A person who is, or who has notified A that the person may be, a candidate for the position.
A position as a partner.	A candidate for the position.
	The partner who holds the position.

Limited liability partnerships (s 45)

Deciding to whom to offer a position as a member.	A person who is, or who has notified A that the person may be, a candidate for the position.
A position as a member.	A candidate for the position.
	The member who holds the position.

Barristers and their clerks (s 47)

Deciding to whom to offer a pupillage or tenancy.	A person who is, or who has notified A that the person may be, an applicant for the pupillage or tenancy.
A pupillage or tenancy.	An applicant for the pupillage or tenancy.
	The pupil or tenant.

Advocates and their clerks (s 48)

| Deciding who to offer to take as a devil or to whom to offer membership of a stable. | A person who applies, or who has notified A that the person may apply, to be taken as a devil or to become a member of the stable. |

The relationship with a devil or membership of a stable.	An applicant to be taken as a devil or to become a member of the stable.
	The devil or member.

Persons making appointments to offices etc (sections 49–51)

Where A is a person who has the power to make an appointment to a personal or public office

Deciding to whom to offer the appointment.	A person who is, or who has notified A that the person may be, seeking the appointment.
	A person who is being considered for the appointment.
Appointment to the office.	A person who is seeking, or who is being considered for, appointment to the office.

Where A is a relevant person in relation to a personal or public office

Appointment to the office.	A person appointed to the office.

Where A is a person who has the power to make a recommendation, or give approval to, an appointment to a public office

Deciding who to recommend or approve of appointment to the office.	A person who is, or who has notified A that the person may be, seeking recommendation or approval to the office.
	A person who is being considered for recommendation or approval for appointment to the office.
An appointment to the office.	A person who is seeking, or who is being considered for, appointment to the office in question.

Qualifications bodies (s 53)

Deciding on whom to confer a relevant qualification.	A person who is, or who has notified A that the person may be, an applicant for the conferment of the qualification.

Conferment by the body of a relevant qualification.	An applicant for the conferment of the qualification.
	A person who holds the qualification.

Employment service-providers (s 55)

Deciding to whom to offer to provide the service.	A person who is, or who has notified A that the person may be, an applicant for the provision of the service.
Provision by A of the service.	A person who applies to A for the provision of the service.
	A person to whom A provides the service.

Trade organisations (s 57)

Deciding to whom to offer membership of the organisation.	A person who is, or who has notified A that the person may be, an applicant for membership.
Membership of the organization.	An applicant for membership.
	A member.

Local authorities (s 58)

A member's carrying-out of official business.	The member.

Occupational pensions (s 61)

Carrying out A's functions in relation to the scheme.	A person who is or who may be a member of the scheme.

If two or more persons are subject to a duty to make reasonable adjustments in relation to the same interested disabled person, each of them must comply with the duty so far as it is reasonable for each of them to do so.[87]

Interested disabled person

7.35 In the context of the duty to make reasonable adjustments, an interested disabled person is a disabled person who, in relation to a relevant matter, is of a description specified in the second column of the applicable table in Part 2 of Sch 8 to the Act.[88] See the second column of the composite table above.

---

[87] EQA 2010, Sch 8, para 2(5).
[88] EQA 2010, Sch 8, para 4.

REASONABLE ADJUSTMENTS: SPECIFIC AREAS

Employers

7.36 A duty to make reasonable adjustments applies to an employer.[89] Where A is an employer, the first and third requirements of the duty apply to deciding to whom to offer employment and to employment by A. The second requirement of the duty only applies to employment by A. In deciding to whom to offer employment, A's duty is owed to a disabled person who is (or who has notified A that the person may be) an applicant for the employment. In relation to employment by A, the duty is owed to a disabled person who is an applicant for employment by A or who is an employee of A's.[90]

Employers and disabled contract workers

7.37 Where A is the employer of a disabled contract worker (B), A must comply with the first, second and third requirements on each occasion when B is supplied to a principal to do contract work.[91]

7.38 In relation to the first requirement as it applies for this purpose, the reference[92] to a provision, criterion or practice is a reference to a provision, criterion or practice applied by or on behalf of all or most of the principals to whom B is or might be supplied.[93] In the same context, the reference to being put at a substantial disadvantage is a reference to being likely to be put at a substantial disadvantage that is the same or similar in the case of each of the principals to whom B is or might be supplied.[94] Similarly, the requirement imposed on A is a requirement to take such steps as it would be reasonable for A to have to take if the provision, criterion or practice were applied by or on behalf of A.[95]

7.39 In relation to the second requirement as it applies for this purpose, the reference[96] to a physical feature is a reference to a physical feature of premises occupied by each of the principals to whom B is or might be supplied.[97] In the same context, the reference to being put at a substantial disadvantage is a reference to being likely to be put at a substantial disadvantage that is the same or similar in the case of each of those principals.[98] Similarly, the requirement imposed on A is a requirement to take such steps as it would be reasonable for A to have to take if the premises were occupied by A.[99]

---

[89] EQA 2010, s 39(5).
[90] EQA 2010, Sch 8, para 5(1).
[91] EQA 2010, Sch 8, para 5(2).
[92] In EQA 2010, s 20(3).
[93] EQA 2010, Sch 8, para 5(3)(a).
[94] EQA 2010, Sch 8, para 5(3)(b).
[95] EQA 2010, Sch 8, para 5(3)(c).
[96] In EQA 2010, s 20(4).
[97] EQA 2010, Sch 8, para 5(4)(a).
[98] EQA 2010, Sch 8, para 5(4)(b).
[99] EQA 2010, Sch 8, para 5(4)(c).

7.40 In relation to the third requirement as it applies for this purpose, the reference[100] to being put at a substantial disadvantage is a reference to being likely to be put at a substantial disadvantage that is the same or similar in the case of each of the principals to whom B is or might be supplied.[101] In the same context, the requirement imposed on A is a requirement to take such steps as it would be reasonable for A to have to take if A were the person to whom B was supplied.[102]

Principals in contract work

7.41 A duty to make reasonable adjustments applies to a principal (as well as to the employer of a contract worker).[103] Where A is a principal, the first and third requirements of the duty apply to contract work that A may make available and to contract work that A makes available. The second requirement of the duty only applies to contract work that A makes available. In relation to contract work that A may make available, A's duty is owed to a disabled person who is (or who has notified A that the person may be) an applicant to do the work. In relation to contract work that A makes available, the duty is owed to a disabled person who is supplied to do the work.[104]

7.42 A (a principal in contract work) is not required to do anything that a disabled person's employer is required to do (see the discussion immediately above).[105] Thus a disabled worker supplied to a principal by the disabled worker's employer enjoys the benefit of a duty owed by the employer and a duty owed by the principal.

Partnerships

7.43 A duty to make reasonable adjustments applies to a firm and to a proposed firm.[106] Where A is a firm or proposed firm, the first and third requirements of the duty apply to deciding to whom to offer a position as a partner. The first and third requirements of the duty also apply to a position as a partner. The second requirement of the duty only applies to a position as a partner. In relation to deciding to whom to offer a position as a partner, A's duty is owed to a disabled person who is (or who has notified A that the person may be) a candidate for the position. In relation to a position as a partner, the duty is owed to a disabled person who is a candidate for the position or the partner who holds the position.[107]

---

[100] In EQA 2010, s 20(5).
[101] EQA 2010, Sch 8, para 5(5)(a).
[102] EQA 2010, Sch 8, para 5(5)(b).
[103] EQA 2010, s 41(4).
[104] EQA 2010, Sch 8, para 6(1).
[105] That is by virtue of EQA 2010, Sch 8, para 5. See EQA 2010, Sch 8, para 6(2).
[106] EQA 2010, s 44(7).
[107] EQA 2010, Sch 8, para 7(1).

7.44   Where a firm or proposed firm (A) is required by Schedule 8 to the Act to take a step in relation to an interested disabled person (B), the cost of taking the step is to be treated as an expense of A.[108] In addition, the extent to which B should (if B is or becomes a partner) bear the cost is not to exceed such amount as is reasonable (having regard in particular to B's entitlement to share in A's profits).[109]

Limited liability partnerships

7.45   A duty to make reasonable adjustments applies to an LLP and a proposed LLP.[110] Where A is an LLP or proposed LLP, the first and third requirements of the duty apply to deciding to whom to offer a position as a member. The first and third requirements of the duty also apply to a position as a member. The second requirement of the duty only applies to a position as a member. In relation to deciding to whom to offer a position as a member, A's duty is owed to a disabled person who is (or who has notified A that the person may be) a candidate for the position. In relation to a position as a member, the duty is owed to a disabled person who is a candidate for the position or the member who holds the position.[111]

7.46   Where an LLP or proposed LLP (A) is required by Sch 8 to the Act to take a step in relation to an interested disabled person (B), the cost of taking the step is to be treated as an expense of A.[112] In addition, the extent to which B should (if B is or becomes a member) bear the cost is not to exceed such amount as is reasonable (having regard in particular to B's entitlement to share in A's profits).[113]

Barristers and their clerks

7.47   A duty to make reasonable adjustments applies to a barrister and to a barrister's clerk.[114] Where A is a barrister or barrister's clerk, the first and third requirements of the duty apply to deciding to whom to offer a pupillage or tenancy. The first and third requirements of the duty also apply to a pupillage or tenancy. The second requirement of the duty only applies to a pupillage or tenancy. In relation to deciding to whom to offer a pupillage or tenancy, A's duty is owed to a disabled person who is (or who has notified A that the person may be) an applicant for the pupillage or tenancy. In relation to a pupillage or tenancy, the duty is owed to a disabled person who is an applicant for the pupillage or tenancy, and to the pupil or tenant.[115]

---

[108]   EQA 2010, Sch 8, para 7(2)(a).
[109]   EQA 2010, Sch 8, para 7(2)(b).
[110]   EQA 2010, s 45(7).
[111]   EQA 2010, Sch 8, para 8(1).
[112]   EQA 2010, Sch 8, para 8(2)(a).
[113]   EQA 2010, Sch 8, para 8(2)(b).
[114]   EQA 2010, s 47(7) and (8).
[115]   EQA 2010, Sch 8, para 9.

Advocates and their clerks

7.48 A duty to make reasonable adjustments applies to an advocate and an advocate's clerk.[116] Where A is an advocate or advocate's clerk, the first and third requirements of the duty apply to deciding to whom to offer to take as a devil or to whom to offer membership of a stable. The first and third requirements of the duty also apply to the relationship with a devil or membership of a stable. The second requirement of the duty only applies to the relationship with a devil or membership of a stable. In relation to deciding to whom to offer to take as a devil or to whom to offer membership of a stable, A's duty is owed to a disabled person who applies (or who has notified A that the person may apply) to be taken as a devil or to become a member of the stable. In relation to the relationship with a devil or membership of a stable, the duty is owed to a disabled person who is an applicant to be taken as a devil or to become a member of the stable, and to the devil or member.[117]

Persons making appointments to offices etc

7.49 A duty to make reasonable adjustments applies to a person who has the power to make an appointment to a personal office and to a relevant person in relation to a personal office.[118] A duty to make reasonable adjustments also applies to a relevant person in relation to a public office.[119] Furthermore, a duty to make reasonable adjustments applies to a person who has the power to make an appointment to a public office which is an office or post, appointment to which is made by a member of the executive; or an office or post, appointment to which is made on the recommendation of (or subject to the approval of) a member of the executive.[120] Moreover, a duty to make reasonable adjustments applies to a person to a person (A) who has the power to make a recommendation for or give approval to an appointment to a public office which is an office or post, appointment to which is made by a member of the executive; or an office or post, appointment to which is made on the recommendation of (or subject to the approval of) a member of the executive.[121]

7.50 Where A is a person who has the power to make an appointment to a personal or public office, the first and third requirements of the duty apply to deciding to whom to offer the appointment. The first and third requirements of the duty also apply to appointment to the office. The second requirement of the duty only applies to appointment to the office. In relation to deciding to whom to offer the appointment, A's duty is owed to a disabled person who is (or who has notified A that the person may be) seeking the appointment and to a disabled person who is being considered for the appointment. In relation to

---

[116] EQA 2010, s 48(7).
[117] EQA 2010, Sch 8, para 10.
[118] EQA 2010, s 49(9).
[119] EQA 2010, s 50(11)(a).
[120] EQA 2010, s 50(11)(b).
[121] EQA 2010, s 51(4).

appointment to the office, A's duty is owed to a disabled person who is seeking (or who is being considered for) appointment to the office.[122]

7.51 Where A is a relevant person in relation to a personal office or public office, the first and third requirements of the duty apply to deciding to whom to offer the appointment. The first, second and third requirements of the duty apply to appointment to the office. The second requirement of the duty only applies to appointment to the office. A's duty is owed to a disabled person appointed to the office.[123]

7.52 Where A is a person who has the power to make a recommendation for (or give approval to) an appointment to a public office, the first and third requirements of the duty apply to deciding who to recommend (or approve) for appointment to the office. The first and third requirements of the duty also apply to an appointment to the office. The second requirement of the duty only applies to an appointment to the office. In relation to deciding who to recommend (or approve) for appointment to the office, A's duty is owed to a disabled person who is (or who has notified A that the person may be) seeking recommendation (or approval) for appointment to the office and to a disabled person who is being considered for recommendation (or approval) for appointment to the office. In relation to an appointment to the office, A's duty is owed to a disabled person who is seeking (or who is being considered for) appointment to the office in question.[124]

7.53 In relation to the second requirement in any of the cases above, the reference in the second requirement to a physical feature being a physical feature of premises occupied by A[125] is to be read as a reference to premises under the control of A and at (or from) which the functions of the office concerned are performed.[126]

Qualifications bodies

7.54 A duty to make reasonable adjustments applies to a qualifications body.[127] Where A is a qualifications body, the first and third requirements of the duty apply to deciding on whom to confer a relevant qualification and to conferment by the body of a relevant qualification. The second requirement of the duty only applies to conferment by the body of a relevant qualification. In relation to deciding on whom to confer a relevant qualification, A's duty is owed to a disabled person who is (or who has notified A that the person may be) an applicant for the conferment of the qualification. In relation to conferment by the body of a relevant qualification, A's duty is owed to a

---

[122] EQA 2010, Sch 8, para 11.
[123] EQA 2010, Sch 8, para 12.
[124] EQA 2010, Sch 8, para 13.
[125] EQA 2010, Sch 8, para 2(2)(b).
[126] EQA 2010, Sch 8, para 14.
[127] EQA 2010, s 53(6).

disabled person who is an applicant for the conferment of the qualification and a disabled person who holds the qualification.[128]

7.55 In this context, a provision, criterion or practice does not include the application of a competence standard.[129] This reflects the fact that the application by a qualifications body of a competence standard to a disabled person is not disability discrimination unless it is discrimination by virtue of s 19 (indirect discrimination).[130] A competence standard is an academic, medical or other standard applied for the purpose of determining whether or not a person has a particular level of competence or ability.[131]

Employment service-providers

7.56 A duty to make reasonable adjustments applies to an employment service-provider, except in relation to the provision of a vocational service.[132] Section 29(7)(a) also imposes a duty to make reasonable adjustments upon a service-provider under Part 3 of the Act (services and public functions) (see Chapter 4 above). However, while the duty imposed by s 29(7)(a) applies to a person concerned with the provision of a vocational service, a failure to comply with that duty in relation to the provision of a vocational service is a contravention of Part 5 (work) for the purposes of Part 9 (enforcement) (see Chapter 12 below).

7.57 A particular provision applies in relation to employment service-providers if a duty to make reasonable adjustments is imposed on A by s 55 of the Act (employment service-providers).[133] It applies except where the employment service which A provides is the provision of vocational training in the form of work experience (including work experience the duration of which is not agreed until after it begins).[134] Where this particular provision applies, the references in the first, second and third requirements[135] to a disabled person are references to an interested disabled person.[136] In relation to each requirement, the relevant matter is the employment service which A provides.[137] If two or more persons are subject to a duty to make reasonable adjustments in

---

128 EQA 2010, Sch 8, para 15(1).
129 EQA 2010, Sch 8, para 15(2).
130 EQA 2010, s 53(7).
131 EQA 2010, s 54(6).
132 EQA 2010, s 55(6). A reference to the provision of a vocational service is a reference to the provision of an employment service within s 56(2)(a)–(d) (or an employment service within s 56(2)(f) or (g) in so far as it is also an employment service within s 56(2)(a)–(d)); and for that purpose (a) the references to an employment service within s 56(2)(a) do not include a reference to vocational training within the meaning given by s 56(6)(b), and (b) the references to an employment service within s 56(2)(d) also include a reference to a service for assisting persons to retain employment: EQA 2010, s 56(7).
133 EQA 2010, Sch 8, para 3(1).
134 EQA 2010, s 56(6)(b).
135 EQA 2010, ss 20(3), 20(4) and 20(5).
136 EQA 2010, Sch 8, para 3(2).
137 EQA 2010, Sch 8, para 3(3).

relation to the same interested disabled person, each of them must comply with the duty so far as it is reasonable for each of them to do so.[138]

7.58   Otherwise, Sch 8 applies where A is an employment service-provider and the employment service which A provides is vocational training in the form of work experience (including work experience the duration of which is not agreed until after it begins).[139] In those limited circumstances, the first and third requirements of the duty apply to deciding to whom to offer to provide the service and to provision by A of the service. The second requirement of the duty only applies to the provision by A of the service. In relation to deciding to whom to offer to provide the service, A's duty is owed to a disabled person who is (or who has notified A that the person may be) an applicant for the provision of the service. In relation to the provision by A of the service, A's duty is owed to a disabled person who applies to A for the provision of the service or a disabled person to whom A provides the service.[140]

Trade organisations

7.59   A duty to make reasonable adjustments applies to a trade organisation.[141] Where A is a trade organisation, the first and third requirements of the duty apply to deciding to whom to offer membership of the organisation and to membership of the organisation. The second requirement of the duty only applies to membership of the organisation. In relation to deciding to whom to offer membership of the organisation, A's duty is owed to a disabled person who is (or who has notified A that the person may be) an applicant for membership. In relation to membership of the organisation, A's duty is owed to a disabled person who is an applicant for membership or who is a member.[142]

Local authorities

7.60   A duty to make reasonable adjustments applies to a local authority in relation to the official business of its members.[143] Where A is a local authority, the first, second and third requirements of the duty apply to a member's carrying-out of official business. A's duty is owed to a disabled person who is a member of the local authority.[144]

7.61   In the present context, regulations may make provision as to circumstances in which a provision, criterion or practice is (or is not) to be taken to put a disabled person at the disadvantage referred to in the first requirement. The regulations may provide as to circumstances in which a

---

[138]   EQA 2010, Sch 8, para 3(4) applying para 2(5).
[139]   EQA 2010, s 56(6)(b).
[140]   EQA 2010, Sch 8, para 16.
[141]   EQA 2010, s 57(6).
[142]   EQA 2010, Sch 8, para 17.
[143]   EQA 2010, s 58(6).
[144]   EQA 2010, Sch 8, para 18(1).

physical feature is (or is not) to be taken to put a disabled person at the disadvantage referred to in the second requirement. They may address the circumstances in which it is (or in which it is not) reasonable for a local authority to be required to take steps of a prescribed description. The regulations might also consider the steps which it is always (or which it is never) reasonable for a local authority to take. No regulations had been made at the time of writing.[145]

Occupational pensions

7.62 A duty to make reasonable adjustments applies to a responsible person in relation to an occupational pension scheme.[146] Where A is a responsible person (within s 61, discussed above) in relation to an occupational pension scheme, the first, second and third requirements of the duty apply to carrying out A's functions in relation to the scheme. A's duty is owed to a disabled person who is or who may be a member of the scheme.[147]

REASONABLE ADJUSTMENTS: LIMITATIONS ON THE DUTY

7.63 Part 3 of Sch 8 to the Equality Act 2010 deals with limitations on the duty to make reasonable adjustments. These are the limitations that arise from a lack of knowledge of disability.

7.64 In the case of an applicant or potential applicant, A is not subject to a duty to make reasonable adjustments if A does not know – and could not reasonably be expected to know – that an interested disabled person is or may be an applicant for the work in question.[148] The following table assists in identifying who is an applicant for the work in question. An applicant is, in relation to the description of A specified in the first column of the table, a person of a description specified in the second column of the table (and the reference to a potential applicant is to be construed accordingly).[149]

Description of A	Applicant
An employer	An applicant for employment
A firm or proposed firm	A candidate for a position as a partner
An LLP or proposed LLP	A candidate for a position as a member

---

[145] EQA 2010, Sch 8, para 18(2).
[146] EQA 2010, s 61(11).
[147] EQA 2010, Sch 8, para 19.
[148] EQA 2010, Sch 8, para 20(1)(a).
[149] EQA 2010, Sch 8, para 20(2).

A barrister or barrister's clerk	An applicant for a pupillage or tenancy
An advocate or advocate's clerk	An applicant for being taken as an advocate's devil or for becoming a member of a stable
A relevant person in relation to a personal or public office	A person who is seeking appointment to, or recommendation or approval for appointment to, the office
A qualifications body	An applicant for the conferment of a relevant qualification
An employment service-provider	An applicant for the provision of an employment service
A trade organisation	An applicant for membership

In any other case referred to in Part 3 of Sch 8,[150] A is not subject to a duty to make reasonable adjustments if A does not know – and could not reasonably be expected to know – that an interested disabled person has a disability and is likely to be placed at the disadvantage referred to in the first, second or third requirement.

7.65 If the duty to make reasonable adjustments is imposed on A by s 55 (employment service-providers), these limitations apply only insofar as the employment service which A provides is vocational training that is training for employment.[151]

OCCUPATIONAL REQUIREMENTS EXCEPTION

7.66 Part 1 of Sch 9 to the Equality Act 2010 deals with the occupational requirements exception. The existing exceptions for occupational requirements are not uniform of principle and are to be found in various sources.[152]

General

7.67 A person (A) does not contravene by way of direct discrimination[153] one of a number of specified provisions in Part 5 of the Act (work) in the following cumulative circumstances.[154] First, A applies a requirement to have a particular

---

[150] EQA 2010, Sch 8, para 20(1)(b).
[151] EQA 2010, s 56(6)(a) and Sch 8, para 20(3).
[152] See the pre-existing legislation: SDA 1975, ss 7–7B; RRA 1976, ss 4A and 5; EE(SO)R 2003, reg 7; EE(RoB)R 2003, reg 7; EE(A)R 2006, reg 8. See Keter, 2009a: 55–56.
[153] A reference to contravening a provision of the Act is a reference to contravening that provision by virtue of s 13 (direct discrimination) only: EQA 2010, Sch 9, para 6(2).
[154] EQA 2010, Sch 9, para 1(1). In the case of gender reassignment, a requirement to have a protected characteristic is to be read as a requirement not to be a transsexual person (and s 7(3) is to be ignored): Sch 9, para 1(3)(a). In the case of marriage and civil partnership, a

protected characteristic in relation to work.[155] Secondly, A then shows that having it is an occupational requirement. Thirdly, A further shows that the application of the requirement is a proportionate means of achieving a legitimate aim. Fourthly, A shows that the person to whom A applies the requirement does not meet it (or A has reasonable grounds for not being satisfied that the person meets it).[156] What A has to show is judged by having regard to the nature or context of the work.

7.68   This is the general occupational requirements exception. It applies only to the following specified forms of direct discrimination by:[157]

- an employer (A) against a person (B) in the arrangements A makes for deciding to whom to offer employment (or by not offering B employment);[158]

- an employer (A) against an employee of A's (B) in the way A affords B access (or by not affording B access) to opportunities for promotion, transfer or training, or (except as relating to sex) by dismissing B;[159]

- a principal against a contract worker by not allowing the worker to do (or to continue to do) the work;[160]

- a firm or proposed firm against a person in the arrangements it makes for deciding to whom to offer a position as a partner (or by not offering the person a position as a partner);[161]

- a firm (A) against a partner (B) in the way A affords B access (or by not affording B access) to opportunities for promotion, transfer or training, or (except as relating to sex) by expelling B;[162]

- an LLP or proposed LLP against a person in the arrangements it makes for deciding to whom to offer a position as a member (or by not offering the person a position as a member);[163]

---

requirement to have a protected characteristic is to be read as a requirement not to be married or a civil partner (and s 8(2) is to be ignored): Sch 9, para 1(3)(b).

[155]   A reference to work is a reference to employment, contract work, a position as a partner or as a member of an LLP, or an appointment to a personal or public office: EQA 2010, Sch 9, para 6(3).

[156]   In the case of a requirement to be of a particular sex, this provision has effect as if the words in parentheses were omitted: EQA 2010, Sch 9, para 1(4).

[157]   EQA 2010, Sch 9, para 1(2).

[158]   EQA 2010, s 39(1)(a) or (c).

[159]   EQA 2010, s 39(2)(b) or (c); Sch 9, para 6(5).

[160]   EQA 2010, s 41(1)(b). So far as relating to sex, the reference to s 41(1)(b) is to be construed as if it read 'by not allowing the worker to do the work': EQA 2010, Sch 9, para 6(7).

[161]   EQA 2010, s 44(1)(a) or (c).

[162]   EQA 2010, s 44(2)(b) or (c); Sch 9, para 6(5).

[163]   EQA 2010, s 45(1)(a) or (c).

- an LLP (A) against a member (B) in the way A affords B access (or by not affording B access) to opportunities for promotion, transfer or training, or (except as relating to sex) by expelling B;[164]

- a person (A) who has the power to make an appointment to a personal office against a person (B) in the arrangements A makes for deciding to whom to offer the appointment (or by not offering B the appointment);[165]

- a person (A) who is a relevant person in relation to a personal office against a person (B) appointed to the office in the way A affords B access (or by not affording B access) to opportunities for promotion, transfer or training, or (except as relating to sex) by terminating B's appointment;[166]

- a person (A) who has the power to make an appointment to a relevant public office against a person (B) in the arrangements A makes for deciding to whom to offer the appointment (or by not offering B the appointment);[167]

- a person (A) who is a relevant person in relation to a relevant public office against a person (B) appointed to the office in the way A affords B access (or by not affording B access) to opportunities for promotion, transfer or training, or (except as relating to sex) by terminating the appointment;[168]

- a person (A) who has the power to make a recommendation for (or give approval to) an appointment to a relevant public office against a person (B) in the arrangements A makes for deciding who to recommend for appointment (or to whose appointment to give approval), by not recommending B for appointment to the office, by making a negative recommendation of B for appointment to the office, or by not giving approval to the appointment of B to the office.[169]

7.69 As the Explanatory Notes elucidate, these otherwise difficult provisions provide a general exception to unlawful direct discrimination in relation to work. The exception applies where being of a particular sex, race, disability, religion or belief, sexual orientation or age (or not being a transsexual person, married or a civil partner) is a requirement for the work. It arises where the person to whom it is applied does not meet it (or, except in the case of sex, does not meet it to the reasonable satisfaction of the person who applied it). The requirement must be crucial to the post and not merely one of several

---

[164]   EQA 2010, s 45(2)(b) or (c); Sch 9, para 6(5).
[165]   EQA 2010, s 49(3)(a) or (c).
[166]   EQA 2010, s 49(6)(b) or (c); Sch 9, para 6(5).
[167]   EQA 2010, s 50(3)(a) or (c) in respect of a relevant public office falling within s 50(2)(a) or (b).
[168]   EQA 2010, s 50(6)(b) or (c) in respect of a relevant public office falling within s 50(2)(a) or (b); Sch 9, para 6(5).
[169]   EQA 2010, s 51(1) in respect of a relevant public office falling within s 50(2)(a) or (b).

important factors. It also must not be a sham or pretext. In addition, applying the requirement must be proportionate so as to achieve a legitimate aim.[170]

7.70 These provisions replicate the effect of exceptions for occupational requirements in previous discrimination legislation.[171] New exceptions are created in relation to disability and to replace the existing exceptions for occupational qualifications in relation to sex, gender reassignment, colour and nationality. The exceptions for occupational requirements make it clear that the requirement must pursue a legitimate aim and that the burden of showing that the exception applies rests on those seeking to rely on it.[172]

7.71 The Explanatory Notes supply the following examples:

• The need for authenticity or realism might require someone of a particular race, sex or age for acting roles (for example, a black man to play the part of Othello) or modelling jobs.

• Considerations of privacy or decency might require a public changing room or lavatory attendant to be of the same sex as those using the facilities.

• An organisation for deaf people might legitimately employ a deaf person who uses British Sign Language to work as a counsellor to other deaf people whose first or preferred language is BSL.

• Unemployed Muslim women might not take advantage of the services of an outreach worker to help them find employment if they were provided by a man.

• A counsellor working with victims of rape might have to be a woman and not a transsexual person, even if she has a gender recognition certificate, in order to avoid causing them further distress.[173]

---

170   EN para 796.
171   SDA 1975, s 7; RRA 1976, ss 4A and 5; EE(RoB)R 2003, reg 7. See: *Timex Corporation v Hodgson* [1981] IRLR 530, EAT; *Sisley v Britannia Security Systems Ltd* [1983] IRLR 404, EAT; *Tottenham Green Under-Fives Centre v Marshall* [1989] IRLR 147, EAT; *Etam plc v Rowan* [1989] IRLR 150, EAT; *Lambeth LBC v CRE* [1989] IRLR 379, EAT and [1990] IRLR 230, CA; *Tottenham Green Under-Fives Centre v Marshall (No.2)* [1991] IRLR 162, EAT; *Lasertop Ltd v Webster* [1997] IRLR 498, EAT.
172   EN para 798.
173   EN para 798.

Religious requirements relating to sex, marriage or sexual orientation

7.72 Subject to certain conditions, a person (A) does not contravene by direct discrimination alone[174] a specified provision by applying in relation to employment an applicable requirement.

7.73 An applicable requirement is a requirement to be of a particular sex;[175] or a requirement not to be a transsexual person; or a requirement not to be married or a civil partner; or a requirement not to be married to (or the civil partner of) a person who has a living former spouse (or civil partner); or a requirement relating to circumstances in which a marriage (or civil partnership) came to an end; or a requirement related to sexual orientation.[176]

7.74 The cumulative conditions are that A must show that the employment is for the purposes of an organised religion. The application of the requirement must engage the compliance principle or the non-conflict principle. The person to whom A applies the requirement does not meet it (or A has reasonable grounds for not being satisfied that the person meets it).[177]

7.75 The specified provisions are direct discrimination by:[178]

- an employer (A) against a person (B) in the arrangements A makes for deciding to whom to offer employment (or by not offering B employment);[179]

- an employer (A) against an employee of A's (B) in the way A affords B access (or by not affording B access) to opportunities for promotion, transfer or training, or (except as relating to sex) by dismissing B;[180]

- a person (A) who has the power to make an appointment to a personal office against a person (B) in the arrangements A makes for deciding to whom to offer the appointment (or by not offering B the appointment);[181]

- a person (A) who is a relevant person in relation to a personal office against a person (B) appointed to the office in the way A affords B access (or by not affording B access) to opportunities for promotion, transfer or training, or (except as relating to sex) by terminating B's appointment;[182]

---

[174] A reference to contravening a provision of the Act is a reference to contravening that provision by virtue of s 13 (direct discrimination) only: EQA 2010, Sch 9, para 6(2).
[175] In the case of this requirement, EQA 2010, Sch 9, para 2(1)(c) has effect as if the words in parentheses were omitted: EQA 2010, Sch 9, para 2(8).
[176] EQA 2010, Sch 9, para 2(4).
[177] EQA 2010, Sch 9, para 2(1).
[178] EQA 2010, Sch 9, para 2(2).
[179] EQA 2010, s 39(1)(a) or (c).
[180] EQA 2010, s 39(2)(b) or (c); Sch 9, para 6(5).
[181] EQA 2010, s 49(3)(a) or (c).
[182] EQA 2010, s 49(6)(b) or (c); Sch 9, para 6(5).

- a person (A) who has the power to make an appointment to a relevant public office against a person (B) in the arrangements A makes for deciding to whom to offer the appointment (or by not offering B the appointment);[183]

- a person (A) who is a relevant person in relation to a relevant public office against a person (B) appointed to the office in the way A affords B access (or by not affording B access) to opportunities for promotion, transfer or training, or (except as relating to sex) by terminating the appointment;[184]

- a person (A) who has the power to make a recommendation for (or give approval to) an appointment to a relevant public office against a person (B) in the arrangements A makes for deciding who to recommend for appointment or to whose appointment to give approval, by not recommending B for appointment to the office, by making a negative recommendation of B for appointment to the office, or by not giving approval to the appointment of B to the office.[185]

7.76 In addition, a person does not contravene by direct discrimination alone[186] the qualifications body provisions in s 53(1)[187] or s 53(2)(a) (except as relating to sex)[188] or s 53(2)(b)[189] by applying in relation to a relevant qualification (within the meaning of s 53) an applicable requirement above if the person shows that the qualification is for the purposes of employment for the purposes of an organised religion, and the application of the requirement engages the compliance principle or the non-conflict principle.[190]

7.77 The application of a requirement engages the compliance principle if the requirement is applied so as to comply with the doctrines of the religion.[191] The application of a requirement engages the non-conflict principle if, because of

---

[183] EQA 2010, s 50(3)(a) or (c) in respect of a relevant public office falling within s 50(2)(a) or (b).

[184] EQA 2010, s 50(6)(b) or (c) in respect of a relevant public office falling within s 50(2)(a) or (b); Sch 9, para 6(5).

[185] EQA 2010, s 51(1) in respect of a relevant public office falling within s 50(2)(a) or (b).

[186] A reference to contravening a provision of the Act is a reference to contravening that provision by virtue of s 13 (direct discrimination) only: EQA 2010, Sch 9, para 6(2).

[187] A qualifications body (A) must not discriminate against a person (B) (a) in the arrangements A makes for deciding upon whom to confer a relevant qualification; or (b) as to the terms on which it is prepared to confer a relevant qualification on B; or (c) by not conferring a relevant qualification on B.

[188] A qualifications body (A) must not discriminate against a person (B) upon whom A has conferred a relevant qualification by withdrawing the qualification from B.

[189] A qualifications body (A) must not discriminate against a person (B) upon whom A has conferred a relevant qualification by varying the terms on which B holds the qualification.

[190] EQA 2010, Sch 9, para 2(3).

[191] EQA 2010, Sch 9, para 2(5). The Government intended that the application of a requirement should engage the compliance principle if the application was a proportionate means of complying with the doctrines of the religion. See EN para 799. However, the present wording was inserted as a result of an Opposition amendment at Committee Stage in the House of Lords.

the nature or context of the employment, the requirement is applied so as to avoid conflicting with the strongly held religious convictions of a significant number of the religion's followers.[192]

7.78 In this context, a reference to employment includes a reference to an appointment to a personal or public office.[193] The Government's drafting of the Bill would have provided that employment is for the purposes of an organised religion only if the employment wholly or mainly involves leading or assisting in the observance of liturgical or ritualistic practices of the religion, or promoting or explaining the doctrine of the religion (whether to followers of the religion or to others).[194] The Government sought to amend that drafting so as to provide that employment is for the purposes of an organised religion only if the employment is as a minister of religion, or the employment is in another post that exists (or, where the post has not previously been filled, that would exist) to promote or represent the religion or to explain the doctrines of the religion (whether to followers of the religion or to others). Not only was the Government's proposed amendment defeated at the Committee Stage in the House of Lords, but its original sub-clause dealing with the limited definition of employment for the purposes of an organised religion was deleted. The exception is thus potentially at large and might now embrace employment generally within an organised religion.

7.79 These provisions (as amended) replace and harmonise pre-existing exceptions.[195] However, what the Government intended to be novel was the emphasis upon the employment in question being closely related to the religious purposes of the organisation.[196] For example, this exception as originally drafted would apply to a requirement that a Catholic priest be a man. However, it would have been unlikely to permit a requirement that a church youth worker who primarily organises sporting activities is celibate if they are gay. Nevertheless, it might have applied if the youth worker mainly teaches Bible classes. The original exception would not apply to a requirement that a church accountant be celibate if they are gay.[197] Nevertheless, the amendments made to the Bill in the House of Lords do not promote the limited exception the Government intended this to be.

---

[192] EQA 2010, Sch 9, para 2(6). The Government intended that the application of a requirement should engage the non-conflict principle if, because of the nature or context of the employment, the application was a proportionate means of avoiding conflict with the strongly held religious convictions of a significant number of the religion's followers. See EN para 799. However, the present wording was inserted as a result of an Opposition amendment at Committee Stage in the House of Lords.

[193] EQA 2010, Sch 9, para 2(7).

[194] EN para 776 (HL Bill 20).

[195] EE(RoB)R 2003, reg 7; EE(SO)R 2003, reg 7. See further: *R (Amicus) v Secretary of State for Trade and Industry* [2004] IRLR 430, HC; *Glasgow City Council v McNab* [2007] IRLR 476, EAT.

[196] EN para 802. See Government Equalities Office, 2009f.

[197] EN para 802. See 'Pope Benedict attacks government over Equality Bill' reported at http://news.bbc.co.uk/1/hi/uk/8492597.stm (last accessed on 2 February 2010) and 'Britain's human rights policies violate natural law, Pope says' reported at http://www.timesonline.co.uk/tol/comment/faith/article7011095.ece (lasted accessed on 2 February 2010).

7.80 This may bring these provisions of the Equality Act 2010 into direct conflict with the EU Equal Treatment Framework Directive. An unpublished, but widely leaked, reasoned opinion was sent to the UK Government on 26 November 2009 by the European Commission. In part, the reasoned opinion asserts that those parts of UK legislation (pre-Equality Act 2010) that permit exceptions for sexual orientation discrimination in the context of religious organisations are potentially in breach of EU law.[198] The Government implicitly attempted to remedy that matter in its original drafting of (and proposed amendments to) the Equality Bill. It does not appear that this has been achieved on the face of the final Act, although its provisions will have to be interpreted by the tribunals and courts in the light of EU law.

Other requirements relating to religion or belief

7.81 An exception applies to a person (A) with an ethos based on religion or belief. A does not contravene by direct discrimination alone[199] a specified provision mentioned above[200] by applying in relation to work a requirement to be of a particular religion or belief in the following circumstance.[201] Having regard to that ethos and to the nature or context of the work, A must be able to show the following. First, that the requirement to be of a particular religion or belief is an occupational requirement. Secondly, that the application of the requirement is a proportionate means of achieving a legitimate aim. Thirdly, that the person to whom A applies the requirement does not meet it (or A has reasonable grounds for not being satisfied that the person meets it).[202]

7.82 The Explanatory Notes posit that this allows an employer with an ethos based on religion or belief to discriminate in relation to work by applying a requirement to be of a particular religion or belief. Nevertheless, this is only if, having regard to that ethos, being of that religion or belief is a requirement for the work. This requirement must not be a sham or pretext. The application of the requirement must be proportionate so as to achieve a legitimate aim.[203] It is for an employer to show that it has an ethos based on religion or belief by reference to such evidence as the organisation's founding constitution.[204]

7.83 These provisions are not new.[205] By way of an example, a religious organisation may wish to restrict applicants for the post of head of its organisation to those people that adhere to that faith. This is because to

---

[198] The challenge is to the compatibility of EE(SO)R 2003, reg 7(3) with Art 4 of the EU Equal Treatment Framework Directive. See Rubenstein, 2010.

[199] A reference to contravening a provision of the Act is a reference to contravening that provision by virtue of s 13 (direct discrimination) only: EQA 2010, Sch 9, para 6(2).

[200] EQA 2010, Sch 9, para 1(2).

[201] A reference to work is a reference to employment, contract work, a position as a partner or as a member of an LLP, or an appointment to a personal or public office: EQA 2010, Sch 9, para 6(3).

[202] EQA 2010, Sch 9, para 3.

[203] EN para 803.

[204] EN para 802.

[205] See EE(RoB)R 2003, reg 7. See further: *Glasgow City Council v McNab* [2007] IRLR 476, EAT.

represent the views of that organisation accurately it is felt that the person in charge of that organisation must have an in-depth understanding of the religion's doctrines. This type of discrimination could be lawful. However, other posts that do not require this kind of in-depth understanding, such as administrative posts, should be open to all people regardless of their religion or belief.[206]

Competing rights: religion or belief and sexual orientation

7.84 When the House of Lords amendments to the Equality Bill were considered by the House of Commons, the Labour Government did not seek to overturn the changes made to the Bill in the Lords in relation to the competing rights of religion or belief and sexual orientation. Its view is that the amendments to the genuine occupational requirement exception for sexual orientation discrimination by religious organisations will not reduce the pre-existing level of protection. This is because the elements removed by the Lords are implicit in the legislation and its associated case law.[207] As for the European Commission's concern that the EE(SO)R 2003 did not properly implement the EU Equal Treatment Framework Directive, it appears to be the Government's position that those Regulations (and, therefore, the EQA 2010) comply with EU law.[208]

7.85 Nothing in the EQA 2010 is designed to change existing case-law principles where the religion or belief of an employee otherwise conflicts with the lawful requirements of his or her employer, especially in the context of providing public services. So, for example, an employer's dress code or uniform policy prohibiting jewellery (including a cross) to be visible is unlikely to be challengeable as indirectly discriminatory on grounds of religion or belief.[209] Similarly, an employee who refuses to carry out (or asks to be excused from) aspects of their employment duties on the ground of their religious beliefs in relation to homosexuality is unlikely to be able to establish unlawful discrimination if their employer reasonably insists that those duties are performed.[210]

---

[206] EN para 805. See Government Equalities Office, 2009f.

[207] HC Deb vol 508 col 931 (Solicitor-General).

[208] HC Deb vol 508 col 931 (Solicitor-General).

[209] *Eweida v British Airways plc* [2010] EWCA Civ 80 [2010] IRLR 322, CA.

[210] *MacFarlane v Relate Avon Ltd* [2010] IRLR 196, EAT (a relationship counsellor asking to be excused working with same sex couples because of his Christian beliefs); *Ladele v London Borough of Islington* [2010] IRLR 211, CA (a registrar who was a committed Christian was disciplined for refusing to conduct civil partnerships). See Rubenstein, 2010a; Webster, 2010. The Supreme Court has refused leave to appeal in *Ladele*. Permission to appeal to the Court of Appeal in *MacFarlane* was refused on 29 April 2010 by Laws LJ.

Armed forces

7.86 A person does not contravene by direct discrimination alone[211] s 39(1)(a)[212] or s 39(1)(c)[213] or s 39(2)(b)[214] by applying in relation to service in the armed forces a relevant requirement if the person shows that the application is a proportionate means of ensuring the combat effectiveness of the armed forces.[215] A relevant requirement is a requirement to be a man and a requirement not to be a transsexual person.[216] The term 'armed forces' means any of the naval, military or air forces of the Crown.[217]

7.87 The prohibition on age discrimination or disability discrimination does not apply to service in the armed forces.[218] Section 55 (employment service-providers), so far as relating to disability, does not apply to work experience in the armed forces.[219]

7.88 In the account of the Explanatory Notes,[220] women and transsexual people are allowed to be excluded from service in the armed forces if this is a proportionate way to ensure the combat effectiveness of the armed forces. The armed forces are also exempted from the work provisions of the Act relating to disability and age. This replicates existing exemptions but narrows the scope of the existing combat effectiveness exception so that this applies only to direct discrimination in relation to recruitment and access to training, promotion and transfer opportunities. Thus, by way of example, only ground close-combat roles requiring service personnel deliberately to close with and kill the enemy face-to-face are confined to men. Women and transsexual people are currently excluded from the Royal Marines General Service, the Household Cavalry and Royal Armoured Corps, the Infantry and the Royal Air Force Regiment only.

7.89 The Joint Committee on Human Rights is of the view that the exemption of the armed forces from the scope of the disability provisions of the Act is unnecessary and incompatible with the UN Convention on the Rights of Persons with Disabilities and with the European Convention on Human Rights.[221]

---

[211] A reference to contravening a provision of the Act is a reference to contravening that provision by virtue of s 13 (direct discrimination) only: EQA 2010, Sch 9, para 6(2).

[212] Discrimination by an employer (A) against a person (B) in the arrangements A makes for deciding to whom to offer employment.

[213] Discrimination by an employer (A) against a person (B) by not offering B employment.

[214] Discrimination by an employer (A) against an employee of A's (B) in the way A affords B access (or by not affording B access) to opportunities for promotion, transfer or training or for receiving any other benefit, facility or service.

[215] EQA 2010, Sch 9, para 4(1).

[216] EQA 2010, Sch 9, para 4(2).

[217] EQA 2010, s 212(1).

[218] EQA 2010, Sch 9, para 4(3).

[219] EQA 2010, Sch 9, para 4(3).

[220] EN paras 806–808.

[221] Joint Committee on Human Rights, 2009: para 182.

Employment services

7.90 First, a person (A) does not contravene by direct discrimination alone[222] the prohibition on discrimination by employment service-providers[223] if A shows that A's treatment of another person relates only to work the offer of which could be refused to that other person in reliance on any of the occupational requirements above.[224] Secondly, a person (A) does not contravene by direct discrimination alone[225] the prohibition on discrimination by employment service-providers[226] if A shows that A's treatment of another person relates only to training for work the offer of which could be refused to that other person in reliance on any of the occupational requirements above.[227] A reference to work is a reference to employment, contract work, a position as a partner or as a member of an LLP, or an appointment to a personal or public office.[228]

7.91 Moreover, a person (A) does not contravene by direct discrimination alone[229] the prohibition on discrimination by employment service-providers[230] if A shows that A acted in reliance on a statement made to A by a person with the power to offer the work in question to the effect that, by virtue of these two exceptions immediately above, A's action would be lawful, and it was reasonable for A to rely on the statement.[231] However, a person commits an offence by knowingly or recklessly making such a statement which in a material respect is false or misleading.[232] A person guilty of this offence is liable on summary conviction to a fine not exceeding level 5 on the standard scale (£5,000).[233]

7.92 The Explanatory Notes rationalise that it is lawful for an employment service-provider to restrict a service to people with a particular protected characteristic if the treatment relates either to work for which having that characteristic is an occupational requirement or to training for such work.[234] A provider of employment services can rely on the exception by showing that he or she reasonably relied on a statement from a person who could offer the work in question that having the particular characteristic was an occupational requirement.[235] These provisions are not new. For example, the provider of a

---

[222] A reference to contravening a provision of the Act is a reference to contravening that provision by virtue of s 13 (direct discrimination) only: EQA 2010, Sch 9, para 6(2).

[223] EQA 2010, ss 55(1) and 55(2) only.

[224] EQA 2010, Sch 9, para 5(1) cross-referring to Sch 9, paras 1–4.

[225] A reference to contravening a provision of the Act is a reference to contravening that provision by virtue of s 13 (direct discrimination) only: EQA 2010, Sch 9, para 6(2).

[226] EQA 2010, ss 55(1) and 55(2) only.

[227] EQA 2010, Sch 9, para 5(2).

[228] EQA 2010, Sch 9, para 6(3).

[229] A reference to contravening a provision of the Act is a reference to contravening that provision by virtue of s 13 (direct discrimination) only: EQA 2010, Sch 9, para 6(2).

[230] EQA 2010, ss 55(1) and 55(2) only.

[231] EQA 2010, Sch 9, para 5(3).

[232] EQA 2010, Sch 9, para 5(4).

[233] EQA 2010, Sch 9, para 5(5).

[234] EN para 809.

[235] EN para 810.

Catholic theological training course required exclusively for those training to be Catholic priests may limit access to the course to Catholics because the training relates to work the offer of which can be limited to Catholics by virtue of an occupational requirement.[236]

Interpretation

7.93 The interpretation of words and phrases in relation to occupational requirements has been noted above.[237] Throughout this discussion a reference to a person includes a reference to an organisation.[238] Unusually, these interpretation provisions are crucial to a proper understanding of the limits of the occupational requirement exceptions. As the Explanatory Notes clarify,[239] the exceptions are only available in respect of direct discrimination in recruitment, access to promotion, transfer or training, or (except in the case of sex discrimination) dismissal. None of these exceptions can be used to justify indirect discrimination or harassment.

Human rights concerns

7.94 The Joint Committee on Human Rights largely welcomed the clarification of the circumstances in which occupational requirements linked to a religious belief or ethos could be imposed by faith-based organisations and organised religious groups. It accepted that some limitations on non-discrimination on grounds of religion or belief may be justified and appropriate in relation to religious organisations. It also considered that in general the provisions of Sch 9 struck the correct balance between the right to equality and non-discrimination and the rights to freedom of religion or belief and association. It stressed the need for such exceptions to the general prohibition on direct discrimination to be construed strictly as a derogation from the principle of equal treatment.[240]

7.95 However, the Joint Committee doubted whether the religious ethos exception permits organisations with a religious ethos to impose wide-ranging requirements on employees to adhere to religious doctrine in their lifestyles and personal relationships. It considered that this should put beyond doubt any suggestion that the exemption could be used to discriminate on the basis of sexual conduct linked to sexual orientation.[241]

7.96 Nevertheless, the Joint Committee remained concerned about the status of employees of organisations with a religious ethos who have been contracted

---

[236] EN para 811.
[237] EQA 2010, Sch 9, para 6. Particularly noteworthy is that a reference to ss 39(2)(c), 44(2)(c), 45(2)(c), 49(6)(c), 50(6)(c), 53(2)(a) or 55(2)(c) (dismissal, etc.) does not include a reference to those provisions so far as relating to sex: EQA 2010, Sch 9, para 6(6).
[238] EQA 2010, Sch 9, para 6(4).
[239] EN para 812.
[240] Joint Committee on Human Rights, 2009: para 175.
[241] Joint Committee on Human Rights, 2009: para 176.

to provide a public service. It noted that such employees have a right not to be subjected to religious discrimination on the basis of the ethos of the contracting organisation if they are otherwise performing their job satisfactorily. However, it was apprehensive that the widespread use of the religious ethos exception by such organisations could result in public functions being discharged by organisations in receipt of public funds that are nevertheless perceived to discriminate on the basis of religion or belief.[242]

EXCEPTIONS RELATING TO AGE

7.97 Part 2 of Sch 9 to the Act is concerned with exceptions to an age contravention: that is, a contravention of Part 5 of the Act (work) so far as relating to age.[243]

Retirement

7.98 It is not an age contravention to dismiss a relevant worker at or over the age of 65 if the reason for the dismissal is retirement.[244] A relevant worker is an employee,[245] a person in Crown employment, a relevant member of the House of Commons staff, or a relevant member of the House of Lords staff.[246] Retirement is a reason for dismissal only if it is a reason for dismissal by virtue of Part 10 of the Employment Rights Act 1996.[247]

7.99 As the Explanatory Notes explain,[248] this allows employers to dismiss employees on the grounds of retirement at the age of 65 or over without this being regarded as age discrimination or unfair dismissal. However, where an employee has a normal retirement age which exceeds the age of 65, if the employee is dismissed on the grounds of retirement before reaching that normal retirement age, this is capable of amounting to age discrimination and/or unfair dismissal. These provisions must be read closely with the amendments to the unfair dismissals provisions in the Employment Rights Act 1996 (as amended by the EE(A)R 2006) which remain in force. Retirement is a reason for dismissal only if it is a reason for a fair dismissal. The 2006 Regulations set out the procedures that need to be followed by an employer in order for the reason for the dismissal to be retirement under unfair dismissal law, and in order for the dismissal to be fair. Thus the existing exception for retirement is preserved.

---

[242] Joint Committee on Human Rights, 2009: para 177.
[243] EQA 2010, Sch 9, para 7.
[244] EQA 2010, Sch 9, para 8(1). See EE(A)R 2006, reg 30 and Sch 6 and 8.
[245] ERA 1996, s 230(1).
[246] EQA 2010, Sch 9, para 8(2).
[247] EQA 2010, Sch 9, para 8(3). Part 10 of the ERA 1996 contains the law relating to the right not to by unfairly dismissed. Sections 98ZA–98ZH of the ERA 1996 contain the provisions on retirement.
[248] EN paras 813–817. See also Keter, 2009a: 131–136.

7.100 Compulsory retirement ages remain a form of direct age discrimination. The Explanatory Notes advise that where the retirement age is below the age of 65 (or the employer's normal retirement age if over the age 65) it will need to be objectively justified.[249] The Explanatory Notes record the Government's view that this exception for retirement ages of 65 and over is within the exemption contained in Art 6(1) of Council Directive 2000/78/EC as being justified by reference to a legitimate aim of social policy.[250] The Government's position is said to be that the default retirement age will remain in place until such point in the future as evidence shows that it may either be raised, or is no longer necessary. The Government has committed to review it in 2010, with any changes being implemented in 2011.[251]

7.101 The Joint Committee on Human Rights was of the view that the default retirement age unduly restricts the rights of older workers to equal treatment and non-discrimination. It recognised that employers have a legitimate interest in workforce planning, but suggested that alternative methods of workforce planning would avoid age discrimination inherent in a default retirement age (for example, performance management techniques and job evaluation and assessment mechanisms).[252]

Employment applicants at or approaching retirement age

7.102 A person does not contravene s 39(1)(a) or s 39(1)(c),[253] so far as relating to age, in a case where the other person has attained the age limit,[254] and would (if recruited for the employment) be a relevant worker (as above).[255] The age limit is whichever is the greater of the age of 65 and the normal retirement age in the case of the employment concerned.[256]

7.103 The Explanatory Notes say that the consequence of this is that it is not unlawful discrimination for an employer to decide not to offer employment to a person where, at the time of the person's application to the employer, he or she is over the employer's normal retirement age or is over the age of 65 (if the employer has no normal retirement age).[257] It is also not unlawful to refuse to offer employment where the applicant will reach the employer's normal

---

[249] EN para 818.
[250] EN para 819.
[251] EN para 820. See the largely unsuccessful judicial review challenge to the default retirement age: *R (Age Concern England) v Secretary of State for Business Enterprise and Regulatory Reform* (Case C-388/07) [2009] All ER (EC) 619, ECJ; *R (Age UK) v Secretary of State for Business, Innovation & Skills* [2009] EWHC 2336 (Admin), HC.
[252] Joint Committee on Human Rights, 2009: para 185. See also: House of Commons Work and Pensions Committee, 2009a: para 122; and 2009b: 7.
[253] An employer (A) must not discriminate against a person (B) (a) in the arrangements A makes for deciding to whom to offer employment; or (c) by not offering B employment.
[254] Or would have attained it before the end of six months beginning with the date on which the application for the employment had to be made.
[255] EQA 2010, Sch 9, para 9(1). See EE(A)R 2006, reg 7(4).
[256] EQA 2010, Sch 9, para 9(2). The reference to the normal retirement age is to be construed in accordance with ERA 1996, s 98ZH: EQA 2010, Sch 9, para 9(3).
[257] EN para 821.

retirement age or the age of 65 (if the employer has no normal retirement age) within six months of the application for employment.[258] For these purposes, the employer's normal retirement age must be 65 or over.[259]

Benefits based on length of service

7.104 It is not an age contravention for a person (A) to put a person (B) at a disadvantage when compared with another (C) in relation to the provision of a benefit, facility or service insofar as the disadvantage is because B has a shorter period of service than C.[260] If B's period of service exceeds 5 years, A may rely on this exception only if A reasonably believes that doing so fulfils a business need.[261] The reference to a benefit, facility or service does not include a reference to a benefit, facility or service which may be provided only by virtue of a person's ceasing to work.[262]

7.105 A person's period of service is whichever of the following A chooses. The first choice is the period for which the person has been working for A at or above a level (assessed by reference to the demands made on the person) that A reasonably regards as appropriate for the present purposes.[263] The second option is the period for which the person has been working for A at any level.[264] The period for which a person has been working for A must be based on the number of weeks during the whole or part of which the person has worked for A.[265] However, for that purpose A may, so far as is reasonable, discount periods of absence (or periods that A reasonably regards as related to periods of absence).[266]

7.106 The Explanatory Notes provide the following explication.[267] An employer does not have to justify paying or providing fewer benefits to a worker with less service than a comparator should such a practice constitute indirect discrimination because of age. The employer can rely on the exception as an absolute defence where the benefit in question was awarded in relation to service of 5 years or less. However, if the length of service exceeds 5 years, the

---

[258] EN para 822.
[259] EN para 823. It has the same meaning as in ERA 1996, s 98ZH.
[260] EQA 2010, Sch 9, para 10(1).
[261] EQA 2010, Sch 9, para 10(2).
[262] EQA 2010, Sch 9, para 10(7).
[263] EQA 2010, Sch 9, para 10(3)(a).
[264] EQA 2010, Sch 9, para 10(3)(b). For the purposes of Sch 9, para 10(3)(b), a person is to be treated as having worked for A during any period in which the person worked for a person other than A if (a) that period counts as a period of employment with A as a result of ERA 1996, s 218, or (b) if that does not apply, that period is treated as a period of employment by an enactment pursuant to which the person's employment was transferred to A: EQA 2010, Sch 9, para 10(6).
[265] EQA 2010, Sch 9, para 10(4).
[266] EQA 2010, Sch 9, para 10(5).
[267] EN paras 828–832.

exception applies only if it reasonably appears to an employer that the way in which it uses length of service to award benefits will fulfil a business need of its undertaking.[268]

7.107 It is suggested by the Explanatory Notes that this provision enables employers to continue to effect employment planning by being able to attract, retain and reward experienced staff through service-related benefits.[269] However, it cannot be used to justify the level of payments when a worker leaves. Service-related termination payments are not a reward for experience from which the employer can benefit. Redundancy payments are dealt with separately.

The national minimum wage: young workers

7.108 It is not an age contravention for a person to pay a young worker (A) at a lower rate than that at which the person pays an older worker (B) if the hourly rate for the national minimum wage for a person of A's age is lower than that for a person of B's age, and the rate at which A is paid is below the single hourly rate.[270] A young worker is a person who qualifies for the national minimum wage at a lower rate than the single hourly rate; and an older worker is a person who qualifies for the national minimum wage at a higher rate than that at which the young worker qualifies for it.[271]

The national minimum wage: apprentices

7.109 It is not an age contravention for a person to pay an apprentice who does not qualify for the national minimum wage at a lower rate than the person pays an apprentice who does.[272] An apprentice is a person who is employed under a contract of apprenticeship, or who is treated as employed under a contract of apprenticeship.[273]

Redundancy

7.110 It is not an age contravention for a person to give a qualifying employee an enhanced redundancy payment of an amount less than that of an enhanced redundancy payment which the person gives to another qualifying employee, if

---

[268] The intent is to replicate the effect of reg 32 of the 2006 Regulations (as amended by the Employment Equality (Age) Regulations 2006 (Amendment) Regulations 2008).

[269] EN para 833.

[270] EQA 2010, Sch 9, para 11(1). See EE(A)R 2006, reg 31 and EN paras 836–838. The single hourly rate is the rate prescribed under National Minimum Wage Act 1998, s 1(3): EQA 2010, Sch 9, para 11(3).

[271] EQA 2010, Sch 9, para 11(2).

[272] EQA 2010, Sch 9, para 12(1). See EE(A)R 2006, reg 31 and EN paras 839–840.

[273] EQA 2010, Sch 9, para 12(2) and National Minimum Wage Act 1998, s 3(2)(a) (persons not qualifying).

each amount is calculated on the same basis.[274] It is not an age contravention to give enhanced redundancy payments only to a person who is entitled to a statutory redundancy payment.[275]

7.111   A person is a qualifying employee if the person is entitled to a statutory redundancy payment;[276] or agrees to the termination of the employment in circumstances where the person would, if dismissed, have been so entitled; or would have been so entitled but for the statutory requirement for 2 years' continuous employment in order to qualify for a statutory redundancy payment;[277] or agrees to the termination of the employment in circumstances where the person would, if dismissed, have been so entitled but for that statutory requirement.[278]

7.112   An enhanced redundancy payment is a payment the amount of which is, subject to what follows, calculated in accordance with the amount of a statutory redundancy payment.[279] A person making a calculation for these purposes may treat a week's pay as not being subject to a maximum amount. They may treat a week's pay as being subject to a maximum amount above that of the statutory maximum of a week's pay.[280] They may multiply the appropriate amount for each year of employment by a figure of more than one.[281] Having made a calculation for these purposes, a person may multiply the amount calculated by a figure of more than one.[282]

Life assurance

7.113   Provision is made where a person (A) takes early retirement because of ill health.[283] It is not an age contravention to provide A with life assurance cover for the period starting when A retires and ending (if there is a normal retirement age) when A attains the normal retirement age or (in any other case) when A attains the age of 65.[284] The normal retirement age in relation to A is

---

[274]   EQA 2010, Sch 9, para 13(1). See EE(A)R 2006, reg 33 and EN paras 841–845.
[275]   EQA 2010, Sch 9, para 13(2).
[276]   Under ERA 1996, s 135.
[277]   ERA 1996, s 155.
[278]   EQA 2010, Sch 9, para 13(3).
[279]   ERA 1996, s 161(1)–(3); EQA 2010, Sch 9, para 13(4).
[280]   ERA 1996, s 227(1), currently £380 per week from 1 October 2009.
[281]   EQA 2010, Sch 9, para 13(5). The term 'the appropriate amount' here has the meaning given in ERA 1996, s 162 (amount of a statutory redundancy pay), and 'a week's pay' is to be read with Chapter 2 of Part 14 of that Act: EQA 2010, Sch 9, para 13(7). For the purposes of EQA 2010, Sch 9, para 13(4)–(6), the reference to 'the relevant date' in ERA 1996, s 162(1)(a) is, in the case of a person who is a qualifying employee by virtue of EQA 2010, Sch 9, para 13(3)(b) or (d), to be read as a reference to the date of the termination of the employment: EQA 2010, Sch 9, para 13(8).
[282]   EQA 2010, Sch 9, para 13(6).
[283]   EQA 2010, Sch 9, para 14(1). See Employment Equality (Age) Regulations 2006, reg 34 and EN paras 846–848.
[284]   EQA 2010, Sch 9, para 14(2).

the age at which, when A retires, persons holding comparable positions in the same undertaking are normally required to retire.[285]

Child care

7.114 A person does not contravene a relevant provision, so far as relating to age, only by providing (or making arrangements for or facilitating the provision of) care for children of a particular age group.[286] Facilitating the provision of care for a child includes paying for some or all of the cost of the provision; helping a parent of the child to find a suitable person to provide care for the child; or enabling a parent of the child to spend more time providing care for the child or otherwise assisting the parent with respect to the care that the parent provides for the child.[287] A child is a person who has not attained the age of 17.[288] A reference to care includes a reference to supervision.[289]

7.115 This exception has been introduced following the ruling of the European Court of Justice in *Coleman v Attridge Law*.[290] Otherwise, it would be direct discrimination for an employer to treat an employee less favourably because of the age of an employee's child. There is a potential impact on the provision of facilities (such as childcare) where access is limited by reference to the child's age. The exception will allow employers to continue to offer employees child care facilities based on the age of a child without being open to a challenge of direct discrimination from other employees.[291]

Contributions to personal pension schemes

7.116 A Minister of the Crown may by order provide that it is not an age contravention for an employer to maintain or use – with respect to contributions to personal pension schemes – practices, actions or decisions relating to age which are of a specified description.[292] An order authorising the

---

[285] EQA 2010, Sch 9, para 14(3).
[286] EQA 2010, Sch 9, para 15(1). The relevant provisions are EQA 2010, ss 39(2)(b), 41(1)(c), 44(2)(b), 45(2)(b), 47(2)(b), 48(2)(b), 49(6)(b), 50(6)(b), 57(2)(a), 58(3)(a): EQA 2010, Sch 9, para 15(2).
[287] EQA 2010, Sch 9, para 15(3).
[288] EQA 2010, Sch 9, para 15(4).
[289] EQA 2010, Sch 9, para 15(5).
[290] [2007] IRLR 88, EAT; (C-303/06) [2008] IRLR 722, ECJ; sub nom *EBR Attridge Law LLP v Coleman* [2010] IRLR 10, EAT.
[291] EN paras 849–852.
[292] EQA 2010, Sch 9, para 16(1). The term 'personal pension scheme' has the meaning given in Pension Schemes Act 1993, s 1; and 'employer', in relation to a personal pension scheme, has the meaning given in Pensions Act 2004, s 318(1): EQA 2010, Sch 9, para 16(3). A personal pension scheme means a pension scheme that is not an occupational pension scheme and which is one that is established by a person within the Finance Act 2004, s 154(1) (that is a person with permission to establish a personal pension scheme in the UK under Financial Services and Markets Act 2000). An employer in relation to a personal pension scheme, where direct payment arrangements exist in respect of one or more members of the scheme who are employees, means an employer with whom those arrangements exist.

use of practices, actions or decisions which are not in use before the order comes into force must not be made unless the Minister consults such persons as the Minister thinks appropriate.[293]

OTHER EXCEPTIONS

Non-contractual payments to women on maternity leave

7.117   An employer (A) must not discriminate against a person (B) as to the terms on which A offers B employment.[294] An employer (A) must not discriminate against an employee of A's (B) as to B's terms of employment; in the way A affords B access (or by not affording B access) to opportunities for promotion, transfer or training or for receiving any other benefit, facility or service; by dismissing B; or by subjecting B to any other detriment.[295] However, a person does not contravene those provisions, so far as relating to pregnancy and maternity, by depriving a woman who is on maternity leave of any benefit from the terms of her employment relating to pay.[296]

7.118   A benefit from the terms of a woman's employment relating to pay does not include a reference to maternity-related pay (including maternity-related pay that is increase-related); pay (including increase-related pay) in respect of times when she is not on maternity leave; or pay by way of bonus in respect of times when she is on compulsory maternity leave.[297] Pay is increase-related insofar as it is to be calculated by reference to increases in pay that the woman would have received had she not been on maternity leave.[298]

7.119   This exception to the prohibitions on pregnancy and maternity discrimination by employers allows an employer not to offer an employment applicant or provide an employee who is on maternity leave the benefits of the non-contractual terms and conditions of her employment.[299] It replicates the effect of provisions in the Sex Discrimination Act 1975. It does for non-contractual terms and conditions of employment relating to pay what is done for contractual terms in s 73 (maternity equality clause) of the EQA 2010. See Chapter 8.

---

[293]   EQA 2010, Sch 9, para 16(2). See EN paras 853–854 and Sch 2 to the EE(A)R 2006.
[294]   EQA 2010, s 39(1)(b).
[295]   EQA 2010, s 39(2).
[296]   EQA 2010, Sch 9, para 17(1). A reference to terms of her employment is a reference to terms of her employment that are not in her contract of employment, her contract of apprenticeship or her contract to do work personally: para 17(4). Pay means benefits that consist of the payment of money to an employee by way of wages or salary and that are not benefits whose provision is regulated by the contract: para 17(5).
[297]   EQA 2010, Sch 9, para 17(2). Maternity–related pay means pay to which a woman is entitled as a result of being pregnant or in respect of times when she is on maternity leave: para 17(6).
[298]   EQA 2010, Sch 9, para 17(3).
[299]   EN para 855.

Benefits dependent on marital status, etc

7.120 A person does not contravene Part 5 of the Act (work), so far as relating to sexual orientation, by doing anything which prevents or restricts a person who is not married from having access to a benefit, facility or service the right to which accrued before 5 December 2005[300] or which is payable in respect of periods of service before that date.[301] A person also does not contravene Part 5, so far as relating to sexual orientation, by providing married persons and civil partners (to the exclusion of all other persons) with access to a benefit, facility or service.[302]

7.121 This concerns a specific exception to the prohibition of discrimination because of sexual orientation in the field of employment and occupation.[303] The exception concerns the provision of benefits by reference to marital status in respect of periods of service before the coming into force of the Civil Partnership Act 2004. It also concerns benefits restricted to married persons and civil partners.

Provision of services etc to the public

7.122 A does not contravene a specified provision[304] in relation to the provision of a benefit, facility or service to B if A is concerned with the provision (for payment or not) of a benefit, facility or service of the same description to the public.[305] However, the exception does not apply if the provision by A to the public differs in a material respect from the provision by A to comparable persons,[306] or the provision to B is regulated by B's terms, or the benefit, facility or service relates to training.[307] B's terms means the terms of B's employment, or the terms on which the principal allows B to do the contract work, or the terms on which B has the position as a partner or member, or the terms of B's appointment to the office.[308] A reference to the public includes a reference to a section of the public which includes B.[309]

7.123 Thus an employer who provides services to the public at large is not liable for claims of discrimination or victimisation by an employee under Part 5 of the Act (work) in relation to those services.[310] Such claims must be brought under Part 3 of the Act (services and public functions). However, if the service

---

[300] The day on which Civil Partnership Act 2004, s 1 (which affords legal recognition to civil partnerships between two people of the same sex) came into force.
[301] EQA 2010, Sch 9, para 18(1).
[302] EQA 2010, Sch 9, para 18(2).
[303] EN paras 857–858. See EE(SO)R 2003, reg 25.
[304] The provisions are EQA 2010, ss 39(2), 39(4), 41(1), 41(3), 44(2), 44(6), 45(2), 45(6), 49(6), 49(8), 50(6), 50(7), 50(9) and 50(10): EQA 2010, Sch 9, para 19(2).
[305] EQA 2010, Sch 9, para 19(1).
[306] As defined in EQA 2010, para 19(4).
[307] EQA 2010, Sch 9, para 19(3).
[308] EQA 2010, Sch 9, para 19(5).
[309] EQA 2010, Sch 9, para 19(6).
[310] EN paras 859–860.

differs from that provided to other employees, or is provided under the terms and conditions of employment, or the service is to do with training, then the claim falls within Part 5 (work). These provisions also apply to services provided by principals, firms, limited liability partnerships and relevant persons (in respect of personal or public office holders). They replace similar provisions in the legacy legislation, except that they have now been extended to partnerships.

Insurance contracts, etc

7.124 It is not a contravention of Part 5 (work), so far as relating to relevant discrimination, to do anything in relation to an annuity, life insurance policy, accident insurance policy or similar matter involving the assessment of risk if the thing is done by reference to actuarial or other data from a source on which it is reasonable to rely and it is reasonable to do the thing.[311] Relevant discrimination here is gender reassignment discrimination; marriage and civil partnership discrimination; pregnancy and maternity discrimination; or sex discrimination.[312]

7.125 Where annuities, life assurance policies, accident insurance policies (or similar matters which involve the assessment of risk) are provided in the field of employment, employers are allowed to provide for payment of premiums or benefits that differ for men and women, persons who are or are not married or in a civil partnership, pregnancy or maternity, or gender reassignment so far as this is reasonable in the light of actuarial or other reliable data.[313] This provision replaces a similar exception in the Sex Discrimination Act 1975. It is designed to ensure that any employment-related insurance benefit is treated similarly to that provided by a financial services-provider relying upon the services exception in Part 5 of Sch 3 (services and public functions exceptions for insurance etc). Where an employer has relied on relevant information, any complaint about discrimination in relation to the policy is to be taken with the insurer in the county court rather than with the employer via the employment tribunal.

SUPPLEMENTARY PROVISIONS

Ships and hovercraft

7.126 Part 5 (work) applies in relation to work on ships, work on hovercraft, and seafarers only in such circumstances as are prescribed.[314] It does not matter

---

[311] EQA 2010, Sch 9, para 20(1).
[312] EQA 2010, Sch 9, para 20(2).
[313] EN paras 861–862.
[314] EQA 2010, s 81(1). 'Ship' has the same meaning as in the Merchant Shipping Act 1995 (that is, a ship includes every description of vessel used in navigation: see s 313(1) of the 1995 Act). 'Hovercraft' has the same meaning as in the Hovercraft Act 1968 (a hovercraft means a vehicle which is designed to be supported when in motion wholly or partly by air expelled from the vehicle to form a cushion of which the boundaries include the ground, water or other surface

whether employment arises or work is carried out within or outside the UK.[315] These provisions do not affect the application of any other provision of the EQA 2010 to conduct outside England and Wales or Scotland.[316]

7.127 The Explanatory Notes state that the employment provisions in Part 5 will apply to seafarers and the crew of hovercraft only in the way set out in regulations made by a Minister of the Crown.[317] The Act is silent on the territorial application of the employment provisions. This approach is thought to be acceptable for most workers, who at any given time are within either the territory of UK or some other territory. However, seafarers work on ships that may be constantly moving between waters under the jurisdiction of different States. Accordingly, the Minister is empowered to say to which seafarers on which ships (and to which crew on which hovercraft) the employment provisions apply in accordance with international law and custom and the global practices of the shipping industry. The Minister may make provision with regard to ships outside Great Britain. This replaces provisions concerning the territorial application and the pay of seafarers in the legacy legislation.

Offshore work

7.128 Her Majesty may by Order in Council provide that in the case of persons in offshore work specified provisions of Part 5 (work) apply (with or without modification).[318] Similarly, an Order in Council may provide that Northern Ireland legislation making provision for purposes corresponding to any of the purposes of Part 5 (work) applies (with or without modification).[319] The Order may provide for these provisions, as applied by the Order, to apply to individuals (whether or not British citizens) and bodies corporate (whether or not incorporated under the law of a part of the UK), whether or not such application affects activities outside the UK.[320] The Order may make provision for conferring jurisdiction on a specified court or class of court or on employment tribunals in respect of offences, causes of action or other matters arising in connection with offshore work.[321]

---

beneath the vehicle: see s 4(1) of the 1968 Act). 'Seafarer' means a person employed or engaged in any capacity on board a ship or hovercraft. See EQA 2010, s 81(3)–(5).

[315] EQA 2010, s 81(2).

[316] EQA 2010, s 81(6).

[317] EN paras 288–290.

[318] EQA 2010, s 82(1)(a).

[319] EQA 2010, s 82(1)(b). Northern Ireland legislation includes an enactment contained in, or in an instrument under, an Act that forms part of the law of Northern Ireland: EQA 2010, s 82(5).

[320] EQA 2010, s 82(2)(a).

[321] EQA 2010, s 82(2)(b). In the application to Northern Ireland of s 82(2)(b), the reference to employment tribunals is to be read as a reference to industrial tribunals: EQA 2010, s 82(8). The Order may exclude from the operation of the Territorial Waters Jurisdiction Act 1878, s 3 (consents required for prosecutions) proceedings for offences under the provisions mentioned in EQA 2010, s 82(1) in connection with offshore work: EQA 2010, s 82(2)(c). The Order may provide that such proceedings must not be brought without such consent as may be required by the Order: EQA 2010, s 82(2)(d).

7.129 Generally, offshore work is work for the purposes of activities in the territorial sea adjacent to the UK.[322] It also includes activities connected with the exploration of (or the exploitation of the natural resources of) the shore or bed of applicable waters or the subsoil beneath it.[323] Without prejudice to that generality, it also includes activities carried on from, by means of or on, or for purposes connected with, installations for the exploration or exploitation of mineral resources and the storage, etc of gas.[324] It also includes activities in relation to renewal energy installations at sea.[325] Work includes employment, contract work, a position as a partner or as a member of an LLP, or an appointment to a personal or public office.[326] Nothing in these provisions affects the application of any other provision of the 2010 Act to conduct outside England and Wales or Scotland.[327]

7.130 These provisions will enable protection to be extended to workers on offshore installations, such as oil and gas rigs and renewable energy installations (generally wind farms), to reflect the extent of current discrimination legislation.[328]

Employment

7.131 For the purposes of Part 5 (work), 'employment' means employment under a contract of employment, a contract of apprenticeship or a contract personally to do work.[329] It also includes Crown employment;[330] employment as a relevant member of the House of Commons staff;[331] and employment as a

---

[322] EQA 2010, s 82(3)(a).

[323] Petroleum Act 1998, s 11(2)(a). The applicable waters are tidal waters and parts of the sea in or adjacent to the UK up to the seaward limits of the territorial sea; waters in an area designated under the Continental Shelf Act 1964, s 1(7); waters in an area specified under the Petroleum Act 1998, s 10(8); and in relation to installations which are or have been maintained (or are intended to be established) in such waters, waters in a foreign sector of the continental shelf which are adjacent to such waters: Petroleum Act 1998, s 11(8). See EQA 2010, s 82(3)(b).

[324] Petroleum Act 1998, s 11(2)(b) and (3). See EQA 2010, s 82(3)(b).

[325] Energy Act 2004, s 87(1)(a) and (b). See EQA 2010, s 82(3)(c).

[326] EQA 2010, s 82(4).

[327] EQA 2010, s 82(9).

[328] EN paras 291–292.

[329] EQA 2010, s 83(1)–(2). See EN para 304. 'Relevant member of the House of Lords staff' has the meaning given in ERA 1996, s 194 (which provides that such a member of staff is an employee of the Corporate Officer of the House of Lords): EQA 2010, s 83(6).

[330] 'Crown employment' has the meaning given in ERA 1996, s 191 (employment under or for the purposes of a government department or any officer or body exercising on behalf of the Crown functions conferred by a statutory provision): EQA 2010, s 83(9).

[331] 'Relevant member of the House of Commons staff' has the meaning given in ERA 1996, s 195 (any person who was appointed by the House of Commons Commission or is employed in the refreshment department or who is a member of the Speaker's personal staff). Such a member of staff is an employee of the person who is the employer of that member under ERA 1996, s 195(6) or, if ERA 1996, s 195(7) applies in the case of that member, the person who is the employer of that member under ERA 1996, s 195(7) (that is where the House of Commons Commission or the Speaker has designated a person as the employer of that member of staff): EQA 2010, s 83(5).

relevant member of the House of Lords staff.[332] This replicates pre-existing definitions of employment in discrimination legislation.[333]

7.132 Part 5 applies to service in the armed forces as it applies to employment by a private person.[334] For that purpose, references to terms of employment, or to a contract of employment, are to be read as including references to terms of service, and references to associated employers are to be ignored.[335]

7.133 A reference to an employer or an employee, or to employing or being employed, generally follows from these core definitions.[336] A reference to an employer also includes a reference to a person who has no employees but is seeking to employ one or more other persons.[337] However, the term 'employer' in relation to an occupational pension scheme means the employer of persons in the description or category of employment to which the scheme in question relates.[338]

7.134 In the case of a person in Crown employment, or in employment as a relevant member of the House of Commons staff, a reference to the person's dismissal is a reference to the termination of the person's employment.[339] A reference to a personal or public office, or to an appointment to a personal or public office, is to be construed in accordance with s 52 (public offices: interpretation and exceptions).[340]

---

[332] EQA 2010, s 83(1)–(2). See EN para 293. 'Relevant member of the House of Lords staff' has the meaning given in ERA 1996, s 194 (which provides that such a member of staff is an employee of the Corporate Officer of the House of Lords): EQA 2010, s 83(6).

[333] SDA 1975, s 82(1); RRA 1976, s 78(1); DDA 1995, s 68(1). See: *Quinnen v Hovells* [1984] IRLR 227, EAT; *Mirror Group Newspapers Ltd v Gunning* [1986] IRLR 27, CA; *BP Chemicals Ltd v Gillick* [1995] IRLR 128, EAT; *Hall v Woolston Hall Leisure Ltd* [2000] IRLR 578, CA; *Burton v Higham t/a Ace Appointments* [2003] IRLR 257, EAT; *South East Sheffield CAB v Grayson* [2004] IRLR 353, EAT; *Mingeley v Pennock and Ivory* [2004] IRLR 373, CA; *Percy v Church of Scotland Board of National Mission* [2006] IRLR 195, HL.

[334] EQA 2010, s 83(3).

[335] EQA 2010, s 83(3).

[336] However, subject to s 212(11), they are to be read with s 83(2) (definition of employment) and s 83(3) (service in the armed forces): EQA 2010, s 83(4).

[337] EQA 2010, s 83(4).

[338] EQA 2010, s 212(11) and Pensions Act 1995, s 124.

[339] EQA 2010, s 83(7).

[340] EQA 2010, s 83(8).

Chapter 8

EQUALITY OF TERMS

INTRODUCTION

8.1 The title of the Equality Act 2010 (EQA 2010), Part 5, Chapter 3 is Equality of Terms. This is a more accurate description of content than its predecessor's title, the Equal Pay Act 1970 (EqPA 1970), since both cover all the terms of the employment contract. However, Chapter 3 relates only to equality on grounds of gender, pregnancy and maternity, rather than all protected characteristics, so there is still potential for confusion. If the complaint is that an employee was paid less because she is black, or contractually entitled to less holiday because he is disabled, the cause of action is under Chapter 1 s 39(2) and not ss 64–83.

8.2 A claim for equality of terms is pursued by enforcing a provision incorporated into the contract of employment to be known as a sex equality clause (or sex equality rule for occupational pension schemes). There is intended to be no overlap between these provisions and those covering gender discrimination which is not governed by the employment contract (for example, non-promotion of a better qualified woman), but one new section may permit or encourage claims to be brought under both chapters.[1]

8.3 The terminology now is that a woman can enforce a sex equality clause or rule where she is engaged on 'equal work'. This is a phrase not previously found in the legislation although it has been in common parlance. It encompasses the three ways in which work can be shown to be equal: that it is like work, work rated as equivalent or work of equal value to that done by the male comparator. There is an important substantive change from the previous law in that a claimant who establishes work rated as equivalent to that performed by her comparator is entitled to equality of terms even where the term was not determined by the evaluation.[2]

8.4 Where there is equal work, the sex equality clause will have no effect if the employer shows that the difference in terms is because of a material factor. This defence is reformulated to merge the different definitions in the EqPA

---

[1] EQA 2010, s 71 providing for hypothetical comparisons where there is direct sex discrimination in pay.

[2] EQA 2010, s 66(4).

1970 and the Pensions Act 1995. It also intends to reflect the effect of European Community (EC) law in respect of the objective justification of indirectly discriminatory factors.[3]

8.5   New provisions which have achieved considerable publicity operate so as to:

- permit actual or potential claimants to talk about their terms of employment with colleagues, despite any prohibition by the employer; and

- empower the minister to make regulations requiring large, private-sector employers to publish information about the gender pay gap.

8.6   EU law is of enormous relevance to any consideration of equal pay law. Article 157 of the Treaty on the Functioning of the European Union (TFEU) creates directly enforceable rights which have effect both horizontally and vertically.[4] This means that individual claimants may rely upon it (and interpretations given to it by the European Court of Justice (ECJ)) in claims against private employers as well as those in the public sector.[5] The prevalent view is that employment tribunals, as creatures of statute,[6] do not have jurisdiction to determine claims founded purely on Art 157. Instead, they operate by disapplying incompatible provisions of English law (for example, limits on the extent of recovery), so as to ensure insofar as possible that domestic law complies with the requirements of EU law.[7] This view has been doubted in respect of specialist employment bodies in consequence of a ruling of the ECJ in the context of the Fixed-Term Workers Directive.[8] The court held that a specialist body must have jurisdiction to determine arguments based on the directive itself. Article 157 was fleshed out by Council Directive 75/117 on the application of the principle of equal pay for men and women. That was replaced from 15 August 2009 when, along with other gender-based equal treatment directives, it was repealed and recast as the Equal Treatment Directive 2006/54. The recasting did not purport to make substantive changes in respect of equal pay law.

8.7   The Equality and Human Rights Commission will publish a statutory code of practice on equal pay to replace that produced by the Equal Opportunities Commission in 2003 for the EqPA 1970. At present there is a draft code, published for consultation purposes on the basis of the Equality Bill

---

3   EN para 243.
4   This revised Treaty is the one agreed at Lisbon which came into effect on 1 December 2009. The relevant provisions were first Art 117 of the Treaty of Rome and later Art 141 of the European Union Treaty.
5   See for example: *Barry v Midland Bank plc* [1997] ICR 192, EAT upheld [1995] IRLR , HL.
6   Deriving their powers from what is now Employment Tribunals Act 1996. This provides for tribunals to have power to determine claims under various statutes and statutory instruments but not the EU Treaty or the TFEU.
7   See for example: *Staffordshire County Council v Barber* [1996] IRLR 209, CA; *Marshall v Southampton and South West Hampshire Area Health Authority (No 2)* [1993] IRLR 445, ECJ.
8   *Impact v Minister for Agriculture and Food* [2008] IRLR 552, ECJ.

as introduced into the House of Lords on 4 December 2009. There will be differences between the current draft and the final version perhaps in consequence of consultation and certainly because the Bill itself underwent some significant amendments in the Lords. For this reason and because the present draft is more like another version of the Explanatory Notes than earlier statutory codes, which concentrated on encouraging good practice, references to the code are not included alongside the discussion of the sections of EQA 2010. When it is published in final form it will have the usual persuasive force of statutory codes so that any breaches may be relied upon as evidence which claimants may ask the tribunal to take into account.

SEX EQUALITY

Relevant types of work

8.8   The head-note to EQA 2010, s 64 ('Relevant types of work') is unhelpful: it really means relevant types of worker, that is, those who are entitled to claim equality of terms. They are identified in s 64(1) as being: (a) persons employed on work equal to that done by a comparator of the opposite sex; (b) persons holding a personal or public office doing work equal to that of a comparator of the opposite sex. This is a new formulation, but makes no change to the previous law.

8.9   Section 64(2) specifies that references in s 64(1) to work done by comparators are not restricted to work done contemporaneously with that of the claimant. This is a new provision, designed to clarify the range of potential comparators in line with existing case law.[9]

Who may claim? The meaning of employment

8.10   The meaning of 'employed' is fleshed out in EQA 2010, s 83(2). It is the usual wide formulation associated with discrimination legislation, rather than the narrower definition associated with unfair dismissal claims. So it covers:

- employment under a contract of employment, a contract of apprenticeship or a contract personally to do any work;

- Crown employment, in accordance with ERA 1996, s 191;

- employment in the Houses of Parliament, in accordance with ERA 1996, ss 194 and 195; and

- service in the armed forces.

---

[9]   EN para 234 enacting the effect of *Macarthys Ltd v Smith* [1979] IRLR 316, CA, although that encompassed only predecessors and the new wording appears potentially wider.

8.11 None of this is new. It comes from the EqPA 1970 as amended over the years to comply with EU law. Some work relationships have been held not to fall within it — for example agency arrangements[10] and franchises[11] — but the definition is broad enough to include some who would be workers or even self-employed rather than true employees. One clear essential is that there must be an obligation of personal performance, in respect of which general employment law principles apply.[12]

8.12 Office-holders were included by an amendment which inserted s 1(6A)–(6C) into the EqPA 1970. Personal office-holders are those appointed to discharge the duties of an office or post personally; public office-holders are those appointed by ministers, government departments or the devolved assemblies.[13] EqPA 1970, s 1(8) expressly excluded people holding statutory office (such as judges), but this was unenforceable as contrary to EC law[14] and is not replicated.[15]

8.13 The wide scope of employment and related provisions means that claims may be brought by building-site labourers, detective constables or judicial office holders as well as those who are more obviously employees. They may compare themselves to persons of the opposite sex engaged in similar roles, vastly different roles ('chalk and cheese' comparisons) and with those who did the job before them.

EQUAL WORK

8.14 EQA 2010, s 65(1) defines the work of a woman (A) as being equal to that of her comparator (B) if it is: (a) like B's work; (b) rated as equivalent to B's work; or (c) of equal value to B's work. These terms are further refined in the section and through case law. None of them is new or changed, although the composite concept of 'equal work' was not previously used in statute.

Like work

8.15 EQA 2010, s 65(2) defines work as like work if: (a) the work done by claimant and comparator is the same or broadly similar; and (b) such differences as there are between their work are not of practical importance in relation to the terms of their work. Section 65(3) provides that in comparing the work it is necessary to have regard to: (a) the frequency with which differences occur in practice, and (b) the nature and extent of the differences.

---

10 *Mirror Group Newspapers Ltd v Gunning* [1986] IRLR 27, CA.
11 *Patterson v Legal Services Commission* [2004] IRLR 153, CA.
12 See for example: *Byrne Brothers (Formwork) Ltd v Baird* [2002] IRLR 96, EAT.
13 See EQA 2010, s 83(8) referring back to s 52 and thence to s 48.
14 *Perceval-Price v Department of Economic Development* [2000] IRLR 380, NICA.
15 See EQA 2010, s 80(2)(b), which makes no exclusions.

8.16 This is unchanged from its original formulation in EqPA 1970. Although it is a limited right, it appears to have been applied with relatively little trouble by tribunals in the 35 years since the EqPA 1970 came into effect and there is delightfully little case-law.

8.17 The leading authorities are still *Capper Pass v Lawton*[16] and *Waddington v Leicester Council for Voluntary Services.*[17] They are relied upon as establishing that the tribunal must undertake a two-stage test:

- The first stage is for the tribunal to consider whether the nature of the work is the same or broadly similar. This requires merely a broad, general consideration, avoiding a pedantic approach;

- The second stage requires the tribunal to analyse the details of the work more closely and to determine:
  - the differences, if any, in the tasks actually performed;[18]
  - the frequency or otherwise with which such differences occur in practice;[19]
  - the nature and extent of any such differences.

In this analysis, the tribunal must carefully scrutinise the whole content of the relevant jobs. The similarities, as well as the dissimilarities, are relevant and over-concentration on the latter would tend to provide a skewed understanding of the roles. It is not simply a question of enumerating the differences (and similarities): the tribunal will need to consider whether the different tasks really make different demands on the employees.[20] If one employee walks to the shops and the other to the bank; one orders furniture and the other stationery and computers, it will be necessary to establish whether this is merely a difference of routes or knowledge of different suppliers and catalogues or whether one of the tasks requires greater responsibility, wider or deeper specialist knowledge and so on. The information is necessary for the next part of the assessment.

8.18 In practice, like work determinations really demand a three-stage test. Once the tribunal has analysed and established the nature and extent of similarities and differences in tasks and demands (the second stage), it must

---

16 [1976] IRLR 366, EAT.
17 [1977] IRLR 32, EAT.
18 Thus the concentration is on the work really done, not that which the contract may theoretically require. See *Shields v Coomes (Holdings) Ltd* [1978] IRLR 263, CA, where the proper approach was to disregard the security function never actually performed by male betting shop employees; *Electrolux Ltd v Hutchinson* [1976] IRLR 410, EAT, correct to regard only the additional duties (for example, overtime) which the employer proved the men were actually required to do.
19 This will include an assessment of the amount of time occupied by the different tasks. See *Redland Roof Tiles Ltd v Harper* [1977] ICR 349, EAT: the fact that the man had acted up to a supervisory role for a few weeks was a matter which the tribunal properly noted, but which did not prevent a finding of like work.
20 *Eaton Ltd v Nuttall* [1977] IRLR 71, CA.

next enquire: are those differences of practical importance in relation to the terms of their work? The tribunal is concerned to decide whether it would expect the differences which it has identified to cause a difference in pay (and/or holidays or other contractual benefits, depending on what is being claimed). One approved approach is to consider whether the differences would be expected to put the jobs in different grades on a job evaluation study.[21] Another might be to look at the breadth of the differences in demands made on the employees which are already encompassed within a particular pay band by the employer, a matter which will not require additional evidence if the claimant has pursued her claim against a few comparators who are paid the same as each other but whose jobs make identifiably varying demands on them. This is an area where representatives (and employment judges) may well consider that the knowledge and experience of the non-legal members of a tribunal could be particularly useful.

8.19 It is proposed to identify, below, the sorts of differences which have and have not been found to be differences of practical importance in respect of pay, but it must be borne in mind that:

- cases in this area are peculiarly fact-sensitive; and

- reported cases often move from a finding that there were some identified differences to a conclusion on like work, without what is described as the stage three analysis above;

- tribunals have not always been particularly skilled at separating the differences which are relevant for the like work analysis from those which are relevant to the material factor defence.

Despite judicial assertion that the same matters can affect both whether there is equal work and whether the material factor defence is established, it seems better to recognise that they are different issues to be determined by different facts (which is not to suggest that an employer who attaches the wrong label should be prevented at any stage from relying on what it has pleaded).

8.20 The following have been held to constitute differences which have not prevented a finding of like work:

- comparator trainee manager acting up into transport manager's role for a few weeks each year when the manager was on holiday whereas the claimant, who had taught him the job, did not;[22]

- claimant driving only inside the factory grounds whereas the comparator sometimes drove outside;[23]

---

[21]   *British Leyland Ltd v Powell* [1978] IRLR 57, EAT, approved by the Court of Appeal in *Shields v Coomes (Holdings) Ltd* [1978] IRLR 263, CA.

[22]   *Redland Roof Tiles* [1977] ICR 349, EAT.

[23]   *British Leyland* [1978] IRLR 57, EAT.

- claimants working a two-shift system whereas comparators were on a three-shift system (including nights, which were not then permissible for women).[24]

8.21 The following have been held to constitute differences which have prevented a finding of like work:

- the exercise of greater responsibility by a senior clerk than a junior clerk[25] and by a man working alone and unsupervised (on night-shift) than women working in the day;[26]

- men working away from the storeroom for more than a day a week whereas women worked there full-time;[27]

- the exercise of greater skill;[28]

- the use of greater physical strength.[29]

8.22 The issue of the time at which work is done has proved tricky, but the settled view now appears to be that it is generally irrelevant to the work done,[30] although it might provide a proper explanation (and thus a material factor defence) for the payment of shift premiums. The time at which the work is done should only be relevant to the like work decision where some other aspect related to it contributes to the demands made on the comparator and so tends to undermine the like work assessment, as in *Thomas v National Coal Board*.[31]

8.23 What happens if the claimant does more work than the comparator? The cases are contradictory. In *Waddington v Leicester Council for Voluntary Service*,[32] the EAT remitted for the consideration of the employment tribunal the question whether the claimant's greater responsibilities meant that she was not employed on like work with the comparator. Yet in *SITA (UK) Ltd v Hope*,[33] the EAT held that the claim of a woman, who had previously been

---

24   *Dugdale v Kraft Foods Ltd* [1977] IRLR 368, EAT.
25   *Eaton Ltd v Nuttall* [1976] IRLR 71, EAT: he was responsible for higher value items, so a mistake would be more significant. See also *Capper Pass Ltd v Allan* [1980] ICR 194, EAT: male canteen assistant handled more money.
26   *Thomas v National Coal Board* [1987] IRLR 368, EAT.
27   *Dorothy Perkins Ltd v Dance* [1977] IRLR 222, EAT.
28   *Brodie v Startrite Engineering Co Ltd* [1976] IRLR 101: male (but not female) drill operator selected his tools, set his machine and did minor repairs.
29   *Noble v David Gold and Son (Holdings) Ltd* [1980] IRLR 252, CA – although this must not be based on mere assumption by the employer.
30   *National Coal Board v Sherwin* [1978] IRLR 122, EAT; *Dugdale v Kraft Foods Ltd* [1976] IRLR 368, EAT.
31   [1987] IRLR 368, EAT.
32   [1977] ICR 32, EAT, where the claimant community leader supervised her comparator, the higher paid male play leader.
33   UKEAT 0787/04.

deputy to a man and was then paid less than his salary when she took over without a deputy, could not be defeated by the fact that she did more work than he had done.

8.24 The practical example of like work given in the Explanatory Notes (at para 225) is that male and female supermarket employees who perform similar tasks which require similar skills will be doing like work even though the men may lift heavier objects from time to time. This is because the differences are not of practical importance in relation to their terms of employment.

Work rated as equivalent

8.25 The second basis upon which a claim for equal pay may be pursued is when the claimant's work is 'rated as equivalent' to that of a man: EQA 2010, s 65(1)(b). Work is rated as equivalent, according to s 65(4), if a job evaluation study: (a) gives an equal value to the jobs in terms of the demands made on the worker, or (b) would give an equal value in those terms if the evaluation were not made on a sex-specific system. A system is sex-specific if, for the purposes of one or more of the demands made on a worker, it sets different values for men from those it sets for women: s 65(5). There is thus room for a tribunal to hold that a claimant succeeds because although her work was given a lower value, it would have been given an equal value on a non-discriminatory scheme.

Definition of job evaluation study

8.26 Section 80 contains the interpretation provisions for this Chapter of the EQA 2010 and s 80(5) provides that a job evaluation study is a study undertaken with a view to evaluating, in terms of the demands made on a person by reference to factors such as effort, skill and decision-making, the jobs done: (a) by some or all of the workers in an undertaking or group of undertakings, or (b) by some or all of the members of the armed forces.

8.27 This is not the place to expound the forms and method of job evaluations:[34] it suffices to say that they are intended for present purposes to be an analytical method for ranking jobs, for pay and/or grading. The aim is that the system, its application and its results will be rational and objective,[35] although it is generally recognised that there is a considerable degree of art

---

[34] There is a short summary in *IDS Employment Law Handbook on Equal Pay* (November 2008) 134–135 taken from the appendix to the judgment in *Eaton Ltd v Nuttall* [1977] IRLR 71, EAT. A fuller, helpful source is Michael Armstrong, Ann Cummins and Sue Hastings, *Job Evaluation Handbook: A Guide to Achieving Equal Pay* (Kogan Page, 2005). The EOC's *Good Practice Guide – Job Evaluation Schemes Free of Sex Bias*, last updated in 2003, is also useful, and the EHRC has similar online Advice and Guidance concerning Job Evaluations. There is also an ACAS guide, *Job Evaluations: Considerations and Risks*.

[35] 'Thorough in analysis and capable of impartial application' per Phillips J in *Eaton Ltd v Nuttall* [1976] IRLR 71, EAT and see also the ECJ in *Rummler v Dato-Druck GmbH* [1987] IRLR 32, ECJ, referring to the requirements of Directive 75/117EC, now recast in 2006/54 EC.

(rather than pure science) in job evaluations.[36] They become less reliable if non-analytical methods are used – for example a straightforward whole job comparison – because the tendency is to be subjective and preserve the status quo, as also happens if a 'felt fair' stage is incorporated into otherwise analytical systems.

8.28 What is here contemplated is a job evaluation study undertaken by an employer, usually with the involvement of relevant trade unions or employees and probably in the absence of a current legal claim for equal pay. The Explanatory Notes suggest that an equality clause would operate in the following circumstances:

'A job evaluation study rated the jobs of women and their better paid male comparators as not equivalent. If the study had not given undue weight to the skills involved in the men's jobs, it would have rated them as equivalent.'[37]

Although there is some variation in terminology in EQA 2010, s 65(4) and (5) from that in EqPA 1970, ss 1(2)(b) and 1(5), no change to the substantive law was intended.[38]

---

[36]   *Arnold v Beecham Group Ltd* [1982] IRLR 307, EAT; *Bromley v H&J Quick Ltd* [1988] IRLR 249, CA.

[37]   EN para 225. It is not clear how this example properly fits the statutory exception which requires the evaluation to have been made on a 'sex-specific system'. EQA 2010, s 65(4)(b) requires the 'system' (presumably the scheme itself, not merely the study – that is, the analysis of the relevant jobs) to be discriminatory, and s 65(5) defines the only manner in which such discrimination can arise. But the example relates to an individual study and does not suggest that the scheme was flawed, merely its application. It is further not apparent why the EQA 2010 has maintained two different definitions of and thus tests for unacceptable sex discrimination in job evaluation studies, namely this 'sex-specific system' test and that set out at s 131(7) in connection with avoiding the early defeat of an equal value claim. See **8.45** and footnotes 86–89.

[38]   EN para 225. This is seen by some as a missed opportunity, because the formulation which seeks to enable a claimant to overcome the problem of the employer's use of a discriminatory job evaluation scheme was too blunt an instrument to achieve its purpose. Job evaluation schemes in the twenty-first century do not usually offend because they set different values on demands for men and women – that would be altogether too crude, although see the positive discrimination ideas mooted in order to achieve equality between men and women for physical effort criteria in *Rummler v Dato-Druck GmbH* [1987] IRLR 32, ECJ. Instead, they err because the factors under which the job demands are analysed are not appropriate, or not appropriately defined, to capture all the demands of all the jobs; or because they capture some of the demands more than once (for example, by attempting to score separately for responsibility and decision-making, but defining them so that they overlap); or because they elide and thus underscore two separate aspects of some of the jobs; or because they are so confused or complex that they cannot be systematically and confidently applied. Further, they may fall into error in application by omitting parts of some jobs from the job description and/or the evaluation; by including tasks no longer performed for others and so on. Where these errors adversely affect the evaluation of the lower-paid job, the leeway permitted by EQA 2010, s 65(5) does not enable an employee to ask a tribunal to correct the defects so as to achieve a proper, fair score which eliminates the discriminatory under-evaluation and award equal pay, if parity is achieved (see *Green v Broxtowe District Council* [1977] IRLR 34, EAT; *England v Bromley London Borough Council* [1978] ICR 1, EAT). Rather, the claimant has to:
– commence a claim under the equal value provisions;
– persuade a tribunal that her claim is a fit one to proceed despite the fact that her work and

8.29 Assuming that there is a satisfactory job evaluation study, the following points are clearly established by case-law:

- a woman is employed on equal work if she actually scores higher than the man;[39]

- a woman will be engaged on equal work if she scores less than the man, but enough to come within the same pre-defined band or score bracket which the job evaluation scheme established for pay purposes;[40]

- absent such a band, coming close will not suffice and the 'near miss' claimant will lose.[41]

Recent developments in this area

8.30 The job evaluation process grew out of the time and motion studies of the 1950s and 1960s which, in effect, persuaded people that the demands of jobs could be enumerated and measured. Under the EqPA 1970 it was intended to encourage employers to move voluntarily to non-discriminatory pay structures in an organised manner. The carrot was that employers would then be less likely to face equal pay claims with their attendant expense and disruption. Through the 1980s and 1990s some large employers, in particular local authorities and health authorities, faced increasing claims from women graded or paid on one system (such as the White Book for local authorities) comparing themselves to men graded under another (the Purple, Green or Red books). This comparison could only be performed through an equal value claim (see following paragraphs). In the hope of avoiding such *ad hoc* claims, these large public employers determined to carry through a sector-wide job evaluation study. In local authorities it is known as Agenda for Change and in health authorities as Single Status. A decade or so on from the initial moves, it appears that the actual schemes may be fine and the outcomes satisfactory.

---

that of her comparator have been given a different value (presumably a lower value) on a job evaluation study. The EQA 2010 here retains the specific provision from EqPA 1970, s 2A(2A), so the claimant must establish that the job evaluation scheme or its application (or both) discriminated 'because of sex' or was otherwise unreliable. See EQA 2010, s 131(6). The phrase 'discriminates because of sex' is different from EqPA 1970, s 2A(2A), which had the more usual 'discriminates on grounds of sex';

– continue through the full rigours of an equal value claim with its attendant delays and multiplicity of hearings.

[39] *Redcar and Cleveland Borough Council v Bainbridge* [2008] IRLR 984, CA. It may appear astonishing that this point was litigated at all (and so recently) but EqPA 1970, s 1(5) provided that a woman was employed on work rated as equivalent 'if, but only if, her job and their job have been given an equal value ...' on a job evaluation study. The new wording omits the caveat, perhaps to accept the *Redcar* point.

[40] *Springboard Sunderland Trust v Robson* [1992] IRLR 261, EAT.

[41] *Home Office v Bailey* [2005] IRLR 757, EAT (reversed on other grounds [2005] IRLR 369, CA). Tribunals cannot engage in setting a 90% wage for the claimant who scores 90%, although where the employer proves that the material factor defence accounts for 10% of the pay difference, they may award a 90% wage for a claimant who scores 100% match with her male comparator: see *Enderby v Frenchay Health Authority* [1993] IRLR 593, ECJ.

However, huge problems have arisen in respect of pay protection and back pay. Tens of thousands of claims have been presented and are still being presented by women who:

- sought to rely on the job evaluation analysis to claim 6 years' arrears of pay at the higher rate which they had achieved under the Agenda for Change or Single Status evaluation;[42] and/or

- claimed that they should receive the same pay as men with whom they were now rated equal but who had previously been rated higher and were either on a protected higher rate or paid a lump sum to buy out their acquired expectations.

These claims are still making their way through the legal system, throwing up numerous procedural and substantive issues in respect of time limits and the effect of TUPE transfers,[43] grievances,[44] sex discrimination by trade unions[45] and by employers in agreement with trade unions,[46] and the overlap or difference between job evaluation and the equal value assessment.[47]

8.31 These latter cases establish that the mere fact that jobs in, say, 2006 have been rated equivalent on a job evaluation scheme:

- cannot be relied upon to claim back pay before the scheme was effective. That is, there is no retrospectivity under this head, even if the jobs have not changed;

- does not mean that the work must be work of equal value now or at any time in the previous 6 years, even if the jobs have not changed. At most, the result of the job evaluation study will be of evidential value.[48]

However, where the woman actually scored slightly fewer points, the tribunal may be able to conclude, even without expert evidence, that the jobs were of

---

[42] That is, relying on the EqPA 1970, ss 2(4),(5) and 2ZA-C remedies provisions, as amended to achieve compliance with EC law in July 2003.

[43] *Gutridge v Sodhexo Ltd* [2009] IRLR 721, CA.

[44] Under the now repealed provisions of the Employment Act 2002 and the Dispute Resolution Regulations 2004. New grievance issues may be expected under TULR(C)A 1992, s 199 and the ACAS Code of Practice on Disciplinary and Grievance Procedures 2009, in force from 6 April 2009, but they will go to remedy only and not to the jurisdiction of the tribunal.

[45] *Allen v GMB* [2008] IRLR 690, CA.

[46] *Redcar and Cleveland Borough Council v Bainbridge, Surtees v Middlesbrough Borough Council* [2008] IRLR 776, CA, in pay protection arrangements for the previously higher-paid male grades which excluded the previously disadvantaged lower paid female grades.

[47] *Redcar and Cleveland Borough Council v Bainbridge* [2007] IRLR 984, CA; *Hovell v Ashford and St Peter's Hospital NHS Trust* [2009] IRLR 734, CA, as to which see the next paragraphs.

[48] Both points from *Redcar and Cleveland Borough Council v Bainbridge* [2007] IRLR 984, CA.

equal value (because of the differences between job evaluation studies and equal value assessments, as to which see below), but it is not bound so to conclude.[49]

Work of equal value

8.32 The third basis for an equal pay claim is where the claimant's work:

- is neither like work nor work rated as equivalent to that of her comparator; but

- is equal to the comparator's in terms of the demands made on the claimant by reference to factors such as effort, skill and decision-making.

This is EQA 2010, s 65(1)(c) read with s 65(6). It is similar to EqPA 1970, s 1(2)(c), inserted in 1983 after the ECJ had held that the failure to permit such a claim unless the employer had voluntarily carried out a job evaluation study left the UK in breach of EC requirements.[50] The only identifiable difference is that 'decision-making' is used instead of 'decision', a sensible linguistic correction.

Distinction between job evaluation studies and equal value assessments

8.33 The equal value claim is for claimants who are not employed on like work with a suitable comparator of the opposite sex[51] and in respect of whom there is no existing job evaluation study or none which compares their work to that of the chosen comparator.[52] It effectively requires an analytical comparison of the work performed by claimants and comparators to be performed on a one-off basis for or by the tribunal, rather than a general comparison across the whole range of jobs (or some identifiable part of the range) such as would be undertaken for a job evaluation study.[53]

---

[49]   The Court of Appeal rejecting what seems a bold submission on behalf of the claimants in *Hovell v Ashford and St Peter's Hospital NHS Trust* [2009] IRLR 734.

[50]   *EC Commission v United Kingdom of Great Britain and Northern Ireland* [1982] IRLR 333, ECJ.

[51]   Claims may be brought by women working alongside an equally poorly paid man: the existence of such a person does not prohibit the choice of a different man employed on other work as the comparator: see *Pickstone v Freemans plc* [1988] IRLR 357, HL.

[52]   Perhaps because clerical jobs have been graded on one study and labouring or technical jobs on another.

[53]   The main differences between job evaluation generally and the equal value assessment are:
– job evaluation is usually done for a wide population of workers, expecting to create a ranking system for many jobs, whereas an equal value assessment is limited to the work of the claimant(s) and any chosen comparator(s). Instead of creating an organised pay and grading structure across the whole or part of the workforce, there is a risk that it will highlight inequalities and create an outcome which leaves the previous pay structure disrupted and out of balance;
– job evaluation is mostly intended to be introduced consensually, so will tend to involve employers and workers, often through unions or other representatives, whereas the equal value

Quality of performance irrelevant (at this stage)

8.34 The quality of an employee's performance is not relevant for equal value purposes (or for like work or work rated as equivalent cases).[54] The work is assessed on the basis of adequate or appropriate performance, for several reasons. First, it is the work not the worker which is being evaluated. If the claimant or comparator left, the evaluation should still hold for their replacement. Secondly, the pay rate or grade will usually have been set before the worker commenced work, so will not have been affected by the performance. Thirdly, if performance is relevant to pay, the proper place to consider it would be as part of the material factor defence.[55] Exceptionally one could envisage that an employer might prove that a particular worker had been given more (or less) work because of earlier exceptional performance. In such circumstances, provided the assessment of performance was not based on discriminatory assumptions, or the increased allocation to the comparator was not made in consequence of preliminary enquiries about equal pay by the claimant,[56] the comparison of the work itself might not meet the equal value test. The quality of performance of the actual jobs done is still irrelevant.

---

claim will usually be resisted by employers – so it is an antagonistic process rather than a co-operative one;

– job evaluation studies are usually conducted on the basis of a pre-existing scheme, whether or not modified for the special circumstances of the jobs being considered. They may use established schemes created by large commercial companies such as Hay or PriceWaterhouseCooper. The equal value assessment (at least where there are not vast numbers of jobs under consideration) lends itself better to a scheme which is devised with the relevant jobs in mind, so that it may more precisely capture the demands than would occur with a scheme which pre-allocated points for factors irrelevant to both or all the jobs in issue. Thus, for example, it can ignore responsibility for cash, adverse physical conditions and so on if concerned solely with clerical or administrative tasks performed in one building;

– large analytical job evaluation studies almost certainly require the use of a points-based scoring system; the use of such a system to compare a few jobs for an equal value assessment (particularly where they are not very dissimilar) may be artificial and may operate so as to highlight insignificant differences which would normally be assessed as equal, so that a simple 'more than/equal to/less than' process may work better;

– job evaluation schemes will usually involve the creation of pay bands, grades or brackets, so that employees with a range of scores may be entitled to equal pay although it is recognised that some have lower demands made on them. For equal value purposes, equal means equal, not substantially or nearly equal. Although a tribunal may be persuaded that a marginal difference in points, where the equal value assessment has used a points-based system, does not mean that the demands are not equal, some explanation (probably from an expert, although the tribunal may fall back on the 'art not science' rationale) will be required;

– job evaluation studies do not usually involve lawyers; equal value assessments almost always do.

54 *E Coomes (Holdings) Ltd v Shields* [1978] IRLR 263, CA at 266.
55 This should be apparent from the terminology of the EQA 2010, but it was reinforced by the ECJ in *Brunnhofer v Bank der österreichischen Postsparkasse AG* [2001] IRLR 571.
56 It may sometimes be appropriate to consider the work done at a period before the claim was commenced if the claimant establishes that her tasks were reduced once she had alerted her boss or the HR department to a breach of the equality clause. The (now repealed) statutory disputes procedure and the promotion within the ACAS Code of Practice on Disciplinary and Grievance Procedures of both informal and formal internal grievances before commencing tribunal claims (for example, at para 31) should not provide a breathing space for employers to undermine equal pay claims.

Practical problems

8.35   The progress of claims brought on the basis of work of equal value has tended to be incredibly complex, prolonged and expensive.[57] There are five main reasons for this:

- the complexity of the procedure;

- the role and use of independent experts;

- the variable experience and expertise and limited resources of employment tribunals. The perception of some users is that tribunals have been overwhelmed by the administrative and judicial demands of equal value claims and have made errors which result in delay and increased expense,[58] sometimes combined with the EAT or higher courts remitting claims for re-hearing a couple of years down the line;[59]

- claims which have been brought on behalf of huge numbers of claimants.[60] Some have representatives, some may not; some withdraw instructions and/or their representatives cease to act mid-claim; some lose contact with their representatives and/or the tribunal. They have proved difficult for representatives, tribunal administration and judiciary;

- successful claims are likely to cost employers large amounts in back-pay and forward pay, for which they have not budgeted and do not have the money, so they have tended to raise every possible technical and substantive defence at every possible level.[61]

---

[57]   See Lord Bridge in *Leverton v Clywd County Council* [1989] IRLR 28 at 33. On the other hand, Peter Allen, a determined TGWU representative in Hull (now retired), brought a series of successful claims for fish packers and processors through the 1980s and claimed never to know what all the fuss was about.

[58]   Andrew Hochhauser QC proposing that 'Tribunals are not fit for purpose' at a debate in the Royal Albert Hall in September 2007; 'Employment Regulation: Up to the Job?' British Chamber of Commerce, 16 March 2010. For example, determining to have an independent expert but failing to require ACAS to instruct one; failing to send the expert's factual findings to the parties in advance of the stage 2 hearing; failing to promulgate orders in time for compliance by the next hearing. The employment tribunal judiciary has taken steps to overcome perceived problems by creating special training programmes for judges who will hear equal pay cases.

[59]   *Home Office v Bailey and others* [2005] IRLR 757, EAT concluding appeals in claims commenced in 1999 and previously remitted in 2002.

[60]   For example, some 2,500 speech and language therapists in the *Enderby v Frenchay Health Authority and Secretary of State for Health* litigation from 1988 to 2003 and the multiple NHS and local authority claims through the first decade of the twenty-first century.

[61]   So that, for example, cases may go to the higher courts and/or the ECJ more than once: see *Enderby* [1993] IRLR 591, ECJ.

8.36 From 1 October 2004 to 6 April 2009 additional delays and complications were caused by challenges to claims in respect of non-compliance with the statutory grievance procedures.[62] And a desire to avoid being accused of selling women short in discriminatory fashion[63] has meant that legal representatives, employers, unions and ACAS are tending to settle fewer cases that might be expected. Finally, the judicial mediation scheme offered through employment tribunals[64] is not available for equal pay claims.

8.37 The procedure has required and continues to permit the appointment of an 'independent expert' to prepare an evaluation of the work of claimant and comparator.[65] Independent experts are appointed by ACAS to a panel: they are not employees and the function is a part-time one.[66] Many have other full-time jobs; some are retired. When an independent expert is required, ACAS officers enquire amongst those on the panel to ascertain who is available; whose geographical area is suited to the work (or who is prepared to travel); whose experience is suited to the task and so on. Thus the actual allocation of task to expert can take a few weeks (or longer in view of the small number of experts, their limited availability and the huge amount of work that has piled up).[67] There are no recognised qualifications[68] and the methods to be used were left largely to the experts, which produced reports of very variable quality.[69] On the other hand, time has moved on: the strictures of tribunals and greater experience undoubtedly mean that standards are now higher.

8.38 The use of an independent expert was essential in claims from 1983–1996 (once they had passed the 'hopeless case?' stage). By amendments to the EqPA 1970, in 1996 tribunals were given greater discretion and could proceed to a substantive decision without an independent expert.[70] Where independent

---

[62] The now repealed parts of the Employment Act 2002 and the associated Dispute Resolution Regulations, SI 2004/752, in respect of which cases are still being litigated.

[63] In the light of *Allen v GMB* [2008] IRLR 690, CA.

[64] Initially in three regions on a trial basis, but nationwide from 5 January 2009. Judicial mediation is regarded as a form of case management, since it is not otherwise established by legislation.

[65] Now EQA 2010, s 131(2). In statutory language, a report on the question whether the jobs are of equal value.

[66] EQA 2010, s 131(8). The Tribunal Service pays their fees and expenses. Communication is between the tribunal clerk (for the Secretary to the Tribunal) and the independent expert, once appointed, as if the expert were a party: Employment Tribunals (Constitution and Rules of Procedure) Regulations 2004 (Employment Tribunal Rules 2004), SI 2004/1861, Sch 6, para 10(4).

[67] A matter not obviously borne in mind by those who devised the indicative timetable which forms part of Employment Tribunal Rules 2004, Sch 6. Additional independent experts have recently been appointed.

[68] Although for a while in the 1990s the Equal Value Advisory Network ran training courses, with input from the TUC (and having invited it from the CBI). ACAS itself provides some training for those whom it has already appointed.

[69] For example, evaluations performed without the independent expert having created a job description (list of tasks) for the jobs under consideration, even where the parties were not in agreement about job content, so that it was impossible to know what was being evaluated; or evaluations which patently omitted some of the tasks that were in the job description.

[70] Which would usually mean that they relied upon experts put forward by one or both parties.

experts were used, the tribunal would accept their factual conclusions (essentially, about job content) as absolute and any report put forward by a party's expert had to be based on the independent expert's facts, unless they were shown to be in error. This meant that in a few cases an additional hearing was required because one (or sometimes both) party disagreed with the independent expert on a significant issue of fact and could only advance its case if the tribunal were persuaded to correct the independent expert's factual conclusions. So there would be evidence, submissions, deliberations, a judgment – and sometimes the expert would have to go away and re-do part of his report.[71] By further amendment to the EqPA 1970 and the Employment Tribunal Rules 2004, Sch 6, the expert's role was very significantly prescribed and the primary right to determine issues of fact was removed from independent experts and given to tribunals.[72]

Present procedure: Employment Tribunal Rules 2004 and EQA 2010, s 131

8.39 Schedule 6 of the Employment Tribunal Rules 2004 applies only to equal value claims. The rules in Sch 6 'modify and complement' those in Sch 1 and if there is a conflict, Sch 6 prevails.[73] They prescribe an intended three-stage procedure.[74] Section 131 of the EQA 2010 sets out additional procedural and substantive law applicable only in equal value claims.

8.40 Stage 1 in most cases is effectively a case management stage.[75] The employment judge will make orders for the conduct of the next part of the proceedings and will usually make the important procedural decision whether or not to appoint an independent expert and, if appointed, whether to order the independent expert to assist in determining the facts on which the equal value report will ultimately be based.[76] In some cases, substantive decisions may be made at stage 1, namely:

---

[71] In its consultation in 2003–04 the Government perceived this to be such a cause of delay that it proposed to remove the fact-finding function from independent experts – and did.

[72] Employment Tribunal Rules 2004, Sch 6, rr 6 and 7(3).

[73] Rule 16(4) and Sch 6, r 1.

[74] And a wonderfully optimistic indicative timetable which aims to have the case completed within 25 weeks if no independent expert is appointed (thus meeting the administrative target for a final Hearing within 26 weeks) or 37 weeks if there is an independent expert.

[75] This has been recognised by an amendment to Employment Tribunal Rules 2004, Sch 6, r 4 with effect from April 2009, enabling employment judges to conduct this stage sitting alone. Either party may still request a full tribunal, as they probably would if any significant substantive matter were to be determined.

[76] Independent experts are very keen to be involved in investigating (interviewing, visiting the premises, reading contemporaneous documents – all as they did for two decades under the previous rules) and fact-finding, rather than having to write a report on the basis of facts found by the tribunal. The analogy is that you would not expect a GP to diagnose a child accurately on the basis of a description of the symptoms from a third party. The harshness of any exclusion of the independent expert from fact-finding is ameliorated somewhat by r 7(6) which permits the independent expert to apply at any stage to have the facts amended, supplemented or omitted.

- whether to strike out the claim (or part of it) where the claimant's work has been given a lower value than that of a comparator on a job evaluation study (a pre-hearing review function);[77]

- the early determination of any material factor defence.

In practice, it is inconceivable that either of these could happen if the stage 1 hearing is held 3 to 4 weeks after the receipt of the response, in accordance with the indicative timetable, because it will first become apparent in the response and will require disclosure of documents, the creation of a bundle, witness statements etc.

8.41 More likely is that there may be a two-part stage 1 hearing or an ordinary case management discussion before the stage 1 hearing, so that the material factor defence can properly be identified and determined before the full rigours of the merits of the equal value aspect are undertaken. This course may commend itself where:

- it could provide a knock-out blow to all or most claims in a short hearing;[78] or

- the equal value aspects appear weak but the material factor potentially has substance.

Of course, some claims look weak only because of ingrained ideas about the value of work which have tended to undervalue 'women's work'[79] and if the defence is considered first it can only be on the basis that the work is assumed to be work of equal value (because it is being used to explain the pay differential).

8.42 Stage 2 is the fact-finding stage at which the tribunal determines any facts not agreed by the parties, on the basis of which the independent expert (if used) will be required to prepare the report on the question of equal value.[80] Subject to the independent expert's right to apply for the facts to be varied,[81] the facts determined at this stage will be the only ones relied upon by the tribunal in respect of the equal value question. It is also at the stage 2 hearing

---

[77] In accordance with EQA 2010, s 131(5)–(7).

[78] Although predicting that is not necessarily easy and some have gone to the ECJ, holding up the assessment of jobs which were finally evaluated about a decade after the case commenced.

[79] For example, Vauxhall Motors assumed that women employees could sew and thus regarded their operation of complex, computerised sewing machines as unskilled work; in another case school welfare assistants were not allocated points that were available for adverse working conditions even though they had to clean premises, toilets and pupils of vomit and faeces, because they were 'only dealing with children': *Lucas, Salter and Stedman v East Sussex County Council* (Southampton ET 1990).

[80] Employment Tribunal Rules 2004, Sch 6, rr 7 and 8.

[81] Employment Tribunal Rules 2004, Sch 6, r 7(6).

that the tribunal may exercise the power to strike out where the claimant's work has been given a lower value than that of her comparator on a job evaluation study.

8.43 Stage 3 (not actually so called) is the Hearing, at which the tribunal will decide whether or not the jobs, or some of them, are of equal value. It does so having received the report of the independent expert and/or any other expert reports as evidence. The report of the independent expert may be excluded from evidence if it is not based on the facts determined in accordance with the rules (that is, those found by the tribunal at stage 2), in which case the tribunal may determine the question without an independent expert or require another from the panel to prepare a report.[82]

8.44 In practice, the procedure seldom occurs as envisaged above. There are several reasons, but one significant issue is that claimants often bring claims in the alternative. 'My work is like work or work of equal value' is a very common pleading. Since the equal value claim may only proceed if the work is not like work,[83] the like work issue has to be determined first. So there will be a case management discussion under Sch 1, r 10, and orders about comparators, disclosure etc, and a Hearing with a full tribunal at which the tribunal will determine any disputed facts in order to decide whether or not there is like work. If the claimant is unsuccessful, the tribunal has already gone past stages 1 and 2 without making any decisions about, or (in principle) having had the opportunity to involve, an independent expert. It may choose not to appoint one[84] or it may then appoint one, send the like work reasons as a summary of the relevant facts and wait to see if the expert applies to have the facts amended.[85]

Effect of previous job evaluation study

8.45 EQA 2010, s 131(5)–(7) provides that the tribunal must determine that the woman's work is not of equal value to that of the male comparator if they have been given different values by a job evaluation study. This is intended to provide a complete defence for an employer who has attempted to do things properly. A claimant may only circumvent it if the tribunal concludes that there are reasonable grounds for suspecting that the evaluation contained in the study: (a) was based on a system that discriminates because of sex; or (b) is otherwise unreliable.[86] The definition of a system that discriminates because of sex is one in which a difference (or coincidence) between values that the system

---

82 Employment Tribunal Rules 2004, Sch 6, r 9. Rules about the expert's conduct, the ability to replace her and the choice of continuing with no independent expert if the first has proved unsatisfactory were introduced from 1 October 2004: SI 2004/2352.

83 EQA 2010, s 65(6).

84 Which is likely only to be wise where the parties (or one of them) will use their own expert, since tribunals are not generally well-versed in assessing the demands of jobs, even if some non-legal members have had some experience.

85 This is a difficult area, since any substantial changes might tend to undermine the tribunal's conclusion on like work.

86 EQA 2010, s 131(6).

sets on different demands is not justifiable regardless of the sex of the person on whom the demands are made.[87] The wording is little changed from EqPA 1970, s 2A(2A), although that used 'on grounds of sex'.[88] The employer bears the burden of persuading the tribunal that the system should not be suspected of discriminating.[89]

8.46 It will probably be easier for a claimant to establish that there were reasonable grounds for concluding that the employer's job evaluation was unreliable because, for example, it did not evaluate the work she actually did, but only a benchmark job so that some of her work was omitted from the evaluation; or the assessment was out of date and did not take account of technological changes in the jobs;[90] or the male comparators no longer do some of the tasks that were attributed to them. A non-analytical job evaluation will not be a reliable one for these purposes.[91]

8.47 One further reason why the procedure becomes protracted is that Sch 6, r 11 makes clear that parties may, with permission from the tribunal, use their own expert evidence instead of, or as well as, any evidence obtained from an independent expert. There are procedural constraints about not challenging the facts and advance disclosure, but these may be relaxed if necessary to do justice.[92] The independent expert's report is not conclusive on any issue, although it is likely to weigh heavily with the tribunal unless its evidential value is undermined because of problems which one or both parties have identified to the tribunal in respect of the system used, the actual evaluations or some failure to incorporate the facts identified by the tribunal. This may be done through cross-examination (the independent expert being in effect the tribunal's witness and thus liable to cross-examination by both parties) and/or the production of different, persuasive expert evidence in accordance with the rules. If three experts (one independent and two called by the parties) each give evidence which attacks that of the others and propounds their own methodology,

---

[87] EQA 2010, s 131(7).

[88] EN para 439 makes nothing of the difference ('This provision replaces similar provisions ...'), implying that no change is intended. It is also unclear why different terminology is used here from that in EQA 2010, s 65(4) and (5), which make provision for a claim to succeed on a work rated as equivalent basis if the work would have been rated equal absent the use of a sex-specific system in the evaluation.

[89] *Bromley v H&J Quick Ltd* [1988] IRLR 249, CA, decided under previous wording when the test was whether there were reasonable grounds for holding that the system was discriminatory (whereas from October 2004 the tribunal only has to have reasonable grounds for suspecting discrimination).

[90] This is the example in EN para 439.

[91] *Bromley v H&J Quick Ltd* [1988] IRLR 249, CA, because it will not properly assess the job under demand heads.

[92] See *Middlesbrough Borough Council v Surtees (No 2)* [2007] IRLR 981, EAT, where the need to challenge the independent expert's methodology only became clear when he presented his report, so that claimants could not have provided a relevant report at the same time as the independent expert, as required by Employment Tribunal Rules 2004, Sch 6, r 11(3) and(4).

particularly if it is done in respect of several jobs, we may easily recognise that there will be numerous multi-day hearings.[93]

8.48 Despite the caveats and criticisms, the equal value provisions have enabled a wide range of comparisons over the years: speech therapists with pharmacists; carers with estate wardens; print-checkers with printers; bank till operators with uniformed guides at bank doors.

Sex equality clause

8.49 The mechanism by which the contractual terms of men and women, relating to work, are equalised is set out at EQA 2010, s 66. Terms of work, if they do not include a sex equality clause, are to be treated as including one.[94] A sex equality clause is a provision which: (a) modifies any term of the woman's which is less favourable than that of the man, to make it not less favourable; (b) modifies the woman's terms so as to include any term she does not have, so that it corresponds to one that the man has.[95]

8.50 This section is designed to replicate the previous EqPA 1970 provisions[96] when read with s 80(2) which defines 'terms' as the terms in a contract of employment or apprenticeship or contract to do work personally. These provisions apply to membership of and rights under an occupational pension scheme only insofar as a sex equality rule would have effect in relation to those terms.[97]

Meaning of a 'term' of the contract

8.51 The question 'what is a term?' is answered by case-law. In *Hayward v Cammell Laird Shipbuilders Ltd*[98] the House of Lords made clear that the law requires a term-by-term comparison. Where men received higher pay, the employer could not claim that it was balanced or equalised by the fact that the women had the benefit of other terms relating to paid meal breaks, sick pay and holidays which the men did not enjoy or not at such good levels. The phrase 'any term' in the EqPA 1970 (repeated in EQA 2010) meant a distinct provision or part of a contract with sufficient content to make it possible to compare it as a benefit with a similar provision in another contract.[99] If there is real difference in the amount of working time (due to longer daily or weekly hours, shorter holidays or term-time only work for example), it will be

---

93   In the *Enderby* speech therapist claims, each of the three lead cases lasted more than a week in the tribunal at this stage.
94   EQA 2010, s 66(1).
95   EQA 2010, s 66(2).
96   EN para 230.
97   EQA 2010, s 66(3).
98   [1988] ICR 464, HL.
99   See also to like effect the ECJ in *Barber,* above, referring to the need for genuine transparency in pay structures, and *Jämställdhetsmbudsmannen v Örebro Läns Landsting* [2000] IRLR 421 refusing to allow the employer of a midwife to count her inconvenient hours supplement as part of the salary for comparison purposes.

appropriate to compare the basic hourly rate, calculating it from the annual salary, if necessary.[100] That will enable a proper comparison of the terms relating to financial remuneration. On the other hand, where bonuses or allowances that were originally for a particular purpose (for example, good performance or 100% attendance) have come to be paid almost automatically to comparators, it will be appropriate to treat them as part of the basic hourly rate for the comparison to be fairly performed.[101]

8.52 In practical terms most cases have been concerned with monetary pay on an hourly or annual basis. Multiple claims against local authorities (even before the single status multiples) focused on male employees who had acquired bonuses and allowances, often in periods of a pay freeze, which had gradually been incorporated into their regular pay. But other benefits may also be pursued. For example, a male employee has a term which permits him to use the employer's vehicle for private purposes outside work hours; a female colleague does not have that term. The sex equality clause will incorporate it into her terms.[102]

Effect of job evaluation study which has not been implemented

8.53 It had been held that in order to have the necessary effect a job evaluation study must be accepted as valid by the employer, although it may not have been implemented.[103] This anomaly is removed by EQA 2010, s 66(4) which provides that in work rated as equivalent cases the claimant may claim equality in respect of terms whether or not they have been determined by the rating of the work. So once the study is complete, whether the employer (and/or union) accepts or implements it is irrelevant: a claimant may rely on it.

Sex equality rule: occupational pension schemes

8.54 In respect of occupational pension schemes,[104] a sex equality rule is to be treated as included if not actually included. It has the effect that it: (a) modifies

---

[100] *Leverton v Clywd County Council* [1989] IRLR 28, HL.

[101] *Degnan v Redcar and Cleveland Borough Council* [2005] IRLR 615, CA, holding that the bonus and allowance had become part of the monetary payment for the performance of the contract during normal working hours. The court noted that, if it were otherwise, the women could claim an equal hourly rate plus the best bonus paid to one comparator and the best allowance paid to another, thus achieving higher pay than, rather than equal pay with, any individual comparator, which was not intended by the EqPA 1970. This potential for 'leapfrogging' was feared after *Hayward* but does not seem to have occurred – and it seems likely that courts will be astute to prevent it.

[102] This is the example at EN para 230.

[103] *O'Brien v Sim-Chem Ltd* [1980] IRLR 373, HL and *Arnold v Beecham Group Ltd* [1982] IRLR 307, EAT. This interpretation was based on an oddity of phrasing in EqPA 1970 whereby s 1(2)(b)(ii) enabled a woman to claim equality on a work rated as equivalent basis only in respect of a term 'determined by the rating of the work'. Lord Russell in *O'Brien* felt compelled to say 'This beats me', when trying to determine what it meant, but both the House of Lords in *O'Brien* and the EAT in *Arnold* decided that the employer had accepted the study and that it should therefore be regarded as determining the pay.

[104] All in EQA 2010, s 67.

any relevant term of the woman's which is less favourable than that of the man, to make it not less favourable; (b) modifies terms relating to the exercise of a relevant discretion so that the discretion cannot be exercised in a way which is less favourable to the woman.

8.55 Relevant terms are those on which persons become members of the scheme and on which members of the scheme are treated (including terms affecting the benefits of dependents) and a relevant discretion is one capable of affecting those things. Where a relevant matter (that is, term, discretion or the exercise of any discretion) has a different effect depending on family, marital or civil partnership status, the comparison must be on a like-for-like basis. All this is designed to replicate Pensions Act 1995, s 62[105] and the temporal limits resulting from ECJ decisions are specifically included, so that terms relating to becoming members of the scheme are only modified from 8 April 1976[106] and those relating to treatment from 17 May 1990.[107]

8.56 In respect of occupational pension schemes, EQA 2010, s 68 empowers trustees or managers by resolution to make sex equality alterations to the scheme, where they could not otherwise do so or only after complex or protracted procedures or with consents which would be unduly difficult or slow to obtain. The permitted alterations are those required to secure conformity with a sex equality rule and the effect may be backdated. All this replaces equivalent provisions in the Pensions Act 1995, s 65.

8.57 If the scheme rules of a large occupational pension scheme require consultation with all the members before the rules can be amended, this will be a complex, time-consuming process. It will be impracticable, particularly where some deferred members cannot be traced. Under EQA 2010, s 68 the trustees may make the alterations needed to comply with a sex equality rule without going through the scheme's procedure.[108]

Material factor defence

8.58 The provisions of EqPA 1970, s 1(3) and Pensions Act 1995, s 62(4) are drawn together into EQA 2010, s 69 which rewrites the material factor defence 'and clarifies the way' it is to be applied.[109] The new section provides that the sex equality clause has no effect in relation to a difference between the claimant's and comparator's terms if the responsible person[110] shows that the difference is because of a material factor reliance on which:

---

[105] EN para 235.
[106] The date of the ECJ ruling in *Defrenne v Sabena (No 2)* [1976] ICR 547 concerning the direct effect of Art 141 (then 117 and now 157).
[107] The date of the ECJ ruling in *Barber v Guardian Royal Exchange Assurance Group* [1990] IRLR 240, to the effect that pensions are pay for Art 141 purposes.
[108] This is the example at EN para 239.
[109] EN para 243.
[110] The phrase 'responsible person' is not defined in the final version of the EQA 2010. In an earlier draft it was the employer (or the person responsible for paying remuneration in respect of a personal or public office holder), with no provision made for anyone else (for example, a

(a) does not involve treating the claimant less favourably because of her sex than the responsible person treats the comparator,[111] (that is, direct sex discrimination must be disproved); and

(b) if the claimant shows that as a result of the factor she and women doing work equal to hers are put at a particular disadvantage when compared to men doing equal work,[112] the responsible person shows that relying on the factor is a proportionate means of achieving a legitimate aim[113] (that is, indirect sex discrimination must be objectively justified).

8.59 The factor is not material unless it is a difference between the claimant's case and that of her comparator.[114] The sex equality clause (for pension schemes) has no effect if the trustees or managers show that the difference in a relevant matter is because of a material factor which is not the difference of sex.[115]

8.60 The law relating to the material factor defence is extensive but the original intention is simple to state. The EqPA 1970 aimed to outlaw sex discrimination in respect of terms and conditions of employment.[116] Not all differences in contractual terms between men and women employed on equal work were prohibited, just those where the employer could not establish some actual reason for the difference (other than sex). In terms of the burden of proof, once a claimant proved equal work, a less favourable term and a difference of gender: 'a rebuttable presumption of sex discrimination arises . . . and . . . the burden passes to the employer to show that the explanation for the variation is not tainted with sex.'[117]

8.61 Section 1(3) of the EqPA 1970 required the employer to establish that the difference was 'genuinely' due to the material factor. 'Genuinely' has been deliberately omitted from the new section: 'because the adverb added nothing to the meaning of the requirement, which is the employer's obligation to show

---

government department or local authority) to be a responsible person. Some aspects of remuneration which the ECJ regards as pay are set by these public authorities, such as provisions in respect of redundancy pay. See *R v Secretary of State for Social Services, ex p Clarke* [1988] IRLR 22 HC. EN paras 240–244 refer only to the employer as the person who may show the reason for the difference (save in respect of pension schemes).

[111] EQA 2010 s 69(1)(a). The different formulation (EqPA 1970 had 'which is not the difference of sex') merely mirrors the change to the definition of direct discrimination generally: see EQA 2010, s 13(1).

[112] EQA 2010, s 69(2).

[113] EQA 2010, s 69(1)(b).

[114] EQA 2010, s 69(6).

[115] EQA 2010, s 69(4).

[116] See the short statement of purpose in the EqPA 1970.

[117] Per Lord Nicholls in *Glasgow City Council v Marshall* [2000] IRLR 272 at 242. See also much older cases, *National Vulcan Engineering Insurance Group Ltd v Wade* [1978] IRLR 225, CA and, clarifying that the employer bore the burden in respect of all aspects of the defence, *Financial Times Ltd v Byrne (No 2)* [1992] IRLR 163, EAT.

that the reason for the difference is genuine and not a sham.'[118] So the analysis of Lord Nicholls in *Marshall* (note 117) is still definitive.

8.62 In order to discharge the burden the employer (or other responsible person) must prove:

- first, that the proffered explanation or reason is genuine and not a sham or pretence;

- secondly, that the less favourable treatment is due to this reason. This is a causal test: the factor must be the cause of the disparity, otherwise it will not be a 'material' factor (meaning a significant and relevant factor), as required by the fourth step below;

- thirdly, that the reason is not 'the difference of sex'. Citing what was EqPA 1970, s 1(3), Lord Nicholls said: 'This phrase is apt to embrace any form of sex discrimination, whether direct or indirect.'

- fourthly, that the factor is a 'material' factor, namely one which is a significant and relevant difference between the woman's case and the man's case.

The corollary of all this is that the employer who satisfies the third requirement is under no obligation to prove a 'good' reason for the pay difference. Absent sex discrimination, the employer is not required to provide objective justification for the pay disparity.[119]

Indirect sex discrimination and the 'taint of sex'

8.63 In dealing with the material factor defence, tribunals and courts have frequently recognised that the employer will be undone if the factor is 'tainted with sex' and that unjustified indirect sex discrimination (as disparate adverse impact or having 'disparately adverse effect', per Lord Nicholls) was as incapable as direct discrimination of founding a defence.[120] Building on the

---

[118] EN para 243. Nonetheless, the removal may well be thought unhelpful to claimants, since 'genuinely' was so recently treated as a very telling and useful concept: see *Hartlepool Borough Council v Dolphin* [2009] IRLR 168, EAT.

[119] Claimants' representatives have subsequently argued that this is wrong because *dicta* of the ECJ in *Brunnhofer v Bank der Österreichischen Postsparkasse AG* [2001] IRLR 571 meant that there had to be objective justification in all cases once the threshold was passed and the burden of proof had shifted. The question has been considered in the EAT in five cases: one division of the EAT in *Sharp v Caledonia Group Services Ltd* [2006] IRLR 4 agreed with the claimant-friendly interpretation; the later four, perhaps most powerfully under Elias P (as he then was) in *Villalba v Merrill Lynch & Co Inc* [2006] IRLR 437 and most recently in *Middlesbrough Borough Council v Surtees (No 2)* [2007] IRLR 981 have all restated the test propounded by Lord Nicholls.

[120] Indirect discrimination was not mentioned in EqPA 1970, s 1(3), so this was entirely a construct of the judiciary, but a necessary one since it was founded on Art 157 (then 119) and decisions of the ECJ: see Lord Keith in *Rainey v Greater Glasgow Health Board* [1987] IRLR 26, HL, following the ECJ in *Bilka Kaufhaus GmbH v Weber von Hartz* [1986] IRLR 317;

'taint of sex' phrase, it was held that the concept of indirect discrimination for equal pay purposes is wider than that for sex discrimination generally: see Cox J in *Ministry of Defence v Armstrong*.[121]

8.64 All the issues which arise in indirect discrimination claims have troubled courts and tribunals in equal pay claims. It will always be useful to cross-check with those chapters, particularly for indirect sex discrimination. What follows is a summary of those issues.

- What is the proper pool for comparison?[122] Broadly speaking, those who have some interest in the advantage or disadvantage in question, rather than the whole of the workforce if they are not potentially touched by it (so, in *Pike*, retired teachers, some of whom would not have their part-time work counted for pension purposes, rather than all teachers);

- What information or statistics show disparate adverse impact?[123] Generally, this will be a matter for the tribunal, which should be clear when the pool is established;

- What does the employer have to do to satisfy the tribunal that indirect sex discrimination was justified? See the cases at footnotes 117–121 and the following discussion.

8.65 EC directives have defined indirect discrimination variably over the years, but gradually settled on the formula now at Art 2(1)(b) of Directive 2006/54/EC (the recast directive), with which our domestic legislation intends to comply. The description of disparate impact is a tight match with EQA 2010, s 19, since both refer to the application of 'provision, criterion or practice' which puts the claimant and her pool at 'a particular disadvantage'. When it comes to proof of objective justification, the EC wording is not followed. The Directive requires that the provision, criterion or practice is objectively justified by:

- a legitimate aim; and

British Coal Corporation v Smith [1994] 342, CA, affirmed [1996] IRLR 404, HL (objective justification required where statistics show a significant difference in pay between a group almost exclusively female and a group almost exclusively male doing equal work); *Bailey v Home Office* [2005] IRLR 369, CA (also where the lower paid group is significantly, but not predominantly, female and the higher paid group is predominantly male).

[121] [2004] IRLR 672, EAT.

[122] *Rutherford v Secretary of State for Trade and Industry (No 2)* [2006] IRLR 551, HL, a decision which has caused much puzzlement: see *British Medical Association v Choudhary* [2007] IRLR 800, CA and *Grundy v British Airways plc* [2008] IRLR 74 CA); *Somerset County Council v Pike* [2009] IRLR 870.

[123] *R v Secretary of State for Trade and Industry, ex p Seymour-Smith* [1999] IRLR 253, ECJ and *Rutherford*, above. See also the difficult case *Armstrong v Newcastle upon Tyne NHS Hospital Trust* [2006] IRLR 124, CA and, recently putting *Armstrong* in its place, *Gibson v Sheffield City Council* [2010] IRLR 311, CA.

- the means of achieving that aim are appropriate; and

- the means are also necessary.

In EC parlance, appropriate carries the connotation of proportionality and balancing. So the EC asserts a clear, three-fold test in which each part is separately identified.

8.66 In respect of justifying indirect discrimination for equal pay at EQA 2010, s 69(2) (as at s 19 for indirect discrimination generally), the EQA 2010 requires the respondent to show only that relying on the material factor is a proportionate means of achieving a legitimate aim. So our domestic legislation establishes just a two-step test: the EC 'necessary' step is omitted. However, the Explanatory Notes assert: 'The section incorporates the effect of EC law in respect of objective justification of indirectly discriminatory factors.'[124] The difference should not matter in practice, because tribunals are bound to apply national law in a manner which conforms with EC law. So the employer must actually show that it is necessary for him to apply the disadvantageous factor and it requires more vigilance by parties, practitioners and the judiciary to ensure that the correct terminology is used, the proper test applied and a correct result achieved (or an unnecessary opportunity for appeal avoided).[125]

8.67 Examples of all this in practice abound. It has been recognised that paying part-timers less (whether directly per hour or by exclusion from pension schemes) is usually a breach of the equal pay provisions which will not be justified unless the objective test is met;[126] the operation of pay protection schemes may be challenged[127] and although occasional personal, red-circling may be objectively justified[128] usually it should be time-limited;[129] separate collective bargaining mechanisms may explain but not without more constitute the cause of pay differentials which are otherwise unjustified[130] and the opposition of unions to steps which would remove pay inequality does not

---

[124] EN para 243. This may seem surprising if we recall how unattractive English courts have found the notion that an employer must show that something is necessary. They have determined that necessary does not mean necessary in the sense of the only way of doing something, but just 'reasonably necessary': see, e g *Hardys and Hansons plc v Lax* [2005] IRLR 726, CA.

[125] See recently the EAT in *Pulham v London Borough of Barking and Dagenham* [2010] IRLR 184, EAT.

[126] *Jenkins v Kingsgate (Clothing Productions) Ltd (No 2)* [1981] IRLR 228, ECJ and the pension litigation, *Vroege v NCIV Instituut voor Volkshuisvesting BV* [1994] IRLR 651, ECJ and *Preston v Wolverhampton Healthcare NHS Trust* [1998] IRLR 197, HL. Claims now could be pursued under the Part-time Workers (Prevention of Less Favourable Treatment) Regulations 2000, SI 2000/1551.

[127] *Redcar and Cleveland Borough Council v Bainbridge* [2008] IRLR 776, CA.

[128] *Methven v Cow Industrial Polymers Ltd* [1980] IRLR 289, CA: long-serving, older, infirm male employee transferred to lighter duties on a protected wage.

[129] In accordance with good industrial practice: *Outlook Supplies Ltd v Parry* [1978] IRLR 12, EAT; *Home Office v Bailey* [2005] IRLR 757, EAT.

[130] *Enderby v Frenchay Health Authority* [1993] IRLR 591, ECJ; *British Airways plc v Grundy (No 2)* [2008] IRLR 815, CA.

establish justification.[131] In the *Danfoss* case,[132] the ECJ held that length of service would automatically constitute a defence and it confirmed the decision recently,[133] but this may change in view of indirect age discrimination law (which might in any event provide an easier claim).

Change in the burden of proof?

8.68 There is one significant change to the formulation of the material factor defence in the EQA 2010. It used to be clear that the burden of proof rested entirely on the employer once the rebuttable presumption of sex discrimination arose.[134] Section 69 partly changes that established position. It does so by separating the material factor defence into two types, namely those where the responsible person proves that the difference is because of a material factor reliance on which does not involve treating the claimant less favourably 'because of her sex' on the one hand and other factors. The first part of the formulation effectively requires the employer to disprove direct discrimination. There is no change here, although it should be remembered that the employer must prove that the reason for less favourable treatment is neither wholly *nor partly* due to gender.[135]

8.69 If the employer disproves direct discrimination, EQA 2010, s 69(2) puts a further burden on claimants. It requires them to prove that: 'as a result of the factor, the claimant and persons of the same sex doing work equal to her are put at a particular disadvantage when compared with persons of the opposite sex doing work equal to her'. They must prove this before the employer is required to justify the discriminatory lower pay. The following problems are identified:

- potential lack of compliance with EC law;

- a formulation of indirect discrimination which is both new and different from that used at EQA 2010, s 19 for all other types of indirect discrimination;[136]

- the exclusion of women who are isolated in the workforce in terms of gender, since the wording appears to prevent reliance on hypothetical further women;[137]

---

[131] *Coventry City Council v Nicholls* [2009] IRLR 345, EAT.
[132] *Danfoss (Handels-og Kontorfunktionoererernes Forbund I Danmark v Dansk Arbejdsverforening)* [1989] IRLR 532.
[133] *Cadman v Health and Safety Executive* [2006] IRLR 969, ECJ.
[134] See Lord Nicholls clear statement in *Glasgow City Council v Marshall* [2000] IRLR 272, HL.
[135] See, for example, in respect of race discrimination, the clear statement in *Owen & Briggs v James* [1982] IRLR 502, CA.
[136] It uses the result of the factor instead of provision, criterion or practice; and it requires comparison only with those proven to be engaged on equal work, instead of allowing a more general comparison.
[137] Cf under the sex discrimination provisions: *London Underground Ltd v Edwards (No 2)* [1999] ICR 494, CA.

- the practical difficulties to which this will give rise for claimants who know so much less about the make-up of the workforce than the employers;

- the awkward fit with established case-law on the 'taint of sex'.

New provision for automatic justification

8.70　In respect of justification EQA 2010, s 69(3) sets out an entirely new provision: the long-term objective of reducing inequality between men's and women's terms is always to be regarded as a legitimate aim. The Explanatory Note gives no indication as to why this was created.[138] The obligation to establish proportionality remains.

EXCLUSION OF SEX DISCRIMINATION PROVISIONS (PREVENTION OF OVERLAPPING CLAIMS)

8.71　The SDA 1975 and EqPA 1970 established a distinction between claims which had to be brought under the sex discrimination provisions and those which had to be brought under the equal pay provisions.[139] The distinction is maintained by EQA 2010, s 70. Sex discrimination provisions relating to less favourable treatment have no effect in relation to a woman's terms insofar as they are modified or included by a sex equality clause or rule or would be save for the material factor defence or certain exceptions in respect of pension benefits.[140] And it is not unlawful sex discrimination for an employer to have provided a claimant with a less favourable term or to have failed to provide a claimant with a term which the comparator has been given[141] – because that would be a breach of the equality of terms provisions. So, although all sex discrimination provisions are now united in one statute, great care is required when commencing tribunal proceedings to avoid bringing the claim under the wrong sections.[142]

SEX DISCRIMINATION IN CONTRACTUAL PAY

8.72　EQA 2010, s 71 sets out an important new provision, which is an exception to the rules described immediately above. Equal pay claims have always required – and will continue to require – a 'real' comparator. Now EQA 2010, s 71 provides for complaints of direct sex discrimination[143] or direct

---

[138]　EN para 244 does set out that it is a new provision. It may be related to the decision in *Allen v GMB* [2008] IRLR 690, CA or to give effect to the submissions of the EHRC to the Court of Appeal in *Redcar & Cleveland Borough Council v Bainbridge* [2008] IRLR 776.

[139]　SDA 1975, ss 6(6), 8(4) and (5).

[140]　EQA 2010, s 67(2) and see in respect of pensions Part 2 of Sch 7.

[141]　EQA 2010, s 63(4).

[142]　The forms of action still rule: see *Hoyland v Asda* [2006] IRLR 468, CS.

[143]　Under EQA 2010, s 13 .

combined discrimination[144] in respect of contractual pay where the sex equality clause or rule has no effect. The obvious application is where the claimant cannot identify a comparator who is engaged on equal work. This will tend to happen either because she is in a gender-segregated workforce or because the only comparable male employees work in different establishments where there are no common terms and conditions of employment.[145]

8.73 This gives rise to interesting tactical choices for claimants or their representatives, who may wish to move straight to the hypothetical direct sex discrimination claim, leaving the employer to assert that it is not available because there is a comparable male employee who has higher pay by virtue of a relevant material factor. The substantive sex discrimination claims will presumably work as they have for years in respect of race discrimination, with female claimants relying on hypothetical comparators perhaps constructed by reference to male colleagues.[146] There are the following limitations:

- indirect discrimination is not covered;

- the provision is limited to 'pay', which will be broadly defined in EC terms but which may not cover all potential contractual disparities.

8.74 The Explanatory Notes give the example of an employer who tells a female employee 'I would pay you more if you were a man.'[147] Real life will probably be less straightforward. It seems more likely that tribunals will be asked to infer direct sex discrimination and shift the burden of disproving it to the employer. One example might be where a new post is created; it is advertised with a salary of '£25–£28,000'; a woman is appointed and she is paid £24,000 a year.

PREGNANCY AND MATERNITY EQUALITY PROVISIONS

Relevant types of work

8.75 EQA 2010, ss 72–76 apply in respect of the pay of female employees or office-holders during periods which are protected for maternity reasons. Everything set out above concerning definitions of employees and office holders applies here too. This is simply a straight replacement of the EqPA 1970 provisions.[148]

---

[144] Under EQA 2010, s 14, namely claims based on sex and one other protected characteristic.
[145] By virtue of EQA 2010, s 71(1)(b), the new provision does not apply where there is a real comparator but the employer establishes a material factor defence such as red-circling.
[146] Or even successors?
[147] EN para 250.
[148] EN para 255.

Maternity equality clause

8.76   Every woman's contract is to be treated as including a maternity equality clause, if it does not actually include one.[149] EQA 2010, s 74 spells out what this means. It is phrased in a convoluted manner, but the intention is to maintain the pre-existing position which itself results from EU case-law, EU Directives and consequential amendments to the EqPA 1970.[150] The effect is that any maternity-related pay must:

- include any increase in pay or bonus to which the woman would have been entitled had she not been pregnant or on maternity leave, in respect of periods before or during the protected period; and

- include any bonus in respect of times after the end of the protected period;

- be paid at the time it would have been paid if the woman were not on maternity leave.

Maternity-related pay is pay (other than statutory maternity pay) to which a woman is entitled as a result of being pregnant or on maternity leave.[151] The protected period is the time when the woman is pregnant or on maternity leave.[152] Further, when the woman returns to work, her pay must include such increases as she would have received had she not been absent on maternity leave.[153]

8.77   An example in the Explanatory Notes is:

> 'Early in her maternity leave, a woman receiving maternity-related pay becomes entitled to an increase in pay. If her terms of employment do not already provide for the increase to be reflected in her maternity-related pay, the employer must recalculate her maternity pay to take account of the increment.'[154]

8.78   EQA 2010, s 73(3) provides that in respect of a term relating to membership of or rights under an occupational pension scheme, the maternity equality clause will only have such effect as would a maternity equality rule.

Maternity equality rule

8.79   EQA 201, s 75 provides that all occupational pension schemes are to be treated as including a maternity equality rule, if they do not actually include one. Such a rule means that:

---

149   EQA 2010, s 73(1).
150   EN para 260.
151   EQA 2010, s 74(9).
152   EQA 2010, s 74(10) referring to s 18.
153   EQA 2010, s 74(8).
154   EN para 260.

- any relevant term in an occupational pension scheme which does not treat time on maternity leave as it treats time not on maternity leave is modified, so that it does;[155]

- any term which confers a relevant discretion and which permits time on maternity leave to be treated differently from time not on maternity leave is modified, so that the discretion cannot be exercised in that way.[156]

A relevant term is one relating to membership of the scheme, accrual of rights under the scheme or the determination of benefits under the scheme.[157] A discretion is relevant if its exercise is capable of affecting membership of the scheme, the accrual of rights under the scheme or the determination of the amount of a benefit payable under the scheme.[158]

8.80 EQA 2010, s 75(7) asserts that s 75 'does not require' a woman on maternity leave to make contributions to the pension scheme otherwise than by reference to the amount she is actually receiving. It does not forbid voluntary additional contributions nor, on a straight reading, does it prohibit the trustees from requiring the woman to pay higher contributions – but that would probably fall foul of s 75(4).

8.81 For the avoidance of doubt, s 75(10) provides that a reference to being on maternity leave includes 'having been' on maternity leave and a reference to being paid by the employer includes receiving statutory maternity pay. There are different dates from which the provisions apply, based on changes to domestic law.[159] Section 75 is not intended to make changes to the substantive law.[160]

8.82 The examples in the Explanatory Notes are as follows:

'A woman who is on maternity leave will be entitled to continuing membership of the pension scheme throughout the period of maternity leave whether she is paid or not.

A woman who is paid whilst on maternity leave will be entitled to accrue rights in a scheme as though she were paid her usual salary but she will be required only to make contributions based on her actual pay.'[161]

---

[155] EQA 2010, s 75(3).
[156] EQA 2010, s 75(4).
[157] EQA 2010, s 75(5).
[158] EQA 2010, s 75(6).
[159] The provisions apply to women on unpaid ordinary maternity leave where the expected week of confinement began on or after 6 April 2003: EQA 2010, s 75(3); and to women on unpaid additional maternity leave only where the expected week of confinement began on or after 5 October 2008.
[160] EN para 268 sets out that the section replaces the 'unfair maternity provisions' in Social Security Act 1989, Sch 5, para 5 and replicates aspects of Maternity and Parental Leave etc Regulations 1999, SI 1999/3312, regs 9 and 18A.
[161] EN para 268.

Exclusion of maternity and discrimination provisions (prevention of overlapping claims)

8.83 EQA 2010, s 76 provides that the relevant pregnancy and maternity discrimination provision has no effect in relation to a term modified by a maternity equality clause or rule. This serves to preserve the contractual/non-contractual distinction between what are essentially gender (pregnancy)-based pay claims, giving 'pay' a very broad meaning, on the one hand, and all other gender(pregnancy)-based claims, for example for promotion, transfer, training and offers of employment or appointment, on the other. It prevents any maternity equality of terms claims overlapping with claims which should properly be brought under other pregnancy and maternity discrimination provisions.[162]

8.84 The example in the Explanatory Notes is that if a woman who is in line for promotion notifies her employer that she is pregnant and is then not considered for promotion, that will be direct pregnancy discrimination, not the breach of a maternity equality clause.[163]

DISCLOSURE OF INFORMATION

Discussions with colleagues

8.85 The entirely new provisions in EQA 2010, s 77 render pay secrecy terms unenforceable in certain relatively limited circumstances. A term of work which seeks to prevent a person from disclosing or seeking to disclose information about the terms of their work is unenforceable against that person insofar as they are making or seeking to make a relevant pay disclosure.[164] And any term which seeks to prevent a person seeking to obtain disclosure from a colleague of information about a person's pay is unenforceable insofar as the person is making or seeking to make a relevant pay disclosure.[165] A disclosure is a relevant pay disclosure if made for the purpose of enabling the person who makes it or the person to whom it is made to find out whether or to what extent there is a connection between pay and having (or not having) a particular protected characteristic.[166]

---

[162] Namely EQA 2010, s 39(2) in respect of employment; s 49(6) in respect of a personal office; and s 50(6) in respect of a public office. The forms of action ruling in the twenty-first century? According to EN para 272 the combined provisions are intended to ensure 'seamless protection' against pregnancy and maternity-related inequality.

[163] EN para 272. This is because promotion is not based on a contractual entitlement.

[164] EQA 2010, s 77(1).

[165] EQA 2010, s 77(2). The term 'colleague' is not defined. It appears to be a leftover from an earlier version of the Bill when comparators had to be colleagues and there was a detailed definition. However, it expressly includes a former colleague, ibid.

[166] EQA 2010, s 77(3).

8.86 Seeking, making or seeking to make and receiving a relevant pay disclosure are protected acts for the relevant victimisation provision.[167] The aim is to protect people who discuss their pay with fellow or former employees or office-holders or with trade union officials with a view to finding out whether there may be unlawful discrimination on grounds of gender or any other protected characteristics. The Explanatory Notes tell us that they are 'intended to ensure that there is greater transparency and dialogue within workplaces about pay'.[168]

8.87 EQA 2010, s 77 is very detailed and precise. It is unclear quite how all aspects of the definition of a relevant disclosure will have to be satisfied in order for the protection to be obtained. Perhaps some parts may just be in the mind of a potential claimant, rather than being uttered aloud or known to the other party to the discussion. Unless it be so, the intended positive example given at EN para 275 does not actually fall within what is required. The example is:

> 'A female employee thinks she is underpaid compared with a male colleague. She asks him what he is paid and he tells her. The employer takes disciplinary action against the man as a result. The man can bring a claim for victimisation against the employer for disciplining him.'

It is not even suggested that the woman thought they were engaged on equal work, let alone that she had said anything to the man about it so as to bring him within EQA 2010, s 77(3), as set out above.

Gender pay gap

8.88 EQA 2010, s 78 provides that a minister may make regulations requiring employers to publish information relating to the pay of employees for the purpose of establishing whether there are pay differences between men and women. The possible ambit of permissible regulations is set out, but so broadly that it is not useful to analyse it.

8.89 This provision has caused considerable public interest, yet:

- the section merely empowers the making of regulations, it does not create an obligation to provide information;

- the Explanatory Notes set out at para 278 that the government does not intend to make use of the power before April 2013 – and it may be anticipated that a government of a different hue would never make use of the power;

- employers with fewer than 250 employees are exempt.[169]

---

[167] EQA 2010, s 77(4).
[168] EN para 277.
[169] EQA 2010, s 78(2)(a).

Local authorities and other public authorities to whom the public sector equality duty applies are also exempt,[170] although the public sector equality duty does not require public authorities to publish gender pay gap information. Nonetheless the government has stated an intention to use its powers to amend the public sector equality duty to require public bodies with 150 or more employees to publish gender pay gap information, together with the same information about ethnic minority and disabled employees, from 2011.[171]

8.90 The regulations made under s 78 may provide for failure to comply to be a criminal offence, punishable on summary conviction by a fine, or for some other means of enforcement.

PERMITTED COMPARATORS

General matters

8.91 The next consideration is the comparisons which the law permits. Employees are defined at EQA 2010, s 79 as comparators only if:

- they are employed by the same employer or an associate employer and they work at the same establishment;[172] or

- they are employed by the same employer or an associate of the claimant's employer and they work at different establishments at which common terms and conditions apply, either generally or as between claimant and comparator.[173]

Case law has made clear that the requirements of s 79(3) and (4) are true alternatives: if the comparator works in the same establishment there is no need to show that he is employed on common terms and conditions.[174] The following subsections define comparators for office holders in a slightly more limited manner: the person responsible for paying the claimant must also be responsible for paying the comparator.[175]

8.92 Employers are defined in s 79(9) as being associated if one is a company of which the other (directly or indirectly) has control or both are companies of which a third person (directly or indirectly) has control, a definition common through employment legislation.[176] There is no change here from the EqPA 1970. It is unclear whether this is intended to be an exclusive definition,

---

[170] EQA 2010, s 78(2)(b) and (c).
[171] Baroness Royall of Blaydon introducing the then Equality Bill for its Second Reading in the House of Lords: HL Deb 15 December 2009, col 1408.
[172] EQA 2010, s 79(3).
[173] EQA 2010, s 79(4).
[174] *Lawson v Britfish Ltd* [1988] IRLR 53, EAT.
[175] EQA 2010, s 79(5). With even more limits in respect of House of Commons and House of Lords staff in the following subsections.
[176] See ERA 1996, s 231.

permitting companies alone to be associated employers. The terminology is not 'if but only if one is a company etc', although that is how it was interpreted in *Halsey v Fair Employment Agency*.[177] The ECJ has treated Art 157 as covering employees 'in the same establishment or service'[178] and the EAT more than a decade ago held that the narrower EqPA 1970 definition must be disapplied so as to permit an interpretation in accordance with Art 157.[179]

Need for a 'single source' for decisions on pay

8.93 Further complications in this area have grown around the ECJ's development of the 'single source' doctrine. The ECJ has held that under Art 157 where claimant and comparator were employed by different bodies (for example, following a TUPE transfer), there can still be a comparison if the pay for both is determined by a single source.[180] This potentially generous notion has been conservatively treated by the English courts.[181]

8.94 One way round this for claimants would be to pursue the hypothetical or 'no actual comparator' approach adopted by the ECJ in the pension part of *Allonby*.[182] Where the challenge was to a scheme contained in national legislation, although it is not entirely clear how significant this was, no male comparator was required if the female claimants could demonstrate by statistical analysis that there was adverse disparate impact on women. This harks back to the early terminology of the ECJ.[183] However, it is trite law that domestic legislation did not permit a hypothetical comparison in an equal pay claim.[184] Alone among discrimination strands, and even amongst contract-based discrimination claims,[185] a woman could not pursue a claim for equal contractual benefits unless she could point to a male comparator who was

---

[177] [1989] IRLR 106, NICA.
[178] See for example: *Defrenne v Sabena Belgian Airlines (No 2)* [1976] ICR 547.
[179] *Scullard v Knowles* [1996] ICR 399.
[180] *Lawrence v Regent Office Care Ltd* [2002] IRLR 822, ECJ, although the claimants failed on the facts. See also *Allonby v Accrington and Rossendale College* [2004] IRLR 224, ECJ, in respect of discriminatory occupational pension scheme provisions established in national legislation.
[181] See *Dumfries and Galloway Council v North* [2009] IRLR 915 (presently on appeal to CA). In *DEFRA v Robertson* [2005] ICR 750, CA it was held that although the Crown was notionally the common employer of all civil servants, the claimants could not compare themselves with comparators employed by another government department. They failed to meet the narrow 'same employment' test and could not show a single source responsible for differences in pay, because the setting of pay was delegated to and done by the various departments. Although the Crown actually retained the right to set pay and could revoke the delegation at any time, this was not enough. In *North Cumbria Acute Hospitals NHS Trust v Potter* [2009] IRLR 176 the EAT rejected an attempt by the Trust to add 'an additional hurdle' for claimants by importing the single source requirement into a case where the claimants and comparators were properly colleagues/in the same employment. The EAT held that the Art 157 test is not added to the s 76 test but an alternative.
[182] [2004] IRLR 224, ECJ.
[183] *Bilka-Kaufhaus GmbH v Weber von Hartz* [1986] IRLR] 317, ECJ.
[184] *Meeks v National Union of Agricultural and Allied Workers* [1976] IRLR 198; *Coloroll Pension Trustees Ltd v Russell* [1994] IRLR 586, ECJ.
[185] Since, for example, a black man can claim equality of contractual terms, including pay, on the basis of a hypothetical white comparator.

employed at the same time (for at least some of the period) or who was her predecessor.[186] This was confirmed recently by Elias P (as he then was) in *Walton Centre for Neurology and Neurosurgery NHS Trust v Bewley*.[187] No provision has been made for the use of hypothetical pay comparisons in the EQA 2010 beyond the limited right in s 71 to claim direct sex discrimination (see **8.71**).

Effect of a TUPE transfer

8.95 This is the place to note a matter which overlaps with what must be considered in respect of time limits and the extent of permissible remedies. Where a TUPE transfer has occurred so that a woman is no longer employed by an employer who also employs suitable male comparators (as may happen when caring services are contracted out by a local authority), the woman may be able to bring an equal work claim based on a comparison with a man alongside whom she used to work. In *Gutridge v Sodexho Ltd*[188] female domestic cleaners, who had transferred from an NHS Trust in June 2001, claimed equal pay in December 2006 from (inter alia) the transferee, comparing themselves to male maintenance assistants who had remained in the employment of the Trust. The claim proceeded on the assumption of equal work and that there was no material factor defence. The Court of Appeal held (unanimously, although they were divided on another point):

- once the women were entitled to equal pay (as they presumptively were here, although they had not claimed whilst still in the Trust's employment), they did not lose the right when they were no longer in the same employment as the men;[189]

- once modified by the operation of a sex equality clause, the contract of employment provides for remuneration at the modified rate until something else happens to change it;

- it would flout the purpose and plain wording of the TUPE regulations[190] if a transfer within the regulations could be the 'something else';

- although the women and the comparators were no longer in the same employment, the comparison was based on the time when both were employed by the Trust;[191]

---

[186] *Macarthys Ltd v Smith* [1979] IRLR 316, CA.
[187] [2008] IRLR 588, EAT. Counsel for the claimants ran a 'successor' comparator case, bolstering his submissions (unsuccessfully) with argument based on EC law, but the EAT rejected it.
[188] [2009] IRLR 721, CA.
[189] This is based on an analysis of how the statutory mechanism operates, as held in *Sorbie v Trust House Forte Hotels Ltd* [1976] IRLR 371, EAT concerning the right of waitresses to continue to be paid at a higher rate after their male comparator had left.
[190] Per Smith LJ at para 24: 'drive a coach and horses through TUPE' per Wall LJ at para 101.
[191] 'The women are not seeking to compare themselves with the men after they have transferred to Sodhexo. They are seeking to rely on a right which has crystallised while they were in the same

- the right was limited to the pay which the men enjoyed at the date of the transfer. That is the pay which was incorporated into their contracts, not a right to continue receiving whatever pay the men (to whom they could no longer compare themselves post transfer) received after June 2001.

This is both obviously correct and likely to be utterly shocking to transferees, who may not know for many years with whom their new female employees may claim comparison and thus at what rate they can require to be paid.

Common terms of employment

8.96 The 'common terms of employment' requirement has been the subject of considerable judicial interpretation, but the position appears now to be reasonably straightforward. The paradigm case is where both establishments are covered by the same terms, for example because there is one collective agreement. The terms do not have to be identical: it suffices if they are broadly similar. The degree of commonality is a question of fact for the tribunal and requires a broad commonsense approach.[192] The terms may be contained in different collective agreements. It suffices if they are 'substantially comparable'.[193] At least where there is one collective agreement, the comparison is of the terms and conditions which the comparator and claimant actually have. Provided they are broadly similar it is not necessary for a claimant to show that if the man were to be employed at the same establishment, it would be on the same terms he already has.[194] Where the terms are not governed by a single agreement, the claimant's terms are not broadly similar to those of the comparator and they work in different establishments, the claimant must prove that if the comparator were employed at her establishment, it would be on terms broadly similar to those he already

---

employment as the men and which they say continued to be their right until validly terminated or varied' (Smith LJ at para 27 and see also para 28).

[192] *Leverton v Clwyd County Council* [1989] IRLR 28, HL (nursery nurses with shorter hours and longer holidays than male clerical staff could proceed).

[193] *British Coal Corporation v Smith* [1996] IRLR 404, HL (canteen workers and cleaners were on common terms and conditions with surface mineworkers and clerical employees who worked at different establishments subject to separate collective bargaining structures which had resulted in differing pay structures).

[194] *South Tyneside Metropolitan Borough Council v Anderson* [2007] IRLR 715, CA: school cooks and cleaners comparing themselves to drivers, a street cleaner, a painter and others. In this case the court appeared to work on the basis that the men would never be required to work at the claimants' schools on account of the nature of their work. The more difficult case, of female employees engaged under differently negotiated terms, was lost in the employment tribunal and not pursued at the EAT. In *Dumfries and Galloway Council v North* [2009] IRLR 915, EAT, Smith J, sitting alone, has held in respect of a similar comparison, that where the terms and conditions of claimants and comparators are in different collective agreements, the claimants cannot be in the same employment unless they prove that the comparators would or could have been employed in their schools and that they would have been so employed on terms broadly similar to those they had when based elsewhere. It is understood that this judgment is on appeal.

enjoys.[195] She may do that, for example, by pointing at others already employed but not suitable to be comparators, being anomalous or not of the opposite sex.

Choice of comparator

8.97 Finally, it is at least clear that the choice of comparator is for the claimant,[196] although the choice must be of a person of the opposite sex.[197] Neither the respondent nor the tribunal may select or substitute a comparator for the one chosen by the claimant,[198] although a claimant runs the risk of losing and being held to have conducted litigation unreasonably, putting herself at risk of a costs order,[199] if she persists with an atypical comparator in respect of whom the employer will obviously establish a material factor defence. In many cases, and especially in the multiple NHS and local authority equal pay claims, it is the norm to identify numerous comparators with a considerable range of pay and contractual benefits. This appears to result from the relative ignorance of claimants, even unionised claimants, about the pay and conditions of those alongside whom they work and an understandable reluctance to limit themselves to those earning only marginally more if they are in jobs which have traditionally been seen as 'women's work' (cleaning, catering and caring, to take just the three 'C's) and, in consequence or anyway, very significantly undervalued. It has been suggested that it will obviously be improper for a woman to compare herself to a man earning somewhat more than her and another earning twice as much as the first,[200] but where there was previously no relevant job comparison it is not necessarily so.[201]

8.98 Examples of permitted comparisons include:

• a female cashier in a Nottingham branch of Boots comparing herself to a male warehouse worker in a branch of Boots in Leeds;

• a male accountant in one company comparing himself to a female finance operative in the parent company;

---

[195] See the words of EQA 2010, s 76(4)(c).

[196] *Ainsworth v Glass Tubes and Components* [1977] IRLR 74, EAT.

[197] See EQA 2010, s 64(1)(a) and (b). But a man may run a 'piggy-back' claim dependent on the success of cases pursued by female claimants: see *South Ayrshire Council v Milligan* [2003] IRLR 153, CS. This has actually been happening for years: in the late 1980s four male sewing machinists employed by Vauxhall achieved equal pay with semi-skilled craft workers on the back of a claim brought and won by 250 women.

[198] But it is likely to be legitimate case management for a tribunal to direct the parties to agree a few 'test' comparators when the assessment or evaluation process is about to get underway and to determine which will be the test cases if the parties cannot agree, in accordance with the Employment Tribunal Rules 2004, reg 3 and Sch 1 and/or 6.

[199] Under Employment Tribunal Rules 2004, Sch 1, rr 38–48.

[200] Lord Bridge in *Leverton v Clywd County Council* [1989] IRLR 28.

[201] Where pay and benefits were not distributed rationally (meaning, here, on the basis of a comparison of the demands made by the work) there is no easily identifiable logical limit to the comparisons which may succeed.

- a female nursery worker in one LEA controlled school comparing herself to male gardeners employed elsewhere by the local authority.

However, job segregation, lack of knowledge and the technicality of this area mean that some employees working on the same job alongside better-paid employees will not be able to claim equal pay with them. Agency workers are perhaps the most obvious example.

ENFORCEMENT AND REMEDIES

8.99 The intention here is to provide a brief overview of enforcement and remedies in respect of the types of claim covered in this chapter. The main analysis is contained in Chapter 12 below.

Jurisdiction of employment tribunals

8.100 EQA 2010, s 127 provides that employment tribunals have jurisdiction to determine complaints relating to breach of an equality clause or rule or for a declaration of relevant rights. Members of the armed forces may also complain to employment tribunals, provided they have first pursued an internal service complaint.[202] Other courts are not prohibited from hearing equal pay claims: they may determine them, strike them out if they think that they could more conveniently be determined by an employment tribunal or may refer relevant questions to the employment tribunal.[203]

8.101 The complex provisions about time limits which were developed in response to delayed pension claim cases through the 1990s into the early twenty-first century have been maintained. They are set out at EQA 2010, ss 129 and 130. Proceedings may not be brought after the end of the qualifying period. The qualifying period is:

- for standard cases (that is, those which are not any other type of case), the period of 6 months beginning with the last day of the employment or appointment;[204]

- for stable work cases,[205] (which are not also concealment or incapacity cases, or both), the period of 6 months beginning with the day on which the stable working relationship ended;

---

[202] EQA 2010, s 127(6).

[203] EQA 2010, s 128.

[204] EQA 2010, s 129(3), as for all the provisions which follow.

[205] 'Stable work cases' have previously been and are again defined as existing 'where the proceedings relate to a period during which there was a stable working relationship between the worker and the responsible person (including any time after the term of work expired)'. The concept was developed by case-law to cover cases where employees worked under a series of contracts, frequently with breaks between them, in the expectation that another contract would be forthcoming after the customary break. Hourly-paid college lecturers are the

- for concealment cases,[206] (which are not also incapacity cases) the period of 6 months beginning with the day on which the worker discovered (or could with due diligence have discovered) the qualifying fact;

- for an incapacity case,[207] (which is not also a concealment case) the period of 6 months from the end of the incapacity;

- for cases which are both incapacity and concealment cases, the period of 6 months beginning with the later of the days on which the period would begin if it were merely a concealment or incapacity case;

- for the armed forces,[208] 3 months is added on in time (to allow for the service complaint).

8.102 It will be noted that although the 6-month limit is more generous than that for other discrimination claims, it is an absolute bar with none of the 'just and equitable' extensions available to the claims for which 3 months is the primary limitation period.

Remedies

8.103 The successful claimant in a non-pension claim may ask the tribunal: (a) to make a declaration as to the rights of the parties; (b) order an award by way of arrears of pay or damages.[209] In England and Wales, the award may be for up to 6 years of arrears in a standard case or from the date of the breach in

---

paradigm example. It seemed unfair to require such employees to bring dozens of pension claim cases, *a fortiori* when many would be out of time, so the ECJ upheld the idea that such employees are in one stable employment from the start of the first contract to the end of the customary break following which no new contract is provided, even where classes, hours and subjects taught have changed throughout the period: see *Preston v Wolverhampton Healthcare NHS Trust and others* [2000] IRLR 506. This has led to the peculiarity that claimants who then exchanged their stable (but actually rather precarious) employment relationship for full-time or fractional salaried permanent (or indefinite) employment found that time ran against them from the change of status. And they found it hard to credit that they had moved out of a stable employment relationship (into a 'standard' employment situation) just as their working life actually became more stable. A glimmer of a way round this has been suggested by Mummery LJ (giving judgment for the CA in *Slack v Cumbria County Council and EHRC intervening* [2009] IRLR 463) who proposed that such claimants might indeed continue in stable employment relationships if the nature of the work done did not change. This has just been followed and reinforced in *Fox v North Cumbria Acute Hospitals NHS Trust (No 2)*, CA (not yet reported) on appeal from *Potter v North Cumbria etc* [2009] IRLR 900: substantial changes made to contracts when implementing Agenda for Change (the large-scale local authority job evaluation programme) did not terminate the stable employment relationship which the permanently employed claimants had with the Trust.

[206] Defined at EQA 2010, s 129(4) for equality clause claims and s 129(5) for equality rule claims. Essentially, where the responsible person deliberately concealed a qualifying (that is, relevant) fact, without knowledge of which the claimant could not reasonably have been expected to bring the proceedings, and the claimant did not discover (or could not with reasonable diligence have discovered) the qualifying fact.

[207] Meaning in the terms used in the Supreme Court Rules, incapable of conducting her affairs.

[208] EQA 2010, s 128(4).

[209] EQA 2010, s 131(2).

a concealment or incapacity case (or where there is both). In Scotland, the maximum award of arrears is 5 years. The difference is because of the different domestic laws applicable to claims for arrears in contract cases.[210] There is no separate provision in respect of stable employment cases. Interest is payable on the award at the special account rate.

8.104 In a pension claim, the only remedy will be a declaration of entitlement, unless the claimant is already a pensioner.[211] Where the declaration relates to:

- the entitlement to be admitted to the pension scheme, the specified date must not be earlier than 8 April 1976;[212]

- terms on which members of the scheme are treated, the specified period must not begin before 17 May 1990.[213]

8.105 Where a pensioner claimant succeeds, EQA 2010, s 133 makes provision for up to 6 years (5 in Scotland) of arrears to be payable. Matters are sometimes complicated by the need for the pensioner (as well as the employer) to make additional contributions to the scheme, so as to avoid unjust enrichment. In practice, any such contribution can often be paid from the enhanced lump sum which is due.

8.106 EQA 2010, s 134 makes further complex provisions in respect of remedies for non-pension claims and pensioner arrears claims where there has been concealment and/or incapacity. No substantive change is made by any of these provisions.

---

[210] Since the ECJ in *Levez v TH Jennings (Harlow Pools) Ltd* [1991] IRLR 764 held that the UK could not artificially keep equal pay claim awards below the comparable domestic law remedy.
[211] EQA 2010, s 132(2) and (3).
[212] EQA 2010, s 132(4), because that was the date fixed by the ECJ in *Defrenne v Sabena (No 2)* [1976] ICR 547, to avoid upsetting the established order too much.
[213] EQA 2010, s 132(7), because that was the date fixed by the ECJ in *Barber v Guardian Royal Exchange Insurance Group* [1990] IRLR 240, ECJ, for similar reasons.

Chapter 9

EDUCATION

INTRODUCTION

9.1   The prohibition of discrimination in relation to the provision of education has given rise to considerably less case-law than the case-law which has arisen from claims of discrimination in, or in relation to, employment. However, the applicable principles are for the most part the same in both areas. In relation to disability, however, perhaps for obvious reasons, there are provisions which are specially 'tuned' to the provision of education.

THE SCOPE OF PART 6 OF THE EQUALITY ACT 2010

9.2   Part 6 of the Equality Act 2010 (EQA 2010) (ss 84–99) prohibits discrimination on most (but not all) grounds in relation to education in schools,[1] further and higher education,[2] and 'general qualifications bodies'.[3] In addition, provision is made affecting educational charities and endowments insofar as they restrict benefits to the members of one sex.[4]

The duty to make reasonable adjustments – general considerations

9.3   Reasonable adjustments are the subject of a Schedule (Sch 13) which applies to all of the kinds of education to which the EQA 2010 applies. In any circumstance in which there may be a need to make such a reasonable adjustment, it will be necessary to have regard to 'relevant provisions of a code of practice issued under s 14 of the Equality Act 2006'.[5] It will also be necessary to have regard to any 'confidentiality request' of which the person or body who or which is said to be under a duty to make a reasonable adjustment, is aware.[6] This is a request 'that the nature or existence of a disabled person's disability be treated as confidential', and which is either made by the person's parent or is made by the person in the circumstance that the person or body who or which is said to be under a duty to make an adjustment 'reasonably believes that the person [who has made the request] has sufficient

---

[1]   EQA 2010, ss 84–89 and Schs 10–11.
[2]   EQA 2010, ss 90–94 and Sch 12.
[3]   EQA 2010, ss 95–97.
[4]   EQA 2010, s 99 and Sch 14.
[5]   EQA 2010, Sch 13, para 7.
[6]   EQA 2010, Sch 13, para 8(1) and (2).

understanding of the nature and effect of the request'.[7] In relation to a student at a further or higher education institution or an applicant for a qualification, a 'confidentiality request' is a request by a disabled person that the nature or existence of the person's disability be treated as confidential.[8]

9.4 In this chapter, the effects of the EQA 2010 on (1) schools, (2) further and higher education providers, (3) general qualifications bodies, and (4) educational charities and endowments are described, in that order.

SCHOOLS

Protected characteristics which do not apply to schools

9.5 In relation to schools, (1) age and (2) marriage and civil partnership are not protected characteristics.[9]

Prohibited activities: the bodies to which the duties apply

9.6 The 'responsible body' of (not 'for', but 'of') certain sorts of school[10] is precluded by the EQA 2010 from doing some things and required by that Act to do others. The 'responsible body' of a school is defined by some complicated provisions in the EQA 2010, which in turn rely on definitions in the Education Acts, ie the statutes concerning the provision of education.[11] The responsible body of a school is essentially the body which has responsibility for the management of the school. By way of example, the responsible body of a maintained school in England or Wales is either the local authority[12] which maintains the school or the governing body of the school.[13]

---

[7] See EQA 2010, Sch 13, para 8(3)–(5).

[8] EQA 2010, Sch 13, para 8(6). A 'student' in relation to an institution means 'a person for whom education is provided by the institution': EQA 2010, s 94(3).

[9] EQA 2010, s 84. The Explanatory Notes explain that this exception merely mirrors that in the prior law.

[10] The term 'school' is defined for this purpose by EQA 2010, s 89(5). In relation to England and Wales, it has the meaning given to it by s 4 of the Education Act 1996 (EA 1996), which is an institution for providing primary or secondary education, or both, whether or not it also provides further education. In relation to Scotland, it has the meaning given in s 135(1) of the Education (Scotland) Act 1980, which is 'an institution for the provision of primary or secondary education or both primary and secondary education being a public school, a grant-aided school or an independent school, and includes a nursery school and a special school'.

[11] See EQA 2010, ss 85(7)–(9) and 89(4)–(11).

[12] This means 'in relation to England, an English local authority within the meaning of section 162 of the Education and Inspections Act 2006' and 'in relation to Wales, a Welsh local authority within the meaning of that section': EQA 2010, s 89(10).

[13] EQA 2010, s 85(9)(a). The term 'responsible body' is defined by s 85(9) generally.

The schools to which the duties apply

9.7   The schools in England and Wales to which the duties in Part 6 of the EQA 2010 apply are:[14]

*   schools maintained by local authorities;

*   independent educational institutions[15] other than special schools; and

*   special schools.[16]

9.8   The schools in Scotland to which the duties in Part 6 of the EQA 2010 apply are:[17]

*   schools managed by an education authority;[18]

*   independent schools;[19] and

*   'a school in respect of which the managers are for the time being receiving grants under section 73(c) or (d) of the Education (Scotland) Act 1980'.[20]

The duties imposed on schools by Part 6 of the EQA 2010

Admissions

9.9   The responsible body of a school to which s 85 of the EQA 2010 applies (in this chapter, 'a relevant school') may not discriminate against persons in the arrangements which it makes for deciding who is offered admission as a pupil,[21] as to the terms on which it offers to admit a person as a pupil,[22] or by not admitting a person to the school.[23]

---

[14]   EQA 2010, s 85(7).
[15]   In England this means an 'independent educational institution' as defined by Ch 1 of Part 4 of the Education and Skills Act 2008: see EQA 2010, s 89(6) and (7). In Wales the term means 'an independent school in Wales', as defined by EA 1996, s 463: see EQA 2010, s 89(7)(b) and (8)(a).
[16]   As defined by EA 1996, s 337: EQA 2010, s 89(9).
[17]   EQA 2010, s 85(8).
[18]   An 'education authority' means 'a council constituted under section 2 of the Local Government etc. (Scotland) Act 1994': see EQA 2010, s 89(11) read with s 135(1) of the Education (Scotland) Act 1980.
[19]   Meaning a school at which full-time education is provided pupils of school age (whether or not education is provided for pupils under or over that age) which is neither a 'public school', which in Scotland means a school under the management of an education authority, nor a 'grant-aided school', which (with exceptions) is a school which is given grants by (now) the Scottish Parliament: see EQA 2010, s 89(8)(b) read with s 135(1) of the Education (Scotland) Act 1980.
[20]   EQA 2010, s 85(8)(c).
[21]   EQA 2010, s 85(1)(a).
[22]   EQA 2010, s 85(1)(b).
[23]   EQA 2010, s 85(1)(c).

Provision of education and services

9.10   The responsible body of a relevant school must not discriminate against a pupil:

'(a)   in the way it provides education for the pupil;
(b)   in the way it affords the pupil access to a benefit, facility or service;
(c)   by not providing education for the pupil;
(d)   by not affording the pupil access to a benefit, facility or service;
(e)   by excluding the pupil from the school;
(f)   by subjecting the pupil to any other detriment.'[24]

Harassment

9.11   The responsible body of a relevant school must not harass (a) a pupil, or (b) a person who has applied for admission as a pupil.[25] However, in regard to harassment in this context, gender reassignment, religion or belief and sexual orientation are not protected characteristics.[26]

Victimisation

9.12   The responsible body of a relevant school must not victimise a person:[27]

'(a)   in the arrangements which it makes for deciding who is to be offered admission as a pupil;
(b)   as to the terms on which it offers to admit the person as a pupil;
(c)   by not admitting the person as a pupil.'[28]

9.13   The responsible body of a relevant school must not victimise a pupil:[29]

'(a)   in the way it provides education for the pupil;
(b)   in the way it affords the pupil access to a benefit, facility or service;
(c)   by not providing education for the pupil;
(d)   by not affording the pupil access to a benefit, facility or service;
(e)   by excluding the pupil from the school;
(f)   by subjecting the pupil to any other detriment.'

9.14   These prohibitions on victimisation extend to victimising a child[30] who is a pupil or who seeks to become a pupil in retaliation for the doing of a protected act by a parent or sibling[31] of the child in question.[32] However, in

---

24   EQA 2010, s 85(2).
25   EQA 2010, s 85(3).
26   EQA 2010, s 85(10).
27   The persons to whom this duty applies are expanded by EQA 2010, s 86: see **9.14**.
28   EQA 2010, s 85(4).
29   The persons to whom this duty applies are expanded by EQA 2010, s 86: see **9.14**.
30   A 'child' is for this purpose a person who has not attained the age of 18: EQA 2010, s 86(5).
31   This means a brother or sister, a half-brother or half-sister, or a stepbrother or stepsister: EQA 2010, s 86(5).
32   See EQA 2010, s 86(1) and (2).

that case, the child must have acted in good faith for the protection against victimisation to apply.[33] Thus, the critical issue in this context will be whether or not the allegation which the child made to his or her parent or sibling, on which the parent or sibling acted, was made in good faith.

Disability

9.15 The responsible body of a relevant school must also make reasonable adjustments of the sort required by s 20 of, and Sch 13 to, the EQA 2010.[34] These are the first and third requirements stated in s 20 of the EQA 2010.[35] Thus, the second requirement stated in that section does not apply. Accordingly, there is no duty 'where a physical feature puts a disabled person at a substantial disadvantage in relation to a relevant matter in comparison with persons who are not disabled, to take such steps as it is reasonable to have to take to avoid the disadvantage'.

9.16 However, a school whose admission arrangements are lawfully selective is not affected by the prohibition of disability discrimination in relation to persons whose admission to the school is sought, as long as the selection is made in accordance with the lawful selection process.[36]

9.17 In *Governing Body of X Endowed Primary School v Mr and Mrs T and the National Autistic Society*,[37] Lloyd-Jones J held that a disability may fall within the exceptions provided for by the Disability Discrimination (Meaning of Disability) Regulations 1996[38] even if it results from a disability. Thus, a tendency to physical abuse of other persons, which was excluded from the definition of a disability for the purposes of the DDA 1995,[39] was not protected by that Act even if it was a manifestation of a condition (for example an autistic spectrum disorder) which *was* protected by that Act. The effect of that ruling may have been negated for the future by the enactment of s 15 of the EQA 2010.[40] Whether it has been so negated remains to be seen, but surely the same difficulties arise even under the wording of s 15.

Enforcement of these duties imposed on the responsible bodies of schools

9.18 The duties imposed by s 85 of the EQA 2010 are enforceable (except as against an independent educational institution other than a special school) by means of a direction given under s 496 or s 497 of the Education Act 1996 (EA

---

[33] EQA 2010, s 86(3) and (4).
[34] EQA 2010, s 85(6) and Sch 13, para 2.
[35] See EQA 2010, Sch 13, para 2(2). See Chapter 3 above for these requirements.
[36] EQA 2010, Sch 11, para 8.
[37] [2009] EWHC 1842 (Admin), [2010] ELR 1. The headnote in the ELR report is slightly erroneous. In holding number (7) the word 'appellant' should have been 'respondent'.
[38] SI 1996/1455.
[39] See reg 4(1)(c) of SI 1996/1455.
[40] See Chapter 3 above concerning s 15 and its likely effect.

1996) by the Secretary of State in relation to a school in England or by the National Assembly in relation to a school in Wales.[41] These are the so-called 'default' powers of the Secretary of State and the National Assembly. Section 496 applies where the Secretary of State is 'satisfied', whether on a complaint by any person or otherwise (so a complaint does not need to have been made by any person for the power in s 496 to arise) that a body to which that section applies has acted or is proposing to act 'unreasonably'. This means irrationality in a public law sense.[42] Section 497 applies where the Secretary of State (or the National Assembly) is 'satisfied (either on a complaint by any person interested or otherwise) that a body to which [that] section applies have failed to discharge any duty imposed on them by or for the purposes of this Act'.

9.19 In both cases, the Secretary of State (or the National Assembly) may give 'such [relevant] directions . . . as appear to him [or it] to be expedient'. Such directions are enforceable ultimately by the High Court.[43]

9.20 Otherwise, enforcement of the duties in Part 6 is by means of a county court action under s 114 of the EQA 2010, unless the claim falls within s 116 of the EQA 2010.[44] Claims which may not be made to a county court because they fall within s 116 include those which may be made to:

(a) the First-tier Tribunal in accordance with Part 2 of Sch 17 to the EQA 2010, which relates to England;

(b) the Special Educational Needs Tribunal for Wales in accordance with Part 2 of that Schedule; or

(c) an Additional Support Needs Tribunal for Scotland in accordance with Part 3 of that Schedule.[45]

These are claims that a responsible body has contravened Chapter 1 of Part 6 because of a person's disability, and may be made in England only by the person's parent.[46] In Scotland, such a claim may also be made by a parent, but in addition may be made by the person concerned if that person 'has the capacity to make the claim'.[47]

---

41   EQA 2010, s 87.
42   See *Secretary of State for Education and Science v Tameside Metropolitan Borough Council* [1977] AC 1014.
43   See EA 1996, s 497(3) concerning s 497 and the *Tameside* case concerning s 496.
44   EQA 2010, s 114(1) and (3).
45   EQA 2010, s 116(1). The powers to make rules governing the procedure for such claims in relation to Wales and Scotland are in Sch 17, paras 6 and 10 respectively. Claims to the First-tier Tribunal (in relation to a claim concerning a school in England) will be governed by the rules made for that tribunal under the legislation under which it was established.
46   See EQA 2010, Sch 17, para 3.
47   EQA 2010, Sch 17, para 8.

9.21 Claims which may also not be made to a county court in respect of Part 6 of the EQA 2010 are certain claims of disability discrimination in relation to admission or exclusion from a maintained school or an Academy.[48] Such claims must instead be made to an independent appeal panel under arrangements made under s 94 of the School Standards and Framework Act 1998 (SSFA 1998) or under an agreement between the responsible body for an Academy and the Secretary of State under s 482 of the EA 1996.[49] These are appeals against refusals of admission to, or permanent exclusion from, maintained schools in England and Wales and Academies in England. The appeal panel may in such an appeal not order that the responsible body pays compensation. Similarly, a claim of disability discrimination (which may be of discrimination in relation to a fixed-period exclusion) on the part of a school, which must be made to a tribunal of the sorts to which reference is made in the preceding paragraph above, may not result in an award of financial compensation even if it is successful.[50]

Accessibility duty

9.22 There is a separate duty imposed on a local authority to prepare an accessibility strategy and on the responsible body of a school to prepare an accessibility plan.[51] The accessibility strategy (which must be in writing[52]) is:

'a strategy for, over a prescribed period –

(a) increasing the extent to which disabled pupils can participate in the schools' curriculums;

(b) improving the physical environment of the schools for the purpose of increasing the extent to which disabled pupils are able to take advantage of education and benefits, facilities or services provided or offered by the schools;

(c) improving the delivery to disabled pupils of information which is readily accessible to pupils who are not disabled.'[53]

9.23 That 'delivery' must be 'within a reasonable time' and 'in ways which are determined after taking account of the pupils' disabilities and any preferences expressed by them or their parents'.[54] A local authority must keep its accessibility strategy under review during the period to which it relates, must if necessary revise it, and must implement it.[55] In preparing the strategy, the authority must have regard to 'the need to allocate adequate resources for

---

[48] See EQA 2010, s 116(2) and Sch 17, paras 13 and 14.

[49] Ibid.

[50] See EQA 2010, Sch 17, paras 5(3)(b) and 9(3)(b).

[51] See EQA 2010, s 88 and Sch 10, paras 1(1) and 3(1). The term 'responsible body' is defined for the purposes of Sch 10 in para 6(5)–(7) of Sch 10; it is in effect the same as it is in s 85(9).

[52] EQA 2010, Sch 10, para 1(4).

[53] EQA 2010, Sch 10, para 1(3). The word 'prescribed' means 'prescribed by regulations': see EQA 2010, s 212(1). Regulations made under the EQA 2010 must be made in accordance with whichever of ss 208–210 applies.

[54] EQA 2010, Sch 10, para 1(3).

[55] EQA 2010, Sch 10, para 1(5) and (6).

implementing the strategy' and when preparing and revising the strategy the authority must have regard to guidance issued for England by a Minister of the Crown or (as the case may be) for Wales by the Welsh Ministers[56] in relation to (1) the content of the strategy, (2) the form in which it is to be produced, and (3) the persons to be consulted in its preparation.[57]

9.24   The accessibility plan which the responsible body of a school in England or Wales must prepare is:

'a plan for, over a prescribed period-

(a)   increasing the extent to which disabled pupils can participate in the school's curriculum,

(b)   improving the physical environment of the school for the purpose of increasing the extent to which disabled pupils are able to take advantage of education and benefits, facilities or services provided or offered by the school, and

(c)   improving the delivery to disabled pupils of information which is readily accessible to pupils who are not disabled.'[58]

9.25   That 'delivery' must be 'within a reasonable time' and 'in ways which are determined after taking account of the pupils' disabilities and any preferences expressed by them or their parents.'[59] The responsible body must keep its accessibility plan under review during the period to which it relates, must if necessary revise it, and must implement it.[60] In preparing the plan, the responsible body must 'have regard to the need to allocate adequate resources for implementing the plan'.[61] An inspection of the sort which Ofsted carries out 'may extend to the performance by the responsible body of its functions in relation to the preparation, publication, review, revision and implementation of its accessibility plan'.[62] The proprietor of an independent educational institution other than an Academy must make the plan available for inspection at reasonable times, and must on request supply a copy of the plan to (in England) a Minister of the Crown or (in Wales) the Welsh Ministers.[63]

Power to direct a responsible body

9.26   There is a power to give a direction to a responsible body in relation to the discharge of a duty imposed by Sch 10 to the EQA 2010. The power is exercisable by the 'appropriate authority', which is the Secretary of State in

---

56   See s 45 of the Government of Wales Act 2006 for the meaning of the term 'the Welsh Ministers'.

57   EQA 2010, Sch 10, para 2(1)–(4).

58   EQA 2010, Sch 10, para 3(2). Regulations may prescribe services which are, or are not, to be regarded as being (a) education, and/or (b) a benefit, facility or service for the purposes of Sch 10: Sch 10, para 6(2) and (3).

59   EQA 2010, Sch 10, para 3(3).

60   EQA 2010, Sch 10, para 3(5) and (6).

61   EQA 2010, Sch 10, para 4(1).

62   EQA 2010, Sch 10, para 3(7) and (8).

63   EQA 2010, Sch 10, para 4(2)–(4).

relation to a school in England and the Welsh Ministers in relation to a school in Wales.[64] It is in the same terms, suitably adapted, as ss 496 and 497 of the EA 1996, and arises where the appropriate authority is satisfied that a responsible body has acted 'unreasonably' in the discharge of a duty under Sch 10 or is proposing to do so, or that it has 'failed to discharge such a duty'.[65] It is enforceable by a mandatory order in the High Court.[66] If a complaint has been made about a matter to a Local Commissioner in accordance with Chapter 2 of Part 10 of the Apprenticeship, Skills, Children and Learning Act 2009 in relation to a responsible body of a school in England, or 'the appropriate authority thinks [that the matter] could have been so complained about', then a direction of the sort described in this paragraph may not be given in relation to that matter unless the Local Commissioner has made a recommendation to the responsible body under s 211(4) of that Act and the responsible body has not complied with the recommendation.[67]

9.27 There is an additional power to give a direction in relation to a school which is approved under s 342 of the EA 1996 (which will be a non-maintained special school) or to an Academy. That power arises where the appropriate authority is satisfied that a responsible body of a school of that sort has acted or is proposing to act unreasonably 'in the discharge of a duty the body has in relation to the provision to the authority of copies of the body's accessibility plan or the inspection of that plan' or has 'failed to discharge the duty'.[68]

9.28 There is a separate power of the same sort to direct a responsible body in relation to compliance with an order made by a tribunal under para 5 of Sch 17 to the EQA 2010 on a claim of disability discrimination (which will in England be made to the First-tier Tribunal, in Wales to the Special Educational Needs Tribunal for Wales, and in Scotland to an Additional Support Needs Tribunal for Scotland).[69]

Exceptions

9.29 There are detailed exceptions to the duty imposed on the responsible body of a school not to discriminate concerning the protected characteristics of sex, religious or belief-related discrimination, and disability discrimination. One is that the content of the curriculum is not affected by ss 84–89.[70]

---

[64]   EQA 2010, Sch 10, para 5(1) and (10).
[65]   EQA 2010, Sch 10, para 5(1) and (5).
[66]   EQA 2010, Sch 10, para 9(b).
[67]   EQA 2010, Sch 10, para 5(7) and (8).
[68]   EQA 2010, Sch 10, para 5(2) and (3).
[69]   EQA 2010, Sch 10, para 5(4), (5) and (9).
[70]   EQA 2010, s 89(2).

Sex discrimination

9.30 In addition, a single-sex school[71] is not affected by the duty imposed by s 85(1) of the EQA 2010 not to discriminate because of sex in relation to admission to the school.[72] Similarly, a school which is not a single-sex school but which admits boarders of one sex only is not obliged to comply with s 85(2)(a)–(d) in relation to boarding facilities.[73]

9.31 Transitional exemption orders may be made where a single-sex school decides to alter its admissions arrangements so that the school will cease to be single-sex, or where a school which has boarders of one sex only decides to admit boarders of both sexes.[74] The order must be made in relation to what may broadly be called a state school (other than an Academy) in accordance with the relevant regime relating to the alteration of a school.[75] In relation to an independent school (including an Academy), the order must be made by the Commission for Equality and Human Rights.[76] The Commission may not make the order unless it is satisfied that the terms of the application are reasonable having regard to '(a) the nature of the school's premises, (b) the accommodation, equipment and facilities available, and (c) the responsible body's financial resources.'[77]

Religious or belief-related discrimination

9.32 Schools which are formally designated as having a religious character or (as the case may be) ethos are exempt from the duty imposed by s 85(1) and 2(a)–(d) so far as relating to religion or belief.[78] Similarly, s 85(2)(a)–(d) so far as relating to religion or belief does not apply in relation to anything done in connection with acts of religious worship or other religious observance organised by or on behalf of a school (whether or not it forms part of the curriculum).[79] There is a power by order made by a Minister of the Crown to add, vary or omit an exception to the duty imposed by s 85 of the EQA 2010, but only in relation to religious or belief-related discrimination.[80] There is also a power by order to amend Sch 11 to the EQA 2010 'so as to make provision about the construction or application of section 19(2)(d) [which is the requirement for a person who is alleged to have discriminated indirectly to show that the provision, criterion or practice in question is 'a proportionate means of achieving a legitimate aim'] in relation to section 85', but, again, only in relation to religious or belief-related discrimination.[81] Before making such an

---

[71]   Defined by EQA 2010, Sch 11, para 1(2)–(4).
[72]   EQA 2010, Sch 11, para 1(1).
[73]   EQA 2010, Sch 11, para 2(1)–(4).
[74]   EQA 2010, Sch 11, para 3.
[75]   See EQA 2010, Sch 11, para 4(1)–(5).
[76]   EQA 2010, Sch 11, para 4(6)–(7).
[77]   EQA 2010, Sch 11, para 6(8).
[78]   EQA 2010, Sch 11, para 5. See **9.9** and **9.10** for the duties in s 85(1) and (2)(a)–(d).
[79]   EQA 2010, Sch 11, para 6.
[80]   EQA 2010, Sch 11, para 7(1)(a) and (2).
[81]   EQA 2010, Sch 11, para 7(1)(b) and (2).

order, the Minister must consult the Welsh Ministers, the Scottish Ministers, and 'such other persons as the Minister thinks appropriate'.[82]

FURTHER AND HIGHER EDUCATION

Protected characteristics which do not apply

9.33 The protected characteristic of marriage and civil partnership does not apply in relation to the provision of further and/or higher education.[83]

Further and higher education institutions

Admission

9.34 The responsible body of a further or higher education institution[84] may not discriminate against persons in the arrangements which it makes for deciding who is offered admission as a student,[85] as to the terms on which it offers to admit a person as a student,[86] or by not admitting a person as a student.[87]

Provision of education and services

9.35 The responsible body of a further or higher education institution must not discriminate against a student:

'(a) in the way it provides education for the student;
(b) in the way it affords the student access to a benefit, facility or service;
(c) by not providing education for the student;
(d) by not affording the student access to a benefit, facility or service;

---

[82] EQA 2010, Sch 11, para 7(3). See s 44(2) of the Scotland Act 1998 for the definition of the term 'Scottish Ministers'.
[83] EQA 2010, s 90.
[84] In this chapter, a reference to a 'further or higher education institution' is to be read as one falling within s 91(10) and (11) of the EQA 2010. In England and Wales those are universities (and the term 'university' in Ch 2 of Part 6 of the EQA 2010 'includes a reference to a university college and a college, school or hall of a university': EQA 2010, s 94(4)), all other institutions in the higher education sector (as defined by s 91 of the Further and Higher Education Act 1992: see EQA 2010, s 94(5)), and institutions in the further education sector (also as so defined). In Scotland, the term 'further or higher education institution' means (1) universities, (2) designated institutions within the meaning of s 44 of the Further and Higher Education (Scotland) Act 1992, and (3) colleges of further education within the meaning of s 36 of that Act: see EQA 2010 ss 91(11) and 94(8) and (9). The 'responsible body' of a 'further or higher education institution' is defined by EQA 2010, s 91(12). It is the governing body, or, in relation to a college of further education, the board of management or (where there is no formally constituted board of management) 'any board of governors of the college or any person responsible for the management of the college, whether or not formally constituted as a governing body or board of governors'.
[85] EQA 2010, s 91(1)(a). The term 'student' means in relation to an institution 'a person for whom education is provided by the institution': s 94(3).
[86] EQA 2010, s 91(1)(b).
[87] EQA 2010, s 91(1)(c).

(e)   by excluding the student;
(f)   by subjecting the student to any other detriment.'[88]

Harassment

9.36   The responsible body of a further or higher education institution must not harass (a) a student, (b) a person who has applied for admission as a student, or (c) a disabled person who holds or has applied for a qualification conferred by the institution.[89]

Victimisation

9.37   The responsible body of a further or higher education institution must not victimise a person:

'(a)   in the arrangements it makes for deciding who is to be offered admission as a student;
(b)   as to the terms on which it offers to admit the person as a student;
(c)   by not admitting the person as a student.'[90]

9.38   The responsible body of a further or higher education institution must not victimise a student:

'(a)   in the way it provides education for the student;
(b)   in the way it affords the student access to a benefit, facility or service;
(c)   by not providing education for the student;
(d)   by not affording the student access to a benefit, facility or service;
(e)   by excluding the student;
(f)   by subjecting the student to any other detriment.'[91]

9.39   The responsible body of a further or higher education institution must not victimise a disabled person:

'(a)   in the arrangements it makes for deciding upon whom to confer a qualification;
(b)   as to the terms on which it is prepared to confer a qualification on the person;
(c)   by not conferring a qualification on the person;
(d)   by withdrawing a qualification from the person or varying the terms on which the person holds it.'[92]

---

[88]   EQA 2010, s 91(2).
[89]   EQA 2010, s 91(5).
[90]   EQA 2010, s 91(6).
[91]   EQA 2010, s 91(7).
[92]   EQA 2010, s 91(8).

Duty to make reasonable adjustments

9.40 The responsible body of a further or higher education institution must make reasonable adjustments for disabled persons by complying with 'the first, second and third requirements' in relation to the manner in which the institution provides tuition and other services.[93]

Competence standards

9.41 However, there is no duty to make a reasonable adjustment where the provision, criterion or practice in question 'include[s] the application of a competence standard'.[94] Such a standard is 'an academic, medical or other standard applied for the purpose of determining whether or not a person has a particular level of competence or ability'.[95] The extent to which there is nevertheless a duty to make adjustments in relation to examinations is not entirely clear. An adjustment which assists a person to take the examination can shade into an adjustment which concerns the application of a competence standard. After all, if a disabled candidate requires more time to take an examination than those who are not disabled, then giving the disabled candidate that extra time may amount to an adjustment which assists the candidate to meet a competence standard. Whether or not it will do so will surely depend on the extent to which the ability to take the examination under timed conditions is an inherent part of a competence standard. However, the very fact that the examination is timed suggests that the ability to complete the examination within a certain period of time will itself be an aspect of the competence assessed by the examination. In addition, the obtaining of a higher education qualification is a sign to employers of a certain level of ability, and ability is shown not just by how well a person can carry out a particular task but also by the time which it takes to carry out that task well. It is therefore suggested that the statement in para 5.74 of the code of practice concerning post-16 education which was current at the time when the EQA 2010 was enacted is at best dubious. That paragraph must be read with those which precede it:

> '5.72 Education providers are likely to impose various requirements and conditions in respect of courses.
>
> 5.73 However, any such requirement or condition only amounts to a competence standard if its purpose is to demonstrate a particular level of a relevant competence or ability. A requirement that a person has a particular level of knowledge of a subject is likely to be a competence standard.
>
> The requirement for students studying for a law degree to demonstrate a particular standard of knowledge of certain areas of law in order to obtain the degree is a competence standard.

---

93   See EQA 2010, s 91(9) and Sch 13, para 3(2). See Chapter 3 above for these requirements. See further Sch 13, paras 3 and 4 in relation to the manner in which the duty to make reasonable adjustments must be complied with.

94   EQA 2010, Sch 13, para 4(2).

95   EQA 2010, Sch 13, para 4(3).

5.74   On the other hand, a condition that a person can, for example, do something within a certain period of time will not be a competence standard if it does not determine a particular level of competence or ability.'

9.42   The one reservation which it is necessary to state is that it is arguable that extra time should be permitted for the taking of an examination if an employer could reasonably be expected to allow an employee performing the same or a similar task more time to carry out that task than persons who are not disabled. However, against that it can reasonably be said that:

- a public qualification is a declaration of a candidate's ability;

- an employer is entitled to know what a prospective employee is able to do when tested under the same conditions as persons who are not disabled;

- the indication by the prospective employee of a disability will put the employer on notice that the candidate's performance may be increased by the making of reasonable adjustments; and

- it would be wrong for examiners to be required to make judgments about a disabled person's likely performance at work if reasonable adjustments are made.

9.43   In addition, and in any event, academic examinations are not a wholly reliable indicator of achievement in practice. It might, however, be said that a disabled candidate is entitled to know that he or she is as knowledgeable as a non-disabled candidate, and is therefore entitled to the same amount of self-esteem of the sort which is gained from the public recognition of that knowledge as that which a non-disabled person with the same level of ability would obtain from the taking of the examination. That, logically, is a valid argument, but it fails to take into account the predominant purpose of examinations, which is to test ability, and that discounting a person's *disability* in determining his or her *ability* could (depending on the circumstances) be illogical.

Further exceptions

9.44   There are further detailed exceptions to the duty imposed on the responsible body of a further or higher education institution not to discriminate. One is that the content of the curriculum is not affected by ss 90–94.[96] Another is that as with schools, there are exceptions concerning admission to single-sex institutions.[97] There is also provision for single-sex

---

[96]   EQA 2010, s 94(2).
[97]   EQA 2010, Sch 12, para 1.

institutions turning co-educational and consequential transitional exemption orders.[98] Such orders must be made by the Commission for Equality and Human Rights.[99]

9.45 A further exception to the duty imposed on the responsible body of a further or higher education institution not to discriminate relates to religion or belief. In the case of a further or higher education institution which a Minister of the Crown has by order designated as having 'a religious ethos', the exception relates to admission to 'a course at the institution' in relation to which the responsible body:

'(a)   gives preference to persons of a particular religion or belief,
(b)   it does so to preserve the institution's religious ethos, and
(c)   the course is not a course of vocational training.'[100]

9.46 There are more exceptions to the duty imposed on the responsible body of a further or higher education institution not to discriminate. One is that a person will not contravene that duty by treatment of another person which relates only to training which would help fit that other person for work for which there is an occupational requirement.[101] Another such exception is that there is no breach of the duty not to discriminate 'so far as relating to sexual orientation, by providing married persons and civil partners (to the exclusion of all other persons) with access to a benefit, facility or service'.[102]

9.47 Furthermore, a further or higher education institution will not contravene the duty not to discriminate so far as relating to age 'only by providing, or making arrangements for or facilitating the provision of, care for children of a particular age group'.[103] For this purpose, a 'child' means a person who has not attained the age of 17, and '[a] reference to care includes a reference to supervision'.[104] Moreover, facilitating the provision of care for a child is stated to include:

'(a)   paying for some or all of the cost of the provision;
(b)   helping a parent of the child to find a suitable person to provide care for the child;
(c)   enabling a parent of the child to spend more time providing care for the child or otherwise assisting the parent with respect to the care that the parent provides for the child.'[105]

---

[98]   EQA 2010, Sch 12, paras 2 and 3.
[99]   EQA 2010, Sch 12, para 3.
[100]   EQA 2010, Sch 12, para 5.
[101]   EQA 2010, Sch 12, para 4.
[102]   EQA 2010, Sch 12, para 6.
[103]   EQA 2010, Sch 12, para 7(1).
[104]   EQA 2010, Sch 12, paras 7(3) and (4).
[105]   EQA 2010, Sch 12, para 7(2).

Further and higher education courses

9.48 There are separate duties imposed by the EQA 2010 on the providers of further and higher education courses other than further and higher education institutions. This is because local authorities and maintained schools[106] may provide further or higher education. The separate duties mirror those imposed on further and higher education institutions. The duties are imposed on the 'responsible body in relation to' a course to which s 92 of the EQA applies. That body will be the local authority[107] or the governing body of the school in question.[108] A course for this purpose 'includes each component part of a course if there is no requirement imposed on persons registered for a component part of the course to register for another component part of the course'.[109]

9.49 The duties imposed on the responsible body include a duty not to discriminate against a person:

'(a) in the arrangements [the responsible body] makes for deciding who is enrolled on the course;
(b) as to the terms on which it offers to enrol the person on the course;
(c) by not accepting the person's application for enrolment.'[110]

9.50 Similarly, the responsible body 'must not discriminate against a person who is enrolled on the course in the services it provides or offers to provide'.[111] It also must not harass a person who '(a) seeks enrolment on the course; (b) is enrolled on the course; [or] (c) is a user of services provided by the body in relation to the course.'[112] It must also not victimise a person '(a) in the arrangements it makes for deciding who is enrolled on the course; (b) as to the terms on which it offers to enrol the person on the course; [or] (c) by not accepting the person's application for enrolment'.[113] In addition, the responsible body must not 'victimise a person who is enrolled on the course in

---

[106] Within the meaning of s 20(7) of the SSFA 1998: EQA 2010, s 92(9).
[107] This means in relation to England an English local authority within the meaning of s 162 of the Education and Inspections Act 2006, in relation to Wales a Welsh local authority within the meaning of that section, and in relation to Scotland it means an 'education authority' as defined by s 135(1) of the Education (Scotland) Act 1980: see EQA 2010, s 94(10) and (11).
[108] EQA 2010, s 92(7) and (8).
[109] EQA 2010, s 92(9). The terms 'further education' and 'higher education' are defined by s 94(6) and (7) respectively. In relation to England and Wales the term 'further education' has the meaning given to it by s 2 of the EA 1996, and in relation to Scotland it has the meaning given in s 1(3) of the Further and Higher Education (Scotland) Act 1992. The term 'higher education' in relation to England and Wales means education provided by means of a course of a description mentioned in Sch 6 to the Education Reform Act 1988. In relation to Scotland, the term 'higher education' has the meaning given in s 38 of the Further and Higher Education (Scotland) Act 1992.
[110] EQA 2010, s 92(1). The word 'enrolment' includes registration for a component part of a course: s 92(9).
[111] EQA 2010, s 92(2). The word 'services' means services of any description which are provided wholly or mainly for persons enrolled on a course to which [s 92] applies: s 92(9).
[112] EQA 2010, s 92(3).
[113] EQA 2010, s 92(4).

the services it provides or offers to provide'.[114] The responsible body must in addition make reasonable adjustments for disabilities by complying with the first, second and third requirements set out in s 20(3), (4) and (5) of the EQA 2010.[115] The 'competence standard' exception does not apply to the responsible body in relation to a course to which s 92 of the EQA 2010 applies. This is presumably because although the courses are provided by the responsible bodies, the qualifications are not awarded by those bodies.

9.51 The content of the curriculum is not affected by s 92.[116] The other exceptions which apply to further and higher education institutions to which reference is made in paras 9.44–9.47 above are not applied to the courses to which s 92 applies. Thus, oddly, the exemption relating to occupational requirements to which reference is made in **9.46** does not apply to the courses to which s 92 applies. Presumably this is because the EQA 2010 was intended merely to replicate the prior provision in this regard.[117]

Recreational and training facilities

9.52 Recreational and training facilities which are provided by (a) a local authority in England under s 507A or 507B of the EA 1996, (b) a local authority in Wales under s 508 of that Act, and (c) an education authority in Scotland, are the subject of s 93 of the EQA 2010. The facilities to which s 93 applies are therefore:

- facilities which are secured by a local authority in England in order to comply with its duty to secure that the facilities for primary and secondary education in its area include adequate facilities for recreation and social and physical training for children who have not attained the age of 13;

- educational and recreational leisure-time activities which are secured by a local authority in England (a) for persons who have attained the age of 13 but not 20 and (b) persons who have attained the age of 20 but not the age of 25 and have a learning difficulty within the meaning of s 13(5)(a) and (6) of the Learning and Skills Act 2000, and which are for the improvement of those young persons' well-being;

- facilities which are secured by a local authority in Wales in order to comply with its duty to secure that the facilities for primary and secondary education in its area include adequate facilities for recreation and social and physical training; and

- any recreational and training facilities provided by an education authority in Scotland.

---

[114] EQA 2010, s 92(5).
[115] EQA 2010, s 92(6) and Sch 13, para 5.
[116] EQA 2010, s 94(2).
[117] See the Explanatory Notes to Sch 12, para 4.

9.53 The responsible body 'in relation to such facilities' (which will be the local authority[118]) must not discriminate against a person:

> '(a) in the arrangements it makes for deciding who is provided with the facilities;
> (b) as to the terms on which it offers to provide the facilities to the person;
> (c) by not accepting the person's application for provision of the facilities.'[119]

9.54 Further, the responsible body in relation to such facilities 'must not discriminate against a person who is provided with the facilities in the services it provides or offers to provide'.[120] Nor may it harass a person who '(a) seeks to have the facilities provided; (b) is provided with the facilities; [or] (c) is a user of services provided by the body in relation to the facilities'.[121] The responsible body in relation to such facilities in addition must not victimise a person '(a) in the arrangements it makes for deciding who is provided with the facilities; (b) as to the terms on which it offers to provide the facilities to the person; [or] (c) by not accepting the person's application for provision of the facilities'.[122] Furthermore, a responsible body in relation to such facilities 'must not victimise a person who is provided with the facilities in the services it provides or offers to provide'.[123]

9.55 The responsible body is also under a duty to make reasonable adjustments in relation to the facilities in question, by complying with all three requirements in s 20(3), (4) and (5).[124]

Exception

9.56 Section 93 'does not apply to the protected characteristic of age, so far as relating to persons who have not attained the age of 18'.[125]

GENERAL QUALIFICATIONS BODIES

What is a 'general qualifications body'?

9.57 The term 'general qualifications body' does not appear in the EQA 2010. The term appears only in the plural and even then appears only in headings or side notes to the EQA 2010. The term 'general' is not used in the provisions of that Act in relation to 'qualifications body'. A 'qualifications body' is 'an authority or body which can confer a relevant qualification'.[126] The term 'relevant qualification' is defined as:

---

[118] See EQA 2010, s 93(8).
[119] EQA 2010, s 93(1).
[120] EQA 2010, s 93(2).
[121] EQA 2010, s 93(3).
[122] EQA 2010, s 93(4).
[123] EQA 2010, s 93(5).
[124] EQA 2010, s 93(6) and Sch 13, para 6.
[125] EQA 2010, s 93(9).
[126] EQA 2010, s 97(2).

'an authorisation, qualification, approval or certification of such description as may be prescribed –

(a)   in relation to conferments in England, by a Minister of the Crown;
(b)   in relation to conferments in Wales, by the Welsh Ministers;
(c)   in relation to conferments in Scotland, by the Scottish Ministers.'[127]

9.58   In addition, a reference to conferring a relevant qualification 'includes a reference' to 'renewing or extending the conferment of a relevant qualification' and to 'authenticating a relevant qualification conferred by another person'.[128]

9.59   A qualifications body does *not* include 'the responsible body of a school to which section 85 applies',[129] 'the governing body of an institution to which section 91 applies',[130] a body insofar as it exercises functions under the Education Acts,[131] or a body insofar as it exercises functions under the Education (Scotland) Act 1980.[132] Nor will it include any authority or body stated to be excluded by regulations made under s 97(5) of the EQA 2010 (none of which have yet been made).

Protected characteristic which does not affect the specific duties owed by qualifications bodies

9.60   For the purposes of the duties owed by qualifications bodies by reason of ss 96 and 97 of the EQA 2010, marriage and civil partnership is not a protected characteristic within the meaning of s 4 of that Act.[133]

The duties owed by qualifications bodies

9.61   A qualifications body must not discriminate against a person:

'(a)   in the arrangements [it] makes for deciding upon whom to confer a relevant qualification;
(b)   as to the terms on which it is prepared to confer a relevant qualification on [that person]; [or]
(c)   by not conferring a relevant qualification on [that person].'[134]

9.62   Further, a qualifications body must not discriminate against a person upon whom the body has conferred a relevant qualification by (a) withdrawing

---

127   EQA 2010, s 97(3). For this purpose, a qualification is conferred in a part of Great Britain if there are, or may reasonably be expected to be, persons seeking to obtain the qualification who are or will be assessed for those purposes wholly or mainly in that part: EQA 2010, ss 96(11) and 97(8).
128   EQA 2010, s 97(6).
129   EQA 2010, s 97(4)(a). See **9.6** for such a body.
130   EQA 2010, s 97(4)(b). See **9.34** above for the meaning of an institution to which s 91 applies.
131   EQA 2010, s 97(4)(c); the term 'Education Acts' has the meaning given it by s 578 of the EA 1996: see EQA 2010, s 212(1).
132   EQA 2010, s 97(4)(d).
133   EQA 2010, s 95.
134   EQA 2010, s 96(1).

the qualification, (b) varying the terms on which that person holds the qualification, or (c) subjecting that person to 'any other detriment'.[135]

9.63 A qualifications body must not, in relation to conferment by it of a relevant qualification, harass (a) a person who holds the qualification or (b) a person who applies for it.[136]

9.64 A qualifications body must also not victimise a person upon whom it has conferred a relevant qualification by (a) withdrawing the qualification, (b) varying the terms on which that person holds the qualification, or (c) subjecting that person to 'any other detriment'.[137] A qualifications body will also act unlawfully if it victimises a person:

> '(a)   in the arrangements [it] makes for deciding upon whom to confer a relevant qualification;
> (b)   as to the terms on which it is prepared to confer a relevant qualification on [that person]; [or]
> (c)   by not conferring a relevant qualification on [that person].'[138]

9.65 A qualifications body is obliged to make reasonable adjustments for disabled persons by complying with all three requirements in s 20(3), (4) and (5) of the EQA 2010.[139] However, this duty may be qualified by a person prescribed in regulations made by (a) a Minister of the Crown in relation to a qualifications body that confers qualifications in England, (b) the Welsh Ministers in relation to a qualifications body that confers qualifications in Wales, and (c) the Scottish Ministers in relation to a qualifications body that confers qualifications in Scotland.[140] Such a person is an 'appropriate regulator' for the purposes of s 96. That regulator may specify:

> 'provisions, criteria or practices in relation to which the [relevant qualifications] body-
>
> (a)   is not subject to a duty to make reasonable adjustments;
> (b)   is subject to a duty to make reasonable adjustments, but in relation to which such adjustments as the regulator specifies should not be made.'[141]

9.66 For these purposes, the appropriate regulator must have regard to:

> '(a)   the need to minimise the extent to which disabled persons are disadvantaged in attaining the qualification because of their disabilities;

---

[135]   EQA 2010, s 96(2).
[136]   EQA 2010, s 96(3).
[137]   EQA 2010, s 96(5).
[138]   EQA 2010, s 96(4).
[139]   EQA 2010, s 96(6) and Sch 13, paras 3, 4(1) and 9(1) and (2).
[140]   EQA 2010, s 96(7) and (10).
[141]   EQA 2010, s 96(7).

(b) the need to secure that the qualification gives a reliable indication of the knowledge, skills and understanding of a person upon whom it is conferred; [and]

(c) the need to maintain public confidence in the qualification.'[142]

9.67 Before specifying any matter for the purpose of s 96(7),[143] the appropriate regulator must consult 'such persons as it thinks appropriate' and 'must publish matters so specified (including the date from which they are to have effect) in such manner as is prescribed'.[144]

9.68 The 'appropriate regulator' is a new body, whose introduction is likely to assist in the resolution of difficulties of the sort to which reference is made in **9.41–9.43**.

EDUCATIONAL CHARITIES AND ENDOWMENTS

9.69 Finally in this chapter, it is necessary to refer to the effect of the EQA 2010 on educational charities and endowments which restrict the benefit of the property held by the charity or the endowment to persons of one sex.

Educational charities in England and Wales

9.70 In England and Wales, if there is a trust deed or other instrument which concerns property which is applicable for or in connection with the provision of education in an establishment in England and Wales to which s 85 or 91 of the EQA 2010 applies (that is, schools and further and higher education institutions) which in any way restricts the benefits available under the instrument to persons of one sex, then, subject to several conditions, a Minister of the Crown may 'by order make such modifications of the instrument as appear to the Minister expedient for removing or modifying the restriction'.[145] Such an order may be made only on the application of the trustees or the responsible body of the school or institution in question.[146] In order to be entitled to make such an order, the Minister must be 'satisfied that the removal or modification of the restriction would be conducive to the advancement of education without sex discrimination'.[147]

9.71 In addition, the Minister must require the applicant for the order to publish (in a manner specified by the Minister[148]) a notice containing particulars of the proposed order and stating that representations may be made

---

[142] EQA 2010, s 96(8).
[143] Concerning which, see **9.65**.
[144] EQA 2010, s 96(9).
[145] EQA 2010, Sch 14, paras 1(1) and (3).
[146] EQA 2010, Sch 14, para 1(2).
[147] Ibid.
[148] EQA 2010, Sch 14, para 1(8).

to the Minister within a period specified in the notice.[149] That period may not be less than a month beginning with the day after the date of the notice.[150] The cost of the publication may be paid out of the property of the trust.[151] The Minister must then before making the order take account of any representations made in accordance with the notice.[152]

9.72 If the trust was created by a gift or bequest, then, unless the donor or personal representatives of the donor or testator consent in writing to making the application for the order, such an order may not be made before the end of the period of 25 years from the date when the gift or bequest took effect.[153]

EDUCATIONAL ENDOWMENTS IN SCOTLAND

9.73 Equivalent provisions apply to Scotland. If there is an educational endowment[154] to which s 104 of the Education (Scotland) Act 1980 applies which in any way restricts the benefit of the endowment to persons of one sex, then, subject to several conditions, the Scottish Ministers may 'by order make such provision as they think expedient for removing or modifying the restriction'.[155] Such an order may be made only on the application of the governing body of the educational endowment in question.[156] In order to be entitled to make such an order, the Ministers must be 'satisfied that the removal or modification of the provision which restricts the benefit of the endowment to persons of one sex would be conducive to the advancement of education without sex discrimination'.[157]

9.74 If the Ministers propose to make such an order then they must publish a notice in such manner as they think sufficient for giving information to persons they think may be interested in the endowment containing particulars of the proposed order and stating that representations may be made with respect to the proposal within such period as is specified in the notice.[158] That period may not be less than a month beginning with the day after the date of the publication of the notice.[159] The cost of the publication may be paid out of the funds of the endowment to which the notice relates.[160] The Ministers must then before making the order take account of any representations made in

---

[149]   EQA 2010, Sch 14, para 1(6).
[150]   EQA 2010, Sch 14, para 1(7).
[151]   EQA 2010, Sch 14, para 1(9).
[152]   EQA 2010, Sch 14, para 1(10).
[153]   EQA 2010, Sch 14, para 1(4) and (5).
[154]   A reference to an educational endowment for this purpose includes a reference to those endowments which are specified in para 2(8) of Sch 14 to the EQA 2010.
[155]   EQA 2010, Sch 14, paras 2(1) and (3); see also para 2(9).
[156]   EQA 2010, Sch 14, para 2(2).
[157]   Ibid.
[158]   EQA 2010, Sch 14, para 2(4).
[159]   EQA 2010, Sch 14, para 2(5).
[160]   EQA 2010, Sch 14, para 2(6).

accordance with the notice.[161] They may also cause a local inquiry to be held into the representations under s 67 of the Education (Scotland) Act 1980.[162]

---

[161] EQA 2010, Sch 14, para 2(7)(a).
[162] EQA 2010, Sch 14, para 2(7)(b).

Chapter 10
ASSOCIATIONS

INTRODUCTION

10.1 Part 7 of the Equality Act 2010 (EQA 2010) applies to all of the protected characteristics apart from marriage and civil partnership.[1] Previous legislation provided protection from discrimination, harassment and victimisation by associations against existing or potential members and associates because of race, disability and sexual orientation.[2] The provisions therefore extend protection to the characteristics of gender, age, religion or belief, pregnancy and maternity, and gender reassignment. The exclusion of marriage and civil partnership is consistent with the fact that they are protected characteristics in respect of the employment provisions in the EQA 2010 only.

10.2 Part 7 also does not apply to discrimination, harassment or victimisation prohibited under Part 3 (services and public functions), Part 4 (premises), Part 5 (work) or Part 6 (education) or that would be prohibited if it were not subject to an express exception.[3] In other words, those provisions would apply – for example – to harassment at work, rather than the provisions under this Part.

ASSOCIATIONS

10.3 The definition of an association is that it must have at least 25 members and admission to membership must be regulated by the association's rules and involve a process of selection.[4] The requirement that the number of members should be 25 can be amended by statutory instrument.[5] It does not matter whether an association is incorporated or whether its activities are carried on for profit.[6]

10.4 Casinos, nightclubs and gyms are not associations for the purposes of this Part, where payment of the requisite 'membership' fee is all that is required

---

1   EQA 2010, s 100(1).
2   Race Relations Act 1976, s 25; the Disability Discrimination (Private Clubs etc.) Regulations 2005, SI 2005/3258; and the Equality Act (Sexual Orientation) Regulations 2007, SI 2007/1263.
3   EQA 2010, s 100(2).
4   EQA 2010, s 107(2).
5   EQA 2010, s 107(3).
6   EQA 2010, s 107(4).

to secure admittance, as there is no process of selection. However, these are covered by the provisions in Part 3 concerning services provided to the public. In contrast, a private members' golf club, would be included in the definition of an association, provided there was a selection process and a minimum membership of 25.[7] Informal associations such as a book club run by a group of friends, where there are no formal rules governing admittance and/or whose membership is less than 25, would therefore not be associations for the purposes of this Part.

DISCRIMINATION AGAINST MEMBERS

10.5 Any kind of membership of an association that falls within the statutory definition is covered by Part 7.[8] This would cover the membership of full members, temporary members and day members, as well as associate members, who are therefore not members of the association, but have some of the rights of members as a consequence of being a member of another association.

10.6 An association must not discriminate against a person in three ways: (a) in the arrangements it makes for deciding who to admit to membership; (b) as to the terms on which it is prepared to admit that person to membership; or (c) by not accepting that person's application for membership.[9] Once that person has become a member, the association must not discriminate against the member: (a) in the way it affords or does not afford the member access to a benefit, facility or service; (b) by depriving the member of membership; (c) by varying the member's terms of membership; or (d) by subjecting the member to any other detriment.[10]

10.7 Similarly, an association must not discriminate against an associate member in the way it affords or does not afford an associate access to a benefit, facility or service; by depriving the associate of rights as an associate or by varying those rights; or by subjecting the associate to any other detriment.[11]

10.8 The Explanatory Notes provide two examples.[12] The first example is of a gentlemen's club that refuses to accept a person's application for membership or charges him a higher subscription rate because he is Muslim.

10.9 Without further explanation, a gentleman's club might seem to be exactly what this Part of the EQA 2010 was seeking to prohibit. However, Sch 16 contains the exceptions, one of which is that an association does not contravene s 101 by restricting membership to persons who share a protected

---

[7]   EN para 356.
[8]   EQA 2010, s 107(5).
[9]   EQA 2010, s 101(1).
[10] EQA 2010, s 101(2).
[11] EQA 2010, s 101(3).
[12] EN para 337.

characteristic.[13] Therefore, a gentleman's club is lawful because it restricts membership to those sharing a protected characteristic, namely being male. Similarly, an association restricted to those of the same religious belief or the same sexual orientation would be lawful. The caveat is colour.[14] An association could restrict membership (for example) to Afro-Caribbean people, because a reference to persons who share the protected characteristic of race is a reference to persons of the same racial group.[15] However, it could not restrict membership to black people.

10.10   Registered political parties are not included within the exception.[16] Therefore, the British National Party – a frequent example at the Committee stages of the Bill – could not rely upon Sch 16 to restrict membership to British members, just as it could not have a 'whites only' membership.

10.11   However, while the gentleman's club can restrict membership to men, it cannot then discriminate against Muslim men by restricting its membership further to exclude another protected characteristic. To take another example, an association for the over-65s would be lawful, but an association for Jewish over-65s would not be lawful, because that would restrict membership to people sharing two protected characteristics: religion and age.

10.12   A club for deaf people can restrict membership to people who are deaf and would not need to admit people with other disabilities, such as a blind person.[17] That is because, in relation to the protected characteristic of disability, a reference to persons who share a protected characteristic is a reference to persons who have the same disability.[18]

10.13   The second example in the EN is of a private members' golf club, which has members of both sexes, but requires its female members to play only on certain days while allowing male members to play at all times. This would be direct discrimination because the club would be denying female members access to the same benefit of membership (unrestricted playing times) as members who are male.[19]

10.14   This example is a reminder that another provision of the EQA may also affect associations and how they treat members.[20] Staying with the example of a private members' golf club, a golf competition would be a 'gender-affected activity', in other words, 'a sport, game or other activity of a competitive nature in circumstances in which the physical strength, stamina or physique of average persons of one sex would put them at a disadvantage compared to

---

13   EQA 2010, Sch 16, para 1(1).
14   EQA 2010, Sch 16, para 1(4).
15   EQA 2010, s 9(2)(b).
16   EQA 2010, Sch 16, para 1(5).
17   EN para 918.
18   EQA 2010, s 6(3)(b).
19   EN para 337.
20   EQA 2010, s 195.

average persons of the other sex as competitors in events involving the activity'.[21] Therefore, holding a competition in which participation is restricted to women would be lawful under the exception for sports (although golf might not be the best example). Holding that competition on a particular day, which meant that men could not play, would also be lawful. However, restricting women members to playing in the mornings when men can play golf at any time would not be lawful.

10.15 Since the protected characteristics of marriage and civil partnerships are excluded, an association for single people would be lawful and restricting that association to single members who share a protected characteristic (such as gender) would also be lawful.

10.16 An association that restricts membership to persons who share a protected characteristic does not breach s 101 by restricting the access by associates to a benefit, facility or service to such persons as share the characteristic.[22]

10.17 Health and safety risks for pregnant women provide an exception for associations. A pregnant woman applies to join a private sports club, but is told that, as a term upon which the association is prepared to admit her to membership, she will not be allowed to use the weights machines beyond 36 weeks into her pregnancy. This would not be discriminatory if that term was intended to remove or reduce a risk to her health and safety and the club reasonably believed that to do otherwise would create such a risk. The association would also have to take similar measures in respect of persons with other physical conditions that it admits to membership, in order to remove or reduce a risk to their health and safety, with the same reasonable belief that to do otherwise would create such a risk.[23]

10.18 Where a pregnant woman is a member of an association, there is a similar exception where the association either restricts her access to a benefit, facility or service or denies such access in order to remove or reduce a risk to her health and safety. It is not discriminatory to do so if there is a reasonable belief that there would otherwise be a risk to her health and safety and an equivalent approach is taken towards those at risk as a result of other physical conditions.[24] Equivalent provision is made in respect of associates and guests.[25]

10.19 Section 101 also includes provisions against harassment and victimisation of members, those seeking membership and associate membership.[26] Victimisation would include depriving someone of membership. However, harassment of members does not extend to the protected

---

[21]   EQA 2010, s 195(3).
[22]   EQA 2010, Sch 16, para 1(2).
[23]   EQA 2010, Sch 16, para 2(1); EN para 898.
[24]   EQA 2010, Sch 16, para 2(3), (4).
[25]   EQA 2010, Sch 16, para 2(3), (4).
[26]   EQA 2010, s 101(4)–(7).

characteristics of religion or belief or sexual orientation.[27] That is because, according to the Solicitor-General '[t]here is no evidence that people are being harassed because of their sexual orientation or religion or belief in situations outside work'.[28]

DISCRIMINATION AGAINST GUESTS

10.20 An association must not discriminate against a person (a) in the arrangements the association makes for deciding who to invite, or who to permit to be invited, as a guest; (b) as to the terms on which it is prepared to invite that person, or to permit them to be invited, as a guest; (c) by not inviting the person, or not permitting them to be invited, as a guest.[29]

10.21 An association must not discriminate against a guest invited by the association or with its permission (whether express or implied) (a) in the way the association affords the guest access, or by not affording the guest access, to a benefit, facility or service; (b) by subjecting the guest to any other detriment.[30] There are also provisions preventing harassment and victimisation of guests or those seeking to be guests.[31] As with members, harassment of guests does not extend to the protected characteristics of religion or belief or sexual orientation.[32]

10.22 For example, the refusal by an association to invite the disabled wife of a member to attend an annual dinner, which is open to all members' partners, simply because she is a wheelchair user, would amount to direct discrimination.[33] That example would have been relevant to the previous legislation, which provided protection for existing and potential guests of associations because of disability only. However, s 102 extends similar protection against discrimination to guests on the basis of all protected characteristics, except marriage and civil partnership.

10.23 An association that restricts membership to persons who share a protected characteristic does not breach s 102 by inviting as guests, or by permitting to be invited as guests, only such persons as share the characteristic.[34]

---

27 EQA 2010, s 103(2).
28 HC Public Committee on Equality Bill (18 June 2009) col 321 (Solicitor-General).
29 EQA 2010, s 102(1).
30 EQA 2010, s 102(2).
31 EQA 2010, s 102(3)–(5).
32 EQA 2010, s 103(2).
33 EN para 347.
34 EQA 2010, Sch 16, para 1(3).

REASONABLE ADJUSTMENTS

10.24 There is a duty on associations to make reasonable adjustments for disabled members, associates and guests and the extent of that duty is set out in Sch 15.[35] An association must comply with the first, second and third requirements under EQA 2010, s 20, namely: where a provision, criterion or practice or a physical feature put a disabled person at a substantial disadvantage, to take reasonable steps to avoid that disadvantage and, where a disabled person, but for the provision of an auxiliary aid, would be put at a substantial disadvantage, to take reasonable steps to provide the auxiliary aid.[36]

10.25 The EN provide two examples.[37] A private club with 30 members usually holds its annual dinner upstairs in a local restaurant. However, as there is no lift, the room is not accessible to two new disabled members who have severe difficulty in climbing stairs. Under the duty, the club would need to think about changing the venue to a downstairs room to accommodate the new members. Secondly, a club has members who cannot read standard print. Under the duty to make reasonable adjustments, it would need to think about providing information in large print and on audio tape for them.

10.26 The association is not required to take a step which would fundamentally alter the nature of the association or the nature of the benefit, facility or service concerned. Therefore, a potholing association, while still under a duty to make reasonable adjustments for disabled members, would not be required to make an adjustment that effectively curtailed the activity itself. Looked at another way, that step would not be reasonable.

10.27 Where an association holds meetings in a member's or an associate's house, there is no requirement to make adjustments to a physical feature of the house.

SELECTION OF CANDIDATES

10.28 Where the association is a registered political party, there are particular provisions relating to the selection of candidates, which allow political parties to address the under-representation of people with particular protected characteristics in elected bodies through making selection arrangements.[38]

10.29 'Selection arrangements' are arrangements which the party makes for regulating the selection of its candidates in a relevant election, the purpose of which is to reduce inequality in the party's representation in the body

---

[35]   EQA 2010, 103(1) and Sch 15, para 1.
[36]   EQA 2010, Sch 15, para 2(1).
[37]   EN para 914.
[38]   EQA 2010, s 104(1) and (2).

concerned, and which are a proportionate means of achieving that purpose.[39] The reference to inequality in a party's representation in a body means the difference between the number of the party's candidates elected to be members of the body who share a protected characteristic, and the number of those who do not share that characteristic.[40] For the purposes of this section, where people share the protected characteristic of disability, this means they are disabled persons, rather than having the same particular disability.[41]

10.30 In practice, this works in two ways. First, for all protected characteristics apart from sex, a party may reserve places on the shortlist for candidates with a particular protected characteristic as a means of addressing inequality in the party's representation, but it may not have a shortlist restricted to that protected characteristic.[42] For example, if the ethnic composition of a party's elected councillors on a particular council shows that there are very few Asian councillors, the party could choose to reserve a specific number of seats for Asian candidates on its by-election shortlist. However, the party could not shortlist only Asian candidates for the by-election.[43]

10.31 Secondly, there is an exception where the protected characteristic is sex.[44] In other words, a political party can have a women-only shortlist of potential candidates to represent a particular constituency in Parliament (for example), provided women remain under-represented in the party's Members of Parliament. Political parties were first allowed to draw up all-women shortlists in 2002, when a 'sunset clause' was included in the legislation, providing for the expiry of that provision in 2015.[45] However, with women only providing 21.9% of MPs after the 2010 election (142 out of 649), there clearly remains room for improvement and the exception where the protected characteristic is sex will now be automatically repealed at the end of 2030, unless an order is made to extend it beyond that date.[46]

10.32 To date, only the Labour Party has had all-women shortlists and 23 out of 30 women candidates chosen from all-women shortlists were elected in the 2005 election. The Conservative Party has so far stopped short of drawing up all-women shortlists, although David Cameron has voiced his support for them.[47] The Conservatives' Priority List (or 'A-List') is also aimed at selecting a

---

[39]   EQA 2010, s 104(3).
[40]   EQA 2010, s 104(4).
[41]   EQA 2010, s 104(5).
[42]   EQA 2010, s 104(6).
[43]   EN para 345.
[44]   EQA 2010, s 104(7).
[45]   Sex Discrimination Act 1975, s 42A, as amended by the Sex Discrimination (Election Candidates) Act 2002.
[46]   EQA 2010, s 105.
[47]   'David Cameron – I will impose all-women shortlists' *The Daily Telegraph*, 18 February 2010.

more representative cross-section of people for selection as candidates. The Liberal Democrats have rejected proposals to select from all-women shortlists.[48]

10.33 These provisions apply to Parliamentary Elections, elections to the European Parliament; elections to the Scottish Parliament and the National Assembly for Wales and to local government elections.[49]

INFORMATION ABOUT DIVERSITY OF CANDIDATES

10.34 Where a party has candidates at an election (excluding local government elections), it must publish information relating to protected characteristics of (a) successful and unsuccessful applicants for nomination as a candidate at the relevant election and (b) candidates at that election, whether elected or not.[50] The protected characteristics in this section do not include marriage and civil partnership or pregnancy and maternity.[51] The rationale for the exclusion of pregnancy and maternity is, 'the relatively temporary nature of such characteristics'.[52]

10.35 Although a political party 'must' publish information about – for example – the sexual orientation of candidates, it cannot require a candidate to provide it with that information.[53] This imbalance is addressed by a requirement that the information is accompanied by a statement showing the proportion of those who provided that information to those who were asked to provide it.[54]

10.36 Regulations will provide for the extent of the information, its timing and the manner in which it is published.[55] The duty applies only insofar as it is possible to publish information in a manner that ensures that no person to whom the information relates can be identified from that information.[56]

---

[48]   'All-women shortlists'; research note SN/PC/5057, 21 October 2009: http://www.parliament.uk/
       commons/lib/research/briefings/snpc-05057.pdf.
[49]   EQA 2010, s 104(8).
[50]   EQA 2010, s 106(1)–(3) and (5).
[51]   EQA 2010, s 106(6).
[52]   HL Committee on Equality Bill (27 January 2010) col 1468 (Baroness Royall of Blaisdon).
[53]   EQA 2010, s 106(11).
[54]   EQA 2010, s 106(7).
[55]   EQA 2010, s 106(2)–(3) and (7)–(10).
[56]   EQA 2010, s 106(4).

Chapter 11

TRANSPORT AND DISABLED PERSONS

INTRODUCTION

11.1 Part 12 of the Equality Act 2010 (EQA 2010) is concerned with the disability accessibility standards that apply in relation to taxis, private hire vehicles, public service vehicles and rail vehicles.[1] To a very large extent, these provisions replicate the comparable sections of Part 5 of the Disability Discrimination Act 1995 (DDA 1995), with some simplification of the statutory language.[2]

11.2 In many ways, Part 12 sits awkwardly beside the provisions on equality and discrimination. It does not provide any directly enforceable rights to disabled persons. It relies upon a combination of regulatory powers, administrative penalties and criminal sanctions. Part 12 does not seek to identify prohibited conduct by reference to a protected characteristic. Its provisions do not rest upon proof of disability or establishing discrimination, harassment or victimisation. Nevertheless, it recognises the disadvantage that disabled persons face in accessing public transport systems and public transport vehicles. Without Part 12 establishing standards for the design, maintenance and accessibility of transport vehicles, the provisions in Part 3 that address discrimination in relation to transport services would be considerably undermined.

11.3 That Part 12 works differently from the remainder of the Act is illustrated by four exceptions afforded its provisions. Part 12 does not apply in relation to a person who has had a disability as it applies in relation to a person who has the disability.[3] Section 109 (liability of employers and principals for the acts of their employees and agents) applies to the criminal offences created by Part 12, whereas it does not apply to offences created by the Act generally.[4] Section 113 (in relation to enforcement and proceedings under the Act) does not apply to proceedings relating to a penalty under Part 12.[5] The provisions of Part 12 (and Sch 20 associated with it) are not subject to the power of a Minister to make a harmonising provision under ss 203 to 204.[6]

---

[1]   EQA 2010, ss 160–188 and Sch 20.
[2]   Keter, 2009a: 92. This chapter draws upon Doyle, 2008: chapter 8.
[3]   EQA 2010, s 6(4).
[4]   EQA 2010, s 109(5).
[5]   EQA 2010, s 113(7)(b).
[6]   EQA 2010, s 203(10) and Sch 24.

11.4 The Government recognised that the provisions of Part 12 might in principle engage Art 1 of Protocol 1 to the European Convention on Human Rights (ECHR) (right to peaceful enjoyment of property).[7] For example, the taxi accessibility regulations below might be said to interfere with the freedom of the owners or operators of taxis to have vehicles designed and fitted out as they please. Nevertheless, the Government's belief is that the regulations would fall within the proviso to Art 1 of Protocol 1, recognising the right of States to enforce such laws as are deemed necessary to control the use of property in accordance with the general interest.[8] Similar considerations arise in relation to public vehicle accessibility regulations[9] and rail vehicle accessibility regulations.[10]

11.5 The duties upon drivers of taxis and private hire vehicles in relation to carrying assistance dogs (discussed below) might also be thought to interfere with the right to respect for private life (ECHR, Art 8) to the extent that the duty might impact upon a driver's physical health. In the Government's view, however, the exemption available to drivers from these duties on medical grounds ensures that these provisions are compatible with Art 8.[11]

TAXIS

Introduction

11.6 The EQA 2010, Part 3 duties in relation to services and public functions (discussed in Chapter 4 above) apply equally to an operator or a driver of a taxi as the provider of a service.[12] As with other transport vehicles, however, the Part 3 duties are not sufficient to overcome the super-structural problems associated with the design, manufacture and accessibility of taxi vehicles.

11.7 Most of the provisions in the EQA 2010 that relate to taxis replicate the similar provisions of the DDA 1995.[13] However, most of the taxi accessibility provisions in the DDA 1995 have never been brought into force.[14] The most

---

[7]   Joint Committee on Human Rights, 2009: Ev 53.
[8]   Joint Committee on Human Rights, 2009: Ev 53, paras 170–172.
[9]   Joint Committee on Human Rights, 2009: Ev 53, paras 181–183.
[10] Joint Committee on Human Rights, 2009: Ev 54, paras 265–271.
[11] Joint Committee on Human Rights, 2009: Ev 53, paras 177–178.
[12] See previously: DDA 1995, ss 19–21 and 21ZA, read with Disability Discrimination (Transport Vehicles) Regulations 2005, SI 2005/3190. See also: DRC, *Provision and Use of Transport Vehicles: Statutory Code of Practice: Supplement to Part 3 Code of Practice* (2006); and DRC, *Avoiding disability discrimination in transport: a practical guide for taxi and private hire services* (2007).
[13] EQA 2010, ss 160–173 (except s 161, which is new) replicate DDA 1995, ss 32–38. See EN paras 530–570.
[14] DDA 1995, ss 32–35 are not in force. DDA 1995, s 36 (carrying of passengers in wheelchairs) (insofar as it applies to designated vehicles) and s 36A (list of wheelchair-accessible vehicles providing local services) came into force on 26 January 2009. DDA 1995, s 37 (carrying of guide dogs and hearing dogs) and s 37A (carrying of assistance dogs in private hire vehicles) came into force fully in England and Wales on 31 March 2001 and 31 March 2004 respectively.

recent developments were triggered by the Local Transport Act 2008 which paved the way to extend to taxi-buses the DDA 1995 duties on the carrying of passengers in wheelchairs in taxis.[15] This resulted in consultation upon how best to bring the taxi accessibility provisions into effect. The consultation ended on 24 April 2009.[16] Subject to the outcome of that consultation, the effect of the EQA 2010 will be to activate the taxi accessibility standards and to apply them also in part to private hire vehicles.[17]

Taxi

11.8 The term taxi is closely defined in the present context.[18] Its primary meaning is a vehicle which is licensed under statute.[19] In no context does it include a vehicle drawn by a horse or other animal. The effect is that the new accessibility standards for taxis will apply only to hackney cabs or so-called black cabs. They will not apply to private hire cars or minicabs unless specifically extended to them. As will be seen below, however, private hire cars are to be increasingly caught by the accessibility provisions. At the same time, it is not intended that the taxi trade will in future be expected to make universal use of the London-style black cab or that the legislation (when in force) will produce a universal purpose-built taxi design.

Taxi accessibility regulations

11.9 The Secretary of State had been given power by the DDA 1995 to make taxi accessibility regulations.[20] By the time of the EQA 2010, however, this power had not been brought into force. No regulations had been made to date. However, these provisions are replicated and simplified in the EQA 2010.[21]

11.10 The purpose of taxi accessibility regulations will be to secure that it is possible for disabled persons (a) to get into and out of taxis in safety; (b) to do so while in wheelchairs; (c) to travel in taxis in safety and reasonable comfort; and (d) to do so while in wheelchairs.[22] The regulations may, in particular,

---

DDA 1995, s 38 (appeals) came into force on various dates. The history of the Government's changing intentions with regard to taxi accessibility is set out in Keter (2009a: 93–95) and Butcher (2009a: 10–12).

[15] Local Transport Act 2008, s 55; DDA 1995, s 36.

[16] Department for Transport (2009).

[17] EQA 2010, s 160 when brought into force.

[18] EQA 2010, s 173(1).

[19] Town Police Clauses Act 1847, s 37; Metropolitan Public Carriage Act 1869, s 6. For the purposes of EQA 2010, s 162 (designated transport facilities) and EQA 2010, ss 165–167 (passengers in wheelchairs and lists of wheelchair-accessible vehicles), the term also includes a taxi licensed under the Civic Government (Scotland) Act 1982, s 10. See Butcher (2009b) for an explanation of the various licensing regimes for taxis and private hire vehicles in London and outside London.

[20] DDA 1995, s 32. A commencement date had not been appointed. In Scotland, the powers to introduce the regulations were contained in the Civic Government (Scotland) Act 1982, s 20 (as amended).

[21] EQA 2010, s 160. See EN paras 530–532. See Butcher, 2009a: 10–12.

[22] EQA 2010, s 160(1).

require a regulated taxi[23] to conform with provision as to (i) the size of a door opening for the use of passengers; (ii) the floor area of the passenger compartment;[24] (iii) the amount of headroom in the passenger compartment; and (iv) the fitting of restraining devices designed to ensure the stability of a wheelchair while the taxi is moving.[25]

11.11 The taxi accessibility regulations may also place requirements upon the driver of a regulated taxi which is plying for hire (or which has been hired). The driver may be required to comply with provisions as to the carrying of ramps or other devices designed to facilitate the loading and unloading of wheelchairs.[26] The regulations may also place requirements upon the driver of a regulated taxi in which a disabled person is being carried while in a wheelchair. The driver may be required to comply with provisions as to the position in which the wheelchair is to be secured.[27]

11.12 The effect of these provisions is that taxi drivers must recognise their duty to carry disabled customers. It would not be lawful for drivers to refuse to pick up a disabled passenger in a wheelchair on the pretext that they are not carrying ramps. The driver of a regulated taxi which is plying for hire (or which has been hired) commits an offence by failing to comply with a requirement of the regulations. An offence is also committed if the taxi fails to conform to any required provision of the regulations.[28] A person guilty of such an offence is liable on summary conviction to a fine not exceeding level 3 on the standard scale (£1,000).[29]

Control of number of licensed taxis: exception

11.13 A new provision was introduced into the Equality Bill at Committee stage in the House of Lords.[30] It applies where an application for a taxi licence is made in respect of a vehicle.[31] Then the question is whether it is possible for a disabled person to get into and out of the vehicle in safety; and to travel in the vehicle in safety and reasonable comfort; and to do those things while in a wheelchair of a prescribed size.[32] An exception to the local authority's control of the number of licensed taxis may then apply if the proportion of taxis licensed in respect of the area to which the licence would (if granted) apply that conform to those requirements is less then the proportion that is prescribed by

---

23   That is, a taxi to which the taxi accessibility regulations are expressed to apply: EQA 2010, s 160(6).
24   The meaning of the term 'passenger compartment' is to be defined in the regulations: EQA 2010, s 160(6).
25   EQA 2010, s 160(2).
26   EQA 2010, s 160(3)(a).
27   EQA 2010, s 160(3)(b).
28   EQA 2010, s 160(4).
29   EQA 2010, s 160(5).
30   EQA 2010, s 161. See EN para 533–535.
31   EQA 2010, s 161(1)(a) and Town Police Clauses Act 1847, s 37.
32   EQA 2010, s 161(1)(b). The size of the wheelchair is to be prescribed by the Secretary of State.

the Secretary of State.[33] In the above circumstances, the modifications to the provisions about hackney carriages to allow a licence to ply for hire to be refused in order to limit the number of licensed carriages do not apply in relation to the vehicle.[34]

11.14 The Minister, in accepting the amendment that resulted in these provisions, explained their effects as follows:

'Taxi licensing and provision is a complicated area, and steps to improve access to taxis for disabled people are always welcome. It is unacceptable that a licensing authority which controls taxi numbers can routinely refuse applications for wheelchair-accessible taxis when it has very few wheelchair-accessible taxis in the district or, indeed, none at all. This new clause provides an ideal means of enhancing accessible taxi provision in these areas. [The amendment] is compatible with the aims of the Bill and has the effect of improving accessibility for disabled people. In making any regulations under this clause, the Government would, of course, consult interested parties before reaching a decision on the proportion of taxis which must be wheelchair accessible and on the specifications of the wheelchair which taxis must be capable of accommodating.'[35]

Put simply, a taxi licensing authority could not refuse to license a wheelchair-accessible taxi simply because it was controlling the number of licensed taxis in its area if, at the time of the application for a licence, the proportion of accessible taxis in the area is less than a prescribed proportion.

Designated transport facilities

11.15 Particular provision is made in respect of the hire of taxis at designated transport facilities.[36] Transport facilities are premises that form part of a port, airport, railway station or bus station.[37] They are designated transport facilities if designated by order made by an appropriate authority.[38] An appropriate authority in relation to transport facilities in England and Wales means the Secretary of State. In relation to transport facilities in Scotland an appropriate authority means the Scottish Ministers.[39] Note the wider meaning of the term taxi in this context.[40]

11.16 The Secretary of State (in Scotland, the Scottish Ministers) may make regulations in the context of designated transport facilities. The regulations

---

[33] EQA 2010, s 161(1)(c).
[34] EQA 2010, s 161(2) cross-referring to Transport Act 1985, s 16 and Town Police Clause Act 1847. Transport Act 1985, s 16 is made expressly subject to EQA 2010, s 161: EQA 2010, s 161(3).
[35] HL Deb vol 717 col 697 (Baroness Thornton).
[36] EQA 2010, s 162. See EN paras 536–538. This replicates provisions found in DDA 1995, s 33.
[37] EQA 2010, s 162(3).
[38] EQA 2010, s 162(3).
[39] EQA 2010, s 162(3).
[40] EQA 2010, s 173(1) (also includes a taxi licensed under Civic Government (Scotland) Act 1982, s 10).

may provide for the application of any taxi provision[41] (with or without modification) to vehicles used for the provision of services under a franchise agreement or to the drivers of such vehicles.[42] A franchise agreement is a contract entered into by the operator of a designated transport facility.[43] That contract is for the provision by the other party to the contract of hire car services for members of the public using any part of the facility and which involve vehicles entering any part of the facility.[44]

11.17 The intention behind this provision is to ensure that taxis that ply for hire at airports, railway stations and other transport termini can be brought within the accessibility regime for taxis. It is not designed to capture those taxis that already fall within the definition of a taxi that is regulated for any of the purposes of the taxi provisions of the EQA 2010. They will be already subject to the new duties and standards. Instead, it is intended to embrace those taxis that are private hire cars or mini-cabs and which are entitled to provide car hire services to passengers under a monopoly contract or franchise with the operator of the transport terminus in question.

Taxi licences

11.18 The EQA 2010 stipulates that a licence for a taxi to ply for hire must not be granted unless the vehicle conforms to the taxi accessibility regulations with which a licensed vehicle is required to conform.[45] However, this does not apply if a licence is in force in relation to the vehicle at any time during the period of 28 days immediately before the day on which the licence is granted.[46]

11.19 It has always been intended to ensure an orderly transition to the new requirements without damaging the viability of the taxi trade. When these provisions are in force, taxi licensing authorities shall not grant a taxi licence unless the taxi conforms to the relevant taxi accessibility regulations. However, these requirements apply only to newly licensed taxis. They do not apply to the renewal of an existing taxi licence. The intention is to regulate only new entrants to the taxi trade or newly acquired taxis. It does not prevent the

---

41   The term 'taxi provision' means any provision of EQA 2010, Part 12, Chapter 1 (disabled persons: transport: taxis etc) or regulations made in pursuance of the Civic Government (Scotland) Act 1982, s 20(2A) which applies in relation to taxis or drivers of taxis: EQA 2010, s 162(3).

42   EQA 2010, s 162(1).

43   An operator in relation to a transport facility means a person who is concerned with the management or operation of the facility: EQA 2010, s 162(3).

44   EQA 2010, s 162(2). The term 'hire car' will have such meaning as is specified in regulations made by the appropriate authority: EQA 2010, s 162(3).

45   EQA 2010, s 163(1). Section 163 of the EQA 2010 replicates DDA 1995, s 34. See EN paras 539–540.

46   EQA 2010, s 163(2). The Secretary of State may by order provide for s 163(2) to cease to have effect on a specified date: s 163(3). The power under s 163(3) may be exercised differently for different areas or localities: s 163(4).

re-licensing of non-accessible taxis provided that – subject to 28 days' grace – the new licence comes into force immediately upon the expiry of the previous licence.

11.20 After a future date yet to be specified, a licensing authority may only license taxis which comply with the construction requirements that will be set out in the regulations. While it is reasonable to expect new taxis to be fully accessible, it would be unreasonable to require someone who had recently purchased and licensed a new non-accessible vehicle to dispose of it prematurely. However, it is not intended that this exceptional treatment should continue indefinitely. It is contemplated that there will be a future date beyond which non-accessible vehicles cannot be re-licensed as taxis. That date is to be the subject of consultation with the taxi trade.

Exemptions

11.21 The EQA 2010 makes provision for exemption from future taxi accessibility regulations.[47] The Secretary of State may by regulations provide for a relevant licensing authority to apply for an exemption order. Such an order will exempt the authority from the provisions that make a taxi licence conditional on compliance with the taxi accessibility regulations.[48] In particular, provision may be made requiring an authority proposing to apply for an exemption order to carry out such consultation as is specified. The authority might be expected to publish its proposals in a specified manner. Before applying for the order, the authority could be required to consider representations made about the proposal. It would also have to make the application in a specified form.[49]

11.22 A relevant licensing authority is an authority responsible for licensing taxis in any area of England and Wales (outside London).[50] An authority may apply for an exemption order only if it is satisfied as to two matters.[51] First, having regard to the circumstances in its area, that it is inappropriate for the provisions that make a taxi licence conditional on compliance with the taxi accessibility regulations to apply. Secondly, that applying those provisions would result in an unacceptable reduction in the number of taxis in its area.

11.23 Before deciding whether to make an exemption order, the Secretary of State must first consult the Disabled Persons Transport Advisory Committee (DPTAC) and such other persons as the Secretary of State thinks appropriate.[52] The Secretary of State may then make an exemption order in the

---

47   EQA 2010, s 164. This replicates the provisions of DDA 1995, s 35. See EN paras 541–543.
48   EQA 2010, ss 163 and 164(1).
49   EQA 2010, s 164(2).
50   EQA 2010, s 164(7) (other than the area to which the Metropolitan Public Carriage Act 1869 applies).
51   EQA 2010, s 164(3).
52   EQA 2010, s 164(4).

terms of the application for the order or in such other terms as the Secretary of State thinks appropriate. Alternatively, the Secretary of State may refuse to make an exemption order.

11.24 As the Explanatory Notes explain,[53] a particular licensing area can apply for an exemption order if it considers that requiring all taxis to comply with the accessibility requirements would mean that licensed taxi drivers in the area would transfer from being hackney carriage drivers to private hire vehicle drivers because the cost of purchasing accessible taxis would make their business unprofitable. The Secretary of State can agree to make an exemption order, but in doing so can require a certain number of accessible taxis to be available in the area.

Swivel seat regulations

11.25 The Secretary of State may make swivel seat regulations.[54] Swivel seat regulations apply to a taxi plying for hire in an area in respect of which an exemption order is in force. Such a taxi must then conform to provisions as to the fitting and use of swivel seats. The swivel seat regulations may provide that a licence for a taxi to ply for hire must not be granted unless the vehicle conforms to the swivel seat regulations.[55]

Passengers in wheelchairs

11.26 The EQA 2010 places duties upon taxi drivers towards passengers in wheelchairs.[56] This largely replicates provisions previously found in the DDA 1995.[57] However, the new section goes further by applying the duties to drivers of both licensed taxis and private hire vehicles[58] that have been designated as being wheelchair accessible by the local licensing authority.[59]

11.27 Duties are imposed on the driver of a designated taxi.[60] The taxi must have been hired by or for a disabled person who is in a wheelchair or by another person who wishes to be accompanied by a disabled person who is in a wheelchair.[61] Duties are also imposed on the driver of a designated private hire

---

53   EN para 543 (example).
54   EQA 2010, s 164(5).
55   EQA 2010, s 164(6).
56   EQA 2010, s 165. See EN paras 544–546.
57   DDA 1995, s 36.
58   For present purposes (EQA 2010, ss 165 (passengers in wheelchairs), 166 (passengers in wheelchairs: exemption certificates) and 167 (lists of wheelchair-accessible vehicles) below), a private hire vehicle is a vehicle licensed under the Local Government (Miscellaneous Provisions) Act 1976, s 48; a vehicle licensed under the Private Hire Vehicles (London) Act 1998, s 7; a vehicle licensed under an equivalent provision of a local enactment; or a private hire car licensed under the Civic Government (Scotland) Act 1982, s 10: EQA 2010, s 165(10).
59   Note also the wider meaning of the term 'taxi' in this context: EQA 2010, s 173(1).
60   A taxi is designated if it appears on a list maintained under s 167 below: EQA 2010, s 165(3)(a).
61   EQA 2010, s 165(1).

vehicle.[62] The duties arise if a disabled person in a wheelchair (or an intended companion) has indicated to the driver that he or she wishes to travel in the vehicle.[63]

11.28 Where these duties are imposed, the driver must carry the disabled passenger concerned while in the wheelchair.[64] The driver may not make any additional charge for doing so.[65] If the passenger chooses to sit in a passenger seat the driver must carry the wheelchair.[66] The driver must take such steps as are necessary to ensure that the passenger is carried in safety and reasonable comfort.[67] He or she must give the passenger such mobility assistance as is reasonably required.[68] Mobility assistance is assistance to enable the passenger to get into or out of the vehicle; to enable the passenger to get into and out of the vehicle while in the wheelchair if the passenger wishes to remain in the wheelchair; to load the passenger's luggage into or out of the vehicle; and to load the wheelchair into or out of the vehicle if the passenger does not wish to remain in the wheelchair.[69] However, the driver is not required to carry more than one person in a wheelchair or more than one wheelchair on any one journey.[70] Moreover, the driver is not obliged to carry a person in circumstances in which it would otherwise be lawful for the driver to refuse to carry the person.[71]

11.29 The Explanatory Notes illustrate these provisions as follows.[72] A person in a wheelchair hires a wheelchair accessible taxi or private hire vehicle. The driver must help the passenger into and out of the vehicle by using a ramp or lift and helping the passenger onto the lift or up the ramp. The driver must ensure the wheelchair is correctly positioned in the vehicle and secured so that the passenger travels safely and in reasonable comfort. If a passenger in a wheelchair wishes to travel in a passenger seat, the driver must assist the passenger into and out of the vehicle and transport the wheelchair. A driver must load a disabled passenger's luggage into and out of the taxi. A driver cannot charge a person in a wheelchair more than any other passenger.

11.30 A driver of a designated taxi or private hire vehicle commits an offence by failing to comply with these duties.[73] A person guilty of such an offence is liable on summary conviction to a fine not exceeding level 3 on the standard

---

[62] A private hire vehicle is designated if it appears on a list maintained under s 167 below: EQA 2010, s 165(3)(a).
[63] EQA 2010, s 165(2).
[64] EQA 2010, ss 165(3)(b) and 165(4)(a).
[65] EQA 2010, s 165(4)(b).
[66] EQA 2010, s 165(4)(c).
[67] EQA 2010, s 165(4)(d).
[68] EQA 2010, s 165(4)(e).
[69] EQA 2010, s 165(5).
[70] EQA 2010, s 165(6)(a), unless the vehicle is of a description specified in regulations.
[71] EQA 2010, s 165(6)(b).
[72] EN para 546.
[73] EQA 2010, s 165(7).

scale (£1,000).[74] Nevertheless, it is a defence to show that at the time of the alleged offence the vehicle conformed to the applicable accessibility requirements,[75] but it would not have been possible for the wheelchair to be carried safely in the vehicle.[76]

Exemption certificates

11.31 A driver is not required to provide physical assistance to help a passenger in a wheelchair into and out of a vehicle if the driver is medically unfit to do so.[77] In certain circumstances a licensing authority must issue a person with an exemption certificate exempting the person from these duties.[78] Those circumstances are where the licensing authority is satisfied that it is appropriate to do so on medical grounds or on the ground that the person's physical condition makes it impossible or unreasonably difficult for the person to comply with those duties.[79] An exemption certificate is valid for such period as is specified in the certificate.[80]

11.32 The driver of a designated taxi or designated private hire vehicle (as the case may be) is exempt from the duties in question if an exemption certificate issued to the driver is in force and the prescribed notice of the exemption is exhibited on the taxi in the prescribed manner.[81] For these purposes, a taxi or private hire vehicle is designated if it appears on a list of wheelchair accessible vehicles maintained under the statutory provisions below.[82] Here, a licensing authority in relation to any area means the authority responsible for licensing taxis or (as the case may be) private hire vehicles in that area.[83]

Wheelchair accessible vehicles

11.33 The EQA 2010 makes provision for maintaining lists of wheelchair accessible vehicles.[84] This replicates some of the provisions in the DDA 1995,[85] but goes further by enabling licensing authorities to designate the taxis and private hire vehicles in their area that are wheelchair accessible.[86]

---

[74] EQA 2010, s 165(8).

[75] Accessibility requirements are requirements for securing that it is possible for disabled persons in wheelchairs (a) to get into and out of vehicles in safety and (b) to travel in vehicles in safety and reasonable comfort, either staying in their wheelchairs or not (depending on which they prefer): EQA 2010, s 167(6) by virtue of s 173(1).

[76] EQA 2010, s 165(9).

[77] EQA 2010, s 166 which replicates DDA 1995, s 36. See EN paras 547–549.

[78] That is, the duties under EQA 2010, s 165.

[79] EQA 2010, s 166(1).

[80] EQA 2010, s 166(2).

[81] EQA 2010, s 166(3) and (4).

[82] EQA 2010, ss 166(5) and 167.

[83] EQA 2010, s 166(6).

[84] EQA 2010, s 167.

[85] DDA 1995, s 36A.

[86] EN paras 550–553. Note the wider meaning of the term 'taxi' in this context: EQA 2010, s 173(1).

11.34 For the purposes of the duties owed by drivers of designated taxis and private hire vehicles,[87] a licensing authority may maintain a list of wheelchair accessible vehicles. These are vehicles that are taxis or private hire vehicles that conform to such accessibility requirements as the licensing authority thinks fit.[88] In this context, accessibility requirements are requirements for securing that it is possible for disabled persons in wheelchairs to get into and out of vehicles in safety, and to travel in vehicles in safety and reasonable comfort, either staying in their wheelchairs or not (depending on which they prefer).[89] The Secretary of State may issue guidance to licensing authorities as to the accessibility requirements which they should apply for these purposes and as to any other aspect of their functions in this context.[90] A licensing authority which maintains a list of wheelchair accessible vehicles must have regard to any such guidance issued.[91]

11.35 A licensing authority may (if it thinks fit) decide that a vehicle may be included on a list of wheelchair accessible vehicles only if it is being used (or is to be used) by the holder of a special licence under that licence.[92]

Assistance dogs in taxis

11.36 Duties are imposed on the driver of a taxi in relation to assistance dogs.[93] The EQA 2010 replicates the similar provisions of the DDA 1995.[94] Those provisions have been in force in England and Wales since 31 March 2001. Comparable provisions have been in force in Scotland since 2 December 2002 and in Northern Ireland since 1 August 2001. They have been supported by regulations.[95]

11.37 The duties arise where the taxi has been hired by or for a disabled person who is accompanied by an assistance dog. They also arise where the taxi has been hired by another person who wishes to be accompanied by a disabled person with an assistance dog.[96] The driver must carry the disabled person's

---

87 EQA 2010, s 165.
88 EQA 2010, s 167(1) and (2).
89 EQA 2010, s 167(5).
90 EQA 2010, s 167(6).
91 EQA 2010, s 167(7).
92 EQA 2010, s 167(3). The term 'special licence' has the meaning given by the Transport Act 1985, s 12 (use of taxis or hire cars in providing local services): EQA 2010, s 167(4).
93 EQA 2010, s 168.
94 DDA 1995, s 37 (in Scotland, the Civic Government (Scotland) Act 1982, s 20, as amended). See EN paras 554–556.
95 Disability Discrimination Act 1995 (Taxis) (Carrying of Guide Dogs etc) (England and Wales) Regulations 2000, SI 2000/2990, as amended by SI 2006/1616; Disability Discrimination Act 1995 (Taxis) (Carrying of Guide Dogs etc) (Northern Ireland) Regulations 2001, SR 2001/169; Taxi Drivers' Licences (Carrying of Guide Dogs and Hearing Dogs) (Scotland) Regulations 2003, SSI 2003/73 (made under s 20(1) and (2A) of the Civic Government (Scotland) Act 1982).
96 EQA 2010, s 168(1). The term 'assistance dog' means (a) a dog which has been trained to guide a blind person; (b) a dog which has been trained to assist a deaf person; (c) a dog which has been trained by a prescribed charity to assist a disabled person who has a disability that

dog and allow it to remain with that person. He or she must not make any additional charge for doing so.[97] The driver of a taxi commits an offence by failing to comply with such a duty.[98] A person guilty of the offence is liable to a fine not exceeding level 3 on the standard scale (£1,000).[99]

11.38 Provision is made for exemption from these duties.[100] A licensing authority must issue a person with an exemption certificate exempting the person from these duties if it is satisfied that it is appropriate so to do on medical grounds.[101] In deciding whether to issue an exemption certificate, the authority must have regard, in particular, to the physical characteristics of the taxi which the person drives or those of any kind of taxi in relation to which the person requires the certificate.[102] An exemption certificate is valid in respect of a specified taxi or a specified kind of taxi; and for such period as is specified in the certificate.[103] The driver of a taxi is exempt from the relevant duties if an exemption certificate issued to the driver is in force with respect to the taxi, and the prescribed notice of the exemption is exhibited on the taxi in the prescribed manner.[104]

Assistance dogs in private hire vehicles

11.39 The EQA 2010 makes similar provision for assistance dogs in private hire vehicles.[105] The previous provisions from which the EQA 2010 provisions derive have been in force since 31 March 2004 in England and Wales, and since 1 June 2008 in Northern Ireland. They were not yet in force in Scotland. There are supporting regulations.[106]

11.40 The duties relating to assistance dogs in private hire vehicles apply to the operator of a private hire vehicle.[107] The operator commits an offence by failing or refusing to accept a booking for the vehicle if the booking is

---

consists of epilepsy or otherwise affects the person's mobility, manual dexterity, physical co-ordination or ability to lift, carry or otherwise move everyday objects; (d) a dog of a prescribed category which has been trained to assist a disabled person who has a disability (other than one falling within paragraph (c)) of a prescribed kind: EQA 2010, s 173(1).

[97] EQA 2010, s 168(2).
[98] EQA 2010, s 168(3).
[99] EQA 2010, s 168(4).
[100] EQA 2010, s 169. This replicates DDA 1995, s 37. See EN paras 557–559.
[101] EQA 2010, s 169(1). In this section, 'licensing authority' means (a) in relation to the area to which the Metropolitan Public Carriage Act 1869 applies, Transport for London; (b) in relation to any other area in England and Wales, the authority responsible for licensing taxis in that area: EQA 2010, 169(5).
[102] EQA 2010, s 169(2).
[103] EQA 2010, s 169(3).
[104] EQA 2010, s 169(4).
[105] EQA 2010, s 170 replicates the main provision in DDA 1995, s 37A, as amended. See EN paras 560–562.
[106] Disability Discrimination Act 1995 (Private Hire Vehicles) (Carriage of Guide Dogs etc) (England and Wales) Regulations 2003, SI 2003/3122, as amended by SI 2006/1617.
[107] The term 'operator' here means a person who holds a licence under Private Hire Vehicles (London) Act 1998, s 3, or Local Government (Miscellaneous Provisions) Act 1976, s 55, or an equivalent provision of a local enactment: EQA 2010, s 170(5).

requested by or on behalf of a disabled person or a person who wishes to be accompanied by a disabled person, and the reason for the failure or refusal is that the disabled person will be accompanied by an assistance dog.[108] The operator also commits an offence by making an additional charge for carrying an assistance dog which is accompanying a disabled person.[109] The driver of a private hire vehicle commits an offence by failing or refusing to carry out a booking accepted by the operator if the booking is made by or on behalf of a disabled person or a person who wishes to be accompanied by a disabled person, and the reason for the failure or refusal is that the disabled person is accompanied by an assistance dog.[110] A person guilty of these offences is liable on summary conviction to a fine not exceeding level 3 on the standard scale (£1,000).[111]

11.41 Provision is made for exemptions from these duties.[112] A licensing authority must issue a driver with an exemption certificate if it is satisfied that it is appropriate to do so on medical grounds.[113] In deciding whether to issue an exemption certificate, the authority must have regard, in particular, to the physical characteristics of the private hire vehicle which the person drives or those of any kind of private hire vehicle in relation to which the person requires the certificate.[114] An exemption certificate is valid in respect of a specified private hire vehicle or a specified kind of private hire vehicle; and for such period as is specified in the certificate.[115] A driver does not commit an offence if an exemption certificate issued to the driver is in force with respect to the private hire vehicle, and the prescribed notice of the exemption is exhibited on the vehicle in the prescribed manner.[116]

Appeals

11.42 A person who is aggrieved by the refusal of a licensing authority in England and Wales to issue an exemption certificate[117] may appeal to a magistrates' court before the end of the period of 28 days beginning with the date of the refusal.[118] A person who is aggrieved by the refusal of a licensing authority in Scotland to issue an exemption certificate[119] may appeal to the sheriff before the end of the period of 28 days beginning with the date of the

---

[108] EQA 2010, s 170(1).
[109] EQA 2010, s 170(2).
[110] EQA 2010, s 170(3). The term 'driver' here means a person who holds a licence under Private Hire Vehicles (London) Act 1998, s 13, or Local Government (Miscellaneous Provisions) Act 1976, s 51, or an equivalent provision of a local enactment: EQA 2010, s 170(5).
[111] EQA 2010, s 170(4).
[112] EQA 2010, s 171. It replicates the remaining provisions in DDA 1995, s 37A. See EN paras 563–565.
[113] EQA 2010, s 171(1).
[114] EQA 2010, s 171(2).
[115] EQA 2010, s 171(3).
[116] EQA 2010, s 171(4).
[117] Under EQA 2010, ss 166, 169 or 171.
[118] EQA 2010, s 172(1).
[119] Under EQA 2010, s 166.

refusal.[120] On an appeal, the magistrates' court or sheriff may direct the licensing authority to issue the exemption certificate to have effect for such period as is specified in the direction.[121] A person who is aggrieved by the decision of a licensing authority to include a vehicle on a maintained list of wheelchair accessible vehicles[122] may appeal to a magistrates' court (or, in Scotland, the sheriff) before the end of the period of 28 days beginning with the date of the inclusion.[123] These provisions replicate similar provisions in the DDA 1995.[124]

PUBLIC SERVICE VEHICLES

PSV accessibility regulations

11.43 The Secretary of State may make public service vehicle (PSV) accessibility regulations.[125] A public service vehicle here is a vehicle which is adapted to carry more than eight passengers and which is also a public service vehicle for the purposes of the Public Passenger Vehicles Act 1981.[126] The Secretary of State must not make PSV accessibility regulations without consulting the Disabled Persons Transport Advisory Committee and such other representative organisations as the Secretary of State thinks fit.[127]

11.44 The purpose of the PSV accessibility regulations will be to secure that it is possible for disabled persons to get on to and off regulated public service vehicles in safety and without unreasonable difficulty. In the case of disabled persons in wheelchairs, they should be enabled to do so while remaining in their wheelchairs. The regulations will also secure that it is possible for disabled persons to travel in such vehicles in safety and reasonable comfort.[128] A regulated public service vehicle is a public service vehicle to which PSV accessibility regulations are expressed to apply.[129]

11.45 In particular, the PSV accessibility regulations may make provision as to the construction, use and maintenance of regulated public service vehicles.[130] This may include provision as to (a) the fitting of equipment to vehicles; (b) equipment to be carried by vehicles; (c) the design of equipment to be fitted to, or carried by, vehicles; (d) the fitting and use of restraining devices designed to ensure the stability of wheelchairs while vehicles are moving; (e) the position in

---

[120] EQA 2010, s 172(2).

[121] EQA 2010, s 172(3).

[122] Under EQA 2010, s 167.

[123] EQA 2010, s 172(4).

[124] DDA 1995, s 38. See EN paras 566–569.

[125] EQA 2010, s 174, replicating DDA 1995, s 40. See EN paras 571–572. See also EQA 2010, s 181 (interpretation). The Public Service Vehicles Accessibility Regulations 2000, SI 2000/1970, came into force on 30 August 2000. See Butcher, 2009a: 8–10.

[126] EQA 2010, s 174(3).

[127] EQA 2010, s 174(5). This requirement also applies to ss 176 and 177.

[128] EQA 2010, s 174(1).

[129] EQA 2010, s 174(3).

[130] EQA 2010, s 174(2).

which wheelchairs are to be secured while vehicles are moving.[131] The regulations may make different provision as respects different classes or descriptions of vehicle; and as respects the same class or description of vehicle in different circumstances.[132]

Contraventions

11.46 A person commits an offence by contravening a provision of PSV accessibility regulations.[133] An offence is also committed if a person uses on a road a regulated public service vehicle which does not conform with a provision of the regulations with which it is required to conform.[134] It is also an offence for a person to cause or permit such a regulated public service vehicle to be used on a road.[135] A person guilty of any such offence is liable on summary conviction to a fine not exceeding level 4 on the standard scale (£2,500).[136]

11.47 If an offence above is committed by a body corporate, and is committed with the consent or connivance of (or is attributable to neglect on the part of), a responsible person, the responsible person as well as the body corporate is guilty of the offence.[137] In this context, a responsible person in relation to a body corporate is a director, manager, secretary or similar officer; or a person purporting to act in such a capacity; or in the case of a body corporate whose affairs are managed by its members, a member.[138] In Scotland, if an offence committed by a partnership or an unincorporated association is committed with the consent or connivance of (or is attributable to neglect on the part of) a partner or person concerned in the management of the association, the partner or person as well as the partnership or association is guilty of the offence.[139]

Accessibility certificates

11.48 A regulated public service vehicle must not be used on a road unless a vehicle examiner has issued an accessibility certificate.[140] An accessibility certificate is a certificate that such provisions of PSV accessibility regulations as are prescribed are satisfied in respect of the vehicle. Regulations may make provision (a) with respect to applications for, and the issue of, accessibility certificates; (b) providing for the examination of vehicles in respect of which

---

[131] EQA 2010, s 174(2).
[132] EQA 2010, s 174(4).
[133] EQA 2010, s 175(1)(a). Section 175 replicates parts of DDA 1995, s 40. See EN paras 573–575. See also EQA 2010, s 181 (interpretation).
[134] EQA 2010, s 175(1)(b).
[135] EQA 2010, s 175(1)(c).
[136] EQA 2010, s 175(2).
[137] EQA 2010, s 175(3).
[138] EQA 2010, s 175(4).
[139] EQA 2010, s 175(4).
[140] EQA 2010, s 176(1)(a). Section 176 replicates DDA 1995, s 41. See EN paras 576–577. See also EQA 2010, s 181 (interpretation).

applications have been made; (c) with respect to the issue of copies of accessibility certificates which have been lost or destroyed.[141]

11.49 The operator of a regulated public service vehicle commits an offence if the vehicle is used in contravention of these provisions.[142] A person guilty of such an offence is liable on summary conviction to a fine not exceeding level 4 on the standard scale (£2,500).[143]

Approval certificates

11.50 A regulated public service vehicle must not be used on a road unless an approval certificate has been issued in respect of the vehicle.[144] The operator of a regulated public service vehicle commits an offence if the vehicle is used in contravention of these provisions.[145] A person guilty of such an offence is liable on summary conviction to a fine not exceeding level 4 on the standard scale (£2,500).[146]

11.51 The Secretary of State may approve a vehicle for present purposes if satisfied that such provisions of PSV accessibility regulations as are prescribed for the purposes of the accessibility certificates provisions above are satisfied in respect of the vehicle.[147] A vehicle which is so approved is referred to as a 'type vehicle'.[148] If a declaration in the prescribed form is made by an authorised person that a particular vehicle conforms in design, construction and equipment with a type vehicle, a vehicle examiner may issue an approval certificate in the prescribed form that the vehicle conforms to the type vehicle.[149]

11.52 Regulations may make provision with respect to applications for and grants of approval of a type vehicle.[150] They may also make provision with respect to applications for and the issue of approval certificates.[151] Such regulations further may be concerned with providing for the examination of

---

[141] EQA 2010, s 176(2). A power to make regulations under this section is exercisable by the Secretary of State: s 176(5).

[142] EQA 2010, s 176(3). In this section 'operator' has the same meaning as in the Public Passenger Vehicles Act 1981: s 176(6).

[143] EQA 2010, s 176(4).

[144] EQA 2010, s 176(1)(b). An approval certificate is a certificate issued under s 177, discussed below.

[145] EQA 2010, s 176(3). In this section 'operator' has the same meaning as in the Public Passenger Vehicles Act 1981: EQA 2010, s 176(6).

[146] EQA 2010, s 176(4).

[147] EQA 2010, ss 176 and 177(1). Section 177 replicates DDA 1995, s 42. See EN paras 578–580. See also EQA 2010, s 181 (interpretation).

[148] EQA 2010, s 177(2).

[149] EQA 2010, s 177(3) and (4). An 'authorised person' means a person authorised by the Secretary of State for this purpose: s 177(9).

[150] EQA 2010, s 177(5)(a). A power to make regulations under this section is exercisable by the Secretary of State: s 177(8).

[151] EQA 2010, s 177(5)(b).

vehicles in respect of which applications have been made and with respect to the issue of copies of approval certificates in place of certificates which have been lost or destroyed.[152]

11.53 The Secretary of State may at any time withdraw approval of a type vehicle.[153] If an approval is withdrawn no further approval certificates are to be issued by reference to the type vehicle. However, an approval certificate issued by reference to the type vehicle before the withdrawal continues to have effect for the present purposes.[154]

Special authorisations

11.54 The Secretary of State may by order authorise the use on roads of (a) a regulated public service vehicle of a class or description specified by the order, or (b) a regulated public service vehicle which is so specified.[155] Nothing in the PSV accessibility regulations or the provisions on accessibility certificates or approval certificates would then prevent the use of a vehicle in accordance with the order.[156] Moreover, the Secretary of State may by order make provision for securing that provisions of PSV accessibility regulations apply to regulated public service vehicles of a description specified by the order, subject to any modifications or exceptions specified by the order.[157] An order of either kind may make the authorisation or provision (as the case may be) subject to such restrictions and conditions as are specified by or under the order.[158]

11.55 The Explanatory Notes offer an example of a special authorisation. A new design of vehicle, which does not conform to the current accessibility regulations, is to be trialled. The Secretary of State makes an order allowing the use of the vehicle in a restricted environment, specifying the permitted areas and times of operation, so that its performance can be tested.[159]

Reviews and appeals

11.56 Provision is made where the Secretary of State refuses an application for the approval of a vehicle as a type vehicle,[160] and before the end of the prescribed period the applicant asks the Secretary of State to review the

---

[152] EQA 2010, s 177(5)(c) and (d).
[153] EQA 2010, s 177(6).
[154] EQA 2010, s 177(7).
[155] EQA 2010, s 178(1). Section 178 replicates DDA 1995, s 43. See EN paras 581–582. See also EQA 2010, s 181 (interpretation).
[156] EQA 2010, s 178(2) cross-referring to ss 174–177.
[157] EQA 2010, s 178(3).
[158] EQA 2010, s 178(4). EQA 2010, s 207(2) (orders, regulations or rules under the Act must be made by statutory instrument) does not require an order under s 178 that applies only to a specified vehicle, or to vehicles of a specified person, to be made by statutory instrument; but such an order is as capable of being amended or revoked as an order made by statutory instrument: EQA 2010, s 178(5).
[159] EN para 582 (example).
[160] EQA 2010, s 177(1).

decision and pays any fee fixed as prescribed.[161] The Secretary of State must review the decision and, in doing so, consider any representations made in writing by the applicant before the end of the prescribed period.[162]

11.57 A person applying for an accessibility certificate or an approval certificate may appeal to the Secretary of State against the refusal of a vehicle examiner to issue the certificate.[163] An appeal must be made within the prescribed time and in the prescribed manner.[164] Regulations made by the Secretary of State may make provision as to the procedure to be followed in connection with appeals.[165] On the determination of an appeal, the Secretary of State may confirm, vary or reverse the decision appealed against and give directions to the vehicle examiner for giving effect to the Secretary of State's decision.[166]

Fees

11.58 The EQA 2010 makes provision for the charging of fees in relation to applications for and grants of approval of a type vehicle, and applications for and the issue of accessibility certificates and approval certificates.[167] This provision (which is also concerned with copies of certificates, and reviews and appeals) is not considered in further detail.

RAIL VEHICLES

Rail vehicle accessibility regulations

11.59 The Secretary of State may make rail vehicle accessibility regulations for securing that it is possible for disabled persons (a) to get on to and off regulated rail vehicles in safety and without unreasonable difficulty; (b) to do so while in wheelchairs; (c) to travel in such vehicles in safety and reasonable comfort; and (d) to do so while in wheelchairs.[168] In this context, a rail vehicle is a vehicle constructed or adapted to carry passengers on a railway, tramway or prescribed system.[169] It does not include a vehicle used in the provision of a

---

[161] EQA 2010, ss 179(1) and 180. Section 179 replicates DDA 1995, s 44. See EN paras 583–584. See also EQA 2010, s 181 (interpretation).

[162] EQA 2010, s 179(2).

[163] EQA 2010, s 179(3).

[164] EQA 2010, s 179(4).

[165] EQA 2010, s 179(5) and (7).

[166] EQA 2010, s 179(6).

[167] EQA 2010, s 180. Section 180 replicates DDA 1995, s 45. See EN paras 585–586. See also EQA 2010, s 181 (interpretation).

[168] EQA 2010, ss 182(1) and 187(1). Section 182 replicates the provisions of DDA 1995, s 46 as amended by DDA 2005. See EN paras 588–592. The Rail Vehicle Accessibility Regulations 1998, SI 1998/2456, apply to all new trains, trams and other track-based systems first brought into use after 1 January 1999. See also the Rail Vehicle Accessibility (Interoperable Rail System) Regulations 2008, SI 2008/1746 implementing Directive 2008/164/EC. See Butcher, 2009a: 4–6.

[169] EQA 2010, ss 182(4) and 187(1). The terms 'railway' and 'tramway' have the same meaning as

service for the carriage of passengers on the high-speed rail system or the conventional TEN rail system.[170] A regulated rail vehicle means a rail vehicle to which provisions of the rail vehicle accessibility regulations are expressed to apply.[171]

11.60 In particular, rail vehicle accessibility regulations may make provision as to the construction, use and maintenance of regulated rail vehicles. This might include provision as to (a) the fitting of equipment to vehicles; (b) equipment to be carried by vehicles; (c) the design of equipment to be fitted to, or carried by, vehicles; (d) the use of equipment fitted to, or carried by, vehicles; (e) the toilet facilities to be provided in vehicles; (f) the location and floor area of the wheelchair accommodation to be provided in vehicles; and (g) assistance to be given to disabled persons.[172]

11.61 The Secretary of State must exercise the power to make rail vehicle accessibility regulations so as to secure that on and after 1 January 2020 every rail vehicle is a regulated rail vehicle.[173] This means that all rail vehicles must comply with accessibility standards, or have an appropriate exemption in place, by no later than 1 January 2020.[174] However, rail vehicle accessibility regulations may contain different provision (a) as respects different classes or descriptions of rail vehicle; (b) as respects the same class or description of rail vehicle in different circumstances; and (c) as respects different networks.[175] Such differential provision is not affected by the requirement that every rail vehicle should be a regulated rail vehicle by 1 January 2020.[176]

11.62 The Explanatory Notes record that these provisions empower the Secretary of State to make regulations to ensure that trains, trams and certain other guided transport systems are accessible to disabled people including wheelchair-users.[177] They make the telling point that the definition of rail vehicle in this context is a limited one. The power to make rail vehicle

---

in the Transport and Works Act 1992: EQA 2010, s 182(5). The term 'prescribed system' means a system using a mode of guided transport (the term 'guided transport' having the same meaning as in the Transport and Works Act 1992) that is specified in the rail vehicle accessibility regulations: EQA 2010, s 182(5).

[170] The terms 'conventional TEN rail system' and 'high-speed rail system' have the meaning given in reg 2(3) of the Railways (Interoperability) Regulations 2006 (SI 2006/397): EQA 2010, s 182(5). The conventional TEN rail system means that part of the trans-European conventional rail system located within the territory of the UK. The high-speed rail system means that part of the trans-European high-speed rail system located within the territory of the UK and identified by reference to the lines specified in Sch 11 to the regulations.

[171] EQA 2010, ss 182(4) and 187(1).

[172] EQA 2010, s 182(2).

[173] EQA 2010, s 182(6). Before making rail vehicle accessibility regulations the Secretary of State must consult the Disabled Persons Transport Advisory Committee and such other representative organisations as the Secretary of State thinks fit: s 182(8).

[174] EN para 590.

[175] EQA 2010, s 182(3). The term 'network' means any permanent way or other means of guiding or supporting rail vehicles, or any section of it: ss 182(4) and 187(1).

[176] EQA 2010, s 182(7). In any event, orders or regulations under the Act may make different provision for different purposes: s 182(7) cross-referring to s 207(4)(a).

[177] EN para 588.

accessibility regulations is limited to rail vehicles that do not operate on the interoperable rail system. Thus any rail vehicle accessibility regulations would only be applicable in general to light rail vehicles (those used on metro, underground and tram systems and prescribed modes of guided transport).[178]

Exemptions

11.63 Provision is made for exemptions from rail vehicle accessibility regulations.[179] The Secretary of State may make an exemption order authorising the use for carriage of a regulated rail vehicle even though the vehicle does not conform with the provisions of rail vehicle accessibility regulations with which it is required to conform.[180] Such an exemption order may also authorise a regulated rail vehicle to be used for carriage otherwise than in conformity with the provisions of rail vehicle accessibility regulations with which use of the vehicle is required to conform.[181] The authorisation of an exemption in either case may be for (a) a regulated rail vehicle that is specified or of a specified description, (b) use in specified circumstances of a regulated rail vehicle, or (c) use in specified circumstances of a regulated rail vehicle that is specified or of a specified description.[182]

11.64 The Secretary of State may by regulations make provision as to exemption orders.[183] In particular, this might include provision as to (a) the persons by whom applications for exemption orders may be made; (b) the form in which applications are to be made; (c) information to be supplied in connection with applications; (d) the period for which exemption orders are to continue in force; (e) the revocation of exemption orders.

11.65 The statutory provisions require the Secretary of State to consult the Disabled Persons Transport Advisory Committee and such other persons as the Secretary of State thinks appropriate before making a decision about an exemption order.[184] Following such consultation, the Secretary of State may (a) make an exemption order in the terms of the application for the order; (b) make an exemption order in such other terms as the Secretary of State thinks

---

[178] EN para 589.
[179] EQA 2010, s 183. It replicates the provisions of DDA 1995, s 47 as amended by DDA 2005. See EN paras 593–596.
[180] EQA 2010, s 183(1)(a). Such provision is not affected by the requirement that every rail vehicle should be a regulated rail vehicle by 1 January 2020: EQA 2010, s 182(7) cross-referring to s 183(1).
[181] EQA 2010, s 183(1)(b). Such provision is not affected by the requirement that every rail vehicle should be a regulated rail vehicle by 1 January 2020: EQA 2010, s 182(7) cross-referring to s 183(1). A vehicle is 'used for carriage' if it is used for the carriage of passengers: EQA 2010, s 187(2).
[182] EQA 2010, s 183(2). A matter is specified if it is specified in the exemption order: s 183(6).
[183] EQA 2010, s 183(3). Before making regulations under EQA 2010, s 183 the Secretary of State must consult the Disabled Persons Transport Advisory Committee and such other representative organisations as the Secretary of State thinks fit: s 182(8).
[184] EQA 2010, s 183(4).

appropriate; or (c) refuse to make an exemption order. The Secretary of State may make an exemption order subject to such conditions and restrictions as are specified in the exemption order.[185]

Procedure

11.66 A statutory procedure is laid down for making exemption orders in relation to rail vehicle accessibility regulations.[186] It is not considered in further detail here. In essence, the Secretary of State has discretion to make proposed exemption orders subject to either the draft affirmative resolution or the negative resolution procedure. It sets out the procedure for the exercise of this discretion and enables regulations to be made setting out the criteria under which a decision will be made. It also provides for consultation before making such regulations, which are in turn subject to the draft affirmative resolution procedure.[187]

Annual reports

11.67 Provision is made for an annual report on exemption orders.[188] In each calendar year the Secretary of State is required to produce such a report on the use of powers to exempt regulated rail vehicles from accessibility requirements. The report must be laid before both Houses of Parliament.[189]

Compliance

11.68 Effect is given to the provisions of Sch 20,[190] which contains powers to introduce compliance certification and a civil enforcement regime with associated penalties in relation to rail vehicle accessibility.[191] These provisions will be repealed automatically at the end of 2010 if the Schedule is not brought into force (either fully or to any extent) before the end of that year.[192]

11.69 The Explanatory Notes make clear why these provisions are necessary.[193] They remark that the Department for Transport has completed a consultation on the reappraisal of the introduction of compliance certification and civil enforcement powers for rail vehicle accessibility. In order to accommodate possible outcomes of the consultation exercise, it has been necessary to include such provisions in the Schedule. The Explanatory Notes

---

[185] EQA 2010, s 183(5) and (6).

[186] EQA 2010, s 184.

[187] See EN paras 597–599. Section 184 replicates DDA 1995, ss 67(5A) and 67A (as inserted by the DDA 2005).

[188] EQA 2010, s 185.

[189] EN paras 600–601. Section 185 replicates DDA 1995, ss 67B (as inserted by the DDA 2005).

[190] EQA 2010, s 186. Schedule 20 replicates the provisions of DDA 1995, ss 47A–47M, as inserted by DDA 2005, but not yet in force: EN para 604.

[191] EQA 2010, s 186(1).

[192] EQA 2010, s 186(2).

[193] EN paras 602–606 and 938–941. For an account of what Sch 20 would have provided for if brought into force, see EN para 942–980.

record that the consultation responses indicate that the Government's preferred option of not commencing the provisions contained in Sch 20 is said to be widely supported by stakeholders. In the event, the government has enacted the Rail Vehicle Accessibility (Non-Interoperable Rail System) Regulations 2010[194] under the DDA 1995. Those Regulations came into force on 6 April 2010. They do not rely upon compliance certification, but instead replace the proposed civil enforcement regime with enforcement by the Office of Rail Regulation under the powers in the Health and Safety at Work etc Act 1974. Therefore, Sch 20 will not be brought into force. Nevertheless, as in the Explanatory Notes, its provisions are outlined here for completeness. What follows in **11.70–11.93** is thus of academic interest only.

Compliance certificates

11.70 A regulated rail vehicle which is prescribed (or which is of a prescribed class or description) must not be used for carriage unless a rail vehicle accessibility compliance certificate is in force for the vehicle.[195] If a regulated rail vehicle is used for carriage in contravention of this prohibition, the Secretary of State may require the operator of the vehicle to pay a penalty.[196]

11.71 A compliance certificate is a certificate that the Secretary of State is satisfied that the regulated rail vehicle conforms with the provisions of rail vehicle accessibility regulations with which it is required to conform.[197] A compliance certificate is subject to such conditions as are specified in it.[198] A compliance certificate may not be issued for a rail vehicle unless the Secretary of State has been provided with a report of a compliance assessment of the vehicle.[199] A compliance assessment is an assessment of a rail vehicle against provisions of rail vehicle accessibility regulations with which the vehicle is required to conform.[200]

11.72 The Secretary of State must review a decision not to issue a compliance certificate if before the end of the prescribed period the applicant asks the Secretary of State to review the decision and pays any fee fixed for this purpose.[201] For the purposes of the review, the Secretary of State must consider any representations made by the applicant in writing before the end of the prescribed period.[202]

---

[194] SI 2010/432.
[195] EQA 2010, Sch 20, para 1(1).
[196] EQA 2010, Sch 20, para 1(6). An 'operator', in relation to a rail vehicle, means the person having the management of the vehicle: EQA 2010, Sch 20, para 15(1).
[197] EQA 2010, Sch 20, para 1(2).
[198] EQA 2010, Sch 20, para 1(3).
[199] EQA 2010, Sch 20, para 1(4).
[200] EQA 2010, Sch 20, para 1(5).
[201] EQA 2010, Sch 20, paras 1(7) and 4.
[202] EQA 2010, Sch 20, para 1(8).

11.73 These provisions introduce compliance certification into the rail vehicle accessibility regime.[203] They prohibit a regulated rail vehicle from being used in passenger service unless a valid compliance certificate has been issued for that rail vehicle. The earlier provisions of the DDA 1995 are thereby replicated.[204]

11.74 Regulations may make provision as to compliance certificates.[205] In particular, such regulations may include provision (a) as to applications for and issue of certificates; (b) specifying conditions to which certificates are subject; (c) as to the period for which a certificate is in force; (d) as to circumstances in which a certificate ceases to be in force; (e) dealing with failure to comply with a specified condition; (f) for the examination of rail vehicles in respect of which applications have been made; and (g) with respect to the issue of copies of certificates in place of those which have been lost or destroyed.[206]

Compliance assessments

11.75 Regulations may make provision as to compliance assessments.[207] Such regulations may make provision as to the person who has to have carried out the assessment. In particular, the regulations may require that the assessment be one carried out by a person who has been appointed by the Secretary of State to carry out compliance assessments (an appointed assessor).[208] In this latter regard, the regulations (a) may make provision about appointments of appointed assessors;[209] (b) may make provision authorising an appointed assessor to charge fees in connection with, or incidental to, the carrying out of a compliance assessment;[210] (c) may make provision requiring an appointed assessor to carry out a compliance assessment, and to do so in accordance with any procedures that may be prescribed, if prescribed conditions (which may include conditions as to the payment of fees to the assessor) are satisfied; and (d) must make provision for the referral to the Secretary of State of disputes between an appointed assessor carrying out a compliance assessment and the person who requested the assessment, relating to which provisions of rail

---

[203] EN paras 942–946.
[204] DDA 1995, ss 47A and 47D, inserted by DDA 2005, but not yet in force.
[205] EQA 2010, Sch 20, para 2(1). See EN paras 947–948. This provision replicates some of the provisions of DDA 1995, s 47B (1)–(3), inserted by DDA 2005, but not yet in force.
[206] EQA 2010, Sch 20, para 2(2).
[207] EQA 2010, Sch 20, para 3(1). See EN paras 949–951. This provision replicates the remaining provisions of DDA 1995, s 47B, inserted by DDA 2005, but not yet in force.
[208] EQA 2010, Sch 20, para 3(2).
[209] Including in particular (i) provision for an appointment to be on application or otherwise than on application; (ii) provision as to who may be appointed; (iii) provision as to the form of applications for appointment; (iv) provision as to information to be supplied with applications for appointment; (v) provision as to terms and conditions, or the period or termination, of an appointment; (vi) provision for terms and conditions of an appointment, including any as to its period or termination, to be as agreed by the Secretary of State when making the appointment.
[210] Including in particular (i) provision restricting the amount of a fee; (ii) provision authorising fees that contain a profit element; (iii) provision for advance payment of fees.

vehicle accessibility regulations the vehicle is to be assessed against or to what amounts to conformity with any of those provisions.[211]

Fees

11.76 The Secretary of State may charge such fees (and payable at such times) as are prescribed in respect of (a) applications for and the issue of compliance certificates; (b) copies of compliance certificates; (c) reviews of decisions not to issue a compliance certificate; and (d) referrals of disputes between an appointed assessor and the person requesting an assessment.[212] Fees received by the Secretary of State must be paid into the Consolidated Fund.[213] Regulations may make provision for the repayment of fees (in whole or in part) in such circumstances as are prescribed.[214] Before making any such regulations the Secretary of State must consult such representative organisations as the Secretary of State thinks fit.[215]

Non-conformity with rail vehicle accessibility regulations

11.77 A penalty may be payable if the Secretary of State thinks that a regulated rail vehicle does not conform with a provision of rail vehicle accessibility regulations with which it is required to conform.[216] If so, the Secretary of State may give the operator of the vehicle a notice (an improvement notice) (a) identifying the vehicle, the provision and how the vehicle fails to conform; and (b) specifying the improvement deadline.[217] The improvement deadline may not be earlier than the end of the prescribed period beginning with the day the notice is given.[218]

11.78 If the Secretary of State has given such an improvement notice, and the improvement deadline specified in the notice has passed, and the Secretary of State thinks that the vehicle still does not conform to the provision identified in the notice, then the Secretary of State may give the operator a further notice (a final notice).[219] That final notice will (i) identify the vehicle, the provision and how the vehicle fails to conform; and (ii) specify the final deadline.[220] The final deadline may not be earlier than the end of the prescribed period beginning

---

[211] EQA 2010, Sch 20, para 3(3). In respect of points (b) to (d) in this paragraph, a compliance assessment here includes pre-assessment activities: EQA 2010, Sch 20, para 3(4).

[212] EQA 2010, Sch 20, para 4(1). See EN paras 952–953. This provision replicates the provisions of DDA 1995, s 47C, inserted by DDA 2005, but not yet in force.

[213] EQA 2010, Sch 20, para 4(2).

[214] EQA 2010, Sch 20, para 4(3).

[215] EQA 2010, Sch 20, para 4(4).

[216] EQA 2010, Sch 20, para 5(1). See EN paras 954–956.

[217] EQA 2010, Sch 20, para 5(1). The term 'improvement notice' appears in EN para 955 rather than in the Act itself.

[218] EQA 2010, Sch 20, para 5(2).

[219] EQA 2010, Sch 20, para 5(3). The term 'final notice' appears in EN para 955 rather than in the Act itself.

[220] EQA 2010, Sch 20, para 5(4).

with the day the further notice is given.[221] The Secretary of State may then require the operator to pay a penalty if the Secretary of State has given the final notice, and the vehicle is used for carriage at a time after the final deadline when the vehicle does not conform to the provision identified in the final notice.[222]

11.79 These provisions establish the procedure to be followed by the Secretary of State in respect of an operator of a regulated rail vehicle which appears not to comply with the construction requirements of rail vehicle accessibility regulations. The procedure involves the issue of improvement notices and final notices. If the vehicle is used despite still being non-compliant with the relevant parts of the rail vehicle accessibility regulations, the Secretary of State may impose a penalty. The timescale leading to a penalty is to be set out in regulations.[223]

11.80 A penalty may also be payable if the Secretary of State thinks that a regulated rail vehicle has been used for carriage otherwise than in conformity with a provision of rail vehicle accessibility regulations with which the use of the vehicle is required to conform.[224] If so, the Secretary of State may give the operator of the vehicle a notice (a) identifying the provision and how it was breached; and (b) identifying each vehicle operated by the operator that is covered by the notice; and (c) specifying the improvement deadline.[225] The improvement deadline may not be earlier than the end of the prescribed period beginning with the day the notice is given.[226] If the Secretary of State has given such a notice, and the improvement deadline specified in the notice has passed, and the Secretary of State thinks that a vehicle covered by the notice has after that deadline been used for carriage otherwise than in conformity with the provision identified in the notice, then the Secretary of State may give the operator a further notice.[227] That second and further notice will (i) identify the provision and how it was breached; (ii) identify each vehicle operated by the operator that is covered by the further notice; and (iii) specify the final deadline.[228] The final deadline may not be earlier than the end of the prescribed period beginning with the day the further notice is given.[229] The Secretary of State may then require the operator to pay a penalty if the Secretary of State has given the second notice, and a vehicle covered by the notice is at a time after the final deadline used for carriage otherwise than in conformity with the provision identified in the notice.[230]

---

[221] EQA 2010, Sch 20, para 5(5).
[222] EQA 2010, Sch 20, para 5(6).
[223] EN paras 955–956. These provisions replicate DDA 1995, s 47E, inserted by DDA 2005, but not yet in force.
[224] EQA 2010, Sch 20, para 6(1).
[225] EQA 2010, Sch 20, para 6(1).
[226] EQA 2010, Sch 20, para 6(2).
[227] EQA 2010, Sch 20, para 6(3).
[228] EQA 2010, Sch 20, para 6(4).
[229] EQA 2010, Sch 20, para 6(5).
[230] EQA 2010, Sch 20, para 6(6).

11.81 The foregoing provisions establish a similar approach in respect of vehicles used in a way which does not comply with the operational requirements of the accessibility regulations as is taken to a vehicle which does not comply with their technical requirements. For example, a regulated rail vehicle may have appropriate equipment to assist a disabled person in getting on or off the vehicle, such as a lift or ramp, but no member of staff is available to operate it.[231]

Inspection of rail vehicles

11.82 An inspector authorised by the Secretary of State may inspect (and test) a regulated rail vehicle for conformity with provisions of the accessibility regulations to which it is required to conform.[232] The exercise of this power is conditional upon the Secretary of State having reasonable grounds for suspecting that the vehicle does not conform with such provisions or having given a notice relating to the vehicle (for using a rail vehicle that does not conform with accessibility regulations).[233]

11.83 For these purposes, an inspector may (a) enter premises if the inspector has reasonable grounds for suspecting that the vehicle is at the premises; (b) enter the vehicle; and (c) require any person to afford such facilities and assistance with respect to matters under the person's control as are necessary to enable the inspector to exercise the power.[234] If required to do so, an inspector must produce evidence of the Secretary of State's authorisation.[235]

11.84 For the purposes of the Secretary of State concluding that a regulated rail vehicle does not conform to a provision of rail vehicle accessibility regulations with which it is required to conform,[236] the Secretary of State may draw such inferences as appear proper from any obstruction of the exercise of the inspection (and testing) power.[237]

11.85 Where the exercise of the power of inspection (and testing) has been conditional upon the Secretary of State having given a notice relating to the vehicle (for using a rail vehicle that does not conform to accessibility regulations),[238] some additional considerations arise.[239] In the following circumstances the Secretary of State may treat as satisfied the requirement that the Secretary of State should conclude that the vehicle still does not conform to

---

[231] EN paras 957–958. These provisions replicate DDA 1995, s 47F, inserted by DDA 2005, but not yet in force.
[232] EQA 2010, Sch 20, para 7(1) and (9) cross-referring to para 5(1) or (4). See EN paras 959–960. These provisions replicate DDA 1995, s 47G, inserted by DDA 2005, but not yet in force.
[233] EQA 2010, Sch 20, para 7(2).
[234] EQA 2010, Sch 20, para 7(3).
[235] EQA 2010, Sch 20, para 7(4).
[236] EQA 2010, Sch 20, para 5(1).
[237] EQA 2010, Sch 20, para 7(5).
[238] EQA 2010, Sch 20, para 7(2)(b).
[239] EQA 2010, Sch 20, para 7(6).

the provision identified in the notice.[240] Those circumstances are where the inspector takes steps to exercise the power after a first notice is given,[241] but before a second and further notice is given,[242] and a person obstructs the exercise of the power.[243] In addition, the Secretary of State may require the operator of a vehicle to pay a penalty if (a) the operator (or a person acting on the operator's behalf) intentionally obstructs the exercise of the power, and (b) the obstruction occurs after a second and further notice has been given in respect of the vehicle.[244]

Supplementary powers

11.86 For the purposes of establishing possible non-conformity with rail vehicle accessibility regulations,[245] the Secretary of State may give notice to a person requiring the person to supply the Secretary of State by a time specified in the notice with a vehicle number or other identifier for a rail vehicle of which the person is the operator, and which is specified in the notice.[246] The time specified may not be earlier than the end of the period of 14 days beginning with the day the notice is given.[247] If the person does not comply with the notice, the Secretary of State may require the person to pay a penalty.[248]

11.87 If the Secretary of State has previously given a notice of non-conformity to a person,[249] the Secretary of State may request the person to supply the Secretary of State, by a time specified in the request, with a statement detailing the steps taken in response to the notice.[250] The time specified may not be earlier than the improvement deadline.[251] If the request is not complied with by the time specified, the Secretary of State may be satisfied without more ado that the vehicle still does not conform with the provision identified in the notice or that a vehicle covered by the notice has after that deadline been used for carriage otherwise than in conformity with the provision identified in the notice.[252]

---

[240] EQA 2010, Sch 20, para 5(3)(c).
[241] EQA 2010, Sch 20, para 5(1).
[242] EQA 2010, Sch 20, para 5(4).
[243] EQA 2010, Sch 20, para 7(7).
[244] EQA 2010, Sch 20, para 7(8) cross-referring to para 5(4).
[245] EQA 2010, Sch 20, para 5.
[246] EQA 2010, Sch 20, para 8(1). EN paras 961–964. These provisions replicate DDA 1995, s 47H, inserted by DDA 2005, but not yet in force.
[247] EQA 2010, Sch 20, para 8(2).
[248] EQA 2010, Sch 20, para 8(3).
[249] EQA 2010, Sch 20, paras 5(1) or 6(1).
[250] EQA 2010, Sch 20, para 8(4).
[251] EQA 2010, Sch 20, para 8(5).
[252] EQA 2010, Sch 20, para 8(6), cross-referring to paras 5(3)(c), 6(3)(c) and 8(4).

Penalties

11.88 The remaining parts of Sch 20 are concerned with penalties.[253] They are not considered in direct detail here.

11.89 The Explanatory Notes[254] explain that provision is made in relation to the amount, due date and recovery of penalties imposed under the provisions discussed above. The maximum penalty cannot exceed the lesser of an amount to be prescribed in regulations or 10 per cent of the turnover of the rail vehicle operator subject to the penalty. The Secretary of State is required to issue a code of practice to set out matters that must be considered in determining the level of a penalty. The Secretary of State is required to take account of the code when imposing a penalty under Sch 20 or in considering any objections received to the imposition of a penalty.

11.90 A procedure is established for the imposition of penalties under the Schedule. In particular, specific information must be provided by the Secretary of State when notifying a rail vehicle operator that it is liable to a penalty. The operator has a right to object to the imposition or amount of a penalty. Should an objection be received, the Secretary of State is under an obligation to consider the objection and take appropriate action. There is a right of appeal to a court by way of re-hearing on the grounds that either the operator is not liable to a penalty or that the amount is too high.

Forgery, etc

11.91 It is a criminal offence for a person (with intent to deceive) to forge, alter, use, or lend a compliance certificate; to allow one to be used by another person; to make or have possession of a document which closely resembles one; or to knowingly make a false statement for the purpose of obtaining one. It is also a criminal offence for a person to impersonate an inspector authorised by the Secretary of State.[255] A person guilty of such offences is liable on summary conviction to a fine not exceeding level 4 on the standard scale (£2,500).

Regulations

11.92 The power to make regulations under Sch 20 is exercisable by the Secretary of State.[256]

---

[253] EQA 2010, Sch 20, paras 9–12. These provisions replicate DDA 1995, ss 47J–47L, inserted by DDA 2005, but not yet in force.

[254] EN paras 965–973.

[255] EQA 2010, s 186 and Sch 20, para 13. See EN paras 974–976. These provisions replicate DDA 1995, s 49, inserted by DDA 2005, but not yet in force.

[256] EQA 2010, Sch 20, para 14.

Exempt rail vehicles

11.93 If a rail vehicle to which Sch 20 would otherwise apply is the subject of an exemption order,[257] then a reference in Sch 20 to a rail vehicle accessibility requirement will not include a requirement from which that vehicle is exempt.[258] As Sch 20 will not be brought into force, the account in **11.70–11.93** is thus of academic interest only.

FORGERY, ETC

11.94 In the context of the transport provisions in Part 12, a person commits an offence if, with intent to deceive, the person (a) forges, alters or uses a relevant document; (b) lends a relevant document to another person; (c) allows a relevant document to be used by another person; (d) makes or has possession of a document which closely resembles a relevant document.[259] For these purposes,[260] a 'relevant document' means an exemption certificate;[261] a notice of a kind mentioned in various statutory provisions;[262] an accessibility certificate;[263] or an approval certificate.[264]

11.95 A person guilty of such an offence is liable, on summary conviction, to a fine not exceeding the statutory maximum; or on conviction on indictment, to imprisonment for a term not exceeding 2 years or to a fine or to both.[265] A person commits an offence by knowingly making a false statement for the purpose of obtaining an accessibility certificate or an approval certificate.[266] A person guilty of this latter offence is liable on summary conviction to a fine not exceeding level 4 on the standard scale (£2,500).[267]

AVIATION AND MARITIME TRANSPORT

11.96 Like the DDA 1995, the EQA 2010 has nothing to say about the design, manufacture and accessibility standards that apply to aviation and maritime transport in relation to disabled passengers. Disabled persons will have rights in relation to transport services providers in these sectors under Part 4 of the Act.

---

[257] Issued under EQA 2010, s 183 above.
[258] EQA 2010, Sch 20, para 15(2). See EN paras 978–980.
[259] EQA 2010, s 188(2).
[260] EQA 2010, s 188(1).
[261] Issued under EQA 2010, ss 165, 168 or 170.
[262] That is, EQA 2010, ss 165(3)(b), 168(4)(b) or 170(4)(b).
[263] See EQA 2010, s 175.
[264] See EQA 2010, s 176.
[265] EQA 2010, s 188(3).
[266] EQA 2010, s 188(4).
[267] EQA 2010, s 188(5).

Chapter 12

ENFORCEMENT

INTRODUCTION

12.1 Part 9 of the Equality Act 2010 (EQA 2010) sets out the provisions for enforcement in either the county court (or sheriff court in Scotland) or the employment tribunal.[1]

12.2 Although proceedings relating to a contravention of the EQA 2010 must be brought in accordance with Part 9, this does not prevent a claim for judicial review.[2] One of the first cases before the Supreme Court was the appeal arising from a judicial review of a faith school's discriminatory admissions policy.[3]

12.3 Similarly, Part 9 does not prevent proceedings under the Immigration Acts or the Special Immigration Appeals Commission Act 1997 or, in Scotland, an application to the supervisory jurisdiction of the Court of Session.[4] There is also a reminder that the enforcement provisions do not apply to Part 1 of the EQA 2010, which is the public sector duty regarding socio-economic equalities and which does not confer a cause of action at private law.[5]

CIVIL COURTS

Jurisdiction

12.4 The jurisdiction of the county court and sheriff court is limited to contraventions of Part 3 of the EQA 2010 (provision of services and the exercise of public functions), Part 4 (premises), Part 6 (education, other than in relation to disability) and Part 7 (associations).[6] The judge must exercise his or her powers under the County Courts Act 1984 'to summon to his assistance, in such manner as may be prescribed, one or more persons of skill and experience in the matter to which the proceedings relate who may be willing to sit with the

---

1   EQA 2010, s 113(1).
2   EQA 2010, s 113(3).
3   *R (on the application of E) v JFS Governing Body* [2009] UKSC 15, [2010] IRLR 136.
4   EQA 2010, s 113(3).
5   EQA 2010, s 113(2).
6   EQA 2010, s 114(1).

judge and act as assessors',[7] unless satisfied there are good reasons for not doing so.[8] The equivalent powers must be exercised in the sheriff court in Scotland.[9]

12.5 The Explanatory Notes provide two examples of claims that might be brought in the county court. A woman joins a golf club, but, because she is a woman, is allowed to play golf only on Tuesday afternoons and she is not allowed access to the club bar. She would bring her discrimination claim in the county or sheriff court, as would a gay man who applies for residential housing in a local authority area, but is told that he can choose from only three housing blocks because all homosexual people are housed together.[10] *Malcolm v Lewisham Borough Council*, which concerned a disabled tenant under a secure tenancy, began life as an application for possession in the county court.[11]

Immigration cases

12.6 The county court and sheriff court can lose their jurisdiction in immigration cases where there are allegations that there has been a breach of Part 3 (services and public functions). This is where an immigration authority takes what is defined as 'a relevant decision', which is a decision under the Immigration Acts relating to a person's entitlement to enter or remain in the UK or a decision on a related appeal. If there is a question over whether the act of the immigration authority in taking that relevant decision amounts to a contravention of Part 3 and that question has been or could be raised on appeal, then the decision is not open to challenge in proceedings under the EQA 2010, nor affected by the decision of the court in such proceedings.[12]

12.7 For example, an immigration officer makes a decision about a person's entitlement to enter the UK. There is a complaint that, in reaching the decision, the immigration officer has discriminated against that person because of his race in contravention of Part 3. The complaint has been raised in an appeal brought under the immigration provisions. Therefore, the decision cannot be challenged in the county court or sheriff court under the enforcement provisions of the EQA 2010.

12.8 Equally, where there has been a decision in an appeal brought under the immigration provisions that there was no contravention of Part 3, the question cannot be raised again in the county court or sheriff court.[13]

---

[7]   County Courts Act 1984, s 63(1).
[8]   EQA 2010, s 114(7).
[9]   Sheriff Court (Scotland) Act 1907, Sch 1, r 44.3; EQA 2010, s 114(8).
[10] EN para 386.
[11] [2008] UKHL 43, [2008] 1 AC 1399.
[12] EQA 2010, s 115.
[13] EQA 2010, s 115(1)(b).

Education cases

12.9 Claims relating to discrimination in schools because of disability are made to specialist tribunals, rather than to the county court or sheriff court. These tribunals are: the First-Tier Tribunal in England, the Special Educational Needs Tribunal for Wales and the Additional Needs Tribunal for Scotland. Schedule 17 to the EQA 2010 (which is the only Schedule referable to enforcement) is headed 'Disabled Pupils: Enforcement'. It sets out the time limit for bringing such a claim (the primary limitation period being 6 months); the powers of the Tribunals and the process for appealing decisions; and the provision to make rules of procedure.[14]

12.10 For instance, the parents of a disabled child believe that the governing body of a school, which is the 'responsible body', has discriminated against their child because of her disability by not admitting her as a pupil, in contravention of Part 6.[15] The claim may be made to the appropriate specialist tribunal, but must be brought within 6 months of the date when the conduct complained of occurred, which in this example would be the decision not to admit the child. If the tribunal finds that the school has acted in contravention of Part 6, it may make such order as it thinks fit (although this does not include an order for compensation).

National security

12.11 Where the interests of national security make it expedient to do so, a county court or sheriff court may, in the interests of national security, exercise powers conferred by rules of court.[16] The court may exclude a claimant and/or their representative or an assessor from all or part of the proceedings.[17] A special advocate may be appointed to represent a claimant's interests where, for example, the claimant's representative has been excluded.[18] The rules may also confer power on the court to take steps to keep secret all or part of the reasons for the court's decision.[19]

12.12 These rules of court are made by the Civil Procedure Rules Committee or the Sheriff Court Rules Council for Scotland. This provision extends to all the protected characteristics.[20]

Time limits

12.13 The primary time limit for bringing a claim to the county court or sheriff court is 6 months starting with the date of the act to which the claim

---

[14] EQA 2010, s 116 and Sch 17.
[15] EQA 2010, s 85(1).
[16] EQA 2010, s 117(1).
[17] EQA 2010, s 117(2).
[18] EQA 2010, s 117(5).
[19] EQA 2010, s 117(4).
[20] EN paras 391–392.

relates, or such other period as the county court thinks just and equitable.[21] This contrasts with the primary time limit of 3 months in the employment tribunal. Conduct extending over a period is treated as done at the end of the period and failure to do something occurs when the decision is made not to do it.[22] That 'decision', in the absence of evidence to the contrary, occurs when the person does something inconsistent with doing it or at the end of whatever period of time in which it might reasonably have been done.[23]

12.14   There is a time limit of 9 months in two different circumstances: where a claim has been referred to a student complaints scheme within 6 months or to the Equality and Human Rights Commission for conciliation.[24] In claims involving the decisions of an immigration authority, where the authority has ruled that there has been a breach of Part 3 and that ruling can no longer be appealed under the immigration provisions (and therefore not falling within s 115), the 6 months begins with the authority's ruling.[25]

Remedies

12.15   Where the county court finds there has been a contravention of the EQA 2010, it has the power to grant any remedy which could be granted by the High Court in proceedings in tort or on a claim for judicial review.[26] The sheriff court has power to make any order which could be made by the Court of Session in proceedings for reparation or on a petition for judicial review. The most likely remedy will be an award of compensation, which may include damages for injured feelings.[27] In a claim for indirect discrimination, if the court is satisfied that the provision, criterion or practice was not applied with the intention of discriminating, then no award of damages can be made unless the court first considers what other remedies are available.[28]

EMPLOYMENT TRIBUNALS

Jurisdiction

12.16   The jurisdiction of the employment tribunal under the EQA 2010 replicates the enforcement provisions under previous legislation.[29] The most significant aspect of that jurisdiction will be the determination of complaints relating to contraventions in the workplace under Part 5. This includes complaints brought by contract workers, partners, office holders, as well as employees.

---

21   EQA 2010, s 118(1).
22   EQA 2010, s 118(6).
23   EQA 2010, s 118(7).
24   EQA 2010, s 118(2)–(4).
25   EQA 2010, s 118(5).
26   EQA 2010, s 119(2).
27   EQA 2010, s 119(4).
28   EQA 2010, s 119(5)–(6).
29   EQA 2010, s 120.

12.17 Where there are disputes relating to occupational pension schemes, an employment tribunal has jurisdiction to determine an application by a 'responsible person' for a declaration as to the rights of that person and worker over the effect of a non-discrimination rule.[30] It also has jurisdiction to determine an application by trustees or managers of a scheme for a declaration as to their rights or those of a member in relation to the effect of a non-discrimination rule, as well as determining questions about a non-discrimination rule referred to the tribunal by a court.[31]

12.18 In armed forces cases, the complainant must first follow the internal armed services complaints procedure and not withdraw that complaint, before bringing a claim to the employment tribunal.[32] So, a black soldier who thinks he has been discriminated against by being passed over for promotion would have to make an internal service complaint before bringing his claim to an employment tribunal.[33]

12.19 Employment tribunals have specialist knowledge of discrimination claims and vastly more experience than the county or sheriff court in dealing with such claims. A court may recognise that a claim relating to the discriminatory manner in which a pension scheme operates may more conveniently be heard by an employment tribunal, in which case the claim may be struck out.[34] The court may also stay the case, while it refers an issue to the tribunal for its determination.[35]

Time limits

12.20 The time limit for bringing a discrimination claim is 3 months, so that proceedings may not be brought after the end of the period of 3 months starting with the date of the act to which the complaint relates, or such other period as the tribunal considers just and equitable.[36] The one exception is armed forces complaints, where the time limit is 6 months, again with a 'just and equitable' discretion to extend time.[37]

12.21 The case-law on the 'just and equitable' discretion establishes that, although the discretion is broad, it should be used exceptionally. It is a broader discretion than that exercised under the 'not reasonably practicable' test for out-of-time unfair dismissal claims.[38] An open-ended checklist of relevant criteria, borrowed from the exercise of discretion by the civil courts under the Limitation Act 1980, was set out in *British Coal Corporation v Keeble*.[39]

---

[30] EQA 2010, s 120(2).
[31] EQA 2010, s 120(3), (4).
[32] EQA 2010, s 121.
[33] EN para 404.
[34] EQA 2010, s 122(1).
[35] EQA 2010, s 122(2).
[36] EQA 2010, s 123(1).
[37] EQA 2010, s 123(2).
[38] *Hawkins v Ball and Barclays Bank plc* [1996] IRLR 258, EAT.
[39] [1997] IRLR 336.

Following the approach taken by the civil courts, an employment tribunal should consider the prejudice which each party would suffer as the result of the decision to be made and also have regard to all the circumstances of the case and in particular to:

(a)   the length of and reasons for the delay;

(b)   the extent to which the cogency of the evidence is likely to be affected by the delay;

(c)   the extent to which the party sued co-operated with any requests for information;

(d)   the promptness with which the claimant acted once he or she knew of the facts giving rise to the cause of action; and

(e)   the steps taken by the claimant to obtain appropriate professional advice once he or she knew of the possibility of taking action.

12.22   The fault of the claimant is a relevant factor for the tribunal when assessing whether time should be extended, but a claimant cannot be held responsible for the failings of his solicitors. Whatever the reason why the legal advisors failed in their duty, and whether any remedy exists against them, would be immaterial in assessing the claimant's culpability.[40]

12.23   A reminder that the discretion to extend time should be exercised exceptionally is provided in *Robertson v Bexley Community Centre*,[41] in which Auld LJ said:

> 'It is also of importance to note that the time limits are exercised strictly in employment and industrial cases. When tribunals consider their discretion to consider a claim out of time on just and equitable grounds there is no presumption that they should do so unless they can justify failure to exercise the discretion. Quite the reverse. A tribunal cannot hear a complaint unless the applicant convinces it that it is just and equitable to extend time. So, the exercise of discretion is the exception rather than the rule.'

12.24   For the purposes of deciding when time 'starts' for the purpose of limitation, conduct extending over a period is to be treated as done at the end of the period, while failure to do a thing is to be treated as occurring when the person in question decided on it.[42] The EQA 2010 uses the single word 'failure', in preference to 'omission' and 'deliberate omission', which were the terms previously used in discrimination legislation in the equivalent provisions. A person is to be taken to decide on failure to do a thing, either (a) when he does

---

[40]   *Virdi v Commissioner of Police of the Metropolis* [2007] IRLR 24.
[41]   [2003] EWCA Civ 576, [2003] IRLR 434.
[42]   EQA 2010, s 123(3).

an act inconsistent with doing the thing, or (b) if he does no inconsistent act, on the expiry of the period in which he might reasonably have been expected to do the thing.[43]

12.25 In *Matuszowicz v Kingston upon Hull City Council* a failure to make reasonable adjustments under the Disability Discrimination Act 1995 (DDA 1995) was held to be an omission, not an act.[44] It is treated as occurring when the person in question decided not to make that adjustment. Where there is no such decision, the tribunal is looking either for an inconsistent act[45] or it will make a finding as to when the person might reasonably have been expected to do the thing he has failed to do.[46]

12.26 For example, a disabled employee with carpal tunnel syndrome returns to work and requires an adapted keyboard, which is a reasonable adjustment for the employer to make. If the employer tells the employee that it has decided not to provide one, then that is when the failure occurs. If there is no such decision, but the employee is provided with a standard keyboard upon his return, that would be an inconsistent act and the failure occurs when that standard keyboard is provided. If there is neither a decision nor an inconsistent act then, in order to decide when the failure occurred, the tribunal must ask itself when was the end of the period in which the employer might reasonably have provided the adapted keyboard.

12.27 Perversely, this will mean that a respondent might argue that it should have made an adjustment earlier, which might mean that a claim is out of time. The EQA 2010 has therefore not simplified a process that Sedley LJ described as demanding a measure of poker-faced insincerity, which only a lawyer could understand or a casuist forgive.[47]

Remedies

12.28 There are three remedies available in employment tribunals where the tribunal finds there has been a relevant contravention of the EQA 2010: a declaration, compensation and an appropriate recommendation.[48]

Declaration

12.29 The first remedy remains the declaration as to the rights of the complainant and the respondent in relation to the matters to which the proceedings relate.[49] This will reflect the finding that, for example, the

---

[43]   EQA 2010, s 123(4).
[44]   [2009] EWCA Civ 22, [2009] IRLR 288.
[45]   EQA 2010, s 123(4)(a).
[46]   EQA 2010, s 123(4)(b).
[47]   *Matuszowicz* para 38.
[48]   EQA 2010, s 124(1).
[49]   EQA 2010, s 124(2)(a).

respondent directly discriminated against a disabled complainant by treating him or her less favourably because of the protected characteristic of disability.

Compensation

12.30 The most frequently sought remedy is an order that the respondent pays compensation to the complainant.[50] The tortious measure of damages is applied, placing the claimant in the same position, as far as possible, as they would have been had the unlawful act not taken place. Compensation can be awarded for pecuniary and non-pecuniary loss.

12.31 The principles behind compensation for non-pecuniary loss are summarised in *Armitage, Marsden and HM Prison Service v Johnson*,[51] where the EAT stated that:

> 'Awards for injury to feelings are compensatory. They should be just to both parties. They should compensate fully without punishing the tortfeasor.'

Awards should neither be too low nor excessive and should bear some broad general similarity to the range of awards in personal injury cases. Tribunals should remind themselves of the value in everyday life of the sum they have in mind and should bear in mind the need for public respect for the level of awards made.

12.32 These principles were applied in *Vento v Chief Constable of West Yorkshire Police (No 2)*,[52] where the Court of Appeal identified three broad bands of compensation for injury to feelings. The figures provided in *Vento* have since been adjusted.[53] A top band, which should normally be between £18,000 and £30,000, applies to the most serious cases, such as where there has been a lengthy campaign of discriminatory harassment. A middle band of between £6,000 and £18,000 should be used for serious cases, 'which do not merit an award in the highest band'. The lowest band of between £600 and £6,000 is appropriate for less serious cases, such as isolated or one-off occurrences. An award exceeding £30,000 should only be made in the most exceptional circumstances, while awards of less than £600 are to be avoided altogether, as they risk being regarded as so low as not to be a proper recognition of injury to feelings.

12.33 The EAT in *Da'Bell* added that disputes about the placement within a band of an award were likely to be about fact and impression and it would be wrong to interfere with those findings unless they were manifestly wrong. They were more likely to raise questions of law if they were about placement in the wrong band or at the extremes.

---

50   EQA 2010, s 124(2)(b).
51   [1997] IRLR 162.
52   [2002] EWCA Civ 1871, [2003] ICR 318.
53   *Da'Bell v National Society for the Prevention of Cruelty to Children* [2010] IRLR 19.

12.34 Where the tribunal has made a finding of indirect discrimination,[54] but is satisfied that the provision, criterion or practice was not applied with the intention of discriminating against the complainant, it cannot make an order for compensation unless it first considers whether to make a declaration or a recommendation.[55]

Aggravated and exemplary damages

12.35 The Tribunal also has power to award aggravated damages in discrimination cases.[56] This is not the case in Scotland, although an award for damages in a Scottish case may reflect the way in which the victim was treated.[57]

12.36 In *Johnson* it was said that the statutory torts may be sufficiently intentional as to enable the claimant to rely upon malice or the respondent's manner of committing the tort or other conduct as aggravating the injury to feelings. In that case, the tribunal had identified in particular the way in which the investigation of the complaints of race discrimination was conducted (described by the tribunal as 'a travesty'), which aggravated the claimant's injury. Other examples of where aggravated damages are available include:

- as compensation for the manner in which a claim for discrimination is defended;[58] if a respondent misconducts himself in the defence of a discrimination case, the claimant could bring a claim for victimisation in respect of the protected act of bringing the claim, so that – in terms – an award of aggravated damages compensates the claimant without the need to commence further proceedings;

- where a respondent has treated a complaint about sexual harassment in a trivial way;[59]

- where a respondent has treated the perpetrator of discrimination in a lenient way.[60]

12.37 In *Ministry of Defence v Fletcher*,[61] the EAT has recently looked at how a tribunal should assess the amount of an award of aggravated damages. Regard should be had to the overall sum awarded in respect of non-pecuniary loss and double recovery should be avoided by taking appropriate account of

---

[54] EQA 2010, s 19.
[55] EQA 2010, s 124(4) and (5).
[56] *Armitage, Marsden and HM Prison Service v Johnson* [1997] IRLR 162.
[57] *D Watt (Shetland) Ltd v Reid* EAT/424/01.
[58] *Zaiwalla & Co v Walia* [2002] IRLR 697.
[59] *HM Prison Service v Salmon* [2001] IRLR 425.
[60] *British Telecommunications plc v Reid* [2003] EWCA Civ 1675, [2004] IRLR 327. In that case, the perpetrator of racial harassment was not punished, remained in post, and was then promoted, even though the charges against him had not been determined.
[61] [2010] IRLR 25.

the overlap between the individual heads of damage. Awards should also bear some broad general similarity to the range of awards in personal injury cases.

12.38　In *Fletcher*, the tribunal awarded £20,000 aggravated damages together with £30,000 for injury to feelings. The EAT took into account an element of double recovery, the totality of the award of £50,000 for non-pecuniary loss, the Judicial Studies Board guidelines in personal injury cases and it then reduced the aggravated damages to £8,000. *Fletcher* also made clear that it is not necessary to establish that the conduct is malicious, although malicious conduct may attract aggravated damages.

12.39　One particular factor that is likely to mitigate an award of aggravated damages is an apology.

12.40　The EAT in *Fletcher* also set aside an award of £50,000 in exemplary damages. Where there has been oppressive, arbitrary or unconstitutional action by the servants of the government or the respondent's conduct has been calculated to make a profit exceeding the likely compensation payable to a claimant, then exemplary damages may be awarded.[62] Such damages are punitive, not compensatory. They are intended to deter and are reserved for the very worst cases.

Recommendations

12.41　The third remedy open to a tribunal is to make an appropriate recommendation.[63] This requires the respondent to take specified steps within a specified period for the purpose of obviating or reducing the adverse effect on either the complainant or any other person of any matter to which the proceedings relate.[64] The power to make recommendations has been used sparingly under discrimination legislation to date and certainly much less than appeared to be the understanding during Parliamentary debate.

12.42　Under previous legislation, the recommendation could only benefit the individual complainant, but this new provision extends the tribunal's power to recommend action that would reduce the impact of the respondent's discriminatory actions on any other person, as well as the complainant, in other words the wider workforce.[65] The term 'specified steps' is also less restricted than the previous requirement that the respondent take action 'appearing to the tribunal to be practicable', which was judicially interpreted as being by reference to the effect upon the complainant.

12.43　The examples of recommendations given are: introducing an equal opportunities policy; ensuring a harassment policy is more effectively implemented; setting up a review panel to deal with equal opportunities and

---

62　*Kuddus v Chief Constable of Leicestershire Constabulary* [2001] UKHL 29.
63　EQA 2010, s 124(2)(c).
64　EQA 2010, s 124(3).
65　EQA 2010, s 124(3).

harassment/grievance procedures; re-training staff; and making public the selection criteria used for transfer of staff.[66]

12.44 As the EAT noted in *Chief Constable of West Yorkshire Police v Vento (No 2)*,[67] the power to make recommendations gives the tribunal an extremely wide discretion. In that case a recommendation that the Deputy Chief Constable should interview named police officers and discuss with them relevant parts of the decisions on liability was approved by the EAT (and not appealed to the Court of Appeal). The employment tribunal had found 'institutional denial', and that finding needed to be addressed. Further, to know that the wrongdoers would be confronted with the findings could reduce injury to the claimant's feelings. However, a recommendation that each of the officers should be invited to apologise in writing to the claimant was not upheld, not least because there was no means of enforcing the recommendation against them.

12.45 In *British Gas plc v Sharma*,[68] the EAT held that a tribunal cannot recommend that a complainant be promoted automatically to the next suitable vacancy. This was because the Race Relations Act 1976 did not allow positive discrimination and to promote the claimant without considering other applicants who might have superior qualifications for the vacancy could amount to discrimination against those other applicants. That remains the case under the EQA 2010.

12.46 The tribunal can only recommend action be taken within a specified time; it cannot enforce the recommendation. If the respondent fails, without reasonable excuse, to comply with the recommendation 'in so far as it relates to the complainant', the tribunal can either make or increase an award of compensation.[69] It follows that there is no sanction for failure to comply with a recommendation aimed at the wider workforce. This reflects the difficulty in mandating an outcome, as well the underlying intention behind this provision, which is not to penalise employers, but to enable them to comply with discrimination legislation.[70] However, no doubt a tribunal would be asked to draw an adverse inference from any such failure in a future case involving that respondent.

12.47 The power to make recommendations does not apply to equal pay claims.[71]

12.48 In national security proceedings, the power to make recommendations is restricted, in that it cannot be made for the benefit of someone other than the

---

[66] EN para 414.
[67] [2002] IRLR 177.
[68] [1991] ICR 19.
[69] EQA 2010, s 124(7).
[70] HL Deb vol 716 col 1471 (27 January 2010) (Chancellor of the Duchy of Lancaster). See also: HC PBC Deb (Equality Bill) 2008–09 (25 June 2009) col 513 (Solicitor General).
[71] EQA 2010, s 113(6).

claimant if that would mean affecting anything done by the Security Service, the Secret Intelligence Service, Government Communications Headquarters or a part of the armed forces assisting Government Communications Headquarters.[72]

Occupational pension schemes

12.49 The employment tribunal's powers in relation to claims involving occupational schemes are different.[73] Compensation may only be awarded for injured feelings or for failure to comply with a recommendation; in other words, it cannot compensate a claimant for financial loss caused by discrimination.[74] There is the same power to make recommendations, but the power to make a declaration is extended to include a declaration that a claimant has a right to be admitted to a scheme or that an existing member has a right to membership without discrimination.[75]

EQUALITY OF TERMS

Jurisdiction

12.50 The provisions relating to the jurisdiction of the courts and tribunals in respect of equality of terms remains the same as contained within previous legislation. Tribunals may hear and decide claims (including those referred to them by courts) involving equality rules in occupational pension schemes and claims relating to an equality clause in the terms of a person's work, including claims relating to pregnancy and maternity equality.[76] A 'responsible person' (such as an employer, or a pension scheme trustee or manager[77]) can also ask a tribunal for a declaration of each party's rights in relation to a dispute or claim about an equality clause or rule. This does not alter any jurisdiction the courts have in relation to an equality clause or rule.[78]

12.51 Members of the armed forces must bring a complaint under service complaints procedures before they can bring a claim to a tribunal.[79]

12.52 A court may decide that a claim or counter-claim relating to an equality clause or rule could more conveniently be dealt with by an employment tribunal, in which case it may strike out the claim or counter-claim or it may stay proceedings.[80] For example, an employer sues an employee in a civil court for breach of her employment contract. In response, the employee

---

[72]　EQA 2010, s 125(1).
[73]　EQA 2010, s 126.
[74]　EQA 2010, s 126(3).
[75]　EQA 2010, s 126(2).
[76]　EQA 2010, s 127.
[77]　EQA 2010, ss 61 and 80.
[78]　EQA 2010, s 127(9).
[79]　EQA 2010, s 127(6).
[80]　EQA 2010, s 128.

counterclaims for breach of an equality clause. The court decides to refer the counterclaim to an employment tribunal and postpones the case until the tribunal's decision.[81]

Time limits

12.53 A claim for breach of an equality clause or rule or to apply for a declaration about the effect of such a clause or rule, must normally be made within 6 months beginning with the last day of the employment or appointment.[82] In certain circumstances, a claimant has more time to make a claim. This applies in non-standard cases where, for example, the employer conceals certain information from the claimant or where the claimant is under an incapacity.[83]

12.54 For example, a woman's employment ends owing to mental health problems that result in her temporary loss of capacity to make decisions for herself (therefore, an incapacity case). She could make a claim for breach of an equality clause to an employment tribunal, but is not well enough to do so. The 6-month time limit will start when she recovers sufficiently to make a claim.[84]

12.55 Members of the armed forces have an additional 3 months in which to bring a claim to allow them time to make a complaint under the service complaints procedures.[85]

Work of equal value

12.56 If an employment tribunal has to decide whether the work of a claimant and a comparator are of equal value in a complaint relating to a breach of an equality clause or rule or on a reference from a court, it may require an independent expert to prepare a report on the question.[86] This is dealt with more fully in Chapter 8.

Remedies in non-pension cases

12.57 In a claim for breach of an equality clause other than in relation to a pension scheme, the court or tribunal may make a declaration clarifying the rights of the parties and/or may order the employer to pay the claimant arrears of pay or damages.[87] The payment may not go back more than 6 years in a standard case.[88] For example, a woman successfully establishes that her work is the same as her male comparator's and that, in addition to a discrepancy

---

[81]   EN para 427.
[82]   EQA 2010, s 129(3).
[83]   As defined in EQA 2010, s 130.
[84]   EQA 2010, ss 129(3) and 130(7); EN para 435.
[85]   EQA 2010, s 129(4); EN para 428.
[86]   EQA 2010, s 131(1), (2).
[87]   EQA 2010, s 132.
[88]   EQA 2010, s 132(3), (4).

between her pay and that of her male colleague, she has been denied access to the benefit of a company car. The claimant is entitled to claim the difference in pay going back up to 6 years from the date of the claim. She is also entitled to monetary compensation for not having had the use of a company car.[89]

12.58 In Scotland, the period of time is 5 years.[90] In both England and Wales and in Scotland, there are particular rules for claims involving concealment or incapacity.[91]

Remedies in pension cases

12.59 In claims relating to a breach of an equality rule or clause with respect to membership of or rights under a pension scheme, a court or tribunal may make a declaration, but must not order arrears of benefits or damages or any other amount to be paid to the complainant.[92] The tribunal may declare that a claimant is entitled to be admitted to a scheme from a date specified by the court or tribunal.[93] It may also declare that a claimant is entitled to have any rights that would have accrued under the scheme from a specified date.[94]

Remedies in claims for arrears brought by pensioners

12.60 On a complaint by a pensioner member of an occupational pension scheme relating to a breach of an equality clause or rule, a court or tribunal may make a declaration and/or order compensation by way of arrears of benefits or damages.[95] The time limit is again 6 years in a standard case in England and Wales, 5 years in Scotland and there are particular rules for claims involving concealment or incapacity.[96]

MISCELLANEOUS PROVISIONS

12.61 The following provisions apply to enforcement in both the county court and sheriff court and the employment tribunal and deal with matters such as the burden of proof, previous findings and statutory questionnaires.

---

[89] EN para 442.
[90] EQA 2010, s 132(5).
[91] EQA 2010, ss 132(4), (5) and 135.
[92] EQA 2010, s 133(2).
[93] EQA 2010, s 133(4), (5); this may not be earlier than 8 April 1976, which was the date of judgment in *Defrenne v Sabena* C 43/75, [1981] 1 All ER 122, [1976] ECR 455, where it was held that the principle of equal pay should not be applied to periods earlier than that judgment.
[94] EQA 2010, s 133(6), (7); this may not be earlier than 17 May 1990, which was the date of judgment in *Barber v Guardian Royal Exchange Assurance Group* C 262/88, [1991] 1 QB 344, [1990] ECR 1-1889, which established that occupational pensions were equal pay for the purposes of Article 119.
[95] EQA 2010, s 134.
[96] EQA 2010, ss 134(5), (6) and 135.

Burden of proof

12.62 The burden of proof provisions apply to any proceedings relating to a contravention of the EQA 2010, apart from offences under the Act.[97]

12.63 Although the wording has been reformulated, the approach reflects the 'reverse burden'. Originally, courts and tribunals followed the guidance provided in *King v Great Britain-China Centre*,[98] which was that claimants who complained of discrimination had to make out their case. If claimants did not prove the case on the balance of probabilities, then they failed. However, the Burden of Proof Directive in 1997[99] led to the various discrimination laws introducing what was termed a reverse burden, which was that, where the complainant proved facts from which the tribunal could conclude in the absence of an adequate explanation that the respondent had committed an act of discrimination, it should uphold the complaint unless the respondent proved that he did not commit that act.[100] That formulation has been extensively considered and refined in the case-law.[101]

12.64 The formulation of the burden of proof under the EQA 2010 is that, if there are facts from which the court could decide, in the absence of any other explanation, that a person (A) contravened the provision concerned, the court must hold that the contravention occurred.[102] However, this does not apply if A shows that A did not contravene the provision.[103]

12.65 As elsewhere in the EQA 2010, the change of wording reflects an attempt to make the law more accessible to the 'ordinary user' of the Act, rather than any subtle shift in meaning.[104] Therefore, although the precise wording has altered, the previous case-law will remain relevant in interpreting the burden of proof.

12.66 That guidance provided in *Igen v Wong*[105] (which related to the Sex Discrimination Act 1975 (SDA 1975)) was as follows:

(1) Pursuant to s 63A of the SDA 1975, it is for the claimant who complains of sex discrimination to prove on the balance of probabilities facts from which the tribunal could conclude, in the absence of an adequate explanation, that the respondent has committed an act of discrimination against the claimant which is unlawful by virtue of Part II or which by

---

[97] EQA 2010, s 136.

[98] [1992] ICR 516.

[99] Council Directive 97/80/EC; now replaced by Council Directive 2006/54/EC.

[100] For example: SDA 1975, s 63A.

[101] See, for example: *Barton v Investec Henderson Crosthwaite Securities Ltd* [2003] ICR 1205; *Igen v Wong* [2005] EWCA Civ 142, [2005] ICR 931; *Madarassy v Nomura International Plc* [2007] EWCA Civ 33, [2007] ICR 867.

[102] EQA 2010, s 136(2).

[103] EQA 2010, s 136(3).

[104] EN para 61.

[105] [2005] EWCA Civ 142, [2005] ICR 931.

virtue of s 41 or s 42 of the SDA 1975 is to be treated as having been committed against the claimant. These are referred to below as 'such facts'.

(2) If the claimant does not prove such facts he or she will fail.

(3) It is important to bear in mind in deciding whether the claimant has proved such facts that it is unusual to find direct evidence of sex discrimination. Few employers would be prepared to admit such discrimination, even to themselves. In some cases the discrimination will not be an intention but merely based on the assumption that 'he or she would not have fitted in'.

(4) In deciding whether the claimant has proved such facts, it is important to remember that the outcome at this stage of the analysis by the tribunal will therefore usually depend on what inferences it is proper to draw from the primary facts found by the tribunal.

(5) It is important to note the word 'could' in s 63A(2). At this stage the tribunal does not have to reach a definitive determination that such facts would lead it to the conclusion that there was an act of unlawful discrimination. At this stage a tribunal is looking at the primary facts before it to see what inferences of secondary fact could be drawn from them.

(6) In considering what inferences or conclusions can be drawn from the primary facts, the tribunal must assume that there is no adequate explanation for those facts.

(7) These inferences can include, in appropriate cases, any inferences that it is just and equitable to draw in accordance with s 74(2)(b) of the SDA 1975 from an evasive or equivocal reply to a questionnaire or any other questions that fall within s 74(2) of the SDA 1975.

(8) Likewise, the tribunal must decide whether any provision of any relevant code of practice is relevant and if so, take it into account in determining such facts pursuant to s 56A(10) of the SDA 1975. This means that inferences may also be drawn from any failure to comply with any relevant code of practice.

(9) Where the claimant has proved facts from which conclusions could be drawn that the respondent has treated the claimant less favourably on the ground of sex, then the burden of proof moves to the respondent.

(10) It is then for the respondent to prove that he did not commit, or as the case may be, is not to be treated as having committed, that act.

(11) To discharge that burden it is necessary for the respondent to prove, on the balance of probabilities, that the treatment was in no sense whatsoever on the grounds of sex, since 'no discrimination whatsoever' is compatible with the Burden of Proof Directive.

(12) That requires a tribunal to assess not merely whether the respondent has proved an explanation for the facts from which such inferences can be drawn, but further that it is adequate to discharge the burden of proof on the balance of probabilities that sex was not a ground for the treatment in question.

(13) Since the facts necessary to prove an explanation would normally be in the possession of the respondent, a tribunal would normally expect cogent evidence to discharge that burden of proof. In particular, the tribunal will need to examine carefully explanations for failure to deal with the questionnaire procedure and/or code of practice.

12.67 The Court of Appeal in *Madarassy*[106] clarified that:

> '"Could conclude" . . . must mean that 'a reasonable tribunal could properly conclude' from all the evidence before it. This would include evidence adduced by the complainant in support of the allegations of sex discrimination, such as evidence of a difference in status, a difference in treatment and the reason for the differential treatment. It would also include evidence adduced by the respondent contesting the complaint.'

As the wording is now 'could decide', that guidance remains relevant.

12.68 The EQA 2010 applies the same rule to all discrimination claims, so that the anomalies that previously existed under discrimination legislation, such as the 'old' burden of proof in race discrimination claims brought on grounds of colour, no longer exist.

12.69 The reference to a 'contravention' includes a reference to a breach of an equality clause or rule. The reference to a 'court' includes an employment tribunal or any other tribunal or commission that has jurisdiction to hear proceedings brought under the EQA 2010.[107]

Previous findings

12.70 If a claimant has brought a case under any of the previous discrimination Acts or Regulations which the EQA 2010 replaces and a tribunal or court has made a final finding, the issues decided in that case cannot be re-opened and litigated again under the provisions of the EQA 2010. The finding becomes 'final' after the appeal process or the time for bringing an

---

[106] [2007] EWCA Civ 33, [2007] ICR 867.
[107] EQA 2010, s 136(6).

appeal have been exhausted.[108] This provision is necessary, because the EQA 2010 is re-enacting many of the provisions in the previous legislation, which should not therefore provide an opportunity to re-open issues that have been decided.

Statutory questionnaires

12.71 Complainants have a right to serve a statutory questionnaire on anyone they think has contravened the EQA 2010.[109] Both the questions and the answers are admissible as evidence. Sometimes with equal importance, the respondent's failure to answer (or answer in time) and/or an evasive or equivocal answer allow the tribunal or court to draw an adverse inference.[110]

12.72 However the court or tribunal cannot draw such adverse inferences in certain specified circumstances. These are if the respondent reasonably asserts that to answer differently or at all would have prejudiced criminal proceedings or revealed the reason for criminal proceedings being withdrawn or not being brought. There is also a power for a Minister of the Crown to specify by order additional circumstances where the adverse inferences would not apply.[111]

12.73 The format of the questionnaire and the time limits for service will be set out in separate orders. Since these provisions replicate the previous provisions, the procedures will remain the same, which means that in employment tribunal proceedings, a questionnaire must be served within 3 months beginning when the act complained of was done. Where a complaint has been presented to the tribunal, the complainant has 21 days to serve the questionnaire or such further time as the tribunal orders. In court proceedings, the time limit is 6 months or with permission of the court. The response should be provided as quickly as possible, but in any event within 8 weeks.[112]

Interest

12.74 The power for an employment tribunal to award interest on amounts awarded in discrimination claims is retained under the EQA 2010.[113] The rates of interest and methods of calculation will be set out in separate regulations.

Conduct giving rise to separate proceedings

12.75 There is a new provision that enables an employment tribunal to transfer a case to a county or sheriff court, or a court to transfer a case to an employment tribunal. This is where the same conduct has given rise to two or more separate claims under the EQA 2010 and one of the claims relates to

---

[108] EQA 2010, s 137.
[109] EQA 2010, s 138.
[110] EQA 2010, s 138(4).
[111] EQA 2010, s 138(5).
[112] For example, Race Relations (Questions and Replies) Order 1977, SI 1977/842.
[113] EQA 2010, s 139.

instructing, causing or inducing a person to discriminate against, harass or victimise another person.[114] It also provides that an employment tribunal or court cannot make a decision about such a case which is inconsistent with an earlier decision about the same conduct.[115]

12.76 For example, an employer instructs an employee to discriminate against a customer by refusing to serve him because of the protected characteristic of race. The customer brings a claim against the employer, which would be in the county court. The employee also brings a case against the employer in an employment tribunal, because he claims that the instruction amounted to harassment. These claims both arise out of the same conduct and so the court and the tribunal can transfer proceedings in order that they can be dealt with together, as this is a better way of managing the cases.[116]

CONTRACTS

Unenforceable terms

12.77 A term of a contract which constitutes, promotes or provides for treatment prohibited under the EQA 2010 is unenforceable in that respect.[117] For disability, this also applies to non-contractual terms relating to the provision of employment services or group insurance arrangements for employees.[118] This clause does not apply to a term of contract modified by an equality clause, because once the term is modified it is no longer discriminatory.[119] Nor does it include contractual terms which may breach the public sector duty regarding socio-economic inequalities or the public sector equality duty, as these do not confer rights at private law.[120]

12.78 The Explanatory Notes provide this example. A term in a franchise agreement which includes a requirement that the franchisee should only employ Asian people could not be enforced by the franchisor unless he could objectively justify it (unless an exception applies). But the franchisee could still obtain any benefit he is due under the term; for example he could continue operating the franchise. However, if the franchisee complied with the discriminatory term, a person discriminated against under it could make a claim against the franchisee for unlawful discrimination under other provisions in the EQA 2010.[121]

---

[114] EQA 2010, s 140(1).
[115] EQA 2010, s 140(5).
[116] EN para 463.
[117] EQA 2010, s 142(1).
[118] EQA 2010, ss 56(2)(a)–(e) and 142(2).
[119] EQA 2010, s 142(4); EN para 467.
[120] EQA 2010, ss 142(5) and 148(2).
[121] EN para 468.

Removal or modification of unenforceable terms

12.79 A county court or sheriff court may, on an application by a person who has an interest in a contract, or other agreement, make an order for an unenforceable term to be removed or modified.[122] Anyone who is affected by a contract has an interest in it. The court may also order that the term is treated as having been modified or removed in respect of a period before the order was made.[123] However, no order can be made unless anyone who would be affected by the order has been given notice and afforded an opportunity to make representations.[124]

12.80 For example, a person renting an office in a serviced office block could ask for a term in the rental contract to be amended if the term discriminated indirectly, for example by including an unjustified requirement that people entering the premises remove any facial covering (thus discriminating against Muslim women). The term could be adjusted by the court to allow special arrangements to be made to satisfy both genuine security needs of other users and the religious needs of Muslim women visiting the claimant.[125]

Contracting out and compromise

12.81 Contractual terms that try to exclude or limit the operation of any provision of the EQA 2010 are unenforceable by the person in whose favour the term operates.[126] The same applies (for disability only) to non-contractual terms relating to the provision of employment services or group insurance arrangements for employees.[127]

12.82 The exceptions are to allow negotiated settlement of claims. Therefore a contract settling a claim in an employment tribunal that has been made with the assistance of a conciliation officer or that is a qualifying compromise contract is permissible.[128] The same applies to a contract settling a county court or sheriff court claim.[129] This includes a contract which settles a complaint relating to a breach of an equality clause or rule or a non-discrimination rule.[130]

12.83 A 'qualifying compromise contract' must meet a number of conditions. These are that:

(a)   the contract is in writing;

---

[122]   EQA 2010, s 143(1).
[123]   EQA 2010, s 143(3).
[124]   EQA 2010, s 143(2).
[125]   EN para 471.
[126]   EQA 2010, s 144(1).
[127]   EQA 2010, s 144(2).
[128]   EQA 2010, s 144(4).
[129]   EQA 2010, s 144(3).
[130]   EQA 2010, s 144(5).

(b)   it relates to the particular complaint;

(c)   the complainant has, before entering into the contract, received advice from an independent adviser about its terms and effect (including, in particular, its effect on the complainant's ability to pursue the complaint before an employment tribunal);

(d)   on the date of the giving of the advice, there is in force a contract of insurance, or an indemnity provided for members of a profession or professional body, covering the risk of a claim by the complainant in respect of loss arising from the advice;

(e)   the contract identifies the adviser; and

(f)   the contract states that the conditions in paragraphs (c) and (d) are met.[131]

12.84   The term 'independent adviser' includes qualified lawyers, but also authorised trade union officials and authorised workers at advice centres.[132] There is a power to add further categories of independent adviser.[133] The provision makes clear that a conflict of interest prevents a person from being an independent adviser.[134] For example, if an employee with a claim at an employment tribunal receives advice about the settlement from a lawyer who works for the same employer, the settlement agreement will be unenforceable.

Void and unenforceable terms in collective agreements

12.85   This provision relates to collective agreements.[135] A term of a collective agreement is void to the extent that it discriminates against a person or would otherwise lead to conduct prohibited under the EQA 2010.[136] The terms are made void, rather than unenforceable, because they are not enforceable in any event unless incorporated into a contract.[137]

12.86   Therefore, for example, a collective agreement which required jobs in a particular part of a factory to be given only to men would be void and a woman who applied could not be refused on that ground.[138]

12.87   Rules made by employers for employees or prospective employees or by trade organisations and qualifications bodies that constitute, promote or provide for treatment prohibited under the EQA 2010 are unenforceable in that

---

[131]   EQA 2010, s 147(3).
[132]   EQA 2010, s 147(4).
[133]   EQA 2010, s 147(4)(d).
[134]   EQA 2010, s 147(5).
[135]   Trade Union & Labour Relations (Consolidation) Act 1992, s 178(1).
[136]   EQA 2010, s 145(1).
[137]   Trade Union & Labour Relations (Consolidation) Act 1992, s 179(1).
[138]   EN para 478.

respect.[139] The example given is of an indirectly discriminatory rule of a qualifications body (providing, for example, a professional qualification for plumbers), which required that applicants must have 2 years' previous experience with a British firm. This would be unenforceable against a person who had the equivalent experience with a foreign firm. It would still be enforceable against a person who did not have the required experience at all (provided it was justified).[140]

12.88 An employment tribunal can declare a term of a collective agreement void, or a rule of an undertaking unenforceable, where a person thinks that it might in the future have the effect of discriminating against him or her. Complaints can be brought by 'qualifying persons', which would include, for example, employees and prospective employees in respect of discriminatory collective agreements and persons seeking or holding relevant qualifications in respect of qualifications bodies.[141]

---

[139] EQA 2010, ss 145(2) and 148(5).
[140] EN para 478.
[141] EQA 2010, s 146.

Chapter 13

ADVANCEMENT OF EQUALITY

INTRODUCTION

13.1 A certain amount of positive action to compensate for disproportionately low representation of, for example, members of a particular racial group was lawful under UK law before the enactment of the Equality Act 2010 (EQA 2010). For example the Race Relations Act 1976 (RRA 1976) provided:

> 'Nothing in Parts II to IV shall render unlawful any act done in affording persons of a particular racial group access to facilities or services to meet the special needs of persons of that group in regard to their education, training or welfare, or any ancillary benefits.'[1]

13.2 In no reported case was this provision considered directly, although in *Lambeth London Borough Council v Commission for Racial Equality*,[2] it was referred to by the Court of Appeal when it decided that positive discrimination was unlawful under the general provisions of the RRA 1976.

13.3 In addition, the RRA 1976 provided that:[3]

'(1) Nothing in Parts II to IV shall render unlawful any act done in relation to particular work by any person in connection with –
    (a) affording only persons of a particular racial group access to facilities for training which would help to fit them for that work; or
    (b) encouraging only persons of a particular racial group to take advantage of opportunities for doing that work,
where it reasonably appears to that person that at any time within the twelve months immediately preceding the doing of the act –
    (i) there were no persons of that group among those doing that work in Great Britain; or
    (ii) the proportion of persons of that group among those doing that work in Great Britain was small in comparison with the proportion of persons of that group among the population of Great Britain.
(2) Where in relation to particular work it reasonably appears to any person that although the condition for the operation of subsection (1) is not met for the

---

[1] RRA 1976, s 35.
[2] [1990] ICR 768.
[3] RRA 1976, s 37.

whole of Great Britain it is met for an area within Great Britain, nothing in
Parts II to IV shall render unlawful any act done by that person in or in
connection with –

(a)   affording persons who are of the racial group in question, and who
      appear likely to take up that work in that area, access to facilities for
      training which would help to fit them for that work; or

(b)   encouraging persons of that group to take advantage of opportunities
      in the area for doing that work.'

13.4   The confinement of this provision to 'particular work' and the need for
there to have been a comparison of the numbers of relevant people able to do
the particular work during the preceding 12 months, meant that the provision
was rarely of any practical value. Any other positive action was prohibited by
the non-discrimination provisions in UK law, although public authorities were,
after the enactment of the Race Relations (Amendment) Act 2000, required to
have due regard to the need to eliminate unlawful racial discrimination and to
act with a view to promoting equality of opportunity and good relations
between persons of different racial groups.[4] Similarly, as a result of the
Equality Act 2006 amending the Sex Discrimination Act 1975 (SDA 1975),
public authorities were under a similar duty in relation to gender.[5]

13.5   In this chapter, the parts of the EQA 2010 which require public
authorities (or bodies which are not public authorities but which exercise public
functions) to act in particular ways, are described first. The two sections (ss 158
and 159) of the EQA 2010 which permit positive action are then examined.
Finally, the effect of the ECJ case law concerning positive action is stated. That
case law will affect the manner in which ss 158 and 159 are applied.

POSITIVE ACTION: AN OVERVIEW OF THE NEW LAW[6]

13.6   The EQA 2010 has three main mechanisms for requiring or enabling
some positive action to combat discrimination. Two relate specifically to the
public sector: one is a new duty requiring public bodies to act with due regard
to the desirability of exercising their functions in a way which is designed to
'reduce the inequalities of outcome which result from socio-economic
disadvantage'.[7] The second is a duty (which is largely equivalent to pre-existing
duties) when exercising its functions to have due regard to the need to:

(1)   eliminate discrimination and other acts prohibited by the EQA 2010;

(2)   advance equality of opportunity; and

---

4   RRA 1976, s 71 as inserted by the 2000 Act.
5   SDA 1975, s 76A.
6   The publication entitled *The Equality Bill: Duty to reduce socio-economic inequalities: A guide*
    published by the London Government Equalities Office is very helpful in describing the
    thinking behind the new law.
7   EQA 2010, ss 1–3. The Explanatory Notes provide some assistance in understanding the
    intention of these new provisions.

(3)   foster good relations between persons who have protected characteristics and those who do not have those characteristics.[8]

13.7   The third means by which the EQA 2010 addresses inequalities otherwise than by a prohibition (ignoring for this purpose the duty to make reasonable adjustments for persons with disabilities) is to make lawful certain positive action.[9] That lawful positive action is more extensive than the positive action which was authorised by the prior legislation.

NEW PUBLIC SECTOR DUTY REGARDING SOCIO-ECONOMIC INEQUALITIES

13.8   The EQA 2010 starts by providing that an authority (essentially public authorities, see below):

> 'when making decisions of a strategic nature about how to exercise its functions [must] have due regard to the desirability of exercising them in a way that is designed to reduce the inequalities of outcome which result from socio-economic disadvantage'.[10]

13.9   In deciding how to fulfil this duty, an authority must 'take into account any guidance issued by a Minister of the Crown'.[11]

13.10   The term 'socio-economic disadvantage' is not defined by the EQA 2010. Presumably the 'elephant test' applies in the application of s 1: one knows socio-economic disadvantage when one sees it. One matter is made clear: the reference to 'inequalities' in s 1(1) 'does not include any inequalities experienced by a person as a result of being a person subject to immigration control within the meaning given by section 115(9) of the Immigration and Asylum Act 1999'.[12] Such a person is one who is not 'a national of an EEA State' (which means 'a State which is a Contracting Party to the Agreement on the European Economic Area signed at Oporto on 2nd May 1992 as it has effect for the time being'[13]) and who:

'(a)   requires leave to enter or remain in the United Kingdom but does not have it;

(b)   has leave to enter or remain in the United Kingdom which is subject to a condition that he or she does not have recourse to public funds;

(c)   has leave to enter or remain in the United Kingdom given as a result of a maintenance undertaking; or

---

8   EQA 2010, ss 149–157 and Schs 18 and 19 (Part 11, Ch 1).
9   EQA 2010, ss 158–159 (Ch 11, Part 2).
10   EQA 2010, s 1(1). See also ss 1(3)–(5) and 2.
11   EQA 2010, s 1(2).
12   EQA 2010, s 1(6).
13   See s 167(1) of the Immigration and Asylum Act 1999 (IAA 1999).

(d)   has leave to enter or remain in the United Kingdom only as a result of paragraph 17 of Schedule 4.'[14]

THE BODIES TO WHICH THE NEW DUTY IMPOSED BY S 1 APPLIES

13.11   The bodies to which the new duty in s 1 applies include those which are set out in s 1(3) of the EQA 2010. They include, as one would expect:

- Ministers of the Crown;

- government departments;[15]

- local authorities in England;

- police authorities in England;

- Strategic Health Authorities;[16]

- Primary Care Trusts;[17] and

- regional development agencies.[18]

The bodies to which the duty imposed by s 1 applies also include[19] a 'partner authority' in relation to a 'responsible local authority',[20] but only in relation to such a partner authority's 'participation in the preparation or modification of a sustainable community strategy'.[21]

13.12   Section 2 empowers a Minister of the Crown by regulations to amend s 1 so as to add or remove a 'public authority' (meaning 'an authority that has functions of a public nature'[22]) to the bodies which are required to comply with s 1(1). Such amendment may also make the duty in that subsection apply in the case of a particular authority only in relation to certain functions that it has, or may remove or alter such a restriction. This power does not extend to imposing a duty on an authority 'in relation to any devolved Scottish functions or

---

[14]   See further the IAA 1999.
[15]   Other than 'the Security Service, the Secret Intelligence Service or the Government Communications Headquarters'.
[16]   Established under s 13 of the National Health Service Act 2006 (NHSA 2006) or continued in existence by virtue of that section.
[17]   Established under s 18 of the NHSA 2006 or continued in existence by virtue of that section.
[18]   Established by the Regional Development Agencies Act 1998.
[19]   See EQA 2010, s 1(4) and (5).
[20]   Within the meaning of (respectively) ss 104 and 103 of the Local Government and Public Involvement in Health Act 2007.
[21]   Prepared under s 4 of the Local Government Act 2000.
[22]   EQA 2010, s 2(2).

devolved Welsh functions'.[23] This means functions (1) which are exercisable 'in or as regards Scotland' and which do not 'relate to reserved matters (within the meaning of the Scotland Act 1998)' or (2) which relate to 'a matter in respect of which functions are exercisable by the Welsh Ministers,[24] the First Minister for Wales or the Counsel General to the Welsh Assembly Government, or to a matter within the legislative competence of the National Assembly for Wales'.[25]

13.13 The Scottish Ministers in relation to Scotland[26] and the Welsh Ministers in relation to Wales may by regulations amend s 1 so as to add an authority to those in s 1.[27] As far as Scotland is concerned, this must be an authority whose functions are (a) exercisable only in or as regards Scotland, (b) are wholly or mainly devolved Scottish functions, and (c) 'correspond or are similar to those of an authority for the time being specified in section 1(3)'.[28] As far as Wales is concerned, the authority to be added must be one whose functions are:

(a)   exercisable only in or as regards Wales;

(b)   are wholly or mainly devolved Welsh functions; and

(c)   'correspond or are similar to those of an authority for the time being specified in subsection (3) of section 1 or referred to in subsection (4) of that section'.[29]

Before making any such regulations, the Scottish Ministers or the Welsh Ministers must consult a Minister of the Crown.[30] The regulations may confer on the Ministers in question a power to issue guidance and may impose on the authorities to which the regulations apply a duty to take that guidance into account.[31] Before issuing any such guidance, the relevant Ministers must take into account any guidance issued by a Minister of the Crown under s 1 and must consult a Minister of the Crown.[32]

Enforcement

13.14 The duty imposed by s 1 does not give rise to a private law cause of action.[33] Presumably, therefore, the duty imposed by s 1 is ultimately enforceable only in public law (ie judicial review) proceedings.

---

23   EQA 2010, s 2(2).
24   See s 45 of the Government of Wales Act 2006 for the meaning of the term 'the Welsh Ministers'.
25   EQA 2010, s 2(11).
26   See s 44(2) of the Scotland Act 1998 for the definition of the term 'Scottish Ministers'.
27   EQA 2010, s 2(4).
28   See EQA 2010, s 2(5).
29   See EQA 2010 s 2(6). The authorities referred to in s 1(4) are partner authorities in relation to responsible local authority: see **13.11**.
30   EQA 2010, s 2(7).
31   EQA 2010, s 2(9).
32   EQA 2010, s 2(10).
33   EQA 2010, s 3.

PART 11 OF THE EQA 2010

13.15 Part 11 of the EQA 2010 (ss 149–159) has two chapters. Chapter 1 (ss 149–157 and Schs 18 and 19) imposes a public sector equality duty and makes related provision. Chapter 2 (ss 158–159) empowers the taking of positive action in some circumstances.

Public sector equality duty

13.16 Section 149 requires a public authority[34] (and a person who is not a public authority but exercises public functions[35]), subject to the exceptions stated in Sch 18 'in the exercise of its functions [to] have due regard to the need to' do three things,[36] namely:

(a) eliminate discrimination, harassment, victimisation and any other conduct that is prohibited by or under the EQA 2010;

(b) advance equality of opportunity between persons who share a 'relevant protected characteristic'[37] and persons who do not share that characteristic; and

(c) 'foster good relations between persons who share a relevant protected characteristic and persons who do not share it'.[38]

13.17
A 'relevant protected characteristic' is defined in alphabetical order as:

- age;

- disability;

- gender reassignment;

- pregnancy and maternity;

- race;

- religion or belief;

- sex; and

---

[34] As defined by or in accordance with ss 150–151 and Sch 19.
[35] The term 'public functions' has the same meaning as that term has in the Human Rights Act 1998: see s 150(5) of the EQA 2010.
[36] See **13.18** for the meaning of the obligation to 'have due regard' in this context.
[37] See **13.17** for the definition of a 'relevant protected characteristic'.
[38] See **13.19** for the meaning of the obligation to 'have due regard' in this context.

- sexual orientation.[39]

13.18 The obligation to 'have due regard to the need to advance equality of opportunity between persons who share a relevant protected characteristic and persons who do not share it *involves*' (emphasis added) 'having due regard, in particular, to the need to' do the following three things:[40]

(a) 'remove or minimise disadvantages suffered by persons who share a relevant protected characteristic that are connected to that characteristic';

(b) 'take steps to meet the needs of persons who share a relevant protected characteristic that are different from the needs of persons who do not share it';[41] and

(c) 'encourage persons who share a relevant protected characteristic to participate in public life or in any other activity in which participation by such persons is disproportionately low'.

13.19 Similarly, having due regard to the need to foster good relations between persons who share a relevant protected characteristic and persons who do not share it involves having due regard, in particular, to the need to (a) tackle prejudice, and (b) promote understanding.[42]

13.20 Section 149 permits treating some persons more favourably than others, but it does not permit conduct which would 'otherwise be prohibited by or under' the EQA 2010, including a breach of:

(1) a sex equality clause within the meaning of s 66;

(2) a maternity equality clause within the meaning of s 73;

(3) a sex equality rule within the meaning of s 67;

(4) a maternity equality rule within the meaning of s 75; or

(5) a breach of a non-discrimination rule within the meaning of s 61.[43]

13.21 The exceptions stated in Sch 18 concern s 149 insofar as it relates to:

(1) age;

---

[39] EQA 2010, s 149(7).
[40] EQA 2010, s 149(3).
[41] 'The steps involved in meeting the needs of disabled persons that are different from the needs of persons who are not disabled include, in particular, steps to take account of disabled persons' disabilities': EQA 2010, s 149(4).
[42] EQA 2010, s 149(5).
[43] EQA 2010, ss 149(6) and (8), and 212(1).

(2)   immigration and nationality functions within the meaning of para 2(2) of
      Sch 18;

(3)   judicial functions; and

(4)   the exercise of public functions by bodies which are not public authorities
      within Sch 19.

13.22   Thus, a public authority (or a body exercising public functions to which
s 149 applies) is not obliged to comply with the duty in s 149(1) in relation to
the exercise of a function relating to (a) the provision of education to pupils in
schools,[44] or (b) the provision of benefits, facilities or services to pupils in
schools.[45] Nor is a public authority obliged to comply with the duty in s 149(1)
in relation to the provision of accommodation, benefits, facilities or services in
community homes pursuant to s 53(1) of the Children Act 1989,[46] the provision
of accommodation, benefits, facilities or services pursuant to arrangements
under s 82(5) of that Act,[47] or the provision of accommodation, benefits,
facilities or services in residential establishments pursuant to s 26(1)(b) of the
Children (Scotland) Act 1995.[48]

13.23   Furthermore, in relation to the exercise of immigration and nationality
functions (as defined by Sch 18, para 2(2)[49]) the duty in s 149(1)(b) (ie to
'advance equality of opportunity between persons who share a relevant
protected characteristic and persons who do not share it') does not apply:

> 'to the protected characteristics of age, race or religion or belief; but for that
> purpose "race" means race so far as relating to –
>
> (a)   nationality, or
> (b)   ethnic or national origins'.[50]

---

[44]   The terms 'pupil' and 'school' have the meanings assigned to them by Ch 1 of Part 6 of the
       EQA 2010: Sch 18, para 1(2).
[45]   EQA 2010, Sch 18, para 1(1)(a) and (b).
[46]   Sch 18, para 1(1)(c). Section 53 of the Children Act 1989 (CA 1989) requires local authorities
       to secure that community homes are available for children looked after by the authorities and
       for purposes connected with the welfare of children, whether or not those children are looked
       after by those authorities.
[47]   Sch 18, para 1(1)(d). Arrangements made under s 82(5) of the CA 1989 are made by the
       Secretary of State for the provision, equipment and maintenance of homes for the
       accommodation of children who are in need of particular facilities and services which (a) are
       or will be provided in those homes and (b) in the opinion of the Secretary of State are unlikely
       to be available in community homes.
[48]   Sch 18, para 1(1)(e). Section 26(1)(b) of the Children (Scotland) Act 1995 empowers a local
       authority to provide accommodation for a child who is looked after by the authority by
       'maintaining him in a residential establishment'.
[49]   This means functions which are exercisable by virtue of the Immigration Acts and related
       enactments concerning immigration and nationality.
[50]   Sch 18, para 2(1).

13.24 Section 149 does not apply to the exercise of any judicial functions (which include judicial functions conferred on any person other than a court or tribunal).[51] Similarly, the exercise of public functions in connection with proceedings in the House of Commons or the House of Lords, the Scottish Parliament (other than a function of the Scottish Parliamentary Corporate Body[52]), or the National Assembly for Wales (other than a function of the Assembly Commission[53]) is not affected by the duty in s 149(1).[54] Moreover, the House of Commons, the House of Lords, the Scottish Parliament, the National Assembly for Wales, the General Synod of the Church of England, the Security Service, the Secret Intelligence Service, the Government Communications Headquarters and any 'part of the armed forces which is, in accordance with a requirement of the Secretary of State, assisting the Government Communications Headquarters', are all excluded from the obligation imposed by s 149(1).[55] Accordingly, although for example the Welsh Ministers[56] are within the definition of a public authority to which s 149(1) applies,[57] the National Assembly for Wales itself is not affected by that subsection.

13.25 Section 151 of the EQA 2010 permits the amendment of Sch 19 to the EQA 2010 so as to alter the application of Sch 19. A Minister of the Crown may 'by order', ie by means of a statutory instrument,[58] amend Part 1, 2, or 3 of Sch 19.[59] A Minister of the Crown may also by order amend Sch 19 'so as to make provision relating to a cross-border Welsh or Scottish authority' which must be placed in a new Part 4 of Sch 19.[60] The Welsh Ministers may by order amend Part 2 of Sch 19.[61] The Scottish Ministers may by order amend Part 3 of Sch 19.[62] However, no order may be made under s 151 of the EQA 2010 so as to extend the application of s 149 to:

(1)   the exercise of a judicial function;

(2)   Parliament, devolved legislatures or the General Synod; or

---

[51]   EQA 2010, Sch 18, para 3.

[52]   The Scottish Parliamentary Corporate Body was established under s 21 of the Scotland Act 1998.

[53]   The Assembly Commission, unlike the Scottish Parliamentary Corporate Body, is defined by the EQA 2010: see s 157(4). The Assembly Commission is the body provided for by s 27 of the Government of Wales Act 2006.

[54]   EQA 2010, Sch 18, para 4(1)(b).

[55]   See EQA 2010, Sch 18, para 4(1)(a) and (2).

[56]   See s 45 of the Government of Wales Act 2006 for the meaning of the term 'the Welsh Ministers'.

[57]   See EQA 2010, Sch 19, Part 2.

[58]   See EQA 2010, s 208.

[59]   EQA 2010, s 151(1).

[60]   EQA 2010, s 151(5)–(7). The definition of a 'cross-border' authority is in s 157(3), (4) and (7).

[61]   EQA 2010, ss 151(2) and 209.

[62]   EQA 2010, ss 151(2) and 210. See s 44(2) of the Scotland Act 1998 for the definition of the term 'Scottish Ministers'.

(3)   proceedings in Parliament or devolved legislatures.[63]

Moreover, no order may be made under s 151 so as to add certain bodies to Sch 19; these are uncontroversial (for example a 'relevant' Welsh or Scottish authority may not be added to Part 1 of Sch 19), but the statutory machinery is necessarily a little convoluted.[64] Furthermore, before any order is made under s 151, the body which is proposing to make the order must consult as required by s 152 and obtain the consents specified by s 152. The obligation imposed by s 152 which is perhaps of most note is the obligation imposed by s 152(1) to consult the Commission for Equality and Human Rights.[65]

13.26   Section 153 of the EQA 2010 permits the imposition by a Minister of the Crown, the Welsh Ministers, and the Scottish Ministers, by regulations of specific duties on public authorities 'for the purpose of enabling the better performance by the authority of the duty imposed by s 149(1)'.[66] Before any such imposition may occur, the body proposing to make the regulations must consult the Commission for Equality and Human Rights.[67]

13.27   There is slightly complicated provision in s 154 of the EQA 2010 concerning the imposition by a Minister of the Crown of specific duties on cross-border authorities. The complications arise from the need to distinguish between functions which are 'devolved' and those which are not.[68]

13.28   The power to make regulations under s 153 or 154 is supplemented by s 155, for example by empowering the imposition of duties on a public authority which is a contracting authority within the meaning of the Public Sector Directive, ie Directive 2004/18/EC, in connection with the functions of that authority which are regulated by that Directive.[69] Those functions concern the procurement of services by public authorities, under what is often called the public procurement regime (which requires that a relevant public authority, within limits, offers for example potential service providers the opportunity to tender for the provision of services to that authority). It is thus possible to envisage the imposition of duties concerning equality of opportunity in connection with public procurement functions.

Enforcement of the public sector equality duty

13.29   A failure by a public authority or a body exercising a public function to which s 149 applies does not give rise to a private law right or cause of action.[70]

---

63   EQA 2010, s 151(9).
64   See EQA 2010, s 151(4) read with s 157(2), (3), (6) and (7).
65   EQA 2010, ss 152(1), (2)(b), (3)(b) and 212(1).
66   See EQA 2010, s 153(1)–(3). Concerning the making of the regulations, see EQA 2010, ss 208, 209 and 210.
67   EQA 2010, s 153(4).
68   See EQA 2010, s 157(5), (8) and (9) for what is a devolved function for this purpose.
69   EQA 2010, s 155(2) and (3).
70   EQA 2010, s 156.

Accordingly, claims to enforce the duty in question will have to be made under any relevant statutory mechanism or by means of an application for judicial review.

POSITIVE ACTION: SS 158 AND 159

Positive action generally

13.30 Section 158 of the EQA 2010 applies, subject to exceptions, if a person 'reasonably thinks that':

'(a) persons who share a protected characteristic suffer a disadvantage connected to the characteristic,

(b) persons who share a protected characteristic have needs that are different from the needs of persons who do not share it, or

(c) participation in an activity by persons who share a protected characteristic is disproportionately low.'[71]

13.31 Section 158(1) does not apply:

(1) to any exceptions specified in regulations made under s 158(3) (which have yet to be made and which will be made only when s 158(3) is in force);

(2) action within s 159(3) (concerning which, see below); and

(3) anything which is permitted by virtue of s 104 of the EQA 2010.[72]

Furthermore, s 158 does not permit anything which is 'prohibited by or under an enactment other than [Part 11 of the EQA 2010]'.[73]

13.32 The requirement for a person reasonably to think that one of the three conditions set out in **13.30** is satisfied means that the judgment of that person will be capable of being reviewed on an objective basis. The extent to which for example in an employment tribunal the judgment will be regarded as being affected by the 'range of reasonable responses of a reasonable employer' test is of course at present unknown. However, the decision of the Court of Appeal in *Smith v Churchill Stairlifts plc*[74] suggests that that test will not be applicable in this context. If that is correct then the test will be whether or not in the view of the tribunal it was reasonable for the person to arrive at the view that the condition was satisfied.

---

[71] EQA 2010, s 158(1).
[72] EQA 2010, s 158(3) and (4). Section 104 concerns the selection of candidates for election to, for example, Parliament by registered political parties and permits selection arrangements (a) whose purpose is 'to reduce inequality in the party's representation in the body concerned' and (b) which are a proportionate means of achieving that purpose. This is only a summary of the effect of s 104. See further that section.
[73] EQA 2010, s 158(6).
[74] [2006] ICR 524.

Positive action in relation to recruitment and promotion

13.33 If a person reasonably thinks that either of the first and third conditions set out in **13.30** is satisfied, ie that:

'(a)   persons who share a protected characteristic suffer a disadvantage connected to the characteristic, or

(b)   participation in an activity by persons who share a protected characteristic is disproportionately low'

then, subject to exceptions, that person may take action of the sorts described in s 159(3) of the EQA 2010[75] 'with the aim of enabling or encouraging persons who share the protected characteristic to . . . (a) overcome or minimise that disadvantage, or (b) participate in that activity'.[76]

13.34 The exceptions to which this permitted derogation from the prohibitions in Part 5 of the EQA 2010 are stated by s 159(4) and (6). Subsection (6) is in the same terms as s 158(6), and is in these terms:

'This section does not enable P to do anything that is prohibited by or under an enactment other than this Act.'

Thus, it is provided by s 159(6) (presumably for the avoidance of doubt) that positive action which is prohibited by or under an enactment other than the EQA 2010 is not authorised by s 159.

13.35   Section 159(4) provides that the positive action which is permitted by s 159(2) and (3) may be taken only if the following three conditions are satisfied:

'(a)   A is as qualified as B to be recruited or promoted,

(b)   P does not have a policy of treating persons who share the protected characteristic more favourably in connection with recruitment or promotion than persons who do not share it, and

(c)   taking the action in question is a proportionate means of achieving the aim referred to in subsection (2).'

Thus, in order for it to be possible lawfully to treat a person more favourably than another under s 159(2) and (3), the person who is treated more favourably must be as well qualified as that other person. In addition, the person taking the positive action must not have a policy of treating persons who share the relevant characteristic more favourably than those who do not share that characteristic. Finally, taking the action in question must be a proportionate means of achieving the aim of enabling or encouraging persons who share the protected characteristic to:

---

[75]   See **13.36** for the sorts of action which fall within s 159(3).
[76]   EQA 2010, s 159(2).

(a) overcome or minimise the disadvantage which the person taking the action has reasonably identified to be connected to that characteristic; or

(b) participate in an activity in which, it reasonably appears to the person taking the action, participation by persons who share the characteristic is disproportionately low.

13.36 The positive action which is permitted by s 159(3) in the circumstances described in the preceding paragraphs above is 'treating a person (A) more favourably in connection with recruitment or promotion than another person (B) because A has the protected characteristic but B does not'. Promotion is not defined for these purposes. Recruitment, however, is so defined. The definition is in s 159(5) and is uncontroversial. It means 'a process for deciding whether to':

- 'offer employment to a person';

- 'make contract work available to a contract worker';

- 'offer a person a position as a partner in a firm or proposed firm';

- 'offer a person a position as a member of an LLP or proposed LLP';

- 'offer a person a pupillage or tenancy in barristers' chambers';

- 'take a person as an advocate's devil or offer a person membership of an advocate's stable';

- 'offer a person an appointment to a personal office';

- 'offer a person an appointment to a public office, recommend a person for such an appointment or approve a person's appointment to a public office'; or

- 'offer a person a service for finding employment'.

EUROPEAN LEGISLATION AND CASE-LAW

13.37 In order for UK legislation concerning a matter which is the subject of EU legislation to be lawful, the UK legislation must be consistent with the EU legislation. In this context the UK legislation (here, the EQA 2010 and any regulations made under it) must not go further by way of positive action than is permitted by EU law. If it goes further, then it will be vulnerable to being declared by the ECJ to be incompatible with EU law, and a UK court or tribunal will probably be enabled, if not obliged, to read it in such a way that it does not contravene EU law.[77]

13.38   It is accordingly necessary to consider the relevant ECJ case-law and the current EU legislation. The current EU legislation which permits positive action is different from (being slightly more favourable than) some of that which was the subject of the existing case-law in the ECJ concerning such action. Some of that case-law accordingly concerned provisions which were less permissive than the current provisions.

Case law

13.39   In *Kalanke v Freie Hansestadt Bremen*,[78] the ECJ decided that a provision of German law to the effect that where a woman and a man were equally qualified for a particular post, the woman was to be given priority for promotion where women were under-represented in the promoted position, was unlawful in that it was contrary to Directive 76/207/EEC. That Directive was the first one made under European Community (now EU) law which required equal treatment, and it applied only to the different treatment of men and women. It was known for a long time as the Equal Treatment Directive. The only basis for positive action under it was Art 2(4) of that Directive, which provided that:

> 'This Directive shall be without prejudice to measures to promote equal opportunity for men and women, in particular by removing existing inequalities which affect women's opportunities in the areas referred to in article 1(1).'

13.40   However, in *Marschall v Land Nordrhein-Westfalen*,[79] which also concerned Art 2(4), the ECJ held that such positive discrimination will be lawful as long as there is:

> 'a guarantee that the candidatures will be the subject of an objective assessment which will take account of all criteria specific to the individual candidates and will override the priority accorded to female candidates where one or more of those criteria tilts the balance in favour of the male candidate. In this respect, however, it should be remembered that those criteria must not be such as to discriminate against female candidates.'

13.41   In *Abrahamsson v Fogelqvist*,[80] where the ECJ decided that the positive action which was challenged in that case was unlawful, the ECJ described the effect of its earlier ruling in *Badeck*[81] in these terms:[82]

---

[77]   See the discussion of the EAT in *EBR Attridge Law LLP v Coleman (No 2)* [2010] ICR 242 which is illuminating in this regard.

[78]   (Case C-450/93) [1996] ICR 314.

[79]   (Case C-409/95) [2001] ICR 45, at 65–6, para 33.

[80]   (Case C-407/98) [2002] ICR 932.

[81]   *Proceedings on an application by Badeck* (Case C-158/97) [2000] ECR I-1875.

[82]   See para 43 of the judgment in *Abrahamsson*.

'in *Proceedings on an application by Badeck (Case C-158/97)* [2000] ECR I-1875, 1919, para 23, the court held that a measure which is intended to give priority in promotion to women in sectors of the public service where they are under-represented must be regarded as compatible with Community law where it does not automatically and unconditionally give priority to women when women and men are equally qualified, and where the candidatures are the subject of an objective assessment which takes account of the specific personal situations of all candidates.'

13.42 *Abrahamsson* concerned in part the application of Art 141(4) of the EC Treaty (which is now Art 157(4) of the revised Treaty), which was (and, as Art 157(4), remains) in these terms:

'With a view to ensuring full equality in practice between men and women in working life, the principle of equal treatment shall not prevent any member state from maintaining or adopting measures providing for specific advantages in order to make it easier for the under-represented sex to pursue a vocational activity or to prevent or compensate for disadvantages in professional careers.'

13.43 The ECJ's analysis in *Abrahamsson* of the three cases mentioned in **13.39–13.41** and of the facts of *Abrahamsson* is instructive. In paras 45–53 of its judgment in *Abrahamsson*, the ECJ said this:

'45   In contrast to the national legislation on positive discrimination examined by the court in *Kalanke v Freie Hansestadt Bremen* (Case C-450/93) [1996] ICR 314, *Marschall v Land Nordrhein-Westfalen* (Case C-409/95) [2001] ICR 45 and *Proceedings on an application by Badeck* (Case C-158/97) [2000] ECR I-1875, the national legislation at issue in the main proceedings enables preference to be given to a candidate of the under-represented sex who, although sufficiently qualified, does not possess qualifications equal to those of other candidates of the opposite sex.

46   As a rule, a procedure for the selection of candidates for a post involves assessment of their qualifications by reference to the requirements of the vacant post or of the duties to be performed.

47   In *Badeck* [2000] ECR I-1875, 1921, paras 31 and 32 the court held that it is legitimate for the purposes of that assessment for certain positive and negative criteria to be taken into account which, although formulated in terms which are neutral as regards sex and thus capable of benefiting men too, in general favour women. Thus, it may be decided that seniority, age and the date of last promotion are to be taken into account only in so far as they are of importance for the suitability, qualifications and professional capability of candidates. Similarly, it may be prescribed that the family status or income of the partner is immaterial and that part-time work, leave and delays in completing training as a result of looking after children or dependants in need of care must not have a negative effect.

48   The clear aim of such criteria is to achieve substantive, rather than formal, equality by reducing de facto inequalities which may arise in society and, thus, in accordance with article 141(4) EC, to prevent or compensate for disadvantages in the professional career of persons belonging to the under-represented sex.

49 It is important to emphasise in that connection that the application of criteria such as those mentioned in paragraph 47 above must be transparent and amenable to review in order to obviate any arbitrary assessment of the qualifications of candidates.

50 As regards the selection procedure at issue in the main proceedings, it does not appear from the relevant Swedish legislation that assessment of the qualifications of candidates by reference to the requirements of the vacant post is based on clear and unambiguous criteria such as to prevent or compensate for disadvantages in the professional career of members of the under-represented sex.

51 On the contrary, under that legislation, a candidate for a public post belonging to the under-represented sex and possessing sufficient qualifications for that post must be chosen in preference to a candidate of the opposite sex who would otherwise have been appointed, where that measure is necessary for a candidate belonging to the under-represented sex to be appointed.

52 It follows that the legislation at issue in the main proceedings automatically grants preference to candidates belonging to the under-represented sex, provided that they are sufficiently qualified, subject only to the proviso that the difference between the merits of the candidates of each sex is not so great as to result in a breach of the requirement of objectivity in making appointments.

53 The scope and effect of that condition cannot be precisely determined, with the result that the selection of a candidate from among those who are sufficiently qualified is ultimately based on the mere fact of belonging to the under-represented sex, and that that is so even if the merits of the candidate so selected are inferior to those of a candidate of the opposite sex. Moreover, candidatures are not subjected to an objective assessment taking account of the specific personal situations of all the candidates. It follows that such a method of selection is not such as to be permitted by article 2(4) of the Directive.'

13.44 However, in *Lommers v Minister van Landbouw*,[83] the ECJ ruled that Art 2(4) of Directive 76/207/EEC permitted the restriction of places in a workplace nursery to the children of women employees. This was because that restriction was a measure which fell:

'in principle into the category of measures designed to eliminate the causes of women's reduced opportunities for access to employment and careers and are intended to improve their ability to compete on the labour market and to pursue a career on an equal footing with men.'[84]

13.45 However, in order to be lawful, it had to be established by the employer that at the time when the measure was adopted and at the time when the claim was made, there was 'a significant underrepresentation of women, both in terms of the number of women working there and their occupation of higher

---

[83] (Case C-476/99) [2002] IRLR 430.
[84] Para 38.

grades', and that 'a proven insufficiency of suitable and affordable nursery facilities [was] likely to induce more particularly female employees to give up their jobs'.[85]

13.46 In *EFTA Surveillance Authority v Norway*[86] the European Free Trade Association Court (EFTA Court), applying EU legislation and case-law, said this:

> 'Under the present state of the law, the criteria for assessing the qualifications of candidates are essential. In such an assessment, there appears to be scope for considering those factors that, on empirical experience, tend to place female candidates in a disadvantaged position in comparison with male candidates. Directing awareness to such factors could reduce actual instances of gender inequality. Furthermore, giving weight to the possibility that in numerous academic disciplines female life experience may be relevant to the determination of the suitability and capability for, and performance in, higher academic positions, could enhance the equality of men and women, which concern lies at the core of the Directive.'[87]

However, that was *obiter*, since the court concluded that the practice which had been adopted in that case was unlawful.

Current EU legislation and its impact

13.47 The current Directive provisions which permit positive action are Art 5 of 2000/43/EC (concerning race discrimination), Art 7 of 2000/78/EC (concerning all other kinds of discrimination except on the ground of sex) and Art 3 of 2006/54/EC (the replacement of 76/207/EEC, concerning sex discrimination). Article 5 provides:

> 'With a view to ensuring full equality in practice, the principle of equal treatment shall not prevent any Member State from maintaining or adopting specific measures to prevent or compensate for disadvantages linked to racial or ethnic origin.'

13.48 Article 7 of Directive 2000/78/EC provides:

> '1   With a view to ensuring full equality in practice, the principle of equal treatment shall not prevent any Member State from maintaining or adopting specific measures to prevent or compensate for disadvantages linked to any of the grounds referred to in Article 1.
> 2   With regard to disabled persons, the principle of equal treatment shall be without prejudice to the right of Member States to maintain or adopt provisions on the protection of health and safety at work or to measures aimed at creating or maintaining provisions or facilities for safeguarding or promoting their integration into the working environment.'

---

[85] See paras 36 and 37 respectively.
[86] (Case E1/02) [2003] IRLR 318.
[87] Para 57.

13.49   Article 3 of Directive 2006/54/EC provides:

> 'Member States may maintain or adopt measures within the meaning of Article 141(4) of the Treaty with a view to ensuring full equality in practice between men and women in working life.'

13.50   It is unlikely that this difference in wording from that which was in the preceding provisions is of major importance. What it does do, however, is make it clear that ss 158 and 159 of the EQA 2010 do not contravene EU law.

13.51   Nevertheless, whatever may be said in any code of practice issued by the Commission for Equality and Human Rights will have to be consistent with the enabling provisions in the Directives mentioned in the preceding paragraphs above and Art 157(4) of the EU Treaty. The approach of the EFTA Court shown by the passage set out in **13.46** is likely to be of some assistance as a kind of touchstone in that regard.

Chapter 14

MISCELLANEOUS PROVISIONS

STATUTORY PROVISIONS

14.1 Provision is made for general exceptions arising from statutory provisions.[1] As the Explanatory Notes explain, these are statutory provisions that allow differential treatment which would otherwise be unlawful under specific parts of the Act.[2] Here also are to be found the provisions that allow differential treatment of pregnant women for their own protection; allow people of particular religions or beliefs to be appointed to specified educational posts; and allow rules about Crown employment to provide for differential treatment on the basis of nationality.

Statutory authority

14.2 A person (P) does not contravene a specified provision, so far as relating to a specified protected characteristic in respect of that provision, if P does anything P must do pursuant to a specified requirement.[3] So far as age is concerned, P will not contravene Parts 3 to 7 of the Act (services and public functions; premises; work; education; and associations) if P does anything P must do pursuant to a requirement of an enactment. So far as disability is concerned, P will not contravene Parts 3 to 7 and Part 12 of the Act (services and public functions; premises; work; education; associations; and transport) if P does anything P must do pursuant to a requirement of an enactment or a relevant requirement or condition imposed by virtue of an enactment.

14.3 So far as religion or belief is concerned, P will not contravene Parts 3, 4, 6 and 7 of the Act (services and public functions; premises; education; and associations) if P does anything P must do pursuant to a requirement of an enactment or a relevant requirement or condition imposed by virtue of an enactment. So far as sex is concerned, P will not contravene s 28(6)[4] and Parts 6 and 7 of the Act (education and associations) if P does anything P must do pursuant to a requirement of an enactment. So far as sexual orientation is concerned, P will not contravene Parts 3, 4, 6 and 7 of the Act (services and public functions; premises; education; and associations) if P does anything P

---

[1]   EQA 2010, s 191 and Sch 22.
[2]   EN para 613.
[3]   EQA 2010, Sch 22, para 1(1).
[4]   In relation to the provision of services, etc, a person must not, in the exercise of a public function that is not the provision of a service to the public or a section of the public, do anything that constitutes discrimination, harassment or victimisation.

must do pursuant to a requirement of an enactment or a relevant requirement or condition imposed by virtue of an enactment.

14.4 References to Part 6 (education) above do not include a reference to Part 6 so far as it relates to vocational training.[5] A reference above to an enactment includes a reference to a Measure of the General Synod of the Church of England; and an enactment passed or made on or after the date on which the Act was passed.[6] A relevant requirement or condition is a requirement or condition imposed (whether before or after the passing of the Act) by a Minister of the Crown; a member of the Scottish Executive; the National Assembly for Wales (constituted by the Government of Wales Act 1998); and the Welsh Ministers, the First Minister for Wales or the Counsel General to the Welsh Assembly Government.[7]

14.5 The Explanatory Notes record that these provisions replace the separate exceptions for statutory authority in current legislation.[8] Thus a shopkeeper can lawfully refuse to sell alcohol to someone under the age of 18; an employer can lawfully dismiss a disabled employee if health and safety regulations leave it with no other choice; and an employer can lawfully refuse to employ someone, who is not old enough to hold a LGV licence, to drive a large goods vehicle.[9] However, the exception in s 41(1) of the Race Relations Act 1976 (RRA 1976), which excuses certain race discrimination done under statutory authority in areas with which European law is not concerned, is removed without replacement.[10]

Protection of women

14.6 A person (P) does not contravene Part 5 (work) or Part 6 (so far as relating to vocational training) of the EQA 2010[11] if all that P does in relation to a woman (W) is anything P is required to do to comply with:

- a pre-1975 Act enactment concerning the protection of women;[12]

---

[5]   EQA 2010, Sch 22, para 1(2).
[6]   EQA 2010, Sch 22, para 1(3).
[7]   EQA 2010, Sch 22, para 1(4).
[8]   EN paras 987–988. See: *Page v Freighhire (Tank Haulage) Ltd* [1981] IRLR 13, EAT; *Hampson v Department of Education & Science* [1990] IRLR 302, HL; *Amnesty International v Ahmed* [2009] IRLR 884, EAT.
[9]   EN para 988.
[10] RRA 1976, s 41(1) contained the statutory authority exception for that Act. However, RRA 1976, s 41(1A) provided that that exception did not apply to an act which was unlawful, on grounds of race or ethnic or national origins, by virtue of a provision referred to in RRA 1976, s 1(1B). Those provisions related to discrimination in the employment field; discrimination in education; discrimination by a public authority in relation to social security, health care, social protection and social advantage; discrimination in relation to the provision of goods, facilities and services; discrimination in relation to barristers and advocates; and discrimination in relation to government offices and other office-holders. See Race Relations Act 1976 (Amendment) Regulations 2003, SI 2003/1626.
[11] EQA 2010, Sch 22, para 2(4).
[12] EQA 2010, Sch 22, para 2(1)(a). A pre-1975 Act enactment is an enactment contained in an

- a relevant statutory provision (within the meaning of Part 1 of the Health and Safety at Work etc. Act 1974) if it is done for the purpose of the protection of W (or a description of women which includes W);[13]

- a requirement of a provision specified in Sch 1 to the Employment Act 1989 (provisions concerned with protection of women at work).[14]

The reference to the protection of women is a reference to protecting women in relation to pregnancy or maternity, or any other circumstances giving rise to risks specifically affecting women.[15] It does not matter whether the protection is restricted to women.[16] This exception applies only to the protected characteristics of pregnancy and maternity, and sex.[17]

14.7 The Explanatory Notes summarise these provisions as allowing such differential treatment based on sex or pregnancy and maternity at work as is required to comply with laws protecting women who are pregnant, who have recently given birth or against risks specific to women. They replace separate exceptions for the protection of women in the Sex Discrimination Act 1975 (SDA 1975) and in the Employment Act 1989. Thus, by way of examples, a care home cannot lawfully dismiss, but can lawfully suspend, a night-shift worker because she is pregnant and her GP has certified that she must not work nights. In addition, it may be lawful for a road haulier to refuse to allow a woman lorry driver to transport chemicals that could harm women of child-bearing age.[18]

Educational appointments, etc: religious belief

14.8 A person does not contravene Part 5 of the EQA 2010 (work) only by doing a relevant act in connection with the employment of another person in a relevant position.[19] A relevant position is the head teacher or principal of an educational establishment;[20] the head, a fellow or other member of the

---

Act passed before the SDA 1975 or an instrument approved or made by or under such an Act (including one approved or made after the passing of the 1975 Act): EQA 2010, Sch 22, para 2(5). If an Act repeals and re-enacts (with or without modification) a pre-1975 enactment then the provision re-enacted must be treated as being in a pre-1975 enactment: EQA 2010, Sch 22, para 2(6).

[13] EQA 2010, Sch 22, para 2(1)(b).
[14] EQA 2010, Sch 22, para 2(1)(c). This includes a reference to a provision for the time being having effect in place of it: EQA 2010, Sch 22, para 2(7).
[15] EQA 2010, Sch 22, para 2(2).
[16] EQA 2010, Sch 22, para 2(3).
[17] EQA 2010, Sch 22, para 2(8).
[18] EN paras 989–990.
[19] EQA 2010, Sch 22, para 3(1). This provision does not affect EQA 2010, Sch 9, para 2 (in the context of the occupational requirements exceptions, religious requirements relating to sex, marriage and civil partnership, and sexual orientation) (discussed in Chapter 7 above): EQA 2010, Sch 22, para 3(7).
[20] An educational establishment is a school within the meaning of the Education Act 1996 or the Education (Scotland) Act 1980; a college (or institution in the nature of a college) in a university; an institution designated by order made (or having effect as if made) under the Education Reform Act 1988, s 129; a college of further education within the meaning of the

academic staff of a college (or institution in the nature of a college) in a university; a professorship of a university which is a canon professorship or one to which a canonry is annexed.[21] A relevant act is anything it is necessary to do to comply with a requirement of an instrument relating to the establishment that the head teacher or principal must be a member of a particular religious order; a requirement of an instrument relating to the college or institution that the holder of the position must be a woman;[22] or an Act or instrument in accordance with which the professorship is a canon professorship or one to which a canonry is annexed.[23]

14.9 In addition, a person does not contravene the EQA 2010 only by doing anything which is permitted for the purposes of s 58(6) or (7) of the School Standards and Framework Act 1998 (dismissal of teachers because of failure to give religious education efficiently); s 60(4) and (5) of that Act (religious considerations relating to certain appointments); or s 124A of that Act (preference for certain teachers at independent schools of a religious character).[24]

14.10 The Explanatory Notes assist here.[25] These are exceptions to the provisions on sex or religious discrimination in relation to relevant posts in schools or further or higher education institutions. For the exception to apply, their governing instrument must require the head teacher or principal to be of a particular religious order or that a particular academic position must be held by a woman. The exception also applies where the legislation or instrument which establishes a professorship requires the holder to be an ordained priest. In the case of academic positions reserved to women, the exception only applies where the governing instrument was made before 16 January 1990. Moreover, it is not unlawful discrimination for faith schools to do certain things which are permitted by the School Standards and Framework Act 1998.

Crown employment, etc

14.11 A person does not contravene the EQA 2010 by making or continuing in force specified rules; by publishing, displaying or implementing such rules; or by publishing the gist of such rules.[26] The specified rules are rules restricting to

---

Further and Higher Education (Scotland) Act 1992, s 36; a university in Scotland; an institution designated by order under the Further and Higher Education Act 1992, s 28 or the Further and Higher Education (Scotland) Act 1992, s 44: EQA 2010, Sch 22, para 3(6).

21   EQA 2010, Sch 22, para 3(2).

22   This does not apply to an instrument taking effect on or after 16 January 1990 (the day on which s 5(3) of the Employment Act 1989 came into force): EQA 2010, Sch 22, para 3(4).

23   EQA 2010, Sch 22, para 3(3). A Minister of the Crown may by order provide that anything in the provisions immediately above does not have effect in relation to a specified educational establishment or university; or a specified description of educational establishments: EQA 2010, Sch 22, para 3(5).

24   EQA 2010, Sch 22, para 4.

25   EN paras 991–996. These provisions replicate existing law to be found in the Employment Act 1989, s 5 and the Employment Equality (Religion or Belief) Regulations 2003, reg 39.

26   EQA 2010, Sch 22, para 5(1).

persons of particular birth, nationality, descent or residence employment in the service of the Crown; employment by a prescribed public body;[27] or holding a public office (within the meaning of s 50 of the Act).[28]

14.12 The Explanatory Notes reveal that this provision allows restrictions on the employment of foreign nationals in the civil service, the diplomatic service, the armed services (with the exception of the Gurkhas) or the security and intelligence services, and by certain public bodies.[29] It also allows restrictions on foreign nationals holding public offices. It replaces similar provisions in the RRA 1976.

GENERAL EXCEPTIONS

14.13 Provision is made for general exceptions to the prohibitions against discrimination and harassment.[30] Here are to be found exceptions covering acts authorised by statute or the Government; organisations relating to religion or belief; communal accommodation; and training provided to people who are not resident in the EEA.[31]

Acts authorised by statute or the executive

14.14 The discussion in this paragraph applies to anything done:

- in pursuance of an enactment;

- in pursuance of an instrument made by a member of the executive under an enactment;

- to comply with a requirement imposed (whether before or after the passing of the EQA 2010) by a member of the executive by virtue of an enactment;

- in pursuance of arrangements made (whether before or after the passing of the Act) by or with the approval of (or for the time being approved by) a Minister of the Crown; or

---

27 The power to make regulations for this purpose is exercisable by the Minister for the Civil Service: EQA 2010, Sch 22, para 5(3). A public body is a body (whether corporate or unincorporated) exercising public functions (within the meaning given by EQA 2010, s 31(4) – that is, a function which is a public function for the purposes of the HRA 1998): EQA 2010, Sch 22, para 5(4).

28 EQA 2010, Sch 22, para 5(2).

29 EN paras 997–998.

30 EQA 2010, s 196 and Sch 23.

31 EN para 625.

- to comply with a condition imposed (whether before or after the passing of the Act) by a Minister of the Crown.[32]

A person does not contravene Part 3 (services and public functions), Part 4 (premises), Part 5 (work) or Part 6 (education) of the EQA 2010 by doing anything to which the above applies and which discriminates against another because of the other's nationality.[33] In addition, a person (A) does not contravene Parts 3–6 if, by doing anything to which the above applies, A discriminates against another (B) by applying to B a provision, criterion or practice which relates to B's place of ordinary residence or the length of time B has been present or resident in or outside the UK or an area within it.[34]

14.15 This provision allows direct nationality discrimination and indirect race discrimination on the basis of residency requirements where the discrimination is required by law, Ministerial arrangements or Ministerial conditions.[35] It replaces a similar exception in the RRA 1976. The examples provided by the Explanatory Notes are helpful. Thus, the points-based system which replaced the former work permit arrangements can discriminate on the basis of nationality in determining whether migrants from outside the EEA and Switzerland should be given permission to work in the UK. Equally, the NHS can charge some people who are not ordinarily resident in the UK for hospital treatment they receive here. Similarly, overseas students at universities in England and Wales can be required to pay higher tuition fees than local students (there are no tuition fees in Scotland).[36]

Organisations relating to religion or belief

14.16 Particular exceptions apply to an organisation the purpose of which is to practise a religion or belief; to advance a religion or belief; to teach the practice or principles of a religion or belief; to enable persons of a religion or belief to receive any benefit (or to engage in any activity) within the framework of that religion or belief; or to foster or to maintain good relations between persons of different religions or beliefs.[37] However, this does not include an organisation whose sole or main purpose is commercial.[38]

14.17 An organisation covered by this provision does not contravene Part 3 (services and public functions), Part 4 (premises) or Part 7 (associations) of the EQA 2010, so far as relating to religion or belief or sexual orientation, only by restricting membership of the organisation; participation in activities

---

[32] EQA 2010, Sch 23, para 1(1).
[33] EQA 2010, Sch 23, para 1(2).
[34] EQA 2010, Sch 23, para 1(3).
[35] EN paras 999–1000.
[36] EN para 1000.
[37] EQA 2010, Sch 23, para 2(1). In the application of Sch 23, para 2 in relation to sexual orientation, the exception for fostering or maintaining good relations between persons of different religions or beliefs must be ignored: EQA 2010, Sch 23, para 2(11). See Government Equalities Office, 2009f.
[38] EQA 2010, Sch 23, para 2(2).

undertaken by the organisation or on its behalf or under its auspices; the provision of goods, facilities or services in the course of activities undertaken by the organisation or on its behalf or under its auspices; or the use or disposal of premises owned or controlled by the organisation.[39] A person does not contravene Part 3, Part 4 or Part 7, so far as relating to religion or belief or sexual orientation, only by doing any of those things on behalf of or under the auspices of the organisation.[40] A minister does not contravene Part 3, Part 4 or Part 7, so far as relating to religion or belief or sexual orientation, only by restricting either participation in activities carried on in the performance of the minister's functions in connection with or in respect of the organisation; or the provision of goods, facilities or services in the course of activities carried on in the performance of the minister's functions in connection with or in respect of the organisation.[41]

14.18 The provisions immediately above permit a restriction relating to religion or belief only if it is imposed because of the purpose of the organisation, or to avoid causing offence (on grounds of the religion or belief to which the organisation relates) to persons of that religion or belief.[42] Those provisions permit a restriction relating to sexual orientation only if it is imposed because it is necessary to comply with the doctrine of the organisation, or to avoid conflict with strongly held convictions.[43] Those strongly held convictions are, in the case of a religion, the strongly held religious convictions of a significant number of the religion's followers. In the case of a belief, they are the strongly held convictions relating to the belief of a significant number of the belief's followers.[44]

14.19 This exception for organisations relating to religion or belief does not permit anything which is prohibited by s 29 of the Act (provision of services

---

[39] EQA 2010, Sch 23, para 2(3). In the application of Sch 23, para 2 in relation to sexual orientation, so far as the exception for the use or disposal of premises owned or controlled by the organisation is concerned, 'disposal' (which must be used in the sense employed in s 38 of the Act – that is, assigning, sub-letting, parting with possession or granting a right to occupy them) does not include disposal of an interest in premises by way of sale if the interest being disposed of is the entirety of the organisation's interest in the premises, or the entirety of the interest in respect of which the organisation has power of disposal: EQA 2010, Sch 23, para 2(12)–(13).

[40] EQA 2010, Sch 23, para 2(4).

[41] EQA 2010, Sch 23, para 2(5). The reference to a minister is a reference to a minister of religion (or other person) who performs functions in connection with a religion or belief to which the organisation relates, and who holds an office or appointment in (or is accredited, approved or recognised for the purposes of) the organisation: EQA 2010, Sch 23, para 2(8).

[42] EQA 2010, Sch 23, para 2(6).

[43] EQA 2010, Sch 23, para 2(7).

[44] EQA 2010, Sch 23, para 2(9).

etc), so far as relating to sexual orientation, if it is done on behalf of a public authority,[45] and under the terms of a contract between the organisation and the public authority.[46]

14.20 The Explanatory Notes provide a useful commentary upon these provisions.[47] The exception allows a religious organisation to impose restrictions on membership of the organisation; participation in its activities; the use of any goods, facilities or services that it provides; and the use of its premises. However, any restriction can only be imposed by reference to a person's religion or belief or their sexual orientation.[48] In relation to religion or belief, the exception can only apply where a restriction is necessary to comply with the purpose of the organisation or to avoid causing offence to members of the religion or belief that the organisation represents.[49] In relation to sexual orientation, the exception can only apply where it is necessary to comply with the doctrine of the organisation or in order to avoid conflict with the strongly held convictions of members of the religion or belief that the organisation represents. However, if an organisation contracts with a public body to carry out an activity on that body's behalf then it cannot discriminate because of sexual orientation in relation to that activity.[50]

14.21 The Explanatory Notes illustrate the exception in the following examples.[51] A Catholic seminary can restrict places for students to those of the Catholic faith. This would not be unlawful religion or belief discrimination. A Church can refuse to let out its hall for a Gay Pride celebration if it considers that it would conflict with the strongly held religious convictions of a significant number of its followers. This would not be unlawful sexual orientation discrimination. However, a religious organisation which has a contract with a local authority to provide meals to elderly and other vulnerable people within the community on behalf of the local authority cannot discriminate because of sexual orientation.

14.22 Human rights concerns and questions of compatibility with the ECHR naturally arise in relation to these provisions. The Government is satisfied that it has considered the need to balance competing human rights in drafting these exceptions and that they strike an appropriate balance.[52] It considers that the exception for religious organisations allowing them to discriminate because of sexual orientation is more narrowly drawn than the exception for discrimination on the basis of religion or belief. The justification offered is that

---

[45]   In the sense explained in EQA 2010, s 150(1) and Sch 19 (essentially, the public bodies which are subject to the public sector equality duty contained in s 149): EQA 2010, Sch 23, para 2(13).

[46]   EQA 2010, Sch 23, para 2(10).

[47]   EN paras 1001–1007. They replicate the effect of similar provisions in Part 2 of the Equality Act 2006 and the Equality Act (Sexual Orientation) Regulations 2007.

[48]   EN paras 1003.

[49]   EN paras 1004.

[50]   EN paras 1005.

[51]   EN para 1007. See Government Equalities Office, 2009f.

[52]   EN para 36 (HL Bill 20).

the religion or belief exception allows otherwise unlawful action provided that the limitation is imposed to comply with the tenets of the organisation or to avoid causing offence on religious grounds to a significant number of persons of the religion to which the organisation relates. To benefit from the exception it must be shown that the restriction is necessary to comply with the doctrine of the organisation or to avoid conflict with the strongly held religious convictions of a significant number of the religion's followers.

14.23 The Government has anticipated the argument that less weight is given to the rights of those of a particular religion or belief (different from that of the religious organisation) than to those of a particular sexual orientation.[53] It counters that the reason for drawing the balance at a different point is because under the religion or belief exception it is open for religious organisations to be ecumenical if they choose. However, in order not to infringe the ECHR Art 9 (freedom of thought, conscience and religion) and Art 11 (freedom of peaceful assembly and freedom of association) rights of such organisations, they should not be required to be ecumenical. In relation to the sexual orientation exception, it is not justified for a religious organisation to discriminate on the basis of a person's sexual orientation unless it can be clearly established that it is intimately linked to the doctrine of the religion.

Communal accommodation

14.24 A person does not contravene the EQA 2010, so far as relating to sex discrimination or gender reassignment discrimination, only because of anything done in relation to the admission of persons to communal accommodation; or the provision of a benefit, facility or service linked to the accommodation.[54] Communal accommodation is residential accommodation which includes dormitories or other shared sleeping accommodation which for reasons of privacy should be used only by persons of the same sex.[55] A benefit, facility or service is linked to communal accommodation if it cannot properly and effectively be provided except for those using the accommodation; and a person could be refused use of the accommodation in reliance on the exception for the admission of persons to communal accommodation.[56]

14.25 The exception for the admission of persons to communal accommodation does not apply unless the accommodation is managed in a way which is as fair as possible to both men and women.[57] In applying that proviso, account must be taken of whether and how far it is reasonable to expect that the accommodation should be altered or extended or that further accommodation

---

[53]   EN para 37 (HL Bill 20).
[54]   EQA 2010, Sch 23, para 3(1).
[55]   EQA 2010, Sch 23, para 3(5). It may include shared sleeping accommodation for men and for women; ordinary sleeping accommodation; and residential accommodation all or part of which should be used only by persons of the same sex because of the nature of the sanitary facilities serving the accommodation: EQA 2010, Sch 23, para 3(6).
[56]   EQA 2010, Sch 23, para 3(7).
[57]   EQA 2010, Sch 23, para 3(2).

should be provided.[58] Account must also be taken of the frequency of the demand or need for use of the accommodation by persons of one sex as compared with those of the other.[59] In relation to gender reassignment, account must also be taken of whether and how far the conduct in question is a proportionate means of achieving a legitimate aim.[60]

14.26 The exception for the admission of persons to communal accommodation does not apply for the purposes of Part 5 (work) unless such arrangements as are reasonably practicable are made to compensate for the refusal of use of the accommodation.[61] The exception for the provision of a benefit, facility or service linked to the accommodation does not apply for the purposes of Part 5 (work) unless such arrangements as are reasonably practicable are made to compensate for the refusal of provision of the benefit, facility or service.[62]

14.27 This exception to the general prohibition of sex discrimination and gender reassignment discrimination allows communal accommodation to be restricted to one sex only, as long as the accommodation is managed as fairly as possible for both men and women.[63] Any discriminatory treatment of transsexual people that results from the exception must be objectively justified. While this exception replaces a similar exception in the SDA 1975, its scope has been extended from employment, education and services to all fields.

14.28 The Explanatory Notes illustrate the exception in the following scenarios.[64] A hostel only accepts male guests. It is not unlawful for it to refuse to accept female guests because the majority of the bedrooms are shared and there is only one communal bathroom. At a worksite the only available sleeping accommodation is communal accommodation occupied by men. A woman employee who wishes to attend a training course at the worksite is refused permission because of the men-only accommodation. Her employer must make alternative arrangements to compensate her where reasonable, for example, by arranging alternative accommodation or an alternative course.

Training provided to non-EEA residents, etc

14.29 A person (A) does not contravene the EQA 2010, so far as relating to nationality, only by providing a non-resident (B) with training,[65] if A thinks

---

58   EQA 2010, Sch 23, para 3(3)(a).
59   EQA 2010, Sch 23, para 3(3)(b).
60   EQA 2010, Sch 23, para 3(4).
61   EQA 2010, Sch 23, para 3(8)(a).
62   EQA 2010, Sch 23, para 3(8)(b).
63   EN paras 1008–1011.
64   EN para 1011.
65   The reference to providing B with training is, if A employs B in relevant employment, a reference to doing anything in or in connection with the employment; if A as a principal allows B to do relevant contract work (in the senses used in s 41 on contract workers), a reference to doing anything in or in connection with allowing B to do the work; in either of those cases or in any other case, a reference to affording B access to facilities for education or training or

that B does not intend to exercise in GB skills B obtains as a result.[66] A non-resident is a person who is not ordinarily resident in an EEA state.[67] This provision is modified (without further explanation here) in the case of training provided by the armed forces or the Secretary of State for purposes relating to defence.[68]

14.30 This exception enables people from developing countries to acquire vital skills which may not be available in their country of residence.[69] It allows less favourable treatment because of a person's nationality in relation to training and associated benefits that are intended for people who do not live in an EEA state. This is conditional upon the training provider believing that the person will not subsequently use the skills obtained in GB. As a result an EEA resident cannot claim to have been discriminated against in relation to this type of activity.[70] However, employment or contract work does not fall within this exception where its sole or main purpose is the provision of training in skills.[71]

14.31 The exception replaces similar provisions in the RRA 1976, but the general rule on non-residence has been extended from GB to include all European Economic Area (EEA) states (except in relation to defence training which is provided to forces from other EEA states as well as those outside the EEA).[72] By way of example, it is not unlawful for a company specialising in sustainable irrigation that offers a training scheme in GB for people who live in Mozambique – who then return home to put the skills learned into practice – to refuse to offer the same training to someone who lives in GB.[73]

OTHER EXCEPTIONS

National security

14.32 A person does not contravene the EQA 2010 only by doing, for the purpose of safeguarding national security, anything it is proportionate to do for that purpose.[74] This is a self-explanatory provision.[75] It replaces similar exceptions in the legacy legislation. However, it narrows the national security

---

ancillary benefits: EQA 2010, Sch 23, para 4(3) and (6). Employment or contract work is relevant if its sole or main purpose is the provision of training in skills: EQA 2010, Sch 23, para 4(4).
[66] EQA 2010, Sch 23, para 4(1).
[67] EQA 2010, Sch 23, para 4(2).
[68] EQA 2010, Sch 23, para 4(5). The Explanatory Notes state that special provision is made in relation to defence training to reflect current arrangements to help provide other nations with the skills to assist the UK in addressing global conflict and supporting the UK on multi-national operations: EN para 1013.
[69] EN para 1014.
[70] EN para 1012.
[71] EN para 1014.
[72] EN para 1013.
[73] EN para 1014.
[74] EQA 2010, s 192.
[75] EN paras 614–615.

exceptions in some areas, while introducing a national security exception in relation to age and sexual orientation discrimination outside work. Thus, denying people of a particular nationality access to sensitive information is not unlawful race discrimination under the Act if it is proportionate in order to guard against terrorist attacks.[76]

Charities

14.33 A number of exceptions arise in respect of charities.[77] However, these provisions and exceptions do not apply to race, so far as relating to colour.[78]

14.34 A person does not contravene the EQA 2010 only by restricting the provision of benefits to persons who share a protected characteristic if the person acts in pursuance of a charitable instrument,[79] and the provision of the benefits is a proportionate means of achieving a legitimate aim, or for the purpose of preventing or compensating for a disadvantage linked to the protected characteristic.[80] However, with the exception of disability,[81] this exception does not apply to a contravention of s 39 (employees and applicants); s 40 (harassment of employees and applicants); s 41 (contract workers); or s 55 (employment services, so far as relating to the provision of vocational training).[82]

14.35 It is not a contravention of the Act for a person who provides supported employment to treat persons who have the same disability or a disability of a prescribed description more favourably than those who do not have that disability or a disability of such a description in providing such employment.[83] Equally, it is not a contravention of the Act for a Minister of the Crown to agree to arrangements for the provision of supported employment which will or may have that effect.[84]

14.36 If a charitable instrument enables the provision of benefits to persons of a class defined by reference to colour, it has effect for all purposes as if it

---

[76] EN para 615.

[77] EQA 2010, s 194 (charities: supplementary) applies for the purposes of s 193 containing the main exceptions for charities: s 194(1). In relation to England and Wales, a 'charity' has the meaning given by the Charities Act 2006 and, in relation to Scotland, means a body entered in the Scottish Charity Register: s 194(3).

[78] EQA 2010, s 194(2).

[79] The term 'charitable instrument' means an instrument establishing or governing a charity (including an instrument made or having effect before the commencement of s 194): EQA 2010, s 194(4).

[80] EQA 2010, s 193(1) and (2).

[81] EQA 2010, s 193(10).

[82] EQA 2010, s 193(9).

[83] EQA 2010, s 193(3)(a). The term 'supported employment' means facilities provided, or in respect of which payments are made, under Disabled Persons (Employment) Act 1944, s 15: EQA 2010, s 194(7).

[84] EQA 2010, s 193(3)(b).

enabled the provision of such benefits to persons of the class which results if the reference to colour is ignored, or if the original class is defined by reference only to colour, to persons generally.[85]

14.37 It is not a contravention of the EQA 2010 for a charity to require members (or persons wishing to become members) to make a statement which asserts or implies membership or acceptance of a religion or belief.[86] For this purpose, restricting the access by members to a benefit, facility or service to those who make such a statement is treated as imposing such a requirement.[87] However, this exception only applies if the charity (or an organisation of which it is part) first imposed such a requirement before 18 May 2005, and the charity (or organisation) has not ceased since that date to impose such a requirement.[88]

14.38 In relation to an activity that is carried on for the purpose of promoting or supporting a charity, it is not a contravention of s 29 of the Act (discrimination in provision of services etc) for a person to restrict participation in the activity to persons of one sex.[89]

14.39 A charity regulator does not contravene the Act only by exercising a function in relation to a charity in a manner which the regulator thinks is expedient in the interests of the charity, having regard to the charitable instrument.[90]

14.40 The Explanatory Notes explain that these provisions[91] allow a charity to provide benefits only to people who share the same protected characteristic if this accords with its charitable instrument. To do so must be objectively justified, or to prevent or compensate for disadvantage. However, it is unlawful for a charity to limit its beneficiaries by reference to colour.[92] This exception does not extend to a charity in respect of employment, contract work or vocational training. However, charities and government may provide arrangements for supported employment based upon a particular disability.[93] A charity may make acceptance of a religion or belief a condition of membership. It may also refuse members access to benefits if they do not accept a religion or belief, where membership itself is not subject to such a condition, provided the charity has done so since before 18 May 2005.

---

[85]   EQA 2010, s 193(4).
[86]   EQA 2010, s 193(5).
[87]   EQA 2010, s 193(5). In relation to members (or persons wishing to become members) of a charity, s 107(5) applies: EQA 2010, 193(6). Thus, 'membership' is membership of any description; and a reference to a 'member' is to be construed accordingly.
[88]   EQA 2010, s 193(6).
[89]   EQA 2010, s 193(7).
[90]   EQA 2010, s 193(8). The charity regulators are the Charity Commission for England and Wales, and the Scottish Charity Regulator: EQA 2010, s 194(5).
[91]   EQA 2010, ss 193–194.
[92]   EN para 616.
[93]   EN para 617.

Single-sex activities are also permitted for the purpose of promoting or supporting a charity (such as women only fun-runs).[94]

14.41 These provisions replace and harmonise separate exceptions in pre-existing discrimination law. The exceptions are now extended to charities benefiting only people of the same age group or with the same disability. A new exception is created[95] so as to allow participation in activities to promote or support charities to be restricted to men or women.[96] The Explanatory Notes clarify that it is lawful for the Womens' Institute to provide educational opportunities only to women or for the Royal National Institute for the Blind to employ (or provide special facilities for) visually impaired people in preference to other disabled people.[97] A charitable instrument enabling the provision of benefits to black members of a community will be treated as enabling the benefits to be provided to all members of that community. The Explanatory Notes also suggest that it is lawful for the Scout Association to require children joining the Scouts to promise to do their best to do their duty to God. Similarly, Race for Life, a women-only event which raises money for Cancer Research UK, remains lawful.[98]

Sport

14.42 A person does not contravene the EQA 2010, so far as relating to sex, only by doing anything in relation to the participation of another as a competitor in a gender-affected activity.[99] A gender-affected activity is a sport, game or other activity of a competitive nature in circumstances in which the physical strength, stamina or physique of average persons of one sex would put them at a disadvantage compared to average persons of the other sex as competitors in events involving the activity.[100] In considering whether a sport, game or other activity is gender-affected in relation to children, it is appropriate to take account of the age and stage of development of children who are likely to be competitors.[101]

14.43 A person does not contravene s 29 (provision of services, etc) and ss 33 to 35 (disposal and management of premises), so far as relating to gender reassignment, only by doing anything in relation to the participation of a transsexual person as a competitor in a gender-affected activity if it is necessary to do so to secure in relation to the activity fair competition or the safety of competitors.[102]

---

[94]   EN para 618.
[95]   EQA 2010, s 193(7).
[96]   EN para 619.
[97]   EN para 619.
[98]   EN para 619.
[99]   EQA 2010, s 195(1).
[100] EQA 2010, s 195(3).
[101] EQA 2010, s 195(4).
[102] EQA 2010, s 195(2).

14.44 Special provision is made for selecting one or more persons to represent a country, place or area or a related association in a sport or game or other activity of a competitive nature.[103] Special provision is also made for doing anything in pursuance of the rules of a competition so far as relating to eligibility to compete in a sport or game or other such activity.[104] A person who does anything in relation to those matters does not contravene the EQA 2010 only because of the nationality or place of birth of another or because of the length of time the other has been resident in a particular area or place.[105]

14.45 Replacing similar provisions in previous discrimination law, the Explanatory Notes say that the 2010 Act continues to allow separate sporting competitions to be organised for men and women where physical strength, stamina or physique are major factors in determining success or failure, and in which one sex is generally at a disadvantage in comparison with the other.[106] It also makes it lawful to restrict participation of transsexual people in such competitions if this is necessary to uphold fair or safe competition, but not otherwise.[107] The Act also allows existing selection arrangements of national sports teams, regional or local clubs, or related associations to continue. It also protects closed competitions where participation is limited to people who meet a requirement relating to nationality, place of birth or residence.[108]

Age

14.46 Drawing in this account upon the Explanatory Notes in preference to the statutory provision itself,[109] the Act enables the Government in future to make orders containing exceptions to the prohibition on discrimination outside the workplace because of age if the persons in question are over 18.[110] Orders can provide for a Minister or the Treasury to issue guidance (after consultation) and can impose requirements that refer to the guidance. Such guidance comes into force on such day as the person who issues the guidance may by order appoint.

14.47 This is a new provision designed to allow exceptions to be made from the new prohibitions on age discrimination in the provision of services and the exercise of public functions. Examples of appropriate age-based treatment are given. They may include concessionary travel for older and young people; disease prevention programmes such as cancer screening targeted at people in particular age groups on the basis of clinical evidence; age differences in the

---

[103] EQA 2010, s 195(6)(a).
[104] EQA 2010, s 195(6)(b).
[105] EQA 2010, s 195(5).
[106] EQA 2010, s 195.
[107] EN para 622.
[108] EN para 623.
[109] EN paras 626–628.
[110] EQA 2010, s 197.

calculation of annuities and insurance programmes which are reasonable and based on adequate evidence of the underlying difference in risk; and holidays for particular age groups.

FAMILY PROPERTY

14.48   As a result of amendments moved by Lord Lester of Herne Hill at the Committee stage in the House of Lords, which the Government then supported, a new Part (now Part 15) was inserted into the Bill that became the EQA 2010.[111] These provisions 'remove three minor rules of law which treat husbands and wives unequally, and they equalise the legal position in respect of civil partners'.[112] They are intended to remove the existing incompatibility of UK law with Art 5 of Protocol 7 to the ECHR (protecting the right to equality between spouses). This may pave the way for the UK to sign and ratify the Protocol.

Abolition of husband's duty to maintain wife

14.49   The rule of common law that a husband must maintain his wife is abolished.[113] This will not affect the wife's statutory remedies for maintenance during a marriage.

Abolition of presumption of advancement

14.50   The presumption of advancement is abolished.[114] This is a rule of evidence. So, for example, if a husband transfers property to his wife, or purchases property in her name, a court will presume that the husband is thereby making a gift to his wife.[115] Conversely, there is no such presumption in favour of the husband. The presumption is now abolished. This does not affect anything done (or anything done pursuant to an obligation incurred) before this provision comes into force.[116]

Amendment of Married Women's Property Act 1964

14.51   The Married Women's Property Act 1964 provides that money and property derived from a housekeeping allowance made by the husband to his wife is to be treated as belonging to the husband and wife in equal shares.[117] Hitherto, this provision has not applied where the wife has made an allowance to the husband. The EQA 2010 amends this so that money and property

---

[111]   EQA 2010, ss 198–201.
[112]   HL Deb vol 717 cols 707–708.
[113]   EQA 2010, s 198.
[114]   EQA 2010, s 199(1). This provision extends to Northern Ireland.
[115]   The rule survived *Stack v Dowden* [2007] UKHL 17, [2007] 2 AC 432 (which was concerned only with ownership of a domestic home and not of other matrimonial property).
[116]   EQA 2010, s 199(2).
[117]   Married Women's Property Act 1964, s 1.

derived from a housekeeping allowance made by either the husband or the wife is to be treated as belonging to them in equal shares.[118] The Married Women's Property Act 1964 will now be cited as the Marital Property Act 1964.[119] This does not affect any allowance made before this new provision comes into force.[120]

Civil partners: housekeeping allowance

14.52 The principle of the Marital Property Act 1964 as it now applies to a housekeeping allowance between a husband and a wife is now extended to civil partners.[121]

GENERAL AND MISCELLANEOUS PROVISIONS

Civil partnerships on religious premises

14.53 The Civil Partnership Act 2004 enables same-sex couples to obtain legal recognition of their relationship by forming a civil partnership. To do so they may register as civil partners of each other. Among other things, that Act provides that the place where the proposed civil partnership is to be registered must not be in religious premises.[122] Religious premises are premises which are used solely or mainly for religious purposes (or which have been so used and have not subsequently been used solely or mainly for other purposes).[123] Otherwise, the place where the proposed civil partnership is to be registered must be on approved premises or in a register office.[124] The Marriages and Civil Partnerships (Approved Premises) Regulations 2005 make provision for and in connection with the approval by registration authorities of premises for these purposes.[125]

14.54 The EQA 2010 prospectively amends the Civil Partnership Act 2004 by abolishing the prohibition on civil partnerships being registered in religious premises.[126] Regulations may in future provide that premises approved for the registration of civil partnerships may differ from those premises approved for the registration of civil marriages.[127] Particular provision may be made to provide that applications for approval of premises may only be made with the consent (whether general or specific) of a person specified (or a person of a

---

[118] EQA 2010, s 200(1).
[119] EQA 2010, s 200(2).
[120] EQA 2010, s 200(3).
[121] EQA 2010, s 201 inserting a new s 70A into the Civil Partnership Act 2004.
[122] Civil Partnership Act 2004, s 6(1)(b).
[123] Civil Partnership Act 2004, s 6(2).
[124] Civil Partnership Act 2004, s 6(3A) as amended by the Civil Partnership (Amendment to Registration Provisions) Order 2005, SI 2005/2000.
[125] SI 2005/3168.
[126] EQA 2010, s 202(1) and (2) omitting Civil Partnership Act 2004, ss 6(1)(b) and 6(2).
[127] EQA 2010, 202(3) inserting s 6A(2A) into the Civil Partnership Act 2004.

description specified) in the provision.[128] There will be a power to provide for different premises to be approved for registration of civil partnerships from those approved for registration of civil marriages.[129]

14.55 However, for the avoidance of doubt, nothing places an obligation on religious organisations to host civil partnerships if they do not wish to do so.[130] Civil marriage means marriage solemnised otherwise than according to the rites of the Church of England or any other religious usages.[131] Religious premises means premises which are used solely or mainly for religious purposes, or have been so used and have not subsequently been used solely or mainly for other purposes.[132]

14.56 This prospective change in the law is as a result of an amendment moved by Lord Alli and approved by a division at the Report stage of the Equality Bill in the House of Lords on a free vote.[133] Civil partnerships and civil marriages are entirely secular. Prior to this prospective change they may not take place on religious premises or contain religious language. The change would result in civil partnerships being treated differently from civil marriages – the former being permitted on religious premises, but the latter not. While the reform would result in civil partnerships being performed on religious premises, the prohibition on any form of religious service or ceremony would remain,[134] thus placing in an ambiguous position the civil registrar performing the registration of the civil partnership in a religious building.

14.57 While the Government did not actively oppose the amendment, neither did it support it, as it could see practical difficulties in making the change work.[135] The Government indicated that there would need to be appropriate consultation (and additional primary or secondary legislation) before this provision could be made to work. The present author agrees. However, various technical amendments were made at Third Reading in the House of Lords and which seem to have met the Government's concerns.[136] This was confirmed when the Lords amendments were considered by the Commons.[137]

Community obligations: harmonisation

14.58 The Government is now enabled to amend the Equality Act 2006 and the EQA 2010 ('the Equality Acts') by order to ensure consistency across the legislation where changes required by European law would otherwise result in

---

[128] EQA 2010, 202(3) inserting s 6A(2B) into the Civil Partnership Act 2004.
[129] EQA 2010, 202(3) inserting s 6A(2C) into the Civil Partnership Act 2004.
[130] EQA 2010, 202(4) inserting s 6A(3A) into the Civil Partnership Act 2004.
[131] EQA 2010, 202(4) inserting s 6A(3B) into the Civil Partnership Act 2004.
[132] EQA 2010, 202(4) inserting s 6A(3C) into the Civil Partnership Act 2004.
[133] HL Deb vol 717 cols 1425–1441.
[134] Civil Partnership Act 2004, s 2(5).
[135] This paragraph draws upon the speech of the Baroness Royall of Blaisdon, the lead Minister on the Bill in the House of Lords: HL Deb vol 717 cols 1437–1440.
[136] HL Deb vol 718 col 870 (Baroness Royall of Blaisdon).
[137] HC Deb vol 508 col 929 (Solicitor-General).

inconsistent provision.[138] This power applies if there is a Community obligation of the UK which a Minister of the Crown thinks relates to the subject-matter of the Equality Acts; and the obligation is to be implemented by the exercise of the power under s 2(2) of the European Communities Act 1972 (the implementing power); and the Minister thinks that it is appropriate to make harmonising provision in the Equality Acts.[139] If so, the Minister may by order make the harmonising provision.[140]

14.59 A harmonising provision is a provision made in relation to relevant subject-matter of the Equality Acts which corresponds to the implementing provision, or which the Minister thinks is necessary or expedient in consequence of or related to that provision or the implementing provision.[141] The implementing provision is a provision made or to be made in exercise of the implementing power in relation to so much of the subject-matter of the Equality Acts as implements a Community obligation.[142] Relevant subject-matter of the Equality Acts is so much of the subject-matter of those Acts as does not implement a Community obligation.[143] A harmonising provision may amend a provision of the Equality Acts.[144]

14.60 As the Explanatory Notes assist in our understanding,[145] this is a new provision designed to ensure that the areas of the Act that are covered by European law and those that are domestic in origin do not get out of step, as was the case with earlier legislation. Where provisions of the EQA 2010 and UK equality law more generally deal with a sector on a single basis, some of the matters covered may not be within the reach of EC law and so outside the scope of s 2(2)(a) of the European Communities Act 1972. This has arisen in the case of nationality and colour, which are not dealt with under the Community law provisions on race discrimination but are covered by the UK provisions. The Government would not be able to use s 2(2)(b) of the European Communities Act 1972 to amend all relevant parts of the legislation in these circumstances. The change required in respect of nationality or colour would not be consequential on or arising out of the Community obligation. This problem is addressed by the new power.

14.61 Before making the order, the Minister must consult persons and organisations the Minister thinks are likely to be affected by the harmonising

---

138 EQA 2010, s 203. See EN paras 638–641.

139 EQA 2010, s 203(1) and (5).

140 EQA 2010, s 203(2). A Minister of the Crown must report to Parliament on the exercise of the power at the end of the period of two years starting on the day this section comes into force and at the end of each succeeding period of two years: EQA 2010, s 203(11).

141 EQA 2010, s 203(6).

142 EQA 2010, s 203(7).

143 EQA 2010, s 203(8).

144 EQA 2010, s 203(9). A harmonising provision may not extend to s 203 itself or to Sch 24 (harmonisation: exceptions) or to a provision specified there: EQA 2010, s 203(10). The reader is referred to Sch 24 for the exceptions themselves.

145 EN paras 642–648.

provision.[146] If, as a result of that consultation, the Minister seeks to change the proposal, the Minister must carry out further consultation as thought appropriate.[147] Once the consultation has been concluded, the Minister must then follow a procedure that leads to the order being made by statutory instrument.[148]

Crown application

14.62 The Crown is bound by Part 1 (public sector duty regarding socio-economic inequalities); Part 3 (services and public functions), so far as relating to the exercise of public functions; and Chapter 1 of Part 11 (public sector equality duty) of the EQA 2010.[149] Part 5 (work) binds the Crown as provided for by that Part (see Chapters 6 and 7 above).[150] The remainder of the Act applies to Crown acts as it applies to acts done by a private person.[151] An act is a Crown act if (and only if) it is done by or on behalf of a member of the executive, or by a statutory body acting on behalf of the Crown, or by or on behalf of the holder of a statutory office acting on behalf of the Crown.[152] A statutory body or office is a body or office established by an enactment.[153]

14.63 The provisions of Parts 2 to 4 of the Crown Proceedings Act 1947 apply to proceedings against the Crown under the EQA 2010 as they apply to proceedings in England and Wales which, as a result of s 23 of the 1947 Act, are treated for the purposes of Part 2 of the 1947 Act as civil proceedings by or against the Crown.[154] The provisions of Part 5 of the Crown Proceedings Act 1947 apply to proceedings against the Crown under the EQA 2010 as they apply to proceedings in Scotland which, as a result of that Part, are treated as civil proceedings by or against the Crown.[155] The proviso to s 44 of the Crown Proceedings Act 1947 (removal of proceedings from the sheriff to the Court of Session) does not apply to proceedings under the EQA 2010.

14.64 These provisions replicate the effect of similar provisions in the legacy legislation. They also replicate the arrangements in earlier discrimination legislation for taking proceedings against the Crown.[156]

---

[146] EQA 2010, s 203(3).
[147] EQA 2010, s 203(4).
[148] EQA 2010, s 204 (which is not considered further here).
[149] EQA 2010, s 205(1).
[150] EQA 2010, s 205(2).
[151] EQA 2010, s 205(3).
[152] EQA 2010, s 205(4).
[153] EQA 2010, s 205(5).
[154] EQA 2010, s 205(6).
[155] EQA 2010, s 205(7).
[156] EN paras 649–650.

Subordinate legislation

14.65 Provision is made for the powers to make secondary legislation under the Act.[157] It is not considered further here.[158] The Act also establishes which Parliamentary procedures apply to the regulations and orders which can be made by Ministers of the Crown under the Act.[159] This is not considered further here.[160] Similar provisions relate to the Welsh Ministers and the Scottish Ministers.[161] These aspects of the Act were heavily amended during the passage of the Bill so as to meet the concerns of the House of Lords Delegated Powers and Regulatory Reform Committee.[162]

Amendments, repeals and revocations

14.66 The Act promotes a number of amendments, repeals and revocations.[163] Amendments to other statutes are necessary as a consequence of the Act's provisions. These amendments are to the Local Government Act 1988, the Employment Act 1989 and the Equality Act 2006. Many provisions in current legislation will cease to have effect when the relevant provisions of the 2010 Act are brought into force.[164]

14.67 Of significance is the prospective repeal of the Equal Pay Act 1970, the SDA 1975, the RRA 1976, the Sex Discrimination Act 1986 and the Disability Discrimination Act 1995.[165] Also to be revoked are the Occupational Pension Schemes (Equal Treatment) Regulations 1995; the Employment Equality (Religion or Belief) Regulations 2003; the Employment Equality (Sexual Orientation) Regulations 2003; the Disability Discrimination Act 1995 (Pensions) Regulations 2003; the Occupational Pension Schemes (Equal Treatment) (Amendment) Regulations 2005; the Employment Equality (Age) Regulations 2006 (other than Schs 6 and 8); the Equality Act (Sexual Orientation) Regulations 2007; and the Sex Discrimination (Amendment of Legislation) Regulations 2008.

INFORMATION SOCIETY SERVICES

Introduction

14.68 The EQA 2010, s 206 provides that Sch 25 (information society services) has effect. Schedule 25 sets out new provisions that address how the sections

---

[157] EQA 2010, s 207.
[158] See EN paras 653–657. See further: House of Lords Delegated Powers and Regulatory Reform Committee, 2010 (especially Appendix 2 which contains a schedule of all the delegated powers in the Act).
[159] EQA 2010, s 208.
[160] See EN paras 658–659.
[161] EQA 2010, ss 209 and 210. See EN paras 660–665.
[162] See House of Lords Delegated Powers and Regulatory Reform Committee, 2010.
[163] EQA 2010, s 211 and Schs 26 and 27.
[164] EN paras 666 and 1018–1025.
[165] The DDA 1995 remains in force so far as it relates to Northern Ireland.

that make it unlawful to discriminate against, harass or victimise a person apply to information society service providers.[166]

14.69 Reference to the explanation provided by the Explanatory Notes will assist the analysis that follows.[167] Schedule 25 ensures that the provisions of the EQA 2010 do not conflict with the requirements of Directive 2000/31/EC (the E-Commerce Directive). Where an information society service provider is established in GB, the provisions of the Act apply to anything done by the provider in providing the information society service in another EEA state. Where the provider is established in an EEA state other than the UK, then the Act does not apply to anything done by the provider in providing the information society service, even within GB. Various exceptions to the provisions of the Act are provided in respect of intermediary internet service providers who carry out activities essential for the operation of the internet.

14.70 The Explanatory Notes provide the following examples:[168]

- An online holiday company established in GB refuses to take bookings for shared accommodation from same-sex couples. In this instance a case of direct sexual orientation discrimination could be brought in the British courts regardless of whether the complainant was in the UK or another EEA member state.

- An online retailer, which provides tickets to major sporting events, provides discounts to large groups of men, but not women, when booking hospitality packages for the 2010 football world cup. The online retailer is established in Germany, so in this instance a case of direct sex discrimination would have to be brought in the German courts regardless of whether the complainant was in the UK or another EEA member state.

These examples are a useful preface to the detail that now follows.

Service providers

14.71 The starting point is where a person concerned with the provision of an information society service[169] (an information society service provider) is

---

[166] EN paras 651–652.
[167] EN paras 1016–1017.
[168] EN para 1017.
[169] The term 'information society service' has the meaning given in Art 2(a) of the E-Commerce Directive (which refers to Art 1(2) of Directive 98/34/EC of the European Parliament and of the Council of 22 June 1998 laying down a procedure for the provision of information in the field of technical standards and regulations), and is summarised in recital 17 of the E-Commerce Directive as covering 'any service normally provided for remuneration, at a distance, by means of electronic equipment for the processing (including digital compression) and storage of data, and at the individual request of a recipient of a service': EQA 2010, Sch 25, para 7(2). The E-Commerce Directive means Directive 2000/31/EC of the European

established in GB.[170] The EQA 2010 applies to anything done by the person in an EEA state (other than the UK) in providing the service as the Act would apply if the act in question were done by the person in GB.[171] If, however, an information society service provider is established in an EEA state (other than the UK),[172] the Act does not apply to anything done by the person in providing the service.[173]

Exceptions for mere conduits

14.72 An information society service provider does not contravene the Act only by providing so much of an information society service as consists in the provision of access to a communication network, or the transmission in a communication network of information provided by the recipient[174] of the service.[175] However, that exception applies only if the service provider does not initiate the transmission, select the recipient of the transmission, or select or modify the information contained in the transmission.[176] For these purposes, the provision of access to a communication network, and the transmission of information in a communication network, includes the automatic, intermediate and transient storage of the information transmitted, so far as the storage is solely for the purpose of carrying out the transmission in the network.[177] However, that gloss on the statute does not apply if the information is stored for longer than is reasonably necessary for the transmission.[178]

Exception for caching

14.73 An exception for caching applies where an information society service consists in the transmission in a communication network of information

---

Parliament and of the Council of 8 June 2000 on certain legal aspects of information society services, in particular electronic commerce, in the Internal Market (directive on electronic commerce): EQA 2010, Sch 25, para 7(3).

[170] EQA 2010, Sch 25, para 1(1). An information society service-provider is 'established' in a country or territory if the service-provider effectively pursues an economic activity using a fixed establishment in that country or territory for an indefinite period, and is a national of an EEA state or a body mentioned in Art 48 of the EEC Treaty: EQA 2010, Sch 25, para 7(5). The presence or use in a particular place of equipment or other technical means of providing an information society service is not itself sufficient to constitute the establishment of a service-provider: EQA 2010, Sch 25, para 7(6). Where it cannot be decided from which of a number of establishments an information society service is provided, the service is to be regarded as provided from the establishment at the centre of the information society service provider's activities relating to that service: EQA 2010, Sch 25, para 7(7).

[171] EQA 2010, Sch 25, para 1(2).
[172] EQA 2010, Sch 25, para 2(1).
[173] EQA 2010, Sch 25, para 2(2). EQA 2010, s 212(4) does not apply to references to providing a service: EQA 2010, Sch 25, para 7(8).
[174] The term 'recipient' means a person who (whether for professional purposes or not) uses an information society service, in particular for seeking information or making it accessible: EQA 2010, Sch 25, para 7(4).
[175] EQA 2010, Sch 25, para 3(1).
[176] EQA 2010, Sch 25, para 3(2).
[177] EQA 2010, Sch 25, para 3(3).
[178] EQA 2010, Sch 25, para 3(4).

provided by a recipient of the service.[179] The information society service provider does not contravene the Act only by doing anything in connection with the automatic, intermediate and temporary storage of information so provided if the storage of the information is solely for the purpose of making more efficient the onward transmission of the information to other recipients of the service at their request, and the following condition is satisfied.[180] That condition is that the service-provider does not modify the information and the service-provider complies with such conditions as are attached to having access to the information.[181] The service-provider must also expeditiously remove the information or disable access to it if the service-provider obtains actual knowledge that the information at the initial source of the transmission has been removed from the network, or access to it has been disabled, or a court or administrative authority has required the removal from the network of (or the disablement of access to) the information.[182]

Exception for hosting

14.74 An information society service provider does not contravene the Act only by doing anything in providing so much of an information society service as consists in the storage of information provided by a recipient of the service in the following circumstances. First, if the service provider had no actual knowledge when the information was provided that its provision amounted to a contravention of the Act.[183] Secondly, if on obtaining actual knowledge that the provision of the information amounted to a contravention of *that section*,[184] the service provider expeditiously removed the information or disabled access to it.[185] However, this provision does not apply if the recipient of the service is acting under the authority of the control of the service provider.[186]

Monitoring obligations

14.75 An injunction (in Scotland, an interdict) under Part 1 of the Equality Act 2006 may not impose on a person concerned with the provision of an information society service[187] a liability the imposition of which would contravene Art 12 (mere conduit), Art 13 (caching) or Art 14 (hosting) of the E-Commerce Directive (which deal with the liability of intermediary service providers); or a general obligation of the description given in Art 15 of that Directive (no general obligation to monitor).[188]

---

179 EQA 2010, Sch 25, para 4(1).
180 EQA 2010, Sch 25, para 4(2).
181 EQA 2010, Sch 25, para 4(3).
182 EQA 2010, Sch 25, para 4(4).
183 EQA 2010, Sch 25, para 5(1)(a).
184 The reference to *that section*, as opposed to *this Act*, appears to be a drafting error.
185 EQA 2010, Sch 25, para 5(1)(b).
186 EQA 2010, Sch 25, para 5(2). It is not clear whether this sub-paragraph contains a drafting error. Should it read 'acting under the authority *or control* of the service-provider'?
187 Of a description given in EQA 2010, Sch 25, paras 3(1), 4(1) or 5(1) above.
188 EQA 2010, Sch 25, para 6.

14.76 A further detailed analysis of the potential interaction between the EQA 2010 and the E-Commerce Directive is beyond the scope of this book.

Appendix

EQUALITY ACT 2010

Chapter 15

CONTENTS

PART 1
SOCIO-ECONOMIC INEQUALITIES

PART 2
EQUALITY: KEY CONCEPTS

Chapter 1
Protected characteristics

Chapter 2
Prohibited conduct

Discrimination

Adjustments for disabled persons

Discrimination: supplementary

Other prohibited conduct

PART 3

SERVICES AND PUBLIC FUNCTIONS

Preliminary

PART 4

PREMISES

Preliminary

PART 5

WORK

Chapter 1

Employment, etc.

Employees

PART 6

EDUCATION

Chapter 1

Schools

Chapter 2

Further and higher education

Chapter 3

General qualifications bodies

Chapter 4

Miscellaneous

PART 7

ASSOCIATIONS

Preliminary

Membership, etc.

Special provision for political parties

Supplementary

PART 8

PROHIBITED CONDUCT: ANCILLARY

PART 9

ENFORCEMENT

Chapter 1

Introductory

PART 10

CONTRACTS, ETC.

Contracts and other agreements

Collective agreements and rules of undertakings

Supplementary

An Act to make provision to require Ministers of the Crown and others when making strategic decisions about the exercise of their functions to have regard to the desirability of reducing socio-economic inequalities; to reform and harmonise equality law and restate the greater part of the enactments relating to discrimination and harassment related to certain personal characteristics; to enable certain employers to be required to publish information about the differences in pay between male and female employees; to prohibit victimisation in certain circumstances; to require the exercise of certain functions to be with regard to the need to eliminate discrimination and other prohibited conduct; to enable duties to be imposed in relation to the exercise of public procurement functions; to increase equality of opportunity; to amend the law relating to rights and responsibilities in family relationships; and for connected purposes. [8th April 2010]

BE IT ENACTED by the Queen's most Excellent Majesty, by and with the advice and consent of the Lords Spiritual and Temporal, and Commons, in this present Parliament assembled, and by the authority of the same, as follows: –

PART 1
SOCIO-ECONOMIC INEQUALITIES

1 Public sector duty regarding socio-economic inequalities

(1) An authority to which this section applies must, when making decisions of a strategic nature about how to exercise its functions, have due regard to the desirability of exercising them in a way that is designed to reduce the inequalities of outcome which result from socio-economic disadvantage.

(2) In deciding how to fulfil a duty to which it is subject under subsection (1), an authority must take into account any guidance issued by a Minister of the Crown.

(3) The authorities to which this section applies are –

(a)   a Minister of the Crown;
(b)   a government department other than the Security Service, the Secret Intelligence Service or the Government Communications Headquarters;
(c)   a county council or district council in England;
(d)   the Greater London Authority;
(e)   a London borough council;
(f)   the Common Council of the City of London in its capacity as a local authority;
(g)   the Council of the Isles of Scilly;
(h)   a Strategic Health Authority established under section 13 of the National Health Service Act 2006, or continued in existence by virtue of that section;
(i)   a Primary Care Trust established under section 18 of that Act, or continued in existence by virtue of that section;
(j)   a regional development agency established by the Regional Development Agencies Act 1998;
(k)   a police authority established for an area in England.

(4) This section also applies to an authority that –

(a)   is a partner authority in relation to a responsible local authority, and
(b)   does not fall within subsection (3),

but only in relation to its participation in the preparation or modification of a sustainable community strategy.

(5) In subsection (4) –

"partner authority" has the meaning given by section 104 of the Local Government and Public Involvement in Health Act 2007;

"responsible local authority" has the meaning given by section 103 of that Act;

"sustainable community strategy" means a strategy prepared under section 4 of the Local Government Act 2000.

(6) The reference to inequalities in subsection (1) does not include any inequalities experienced by a person as a result of being a person subject to immigration control within the meaning given by section 115(9) of the Immigration and Asylum Act 1999.

2 Power to amend section 1

(1) A Minister of the Crown may by regulations amend section 1 so as to –

(a)   add a public authority to the authorities that are subject to the duty under subsection (1) of that section;

(b)   remove an authority from those that are subject to the duty;

(c)   make the duty apply, in the case of a particular authority, only in relation to certain functions that it has;

(d)   in the case of an authority to which the application of the duty is already restricted to certain functions, remove or alter the restriction.

(2) In subsection (1) "public authority" means an authority that has functions of a public nature.

(3) Provision made under subsection (1) may not impose a duty on an authority in relation to any devolved Scottish functions or devolved Welsh functions.

(4) The Scottish Ministers or the Welsh Ministers may by regulations amend section 1 so as to –

(a)   add a relevant authority to the authorities that are subject to the duty under subsection (1) of that section;

(b)   remove a relevant authority from those that are subject to the duty;

(c)   make the duty apply, in the case of a particular relevant authority, only in relation to certain functions that it has;

(d)   in the case of a relevant authority to which the application of the duty is already restricted to certain functions, remove or alter the restriction.

(5) For the purposes of the power conferred by subsection (4) on the Scottish Ministers, "relevant authority" means an authority whose functions –

(a)   are exercisable only in or as regards Scotland,

(b)   are wholly or mainly devolved Scottish functions, and

(c)   correspond or are similar to those of an authority for the time being specified in section 1(3).

(6) For the purposes of the power conferred by subsection (4) on the Welsh Ministers, "relevant authority" means an authority whose functions –

(a)   are exercisable only in or as regards Wales,

(b)   are wholly or mainly devolved Welsh functions, and

(c)   correspond or are similar to those of an authority for the time being specified in subsection (3) of section 1 or referred to in subsection (4) of that section.

(7) Before making regulations under this section, the Scottish Ministers or the Welsh Ministers must consult a Minister of the Crown.

(8) Regulations under this section may make any amendments of section 1 that appear to the Minister or Ministers to be necessary or expedient in consequence of provision made under subsection (1) or (as the case may be) subsection (4).

(9) Provision made by the Scottish Ministers or the Welsh Ministers in reliance on subsection (8) may, in particular, amend section 1 so as to –

    (a)   confer on the Ministers a power to issue guidance;

    (b)   require a relevant authority to take into account any guidance issued under a power conferred by virtue of paragraph (a);

    (c)   disapply section 1(2) in consequence of the imposition of a requirement by virtue of paragraph (b).

(10) Before issuing guidance under a power conferred by virtue of subsection (9)(a), the Ministers must –

    (a)   take into account any guidance issued by a Minister of the Crown under section 1;

    (b)   consult a Minister of the Crown.

(11) For the purposes of this section –

    (a)   a function is a devolved Scottish function if it is exercisable in or as regards Scotland and it does not relate to reserved matters (within the meaning of the Scotland Act 1998);

    (b)   a function is a devolved Welsh function if it relates to a matter in respect of which functions are exercisable by the Welsh Ministers, the First Minister for Wales or the Counsel General to the Welsh Assembly Government, or to a matter within the legislative competence of the National Assembly for Wales.

3 Enforcement

A failure in respect of a performance of a duty under section 1 does not confer a cause of action at private law.

PART 2
EQUALITY: KEY CONCEPTS

Chapter 1
Protected characteristics

4 The protected characteristics

The following characteristics are protected characteristics –

    age;
    disability;
    gender reassignment;
    marriage and civil partnership;
    pregnancy and maternity;
    race;
    religion or belief;
    sex;
    sexual orientation.

5 Age

(1) In relation to the protected characteristic of age –

   (a)   a reference to a person who has a particular protected characteristic is a reference to a person of a particular age group;

   (b)   a reference to persons who share a protected characteristic is a reference to persons of the same age group.

(2) A reference to an age group is a reference to a group of persons defined by reference to age, whether by reference to a particular age or to a range of ages.

6 Disability

(1) A person (P) has a disability if –

   (a)   P has a physical or mental impairment, and

   (b)   the impairment has a substantial and long-term adverse effect on P's ability to carry out normal day-to-day activities.

(2) A reference to a disabled person is a reference to a person who has a disability.

(3) In relation to the protected characteristic of disability –

   (a)   a reference to a person who has a particular protected characteristic is a reference to a person who has a particular disability;

   (b)   a reference to persons who share a protected characteristic is a reference to persons who have the same disability.

(4) This Act (except Part 12 and section 190) applies in relation to a person who has had a disability as it applies in relation to a person who has the disability; accordingly (except in that Part and that section) –

   (a)   a reference (however expressed) to a person who has a disability includes a reference to a person who has had the disability, and

   (b)   a reference (however expressed) to a person who does not have a disability includes a reference to a person who has not had the disability.

(5) A Minister of the Crown may issue guidance about matters to be taken into account in deciding any question for the purposes of subsection (1).

(6) Schedule 1 (disability: supplementary provision) has effect.

7 Gender reassignment

(1) A person has the protected characteristic of gender reassignment if the person is proposing to undergo, is undergoing or has undergone a process (or part of a process) for the purpose of reassigning the person's sex by changing physiological or other attributes of sex.

(2) A reference to a transsexual person is a reference to a person who has the protected characteristic of gender reassignment.

(3) In relation to the protected characteristic of gender reassignment –

   (a)   a reference to a person who has a particular protected characteristic is a reference to a transsexual person;

   (b)   a reference to persons who share a protected characteristic is a reference to transsexual persons.

8 Marriage and civil partnership

(1) A person has the protected characteristic of marriage and civil partnership if the person is married or is a civil partner.

(2) In relation to the protected characteristic of marriage and civil partnership –

(a)   a reference to a person who has a particular protected characteristic is a reference to a person who is married or is a civil partner;

(b)   a reference to persons who share a protected characteristic is a reference to persons who are married or are civil partners.

9 Race

(1) Race includes –

(a)   colour;

(b)   nationality;

(c)   ethnic or national origins.

(2) In relation to the protected characteristic of race –

(a)   a reference to a person who has a particular protected characteristic is a reference to a person of a particular racial group;

(b)   a reference to persons who share a protected characteristic is a reference to persons of the same racial group.

(3) A racial group is a group of persons defined by reference to race; and a reference to a person's racial group is a reference to a racial group into which the person falls.

(4) The fact that a racial group comprises two or more distinct racial groups does not prevent it from constituting a particular racial group.

(5) A Minister of the Crown may by order –

(a)   amend this section so as to provide for caste to be an aspect of race;

(b)   amend this Act so as to provide for an exception to a provision of this Act to apply, or not to apply, to caste or to apply, or not to apply, to caste in specified circumstances.

(6) The power under section 207(4)(b), in its application to subsection (5), includes power to amend this Act.

10 Religion or belief

(1) Religion means any religion and a reference to religion includes a reference to a lack of religion.

(2) Belief means any religious or philosophical belief and a reference to belief includes a reference to a lack of belief.

(3) In relation to the protected characteristic of religion or belief –

(a)   a reference to a person who has a particular protected characteristic is a reference to a person of a particular religion or belief;

(b)   a reference to persons who share a protected characteristic is a reference to persons who are of the same religion or belief.

11 Sex

In relation to the protected characteristic of sex –

(a) a reference to a person who has a particular protected characteristic is a reference to a man or to a woman;

(b) a reference to persons who share a protected characteristic is a reference to persons of the same sex.

12 Sexual orientation

(1) Sexual orientation means a person's sexual orientation towards –

    (a)   persons of the same sex,
    (b)   persons of the opposite sex, or
    (c)   persons of either sex.

(2) In relation to the protected characteristic of sexual orientation –

    (a)   a reference to a person who has a particular protected characteristic is a reference to a person who is of a particular sexual orientation;
    (b)   a reference to persons who share a protected characteristic is a reference to persons who are of the same sexual orientation.

Chapter 2
Prohibited conduct

Discrimination

13 Direct discrimination

(1) A person (A) discriminates against another (B) if, because of a protected characteristic, A treats B less favourably than A treats or would treat others.

(2) If the protected characteristic is age, A does not discriminate against B if A can show A's treatment of B to be a proportionate means of achieving a legitimate aim.

(3) If the protected characteristic is disability, and B is not a disabled person, A does not discriminate against B only because A treats or would treat disabled persons more favourably than A treats B.

(4) If the protected characteristic is marriage and civil partnership, this section applies to a contravention of Part 5 (work) only if the treatment is because it is B who is married or a civil partner.

(5) If the protected characteristic is race, less favourable treatment includes segregating B from others.

(6) If the protected characteristic is sex –

    (a)   less favourable treatment of a woman includes less favourable treatment of her because she is breast-feeding;
    (b)   in a case where B is a man, no account is to be taken of special treatment afforded to a woman in connection with pregnancy or childbirth.

(7) Subsection (6)(a) does not apply for the purposes of Part 5 (work).

(8) This section is subject to sections 17(6) and 18(7).

14 Combined discrimination: dual characteristics

(1) A person (A) discriminates against another (B) if, because of a combination of two relevant protected characteristics, A treats B less favourably than A treats or would treat a person who does not share either of those characteristics.

(2) The relevant protected characteristics are –

   (a)   age;
   (b)   disability;
   (c)   gender reassignment;
   (d)   race;
   (e)   religion or belief;
   (f)   sex;
   (g)   sexual orientation.

(3) For the purposes of establishing a contravention of this Act by virtue of subsection (1), B need not show that A's treatment of B is direct discrimination because of each of the characteristics in the combination (taken separately).

(4) But B cannot establish a contravention of this Act by virtue of subsection (1) if, in reliance on another provision of this Act or any other enactment, A shows that A's treatment of B is not direct discrimination because of either or both of the characteristics in the combination.

(5) Subsection (1) does not apply to a combination of characteristics that includes disability in circumstances where, if a claim of direct discrimination because of disability were to be brought, it would come within section 116 (special educational needs).

(6) A Minister of the Crown may by order amend this section so as to –

   (a)   make further provision about circumstances in which B can, or in which B cannot, establish a contravention of this Act by virtue of subsection (1);
   (b)   specify other circumstances in which subsection (1) does not apply.

(7) The references to direct discrimination are to a contravention of this Act by virtue of section 13.

15 Discrimination arising from disability

(1) A person (A) discriminates against a disabled person (B) if –

   (a)   A treats B unfavourably because of something arising in consequence of B's disability, and
   (b)   A cannot show that the treatment is a proportionate means of achieving a legitimate aim.

(2) Subsection (1) does not apply if A shows that A did not know, and could not reasonably have been expected to know, that B had the disability.

16 Gender reassignment discrimination: cases of absence from work

(1) This section has effect for the purposes of the application of Part 5 (work) to the protected characteristic of gender reassignment.

(2) A person (A) discriminates against a transsexual person (B) if, in relation to an absence of B's that is because of gender reassignment, A treats B less favourably than A would treat B if –

(a)   B's absence was because of sickness or injury, or
(b)   B's absence was for some other reason and it is not reasonable for B to be treated less favourably.

(3) A person's absence is because of gender reassignment if it is because the person is proposing to undergo, is undergoing or has undergone the process (or part of the process) mentioned in section 7(1).

17 Pregnancy and maternity discrimination: non-work cases

(1) This section has effect for the purposes of the application to the protected characteristic of pregnancy and maternity of –

(a)   Part 3 (services and public functions);
(b)   Part 4 (premises);
(c)   Part 6 (education);
(d)   Part 7 (associations).

(2) A person (A) discriminates against a woman if A treats her unfavourably because of a pregnancy of hers.

(3) A person (A) discriminates against a woman if, in the period of 26 weeks beginning with the day on which she gives birth, A treats her unfavourably because she has given birth.

(4) The reference in subsection (3) to treating a woman unfavourably because she has given birth includes, in particular, a reference to treating her unfavourably because she is breast-feeding.

(5) For the purposes of this section, the day on which a woman gives birth is the day on which –

(a)   she gives birth to a living child, or
(b)   she gives birth to a dead child (more than 24 weeks of the pregnancy having passed).

(6) Section 13, so far as relating to sex discrimination, does not apply to anything done in relation to a woman in so far as –

(a)   it is for the reason mentioned in subsection (2), or
(b)   it is in the period, and for the reason, mentioned in subsection (3).

18 Pregnancy and maternity discrimination: work cases

(1) This section has effect for the purposes of the application of Part 5 (work) to the protected characteristic of pregnancy and maternity.

(2) A person (A) discriminates against a woman if, in the protected period in relation to a pregnancy of hers, A treats her unfavourably –

(a)   because of the pregnancy, or
(b)   because of illness suffered by her as a result of it.

(3) A person (A) discriminates against a woman if A treats her unfavourably because she is on compulsory maternity leave.

(4) A person (A) discriminates against a woman if A treats her unfavourably because she is exercising or seeking to exercise, or has exercised or sought to exercise, the right to ordinary or additional maternity leave.

(5) For the purposes of subsection (2), if the treatment of a woman is in implementation of a decision taken in the protected period, the treatment is to be regarded as occurring in that period (even if the implementation is not until after the end of that period).

(6) The protected period, in relation to a woman's pregnancy, begins when the pregnancy begins, and ends –

    (a)   if she has the right to ordinary and additional maternity leave, at the end of the additional maternity leave period or (if earlier) when she returns to work after the pregnancy;

    (b)   if she does not have that right, at the end of the period of 2 weeks beginning with the end of the pregnancy.

(7) Section 13, so far as relating to sex discrimination, does not apply to treatment of a woman in so far as –

    (a)   it is in the protected period in relation to her and is for a reason mentioned in paragraph (a) or (b) of subsection (2), or

    (b)   it is for a reason mentioned in subsection (3) or (4).

19 Indirect discrimination

(1) A person (A) discriminates against another (B) if A applies to B a provision, criterion or practice which is discriminatory in relation to a relevant protected characteristic of B's.

(2) For the purposes of subsection (1), a provision, criterion or practice is discriminatory in relation to a relevant protected characteristic of B's if –

    (a)   A applies, or would apply, it to persons with whom B does not share the characteristic,

    (b)   it puts, or would put, persons with whom B shares the characteristic at a particular disadvantage when compared with persons with whom B does not share it,

    (c)   it puts, or would put, B at that disadvantage, and

    (d)   A cannot show it to be a proportionate means of achieving a legitimate aim.

(3) The relevant protected characteristics are –

age;
disability;
gender reassignment;
marriage and civil partnership;
race;
religion or belief;
sex;
sexual orientation.

Adjustments for disabled persons

20 Duty to make adjustments

(1) Where this Act imposes a duty to make reasonable adjustments on a person, this section, sections 21 and 22 and the applicable Schedule apply; and for those purposes, a person on whom the duty is imposed is referred to as A.

(2) The duty comprises the following three requirements.

(3) The first requirement is a requirement, where a provision, criterion or practice of A's puts a disabled person at a substantial disadvantage in relation to a relevant matter in comparison with persons who are not disabled, to take such steps as it is reasonable to have to take to avoid the disadvantage.

(4) The second requirement is a requirement, where a physical feature puts a disabled person at a substantial disadvantage in relation to a relevant matter in comparison with persons who are not disabled, to take such steps as it is reasonable to have to take to avoid the disadvantage.

(5) The third requirement is a requirement, where a disabled person would, but for the provision of an auxiliary aid, be put at a substantial disadvantage in relation to a relevant matter in comparison with persons who are not disabled, to take such steps as it is reasonable to have to take to provide the auxiliary aid.

(6) Where the first or third requirement relates to the provision of information, the steps which it is reasonable for A to have to take include steps for ensuring that in the circumstances concerned the information is provided in an accessible format.

(7) A person (A) who is subject to a duty to make reasonable adjustments is not (subject to express provision to the contrary) entitled to require a disabled person, in relation to whom A is required to comply with the duty, to pay to any extent A's costs of complying with the duty.

(8) A reference in section 21 or 22 or an applicable Schedule to the first, second or third requirement is to be construed in accordance with this section.

(9) In relation to the second requirement, a reference in this section or an applicable Schedule to avoiding a substantial disadvantage includes a reference to –

(a)   removing the physical feature in question,
(b)   altering it, or
(c)   providing a reasonable means of avoiding it.

(10) A reference in this section, section 21 or 22 or an applicable Schedule (apart from paragraphs 2 to 4 of Schedule 4) to a physical feature is a reference to –

(a)   a feature arising from the design or construction of a building,
(b)   a feature of an approach to, exit from or access to a building,
(c)   a fixture or fitting, or furniture, furnishings, materials, equipment or other chattels, in or on premises, or
(d)   any other physical element or quality.

(11) A reference in this section, section 21 or 22 or an applicable Schedule to an auxiliary aid includes a reference to an auxiliary service.

(12) A reference in this section or an applicable Schedule to chattels is to be read, in relation to Scotland, as a reference to moveable property.

(13) The applicable Schedule is, in relation to the Part of this Act specified in the first column of the Table, the Schedule specified in the second column.

Part of this Act	*Applicable Schedule*
Part 3 (services and public functions)	Schedule 2
Part 4 (premises)	Schedule 4
Part 5 (work)	Schedule 8

Part 6 (education)   Schedule 13

Part 7 (associations)   Schedule 15

Each of the Parts mentioned above   Schedule 21

21 Failure to comply with duty

(1) A failure to comply with the first, second or third requirement is a failure to comply with a duty to make reasonable adjustments.

(2) A discriminates against a disabled person if A fails to comply with that duty in relation to that person.

(3) A provision of an applicable Schedule which imposes a duty to comply with the first, second or third requirement applies only for the purpose of establishing whether A has contravened this Act by virtue of subsection (2); a failure to comply is, accordingly, not actionable by virtue of another provision of this Act or otherwise.

22 Regulations

(1) Regulations may prescribe –

   (a)   matters to be taken into account in deciding whether it is reasonable for A to take a step for the purposes of a prescribed provision of an applicable Schedule;
   (b)   descriptions of persons to whom the first, second or third requirement does not apply.

(2) Regulations may make provision as to –

   (a)   circumstances in which it is, or in which it is not, reasonable for a person of a prescribed description to have to take steps of a prescribed description;
   (b)   what is, or what is not, a provision, criterion or practice;
   (c)   things which are, or which are not, to be treated as physical features;
   (d)   things which are, or which are not, to be treated as alterations of physical features;
   (e)   things which are, or which are not, to be treated as auxiliary aids.

(3) Provision made by virtue of this section may amend an applicable Schedule.

Discrimination: supplementary

23 Comparison by reference to circumstances

(1) On a comparison of cases for the purposes of section 13, 14, or 19 there must be no material difference between the circumstances relating to each case.

(2) The circumstances relating to a case include a person's abilities if –

   (a)   on a comparison for the purposes of section 13, the protected characteristic is disability;
   (b)   on a comparison for the purposes of section 14, one of the protected characteristics in the combination is disability.

(3) If the protected characteristic is sexual orientation, the fact that one person (whether or not the person referred to as B) is a civil partner while another is married is not a material difference between the circumstances relating to each case.

24 Irrelevance of alleged discriminator's characteristics

(1) For the purpose of establishing a contravention of this Act by virtue of section 13(1), it does not matter whether A has the protected characteristic.

(2) For the purpose of establishing a contravention of this Act by virtue of section 14(1), it does not matter –

    (a)   whether A has one of the protected characteristics in the combination;
    (b)   whether A has both.

25 References to particular strands of discrimination

(1) Age discrimination is –

    (a)   discrimination within section 13 because of age;
    (b)   discrimination within section 19 where the relevant protected characteristic is age.

(2) Disability discrimination is –

    (a)   discrimination within section 13 because of disability;
    (b)   discrimination within section 15;
    (c)   discrimination within section 19 where the relevant protected characteristic is disability;
    (d)   discrimination within section 21.

(3) Gender reassignment discrimination is –

    (a)   discrimination within section 13 because of gender reassignment;
    (b)   discrimination within section 16;
    (c)   discrimination within section 19 where the relevant protected characteristic is gender reassignment.

(4) Marriage and civil partnership discrimination is –

    (a)   discrimination within section 13 because of marriage and civil partnership;
    (b)   discrimination within section 19 where the relevant protected characteristic is marriage and civil partnership.

(5) Pregnancy and maternity discrimination is discrimination within section 17 or 18.

(6) Race discrimination is –

    (a)   discrimination within section 13 because of race;
    (b)   discrimination within section 19 where the relevant protected characteristic is race.

(7) Religious or belief-related discrimination is –

    (a)   discrimination within section 13 because of religion or belief;
    (b)   discrimination within section 19 where the relevant protected characteristic is religion or belief.

(8) Sex discrimination is –

    (a)   discrimination within section 13 because of sex;
    (b)   discrimination within section 19 where the relevant protected characteristic is sex.

(9) Sexual orientation discrimination is –

(a) discrimination within section 13 because of sexual orientation;
(b) discrimination within section 19 where the relevant protected characteristic is sexual orientation.

Other prohibited conduct

26 Harassment

(1) A person (A) harasses another (B) if –

(a) A engages in unwanted conduct related to a relevant protected characteristic, and
(b) the conduct has the purpose or effect of –
  (i) violating B's dignity, or
  (ii) creating an intimidating, hostile, degrading, humiliating or offensive environment for B.

(2) A also harasses B if –

(a) A engages in unwanted conduct of a sexual nature, and
(b) the conduct has the purpose or effect referred to in subsection (1)(b).

(3) A also harasses B if –

(a) A or another person engages in unwanted conduct of a sexual nature or that is related to gender reassignment or sex,
(b) the conduct has the purpose or effect referred to in subsection (1)(b), and
(c) because of B's rejection of or submission to the conduct, A treats B less favourably than A would treat B if B had not rejected or submitted to the conduct.

(4) In deciding whether conduct has the effect referred to in subsection (1)(b), each of the following must be taken into account –

(a) the perception of B;
(b) the other circumstances of the case;
(c) whether it is reasonable for the conduct to have that effect.

(5) The relevant protected characteristics are –

age;
disability;
gender reassignment;
race;
religion or belief;
sex;
sexual orientation.

27 Victimisation

(1) A person (A) victimises another person (B) if A subjects B to a detriment because –

(a) B does a protected act, or
(b) A believes that B has done, or may do, a protected act.

(2) Each of the following is a protected act –

(a) bringing proceedings under this Act;
(b) giving evidence or information in connection with proceedings under this Act;

(c)   doing any other thing for the purposes of or in connection with this Act;

(d)   making an allegation (whether or not express) that A or another person has contravened this Act.

(3) Giving false evidence or information, or making a false allegation, is not a protected act if the evidence or information is given, or the allegation is made, in bad faith.

(4) This section applies only where the person subjected to a detriment is an individual.

(5) The reference to contravening this Act includes a reference to committing a breach of an equality clause or rule.

PART 3
SERVICES AND PUBLIC FUNCTIONS

Preliminary

28 Application of this Part

(1) This Part does not apply to the protected characteristic of –

(a)   age, so far as relating to persons who have not attained the age of 18;

(b)   marriage and civil partnership.

(2) This Part does not apply to discrimination, harassment or victimisation –

(a)   that is prohibited by Part 4 (premises), 5 (work) or 6 (education), or

(b)   that would be so prohibited but for an express exception.

(3) This Part does not apply to –

(a)   a breach of an equality clause or rule;

(b)   anything that would be a breach of an equality clause or rule but for section 69 or Part 2 of Schedule 7;

(c)   a breach of a non-discrimination rule.

Provision of services, etc.

29 Provision of services, etc.

(1) A person (a "service-provider") concerned with the provision of a service to the public or a section of the public (for payment or not) must not discriminate against a person requiring the service by not providing the person with the service.

(2) A service-provider (A) must not, in providing the service, discriminate against a person (B) –

(a)   as to the terms on which A provides the service to B;

(b)   by terminating the provision of the service to B;

(c)   by subjecting B to any other detriment.

(3) A service-provider must not, in relation to the provision of the service, harass –

(a)   a person requiring the service, or

(b)   a person to whom the service-provider provides the service.

(4) A service-provider must not victimise a person requiring the service by not providing the person with the service.

(5) A service-provider (A) must not, in providing the service, victimise a person (B) –

(a)   as to the terms on which A provides the service to B;

(b)   by terminating the provision of the service to B;

(c)   by subjecting B to any other detriment.

(6) A person must not, in the exercise of a public function that is not the provision of a service to the public or a section of the public, do anything that constitutes discrimination, harassment or victimisation.

(7) A duty to make reasonable adjustments applies to –

(a)   a service-provider (and see also section 55(7));

(b)   a person who exercises a public function that is not the provision of a service to the public or a section of the public.

(8) In the application of section 26 for the purposes of subsection (3), and subsection (6) as it relates to harassment, neither of the following is a relevant protected characteristic –

(a)   religion or belief;

(b)   sexual orientation.

(9) In the application of this section, so far as relating to race or religion or belief, to the granting of entry clearance (within the meaning of the Immigration Act 1971), it does not matter whether an act is done within or outside the United Kingdom.

(10) Subsection (9) does not affect the application of any other provision of this Act to conduct outside England and Wales or Scotland.

Supplementary

30 Ships and hovercraft

(1) This Part (subject to subsection (2)) applies only in such circumstances as are prescribed in relation to –

(a)   transporting people by ship or hovercraft;

(b)   a service provided on a ship or hovercraft.

(2) Section 29(6) applies in relation to the matters referred to in paragraphs (a) and (b) of subsection (1); but in so far as it relates to disability discrimination, section 29(6) applies to those matters only in such circumstances as are prescribed.

(3) It does not matter whether the ship or hovercraft is within or outside the United Kingdom.

(4) "Ship" has the same meaning as in the Merchant Shipping Act 1995.

(5) "Hovercraft" has the same meaning as in the Hovercraft Act 1968.

(6) Nothing in this section affects the application of any other provision of this Act to conduct outside England and Wales or Scotland.

31 Interpretation and exceptions

(1) This section applies for the purposes of this Part.

(2) A reference to the provision of a service includes a reference to the provision of goods or facilities.

(3) A reference to the provision of a service includes a reference to the provision of a service in the exercise of a public function.

(4) A public function is a function that is a function of a public nature for the purposes of the Human Rights Act 1998.

(5) Where an employer arranges for another person to provide a service only to the employer's employees –

    (a)   the employer is not to be regarded as the service-provider, but
    (b)   the employees are to be regarded as a section of the public.

(6) A reference to a person requiring a service includes a reference to a person who is seeking to obtain or use the service.

(7) A reference to a service-provider not providing a person with a service includes a reference to –

    (a)   the service-provider not providing the person with a service of the quality that the service-provider usually provides to the public (or the section of it which includes the person), or
    (b)   the service-provider not providing the person with the service in the manner in which, or on the terms on which, the service-provider usually provides the service to the public (or the section of it which includes the person).

(8) In relation to the provision of a service by either House of Parliament, the service-provider is the Corporate Officer of the House concerned; and if the service involves access to, or use of, a place in the Palace of Westminster which members of the public are allowed to enter, both Corporate Officers are jointly the service-provider.

(9) Schedule 2 (reasonable adjustments) has effect.

(10) Schedule 3 (exceptions) has effect.

PART 4
PREMISES

Preliminary

32 Application of this Part

(1) This Part does not apply to the following protected characteristics –

    (a)   age;
    (b)   marriage and civil partnership.

(2) This Part does not apply to discrimination, harassment or victimisation –

    (a)   that is prohibited by Part 5 (work) or Part 6 (education), or
    (b)   that would be so prohibited but for an express exception.

(3) This Part does not apply to the provision of accommodation if the provision –

    (a)   is generally for the purpose of short stays by individuals who live elsewhere, or
    (b)   is for the purpose only of exercising a public function or providing a service to the public or a section of the public.

(4) The reference to the exercise of a public function, and the reference to the provision of a service, are to be construed in accordance with Part 3.

(5) This Part does not apply to –

    (a)   a breach of an equality clause or rule;

(b)   anything that would be a breach of an equality clause or rule but for section 69 or Part 2 of Schedule 7;

(c)   a breach of a non-discrimination rule.

Disposal and management

33 Disposals, etc.

(1) A person (A) who has the right to dispose of premises must not discriminate against another (B) –

(a)   as to the terms on which A offers to dispose of the premises to B;

(b)   by not disposing of the premises to B;

(c)   in A's treatment of B with respect to things done in relation to persons seeking premises.

(2) Where an interest in a commonhold unit cannot be disposed of unless a particular person is a party to the disposal, that person must not discriminate against a person by not being a party to the disposal.

(3) A person who has the right to dispose of premises must not, in connection with anything done in relation to their occupation or disposal, harass –

(a)   a person who occupies them;

(b)   a person who applies for them.

(4) A person (A) who has the right to dispose of premises must not victimise another (B) –

(a)   as to the terms on which A offers to dispose of the premises to B;

(b)   by not disposing of the premises to B;

(c)   in A's treatment of B with respect to things done in relation to persons seeking premises.

(5) Where an interest in a commonhold unit cannot be disposed of unless a particular person is a party to the disposal, that person must not victimise a person by not being a party to the disposal.

(6) In the application of section 26 for the purposes of subsection (3), neither of the following is a relevant protected characteristic –

(a)   religion or belief;

(b)   sexual orientation.

34 Permission for disposal

(1) A person whose permission is required for the disposal of premises must not discriminate against another by not giving permission for the disposal of the premises to the other.

(2) A person whose permission is required for the disposal of premises must not, in relation to an application for permission to dispose of the premises, harass a person –

(a)   who applies for permission to dispose of the premises, or

(b)   to whom the disposal would be made if permission were given.

(3) A person whose permission is required for the disposal of premises must not victimise another by not giving permission for the disposal of the premises to the other.

(4) In the application of section 26 for the purposes of subsection (2), neither of the following is a relevant protected characteristic –

 (a)   religion or belief;
 (b)   sexual orientation.

(5) This section does not apply to anything done in the exercise of a judicial function.

35 Management

(1) A person (A) who manages premises must not discriminate against a person (B) who occupies the premises –

 (a)   in the way in which A allows B, or by not allowing B, to make use of a benefit or facility;
 (b)   by evicting (or taking steps for the purpose of securing B's eviction);
 (c)   by subjecting to any other detriment.

(2) A person who manages premises must not, in relation to their management, harass –

 (a)   a person who occupies them;
 (b)   a person who applies for them.

(3) A person (A) who manages premises must not victimise a person (B) who occupies the premises –

 (a)   in the way in which A allows B, or by not allowing B, to make use of a benefit or facility;
 (b)   by evicting (or taking steps for the purpose of securing B's eviction);
 (c)   by subjecting B to any other detriment.

(4) In the application of section 26 for the purposes of subsection (2), neither of the following is a relevant protected characteristic –

 (a)   religion or belief;
 (b)   sexual orientation.

Reasonable adjustments

36 Leasehold and commonhold premises and common parts

(1) A duty to make reasonable adjustments applies to –

 (a)   a controller of let premises;
 (b)   a controller of premises to let;
 (c)   a commonhold association;
 (d)   a responsible person in relation to common parts.

(2) A controller of let premises is –

 (a)   a person by whom premises are let, or
 (b)   a person who manages them.

(3) A controller of premises to let is –

 (a)   a person who has premises to let, or
 (b)   a person who manages them.

(4) The reference in subsection (1)(c) to a commonhold association is a reference to the association in its capacity as the person who manages a commonhold unit.

(5) A responsible person in relation to common parts is –

(a) where the premises to which the common parts relate are let (and are not part of commonhold land or in Scotland), a person by whom the premises are let;

(b) where the premises to which the common parts relate are part of commonhold land, the commonhold association.

(6) Common parts are –

(a) in relation to let premises (which are not part of commonhold land or in Scotland), the structure and exterior of, and any common facilities within or used in connection with, the building or part of a building which includes the premises;

(b) in relation to commonhold land, every part of the commonhold which is not for the time being a commonhold unit in accordance with the commonhold community statement.

(7) A reference to letting includes a reference to sub-letting; and for the purposes of subsection (1)(a) and (b), a reference to let premises includes premises subject to a right to occupy.

(8) This section does not apply to premises of such description as may be prescribed.

37 Adjustments to common parts in Scotland

(1) The Scottish Ministers may by regulations provide that a disabled person is entitled to make relevant adjustments to common parts in relation to premises in Scotland.

(2) The reference in subsection (1) to a disabled person is a reference to a disabled person who –

(a) is a tenant of the premises,

(b) is an owner of the premises, or

(c) is otherwise entitled to occupy the premises,

and uses or intends to use the premises as the person's only or main home.

(3) Before making regulations under subsection (1), the Scottish Ministers must consult a Minister of the Crown.

(4) Regulations under subsection (1) may, in particular –

(a) prescribe things which are, or which are not, to be treated as relevant adjustments;

(b) prescribe circumstances in which the consent of an owner of the common parts is required before a disabled person may make an adjustment;

(c) provide that the consent to adjustments is not to be withheld unreasonably;

(d) prescribe matters to be taken into account, or to be disregarded, in deciding whether it is reasonable to consent to adjustments;

(e) prescribe circumstances in which consent to adjustments is to be taken to be withheld;

(f) make provision about the imposition of conditions on consent to adjustments;

(g) make provision as to circumstances in which the sheriff may make an order authorising a disabled person to carry out adjustments;

(h) make provision about the responsibility for costs arising (directly or indirectly) from an adjustment;

(i) make provision about the reinstatement of the common parts to the condition they were in before an adjustment was made;

(j)   make provision about the giving of notice to the owners of the common parts and other persons;

(k)   make provision about agreements between a disabled person and an owner of the common parts;

(l)   make provision about the registration of information in the Land Register of Scotland or the recording of documents in the Register of Sasines relating to an entitlement of a disabled person or an obligation on an owner of the common parts;

(m)   make provision about the effect of such registration or recording;

(n)   make provision about who is to be treated as being, or as not being, a person entitled to occupy premises otherwise than as tenant or owner.

(5) In this section –

"common parts" means, in relation to premises, the structure and exterior of, and any common facilities within or used in connection with, the building or part of a building which includes the premises but only in so far as the structure, exterior and common facilities are not solely owned by the owner of the premises;

"relevant adjustments" means, in relation to a disabled person, alterations or additions which are likely to avoid a substantial disadvantage to which the disabled person is put in using the common parts in comparison with persons who are not disabled.

Supplementary

38 Interpretation and exceptions

(1) This section applies for the purposes of this Part.

(2) A reference to premises is a reference to the whole or part of the premises.

(3) A reference to disposing of premises includes, in the case of premises subject to a tenancy, a reference to –

(a)   assigning the premises,
(b)   sub-letting them, or
(c)   parting with possession of them.

(4) A reference to disposing of premises also includes a reference to granting a right to occupy them.

(5) A reference to disposing of an interest in a commonhold unit includes a reference to creating an interest in a commonhold unit.

(6) A reference to a tenancy is to a tenancy created (whether before or after the passing of this Act) –

(a)   by a lease or sub-lease,
(b)   by an agreement for a lease or sub-lease,
(c)   by a tenancy agreement, or
(d)   in pursuance of an enactment,

and a reference to a tenant is to be construed accordingly.

(7) A reference to commonhold land, a commonhold association, a commonhold community statement, a commonhold unit or a unit-holder is to be construed in accordance with the Commonhold and Leasehold Reform Act 2002.

(8) Schedule 4 (reasonable adjustments) has effect.

(9) Schedule 5 (exceptions) has effect.

PART 5
WORK

Chapter 1
Employment, etc.

Employees

39 Employees and applicants

(1) An employer (A) must not discriminate against a person (B) –

    (a)   in the arrangements A makes for deciding to whom to offer employment;
    (b)   as to the terms on which A offers B employment;
    (c)   by not offering B employment.

(2) An employer (A) must not discriminate against an employee of A's (B) –

    (a)   as to B's terms of employment;
    (b)   in the way A affords B access, or by not affording B access, to opportunities for promotion, transfer or training or for receiving any other benefit, facility or service;
    (c)   by dismissing B;
    (d)   by subjecting B to any other detriment.

(3) An employer (A) must not victimise a person (B) –

    (a)   in the arrangements A makes for deciding to whom to offer employment;
    (b)   as to the terms on which A offers B employment;
    (c)   by not offering B employment.

(4) An employer (A) must not victimise an employee of A's (B) –

    (a)   as to B's terms of employment;
    (b)   in the way A affords B access, or by not affording B access, to opportunities for promotion, transfer or training or for any other benefit, facility or service;
    (c)   by dismissing B;
    (d)   by subjecting B to any other detriment.

(5) A duty to make reasonable adjustments applies to an employer.

(6) Subsection (1)(b), so far as relating to sex or pregnancy and maternity, does not apply to a term that relates to pay –

    (a)   unless, were B to accept the offer, an equality clause or rule would have effect in relation to the term, or
    (b)   if paragraph (a) does not apply, except in so far as making an offer on terms including that term amounts to a contravention of subsection (1)(b) by virtue of section 13, 14 or 18.

(7) In subsections (2)(c) and (4)(c), the reference to dismissing B includes a reference to the termination of B's employment –

    (a)   by the expiry of a period (including a period expiring by reference to an event or circumstance);
    (b)   by an act of B's (including giving notice) in circumstances such that B is entitled, because of A's conduct, to terminate the employment without notice.

(8) Subsection (7)(a) does not apply if, immediately after the termination, the employment is renewed on the same terms.

40 Employees and applicants: harassment

(1) An employer (A) must not, in relation to employment by A, harass a person (B) –

  (a)   who is an employee of A's;
  (b)   who has applied to A for employment.

(2) The circumstances in which A is to be treated as harassing B under subsection (1) include those where –

  (a)   a third party harasses B in the course of B's employment, and
  (b)   A failed to take such steps as would have been reasonably practicable to prevent the third party from doing so.

(3) Subsection (2) does not apply unless A knows that B has been harassed in the course of B's employment on at least two other occasions by a third party; and it does not matter whether the third party is the same or a different person on each occasion.

(4) A third party is a person other than –

  (a)   A, or
  (b)   an employee of A's.

41 Contract workers

(1) A principal must not discriminate against a contract worker –

  (a)   as to the terms on which the principal allows the worker to do the work;
  (b)   by not allowing the worker to do, or to continue to do, the work;
  (c)   in the way the principal affords the worker access, or by not affording the worker access, to opportunities for receiving a benefit, facility or service;
  (d)   by subjecting the worker to any other detriment.

(2) A principal must not, in relation to contract work, harass a contract worker.

(3) A principal must not victimise a contract worker –

  (a)   as to the terms on which the principal allows the worker to do the work;
  (b)   by not allowing the worker to do, or to continue to do, the work;
  (c)   in the way the principal affords the worker access, or by not affording the worker access, to opportunities for receiving a benefit, facility or service;
  (d)   by subjecting the worker to any other detriment.

(4) A duty to make reasonable adjustments applies to a principal (as well as to the employer of a contract worker).

(5) A "principal" is a person who makes work available for an individual who is –

  (a)   employed by another person, and
  (b)   supplied by that other person in furtherance of a contract to which the principal is a party (whether or not that other person is a party to it).

(6) "Contract work" is work such as is mentioned in subsection (5).

(7) A "contract worker" is an individual supplied to a principal in furtherance of a contract such as is mentioned in subsection (5)(b).

Police officers

42 Identity of employer

(1) For the purposes of this Part, holding the office of constable is to be treated as employment –

(a) by the chief officer, in respect of any act done by the chief officer in relation to a constable or appointment to the office of constable;

(b) by the responsible authority, in respect of any act done by the authority in relation to a constable or appointment to the office of constable.

(2) For the purposes of this Part, holding an appointment as a police cadet is to be treated as employment –

(a) by the chief officer, in respect of any act done by the chief officer in relation to a police cadet or appointment as one;

(b) by the responsible authority, in respect of any act done by the authority in relation to a police cadet or appointment as one.

(3) Subsection (1) does not apply to service with the Civil Nuclear Constabulary (as to which, see section 55(2) of the Energy Act 2004).

(4) Subsection (1) does not apply to a constable at SOCA, SPSA or SCDEA.

(5) A constable at SOCA or SPSA is to be treated as employed by it, in respect of any act done by it in relation to the constable.

(6) A constable at SCDEA is to be treated as employed by the Director General of SCDEA, in respect of any act done by the Director General in relation to the constable.

43 Interpretation

(1) This section applies for the purposes of section 42.

(2) "Chief officer" means –

(a) in relation to an appointment under a relevant Act, the chief officer of police for the police force to which the appointment relates;

(b) in relation to any other appointment, the person under whose direction and control the body of constables or other persons to which the appointment relates is;

(c) in relation to a constable or other person under the direction and control of a chief officer of police, that chief officer of police;

(d) in relation to any other constable or any other person, the person under whose direction and control the constable or other person is.

(3) "Responsible authority" means –

(a) in relation to an appointment under a relevant Act, the police authority that maintains the police force to which the appointment relates;

(b) in relation to any other appointment, the person by whom a person would (if appointed) be paid;

(c) in relation to a constable or other person under the direction and control of a chief officer of police, the police authority that maintains the police force for which that chief officer is the chief officer of police;

(d) in relation to any other constable or any other person, the person by whom the constable or other person is paid.

(4) "Police cadet" means a person appointed to undergo training with a view to becoming a constable.

(5) "SOCA" means the Serious Organised Crime Agency; and a reference to a constable at SOCA is a reference to a constable seconded to it to serve as a member of its staff.

(6) "SPSA" means the Scottish Police Services Authority; and a reference to a constable at SPSA is a reference to a constable –

(a)   seconded to it to serve as a member of its staff, and
(b)   not at SCDEA.

(7) "SCDEA" means the Scottish Crime and Drugs Enforcement Agency; and a reference to a constable at SCDEA is a reference to a constable who is a police member of it by virtue of paragraph 7(2)(a) or (b) of Schedule 2 to the Police, Public Order and Criminal Justice (Scotland) Act 2006 (asp 10) (secondment).

(8) For the purposes of this section, the relevant Acts are –

(a)   the Metropolitan Police Act 1829;
(b)   the City of London Police Act 1839;
(c)   the Police (Scotland) Act 1967;
(d)   the Police Act 1996.

(9) A reference in subsection (2) or (3) to a chief officer of police includes, in relation to Scotland, a reference to a chief constable.

Partners

44 Partnerships

(1) A firm or proposed firm must not discriminate against a person –

(a)   in the arrangements it makes for deciding to whom to offer a position as a partner;
(b)   as to the terms on which it offers the person a position as a partner;
(c)   by not offering the person a position as a partner.

(2) A firm (A) must not discriminate against a partner (B) –

(a)   as to the terms on which B is a partner;
(b)   in the way A affords B access, or by not affording B access, to opportunities for promotion, transfer or training or for receiving any other benefit, facility or service;
(c)   by expelling B;
(d)   by subjecting B to any other detriment.

(3) A firm must not, in relation to a position as a partner, harass –

(a)   a partner;
(b)   a person who has applied for the position.

(4) A proposed firm must not, in relation to a position as a partner, harass a person who has applied for the position.

(5) A firm or proposed firm must not victimise a person –

(a)   in the arrangements it makes for deciding to whom to offer a position as a partner;
(b)   as to the terms on which it offers the person a position as a partner;

(c)   by not offering the person a position as a partner.

(6) A firm (A) must not victimise a partner (B) –

(a)   as to the terms on which B is a partner;
(b)   in the way A affords B access, or by not affording B access, to opportunities for promotion, transfer or training or for receiving any other benefit, facility or service;
(c)   by expelling B;
(d)   by subjecting to any other detriment.

(7) A duty to make reasonable adjustments applies to –

(a)   a firm;
(b)   a proposed firm.

(8) In the application of this section to a limited partnership within the meaning of the Limited Partnerships Act 1907, "partner" means a general partner within the meaning of that Act.

45 Limited liability partnerships

(1) An LLP or proposed LLP must not discriminate against a person –

(a)   in the arrangements it makes for deciding to whom to offer a position as a member;
(b)   as to the terms on which it offers the person a position as a member;
(c)   by not offering the person a position as a member.

(2) An LLP (A) must not discriminate against a member (B) –

(a)   as to the terms on which B is a member;
(b)   in the way A affords B access, or by not affording B access, to opportunities for promotion, transfer or training or for receiving any other benefit, facility or service;
(c)   by expelling B;
(d)   by subjecting B to any other detriment.

(3) An LLP must not, in relation to a position as a member, harass –

(a)   a member;
(b)   a person who has applied for the position.

(4) A proposed LLP must not, in relation to a position as a member, harass a person who has applied for the position.

(5) An LLP or proposed LLP must not victimise a person –

(a)   in the arrangements it makes for deciding to whom to offer a position as a member;
(b)   as to the terms on which it offers the person a position as a member;
(c)   by not offering the person a position as a member.

(6) An LLP (A) must not victimise a member (B) –

(a)   as to the terms on which B is a member;
(b)   in the way A affords B access, or by not affording B access, to opportunities for promotion, transfer or training or for receiving any other benefit, facility or service;
(c)   by expelling B;

(d)   by subjecting B to any other detriment.

(7) A duty to make reasonable adjustments applies to –

(a)   an LLP;
(b)   a proposed LLP.

46 Interpretation

(1) This section applies for the purposes of sections 44 and 45.

(2) "Partnership" and "firm" have the same meaning as in the Partnership Act 1890.

(3) "Proposed firm" means persons proposing to form themselves into a partnership.

(4) "LLP" means a limited liability partnership (within the meaning of the Limited Liability Partnerships Act 2000).

(5) "Proposed LLP" means persons proposing to incorporate an LLP with themselves as members.

(6) A reference to expelling a partner of a firm or a member of an LLP includes a reference to the termination of the person's position as such –

(a)   by the expiry of a period (including a period expiring by reference to an event or circumstance);
(b)   by an act of the person (including giving notice) in circumstances such that the person is entitled, because of the conduct of other partners or members, to terminate the position without notice;
(c)   (in the case of a partner of a firm) as a result of the dissolution of the partnership.

(7) Subsection (6)(a) and (c) does not apply if, immediately after the termination, the position is renewed on the same terms.

The Bar

47 Barristers

(1) A barrister (A) must not discriminate against a person (B) –

(a)   in the arrangements A makes for deciding to whom to offer a pupillage or tenancy;
(b)   as to the terms on which A offers B a pupillage or tenancy;
(c)   by not offering B a pupillage or tenancy.

(2) A barrister (A) must not discriminate against a person (B) who is a pupil or tenant –

(a)   as to the terms on which B is a pupil or tenant;
(b)   in the way A affords B access, or by not affording B access, to opportunities for training or gaining experience or for receiving any other benefit, facility or service;
(c)   by terminating the pupillage;
(d)   by subjecting B to pressure to leave chambers;
(e)   by subjecting B to any other detriment.

(3) A barrister must not, in relation to a pupillage or tenancy, harass –

(a)   the pupil or tenant;
(b)   a person who has applied for the pupillage or tenancy.

(4) A barrister (A) must not victimise a person (B) –

    (a)   in the arrangements A makes for deciding to whom to offer a pupillage or tenancy;

    (b)   as to the terms on which A offers B a pupillage or tenancy;

    (c)   by not offering B a pupillage or tenancy.

(5) A barrister (A) must not victimise a person (B) who is a pupil or tenant –

    (a)   as to the terms on which B is a pupil or tenant;

    (b)   in the way A affords B access, or by not affording B access, to opportunities for training or gaining experience or for receiving any other benefit, facility or service;

    (c)   by terminating the pupillage;

    (d)   by subjecting B to pressure to leave chambers;

    (e)   by subjecting B to any other detriment.

(6) A person must not, in relation to instructing a barrister –

    (a)   discriminate against a barrister by subjecting the barrister to a detriment;

    (b)   harass the barrister;

    (c)   victimise the barrister.

(7) A duty to make reasonable adjustments applies to a barrister.

(8) The preceding provisions of this section (apart from subsection (6)) apply in relation to a barrister's clerk as they apply in relation to a barrister; and for that purpose the reference to a barrister's clerk includes a reference to a person who carries out the functions of a barrister's clerk.

(9) A reference to a tenant includes a reference to a barrister who is permitted to work in chambers (including as a squatter or door tenant); and a reference to a tenancy is to be construed accordingly.

48 Advocates

(1) An advocate (A) must not discriminate against a person (B) –

    (a)   in the arrangements A makes for deciding who to take as A's devil or to whom to offer membership of a stable;

    (b)   as to the terms on which A offers to take B as A's devil or offers B membership of a stable;

    (c)   by not offering to take B as A's devil or not offering B membership of a stable.

(2) An advocate (A) must not discriminate against a person (B) who is a devil or a member of a stable –

    (a)   as to the terms on which B is a devil or a member of the stable;

    (b)   in the way A affords B access, or by not affording B access, to opportunities for training or gaining experience or for receiving any other benefit, facility or service;

    (c)   by terminating A's relationship with B (where B is a devil);

    (d)   by subjecting B to pressure to leave the stable;

    (e)   by subjecting B to any other detriment.

(3) An advocate must not, in relation to a relationship with a devil or membership of a stable, harass –

    (a)   a devil or member;

(b)   a person who has applied to be taken as the advocate's devil or to become a member of the stable.

(4) An advocate (A) must not victimise a person (B) –

(a)   in the arrangements A makes for deciding who to take as A's devil or to whom to offer membership of a stable;

(b)   as to the terms on which A offers to take B as A's devil or offers B membership of a stable;

(c)   by not offering to take B as A's devil or not offering B membership of a stable.

(5) An advocate (A) must not victimise a person (B) who is a devil or a member of a stable –

(a)   as to the terms on which B is a devil or a member of the stable;

(b)   in the way A affords B access, or by not affording B access, to opportunities for training or gaining experience or for receiving any other benefit, facility or service;

(c)   by terminating A's relationship with B (where B is a devil);

(d)   by subjecting B to pressure to leave the stable;

(e)   by subjecting B to any other detriment.

(6) A person must not, in relation to instructing an advocate –

(a)   discriminate against the advocate by subjecting the advocate to a detriment;

(b)   harass the advocate;

(c)   victimise the advocate.

(7) A duty to make reasonable adjustments applies to an advocate.

(8) This section (apart from subsection (6)) applies in relation to an advocate's clerk as it applies in relation to an advocate; and for that purpose the reference to an advocate's clerk includes a reference to a person who carries out the functions of an advocate's clerk.

(9) "Advocate" means a practising member of the Faculty of Advocates.

Office-holders

49 Personal offices: appointments, etc.

(1) This section applies in relation to personal offices.

(2) A personal office is an office or post –

(a)   to which a person is appointed to discharge a function personally under the direction of another person, and

(b)   in respect of which an appointed person is entitled to remuneration.

(3) A person (A) who has the power to make an appointment to a personal office must not discriminate against a person (B) –

(a)   in the arrangements A makes for deciding to whom to offer the appointment;

(b)   as to the terms on which A offers B the appointment;

(c)   by not offering B the appointment.

(4) A person who has the power to make an appointment to a personal office must not, in relation to the office, harass a person seeking, or being considered for, the appointment.

(5) A person (A) who has the power to make an appointment to a personal office must not victimise a person (B) –

(a) in the arrangements A makes for deciding to whom to offer the appointment;
(b) as to the terms on which A offers B the appointment;
(c) by not offering B the appointment.

(6) A person (A) who is a relevant person in relation to a personal office must not discriminate against a person (B) appointed to the office –

(a) as to the terms of B's appointment;
(b) in the way A affords B access, or by not affording B access, to opportunities for promotion, transfer or training or for receiving any other benefit, facility or service;
(c) by terminating B's appointment;
(d) by subjecting B to any other detriment.

(7) A relevant person in relation to a personal office must not, in relation to that office, harass a person appointed to it.

(8) A person (A) who is a relevant person in relation to a personal office must not victimise a person (B) appointed to the office –

(a) as to the terms of B's appointment;
(b) in the way A affords B access, or by not affording B access, to opportunities for promotion, transfer or training or for receiving any other benefit, facility or service;
(c) by terminating B's appointment;
(d) by subjecting B to any other detriment.

(9) A duty to make reasonable adjustments applies to –

(a) a person who has the power to make an appointment to a personal office;
(b) a relevant person in relation to a personal office.

(10) For the purposes of subsection (2)(a), a person is to be regarded as discharging functions personally under the direction of another person if that other person is entitled to direct the person as to when and where to discharge the functions.

(11) For the purposes of subsection (2)(b), a person is not to be regarded as entitled to remuneration merely because the person is entitled to payments –

(a) in respect of expenses incurred by the person in discharging the functions of the office or post, or
(b) by way of compensation for the loss of income or benefits the person would or might have received had the person not been discharging the functions of the office or post.

(12) Subsection (3)(b), so far as relating to sex or pregnancy and maternity, does not apply to a term that relates to pay –

(a) unless, were B to accept the offer, an equality clause or rule would have effect in relation to the term, or
(b) if paragraph (a) does not apply, except in so far as making an offer on terms including that term amounts to a contravention of subsection (3)(b) by virtue of section 13, 14 or 18.

50 Public offices: appointments, etc.

(1) This section and section 51 apply in relation to public offices.

(2) A public office is –

    (a)   an office or post, appointment to which is made by a member of the executive;

    (b)   an office or post, appointment to which is made on the recommendation of, or subject to the approval of, a member of the executive;

    (c)   an office or post, appointment to which is made on the recommendation of, or subject to the approval of, the House of Commons, the House of Lords, the National Assembly for Wales or the Scottish Parliament.

(3) A person (A) who has the power to make an appointment to a public office within subsection (2)(a) or (b) must not discriminate against a person (B) –

    (a)   in the arrangements A makes for deciding to whom to offer the appointment;

    (b)   as to the terms on which A offers B the appointment;

    (c)   by not offering B the appointment.

(4) A person who has the power to make an appointment to a public office within subsection (2)(a) or (b) must not, in relation to the office, harass a person seeking, or being considered for, the appointment.

(5) A person (A) who has the power to make an appointment to a public office within subsection (2)(a) or (b) must not victimise a person (B) –

    (a)   in the arrangements A makes for deciding to whom to offer the appointment;

    (b)   as to the terms on which A offers B the appointment;

    (c)   by not offering B the appointment.

(6) A person (A) who is a relevant person in relation to a public office within subsection (2)(a) or (b) must not discriminate against a person (B) appointed to the office –

    (a)   as to B's terms of appointment;

    (b)   in the way A affords B access, or by not affording B access, to opportunities for promotion, transfer or training or for receiving any other benefit, facility or service;

    (c)   by terminating the appointment;

    (d)   by subjecting B to any other detriment.

(7) A person (A) who is a relevant person in relation to a public office within subsection (2)(c) must not discriminate against a person (B) appointed to the office –

    (a)   as to B's terms of appointment;

    (b)   in the way A affords B access, or by not affording B access, to opportunities for promotion, transfer or training or for receiving any other benefit, facility or service;

    (c)   by subjecting B to any other detriment (other than by terminating the appointment).

(8) A relevant person in relation to a public office must not, in relation to that office, harass a person appointed to it.

(9) A person (A) who is a relevant person in relation to a public office within subsection (2)(a) or (b) must not victimise a person (B) appointed to the office –

    (a)   as to B's terms of appointment;

(b)   in the way A affords B access, or by not affording B access, to opportunities for promotion, transfer or training or for receiving any other benefit, facility or service;

(c)   by terminating the appointment;

(d)   by subjecting B to any other detriment.

(10) A person (A) who is a relevant person in relation to a public office within subsection (2)(c) must not victimise a person (B) appointed to the office –

(a)   as to B's terms of appointment;

(b)   in the way A affords B access, or by not affording B access, to opportunities for promotion, transfer or training or for receiving any other benefit, facility or service;

(c)   by subjecting B to any other detriment (other than by terminating the appointment).

(11) A duty to make reasonable adjustments applies to –

(a)   a relevant person in relation to a public office;

(b)   a person who has the power to make an appointment to a public office within subsection (2)(a) or (b).

(12) Subsection (3)(b), so far as relating to sex or pregnancy and maternity, does not apply to a term that relates to pay –

(a)   unless, were B to accept the offer, an equality clause or rule would have effect in relation to the term, or

(b)   if paragraph (a) does not apply, except in so far as making an offer on terms including that term amounts to a contravention of subsection (3)(b) by virtue of section 13, 14 or 18.

51 Public offices: recommendations for appointments, etc.

(1) A person (A) who has the power to make a recommendation for or give approval to an appointment to a public office within section 50(2)(a) or (b), must not discriminate against a person (B) –

(a)   in the arrangements A makes for deciding who to recommend for appointment or to whose appointment to give approval;

(b)   by not recommending B for appointment to the office;

(c)   by making a negative recommendation of B for appointment to the office;

(d)   by not giving approval to the appointment of B to the office.

(2) A person who has the power to make a recommendation for or give approval to an appointment to a public office within section 50(2)(a) or (b) must not, in relation to the office, harass a person seeking or being considered for the recommendation or approval.

(3) A person (A) who has the power to make a recommendation for or give approval to an appointment to a public office within section 50(2)(a) or (b), must not victimise a person (B) –

(a)   in the arrangements A makes for deciding who to recommend for appointment or to whose appointment to give approval;

(b)   by not recommending B for appointment to the office;

(c)   by making a negative recommendation of B for appointment to the office;

(d)   by not giving approval to the appointment of B to the office.

(4) A duty to make reasonable adjustments applies to a person who has the power to make a recommendation for or give approval to an appointment to a public office within section 50(2)(a) or (b).

(5) A reference in this section to a person who has the power to make a recommendation for or give approval to an appointment to a public office within section 50(2)(a) is a reference only to a relevant body which has that power; and for that purpose "relevant body" means a body established –

    (a)   by or in pursuance of an enactment, or
    (b)   by a member of the executive.

52 Interpretation and exceptions

(1) This section applies for the purposes of sections 49 to 51.

(2) "Personal office" has the meaning given in section 49.

(3) "Public office" has the meaning given in section 50.

(4) An office or post which is both a personal office and a public office is to be treated as being a public office only.

(5) Appointment to an office or post does not include election to it.

(6) "Relevant person", in relation to an office, means the person who, in relation to a matter specified in the first column of the table, is specified in the second column (but a reference to a relevant person does not in any case include the House of Commons, the House of Lords, the National Assembly for Wales or the Scottish Parliament).

Matter	*Relevant person*
A term of appointment	The person who has the power to set the term.
Access to an opportunity	The person who has the power to afford access to the opportunity (or, if there is no such person, the person who has the power to make the appointment).
Terminating an appointment	The person who has the power to terminate the appointment.
Subjecting an appointee to any other detriment	The person who has the power in relation to the matter to which the conduct in question relates (or, if there is no such person, the person who has the power to make the appointment).
Harassing an appointee	The person who has the power in relation to the matter to which the conduct in question relates.

(7) A reference to terminating a person's appointment includes a reference to termination of the appointment –

    (a)   by the expiry of a period (including a period expiring by reference to an event or circumstance);

(b) by an act of the person (including giving notice) in circumstances such that the person is entitled, because of the relevant person's conduct, to terminate the appointment without notice.

(8) Subsection (7)(a) does not apply if, immediately after the termination, the appointment is renewed on the same terms.

(9) Schedule 6 (excluded offices) has effect.

Qualifications

53 Qualifications bodies

(1) A qualifications body (A) must not discriminate against a person (B) –

(a) in the arrangements A makes for deciding upon whom to confer a relevant qualification;
(b) as to the terms on which it is prepared to confer a relevant qualification on B;
(c) by not conferring a relevant qualification on B.

(2) A qualifications body (A) must not discriminate against a person (B) upon whom A has conferred a relevant qualification –

(a) by withdrawing the qualification from B;
(b) by varying the terms on which B holds the qualification;
(c) by subjecting B to any other detriment.

(3) A qualifications body must not, in relation to conferment by it of a relevant qualification, harass –

(a) a person who holds the qualification, or
(b) a person who applies for it.

(4) A qualifications body (A) must not victimise a person (B) –

(a) in the arrangements A makes for deciding upon whom to confer a relevant qualification;
(b) as to the terms on which it is prepared to confer a relevant qualification on B;
(c) by not conferring a relevant qualification on B.

(5) A qualifications body (A) must not victimise a person (B) upon whom A has conferred a relevant qualification –

(a) by withdrawing the qualification from B;
(b) by varying the terms on which B holds the qualification;
(c) by subjecting B to any other detriment.

(6) A duty to make reasonable adjustments applies to a qualifications body.

(7) The application by a qualifications body of a competence standard to a disabled person is not disability discrimination unless it is discrimination by virtue of section 19.

54 Interpretation

(1) This section applies for the purposes of section 53.

(2) A qualifications body is an authority or body which can confer a relevant qualification.

(3) A relevant qualification is an authorisation, qualification, recognition, registration, enrolment, approval or certification which is needed for, or facilitates engagement in, a particular trade or profession.

(4) An authority or body is not a qualifications body in so far as –

(a)   it can confer a qualification to which section 96 applies,
(b)   it is the responsible body of a school to which section 85 applies,
(c)   it is the governing body of an institution to which section 91 applies,
(d)   it exercises functions under the Education Acts, or
(e)   it exercises functions under the Education (Scotland) Act 1980.

(5) A reference to conferring a relevant qualification includes a reference to renewing or extending the conferment of a relevant qualification.

(6) A competence standard is an academic, medical or other standard applied for the purpose of determining whether or not a person has a particular level of competence or ability.

Employment services

55 Employment service-providers

(1) A person (an "employment service-provider") concerned with the provision of an employment service must not discriminate against a person –

(a)   in the arrangements the service-provider makes for selecting persons to whom to provide, or to whom to offer to provide, the service;
(b)   as to the terms on which the service-provider offers to provide the service to the person;
(c)   by not offering to provide the service to the person.

(2) An employment service-provider (A) must not, in relation to the provision of an employment service, discriminate against a person (B) –

(a)   as to the terms on which A provides the service to B;
(b)   by not providing the service to B;
(c)   by terminating the provision of the service to B;
(d)   by subjecting B to any other detriment.

(3) An employment service-provider must not, in relation to the provision of an employment service, harass –

(a)   a person who asks the service-provider to provide the service;
(b)   a person for whom the service-provider provides the service.

(4) An employment service-provider (A) must not victimise a person (B) –

(a)   in the arrangements A makes for selecting persons to whom to provide, or to whom to offer to provide, the service;
(b)   as to the terms on which A offers to provide the service to B;
(c)   by not offering to provide the service to B.

(5) An employment service-provider (A) must not, in relation to the provision of an employment service, victimise a person (B) –

(a)   as to the terms on which A provides the service to B;
(b)   by not providing the service to B;
(c)   by terminating the provision of the service to B;

(d)   by subjecting B to any other detriment.

(6) A duty to make reasonable adjustments applies to an employment service-provider, except in relation to the provision of a vocational service.

(7) The duty imposed by section 29(7)(a) applies to a person concerned with the provision of a vocational service; but a failure to comply with that duty in relation to the provision of a vocational service is a contravention of this Part for the purposes of Part 9 (enforcement).

56 Interpretation

(1) This section applies for the purposes of section 55.

(2) The provision of an employment service includes –

(a)   the provision of vocational training;
(b)   the provision of vocational guidance;
(c)   making arrangements for the provision of vocational training or vocational guidance;
(d)   the provision of a service for finding employment for persons;
(e)   the provision of a service for supplying employers with persons to do work;
(f)   the provision of a service in pursuance of arrangements made under section 2 of the Employment and Training Act 1973 (functions of the Secretary of State relating to employment);
(g)   the provision of a service in pursuance of arrangements made or a direction given under section 10 of that Act (careers services);
(h)   the exercise of a function in pursuance of arrangements made under section 2(3) of the Enterprise and New Towns (Scotland) Act 1990 (functions of Scottish Enterprise, etc. relating to employment);
(i)   an assessment related to the conferment of a relevant qualification within the meaning of section 53 above (except in so far as the assessment is by the qualifications body which confers the qualification).

(3) This section does not apply in relation to training or guidance in so far as it is training or guidance in relation to which another provision of this Part applies.

(4) This section does not apply in relation to training or guidance for pupils of a school to which section 85 applies in so far as it is training or guidance to which the responsible body of the school has power to afford access (whether as the responsible body of that school or as the responsible body of any other school at which the training or guidance is provided).

(5) This section does not apply in relation to training or guidance for students of an institution to which section 91 applies in so far as it is training or guidance to which the governing body of the institution has power to afford access.

(6) "Vocational training" means –

(a)   training for employment, or
(b)   work experience (including work experience the duration of which is not agreed until after it begins).

(7) A reference to the provision of a vocational service is a reference to the provision of an employment service within subsection (2)(a) to (d) (or an employment service within subsection (2)(f) or (g) in so far as it is also an employment service within subsection (2)(a) to (d)); and for that purpose –

(a) the references to an employment service within subsection (2)(a) do not include a reference to vocational training within the meaning given by subsection (6)(b), and

(b) the references to an employment service within subsection (2)(d) also include a reference to a service for assisting persons to retain employment.

(8) A reference to training includes a reference to facilities for training.

Trade organisations

57 Trade organisations

(1) A trade organisation (A) must not discriminate against a person (B) –

(a) in the arrangements A makes for deciding to whom to offer membership of the organisation;

(b) as to the terms on which it is prepared to admit B as a member;

(c) by not accepting B's application for membership.

(2) A trade organisation (A) must not discriminate against a member (B) –

(a) in the way it affords B access, or by not affording B access, to opportunities for receiving a benefit, facility or service;

(b) by depriving B of membership;

(c) by varying the terms on which B is a member;

(d) by subjecting B to any other detriment.

(3) A trade organisation must not, in relation to membership of it, harass –

(a) a member, or

(b) an applicant for membership.

(4) A trade organisation (A) must not victimise a person (B) –

(a) in the arrangements A makes for deciding to whom to offer membership of the organisation;

(b) as to the terms on which it is prepared to admit B as a member;

(c) by not accepting B's application for membership.

(5) A trade organisation (A) must not victimise a member (B) –

(a) in the way it affords B access, or by not affording B access, to opportunities for receiving a benefit, facility or service;

(b) by depriving B of membership;

(c) by varying the terms on which B is a member;

(d) by subjecting B to any other detriment.

(6) A duty to make reasonable adjustments applies to a trade organisation.

(7) A trade organisation is –

(a) an organisation of workers,

(b) an organisation of employers, or

(c) any other organisation whose members carry on a particular trade or profession for the purposes of which the organisation exists.

Local authority members

58 Official business of members

(1) A local authority must not discriminate against a member of the authority in relation to the member's carrying out of official business –

    (a)   in the way the authority affords the member access, or by not affording the member access, to opportunities for training or for receiving any other facility;

    (b)   by subjecting the member to any other detriment.

(2) A local authority must not, in relation to a member's carrying out of official business, harass the member.

(3) A local authority must not victimise a member of the authority in relation to the member's carrying out of official business –

    (a)   in the way the authority affords the member access, or by not affording the member access, to opportunities for training or for receiving any other facility;

    (b)   by subjecting the member to any other detriment.

(4) A member of a local authority is not subjected to a detriment for the purposes of subsection (1)(b) or (3)(b) only because the member is –

    (a)   not appointed or elected to an office of the authority,

    (b)   not appointed or elected to, or to an office of, a committee or subcommittee of the authority, or

    (c)   not appointed or nominated in exercise of an appointment power of the authority.

(5) In subsection (4)(c), an appointment power of a local authority is a power of the authority, or of a group of bodies including the authority, to make –

    (a)   appointments to a body;

    (b)   nominations for appointment to a body.

(6) A duty to make reasonable adjustments applies to a local authority.

59 Interpretation

(1) This section applies for the purposes of section 58.

(2) "Local authority" means –

    (a)   a county council in England;

    (b)   a district council in England;

    (c)   the Greater London Authority;

    (d)   a London borough council;

    (e)   the Common Council of the City of London;

    (f)   the Council of the Isles of Scilly;

    (g)   a parish council in England;

    (h)   a county council in Wales;

    (i)   a community council in Wales;

    (j)   a county borough council in Wales;

    (k)   a council constituted under section 2 of the Local Government etc. (Scotland) Act 1994;

    (l)   a community council in Scotland.

(3) A Minister of the Crown may by order amend subsection (2) so as to add, vary or omit a reference to a body which exercises functions that have been conferred on a local authority within paragraph (a) to (l).

(4) A reference to the carrying-out of official business by a person who is a member of a local authority is a reference to the doing of anything by the person –

    (a)   as a member of the authority,

    (b)   as a member of a body to which the person is appointed by, or appointed following nomination by, the authority or a group of bodies including the authority, or

    (c)   as a member of any other public body.

(5) "Member", in relation to the Greater London Authority, means –

    (a)   the Mayor of London;

    (b)   a member of the London Assembly.

Recruitment

60 Enquiries about disability and health

(1) A person (A) to whom an application for work is made must not ask about the health of the applicant (B) –

    (a)   before offering work to B, or

    (b)   where A is not in a position to offer work to B, before including B in a pool of applicants from whom A intends (when in a position to do so) to select a person to whom to offer work.

(2) A contravention of subsection (1) (or a contravention of section 111 or 112 that relates to a contravention of subsection (1)) is enforceable as an unlawful act under Part 1 of the Equality Act 2006 (and, by virtue of section 120(8), is enforceable only by the Commission under that Part).

(3) A does not contravene a relevant disability provision merely by asking about B's health; but A's conduct in reliance on information given in response may be a contravention of a relevant disability provision.

(4) Subsection (5) applies if B brings proceedings before an employment tribunal on a complaint that A's conduct in reliance on information given in response to a question about B's health is a contravention of a relevant disability provision.

(5) In the application of section 136 to the proceedings, the particulars of the complaint are to be treated for the purposes of subsection (2) of that section as facts from which the tribunal could decide that A contravened the provision.

(6) This section does not apply to a question that A asks in so far as asking the question is necessary for the purpose of –

    (a)   establishing whether B will be able to comply with a requirement to undergo an assessment or establishing whether a duty to make reasonable adjustments is or will be imposed on A in relation to B in connection with a requirement to undergo an assessment,

    (b)   establishing whether B will be able to carry out a function that is intrinsic to the work concerned,

    (c)   monitoring diversity in the range of persons applying to A for work,

(d)   taking action to which section 158 would apply if references in that section to persons who share (or do not share) a protected characteristic were references to disabled persons (or persons who are not disabled) and the reference to the characteristic were a reference to disability, or

(e)   if A applies in relation to the work a requirement to have a particular disability, establishing whether B has that disability.

(7) In subsection (6)(b), where A reasonably believes that a duty to make reasonable adjustments would be imposed on A in relation to B in connection with the work, the reference to a function that is intrinsic to the work is to be read as a reference to a function that would be intrinsic to the work once A complied with the duty.

(8) Subsection (6)(e) applies only if A shows that, having regard to the nature or context of the work –

(a)   the requirement is an occupational requirement, and

(b)   the application of the requirement is a proportionate means of achieving a legitimate aim.

(9) "Work" means employment, contract work, a position as a partner, a position as a member of an LLP, a pupillage or tenancy, being taken as a devil, membership of a stable, an appointment to a personal or public office, or the provision of an employment service; and the references in subsection (1) to offering a person work are, in relation to contract work, to be read as references to allowing a person to do the work.

(10) A reference to offering work is a reference to making a conditional or unconditional offer of work (and, in relation to contract work, is a reference to allowing a person to do the work subject to fulfilment of one or more conditions).

(11) The following, so far as relating to discrimination within section 13 because of disability, are relevant disability provisions –

(a)   section 39(1)(a) or (c);
(b)   section 41(1)(b);
(c)   section 44(1)(a) or (c);
(d)   section 45(1)(a) or (c);
(e)   section 47(1)(a) or (c);
(f)   section 48(1)(a) or (c);
(g)   section 49(3)(a) or (c);
(h)   section 50(3)(a) or (c);
(i)   section 51(1);
(j)   section 55(1)(a) or (c).

(12) An assessment is an interview or other process designed to give an indication of a person's suitability for the work concerned.

(13) For the purposes of this section, whether or not a person has a disability is to be regarded as an aspect of that person's health.

(14) This section does not apply to anything done for the purpose of vetting applicants for work for reasons of national security.

Chapter 2
Occupational pension schemes

61 Non-discrimination rule

(1) An occupational pension scheme must be taken to include a non-discrimination rule.

(2) A non-discrimination rule is a provision by virtue of which a responsible person (A) –

    (a)   must not discriminate against another person (B) in carrying out any of A's functions in relation to the scheme;

    (b)   must not, in relation to the scheme, harass B;

    (c)   must not, in relation to the scheme, victimise B.

(3) The provisions of an occupational pension scheme have effect subject to the non-discrimination rule.

(4) The following are responsible persons –

    (a)   the trustees or managers of the scheme;

    (b)   an employer whose employees are, or may be, members of the scheme;

    (c)   a person exercising an appointing function in relation to an office the holder of which is, or may be, a member of the scheme.

(5) A non-discrimination rule does not apply in relation to a person who is a pension credit member of a scheme.

(6) An appointing function is any of the following –

    (a)   the function of appointing a person;

    (b)   the function of terminating a person's appointment;

    (c)   the function of recommending a person for appointment;

    (d)   the function of approving an appointment.

(7) A breach of a non-discrimination rule is a contravention of this Part for the purposes of Part 9 (enforcement).

(8) It is not a breach of a non-discrimination rule for the employer or the trustees or managers of a scheme to maintain or use in relation to the scheme rules, practices, actions or decisions relating to age which are of a description specified by order by a Minister of the Crown.

(9) An order authorising the use of rules, practices, actions or decisions which are not in use before the order comes into force must not be made unless the Minister consults such persons as the Minister thinks appropriate.

(10) A non-discrimination rule does not have effect in relation to an occupational pension scheme in so far as an equality rule has effect in relation to it (or would have effect in relation to it but for Part 2 of Schedule 7).

(11) A duty to make reasonable adjustments applies to a responsible person.

62 Non-discrimination alterations

(1) This section applies if the trustees or managers of an occupational pension scheme do not have power to make non-discrimination alterations to the scheme.

(2) This section also applies if the trustees or managers of an occupational pension scheme have power to make non-discrimination alterations to the scheme but the procedure for doing so –

(a)   is liable to be unduly complex or protracted, or

(b)   involves obtaining consents which cannot be obtained or which can be obtained only with undue delay or difficulty.

(3) The trustees or managers may by resolution make non-discrimination alterations to the scheme.

(4) Non-discrimination alterations may have effect in relation to a period before the date on which they are made.

(5) Non-discrimination alterations to an occupational pension scheme are such alterations to the scheme as may be required for the provisions of the scheme to have the effect that they have in consequence of section 61(3).

63 Communications

(1) In their application to communications the following provisions apply in relation to a disabled person who is a pension credit member of an occupational pension scheme as they apply in relation to a disabled person who is a deferred member or pensioner member of the scheme –

(a)   section 61;

(b)   section 120;

(c)   section 126;

(d)   paragraph 19 of Schedule 8 (and such other provisions of that Schedule as apply for the purposes of that paragraph).

(2) Communications include –

(a)   the provision of information;

(b)   the operation of a dispute resolution procedure.

Chapter 3
Equality of terms

Sex equality

64 Relevant types of work

(1) Sections 66 to 70 apply where –

(a)   a person (A) is employed on work that is equal to the work that a comparator of the opposite sex (B) does;

(b)   a person (A) holding a personal or public office does work that is equal to the work that a comparator of the opposite sex (B) does.

(2) The references in subsection (1) to the work that B does are not restricted to work done contemporaneously with the work done by A.

65 Equal work

(1) For the purposes of this Chapter, A's work is equal to that of B if it is –

(a)   like B's work,

(b)   rated as equivalent to B's work, or

(c)   of equal value to B's work.

(2) A's work is like B's work if –

(a)   A's work and B's work are the same or broadly similar, and
(b)   such differences as there are between their work are not of practical importance in relation to the terms of their work.

(3) So on a comparison of one person's work with another's for the purposes of subsection (2), it is necessary to have regard to –

(a)   the frequency with which differences between their work occur in practice, and
(b)   the nature and extent of the differences.

(4) A's work is rated as equivalent to B's work if a job evaluation study –

(a)   gives an equal value to A's job and B's job in terms of the demands made on a worker, or
(b)   would give an equal value to A's job and B's job in those terms were the evaluation not made on a sex-specific system.

(5) A system is sex-specific if, for the purposes of one or more of the demands made on a worker, it sets values for men different from those it sets for women.

(6) A's work is of equal value to B's work if it is –

(a)   neither like B's work nor rated as equivalent to B's work, but
(b)   nevertheless equal to B's work in terms of the demands made on A by reference to factors such as effort, skill and decision-making.

66 Sex equality clause

(1) If the terms of A's work do not (by whatever means) include a sex equality clause, they are to be treated as including one.

(2) A sex equality clause is a provision that has the following effect –

(a)   if a term of A's is less favourable to A than a corresponding term of B's is to B, A's term is modified so as not to be less favourable;
(b)   if A does not have a term which corresponds to a term of B's that benefits B, A's terms are modified so as to include such a term.

(3) Subsection (2)(a) applies to a term of A's relating to membership of or rights under an occupational pension scheme only in so far as a sex equality rule would have effect in relation to the term.

(4) In the case of work within section 65(1)(b), a reference in subsection (2) above to a term includes a reference to such terms (if any) as have not been determined by the rating of the work (as well as those that have).

67 Sex equality rule

(1) If an occupational pension scheme does not include a sex equality rule, it is to be treated as including one.

(2) A sex equality rule is a provision that has the following effect –

(a)   if a relevant term is less favourable to A than it is to B, the term is modified so as not to be less favourable;

(b)   if a term confers a relevant discretion capable of being exercised in a way that would be less favourable to A than to B, the term is modified so as to prevent the exercise of the discretion in that way.

(3) A term is relevant if it is –

(a)   a term on which persons become members of the scheme, or
(b)   a term on which members of the scheme are treated.

(4) A discretion is relevant if its exercise in relation to the scheme is capable of affecting –

(a)   the way in which persons become members of the scheme, or
(b)   the way in which members of the scheme are treated.

(5) The reference in subsection (3)(b) to a term on which members of a scheme are treated includes a reference to the term as it has effect for the benefit of dependants of members.

(6) The reference in subsection (4)(b) to the way in which members of a scheme are treated includes a reference to the way in which they are treated as the scheme has effect for the benefit of dependants of members.

(7) If the effect of a relevant matter on persons of the same sex differs according to their family, marital or civil partnership status, a comparison for the purposes of this section of the effect of that matter on persons of the opposite sex must be with persons who have the same status.

(8) A relevant matter is –

(a)   a relevant term;
(b)   a term conferring a relevant discretion;
(c)   the exercise of a relevant discretion in relation to an occupational pension scheme.

(9) This section, so far as relating to the terms on which persons become members of an occupational pension scheme, does not have effect in relation to pensionable service before 8 April 1976.

(10) This section, so far as relating to the terms on which members of an occupational pension scheme are treated, does not have effect in relation to pensionable service before 17 May 1990.

68 Sex equality rule: consequential alteration of schemes

(1) This section applies if the trustees or managers of an occupational pension scheme do not have power to make sex equality alterations to the scheme.

(2) This section also applies if the trustees or managers of an occupational pension scheme have power to make sex equality alterations to the scheme but the procedure for doing so –

(a)   is liable to be unduly complex or protracted, or
(b)   involves obtaining consents which cannot be obtained or which can be obtained only with undue delay or difficulty.

(3) The trustees or managers may by resolution make sex equality alterations to the scheme.

(4) Sex equality alterations may have effect in relation to a period before the date on which they are made.

(5) Sex equality alterations to an occupational pension scheme are such alterations to the scheme as may be required to secure conformity with a sex equality rule.

69 Defence of material factor

(1) The sex equality clause in A's terms has no effect in relation to a difference between A's terms and B's terms if the responsible person shows that the difference is because of a material factor reliance on which –

(a)   does not involve treating A less favourably because of A's sex than the responsible person treats B, and
(b)   if the factor is within subsection (2), is a proportionate means of achieving a legitimate aim.

(2) A factor is within this subsection if A shows that, as a result of the factor, A and persons of the same sex doing work equal to A's are put at a particular disadvantage when compared with persons of the opposite sex doing work equal to A's.

(3) For the purposes of subsection (1), the long-term objective of reducing inequality between men's and women's terms of work is always to be regarded as a legitimate aim.

(4) A sex equality rule has no effect in relation to a difference between A and B in the effect of a relevant matter if the trustees or managers of the scheme in question show that the difference is because of a material factor which is not the difference of sex.

(5) "Relevant matter" has the meaning given in section 67.

(6) For the purposes of this section, a factor is not material unless it is a material difference between A's case and B's.

70 Exclusion of sex discrimination provisions

(1) The relevant sex discrimination provision has no effect in relation to a term of A's that –

(a)   is modified by, or included by virtue of, a sex equality clause or rule, or
(b)   would be so modified or included but for section 69 or Part 2 of Schedule 7.

(2) Neither of the following is sex discrimination for the purposes of the relevant sex discrimination provision –

(a)   the inclusion in A's terms of a term that is less favourable as referred to in section 66(2)(a);
(b)   the failure to include in A's terms a corresponding term as referred to in section 66(2)(b).

(3) The relevant sex discrimination provision is, in relation to work of a description given in the first column of the table, the provision referred to in the second column so far as relating to sex.

Description of work	Provision
Employment	Section 39(2)
Appointment to a personal office	Section 49(6)
Appointment to a public office	Section 50(6)

71 Sex discrimination in relation to contractual pay

(1) This section applies in relation to a term of a person's work –

(a)   that relates to pay, but

(b)   in relation to which a sex equality clause or rule has no effect.

(2) The relevant sex discrimination provision (as defined by section 70) has no effect in relation to the term except in so far as treatment of the person amounts to a contravention of the provision by virtue of section 13 or 14.

Pregnancy and maternity equality

72 Relevant types of work

Sections 73 to 76 apply where a woman –

(a)   is employed, or

(b)   holds a personal or public office.

73 Maternity equality clause

(1) If the terms of the woman's work do not (by whatever means) include a maternity equality clause, they are to be treated as including one.

(2) A maternity equality clause is a provision that, in relation to the terms of the woman's work, has the effect referred to in section 74(1), (6) and (8).

(3) In the case of a term relating to membership of or rights under an occupational pension scheme, a maternity equality clause has only such effect as a maternity equality rule would have.

74 Maternity equality clause: pay

(1) A term of the woman's work that provides for maternity-related pay to be calculated by reference to her pay at a particular time is, if each of the following three conditions is satisfied, modified as mentioned in subsection (5).

(2) The first condition is that, after the time referred to in subsection (1) but before the end of the protected period –

(a)   her pay increases, or

(b)   it would have increased had she not been on maternity leave.

(3) The second condition is that the maternity-related pay is not –

(a)   what her pay would have been had she not been on maternity leave, or

(b)   the difference between the amount of statutory maternity pay to which she is entitled and what her pay would have been had she not been on maternity leave.

(4) The third condition is that the terms of her work do not provide for the maternity-related pay to be subject to –

(a)   an increase as mentioned in subsection (2)(a), or

(b)   an increase that would have occurred as mentioned in subsection (2)(b).

(5) The modification referred to in subsection (1) is a modification to provide for the maternity-related pay to be subject to –

(a)   any increase as mentioned in subsection (2)(a), or

(b)   any increase that would have occurred as mentioned in subsection (2)(b).

(6) A term of her work that –

(a)   provides for pay within subsection (7), but

(b)   does not provide for her to be given the pay in circumstances in which she would have been given it had she not been on maternity leave,

is modified so as to provide for her to be given it in circumstances in which it would normally be given.

(7) Pay is within this subsection if it is –

(a)   pay (including pay by way of bonus) in respect of times before the woman is on maternity leave,

(b)   pay by way of bonus in respect of times when she is on compulsory maternity leave, or

(c)   pay by way of bonus in respect of times after the end of the protected period.

(8) A term of the woman's work that –

(a)   provides for pay after the end of the protected period, but

(b)   does not provide for it to be subject to an increase to which it would have been subject had she not been on maternity leave,

is modified so as to provide for it to be subject to the increase.

(9) Maternity-related pay is pay (other than statutory maternity pay) to which a woman is entitled –

(a)   as a result of being pregnant, or

(b)   in respect of times when she is on maternity leave.

(10) A reference to the protected period is to be construed in accordance with section 18.

75 Maternity equality rule

(1) If an occupational pension scheme does not include a maternity equality rule, it is to be treated as including one.

(2) A maternity equality rule is a provision that has the effect set out in subsections (3) and (4).

(3) If a relevant term does not treat time when the woman is on maternity leave as it treats time when she is not, the term is modified so as to treat time when she is on maternity leave as time when she is not.

(4) If a term confers a relevant discretion capable of being exercised so that time when she is on maternity leave is treated differently from time when she is not, the term is modified so as not to allow the discretion to be exercised in that way.

(5) A term is relevant if it is –

(a)   a term relating to membership of the scheme,

(b)   a term relating to the accrual of rights under the scheme, or

(c)   a term providing for the determination of the amount of a benefit payable under the scheme.

(6) A discretion is relevant if its exercise is capable of affecting –

   (a)   membership of the scheme,

   (b)   the accrual of rights under the scheme, or

   (c)   the determination of the amount of a benefit payable under the scheme.

(7) This section does not require the woman's contributions to the scheme in respect of time when she is on maternity leave to be determined otherwise than by reference to the amount she is paid in respect of that time.

(8) This section, so far as relating to time when she is on ordinary maternity leave but is not being paid by her employer, applies only in a case where the expected week of childbirth began on or after 6 April 2003.

(9) This section, so far as relating to time when she is on additional maternity leave but is not being paid by her employer –

   (a)   does not apply to the accrual of rights under the scheme in any case;

   (b)   applies for other purposes only in a case where the expected week of childbirth began on or after 5 October 2008.

(10) In this section –

   (a)   a reference to being on maternity leave includes a reference to having been on maternity leave, and

   (b)   a reference to being paid by the employer includes a reference to receiving statutory maternity pay from the employer.

76 Exclusion of pregnancy and maternity discrimination provisions

(1) The relevant pregnancy and maternity discrimination provision has no effect in relation to a term of the woman's work that is modified by a maternity equality clause or rule.

(2) The inclusion in the woman's terms of a term that requires modification by virtue of section 73(2) or (3) is not pregnancy and maternity discrimination for the purposes of the relevant pregnancy and maternity discrimination provision.

(3) The relevant pregnancy and maternity discrimination provision is, in relation to a description of work given in the first column of the table, the provision referred to in the second column so far as relating to pregnancy and maternity.

Description of work	*Provision*
Employment	Section 39(2)
Appointment to a personal office	Section 49(6)
Appointment to a public office	Section 50(6)

Disclosure of information

77 Discussions about pay

(1) A term of a person's work that purports to prevent or restrict the person (P) from disclosing or seeking to disclose information about the terms of P's work is unenforceable against P in so far as P makes or seeks to make a relevant pay disclosure.

(2) A term of a person's work that purports to prevent or restrict the person (P) from seeking disclosure of information from a colleague about the terms of the colleague's

work is unenforceable against P in so far as P seeks a relevant pay disclosure from the colleague; and "colleague" includes a former colleague in relation to the work in question.

(3) A disclosure is a relevant pay disclosure if made for the purpose of enabling the person who makes it, or the person to whom it is made, to find out whether or to what extent there is, in relation to the work in question, a connection between pay and having (or not having) a particular protected characteristic.

(4) The following are to be treated as protected acts for the purposes of the relevant victimisation provision –

    (a)   seeking a disclosure that would be a relevant pay disclosure;
    (b)   making or seeking to make a relevant pay disclosure;
    (c)   receiving information disclosed in a relevant pay disclosure.

(5) The relevant victimisation provision is, in relation to a description of work specified in the first column of the table, section 27 so far as it applies for the purposes of a provision mentioned in the second column.

Description of work	*Provision by virtue of which section 27 has effect*
Employment	Section 39(3) or (4)
Appointment to a personal office	Section 49(5) or (8)
Appointment to a public office	Section 50(5) or (9)

78 Gender pay gap information

(1) Regulations may require employers to publish information relating to the pay of employees for the purpose of showing whether, by reference to factors of such description as is prescribed, there are differences in the pay of male and female employees.

(2) This section does not apply to –

    (a)   an employer who has fewer than 250 employees;
    (b)   a person specified in Schedule 19;
    (c)   a government department or part of the armed forces not specified in that Schedule.

(3) The regulations may prescribe –

    (a)   descriptions of employer;
    (b)   descriptions of employee;
    (c)   how to calculate the number of employees that an employer has;
    (d)   descriptions of information;
    (e)   the time at which information is to be published;
    (f)   the form and manner in which it is to be published.

(4) Regulations under subsection (3)(e) may not require an employer, after the first publication of information, to publish information more frequently than at intervals of 12 months.

(5) The regulations may make provision for a failure to comply with the regulations –

    (a)   to be an offence punishable on summary conviction by a fine not exceeding level 5 on the standard scale;
    (b)   to be enforced, otherwise than as an offence, by such means as are prescribed.

(6) The reference to a failure to comply with the regulations includes a reference to a failure by a person acting on behalf of an employer.

Supplementary

79 Comparators

(1) This section applies for the purposes of this Chapter.

(2) If A is employed, B is a comparator if subsection (3) or (4) applies.

(3) This subsection applies if –

    (a)   B is employed by A's employer or by an associate of A's employer, and
    (b)   A and B work at the same establishment.

(4) This subsection applies if –

    (a) B is employed by A's employer or an associate of A's employer,
    (b)   B works at an establishment other than the one at which A works, and
    (c)   common terms apply at the establishments (either generally or as between A and B).

(5) If A holds a personal or public office, B is a comparator if –

    (a)   B holds a personal or public office, and
    (b)   the person responsible for paying A is also responsible for paying B.

(6) If A is a relevant member of the House of Commons staff, B is a comparator if –

    (a)   B is employed by the person who is A's employer under subsection (6) of section 195 of the Employment Rights Act 1996, or
    (b)   if subsection (7) of that section applies in A's case, B is employed by the person who is A's employer under that subsection.

(7) If A is a relevant member of the House of Lords staff, B is a comparator if B is also a relevant member of the House of Lords staff.

(8) Section 42 does not apply to this Chapter; accordingly, for the purposes of this Chapter only, holding the office of constable is to be treated as holding a personal office.

(9) For the purposes of this section, employers are associated if –

    (a)   one is a company of which the other (directly or indirectly) has control, or
    (b)   both are companies of which a third person (directly or indirectly) has control.

80 Interpretation and exceptions

(1) This section applies for the purposes of this Chapter.

(2) The terms of a person's work are –

    (a)   if the person is employed, the terms of the person's employment that are in the person's contract of employment, contract of apprenticeship or contract to do work personally;
    (b)   if the person holds a personal or public office, the terms of the person's appointment to the office.

(3) If work is not done at an establishment, it is to be treated as done at the establishment with which it has the closest connection.

(4) A person (P) is the responsible person in relation to another person if –

    (a)   P is the other's employer;

    (b)   P is responsible for paying remuneration in respect of a personal or public office that the other holds.

(5) A job evaluation study is a study undertaken with a view to evaluating, in terms of the demands made on a person by reference to factors such as effort, skill and decision-making, the jobs to be done –

    (a)   by some or all of the workers in an undertaking or group of undertakings, or

    (b)   in the case of the armed forces, by some or all of the members of the armed forces.

(6) In the case of Crown employment, the reference in subsection (5)(a) to an undertaking is to be construed in accordance with section 191(4) of the Employment Rights Act 1996.

(7) "Civil partnership status" has the meaning given in section 124(1) of the Pensions Act 1995.

(8) Schedule 7 (exceptions) has effect.

Chapter 4
Supplementary

81 Ships and hovercraft

(1) This Part applies in relation to –

    (a)   work on ships,

    (b)   work on hovercraft, and

    (c)   seafarers,

only in such circumstances as are prescribed.

(2) For the purposes of this section, it does not matter whether employment arises or work is carried out within or outside the United Kingdom.

(3) "Ship" has the same meaning as in the Merchant Shipping Act 1995.

(4) "Hovercraft" has the same meaning as in the Hovercraft Act 1968.

(5) "Seafarer" means a person employed or engaged in any capacity on board a ship or hovercraft.

(6) Nothing in this section affects the application of any other provision of this Act to conduct outside England and Wales or Scotland.

82 Offshore work

(1) Her Majesty may by Order in Council provide that in the case of persons in offshore work –

    (a)   specified provisions of this Part apply (with or without modification);

    (b)   Northern Ireland legislation making provision for purposes corresponding to any of the purposes of this Part applies (with or without modification).

(2) The Order may –

(a)   provide for these provisions, as applied by the Order, to apply to individuals (whether or not British citizens) and bodies corporate (whether or not incorporated under the law of a part of the United Kingdom), whether or not such application affects activities outside the United Kingdom;

(b)   make provision for conferring jurisdiction on a specified court or class of court or on employment tribunals in respect of offences, causes of action or other matters arising in connection with offshore work;

(c)   exclude from the operation of section 3 of the Territorial Waters Jurisdiction Act 1878 (consents required for prosecutions) proceedings for offences under the provisions mentioned in subsection (1) in connection with offshore work;

(d)   provide that such proceedings must not be brought without such consent as may be required by the Order.

(3) "Offshore work" is work for the purposes of –

(a)   activities in the territorial sea adjacent to the United Kingdom,

(b)   activities such as are mentioned in subsection (2) of section 11 of the Petroleum Act 1998 in waters within subsection (8)(b) or (c) of that section, or

(c)   activities mentioned in paragraphs (a) and (b) of section 87(1) of the Energy Act 2004 in waters to which that section applies.

(4) Work includes employment, contract work, a position as a partner or as a member of an LLP, or an appointment to a personal or public office.

(5) Northern Ireland legislation includes an enactment contained in, or in an instrument under, an Act that forms part of the law of Northern Ireland.

(6) In the application to Northern Ireland of subsection (2)(b), the reference to employment tribunals is to be read as a reference to industrial tribunals.

(7) Nothing in this section affects the application of any other provision of this Act to conduct outside England and Wales or Scotland.

83 Interpretation and exceptions

(1) This section applies for the purposes of this Part.

(2) "Employment" means –

(a)   employment under a contract of employment, a contract of apprenticeship or a contract personally to do work;

(b)   Crown employment;

(c)   employment as a relevant member of the House of Commons staff;

(d)   employment as a relevant member of the House of Lords staff.

(3) This Part applies to service in the armed forces as it applies to employment by a private person; and for that purpose –

(a)   references to terms of employment, or to a contract of employment, are to be read as including references to terms of service;

(b)   references to associated employers are to be ignored.

(4) A reference to an employer or an employee, or to employing or being employed, is (subject to section 212(11)) to be read with subsections (2) and (3); and a reference to an employer also includes a reference to a person who has no employees but is seeking to employ one or more other persons.

(5) "Relevant member of the House of Commons staff" has the meaning given in section 195 of the Employment Rights Act 1996; and such a member of staff is an employee of –

    (a)   the person who is the employer of that member under subsection (6) of that section, or

    (b)   if subsection (7) of that section applies in the case of that member, the person who is the employer of that member under that subsection.

(6) "Relevant member of the House of Lords staff" has the meaning given in section 194 of that Act (which provides that such a member of staff is an employee of the Corporate Officer of the House of Lords).

(7) In the case of a person in Crown employment, or in employment as a relevant member of the House of Commons staff, a reference to the person's dismissal is a reference to the termination of the person's employment.

(8) A reference to a personal or public office, or to an appointment to a personal or public office, is to be construed in accordance with section 52.

(9) "Crown employment" has the meaning given in section 191 of the Employment Rights Act 1996.

(10) Schedule 8 (reasonable adjustments) has effect.

(11) Schedule 9 (exceptions) has effect.

PART 6
EDUCATION

Chapter 1
Schools

84 Application of this Chapter

This Chapter does not apply to the following protected characteristics –

    (a)   age;
    (b)   marriage and civil partnership.

85 Pupils: admission and treatment, etc.

(1) The responsible body of a school to which this section applies must not discriminate against a person –

    (a)   in the arrangements it makes for deciding who is offered admission as a pupil;
    (b)   as to the terms on which it offers to admit the person as a pupil;
    (c)   by not admitting the person as a pupil.

(2) The responsible body of such a school must not discriminate against a pupil –

    (a)   in the way it provides education for the pupil;
    (b)   in the way it affords the pupil access to a benefit, facility or service;
    (c)   by not providing education for the pupil;
    (d)   by not affording the pupil access to a benefit, facility or service;
    (e)   by excluding the pupil from the school;
    (f)   by subjecting the pupil to any other detriment.

(3) The responsible body of such a school must not harass –

(a)   a pupil;

(b)   a person who has applied for admission as a pupil.

(4) The responsible body of such a school must not victimise a person –

(a)   in the arrangements it makes for deciding who is offered admission as a pupil;

(b)   as to the terms on which it offers to admit the person as a pupil;

(c)   by not admitting the person as a pupil.

(5) The responsible body of such a school must not victimise a pupil –

(a)   in the way it provides education for the pupil;

(b)   in the way it affords the pupil access to a benefit, facility or service;

(c)   by not providing education for the pupil;

(d)   by not affording the pupil access to a benefit, facility or service;

(e)   by excluding the pupil from the school;

(f)   by subjecting the pupil to any other detriment.

(6) A duty to make reasonable adjustments applies to the responsible body of such a school.

(7) In relation to England and Wales, this section applies to –

(a)   a school maintained by a local authority;

(b)   an independent educational institution (other than a special school);

(c)   a special school (not maintained by a local authority).

(8) In relation to Scotland, this section applies to –

(a)   a school managed by an education authority;

(b)   an independent school;

(c)   a school in respect of which the managers are for the time being receiving grants under section 73(c) or (d) of the Education (Scotland) Act 1980.

(9) The responsible body of a school to which this section applies is –

(a)   if the school is within subsection (7)(a), the local authority or governing body;

(b)   if it is within subsection (7)(b) or (c), the proprietor;

(c)   if it is within subsection (8)(a), the education authority;

(d)   if it is within subsection (8)(b), the proprietor;

(e)   if it is within subsection (8)(c), the managers.

(10) In the application of section 26 for the purposes of subsection (3), none of the following is a relevant protected characteristic –

(a)   gender reassignment;

(b)   religion or belief;

(c)   sexual orientation.

86 Victimisation of pupils, etc. for conduct of parents, etc.

(1) This section applies for the purposes of section 27 in its application to section 85(4) or (5).

(2) The references to B in paragraphs (a) and (b) of subsection (1) of section 27 include a reference to a parent or sibling of the child in question.

(3) Giving false evidence or information, or making a false allegation, in good faith is not a protected act in a case where –

(a)   the evidence or information is given, or the allegation is made, by a parent or sibling of the child, and

(b)   the child has acted in bad faith.

(4) Giving false evidence or information, or making a false allegation, in bad faith, is a protected act in a case where –

(a)   the evidence or information is given, or the allegation is made, by a parent or sibling of the child, and

(b)   the child has acted in good faith.

(5) In this section –

"child" means a person who has not attained the age of 18;

"sibling" means a brother or sister, a half-brother or half-sister, or a stepbrother or stepsister.

87 Application of certain powers under Education Act 1996

(1) Sections 496 and 497 of the Education Act 1996 (powers to give directions where responsible body of school in default of obligations, etc.) apply to the performance of a duty under section 85.

(2) But neither of sections 496 and 497 of that Act applies to the performance of a duty under that section by the proprietor of an independent educational institution (other than a special school).

88 Disabled pupils: accessibility

Schedule 10 (accessibility) has effect.

89 Interpretation and exceptions

(1) This section applies for the purposes of this Chapter.

(2) Nothing in this Chapter applies to anything done in connection with the content of the curriculum.

(3) "Pupil" –

(a)   in relation to England and Wales, has the meaning given in section 3(1) of the Education Act 1996;

(b)   in relation to Scotland, has the meaning given in section 135(1) of the Education (Scotland) Act 1980.

(4) "Proprietor" –

(a)   in relation to a school in England and Wales, has the meaning given in section 579(1) of the Education Act 1996;

(b)   in relation to a school in Scotland, has the meaning given in section 135(1) of the Education (Scotland) Act 1980.

(5) "School" –

(a)   in relation to England and Wales, has the meaning given in section 4 of the Education Act 1996;

(b)   in relation to Scotland, has the meaning given in section 135(1) of the Education (Scotland) Act 1980.

(6) A reference to a school includes a reference to an independent educational institution in England; and a reference to an independent educational institution in England is to be construed in accordance with Chapter 1 of Part 4 of the Education and Skills Act 2008.

(7) A reference to an independent educational institution is a reference to –

(a)   an independent educational institution in England, or

(b)   an independent school in Wales.

(8) "Independent school" –

(a)   in relation to Wales, has the meaning given in section 463 of the Education Act 1996;

(b)   in relation to Scotland, has the meaning given in section 135(1) of the Education (Scotland) Act 1980.

(9) "Special school" has the meaning given in section 337 of the Education Act 1996.

(10) "Local authority" means –

(a)   in relation to England, an English local authority within the meaning of section 162 of the Education and Inspections Act 2006;

(b)   in relation to Wales, a Welsh local authority within the meaning of that section.

(11) "Education authority", in relation to Scotland, has the meaning given in section 135(1) of the Education (Scotland) Act 1980.

(12) Schedule 11 (exceptions) has effect.

Chapter 2
Further and higher education

90 Application of this Chapter

This Chapter does not apply to the protected characteristic of marriage and civil partnership.

91 Students: admission and treatment, etc.

(1) The responsible body of an institution to which this section applies must not discriminate against a person –

(a)   in the arrangements it makes for deciding who is offered admission as a student;

(b)   as to the terms on which it offers to admit the person as a student;

(c)   by not admitting the person as a student.

(2) The responsible body of such an institution must not discriminate against a student –

(a)   in the way it provides education for the student;

(b)   in the way it affords the student access to a benefit, facility or service;

(c)   by not providing education for the student;

(d)   by not affording the student access to a benefit, facility or service;

(e)   by excluding the student;

(f)   by subjecting the student to any other detriment.

(3) The responsible body of such an institution must not discriminate against a disabled person –

    (a)   in the arrangements it makes for deciding upon whom to confer a qualification;

    (b)   as to the terms on which it is prepared to confer a qualification on the person;

    (c)   by not conferring a qualification on the person;

    (d)   by withdrawing a qualification from the person or varying the terms on which the person holds it.

(4) Subsection (3) applies only to disability discrimination.

(5) The responsible body of such an institution must not harass –

    (a)   a student;

    (b)   a person who has applied for admission as a student;

    (c)   a disabled person who holds or has applied for a qualification conferred by the institution.

(6) The responsible body of such an institution must not victimise a person –

    (a)   in the arrangements it makes for deciding who is offered admission as a student;

    (b)   as to the terms on which it offers to admit the person as a student;

    (c)   by not admitting the person as a student.

(7) The responsible body of such an institution must not victimise a student –

    (a)   in the way it provides education for the student;

    (b)   in the way it affords the student access to a benefit, facility or service;

    (c)   by not providing education for the student;

    (d)   by not affording the student access to a benefit, facility or service;

    (e)   by excluding the student;

    (f)   by subjecting the student to any other detriment.

(8) The responsible body of such an institution must not victimise a disabled person –

    (a)   in the arrangements it makes for deciding upon whom to confer a qualification;

    (b)   as to the terms on which it is prepared to confer a qualification on the person;

    (c)   by not conferring a qualification on the person;

    (d)   by withdrawing a qualification from the person or varying the terms on which the person holds it.

(9) A duty to make reasonable adjustments applies to the responsible body of such an institution.

(10) In relation to England and Wales, this section applies to –

    (a)   a university;

    (b)   any other institution within the higher education sector;

    (c)   an institution within the further education sector.

(11) In relation to Scotland, this section applies to –

    (a)   a university;

    (b)   a designated institution;

    (c)   a college of further education.

(12) A responsible body is –

(a) in the case of an institution within subsection (10)(a), (b) or (c), the governing body;

(b) in the case of an institution within subsection (11)(a) or (b), the governing body;

(c) in the case of a college of further education under the management of a board of management, the board of management;

(d) in the case of any other college of further education, any board of governors of the college or any person responsible for the management of the college, whether or not formally constituted as a governing body or board of governors.

92 Further and higher education courses

(1) The responsible body in relation to a course to which this section applies must not discriminate against a person –

(a) in the arrangements it makes for deciding who is enrolled on the course;

(b) as to the terms on which it offers to enrol the person on the course;

(c) by not accepting the person's application for enrolment.

(2) The responsible body in relation to such a course must not discriminate against a person who is enrolled on the course in the services it provides or offers to provide.

(3) The responsible body in relation to such a course must not harass a person who –

(a) seeks enrolment on the course;

(b) is enrolled on the course;

(c) is a user of services provided by the body in relation to the course.

(4) The responsible body in relation to such a course must not victimise a person –

(a) in the arrangements it makes for deciding who is enrolled on the course;

(b) as to the terms on which it offers to enrol the person on the course;

(c) by not accepting the person's application for enrolment.

(5) The responsible body in relation to such a course must not victimise a person who is enrolled on the course in the services it provides or offers to provide.

(6) A duty to make reasonable adjustments applies to the responsible body.

(7) This section applies to –

(a) a course of further or higher education secured by a responsible body in England or Wales;

(b) a course of education provided by the governing body of a maintained school under section 80 of the School Standards and Framework Act 1998;

(c) a course of further education secured by an education authority in Scotland.

(8) A responsible body is –

(a) a local authority in England or Wales, for the purposes of subsection (7)(a);

(b) the governing body of a maintained school, for the purposes of subsection (7)(b);

(c) an education authority in Scotland, for the purposes of subsection (7)(c).

(9) In this section –

"course", in relation to further education, includes each component part of a course if there is no requirement imposed on persons registered for a component part of the course to register for another component part of the course;

"enrolment" includes registration for a component part of a course;

"maintained school" has the meaning given in section 20(7) of the School Standards and Framework Act 1998;

"services" means services of any description which are provided wholly or mainly for persons enrolled on a course to which this section applies.

93 Recreational or training facilities

(1) The responsible body in relation to facilities to which this section applies must not discriminate against a person –

    (a)   in the arrangements it makes for deciding who is provided with the facilities;

    (b)   as to the terms on which it offers to provide the facilities to the person;

    (c)   by not accepting the person's application for provision of the facilities.

(2) The responsible body in relation to such facilities must not discriminate against a person who is provided with the facilities in the services it provides or offers to provide.

(3) The responsible body in relation to such facilities must not harass a person who –

    (a)   seeks to have the facilities provided;

    (b)   is provided with the facilities;

    (c)   is a user of services provided by the body in relation to the facilities.

(4) The responsible body in relation to such facilities must not victimise a person –

    (a)   in the arrangements it makes for deciding who is provided with the facilities;

    (b)   as to the terms on which it offers to provide the facilities to the person;

    (c)   by not accepting the person's application for provision of the facilities.

(5) The responsible body in relation to such facilities must not victimise a person who is provided with the facilities in the services it provides or offers to provide.

(6) A duty to make reasonable adjustments applies to the responsible body.

(7) This section applies to –

    (a)   facilities secured by a local authority in England under section 507A or 507B of the Education Act 1996;

    (b)   facilities secured by a local authority in Wales under section 508 of that Act;

    (c)   recreational or training facilities provided by an education authority in Scotland.

(8) A responsible body is –

    (a)   a local authority in England, for the purposes of subsection (7)(a);

    (b)   a local authority in Wales, for the purposes of subsection (7)(b);

    (c)   an education authority in Scotland, for the purposes of subsection (7)(c).

(9) This section does not apply to the protected characteristic of age, so far as relating to persons who have not attained the age of 18.

94 Interpretation and exceptions

(1) This section applies for the purposes of this Chapter.

(2) Nothing in this Chapter applies to anything done in connection with the content of the curriculum.

(3) A reference to a student, in relation to an institution, is a reference to a person for whom education is provided by the institution.

(4) A reference to a university includes a reference to a university college and a college, school or hall of a university.

(5) A reference to an institution within the further or higher education sector is to be construed in accordance with section 91 of the Further and Higher Education Act 1992.

(6) "Further education" –

   (a)   in relation to England and Wales, has the meaning given in section 2 of the Education Act 1996;
   (b)   in relation to Scotland, has the meaning given in section 1(3) of the Further and Higher Education (Scotland) Act 1992.

(7) "Higher education" –

   (a)   in relation to England and Wales, means education provided by means of a course of a description mentioned in Schedule 6 to the Education Reform Act 1988;
   (b)   in relation to Scotland, has the meaning given in section 38 of the Further and Higher Education (Scotland) Act 1992.

(8) "College of further education" has the meaning given in section 36 of the Further and Higher Education (Scotland) Act 1992.

(9) "Designated institution" has the meaning given in section 44 of that Act.

(10) "Local authority" means –

   (a)   in relation to England, an English local authority within the meaning of section 162 of the Education and Inspections Act 2006;
   (b)   in relation to Wales, a Welsh local authority within the meaning of that section.

(11) "Education authority" has the meaning given by section 135(1) of the Education (Scotland) Act 1980.

(12) Schedule 12 (exceptions) has effect.

Chapter 3
General qualifications bodies

95 Application of this Chapter

This Chapter does not apply to the protected characteristic of marriage and civil partnership.

96 Qualifications bodies

(1) A qualifications body (A) must not discriminate against a person (B) –

   (a)   in the arrangements A makes for deciding upon whom to confer a relevant qualification;
   (b)   as to the terms on which it is prepared to confer a relevant qualification on B;
   (c)   by not conferring a relevant qualification on B.

(2) A qualifications body (A) must not discriminate against a person (B) upon whom A has conferred a relevant qualification –

    (a)   by withdrawing the qualification from B;

    (b)   by varying the terms on which B holds the qualification;

    (c)   by subjecting B to any other detriment.

(3) A qualifications body must not, in relation to conferment by it of a relevant qualification, harass –

    (a)   a person who holds the qualification, or

    (b)   a person who applies for it.

(4) A qualifications body (A) must not victimise a person (B) –

    (a)   in the arrangements A makes for deciding upon whom to confer a relevant qualification;

    (b)   as to the terms on which it is prepared to confer a relevant qualification on B;

    (c)   by not conferring a relevant qualification on B.

(5) A qualifications body (A) must not victimise a person (B) upon whom A has conferred a relevant qualification –

    (a)   by withdrawing the qualification from B;

    (b)   by varying the terms on which B holds the qualification;

    (c)   by subjecting B to any other detriment.

(6) A duty to make reasonable adjustments applies to a qualifications body.

(7) Subsection (6) does not apply to the body in so far as the appropriate regulator specifies provisions, criteria or practices in relation to which the body –

    (a)   is not subject to a duty to make reasonable adjustments;

    (b)   is subject to a duty to make reasonable adjustments, but in relation to which such adjustments as the regulator specifies should not be made.

(8) For the purposes of subsection (7) the appropriate regulator must have regard to –

    (a)   the need to minimise the extent to which disabled persons are disadvantaged in attaining the qualification because of their disabilities;

    (b)   the need to secure that the qualification gives a reliable indication of the knowledge, skills and understanding of a person upon whom it is conferred;

    (c)   the need to maintain public confidence in the qualification.

(9) The appropriate regulator –

    (a)   must not specify any matter for the purposes of subsection (7) unless it has consulted such persons as it thinks appropriate;

    (b)   must publish matters so specified (including the date from which they are to have effect) in such manner as is prescribed.

(10) The appropriate regulator is –

    (a)   in relation to a qualifications body that confers qualifications in England, a person prescribed by a Minister of the Crown;

    (b)   in relation to a qualifications body that confers qualifications in Wales, a person prescribed by the Welsh Ministers;

    (c)   in relation to a qualifications body that confers qualifications in Scotland, a person prescribed by the Scottish Ministers.

(11) For the purposes of subsection (10), a qualification is conferred in a part of Great Britain if there are, or may reasonably be expected to be, persons seeking to obtain the qualification who are or will be assessed for those purposes wholly or mainly in that part.

97 Interpretation

(1) This section applies for the purposes of section 96.

(2) A qualifications body is an authority or body which can confer a relevant qualification.

(3) A relevant qualification is an authorisation, qualification, approval or certification of such description as may be prescribed –

(a) in relation to conferments in England, by a Minister of the Crown;
(b) in relation to conferments in Wales, by the Welsh Ministers;
(c) in relation to conferments in Scotland, by the Scottish Ministers.

(4) An authority or body is not a qualifications body in so far as –

(a) it is the responsible body of a school to which section 85 applies,
(b) it is the governing body of an institution to which section 91 applies,
(c) it exercises functions under the Education Acts, or
(d) it exercises functions under the Education (Scotland) Act 1980.

(5) A qualifications body does not include an authority or body of such description, or in such circumstances, as may be prescribed.

(6) A reference to conferring a relevant qualification includes a reference –

(a) to renewing or extending the conferment of a relevant qualification;
(b) to authenticating a relevant qualification conferred by another person.

(7) A reference in section 96(8), (10) or (11) to a qualification is a reference to a relevant qualification.

(8) Subsection (11) of section 96 applies for the purposes of subsection (3) of this section as it applies for the purposes of subsection (10) of that section.

Chapter 4
Miscellaneous

98 Reasonable adjustments

Schedule 13 (reasonable adjustments) has effect.

99 Educational charities and endowments

Schedule 14 (educational charities and endowments) has effect.

PART 7
ASSOCIATIONS

Preliminary

100 Application of this Part

(1) This Part does not apply to the protected characteristic of marriage and civil partnership.

(2) This Part does not apply to discrimination, harassment or victimisation –

(a) that is prohibited by Part 3 (services and public functions), Part 4 (premises), Part 5 (work) or Part 6 (education), or

(b) that would be so prohibited but for an express exception.

Membership, etc.

101 Members and associates

(1) An association (A) must not discriminate against a person (B) –

(a) in the arrangements A makes for deciding who to admit to membership;

(b) as to the terms on which A is prepared to admit B to membership;

(c) by not accepting B's application for membership.

(2) An association (A) must not discriminate against a member (B) –

(a) in the way A affords B access, or by not affording B access, to a benefit, facility or service;

(b) by depriving B of membership;

(c) by varying B's terms of membership;

(d) by subjecting B to any other detriment.

(3) An association (A) must not discriminate against an associate (B) –

(a) in the way A affords B access, or by not affording B access, to a benefit, facility or service;

(b) by depriving B of B's rights as an associate;

(c) by varying B's rights as an associate;

(d) by subjecting B to any other detriment.

(4) An association must not harass –

(a) a member;

(b) a person seeking to become a member;

(c) an associate.

(5) An association (A) must not victimise a person (B) –

(a) in the arrangements A makes for deciding who to admit to membership;

(b) as to the terms on which A is prepared to admit B to membership;

(c) by not accepting B's application for membership.

(6) An association (A) must not victimise a member (B) –

(a) in the way A affords B access, or by not affording B access, to a benefit, facility or service;

(b) by depriving B of membership;

(c) by varying B's terms of membership;

(d) by subjecting B to any other detriment.

(7) An association (A) must not victimise an associate (B) –

(a) in the way A affords B access, or by not affording B access, to a benefit, facility or service;

(b) by depriving B of B's rights as an associate;

(c) by varying B's rights as an associate;

(d) by subjecting B to any other detriment.

102 Guests

(1) An association (A) must not discriminate against a person (B) –

    (a)   in the arrangements A makes for deciding who to invite, or who to permit to be invited, as a guest;

    (b)   as to the terms on which A is prepared to invite B, or to permit B to be invited, as a guest;

    (c)   by not inviting B, or not permitting B to be invited, as a guest.

(2) An association (A) must not discriminate against a guest (B) invited by A or with A's permission (whether express or implied) –

    (a)   in the way A affords B access, or by not affording B access, to a benefit, facility or service;

    (b)   by subjecting B to any other detriment.

(3) An association must not harass –

    (a)   a guest;

    (b)   a person seeking to be a guest.

(4) An association (A) must not victimise a person (B) –

    (a)   in the arrangements A makes for deciding who to invite, or who to permit to be invited, as a guest;

    (b)   as to the terms on which A is prepared to invite B, or to permit B to be invited, as a guest;

    (c)   by not inviting B, or not permitting B to be invited, as a guest.

(5) An association (A) must not victimise a guest (B) invited by A or with A's permission (whether express or implied) –

    (a)   in the way A affords B access, or by not affording B access, to a benefit, facility or service;

    (b)   by subjecting B to any other detriment.

103 Sections 101 and 102: further provision

(1) A duty to make reasonable adjustments applies to an association.

(2) In the application of section 26 for the purposes of section 101(4) or 102(3), neither of the following is a relevant protected characteristic –

    (a)   religion or belief;

    (b)   sexual orientation.

Special provision for political parties

104 Selection of candidates

(1) This section applies to an association which is a registered political party.

(2) A person does not contravene this Part only by acting in accordance with selection arrangements.

(3) Selection arrangements are arrangements –

    (a)   which the party makes for regulating the selection of its candidates in a relevant election,

(b)   the purpose of which is to reduce inequality in the party's representation in the body concerned, and

(c)   which, subject to subsection (7), are a proportionate means of achieving that purpose.

(4) The reference in subsection (3)(b) to inequality in a party's representation in a body is a reference to inequality between –

(a)   the number of the party's candidates elected to be members of the body who share a protected characteristic, and

(b)   the number of the party's candidates so elected who do not share that characteristic.

(5) For the purposes of subsection (4), persons share the protected characteristic of disability if they are disabled persons (and section 6(3)(b) is accordingly to be ignored).

(6) Selection arrangements do not include short-listing only such persons as have a particular protected characteristic.

(7) But subsection (6) does not apply to the protected characteristic of sex; and subsection (3)(c) does not apply to short-listing in reliance on this subsection.

(8) The following elections are relevant elections –

(a)   Parliamentary Elections;
(b)   elections to the European Parliament;
(c)   elections to the Scottish Parliament;
(d)   elections to the National Assembly for Wales;
(e)   local government elections within the meaning of section 191, 203 or 204 of the Representation of the People Act 1983 (excluding elections for the Mayor of London).

105 Time-limited provision

(1) Section 104(7) and the words, "subject to subsection (7)," in section 104(3)(c) are repealed at the end of 2030 unless an order is made under subsection (2).

(2) At any time before the end of 2030, a Minister of the Crown may by order provide that subsection (1) is to have effect with the substitution of a later time for that for the time being specified there.

(3) In section 3 of the Sex Discrimination (Election Candidates) Act 2002 (expiry of that Act), in subsection (1) for "2015" substitute "2030".

(4) The substitution made by subsection (3) does not affect the power to substitute a later time by order under section 3 of that Act.

106 Information about diversity in range of candidates, etc.

(1) This section applies to an association which is a registered political party.

(2) If the party had candidates at a relevant election, the party must, in accordance with regulations, publish information relating to protected characteristics of persons who come within a description prescribed in the regulations in accordance with subsection (3).

(3) One or more of the following descriptions may be prescribed for the purposes of subsection (2) –

(a)   successful applicants for nomination as a candidate at the relevant election;
(b)   unsuccessful applicants for nomination as a candidate at that election;
(c)   candidates elected at that election;
(d)   candidates who are not elected at that election.

(4) The duty imposed by subsection (2) applies only in so far as it is possible to publish information in a manner that ensures that no person to whom the information relates can be identified from that information.

(5) The following elections are relevant elections –

(a)   Parliamentary Elections;
(b)   elections to the European Parliament;
(c)   elections to the Scottish Parliament;
(d)   elections to the National Assembly for Wales.

(6) This section does not apply to the following protected characteristics –

(a)   marriage and civil partnership;
(b)   pregnancy and maternity.

(7) The regulations may provide that the information to be published –

(a)   must (subject to subsection (6)) relate to all protected characteristics or only to such as are prescribed;
(b)   must include a statement, in respect of each protected characteristic to which the information relates, of the proportion that the number of persons who provided the information to the party bears to the number of persons who were asked to provide it.

(8) Regulations under this section may prescribe –

(a)   descriptions of information;
(b)   descriptions of political party to which the duty is to apply;
(c)   the time at which information is to be published;
(d)   the form and manner in which information is to be published;
(e)   the period for which information is to be published.

(9) Provision by virtue of subsection (8)(b) may, in particular, provide that the duty imposed by subsection (2) does not apply to a party which had candidates in fewer constituencies in the election concerned than a prescribed number.

(10) Regulations under this section –

(a)   may provide that the duty imposed by subsection (2) applies only to such relevant elections as are prescribed;
(b)   may provide that a by-election or other election to fill a vacancy is not to be treated as a relevant election or is to be so treated only to a prescribed extent;
(c)   may amend this section so as to provide for the duty imposed by subsection (2) to apply in the case of additional descriptions of election.

(11) Nothing in this section authorises a political party to require a person to provide information to it.

Supplementary

107 Interpretation and exceptions

(1) This section applies for the purposes of this Part.

(2) An "association" is an association of persons –

(a)   which has at least 25 members, and

(b)   admission to membership of which is regulated by the association's rules and involves a process of selection.

(3) A Minister of the Crown may by order amend subsection (2)(a) so as to substitute a different number for that for the time being specified there.

(4) It does not matter –

(a)   whether an association is incorporated;

(b)   whether its activities are carried on for profit.

(5) Membership is membership of any description; and a reference to a member is to be construed accordingly.

(6) A person is an "associate", in relation to an association, if the person –

(a)   is not a member of the association, but

(b)   in accordance with the association's rules, has some or all of the rights as a member as a result of being a member of another association.

(7) A reference to a registered political party is a reference to a party registered in the Great Britain register under Part 2 of the Political Parties, Elections and Referendums Act 2000.

(8) Schedule 15 (reasonable adjustments) has effect.

(9) Schedule 16 (exceptions) has effect.

PART 8
PROHIBITED CONDUCT: ANCILLARY

108 Relationships that have ended

(1) A person (A) must not discriminate against another (B) if –

(a)   the discrimination arises out of and is closely connected to a relationship which used to exist between them, and

(b)   conduct of a description constituting the discrimination would, if it occurred during the relationship, contravene this Act.

(2) A person (A) must not harass another (B) if –

(a)   the harassment arises out of and is closely connected to a relationship which used to exist between them, and

(b)   conduct of a description constituting the harassment would, if it occurred during the relationship, contravene this Act.

(3) It does not matter whether the relationship ends before or after the commencement of this section.

(4) A duty to make reasonable adjustments applies to A in so far as B continues to be placed at a substantial disadvantage as mentioned in section 20.

(5) For the purposes of subsection (4), sections 20, 21 and 22 and the applicable Schedules are to be construed as if the relationship had not ended.

(6) For the purposes of Part 9 (enforcement), a contravention of this section relates to the Part of this Act that would have been contravened if the relationship had not ended.

(7) But conduct is not a contravention of this section in so far as it also amounts to victimisation of B by A.

109 Liability of employers and principals

(1) Anything done by a person (A) in the course of A's employment must be treated as also done by the employer.

(2) Anything done by an agent for a principal, with the authority of the principal, must be treated as also done by the principal.

(3) It does not matter whether that thing is done with the employer's or principal's knowledge or approval.

(4) In proceedings against A's employer (B) in respect of anything alleged to have been done by A in the course of A's employment it is a defence for B to show that B took all reasonable steps to prevent A –

    (a)   from doing that thing, or

    (b)   from doing anything of that description.

(5) This section does not apply to offences under this Act (other than offences under Part 12 (disabled persons: transport)).

110 Liability of employees and agents

(1) A person (A) contravenes this section if –

    (a)   A is an employee or agent,

    (b)   A does something which, by virtue of section 109(1) or (2), is treated as having been done by A's employer or principal (as the case may be), and

    (c)   the doing of that thing by A amounts to a contravention of this Act by the employer or principal (as the case may be).

(2) It does not matter whether, in any proceedings, the employer is found not to have contravened this Act by virtue of section 109(4).

(3) A does not contravene this section if –

    (a)   A relies on a statement by the employer or principal that doing that thing is not a contravention of this Act, and

    (b)   it is reasonable for A to do so.

(4) A person (B) commits an offence if B knowingly or recklessly makes a statement mentioned in subsection (3)(a) which is false or misleading in a material respect.

(5) A person guilty of an offence under subsection (4) is liable on summary conviction to a fine not exceeding level 5 on the standard scale.

(6) Part 9 (enforcement) applies to a contravention of this section by A as if it were the contravention mentioned in subsection (1)(c).

(7) The reference in subsection (1)(c) to a contravention of this Act does not include a reference to disability discrimination in contravention of Chapter 1 of Part 6 (schools).

111 Instructing, causing or inducing contraventions

(1) A person (A) must not instruct another (B) to do in relation to a third person (C) anything which contravenes Part 3, 4, 5, 6 or 7 or section 108(1) or (2) or 112(1) (a basic contravention).

(2) A person (A) must not cause another (B) to do in relation to a third person (C) anything which is a basic contravention.

(3) A person (A) must not induce another (B) to do in relation to a third person (C) anything which is a basic contravention.

(4) For the purposes of subsection (3), inducement may be direct or indirect.

(5) Proceedings for a contravention of this section may be brought –

(a)　　by B, if B is subjected to a detriment as a result of A's conduct;
(b)　　by C, if C is subjected to a detriment as a result of A's conduct;
(c)　　by the Commission.

(6) For the purposes of subsection (5), it does not matter whether –

(a)　　the basic contravention occurs;
(b)　　any other proceedings are, or may be, brought in relation to A's conduct.

(7) This section does not apply unless the relationship between A and B is such that A is in a position to commit a basic contravention in relation to B.

(8) A reference in this section to causing or inducing a person to do something includes a reference to attempting to cause or induce the person to do it.

(9) For the purposes of Part 9 (enforcement), a contravention of this section is to be treated as relating –

(a)　　in a case within subsection (5)(a), to the Part of this Act which, because of the relationship between A and B, A is in a position to contravene in relation to B;
(b)　　in a case within subsection (5)(b), to the Part of this Act which, because of the relationship between B and C, B is in a position to contravene in relation to C.

112 Aiding contraventions

(1) A person (A) must not knowingly help another (B) to do anything which contravenes Part 3, 4, 5, 6 or 7 or section 108(1) or (2) or 111 (a basic contravention).

(2) It is not a contravention of subsection (1) if –

(a)　　A relies on a statement by B that the act for which the help is given does not contravene this Act, and
(b)　　it is reasonable for A to do so.

(3) B commits an offence if B knowingly or recklessly makes a statement mentioned in subsection (2)(a) which is false or misleading in a material respect.

(4) A person guilty of an offence under subsection (3) is liable on summary conviction to a fine not exceeding level 5 on the standard scale.

(5) For the purposes of Part 9 (enforcement), a contravention of this section is to be treated as relating to the provision of this Act to which the basic contravention relates.

(6) The reference in subsection (1) to a basic contravention does not include a reference to disability discrimination in contravention of Chapter 1 of Part 6 (schools).

PART 9
ENFORCEMENT

Chapter 1
Introductory

113 Proceedings

(1) Proceedings relating to a contravention of this Act must be brought in accordance with this Part.

(2) Subsection (1) does not apply to proceedings under Part 1 of the Equality Act 2006.

(3) Subsection (1) does not prevent –

(a)   a claim for judicial review;
(b)   proceedings under the Immigration Acts;
(c)   proceedings under the Special Immigration Appeals Commission Act 1997;
(d)   in Scotland, an application to the supervisory jurisdiction of the Court of Session.

(4) This section is subject to any express provision of this Act conferring jurisdiction on a court or tribunal.

(5) The reference to a contravention of this Act includes a reference to a breach of an equality clause or rule.

(6) Chapters 2 and 3 do not apply to proceedings relating to an equality clause or rule except in so far as Chapter 4 provides for that.

(7) This section does not apply to –

(a)   proceedings for an offence under this Act;
(b)   proceedings relating to a penalty under Part 12 (disabled persons: transport).

Chapter 2
Civil courts

114 Jurisdiction

(1) A county court or, in Scotland, the sheriff has jurisdiction to determine a claim relating to –

(a)   a contravention of Part 3 (services and public functions);
(b)   a contravention of Part 4 (premises);
(c)   a contravention of Part 6 (education);
(d)   a contravention of Part 7 (associations);
(e)   a contravention of section 108, 111 or 112 that relates to Part 3,4,6 or 7.

(2) Subsection (1)(a) does not apply to a claim within section 115.

(3) Subsection (1)(c) does not apply to a claim within section 116.

(4) Subsection (1)(d) does not apply to a contravention of section 106.

(5) For the purposes of proceedings on a claim within subsection (1)(a) –

(a)   a decision in proceedings on a claim mentioned in section 115(1) that an act is a contravention of Part 3 is binding;
(b)   it does not matter whether the act occurs outside the United Kingdom.

(6) The county court or sheriff –

(a) must not grant an interim injunction or interdict unless satisfied that no criminal matter would be prejudiced by doing so;

(b) must grant an application to stay or sist proceedings under subsection (1) on grounds of prejudice to a criminal matter unless satisfied the matter will not be prejudiced.

(7) In proceedings in England and Wales on a claim within subsection (1), the power under section 63(1) of the County Courts Act 1984 (appointment of assessors) must be exercised unless the judge is satisfied that there are good reasons for not doing so.

(8) In proceedings in Scotland on a claim within subsection (1), the power under rule 44.3 of Schedule 1 to the Sheriff Court (Scotland) Act 1907 (appointment of assessors) must be exercised unless the sheriff is satisfied that there are good reasons for not doing so.

(9) The remuneration of an assessor appointed by virtue of subsection (8) is to be at a rate determined by the Lord President of the Court of Session.

115 Immigration cases

(1) A claim is within this section if it relates to the act of an immigration authority in taking a relevant decision and –

(a) the question whether the act is a contravention of Part 3 has been or could be raised on an appeal which is pending, or could be brought, under the immigration provisions, or

(b) it has been decided on an appeal under those provisions that the act is not a contravention of Part 3.

(2) The relevant decision is not –

(a) subject to challenge in proceedings on a claim within section 114(1)(a), or

(b) affected by the decision of a court in such proceedings.

(3) For the purposes of subsection (1)(a) a power to grant permission to appeal out of time must be ignored.

(4) Each of the following is an immigration authority –

(a) the Secretary of State;

(b) an immigration officer;

(c) a person responsible for the grant or refusal of entry clearance (within the meaning of section 33(1) of the Immigration Act 1971).

(5) The immigration provisions are –

(a) the Special Immigration Appeals Commission Act 1997, or

(b) Part 5 of the Nationality, Immigration and Asylum Act 2002.

(6) A relevant decision is –

(a) a decision under the Immigration Acts relating to the entitlement of a person to enter or remain in the United Kingdom;

(b) a decision on an appeal under the immigration provisions relating to a decision within paragraph (a).

(7) An appeal is pending if it is pending for the purposes of section 104 of the Nationality, Immigration and Asylum Act 2002 or (as the case may be) for the purposes of that section as it is applied by section 2(2)(j) of the Special Immigration Appeals Commission Act 1997.

116 Education cases

(1) A claim is within this section if it may be made to –

    (a)   the First-tier Tribunal in accordance with Part 2 of Schedule 17,

    (b)   the Special Educational Needs Tribunal for Wales in accordance with Part 2 of that Schedule, or

    (c)   an Additional Support Needs Tribunal for Scotland in accordance with Part 3 of that Schedule.

(2) A claim is also within this section if it must be made in accordance with appeal arrangements within the meaning of Part 4 of that Schedule.

(3) Schedule 17 (disabled pupils: enforcement) has effect.

117 National security

(1) Rules of court may, in relation to proceedings on a claim within section 114, confer power as mentioned in subsections (2) to (4); but a power so conferred is exercisable only if the court thinks it expedient to do so in the interests of national security.

(2) The rules may confer power to exclude from all or part of the proceedings –

    (a)   the claimant or pursuer;

    (b)   a representative of the claimant or pursuer;

    (c)   an assessor.

(3) The rules may confer power to permit a claimant, pursuer or representative who has been excluded to make a statement to the court before the commencement of the proceedings, or part of the proceedings, to which the exclusion relates.

(4) The rules may confer power to take steps to keep secret all or part of the reasons for the court's decision.

(5) The Attorney General or, in Scotland, the Advocate General for Scotland may appoint a person to represent the interests of a claimant or pursuer in, or in any part of, proceedings to which an exclusion by virtue of subsection (2)(a) or (b) relates.

(6) A person (P) may be appointed under subsection (5) only if –

    (a)   in relation to proceedings in England and Wales, P is a person who, for the purposes of the Legal Services Act 2007, is an authorised person in relation to an activity which constitutes the exercise of a right of audience or the conduct of litigation;

    (b)   in relation to proceedings in Scotland, P is an advocate or qualified to practice as a solicitor in Scotland.

(7) P is not responsible to the person whose interests P is appointed to represent.

118 Time limits

(1) Proceedings on a claim within section 114 may not be brought after the end of –

(a)   the period of 6 months starting with the date of the act to which the claim relates, or

(b)   such other period as the county court or sheriff thinks just and equitable.

(2) If subsection (3) or (4) applies, subsection (1)(a) has effect as if for "6 months" there were substituted "9 months".

(3) This subsection applies if –

(a)   the claim relates to the act of a qualifying institution, and

(b)   a complaint relating to the act is referred under the student complaints scheme before the end of the period of 6 months starting with the date of the act.

(4) This subsection applies if –

(a)   the claim relates to a dispute referred for conciliation in pursuance of arrangements under section 27 of the Equality Act 2006, and

(b)   subsection (3) does not apply.

(5) If it has been decided under the immigration provisions that the act of an immigration authority in taking a relevant decision is a contravention of Part 3 (services and public functions), subsection (1) has effect as if for paragraph (a) there were substituted –

"(a)the period of 6 months starting with the day after the expiry of the period during which, as a result of section 114(2), proceedings could not be brought in reliance on section 114(1)(a);"

(6) For the purposes of this section –

(a)   conduct extending over a period is to be treated as done at the end of the period;

(b)   failure to do something is to be treated as occurring when the person in question decided on it.

(7) In the absence of evidence to the contrary, a person (P) is to be taken to decide on failure to do something –

(a)   when P does an act inconsistent with doing it, or

(b)   if P does no inconsistent act, on the expiry of the period in which P might reasonably have been expected to do it.

(8) In this section –

"immigration authority", "immigration provisions" and "relevant decision" each have the meaning given in section 115;

"qualifying institution" has the meaning given in section 11 of the Higher Education Act 2004;

"the student complaints scheme" means a scheme for the review of qualifying complaints (within the meaning of section 12 of that Act) that is provided by the designated operator (within the meaning of section 13(5)(b) of that Act).

119 Remedies

(1) This section applies if a county court or the sheriff finds that there has been a contravention of a provision referred to in section 114(1).

(2) The county court has power to grant any remedy which could be granted by the High Court –

(a)   in proceedings in tort;

(b)   on a claim for judicial review.

(3) The sheriff has power to make any order which could be made by the Court of Session –

(a)   in proceedings for reparation;

(b)   on a petition for judicial review.

(4) An award of damages may include compensation for injured feelings (whether or not it includes compensation on any other basis).

(5) Subsection (6) applies if the county court or sheriff –

(a)   finds that a contravention of a provision referred to in section 114(1) is established by virtue of section 19, but

(b)   is satisfied that the provision, criterion or practice was not applied with the intention of discriminating against the claimant or pursuer.

(6) The county court or sheriff must not make an award of damages unless it first considers whether to make any other disposal.

(7) The county court or sheriff must not grant a remedy other than an award of damages or the making of a declaration unless satisfied that no criminal matter would be prejudiced by doing so.

Chapter 3
Employment tribunals

120 Jurisdiction

(1) An employment tribunal has, subject to section 121, jurisdiction to determine a complaint relating to –

(a)   a contravention of Part 5 (work);

(b)   a contravention of section 108, 111 or 112 that relates to Part 5.

(2) An employment tribunal has jurisdiction to determine an application by a responsible person (as defined by section 61) for a declaration as to the rights of that person and a worker in relation to a dispute about the effect of a non-discrimination rule.

(3) An employment tribunal also has jurisdiction to determine an application by the trustees or managers of an occupational pension scheme for a declaration as to their rights and those of a member in relation to a dispute about the effect of a non-discrimination rule.

(4) An employment tribunal also has jurisdiction to determine a question that –

(a)   relates to a non-discrimination rule, and

(b)   is referred to the tribunal by virtue of section 122.

(5) In proceedings before an employment tribunal on a complaint relating to a breach of a non-discrimination rule, the employer –

(a)   is to be treated as a party, and

(b)   is accordingly entitled to appear and be heard.

(6) Nothing in this section affects such jurisdiction as the High Court, a county court, the Court of Session or the sheriff has in relation to a non-discrimination rule.

(7) Subsection (1)(a) does not apply to a contravention of section 53 in so far as the act complained of may, by virtue of an enactment, be subject to an appeal or proceedings in the nature of an appeal.

(8) In subsection (1), the references to Part 5 do not include a reference to section 60(1).

121 Armed forces cases

(1) Section 120(1) does not apply to a complaint relating to an act done when the complainant was serving as a member of the armed forces unless –

(a)   the complainant has made a service complaint about the matter, and
(b)   the complaint has not been withdrawn.

(2) If the complaint is made under the service complaint procedures, it is to be treated for the purposes of subsection (1)(b) as withdrawn if –

(a)   neither the officer to whom it is made nor a superior officer refers it to the Defence Council, and
(b)   the complainant does not apply for it to be referred to the Defence Council.

(3) If the complaint is made under the old service redress procedures, it is to be treated for the purposes of subsection (1)(b) as withdrawn if the complainant does not submit it to the Defence Council under those procedures.

(4) The reference in subsection (3) to the old service redress procedures is a reference to the procedures (other than those relating to the making of a report on a complaint to Her Majesty) referred to in –

(a)   section 180 of the Army Act 1955,
(b)   section 180 of the Air Force Act 1955, or
(c)   section 130 of the Naval Discipline Act 1957.

(5) The making of a complaint to an employment tribunal in reliance on subsection (1) does not affect the continuation of the service complaint procedures or (as the case may be) the old service redress procedures.

122 References by court to tribunal, etc.

(1) If it appears to a court in which proceedings are pending that a claim or counter-claim relating to a non-discrimination rule could more conveniently be determined by an employment tribunal, the court may strike out the claim or counter-claim.

(2) If in proceedings before a court a question arises about a non-discrimination rule, the court may (whether or not on an application by a party to the proceedings) –

(a)   refer the question, or direct that it be referred by a party to the proceedings, to an employment tribunal for determination, and
(b)   stay or sist the proceedings in the meantime.

123 Time limits

(1) Proceedings on a complaint within section 120 may not be brought after the end of –

(a)   the period of 3 months starting with the date of the act to which the complaint relates, or
(b)   such other period as the employment tribunal thinks just and equitable.

(2) Proceedings may not be brought in reliance on section 121(1) after the end of –

    (a)   the period of 6 months starting with the date of the act to which the proceedings relate, or

    (b)   such other period as the employment tribunal thinks just and equitable.

(3) For the purposes of this section –

    (a)   conduct extending over a period is to be treated as done at the end of the period;

    (b)   failure to do something is to be treated as occurring when the person in question decided on it.

(4) In the absence of evidence to the contrary, a person (P) is to be taken to decide on failure to do something –

    (a)   when P does an act inconsistent with doing it, or

    (b)   if P does no inconsistent act, on the expiry of the period in which P might reasonably have been expected to do it.

124 Remedies: general

(1) This section applies if an employment tribunal finds that there has been a contravention of a provision referred to in section 120(1).

(2) The tribunal may –

    (a)   make a declaration as to the rights of the complainant and the respondent in relation to the matters to which the proceedings relate;

    (b)   order the respondent to pay compensation to the complainant;

    (c)   make an appropriate recommendation.

(3) An appropriate recommendation is a recommendation that within a specified period the respondent takes specified steps for the purpose of obviating or reducing the adverse effect of any matter to which the proceedings relate –

    (a)   on the complainant;

    (b)   on any other person.

(4) Subsection (5) applies if the tribunal –

    (a)   finds that a contravention is established by virtue of section 19, but

    (b)   is satisfied that the provision, criterion or practice was not applied with the intention of discriminating against the complainant.

(5) It must not make an order under subsection (2)(b) unless it first considers whether to act under subsection (2)(a) or (c).

(6) The amount of compensation which may be awarded under subsection (2)(b) corresponds to the amount which could be awarded by a county court or the sheriff under section 119.

(7) If a respondent fails, without reasonable excuse, to comply with an appropriate recommendation in so far as it relates to the complainant, the tribunal may –

    (a)   if an order was made under subsection (2)(b), increase the amount of compensation to be paid;

    (b)   if no such order was made, make one.

125 Remedies: national security

(1) In national security proceedings, an appropriate recommendation (as defined by section 124) must not be made in relation to a person other than the complainant if the recommendation would affect anything done by –

    (a)   the Security Service,
    (b)   the Secret Intelligence Service,
    (c)   the Government Communications Headquarters, or
    (d)   a part of the armed forces which is, in accordance with a requirement of the Secretary of State, assisting the Government Communications Headquarters.

(2) National security proceedings are –

    (a)   proceedings to which a direction under section 10(3) of the Employment Tribunals Act 1996 (national security) relates;
    (b)   proceedings to which an order under section 10(4) of that Act relates;
    (c)   proceedings (or the part of proceedings) to which a direction pursuant to regulations made under section 10(5) of that Act relates;
    (d)   proceedings (or the part of proceedings) in relation to which an employment tribunal acts pursuant to regulations made under section 10(6) of that Act.

126 Remedies: occupational pension schemes

(1) This section applies if an employment tribunal finds that there has been a contravention of a provision referred to in section 120(1) in relation to –

    (a)   the terms on which persons become members of an occupational pension scheme, or
    (b)   the terms on which members of an occupational pension scheme are treated.

(2) In addition to anything which may be done by the tribunal under section 124 the tribunal may also by order declare –

    (a)   if the complaint relates to the terms on which persons become members of a scheme, that the complainant has a right to be admitted to the scheme;
    (b)   if the complaint relates to the terms on which members of the scheme are treated, that the complainant has a right to membership of the scheme without discrimination.

(3) The tribunal may not make an order under subsection (2)(b) of section 124 unless –

    (a)   the compensation is for injured feelings, or
    (b)   the order is made by virtue of subsection (7) of that section.

(4) An order under subsection (2) –

    (a)   may make provision as to the terms on which or the capacity in which the claimant is to enjoy the admission or membership;
    (b)   may have effect in relation to a period before the order is made.

Chapter 4
Equality of terms

127 Jurisdiction

(1) An employment tribunal has, subject to subsection (6), jurisdiction to determine a complaint relating to a breach of an equality clause or rule.

(2) The jurisdiction conferred by subsection (1) includes jurisdiction to determine a complaint arising out of a breach of an equality clause or rule; and a reference in this Chapter to a complaint relating to such a breach is to be read accordingly.

(3) An employment tribunal also has jurisdiction to determine an application by a responsible person for a declaration as to the rights of that person and a worker in relation to a dispute about the effect of an equality clause or rule.

(4) An employment tribunal also has jurisdiction to determine an application by the trustees or managers of an occupational pension scheme for a declaration as to their rights and those of a member in relation to a dispute about the effect of an equality rule.

(5) An employment tribunal also has jurisdiction to determine a question that –

(a)   relates to an equality clause or rule, and
(b)   is referred to the tribunal by virtue of section 128(2).

(6) This section does not apply to a complaint relating to an act done when the complainant was serving as a member of the armed forces unless –

(a)   the complainant has made a service complaint about the matter, and
(b)   the complaint has not been withdrawn.

(7) Subsections (2) to (5) of section 121 apply for the purposes of subsection (6) of this section as they apply for the purposes of subsection (1) of that section.

(8) In proceedings before an employment tribunal on a complaint relating to a breach of an equality rule, the employer –

(a)   is to be treated as a party, and
(b)   is accordingly entitled to appear and be heard.

(9) Nothing in this section affects such jurisdiction as the High Court, a county court, the Court of Session or the sheriff has in relation to an equality clause or rule.

128 References by court to tribunal, etc.

(1) If it appears to a court in which proceedings are pending that a claim or counter-claim relating to an equality clause or rule could more conveniently be determined by an employment tribunal, the court may strike out the claim or counter-claim.

(2) If in proceedings before a court a question arises about an equality clause or rule, the court may (whether or not on an application by a party to the proceedings) –

(a)   refer the question, or direct that it be referred by a party to the proceedings, to an employment tribunal for determination, and
(b)   stay or sist the proceedings in the meantime.

129 Time limits

(1) This section applies to –

(a)   a complaint relating to a breach of an equality clause or rule;
(b)   an application for a declaration referred to in section 127(3) or (4).

(2) Proceedings on the complaint or application may not be brought in an employment tribunal after the end of the qualifying period.

(3) If the complaint or application relates to terms of work other than terms of service in the armed forces, the qualifying period is, in a case mentioned in the first column of the table, the period mentioned in the second column.

Case	Qualifying period
A standard case	The period of 6 months beginning with the last day of the employment or appointment.
A stable work case (but not if it is also a concealment or incapacity case (or both))	The period of 6 months beginning with the day on which the stable working relationship ended.
A concealment case (but not if it is also an incapacity case)	The period of 6 months beginning with the day on which the worker discovered (or could with reasonable diligence have discovered) the qualifying fact.
An incapacity case (but not if it is also a concealment case)	The period of 6 months beginning with the day on which the worker ceased to have the incapacity.
A case which is a concealment case and an incapacity case.	The period of 6 months beginning with the later of the days on which the period would begin if the case were merely a concealment or incapacity case.

(4) If the complaint or application relates to terms of service in the armed forces, the qualifying period is, in a case mentioned in the first column of the table, the period mentioned in the second column.

Case	Qualifying period
A standard case	The period of 9 months beginning with the last day of the period of service during which the complaint arose.
A concealment case (but not if it is also an incapacity case)	The period of 9 months beginning with the day on which the worker discovered (or could with reasonable diligence have discovered) the qualifying fact.
An incapacity case (but not if it is also a concealment case)	The period of 9 months beginning with the day on which the worker ceased to have the incapacity.
A case which is a concealment case and an incapacity case.	The period of 9 months beginning with the later of the days on which the period would begin if the case were merely a concealment or incapacity case.

130 Section 129: supplementary

(1) This section applies for the purposes of section 129.

(2) A standard case is a case which is not –

    (a)   a stable work case,

    (b)   a concealment case,

    (c)   an incapacity case, or

    (d)   a concealment case and an incapacity case.

(3) A stable work case is a case where the proceedings relate to a period during which there was a stable working relationship between the worker and the responsible person (including any time after the terms of work had expired).

(4) A concealment case in proceedings relating to an equality clause is a case where –

    (a)   the responsible person deliberately concealed a qualifying fact from the worker, and

    (b)   the worker did not discover (or could not with reasonable diligence have discovered) the qualifying fact until after the relevant day.

(5) A concealment case in proceedings relating to an equality rule is a case where –

    (a)   the employer or the trustees or managers of the occupational pension scheme in question deliberately concealed a qualifying fact from the member, and

    (b)   the member did not discover (or could not with reasonable diligence have discovered) the qualifying fact until after the relevant day.

(6) A qualifying fact for the purposes of subsection (4) or (5) is a fact –

    (a)   which is relevant to the complaint, and

    (b)   without knowledge of which the worker or member could not reasonably have been expected to bring the proceedings.

(7) An incapacity case in proceedings relating to an equality clause with respect to terms of work other than terms of service in the armed forces is a case where the worker had an incapacity during the period of 6 months beginning with the later of –

    (a)   the relevant day, or

    (b)   the day on which the worker discovered (or could with reasonable diligence have discovered) the qualifying fact deliberately concealed from the worker by the responsible person.

(8) An incapacity case in proceedings relating to an equality clause with respect to terms of service in the armed forces is a case where the worker had an incapacity during the period of 9 months beginning with the later of –

    (a)   the last day of the period of service during which the complaint arose, or

    (b)   the day on which the worker discovered (or could with reasonable diligence have discovered) the qualifying fact deliberately concealed from the worker by the responsible person.

(9) An incapacity case in proceedings relating to an equality rule is a case where the member of the occupational pension scheme in question had an incapacity during the period of 6 months beginning with the later of –

    (a)   the relevant day, or

    (b)   the day on which the member discovered (or could with reasonable diligence have discovered) the qualifying fact deliberately concealed from the member by the employer or the trustees or managers of the scheme.

(10) The relevant day for the purposes of this section is –

    (a)   the last day of the employment or appointment, or

(b)   the day on which the stable working relationship between the worker and the responsible person ended.

131 Assessment of whether work is of equal value

(1) This section applies to proceedings before an employment tribunal on –

(a)   a complaint relating to a breach of an equality clause or rule, or
(b)   a question referred to the tribunal by virtue of section 128(2).

(2) Where a question arises in the proceedings as to whether one person's work is of equal value to another's, the tribunal may, before determining the question, require a member of the panel of independent experts to prepare a report on the question.

(3) The tribunal may withdraw a requirement that it makes under subsection (2); and, if it does so, it may –

(a)   request the panel member to provide it with specified documentation;
(b)   make such other requests to that member as are connected with the withdrawal of the requirement.

(4) If the tribunal requires the preparation of a report under subsection (2) (and does not withdraw the requirement), it must not determine the question unless it has received the report.

(5) Subsection (6) applies where –

(a)   a question arises in the proceedings as to whether the work of one person (A) is of equal value to the work of another (B), and
(b)   A's work and B's work have been given different values by a job evaluation study.

(6) The tribunal must determine that A's work is not of equal value to B's work unless it has reasonable grounds for suspecting that the evaluation contained in the study –

(a)   was based on a system that discriminates because of sex, or
(b)   is otherwise unreliable.

(7) For the purposes of subsection (6)(a), a system discriminates because of sex if a difference (or coincidence) between values that the system sets on different demands is not justifiable regardless of the sex of the person on whom the demands are made.

(8) A reference to a member of the panel of independent experts is a reference to a person –

(a)   who is for the time being designated as such by the Advisory, Conciliation and Arbitration Service (ACAS) for the purposes of this section, and
(b)   who is neither a member of the Council of ACAS nor one of its officers or members of staff.

(9) "Job evaluation study" has the meaning given in section 80(5).

132 Remedies in non-pensions cases

(1) This section applies to proceedings before a court or employment tribunal on a complaint relating to a breach of an equality clause, other than a breach with respect to membership of or rights under an occupational pension scheme.

(2) If the court or tribunal finds that there has been a breach of the equality clause, it may –

(a) make a declaration as to the rights of the parties in relation to the matters to which the proceedings relate;

(b) order an award by way of arrears of pay or damages in relation to the complainant.

(3) The court or tribunal may not order a payment under subsection (2)(b) in respect of a time before the arrears day.

(4) In relation to proceedings in England and Wales, the arrears day is, in a case mentioned in the first column of the table, the day mentioned in the second column.

Case	Arrears day
A standard case	The day falling 6 years before the day on which the proceedings were instituted.
A concealment case or an incapacity case (or a case which is both).	The day on which the breach first occurred.

(5) In relation to proceedings in Scotland, the arrears day is the first day of –

(a) the period of 5 years ending with the day on which the proceedings were commenced, or

(b) if the case involves a relevant incapacity, or a relevant fraud or error, the period of 20 years ending with that day.

133 Remedies in pensions cases

(1) This section applies to proceedings before a court or employment tribunal on a complaint relating to –

(a) a breach of an equality rule, or

(b) a breach of an equality clause with respect to membership of, or rights under, an occupational pension scheme.

(2) If the court or tribunal finds that there has been a breach as referred to in subsection (1) –

(a) it may make a declaration as to the rights of the parties in relation to the matters to which the proceedings relate;

(b) it must not order arrears of benefits or damages or any other amount to be paid to the complainant.

(3) Subsection (2)(b) does not apply if the proceedings are proceedings to which section 134 applies.

(4) If the breach relates to a term on which persons become members of the scheme, the court or tribunal may declare that the complainant is entitled to be admitted to the scheme with effect from a specified date.

(5) A date specified for the purposes of subsection (4) must not be before 8 April 1976.

(6) If the breach relates to a term on which members of the scheme are treated, the court or tribunal may declare that the complainant is, in respect of a specified period, entitled to secure the rights that would have accrued if the breach had not occurred.

(7) A period specified for the purposes of subsection (6) must not begin before 17 May 1990.

(8) If the court or tribunal makes a declaration under subsection (6), the employer must provide such resources to the scheme as are necessary to secure for the complainant (without contribution or further contribution by the complainant or other members) the rights referred to in that subsection.

134 Remedies in claims for arrears brought by pensioner members

(1) This section applies to proceedings before a court or employment tribunal on a complaint by a pensioner member of an occupational pension scheme relating to a breach of an equality clause or rule with respect to a term on which the member is treated.

(2) If the court or tribunal finds that there has been a breach referred to in subsection (1), it may –

   (a)   make a declaration as to the rights of the complainant and the respondent in relation to the matters to which the proceedings relate;
   (b)   order an award by way of arrears of benefits or damages or of any other amount in relation to the complainant.

(3) The court or tribunal must not order an award under subsection (2)(b) in respect of a time before the arrears day.

(4) If the court or tribunal orders an award under subsection (2)(b), the employer must provide such resources to the scheme as are necessary to secure for the complainant (without contribution or further contribution by the complainant or other members) the amount of the award.

(5) In relation to proceedings in England and Wales, the arrears day is, in a case mentioned in the first column of the table, the day mentioned in the second column.

Case	*Arrears day*
A standard case	The day falling 6 years before the day on which the proceedings were commenced.
A concealment case or an incapacity case (or a case which is both).	The day on which the breach first occurred.

(6) In relation to proceedings in Scotland, the arrears day is the first day of –

   (a)   the period of 5 years ending with the day on which the proceedings were commenced, or
   (b)   if the case involves a relevant incapacity, or a relevant fraud or error, the period of 20 years ending with that day.

135 Supplementary

(1) This section applies for the purposes of sections 132 to 134.

(2) A standard case is a case which is not –

   (a)   a concealment case,
   (b)   an incapacity case, or
   (c)   a concealment case and an incapacity case.

(3) A concealment case in relation to an equality clause is a case where –

(a)   the responsible person deliberately concealed a qualifying fact (as defined by section 130) from the worker, and

(b)   the worker commenced the proceedings before the end of the period of 6 years beginning with the day on which the worker discovered (or could with reasonable diligence have discovered) the qualifying fact.

(4) A concealment case in relation to an equality rule is a case where –

(a)   the employer or the trustees or managers of the occupational pension scheme in question deliberately concealed a qualifying fact (as defined by section 130) from the member, and

(b)   the member commenced the proceedings before the end of the period of 6 years beginning with the day on which the member discovered (or could with reasonable diligence have discovered) the qualifying fact.

(5) An incapacity case is a case where the worker or member –

(a)   had an incapacity when the breach first occurred, and

(b)   commenced the proceedings before the end of the period of 6 years beginning with the day on which the worker or member ceased to have the incapacity.

(6) A case involves a relevant incapacity or a relevant fraud or error if the period of 5 years referred to in section 132(5)(a) is, as a result of subsection (7) below, reckoned as a period of more than 20 years.

(7) For the purposes of the reckoning referred to in subsection (6), no account is to be taken of time when the worker or member –

(a)   had an incapacity, or

(b)   was induced by a relevant fraud or error to refrain from commencing proceedings (not being a time after the worker or member could with reasonable diligence have discovered the fraud or error).

(8) For the purposes of subsection (7) –

(a)   a fraud is relevant in relation to an equality clause if it is a fraud on the part of the responsible person;

(b)   an error is relevant in relation to an equality clause if it is induced by the words or conduct of the responsible person;

(c)   a fraud is relevant in relation to an equality rule if it is a fraud on the part of the employer or the trustees or managers of the scheme;

(d)   an error is relevant in relation to an equality rule if it is induced by the words or conduct of the employer or the trustees or managers of the scheme.

(9) A reference in subsection (8) to the responsible person, the employer or the trustees or managers includes a reference to a person acting on behalf of the person or persons concerned.

(10) In relation to terms of service, a reference in section 132(5) or subsection (3) or (5)(b) of this section to commencing proceedings is to be read as a reference to making a service complaint.

(11) A reference to a pensioner member of a scheme includes a reference to a person who is entitled to the present payment of pension or other benefits derived through a member.

(12) In relation to proceedings before a court –

(a)   a reference to a complaint is to be read as a reference to a claim, and

(b)   a reference to a complainant is to be read as a reference to a claimant.

Chapter 5
Miscellaneous

136 Burden of proof

(1) This section applies to any proceedings relating to a contravention of this Act.

(2) If there are facts from which the court could decide, in the absence of any other explanation, that a person (A) contravened the provision concerned, the court must hold that the contravention occurred.

(3) But subsection (2) does not apply if A shows that A did not contravene the provision.

(4) The reference to a contravention of this Act includes a reference to a breach of an equality clause or rule.

(5) This section does not apply to proceedings for an offence under this Act.

(6) A reference to the court includes a reference to –

(a)   an employment tribunal;
(b)   the Asylum and Immigration Tribunal;
(c)   the Special Immigration Appeals Commission;
(d)   the First-tier Tribunal;
(e)   the Special Educational Needs Tribunal for Wales;
(f)   an Additional Support Needs Tribunal for Scotland.

137 Previous findings

(1) A finding in relevant proceedings in respect of an act which has become final is to be treated as conclusive in proceedings under this Act.

(2) Relevant proceedings are proceedings before a court or employment tribunal under any of the following –

(a)   section 19 or 20 of the Race Relations Act 1968;
(b)   the Equal Pay Act 1970;
(c)   the Sex Discrimination Act 1975;
(d)   the Race Relations Act 1976;
(e)   section 6(4A) of the Sex Discrimination Act 1986;
(f)   the Disability Discrimination Act 1995;
(g)   Part 2 of the Equality Act 2006;
(h)   the Employment Equality (Religion and Belief) Regulations 2003 (S.I. 2003/1660);
(i)   the Employment Equality (Sexual Orientation) Regulations 2003 (S.I. 2003/1661);
(j)   the Employment Equality (Age) Regulations 2006 (S.I. 2006/1031);
(k)   the Equality Act (Sexual Orientation) Regulations 2007 (S.I. 2007/1263).

(3) A finding becomes final –

(a)   when an appeal against the finding is dismissed, withdrawn or abandoned, or
(b)   when the time for appealing expires without an appeal having been brought.

138 Obtaining information, etc.

(1) In this section –

    (a)   P is a person who thinks that a contravention of this Act has occurred in relation to P;

    (b)   R is a person who P thinks has contravened this Act.

(2) A Minister of the Crown must by order prescribe –

    (a)   forms by which P may question R on any matter which is or may be relevant;

    (b)   forms by which R may answer questions by P.

(3) A question by P or an answer by R is admissible as evidence in proceedings under this Act (whether or not the question or answer is contained in a prescribed form).

(4) A court or tribunal may draw an inference from –

    (a)   a failure by R to answer a question by P before the end of the period of 8 weeks beginning with the day on which the question is served;

    (b)   an evasive or equivocal answer.

(5) Subsection (4) does not apply if –

    (a)   R reasonably asserts that to have answered differently or at all might have prejudiced a criminal matter;

    (b)   R reasonably asserts that to have answered differently or at all would have revealed the reason for not commencing or not continuing criminal proceedings;

    (c)   R's answer is of a kind specified for the purposes of this paragraph by order of a Minister of the Crown;

    (d)   R's answer is given in circumstances specified for the purposes of this paragraph by order of a Minister of the Crown;

    (e)   R's failure to answer occurs in circumstances specified for the purposes of this paragraph by order of a Minister of the Crown.

(6) The reference to a contravention of this Act includes a reference to a breach of an equality clause or rule.

(7) A Minister of the Crown may by order –

    (a)   prescribe the period within which a question must be served to be admissible under subsection (3);

    (b)   prescribe the manner in which a question by P, or an answer by R, may be served.

(8) This section –

    (a)   does not affect any other enactment or rule of law relating to interim or preliminary matters in proceedings before a county court, the sheriff or an employment tribunal, and

    (b)   has effect subject to any enactment or rule of law regulating the admissibility of evidence in such proceedings.

139 Interest

(1) Regulations may make provision –

    (a)   for enabling an employment tribunal to include interest on an amount awarded by it in proceedings under this Act;

(b) specifying the manner in which, and the periods and rate by reference to which, the interest is to be determined.

(2) Regulations may modify the operation of an order made under section 14 of the Employment Tribunals Act 1996 (power to make provision as to interest on awards) in so far as it relates to an award in proceedings under this Act.

140 Conduct giving rise to separate proceedings

(1) This section applies in relation to conduct which has given rise to two or more separate proceedings under this Act, with at least one being for a contravention of section 111 (instructing, causing or inducing contraventions).

(2) A court may transfer proceedings to an employment tribunal.

(3) An employment tribunal may transfer proceedings to a court.

(4) A court or employment tribunal is to be taken for the purposes of this Part to have jurisdiction to determine a claim or complaint transferred to it under this section; accordingly –

(a) a reference to a claim within section 114(1) includes a reference to a claim transferred to a court under this section, and
(b) a reference to a complaint within section 120(1) includes a reference to a complaint transferred to an employment tribunal under this section.

(5) A court or employment tribunal may not make a decision that is inconsistent with an earlier decision in proceedings arising out of the conduct.

(6) "Court" means –

(a) in relation to proceedings in England and Wales, a county court;
(b) in relation to proceedings in Scotland, the sheriff.

141 Interpretation, etc.

(1) This section applies for the purposes of this Part.

(2) A reference to the responsible person, in relation to an equality clause or rule, is to be construed in accordance with Chapter 3 of Part 5.

(3) A reference to a worker is a reference to the person to the terms of whose work the proceedings in question relate; and, for the purposes of proceedings relating to an equality rule or a non-discrimination rule, a reference to a worker includes a reference to a member of the occupational pension scheme in question.

(4) A reference to the terms of a person's work is to be construed in accordance with Chapter 3 of Part 5.

(5) A reference to a member of an occupational pension scheme includes a reference to a prospective member.

(6) In relation to proceedings in England and Wales, a person has an incapacity if the person –

(a) has not attained the age of 18, or
(b) lacks capacity (within the meaning of the Mental Capacity Act 2005).

(7) In relation to proceedings in Scotland, a person has an incapacity if the person –

(a) has not attained the age of 16, or

(b)   is incapable (within the meaning of the Adults with Incapacity (Scotland) Act 2000 (asp 4)).

(8) "Service complaint" means a complaint under section 334 of the Armed Forces Act 2006; and "service complaint procedures" means the procedures prescribed by regulations under that section (except in so far as relating to references under section 337 of that Act).

(9) "Criminal matter" means –

(a)   an investigation into the commission of an alleged offence;
(b)   a decision whether to commence criminal proceedings;
(c)   criminal proceedings.

PART 10
CONTRACTS, ETC.

Contracts and other agreements

142 Unenforceable terms

(1) A term of a contract is unenforceable against a person in so far as it constitutes, promotes or provides for treatment of that or another person that is of a description prohibited by this Act.

(2) A relevant non-contractual term is unenforceable against a person in so far as it constitutes, promotes or provides for treatment of that or another person that is of a description prohibited by this Act, in so far as this Act relates to disability.

(3) A relevant non-contractual term is a term which –

(a)   is a term of an agreement that is not a contract, and
(b)   relates to the provision of an employment service within section 56(2)(a) to (e) or to the provision under a group insurance arrangement of facilities by way of insurance.

(4) A reference in subsection (1) or (2) to treatment of a description prohibited by this Act does not include –

(a)   a reference to the inclusion of a term in a contract referred to in section 70(2)(a) or 76(2), or
(b)   a reference to the failure to include a term in a contract as referred to in section 70(2)(b).

(5) Subsection (4) does not affect the application of section 148(2) to this section.

143 Removal or modification of unenforceable terms

(1) A county court or the sheriff may, on an application by a person who has an interest in a contract or other agreement which includes a term that is unenforceable as a result of section 142, make an order for the term to be removed or modified.

(2) An order under this section must not be made unless every person who would be affected by it –

(a)   has been given notice of the application (except where notice is dispensed with in accordance with rules of court), and
(b)   has been afforded an opportunity to make representations to the county court or sheriff.

(3) An order under this section may include provision in respect of a period before the making of the order.

144 Contracting out

(1) A term of a contract is unenforceable by a person in whose favour it would operate in so far as it purports to exclude or limit a provision of or made under this Act.

(2) A relevant non-contractual term (as defined by section 142) is unenforceable by a person in whose favour it would operate in so far as it purports to exclude or limit a provision of or made under this Act, in so far as the provision relates to disability.

(3) This section does not apply to a contract which settles a claim within section 114.

(4) This section does not apply to a contract which settles a complaint within section 120 if the contract –

(a)   is made with the assistance of a conciliation officer, or
(b)   is a qualifying compromise contract.

(5) A contract within subsection (4) includes a contract which settles a complaint relating to a breach of an equality clause or rule or of a non-discrimination rule.

(6) A contract within subsection (4) includes an agreement by the parties to a dispute to submit the dispute to arbitration if –

(a)   the dispute is covered by a scheme having effect by virtue of an order under section 212A of the Trade Union and Labour Relations (Consolidation) Act 1992, and
(b)   the agreement is to submit the dispute to arbitration in accordance with the scheme.

Collective agreements and rules of undertakings

145 Void and unenforceable terms

(1) A term of a collective agreement is void in so far as it constitutes, promotes or provides for treatment of a description prohibited by this Act.

(2) A rule of an undertaking is unenforceable against a person in so far as it constitutes, promotes or provides for treatment of the person that is of a description prohibited by this Act.

146 Declaration in respect of void term, etc.

(1) A qualifying person (P) may make a complaint to an employment tribunal that a term is void, or that a rule is unenforceable, as a result of section 145.

(2) But subsection (1) applies only if –

(a)   the term or rule may in the future have effect in relation to P, and
(b)   where the complaint alleges that the term or rule provides for treatment of a description prohibited by this Act, P may in the future be subjected to treatment that would (if P were subjected to it in present circumstances) be of that description.

(3) If the tribunal finds that the complaint is well-founded, it must make an order declaring that the term is void or the rule is unenforceable.

(4) An order under this section may include provision in respect of a period before the making of the order.

(5) In the case of a complaint about a term of a collective agreement, where the term is one made by or on behalf of a person of a description specified in the first column of the table, a qualifying person is a person of a description specified in the second column.

Description of person who made collective agreement	*Qualifying person*
Employer	A person who is, or is seeking to be, an employee of that employer
Organisation of employers	A person who is, or is seeking to be, an employee of an employer who is a member of that organisation
Association of organisations of employers	A person who is, or is seeking to be, an employee of an employer who is a member of an organisation in that association

(6) In the case of a complaint about a rule of an undertaking, where the rule is one made by or on behalf of a person of a description specified in the first column of the table, a qualifying person is a person of a description specified in the second column.

Description of person who made rule of undertaking	*Qualifying person*
Employer	A person who is, or is seeking to be, an employee of that employer
Trade organisation or qualifications body	A person who is, or is seeking to be, a member of the organisation or body
	A person upon whom the body has conferred a relevant qualification
	A person seeking conferment by the body of a relevant qualification

Supplementary

147 Meaning of "qualifying compromise contract"

(1) This section applies for the purposes of this Part.

(2) A qualifying compromise contract is a contract in relation to which each of the conditions in subsection (3) is met.

(3) Those conditions are that –

    (a)   the contract is in writing,

    (b)   the contract relates to the particular complaint,

    (c)   the complainant has, before entering into the contract, received advice from an independent adviser about its terms and effect (including, in particular, its effect on the complainant's ability to pursue the complaint before an employment tribunal),

(d)   on the date of the giving of the advice, there is in force a contract of insurance, or an indemnity provided for members of a profession or professional body, covering the risk of a claim by the complainant in respect of loss arising from the advice,

(e)   the contract identifies the adviser, and

(f)   the contract states that the conditions in paragraphs (c) and (d) are met.

(4) Each of the following is an independent adviser –

(a)   a qualified lawyer;

(b)   an officer, official, employee or member of an independent trade union certified in writing by the trade union as competent to give advice and as authorised to do so on its behalf;

(c)   a worker at an advice centre (whether as an employee or a volunteer) certified in writing by the centre as competent to give advice and as authorised to do so on its behalf;

(d)   a person of such description as may be specified by order.

(5) Despite subsection (4), none of the following is an independent adviser in relation to a qualifying compromise contract –

(a)   a person who is a party to the contract or the complaint;

(b)   a person who is connected to a person within paragraph (a);

(c)   a person who is employed by a person within paragraph (a) or (b);

(d)   a person who is acting for a person within paragraph (a) or (b) in relation to the contract or the complaint;

(e)   a person within subsection (4)(b) or (c), if the trade union or advice centre is a person within paragraph (a) or (b);

(f)   a person within subsection (4)(c) to whom the complainant makes a payment for the advice.

(6) A "qualified lawyer", for the purposes of subsection (4)(a), is –

(a)   in relation to England and Wales, a person who, for the purposes of the Legal Services Act 2007, is an authorised person in relation to an activity which constitutes the exercise of a right of audience or the conduct of litigation;

(b)   in relation to Scotland, an advocate (whether in practice as such or employed to give legal advice) or a solicitor who holds a practising certificate.

(7) "Independent trade union" has the meaning given in section 5 of the Trade Union and Labour Relations (Consolidation) Act 1992.

(8) Two persons are connected for the purposes of subsection (5) if –

(a)   one is a company of which the other (directly or indirectly) has control, or

(b)   both are companies of which a third person (directly or indirectly) has control.

(9) Two persons are also connected for the purposes of subsection (5) in so far as a connection between them gives rise to a conflict of interest in relation to the contract or the complaint.

148 Interpretation

(1) This section applies for the purposes of this Part.

(2) A reference to treatment of a description prohibited by this Act does not include treatment in so far as it is treatment that would contravene –

(a) Part 1 (public sector duty regarding socio-economic inequalities), or

(b) Chapter 1 of Part 11 (public sector equality duty).

(3) "Group insurance arrangement" means an arrangement between an employer and another person for the provision by that other person of facilities by way of insurance to the employer's employees (or a class of those employees).

(4) "Collective agreement" has the meaning given in section 178 of the Trade Union and Labour Relations (Consolidation) Act 1992.

(5) A rule of an undertaking is a rule within subsection (6) or (7).

(6) A rule within this subsection is a rule made by a trade organisation or a qualifications body for application to –

(a) its members or prospective members,

(b) persons on whom it has conferred a relevant qualification, or

(c) persons seeking conferment by it of a relevant qualification.

(7) A rule within this subsection is a rule made by an employer for application to –

(a) employees,

(b) persons who apply for employment, or

(c) persons the employer considers for employment.

(8) "Trade organisation", "qualifications body" and "relevant qualification" each have the meaning given in Part 5 (work).

PART 11
ADVANCEMENT OF EQUALITY

Chapter 1
Public sector equality duty

149 Public sector equality duty

(1) A public authority must, in the exercise of its functions, have due regard to the need to –

(a) eliminate discrimination, harassment, victimisation and any other conduct that is prohibited by or under this Act;

(b) advance equality of opportunity between persons who share a relevant protected characteristic and persons who do not share it;

(c) foster good relations between persons who share a relevant protected characteristic and persons who do not share it.

(2) A person who is not a public authority but who exercises public functions must, in the exercise of those functions, have due regard to the matters mentioned in subsection (1).

(3) Having due regard to the need to advance equality of opportunity between persons who share a relevant protected characteristic and persons who do not share it involves having due regard, in particular, to the need to –

(a) remove or minimise disadvantages suffered by persons who share a relevant protected characteristic that are connected to that characteristic;

(b) take steps to meet the needs of persons who share a relevant protected characteristic that are different from the needs of persons who do not share it;

(c)   encourage persons who share a relevant protected characteristic to participate in public life or in any other activity in which participation by such persons is disproportionately low.

(4) The steps involved in meeting the needs of disabled persons that are different from the needs of persons who are not disabled include, in particular, steps to take account of disabled persons' disabilities.

(5) Having due regard to the need to foster good relations between persons who share a relevant protected characteristic and persons who do not share it involves having due regard, in particular, to the need to –

(a)   tackle prejudice, and
(b)   promote understanding.

(6) Compliance with the duties in this section may involve treating some persons more favourably than others; but that is not to be taken as permitting conduct that would otherwise be prohibited by or under this Act.

(7) The relevant protected characteristics are –

age;
disability;
gender reassignment;
pregnancy and maternity;
race;
religion or belief;
sex;
sexual orientation.

(8) A reference to conduct that is prohibited by or under this Act includes a reference to –

(a)   a breach of an equality clause or rule;
(b)   a breach of a non-discrimination rule.

(9) Schedule 18 (exceptions) has effect.

150 Public authorities and public functions

(1) A public authority is a person who is specified in Schedule 19.

(2) In that Schedule –

Part 1 specifies public authorities generally;
Part 2 specifies relevant Welsh authorities;
Part 3 specifies relevant Scottish authorities.

(3) A public authority specified in Schedule 19 is subject to the duty imposed by section 149(1) in relation to the exercise of all of its functions unless subsection (4) applies.

(4) A public authority specified in that Schedule in respect of certain specified functions is subject to that duty only in respect of the exercise of those functions.

(5) A public function is a function that is a function of a public nature for the purposes of the Human Rights Act 1998.

151 Power to specify public authorities

(1) A Minister of the Crown may by order amend Part 1, 2 or 3 of Schedule 19.

(2) The Welsh Ministers may by order amend Part 2 of Schedule 19.

(3) The Scottish Ministers may by order amend Part 3 of Schedule 19.

(4) The power under subsection (1), (2) or (3) may not be exercised so as to –

    (a) add an entry to Part 1 relating to a relevant Welsh or Scottish authority or a cross-border Welsh or Scottish authority;

    (b) add an entry to Part 2 relating to a person who is not a relevant Welsh authority;

    (c) add an entry to Part 3 relating to a person who is not a relevant Scottish authority.

(5) A Minister of the Crown may by order amend Schedule 19 so as to make provision relating to a cross-border Welsh or Scottish authority.

(6) On the first exercise of the power under subsection (5) to add an entry relating to a cross-border Welsh or Scottish authority to Schedule 19, a Minister of the Crown must –

    (a) add a Part 4 to the Schedule for cross-border authorities, and

    (b) add the cross-border Welsh or Scottish authority to that Part.

(7) Any subsequent exercise of the power under subsection (5) to add an entry relating to a cross-border Welsh or Scottish authority to Schedule 19 must add that entry to Part 4 of the Schedule.

(8) An order may not be made under this section so as to extend the application of section 149 unless the person making it considers that the extension relates to a person by whom a public function is exercisable.

(9) An order may not be made under this section so as to extend the application of section 149 to –

    (a) the exercise of a function referred to in paragraph 3 of Schedule 18 (judicial functions, etc);

    (b) a person listed in paragraph 4(2)(a) to (e) of that Schedule (Parliament, devolved legislatures and General Synod);

    (c) the exercise of a function listed in paragraph 4(3) of that Schedule (proceedings in Parliament or devolved legislatures).

152 Power to specify public authorities: consultation and consent

(1) Before making an order under a provision specified in the first column of the Table, a Minister of the Crown must consult the person or persons specified in the second column.

Provision	Consultees
Section 151(1)	The Commission
Section 151(1), so far as relating to a relevant Welsh authority	The Welsh Ministers
Section 151(1), so far as relating to a relevant Scottish authority	The Scottish Ministers

Section 151(5)	The Commission
Section 151(5), so far as relating to a cross-border Welsh authority	The Welsh Ministers
Section 151(5), so far as relating to a cross-border Scottish authority	The Scottish Ministers

(2) Before making an order under section 151(2), the Welsh Ministers must –

    (a)   obtain the consent of a Minister of the Crown, and

    (b)   consult the Commission.

(3) Before making an order under section 151(3), the Scottish Ministers must –

    (a)   obtain the consent of a Minister of the Crown, and

    (b)   consult the Commission.

153 Power to impose specific duties

(1) A Minister of the Crown may by regulations impose duties on a public authority specified in Part 1 of Schedule 19 for the purpose of enabling the better performance by the authority of the duty imposed by section 149(1).

(2) The Welsh Ministers may by regulations impose duties on a public authority specified in Part 2 of Schedule 19 for that purpose.

(3) The Scottish Ministers may by regulations impose duties on a public authority specified in Part 3 of Schedule 19 for that purpose.

(4) Before making regulations under this section, the person making them must consult the Commission.

154 Power to impose specific duties: cross-border authorities

(1) If a Minister of the Crown exercises the power in section 151(5) to add an entry for a public authority to Part 4 of Schedule 19, the Minister must include after the entry a letter specified in the first column of the Table in subsection (3).

(2) Where a letter specified in the first column of the Table in subsection (3) is included after an entry for a public authority in Part 4 of Schedule 19, the person specified in the second column of the Table –

    (a)   may by regulations impose duties on the authority for the purpose of enabling the better performance by the authority of the duty imposed by section 149(1), subject to such limitations as are specified in that column;

    (b)   must in making the regulations comply with the procedural requirement specified in that column.

(3) This is the Table –

Letter	*Person by whom regulations may he made and procedural requirements*
A	Regulations may be made by a Minister of the Crown in relation to the authority's functions that are not devolved Welsh functions.
	The Minister of the Crown must consult the Welsh Ministers before making the regulations.

Regulations may be made by the Welsh Ministers in relation to the authority's devolved Welsh functions.

The Welsh Ministers must consult a Minister of the Crown before making the regulations.

B   Regulations may be made by a Minister of the Crown in relation to the authority's functions that are not devolved Scottish functions.

The Minister of the Crown must consult the Scottish Ministers before making the regulations.

Regulations may be made by the Scottish Ministers in relation to the authority's devolved Scottish functions.

The Scottish Ministers must consult a Minister of the Crown before making the regulations.

C   Regulations may be made by a Minister of the Crown in relation to the authority's functions that are neither devolved Welsh functions nor devolved Scottish functions.

The Minister of the Crown must consult the Welsh Ministers and the Scottish Ministers before making the regulations.

Regulations may be made by the Welsh Ministers in relation to the authority's devolved Welsh functions.

The Welsh Ministers must consult a Minister of the Crown before making the regulations.

Regulations may be made by the Scottish Ministers in relation to the authority's devolved Scottish functions.

The Scottish Ministers must consult a Minister of the Crown before making the regulations.

D   The regulations may be made by a Minister of the Crown.

The Minister of the Crown must consult the Welsh Ministers before making the regulations.

(4) Before making regulations under subsection (2), the person making them must consult the Commission.

155 Power to impose specific duties: supplementary

(1) Regulations under section 153 or 154 may require a public authority to consider such matters as may be specified from time to time by –

(a)   a Minister of the Crown, where the regulations are made by a Minister of the Crown;
(b)   the Welsh Ministers, where the regulations are made by the Welsh Ministers;
(c)   the Scottish Ministers, where the regulations are made by the Scottish Ministers.

(2) Regulations under section 153 or 154 may impose duties on a public authority that is a contracting authority within the meaning of the Public Sector Directive in connection with its public procurement functions.

(3) In subsection (2) –

"public procurement functions" means functions the exercise of which is regulated by the Public Sector Directive;

"the Public Sector Directive" means Directive 2004/18/EC of the European Parliament and of the Council of 31 March 2004 on the coordination of procedures for the award of public works contracts, public supply contracts and public service contracts, as amended from time to time.

(4) Subsections (1) and (2) do not affect the generality of section 153 or 154(2)(a).

(5) A duty imposed on a public authority under section 153 or 154 may be modified or removed by regulations made by –

(a) a Minister of the Crown, where the original duty was imposed by regulations made by a Minister of the Crown;

(b) the Welsh Ministers, where the original duty was imposed by regulations made by the Welsh Ministers;

(c) the Scottish Ministers, where the original duty was imposed by regulations made by the Scottish Ministers.

156 Enforcement

A failure in respect of a performance of a duty imposed by or under this Chapter does not confer a cause of action at private law.

157 Interpretation

(1) This section applies for the purposes of this Chapter.

(2) A relevant Welsh authority is a person (other than the Assembly Commission) whose functions –

(a) are exercisable only in or as regards Wales, and

(b) are wholly or mainly devolved Welsh functions.

(3) A cross-border Welsh authority is a person other than a relevant Welsh authority (or the Assembly Commission) who has any function that –

(a) is exercisable in or as regards Wales, and

(b) is a devolved Welsh function.

(4) The Assembly Commission has the same meaning as in the Government of Wales Act 2006.

(5) A function is a devolved Welsh function if it relates to –

(a) a matter in respect of which functions are exercisable by the Welsh Ministers, the First Minister for Wales or the Counsel General to the Welsh Assembly Government, or

(b) a matter within the legislative competence of the National Assembly for Wales.

(6) A relevant Scottish authority is a public body, public office or holder of a public office –

(a) which is not a cross-border Scottish authority or the Scottish Parliamentary Corporate Body,

(b) whose functions are exercisable only in or as regards Scotland, and

(c) at least some of whose functions do not relate to reserved matters.

(7) A cross-border Scottish authority is a cross-border public authority within the meaning given by section 88(5) of the Scotland Act 1998.

(8) A function is a devolved Scottish function if it –

    (a)   is exercisable in or as regards Scotland, and

    (b)   does not relate to reserved matters.

(9) Reserved matters has the same meaning as in the Scotland Act 1998.

Chapter 2
Positive action

158 Positive action: general

(1) This section applies if a person (P) reasonably thinks that –

    (a)   persons who share a protected characteristic suffer a disadvantage connected to the characteristic,

    (b)   persons who share a protected characteristic have needs that are different from the needs of persons who do not share it, or

    (c)   participation in an activity by persons who share a protected characteristic is disproportionately low.

(2) This Act does not prohibit P from taking any action which is a proportionate means of achieving the aim of –

    (a)   enabling or encouraging persons who share the protected characteristic to overcome or minimise that disadvantage,

    (b)   meeting those needs, or

    (c)   enabling or encouraging persons who share the protected characteristic to participate in that activity.

(3) Regulations may specify action, or descriptions of action, to which subsection (2) does not apply.

(4) This section does not apply to –

    (a)   action within section 159(3), or

    (b)   anything that is permitted by virtue of section 104.

(5) If section 104(7) is repealed by virtue of section 105, this section will not apply to anything that would have been so permitted but for the repeal.

(6) This section does not enable P to do anything that is prohibited by or under an enactment other than this Act.

159 Positive action: recruitment and promotion

(1) This section applies if a person (P) reasonably thinks that –

    (a)   persons who share a protected characteristic suffer a disadvantage connected to the characteristic, or

    (b)   participation in an activity by persons who share a protected characteristic is disproportionately low.

(2) Part 5 (work) does not prohibit P from taking action within subsection (3) with the aim of enabling or encouraging persons who share the protected characteristic to –

    (a)   overcome or minimise that disadvantage, or

(b)　participate in that activity.

(3) That action is treating a person (A) more favourably in connection with recruitment or promotion than another person (B) because A has the protected characteristic but B does not.

(4) But subsection (2) applies only if –

(a)　A is as qualified as B to be recruited or promoted,

(b)　P does not have a policy of treating persons who share the protected characteristic more favourably in connection with recruitment or promotion than persons who do not share it, and

(c)　taking the action in question is a proportionate means of achieving the aim referred to in subsection (2).

(5) "Recruitment" means a process for deciding whether to –

(a)　offer employment to a person,

(b)　make contract work available to a contract worker,

(c)　offer a person a position as a partner in a firm or proposed firm,

(d)　offer a person a position as a member of an LLP or proposed LLP,

(e)　offer a person a pupillage or tenancy in barristers' chambers,

(f)　take a person as an advocate's devil or offer a person membership of an advocate's stable,

(g)　offer a person an appointment to a personal office,

(h)　offer a person an appointment to a public office, recommend a person for such an appointment or approve a person's appointment to a public office, or

(i)　offer a person a service for finding employment.

(6) This section does not enable P to do anything that is prohibited by or under an enactment other than this Act.

PART 12
DISABLED PERSONS: TRANSPORT

Chapter 1
Taxis, etc.

160 Taxi accessibility regulations

(1) The Secretary of State may make regulations (in this Chapter referred to as "taxi accessibility regulations") for securing that it is possible for disabled persons –

(a)　to get into and out of taxis in safety;

(b)　to do so while in wheelchairs;

(c)　to travel in taxis in safety and reasonable comfort;

(d)　to do so while in wheelchairs.

(2) The regulations may, in particular, require a regulated taxi to conform with provision as to –

(a)　the size of a door opening for the use of passengers;

(b)　the floor area of the passenger compartment;

(c)　the amount of headroom in the passenger compartment;

(d)　the fitting of restraining devices designed to ensure the stability of a wheelchair while the taxi is moving.

(3) The regulations may also –

(a)   require the driver of a regulated taxi which is plying for hire, or which has been hired, to comply with provisions as to the carrying of ramps or other devices designed to facilitate the loading and unloading of wheelchairs;

(b)   require the driver of a regulated taxi in which a disabled person is being carried while in a wheelchair to comply with provisions as to the position in which the wheelchair is to be secured.

(4) The driver of a regulated taxi which is plying for hire or has been hired commits an offence –

(a)   by failing to comply with a requirement of the regulations, or

(b)   if the taxi fails to conform with any provision of the regulations with which it is required to conform.

(5) A person guilty of an offence under subsection (4) is liable on summary conviction to a fine not exceeding level 3 on the standard scale.

(6) In this section –

"passenger compartment" has such meaning as is specified in taxi accessibility regulations;

"regulated taxi" means a taxi to which taxi accessibility regulations are expressed to apply.

161 Control of numbers of licensed taxis: exception

(1) This section applies if –

(a)   an application for a licence in respect of a vehicle is made under section 37 of the Town Police Clauses Act 1847,

(b)   it is possible for a disabled person –

    (i)   to get into and out of the vehicle in safety,

    (ii)   to travel in the vehicle in safety and reasonable comfort, and

    (iii)   to do the things mentioned in sub-paragraphs (i) and (ii) while in a wheelchair of a size prescribed by the Secretary of State, and

(c)   the proportion of taxis licensed in respect of the area to which the licence would (if granted) apply that conform to the requirement in paragraph (b) is less than the proportion that is prescribed by the Secretary of State.

(2) Section 16 of the Transport Act 1985 (which modifies the provisions of the Town Police Clauses Act 1847 about hackney carriages to allow a licence to ply for hire to be refused in order to limit the number of licensed carriages) does not apply in relation to the vehicle; and those provisions of the Town Police Clauses Act 1847 are to have effect subject to this section.

(3) In section 16 of the Transport Act 1985, after "shall" insert "(subject to section 161 of the Equality Act 2010)".

162 Designated transport facilities

(1) The appropriate authority may by regulations provide for the application of any taxi provision (with or without modification) to –

(a)   vehicles used for the provision of services under a franchise agreement, or

(b)   drivers of such vehicles.

(2) A franchise agreement is a contract entered into by the operator of a designated transport facility for the provision, by the other party to the contract, of hire car services –

    (a)   for members of the public using any part of the facility, and
    (b)   which involve vehicles entering any part of the facility.

(3) In this section –

"appropriate authority" means –
    (a)   in relation to transport facilities in England and Wales, the Secretary of State;
    (b)   in relation to transport facilities in Scotland, the Scottish Ministers;

"designated" means designated by order made by the appropriate authority;
"hire car" has such meaning as is prescribed by the appropriate authority;
"operator", in relation to a transport facility, means a person who is concerned with the management or operation of the facility;
"taxi provision" means a provision of –
    (a)   this Chapter, or
    (b)   regulations made in pursuance of section 20(2A) of the Civic Government (Scotland) Act 1982,

which applies in relation to taxis or drivers of taxis;
"transport facility" means premises which form part of a port, airport, railway station or bus station.

(4) For the purposes of section 2(2) of the European Communities Act 1972 (implementation of EU obligations), the Secretary of State may exercise a power conferred by this section on the Scottish Ministers.

163 Taxi licence conditional on compliance with taxi accessibility regulations

(1) A licence for a taxi to ply for hire must not be granted unless the vehicle conforms with the provisions of taxi accessibility regulations with which a vehicle is required to conform if it is licensed.

(2) Subsection (1) does not apply if a licence is in force in relation to the vehicle at any time during the period of 28 days immediately before the day on which the licence is granted.

(3) The Secretary of State may by order provide for subsection (2) to cease to have effect on a specified date.

(4) The power under subsection (3) may be exercised differently for different areas or localities.

164 Exemption from taxi accessibility regulations

(1) The Secretary of State may by regulations provide for a relevant licensing authority to apply for an order (an "exemption order") exempting the authority from the requirements of section 163.

(2) Regulations under subsection (1) may, in particular, make provision requiring an authority proposing to apply for an exemption order –

    (a)   to carry out such consultation as is specified;
    (b)   to publish its proposals in the specified manner;

(c)   before applying for the order, to consider representations made about the proposal;

(d)   to make the application in the specified form.

In this subsection "specified" means specified in the regulations.

(3) An authority may apply for an exemption order only if it is satisfied –

(a)   that, having regard to the circumstances in its area, it is inappropriate for section 163 to apply, and

(b)   that the application of that section would result in an unacceptable reduction in the number of taxis in its area.

(4) After consulting the Disabled Persons Transport Advisory Committee and such other persons as the Secretary of State thinks appropriate, the Secretary of State may –

(a)   make an exemption order in the terms of the application for the order;

(b)   make an exemption order in such other terms as the Secretary of State thinks appropriate;

(c)   refuse to make an exemption order.

(5) The Secretary of State may by regulations make provision requiring a taxi plying for hire in an area in respect of which an exemption order is in force to conform with provisions of the regulations as to the fitting and use of swivel seats.

(6) Regulations under subsection (5) may make provision corresponding to section 163.

(7) In this section –

"relevant licensing authority" means an authority responsible for licensing taxis in any area of England and Wales other than the area to which the Metropolitan Public Carriage Act 1869 applies;

"swivel seats" has such meaning as is specified in regulations under subsection (5).

165 Passengers in wheelchairs

(1) This section imposes duties on the driver of a designated taxi which has been hired –

(a)   by or for a disabled person who is in a wheelchair, or

(b)   by another person who wishes to be accompanied by a disabled person who is in a wheelchair.

(2) This section also imposes duties on the driver of a designated private hire vehicle, if a person within paragraph (a) or (b) of subsection (1) has indicated to the driver that the person wishes to travel in the vehicle.

(3) For the purposes of this section –

(a)   a taxi or private hire vehicle is "designated" if it appears on a list maintained under section 167;

(b)   "the passenger" means the disabled person concerned.

(4) The duties are –

(a)   to carry the passenger while in the wheelchair;

(b)   not to make any additional charge for doing so;

(c)   if the passenger chooses to sit in a passenger seat, to carry the wheelchair;

(d)   to take such steps as are necessary to ensure that the passenger is carried in safety and reasonable comfort;

(e)   to give the passenger such mobility assistance as is reasonably required.

(5) Mobility assistance is assistance –

(a) to enable the passenger to get into or out of the vehicle;
(b) if the passenger wishes to remain in the wheelchair, to enable the passenger to get into and out of the vehicle while in the wheelchair;
(c) to load the passenger's luggage into or out of the vehicle;
(d) if the passenger does not wish to remain in the wheelchair, to load the wheelchair into or out of the vehicle.

(6) This section does not require the driver –

(a) unless the vehicle is of a description prescribed by the Secretary of State, to carry more than one person in a wheelchair, or more than one wheelchair, on any one journey;
(b) to carry a person in circumstances in which it would otherwise be lawful for the driver to refuse to carry the person.

(7) A driver of a designated taxi or designated private hire vehicle commits an offence by failing to comply with a duty imposed on the driver by this section.

(8) A person guilty of an offence under subsection (7) is liable on summary conviction to a fine not exceeding level 3 on the standard scale.

(9) It is a defence for a person charged with the offence to show that at the time of the alleged offence –

(a) the vehicle conformed to the accessibility requirements which applied to it, but
(b) it would not have been possible for the wheelchair to be carried safely in the vehicle.

(10) In this section and sections 166 and 167 "private hire vehicle" means –

(a) a vehicle licensed under section 48 of the Local Government (Miscellaneous Provisions) Act 1976;
(b) a vehicle licensed under section 7 of the Private Hire Vehicles (London) Act 1998;
(c) a vehicle licensed under an equivalent provision of a local enactment;
(d) a private hire car licensed under section 10 of the Civic Government (Scotland) Act 1982.

166 Passengers in wheelchairs: exemption certificates

(1) A licensing authority must issue a person with a certificate exempting the person from the duties imposed by section 165 (an "exemption certificate") if satisfied that it is appropriate to do so –

(a) on medical grounds, or
(b) on the ground that the person's physical condition makes it impossible or unreasonably difficult for the person to comply with those duties.

(2) An exemption certificate is valid for such period as is specified in the certificate.

(3) The driver of a designated taxi is exempt from the duties imposed by section 165 if –

(a) an exemption certificate issued to the driver is in force, and
(b) the prescribed notice of the exemption is exhibited on the taxi in the prescribed manner.

(4) The driver of a designated private hire vehicle is exempt from the duties imposed by section 165 if –

(a)   an exemption certificate issued to the driver is in force, and
(b)   the prescribed notice of the exemption is exhibited on the vehicle in the prescribed manner.

(5) For the purposes of this section, a taxi or private hire vehicle is "designated" if it appears on a list maintained under section 167.

(6) In this section and section 167 "licensing authority", in relation to any area, means the authority responsible for licensing taxis or, as the case may be, private hire vehicles in that area.

167 Lists of wheelchair-accessible vehicles

(1) For the purposes of section 165, a licensing authority may maintain a list of vehicles falling within subsection (2).

(2) A vehicle falls within this subsection if –

(a)   it is either a taxi or a private hire vehicle, and
(b)   it conforms to such accessibility requirements as the licensing authority thinks fit.

(3) A licensing authority may, if it thinks fit, decide that a vehicle may be included on a list maintained under this section only if it is being used, or is to be used, by the holder of a special licence under that licence.

(4) In subsection (3) "special licence" has the meaning given by section 12 of the Transport Act 1985 (use of taxis or hire cars in providing local services).

(5) "Accessibility requirements" are requirements for securing that it is possible for disabled persons in wheelchairs –

(a)   to get into and out of vehicles in safety, and
(b)   to travel in vehicles in safety and reasonable comfort,

either staying in their wheelchairs or not (depending on which they prefer).

(6) The Secretary of State may issue guidance to licensing authorities as to –

(a)   the accessibility requirements which they should apply for the purposes of this section;
(b)   any other aspect of their functions under or by virtue of this section.

(7) A licensing authority which maintains a list under subsection (1) must have regard to any guidance issued under subsection (6).

168 Assistance dogs in taxis

(1) This section imposes duties on the driver of a taxi which has been hired –

(a)   by or for a disabled person who is accompanied by an assistance dog, or
(b)   by another person who wishes to be accompanied by a disabled person with an assistance dog.

(2) The driver must –

(a)   carry the disabled person's dog and allow it to remain with that person;
(b)   not make any additional charge for doing so.

(3) The driver of a taxi commits an offence by failing to comply with a duty imposed by this section.

(4) A person guilty of an offence under this section is liable on summary conviction to a fine not exceeding level 3 on the standard scale.

169 Assistance dogs in taxis: exemption certificates

(1) A licensing authority must issue a person with a certificate exempting the person from the duties imposed by section 168 (an "exemption certificate") if satisfied that it is appropriate to do so on medical grounds.

(2) In deciding whether to issue an exemption certificate the authority must have regard, in particular, to the physical characteristics of the taxi which the person drives or those of any kind of taxi in relation to which the person requires the certificate.

(3) An exemption certificate is valid –

    (a)   in respect of a specified taxi or a specified kind of taxi;
    (b)   for such period as is specified in the certificate.

(4) The driver of a taxi is exempt from the duties imposed by section 168 if –

    (a)   an exemption certificate issued to the driver is in force with respect to the taxi, and
    (b)   the prescribed notice of the exemption is exhibited on the taxi in the prescribed manner.

The power to make regulations under paragraph (b) is exercisable by the Secretary of State.

(5) In this section "licensing authority" means –

    (a)   in relation to the area to which the Metropolitan Public Carriage Act 1869 applies, Transport for London;
    (b)   in relation to any other area in England and Wales, the authority responsible for licensing taxis in that area.

170 Assistance dogs in private hire vehicles

(1) The operator of a private hire vehicle commits an offence by failing or refusing to accept a booking for the vehicle –

    (a)   if the booking is requested by or on behalf of a disabled person or a person who wishes to be accompanied by a disabled person, and
    (b)   the reason for the failure or refusal is that the disabled person will be accompanied by an assistance dog.

(2) The operator commits an offence by making an additional charge for carrying an assistance dog which is accompanying a disabled person.

(3) The driver of a private hire vehicle commits an offence by failing or refusing to carry out a booking accepted by the operator –

    (a)   if the booking is made by or on behalf of a disabled person or a person who wishes to be accompanied by a disabled person, and
    (b)   the reason for the failure or refusal is that the disabled person is accompanied by an assistance dog.

(4) A person guilty of an offence under this section is liable on summary conviction to a fine not exceeding level 3 on the standard scale.

(5) In this section –

"driver" means a person who holds a licence under –
    (a)   section 13 of the Private Hire Vehicles (London) Act 1998 ("the 1998 Act"),
    (b)   section 51 of the Local Government (Miscellaneous Provisions) Act 1976 ("the 1976 Act"), or
    (c)   an equivalent provision of a local enactment;

"licensing authority", in relation to any area in England and Wales, means the authority responsible for licensing private hire vehicles in that area;

"operator" means a person who holds a licence under –
    (a)   section 3 of the 1998 Act,
    (b)   section 55 of the 1976 Act, or
    (c)   an equivalent provision of a local enactment;

"private hire vehicle" means a vehicle licensed under –
    (a)   section 6 of the 1998 Act,
    (b)   section 48 of the 1976 Act, or
    (c)   an equivalent provision of a local enactment.

171 Assistance dogs in private hire vehicles: exemption certificates

(1) A licensing authority must issue a driver with a certificate exempting the driver from the offence under section 170(3) (an "exemption certificate") if satisfied that it is appropriate to do so on medical grounds.

(2) In deciding whether to issue an exemption certificate the authority must have regard, in particular, to the physical characteristics of the private hire vehicle which the person drives or those of any kind of private hire vehicle in relation to which the person requires the certificate.

(3) An exemption certificate is valid –

    (a)   in respect of a specified private hire vehicle or a specified kind of private hire vehicle;
    (b)   for such period as is specified in the certificate.

(4) A driver does not commit an offence under section 170(3) if –

    (a)   an exemption certificate issued to the driver is in force with respect to the private hire vehicle, and
    (b)   the prescribed notice of the exemption is exhibited on the vehicle in the prescribed manner.

The power to make regulations under paragraph (b) is exercisable by the Secretary of State.

(5) In this section "driver", "licensing authority" and "private hire vehicle" have the same meaning as in section 170.

172 Appeals

(1) A person who is aggrieved by the refusal of a licensing authority in England and Wales to issue an exemption certificate under section 166, 169 or 171 may appeal to a magistrates' court before the end of the period of 28 days beginning with the date of the refusal.

(2) A person who is aggrieved by the refusal of a licensing authority in Scotland to issue an exemption certificate under section 166 may appeal to the sheriff before the end of the period of 28 days beginning with the date of the refusal.

(3) On an appeal under subsection (1) or (2), the magistrates' court or sheriff may direct the licensing authority to issue the exemption certificate to have effect for such period as is specified in the direction.

(4) A person who is aggrieved by the decision of a licensing authority to include a vehicle on a list maintained under section 167 may appeal to a magistrates' court or, in Scotland, the sheriff before the end of the period of 28 days beginning with the date of the inclusion.

173 Interpretation

(1) In this Chapter –

"accessibility requirements" has the meaning given in section 167(5);
"assistance dog" means –
    (a)   a dog which has been trained to guide a blind person;
    (b)   a dog which has been trained to assist a deaf person;
    (c)   a dog which has been trained by a prescribed charity to assist a disabled person who has a disability that consists of epilepsy or otherwise affects the person's mobility, manual dexterity, physical co-ordination or ability to lift, carry or otherwise move everyday objects;
    (d)   a dog of a prescribed category which has been trained to assist a disabled person who has a disability (other than one falling within paragraph (c)) of a prescribed kind;
"taxi" –
    (a)   means a vehicle which is licensed under section 37 of the Town Police Clauses Act 1847 or section 6 of the Metropolitan Public Carriage Act 1869, and
    (b)   in sections 162 and 165 to 167, also includes a taxi licensed under section 10 of the Civic Government (Scotland) Act 1982,
but does not include a vehicle drawn by a horse or other animal;
"taxi accessibility regulations" has the meaning given by section 160(1).

(2) A power to make regulations under paragraph (c) or (d) of the definition of "assistance dog" in subsection (1) is exercisable by the Secretary of State.

Chapter 2
Public service vehicles

174 PSV accessibility regulations

(1) The Secretary of State may make regulations (in this Chapter referred to as "PSV accessibility regulations") for securing that it is possible for disabled persons –

(a)   to get on to and off regulated public service vehicles in safety and without unreasonable difficulty (and, in the case of disabled persons in wheelchairs, to do so while remaining in their wheelchairs), and

(b)   to travel in such vehicles in safety and reasonable comfort.

(2) The regulations may, in particular, make provision as to the construction, use and maintenance of regulated public service vehicles, including provision as to –

(a)   the fitting of equipment to vehicles;

(b)   equipment to be carried by vehicles;

(c)   the design of equipment to be fitted to, or carried by, vehicles;

(d)   the fitting and use of restraining devices designed to ensure the stability of wheelchairs while vehicles are moving;

(e)   the position in which wheelchairs are to be secured while vehicles are moving.

(3) In this section "public service vehicle" means a vehicle which is –

(a)   adapted to carry more than 8 passengers, and

(b)   a public service vehicle for the purposes of the Public Passenger Vehicles Act 1981;

and in this Chapter "regulated public service vehicle" means a public service vehicle to which PSV accessibility regulations are expressed to apply.

(4) The regulations may make different provision –

(a)   as respects different classes or descriptions of vehicle;

(b)   as respects the same class or description of vehicle in different circumstances.

(5) The Secretary of State must not make regulations under this section or section 176 or 177 without consulting –

(a)   the Disabled Persons Transport Advisory Committee, and

(b)   such other representative organisations as the Secretary of State thinks fit.

175 Offence of contravening PSV accessibility regulations

(1) A person commits an offence by –

(a)   contravening a provision of PSV accessibility regulations;

(b)   using on a road a regulated public service vehicle which does not conform with a provision of the regulations with which it is required to conform;

(c)   causing or permitting such a regulated public service vehicle to be used on a road.

(2) A person guilty of an offence under this section is liable on summary conviction to a fine not exceeding level 4 on the standard scale.

(3) If an offence under this section committed by a body corporate is committed with the consent or connivance of, or is attributable to neglect on the part of, a responsible person, the responsible person as well as the body corporate is guilty of the offence.

(4) In subsection (3) a responsible person, in relation to a body corporate, is –

(a)   a director, manager, secretary or similar officer;

(b)   a person purporting to act in the capacity of a person mentioned in paragraph (a);

(c)   in the case of a body corporate whose affairs are managed by its members, a member.

(5) If, in Scotland, an offence committed by a partnership or an unincorporated association is committed with the consent or connivance of, or is attributable to neglect on the part of, a partner or person concerned in the management of the association, the partner or person as well as the partnership or association is guilty of the offence.

176 Accessibility certificates

(1) A regulated public service vehicle must not be used on a road unless –

(a)   a vehicle examiner has issued a certificate (an "accessibility certificate") that such provisions of PSV accessibility regulations as are prescribed are satisfied in respect of the vehicle, or

(b)   an approval certificate has been issued under section 177 in respect of the vehicle.

(2) Regulations may make provision –

(a)   with respect to applications for, and the issue of, accessibility certificates;

(b)   providing for the examination of vehicles in respect of which applications have been made;

(c)   with respect to the issue of copies of accessibility certificates which have been lost or destroyed.

(3) The operator of a regulated public service vehicle commits an offence if the vehicle is used in contravention of this section.

(4) A person guilty of an offence under this section is liable on summary conviction to a fine not exceeding level 4 on the standard scale.

(5) A power to make regulations under this section is exercisable by the Secretary of State.

(6) In this section "operator" has the same meaning as in the Public Passenger Vehicles Act 1981.

177 Approval certificates

(1) The Secretary of State may approve a vehicle for the purposes of this section if satisfied that such provisions of PSV accessibility regulations as are prescribed for the purposes of section 176 are satisfied in respect of the vehicle.

(2) A vehicle which is so approved is referred to in this section as a "type vehicle".

(3) Subsection (4) applies if a declaration in the prescribed form is made by an authorised person that a particular vehicle conforms in design, construction and equipment with a type vehicle.

(4) A vehicle examiner may issue a certificate in the prescribed form (an "approval certificate") that it conforms to the type vehicle.

(5) Regulations may make provision –

(a)   with respect to applications for, and grants of, approval under subsection (1);

(b)   with respect to applications for, and the issue of, approval certificates;

(c)   providing for the examination of vehicles in respect of which applications have been made;

(d)   with respect to the issue of copies of approval certificates in place of certificates which have been lost or destroyed.

(6) The Secretary of State may at any time withdraw approval of a type vehicle.

(7) If an approval is withdrawn –

(a) no further approval certificates are to be issued by reference to the type vehicle; but

(b) an approval certificate issued by reference to the type vehicle before the withdrawal continues to have effect for the purposes of section 176.

(8) A power to make regulations under this section is exercisable by the Secretary of State.

(9) In subsection (3) "authorised person" means a person authorised by the Secretary of State for the purposes of that subsection.

178 Special authorisations

(1) The Secretary of State may by order authorise the use on roads of –

(a) a regulated public service vehicle of a class or description specified by the order, or

(b) a regulated public service vehicle which is so specified.

(2) Nothing in sections 174 to 177 prevents the use of a vehicle in accordance with the order.

(3) The Secretary of State may by order make provision for securing that provisions of PSV accessibility regulations apply to regulated public service vehicles of a description specified by the order, subject to any modifications or exceptions specified by the order.

(4) An order under subsection (1) or (3) may make the authorisation or provision (as the case may be) subject to such restrictions and conditions as are specified by or under the order.

(5) Section 207(2) does not require an order under this section that applies only to a specified vehicle, or to vehicles of a specified person, to be made by statutory instrument; but such an order is as capable of being amended or revoked as an order made by statutory instrument.

179 Reviews and appeals

(1) Subsection (2) applies if the Secretary of State refuses an application for the approval of a vehicle under section 177(1) and, before the end of the prescribed period, the applicant –

(a) asks the Secretary of State to review the decision, and

(b) pays any fee fixed under section 180.

(2) The Secretary of State must –

(a) review the decision, and

(b) in doing so, consider any representations made in writing by the applicant before the end of the prescribed period.

(3) A person applying for an accessibility certificate or an approval certificate may appeal to the Secretary of State against the refusal of a vehicle examiner to issue the certificate.

(4) An appeal must be made within the prescribed time and in the prescribed manner.

(5) Regulations may make provision as to the procedure to be followed in connection with appeals.

(6) On the determination of an appeal, the Secretary of State may –

    (a)   confirm, vary or reverse the decision appealed against;

    (b)   give directions to the vehicle examiner for giving effect to the Secretary of State's decision.

(7) A power to make regulations under this section is exercisable by the Secretary of State.

180 Fees

(1) The Secretary of State may charge such fees, payable at such times, as are prescribed in respect of –

    (a)   applications for, and grants of, approval under section 177(1);

    (b)   applications for, and the issue of, accessibility certificates and approval certificates;

    (c)   copies of such certificates;

    (d)   reviews and appeals under section 179.

(2) Fees received by the Secretary of State must be paid into the Consolidated Fund.

(3) The power to make regulations under subsection (1) is exercisable by the Secretary of State.

(4) The regulations may make provision for the repayment of fees, in whole or in part, in such circumstances as are prescribed.

(5) Before making the regulations the Secretary of State must consult such representative organisations as the Secretary of State thinks fit.

181 Interpretation

In this Chapter –

    "accessibility certificate" has the meaning given in section 176(1);
    "approval certificate" has the meaning given in section 177(4);
    "PSV accessibility regulations" has the meaning given in section 174(1);
    "regulated public service vehicle" has the meaning given in section 174(3).

Chapter 3
Rail vehicles

182 Rail vehicle accessibility regulations

(1) The Secretary of State may make regulations (in this Chapter referred to as "rail vehicle accessibility regulations") for securing that it is possible for disabled persons –

    (a)   to get on to and off regulated rail vehicles in safety and without unreasonable difficulty;

    (b)   to do so while in wheelchairs;

    (c)   to travel in such vehicles in safety and reasonable comfort;

    (d)   to do so while in wheelchairs.

(2) The regulations may, in particular, make provision as to the construction, use and maintenance of regulated rail vehicles including provision as to –

(a)   the fitting of equipment to vehicles;

(b)   equipment to be carried by vehicles;

(c)   the design of equipment to be fitted to, or carried by, vehicles;

(d)   the use of equipment fitted to, or carried by, vehicles;

(e)   the toilet facilities to be provided in vehicles;

(f)   the location and floor area of the wheelchair accommodation to be provided in vehicles;

(g)   assistance to be given to disabled persons.

(3) The regulations may contain different provision –

(a)   as respects different classes or descriptions of rail vehicle;

(b)   as respects the same class or description of rail vehicle in different circumstances;

(c)   as respects different networks.

(4) In this section –

"network" means any permanent way or other means of guiding or supporting rail vehicles, or any section of it;

"rail vehicle" means a vehicle constructed or adapted to carry passengers on a railway, tramway or prescribed system other than a vehicle used in the provision of a service for the carriage of passengers on the highspeed rail system or the conventional TEN rail system;

"regulated rail vehicle" means a rail vehicle to which provisions of rail vehicle accessibility regulations are expressed to apply.

(5) In subsection (4) –

"conventional TEN rail system" and "high-speed rail system" have the meaning given in regulation 2(3) of the Railways (Interoperability) Regulations 2006 (S.I. 2006/397);

"prescribed system" means a system using a mode of guided transport ("guided transport" having the same meaning as in the Transport and Works Act 1992) that is specified in rail vehicle accessibility regulations;

"railway" and "tramway" have the same meaning as in the Transport and Works Act 1992.

(6) The Secretary of State must exercise the power to make rail vehicle accessibility regulations so as to secure that on and after 1 January 2020 every rail vehicle is a regulated rail vehicle.

(7) Subsection (6) does not affect subsection (3), section 183(1) or section 207(4)(a).

(8) Before making regulations under subsection (1) or section 183, the Secretary of State must consult –

(a)   the Disabled Persons Transport Advisory Committee, and

(b)   such other representative organisations as the Secretary of State thinks fit.

183 Exemptions from rail vehicle accessibility regulations

(1) The Secretary of State may by order (an "exemption order") –

(a)   authorise the use for carriage of a regulated rail vehicle even though the vehicle does not conform with the provisions of rail vehicle accessibility regulations with which it is required to conform;

(b)   authorise a regulated rail vehicle to be used for carriage otherwise than in conformity with the provisions of rail vehicle accessibility regulations with which use of the vehicle is required to conform.

(2) Authority under subsection (1)(a) or (b) may be for –

(a)   a regulated rail vehicle that is specified or of a specified description,
(b)   use in specified circumstances of a regulated rail vehicle, or
(c)   use in specified circumstances of a regulated rail vehicle that is specified or of a specified description.

(3) The Secretary of State may by regulations make provision as to exemption orders including, in particular, provision as to –

(a)   the persons by whom applications for exemption orders may be made;
(b)   the form in which applications are to be made;
(c)   information to be supplied in connection with applications;
(d)   the period for which exemption orders are to continue in force;
(e)   the revocation of exemption orders.

(4) After consulting the Disabled Persons Transport Advisory Committee and such other persons as the Secretary of State thinks appropriate, the Secretary of State may –

(a)   make an exemption order in the terms of the application for the order;
(b)   make an exemption order in such other terms as the Secretary of State thinks appropriate;
(c)   refuse to make an exemption order.

(5) The Secretary of State may make an exemption order subject to such conditions and restrictions as are specified.

(6) "Specified" means specified in an exemption order.

184 Procedure for making exemption orders

(1) A statutory instrument that contains an order under section 183(1), if made without a draft having been laid before and approved by a resolution of each House of Parliament, is subject to annulment in pursuance of a resolution of either House.

(2) The Secretary of State must consult the Disabled Persons Transport Advisory Committee before deciding which of the parliamentary procedures available under subsection (1) is to be adopted in connection with the making of any particular order under section 183(1).

(3) An order under section 183(1) may be made without a draft of the instrument that contains it having been laid before and approved by a resolution of each House of Parliament only if –

(a)   regulations under subsection (4) are in force; and
(b)   the making of the order without such laying and approval is in accordance with the regulations.

(4) The Secretary of State may by regulations set out the basis on which the Secretary of State, when making an order under section 183(1), will decide which of the parliamentary procedures available under subsection (1) is to be adopted in connection with the making of the order.

(5) Before making regulations under subsection (4), the Secretary of State must consult –

(a)   the Disabled Persons Transport Advisory Committee; and

(b)   such other persons as the Secretary of State considers appropriate.

185 Annual report on exemption orders

(1) After the end of each calendar year the Secretary of State must prepare a report on –

(a)   the exercise in that year of the power to make orders under section 183(1);

(b)   the exercise in that year of the discretion under section 184(1).

(2) A report under subsection (1) must (in particular) contain –

(a)   details of each order made under section 183(1) in the year in question;

(b)   details of consultation carried out under sections 183(4) and 184(2) in connection with orders made in that year under section 183(1).

(3) The Secretary of State must lay before Parliament each report prepared under this section.

186 Rail vehicle accessibility: compliance

(1) Schedule 20 (rail vehicle accessibility: compliance) has effect.

(2) This section and that Schedule are repealed at the end of 2010 if the Schedule is not brought into force (either fully or to any extent) before the end of that year.

187 Interpretation

(1) In this Chapter –

"rail vehicle" and "regulated rail vehicle" have the meaning given in section 182(4);
"rail vehicle accessibility regulations" has the meaning given in section 182(1).

(2) For the purposes of this Chapter a vehicle is used "for carriage" if it is used for the carriage of passengers.

Chapter 4
Supplementary

188 Forgery, etc.

(1) In this section "relevant document" means –

(a)   an exemption certificate issued under section 166, 169 or 171;

(b)   a notice of a kind mentioned in section 166(3)(b), 169(4)(b) or 171(4)(b);

(c)   an accessibility certificate (see section 176);

(d)   an approval certificate (see section 177).

(2) A person commits an offence if, with intent to deceive, the person –

(a)   forges, alters or uses a relevant document;

(b)   lends a relevant document to another person;

(c)   allows a relevant document to be used by another person;

(d)   makes or has possession of a document which closely resembles a relevant document.

(3) A person guilty of an offence under subsection (2) is liable –

(a)   on summary conviction, to a fine not exceeding the statutory maximum;

(b)   on conviction on indictment, to imprisonment for a term not exceeding 2 years or to a fine or to both.

(4) A person commits an offence by knowingly making a false statement for the purpose of obtaining an accessibility certificate or an approval certificate.

(5) A person guilty of an offence under subsection (4) is liable on summary conviction to a fine not exceeding level 4 on the standard scale.

PART 13
DISABILITY: MISCELLANEOUS

189 Reasonable adjustments

Schedule 21 (reasonable adjustments: supplementary) has effect.

190 Improvements to let dwelling houses

(1) This section applies in relation to a lease of a dwelling house if each of the following applies –

(a)   the tenancy is not a protected tenancy, a statutory tenancy or a secure tenancy;
(b)   the tenant or another person occupying or intending to occupy the premises is a disabled person;
(c)   the disabled person occupies or intends to occupy the premises as that person's only or main home;
(d)   the tenant is entitled, with the consent of the landlord, to make improvements to the premises;
(e)   the tenant applies to the landlord for consent to make a relevant improvement.

(2) Where the tenant applies in writing for the consent –

(a)   if the landlord refuses to give consent, the landlord must give the tenant a written statement of the reason why the consent was withheld;
(b)   if the landlord neither gives nor refuses to give consent within a reasonable time, consent must be taken to have been unreasonably withheld.

(3) If the landlord gives consent subject to a condition which is unreasonable, the consent must be taken to have been unreasonably withheld.

(4) If the landlord's consent is unreasonably withheld, it must be taken to have been given.

(5) On any question as to whether –

(a)   consent was unreasonably withheld, or
(b)   a condition imposed was unreasonable,

it is for the landlord to show that it was not.

(6) If the tenant fails to comply with a reasonable condition imposed by the landlord on the making of a relevant improvement, the failure is to be treated as a breach by the tenant of an obligation of the tenancy.

(7) An improvement to premises is a relevant improvement if, having regard to the disabled peron's disability, it is likely to facilitate that person's enjoyment of the premises.

(8) Subsections (2) to (7) apply only in so far as provision of a like nature is not made by the lease.

(9) In this section –

"improvement" means an alteration in or addition to the premises and includes –
   (a)   an addition to or alteration in the landlord's fittings and fixtures;
   (b)   an addition or alteration connected with the provision of services to the premises;
   (c)the erection of a wireless or television aerial;
   (d)   carrying out external decoration;

"lease" includes a sub-lease or other tenancy, and "landlord" and "tenant" are to be construed accordingly;
"protected tenancy" has the same meaning as in section 1 of the Rent Act 1977;
"statutory tenancy" is to be construed in accordance with section 2 of that Act;
"secure tenancy" has the same meaning as in section 79 of the Housing Act 1985.

PART 14
GENERAL EXCEPTIONS

191 Statutory provisions

Schedule 22 (statutory provisions) has effect.

192 National security

A person does not contravene this Act only by doing, for the purpose of safeguarding national security, anything it is proportionate to do for that purpose.

193 Charities

(1) A person does not contravene this Act only by restricting the provision of benefits to persons who share a protected characteristic if –

   (a)   the person acts in pursuance of a charitable instrument, and
   (b)   the provision of the benefits is within subsection (2).

(2) The provision of benefits is within this subsection if it is –

   (a)   a proportionate means of achieving a legitimate aim, or
   (b)   for the purpose of preventing or compensating for a disadvantage linked to the protected characteristic.

(3) It is not a contravention of this Act for –

   (a)   a person who provides supported employment to treat persons who have the same disability or a disability of a prescribed description more favourably than those who do not have that disability or a disability of such a description in providing such employment;
   (b)   a Minister of the Crown to agree to arrangements for the provision of supported employment which will, or may, have that effect.

(4) If a charitable instrument enables the provision of benefits to persons of a class defined by reference to colour, it has effect for all purposes as if it enabled the provision of such benefits –

   (a)   to persons of the class which results if the reference to colour is ignored, or

(b)   if the original class is defined by reference only to colour, to persons generally.

(5) It is not a contravention of this Act for a charity to require members, or persons wishing to become members, to make a statement which asserts or implies membership or acceptance of a religion or belief; and for this purpose restricting the access by members to a benefit, facility or service to those who make such a statement is to be treated as imposing such a requirement.

(6) Subsection (5) applies only if –

(a)   the charity, or an organisation of which it is part, first imposed such a requirement before 18 May 2005, and

(b)   the charity or organisation has not ceased since that date to impose such a requirement.

(7) It is not a contravention of section 29 for a person, in relation to an activity which is carried on for the purpose of promoting or supporting a charity, to restrict participation in the activity to persons of one sex.

(8) A charity regulator does not contravene this Act only by exercising a function in relation to a charity in a manner which the regulator thinks is expedient in the interests of the charity, having regard to the charitable instrument.

(9) Subsection (1) does not apply to a contravention of –

(a)   section 39;
(b)   section 40;
(c)   section 41;
(d)   section 55, so far as relating to the provision of vocational training.

(10) Subsection (9) does not apply in relation to disability.

194 Charities: supplementary

(1) This section applies for the purposes of section 193.

(2) That section does not apply to race, so far as relating to colour.

(3) "Charity" –

(a)   in relation to England and Wales, has the meaning given by section 1(1) of the Charities Act 2006;

(b)   in relation to Scotland, means a body entered in the Scottish Charity Register.

(4) "Charitable instrument" means an instrument establishing or governing a charity (including an instrument made or having effect before the commencement of this section).

(5) The charity regulators are –

(a)   the Charity Commission for England and Wales;
(b)   the Scottish Charity Regulator.

(6) Section 107(5) applies to references in subsection (5) of section 193 to members, or persons wishing to become members, of a charity.

(7) "Supported employment" means facilities provided, or in respect of which payments are made, under section 15 of the Disabled Persons (Employment) Act 1944.

195 Sport

(1) A person does not contravene this Act, so far as relating to sex, only by doing anything in relation to the participation of another as a competitor in a gender-affected activity.

(2) A person does not contravene section 29, 33, 34 or 35, so far as relating to gender reassignment, only by doing anything in relation to the participation of a transsexual person as a competitor in a gender-affected activity if it is necessary to do so to secure in relation to the activity –

    (a)   fair competition, or
    (b)   the safety of competitors.

(3) A gender-affected activity is a sport, game or other activity of a competitive nature in circumstances in which the physical strength, stamina or physique of average persons of one sex would put them at a disadvantage compared to average persons of the other sex as competitors in events involving the activity.

(4) In considering whether a sport, game or other activity is gender-affected in relation to children, it is appropriate to take account of the age and stage of development of children who are likely to be competitors.

(5) A person who does anything to which subsection (6) applies does not contravene this Act only because of the nationality or place of birth of another or because of the length of time the other has been resident in a particular area or place.

(6) This subsection applies to –

    (a)   selecting one or more persons to represent a country, place or area or a related association, in a sport or game or other activity of a competitive nature;
    (b)   doing anything in pursuance of the rules of a competition so far as relating to eligibility to compete in a sport or game or other such activity.

196 General

Schedule 23 (general exceptions) has effect.

197 Age

(1) A Minister of the Crown may by order amend this Act to provide that any of the following does not contravene this Act so far as relating to age –

    (a)   specified conduct;
    (b)   anything done for a specified purpose;
    (c)   anything done in pursuance of arrangements of a specified description.

(2) Specified conduct is conduct –

    (a)   of a specified description,
    (b)   carried out in specified circumstances, or
    (c)   by or in relation to a person of a specified description.

(3) An order under this section may –

    (a)   confer on a Minister of the Crown or the Treasury a power to issue guidance about the operation of the order (including, in particular, guidance about the steps that may be taken by persons wishing to rely on an exception provided for by the order);

(b)   require the Minister or the Treasury to carry out consultation before issuing guidance under a power conferred by virtue of paragraph (a);

(c)   make provision (including provision to impose a requirement) that refers to guidance issued under a power conferred by virtue of paragraph (a).

(4) Guidance given by a Minister of the Crown or the Treasury in anticipation of the making of an order under this section is, on the making of the order, to be treated as if it has been issued in accordance with the order.

(5) For the purposes of satisfying a requirement imposed by virtue of subsection (3)(b), the Minister or the Treasury may rely on consultation carried out before the making of the order that imposes the requirement (including consultation carried out before the commencement of this section).

(6) Provision by virtue of subsection (3)(c) may, in particular, refer to provisions of the guidance that themselves refer to a document specified in the guidance.

(7) Guidance issued (or treated as issued) under a power conferred by virtue of subsection (3)(a) comes into force on such day as the person who issues the guidance may by order appoint; and an order under this subsection may include the text of the guidance or of extracts from it.

(8) This section is not affected by any provision of this Act which makes special provision in relation to age.

(9) The references to this Act in subsection (1) do not include references to –

(a)   Part 5 (work);

(b)   Chapter 2 of Part 6 (further and higher education).

PART 15
FAMILY PROPERTY

198 Abolition of husband's duty to maintain wife

The rule of common law that a husband must maintain his wife is abolished.

199 Abolition of presumption of advancement

(1) The presumption of advancement (by which, for example, a husband is presumed to be making a gift to his wife if he transfers property to her, or purchases property in her name) is abolished.

(2) The abolition by subsection (1) of the presumption of advancement does not have effect in relation to –

(a)   anything done before the commencement of this section, or

(b)   anything done pursuant to any obligation incurred before the commencement of this section.

200 Amendment of Married Women's Property Act 1964

(1) In section 1 of the Married Women's Property Act 1964 (money and property derived from housekeeping allowance made by husband to be treated as belonging to husband and wife in equal shares) –

(a)   for "the husband for" substitute "either of them for", and

(b)   for "the husband and the wife" substitute "them".

(2) Accordingly, that Act may be cited as the Matrimonial Property Act 1964.

(3) The amendments made by this section do not have effect in relation to any allowance made before the commencement of this section.

201 Civil partners: housekeeping allowance

(1) After section 70 of the Civil Partnership Act 2004 insert –

> **"70A Money and property derived from housekeeping allowance**
>
> Section 1 of the Matrimonial Property Act 1964 (money and property derived from housekeeping allowance to be treated as belonging to husband and wife in equal shares) applies in relation to –
>
> > (a) money derived from any allowance made by a civil partner for the expenses of the civil partnership home or for similar purposes, and
> >
> > (b) any property acquired out of such money,
>
> as it applies in relation to money derived from any allowance made by a husband or wife for the expenses of the matrimonial home or for similar purposes, and any property acquired out of such money."

(2) The amendment made by this section does not have effect in relation to any allowance made before the commencement of this section.

PART 16
GENERAL AND MISCELLANEOUS

Civil partnerships

202 Civil partnerships on religious premises

(1) The Civil Partnership Act 2004 is amended as follows.

(2) Omit section 6(1)(b) and (2) (prohibition on use of religious premises for registration of civil partnership).

(3) In section 6A (power to approve premises for registration of civil partnership), after subsection (2), insert –

> "(2A) Regulations under this section may provide that premises approved for the registration of civil partnerships may differ from those premises approved for the registration of civil marriages.
>
> (2B) Provision by virtue of subsection (2)(b) may, in particular, provide that applications for approval of premises may only be made with the consent (whether general or specific) of a person specified, or a person of a description specified, in the provision.
>
> (2C) The power conferred by section 258(2), in its application to the power conferred by this section, includes in particular –
>
> > (a) power to make provision in relation to religious premises that differs from provision in relation to other premises;
> >
> > (b) power to make different provision for different kinds of religious premises."

(4) In that section, after subsection (3), insert –

> "(3A) For the avoidance of doubt, nothing in this Act places an obligation on religious organisations to host civil partnerships if they do not wish to do so.
>
> (3B) "Civil marriage" means marriage solemnised otherwise than according to the rites of the Church of England or any other religious usages.

(3C) "Religious premises" means premises which –
  (a)   are used solely or mainly for religious purposes, or
  (b)   have been so used and have not subsequently been used solely or mainly for other purposes."

EU obligations

203 Harmonisation

(1) This section applies if –

  (a)   there is a Community obligation of the United Kingdom which a Minister of the Crown thinks relates to the subject matter of the Equality Acts,
  (b)   the obligation is to be implemented by the exercise of the power under section 2(2) of the European Communities Act 1972 (the implementing power), and
  (c)   the Minister thinks that it is appropriate to make harmonising provision in the Equality Acts.

(2) The Minister may by order make the harmonising provision.

(3) If the Minister proposes to make an order under this section, the Minister must consult persons and organisations the Minister thinks are likely to be affected by the harmonising provision.

(4) If, as a result of the consultation under subsection (3), the Minister thinks it appropriate to change the whole or part of the proposal, the Minister must carry out such further consultation with respect to the changes as the Minister thinks appropriate.

(5) The Equality Acts are the Equality Act 2006 and this Act.

(6) Harmonising provision is provision made in relation to relevant subject matter of the Equality Acts –

  (a)   which corresponds to the implementing provision, or
  (b)   which the Minister thinks is necessary or expedient in consequence of or related to provision made in pursuance of paragraph (a) or the implementing provision.

(7) The implementing provision is provision made or to be made in exercise of the implementing power in relation to so much of the subject matter of the Equality Acts as implements a Community obligation.

(8) Relevant subject matter of the Equality Acts is so much of the subject matter of those Acts as does not implement a Community obligation.

(9) A harmonising provision may amend a provision of the Equality Acts.

(10) The reference to this Act does not include a reference to this section or Schedule 24 or to a provision specified in that Schedule.

(11) A Minister of the Crown must report to Parliament on the exercise of the power under subsection (2) –

  (a)   at the end of the period of 2 years starting on the day this section comes into force;
  (b)   at the end of each succeeding period of 2 years.

204 Harmonisation: procedure

(1) If, after the conclusion of the consultation required under section 203, the Minister thinks it appropriate to proceed with the making of an order under that section, the Minister must lay before Parliament –

    (a)   a draft of a statutory instrument containing the order, together with

    (b)   an explanatory document.

(2) The explanatory document must –

    (a)   introduce and give reasons for the harmonising provision;

    (b)   explain why the Minister thinks that the conditions in subsection (1) of section 203 are satisfied;

    (c)   give details of the consultation carried out under that section;

    (d)   give details of the representations received as a result of the consultation;

    (e)   give details of such changes as were made as a result of the representations.

(3) Where a person making representations in response to the consultation has requested the Minister not to disclose them, the Minister must not disclose them under subsection (2)(d) if, or to the extent that, to do so would (disregarding any connection with proceedings in Parliament) constitute an actionable breach of confidence.

(4) If information in representations made by a person in response to consultation under section 203 relates to another person, the Minister need not disclose the information under subsection (2)(d) if or to the extent that –

    (a)   the Minister thinks that the disclosure of information could adversely affect the interests of that other person, and

    (b)   the Minister has been unable to obtain the consent of that other person to the disclosure.

(5) The Minister may not act under subsection (1) before the end of the period of 12 weeks beginning with the day on which the consultation under section 203(3) begins.

(6) Laying a draft of a statutory instrument in accordance with subsection (1) satisfies the condition as to laying imposed by subsection (8) of section 208, in so far as that subsection applies in relation to orders under section 203.

Application

205 Crown application

(1) The following provisions of this Act bind the Crown –

    (a)   Part 1 (public sector duty regarding socio-economic inequalities);

    (b)   Part 3 (services and public functions), so far as relating to the exercise of public functions;

    (c)   Chapter 1 of Part 11 (public sector equality duty).

(2) Part 5 (work) binds the Crown as provided for by that Part.

(3) The remainder of this Act applies to Crown acts as it applies to acts done by a private person.

(4) For the purposes of subsection (3), an act is a Crown act if (and only if) it is done –

    (a)   by or on behalf of a member of the executive,

    (b)   by a statutory body acting on behalf of the Crown, or

(c)   by or on behalf of the holder of a statutory office acting on behalf of the Crown.

(5) A statutory body or office is a body or office established by an enactment.

(6) The provisions of Parts 2 to 4 of the Crown Proceedings Act 1947 apply to proceedings against the Crown under this Act as they apply to proceedings in England and Wales which, as a result of section 23 of that Act, are treated for the purposes of Part 2 of that Act as civil proceedings by or against the Crown.

(7) The provisions of Part 5 of that Act apply to proceedings against the Crown under this Act as they apply to proceedings in Scotland which, as a result of that Part, are treated as civil proceedings by or against the Crown.

(8) But the proviso to section 44 of that Act (removal of proceedings from the sheriff to the Court of Session) does not apply to proceedings under this Act.

206 Information society services

Schedule 25 (information society services) has effect.

Subordinate legislation

207 Exercise of power

(1) A power to make an order or regulations under this Act is exercisable by a Minister of the Crown, unless there is express provision to the contrary.

(2) Orders, regulations or rules under this Act must be made by statutory instrument.

(3) Subsection (2) does not apply to –

(a)   a transitional exemption order under Part 1 of Schedule 11,
(b)   a transitional exemption order under Part 1 of Schedule 12, or
(c)   an order under paragraph 1(3) of Schedule 14 that does not modify an enactment.

(4) Orders or regulations under this Act –

(a)   may make different provision for different purposes;
(b)   may include consequential, incidental, supplementary, transitional, transitory or saving provision.

(5) Nothing in section 163(4), 174(4) or 182(3) affects the generality of the power under subsection (4)(a).

(6) The power under subsection (4)(b), in its application to section 37, 153, 154(2), 155(5), 197 or 216 or to paragraph 7(1) of Schedule 11 or paragraph 1(3) or 2(3) of Schedule 14, includes power to amend an enactment (including, in the case of section 197 or 216, this Act).

(7) In the case of section 216 (commencement), provision by virtue of subsection (4)(b) may be included in a separate order from the order that provides for the commencement to which the provision relates; and, for that purpose, it does not matter –

(a)   whether the order providing for the commencement includes provision by virtue of subsection (4)(b);
(b)   whether the commencement has taken place.

(8) A statutory instrument containing an Order in Council under section 82 (offshore work) is subject to annulment in pursuance of a resolution of either House of Parliament.

208 Ministers of the Crown, etc.

(1) This section applies where the power to make an order or regulations under this Act is exercisable by a Minister of the Crown or the Treasury.

(2) A statutory instrument containing (whether alone or with other provision) an order or regulations that amend this Act or another Act of Parliament, or an Act of the Scottish Parliament or an Act or Measure of the National Assembly for Wales, is subject to the affirmative procedure.

(3) But a statutory instrument is not subject to the affirmative procedure by virtue of subsection (2) merely because it contains –

    (a)   an order under section 59 (local authority functions);

    (b)   an order under section 151 (power to amend list of public authorities for the purposes of the public sector equality duty) that provides for the omission of an entry where the authority concerned has ceased to exist or the variation of an entry where the authority concerned has changed its name;

    (c)   an order under paragraph 1(3) of Schedule 14 (educational charities and endowments) that modifies an enactment.

(4) A statutory instrument containing (whether alone or with other provision) an order or regulations mentioned in subsection (5) is subject to the affirmative procedure.

(5) The orders and regulations referred to in subsection (4) are –

    (a)   regulations under section 30 (services: ships and hovercraft);

    (b)   regulations under section 78 (gender pay gap information);

    (c)   regulations under section 81 (work: ships and hovercraft);

    (d)   an order under section 105 (election candidates: expiry of provision);

    (e)   regulations under section 106 (election candidates: diversity information);

    (f)   regulations under section 153 or 154(2) (public sector equality duty: powers to impose specific duties);

    (g)   regulations under section 184(4) (rail vehicle accessibility: procedure for exemption orders);

    (h)   an order under section 203 (EU obligations: harmonisation);

    (i)   regulations under paragraph 9(3) of Schedule 20 (rail vehicle accessibility: determination of turnover for purposes of penalties).

(6) A statutory instrument that is not subject to the affirmative procedure by virtue of subsection (2) or (4) is subject to the negative procedure.

(7) But a statutory instrument is not subject to the negative procedure by virtue of subsection (6) merely because it contains –

    (a)   an order under section 183(1) (rail vehicle accessibility: exemptions);

    (b)   an order under section 216 (commencement) that –

        (i)   does not amend an Act of Parliament, an Act of the Scottish Parliament or an Act or Measure of the National Assembly for Wales, and

        (ii)   is not made in reliance on section 207(7).

(8) If a statutory instrument is subject to the affirmative procedure, the order or regulations contained in it must not be made unless a draft of the instrument is laid before and approved by a resolution of each House of Parliament.

(9) If a statutory instrument is subject to the negative procedure, it is subject to annulment in pursuance of a resolution of either House of Parliament.

(10) If a draft of a statutory instrument containing an order or regulations under section 2, 151, 153, 154(2) or 155(5) would, apart from this subsection, be treated for the purposes of the Standing Orders of either House of Parliament as a hybrid instrument, it is to proceed in that House as if it were not a hybrid instrument.

209 The Welsh Ministers

(1) This section applies where the power to make an order or regulations under this Act is exercisable by the Welsh Ministers.

(2) A statutory instrument containing (whether alone or with other provision) an order or regulations mentioned in subsection (3) is subject to the affirmative procedure.

(3) The orders and regulations referred to in subsection (2) are –

- (a) regulations under section 2 (socio-economic inequalities);
- (b) an order under section 151 (power to amend list of public authorities for the purposes of the public sector equality duty);
- (c) regulations under section 153 or 154(2) (public sector equality duty: powers to impose specific duties);
- (d) regulations under section 155(5) that amend an Act of Parliament or an Act or Measure of the National Assembly for Wales (public sector equality duty: power to modify or remove specific duties).

(4) But a statutory instrument is not subject to the affirmative procedure by virtue of subsection (2) merely because it contains an order under section 151 that provides for –

- (a) the omission of an entry where the authority concerned has ceased to exist, or
- (b) the variation of an entry where the authority concerned has changed its name.

(5) A statutory instrument that is not subject to the affirmative procedure by virtue of subsection (2) is subject to the negative procedure.

(6) If a statutory instrument is subject to the affirmative procedure, the order or regulations contained in it must not be made unless a draft of the instrument is laid before and approved by a resolution of the National Assembly for Wales.

(7) If a statutory instrument is subject to the negative procedure, it is subject to annulment in pursuance of a resolution of the National Assembly for Wales.

210 The Scottish Ministers

(1) This section applies where the power to make an order, regulations or rules under this Act is exercisable by the Scottish Ministers.

(2) A statutory instrument containing (whether alone or with other provision) an order or regulations mentioned in subsection (3) is subject to the affirmative procedure.

(3) The orders and regulations referred to in subsection (2) are –

- (a) regulations under section 2 (socio-economic inequalities);

(b)   regulations under section 37 (power to make provision about adjustments to common parts in Scotland);

(c)   an order under section 151 (power to amend list of public authorities for the purposes of the public sector equality duty);

(d)   regulations under section 153 or 154(2) (public sector equality duty: powers to impose specific duties);

(e)   regulations under section 155(5) that amend an Act of Parliament or an Act of the Scottish Parliament (public sector equality duty: power to modify or remove specific duties).

(4) But a statutory instrument is not subject to the affirmative procedure by virtue of subsection (2) merely because it contains an order under section 151 that provides for –

(a)   the omission of an entry where the authority concerned has ceased to exist, or

(b)   the variation of an entry where the authority concerned has changed its name.

(5) A statutory instrument that is not subject to the affirmative procedure by virtue of subsection (2) is subject to the negative procedure.

(6) If a statutory instrument is subject to the affirmative procedure, the order or regulations contained in it must not be made unless a draft of the instrument is laid before and approved by a resolution of the Scottish Parliament.

(7) If a statutory instrument is subject to the negative procedure, it is subject to annulment in pursuance of a resolution of the Scottish Parliament.

Amendments, etc.

211 Amendments, repeals and revocations

(1) Schedule 26 (amendments) has effect.

(2) Schedule 27 (repeals and revocations) has effect.

Interpretation

212 General interpretation

(1) In this Act –

"armed forces" means any of the naval, military or air forces of the Crown;

"the Commission" means the Commission for Equality and Human Rights;

"detriment" does not, subject to subsection (5), include conduct which amounts to harassment;

"the Education Acts" has the meaning given in section 578 of the Education Act 1996;

"employment" and related expressions are (subject to subsection (11)) to be read with section 83;

"enactment" means an enactment contained in –

(a)   an Act of Parliament,

(b)   an Act of the Scottish Parliament,

(c)   an Act or Measure of the National Assembly for Wales, or

(d)   subordinate legislation;

"equality clause" means a sex equality clause or maternity equality clause;

"equality rule" means a sex equality rule or maternity equality rule;

"man" means a male of any age;

"maternity equality clause" has the meaning given in section 73;

"maternity equality rule" has the meaning given in section 75;

"non-discrimination rule" has the meaning given in section 61;

"occupational pension scheme" has the meaning given in section 1 of the Pension Schemes Act 1993;

"parent" has the same meaning as in –

    (a)   the Education Act 1996 (in relation to England and Wales);

    (b)   the Education (Scotland) Act 1980 (in relation to Scotland);

"prescribed" means prescribed by regulations;

"profession" includes a vocation or occupation;

"sex equality clause" has the meaning given in section 66;

"sex equality rule" has the meaning given in section 67;

"subordinate legislation" means –

    (a)   subordinate legislation within the meaning of the Interpretation Act 1978, or

    (b)   an instrument made under an Act of the Scottish Parliament or an Act or Measure of the National Assembly for Wales;

"substantial" means more than minor or trivial;

"trade" includes any business;

"woman" means a female of any age.

(2) A reference (however expressed) to an act includes a reference to an omission.

(3) A reference (however expressed) to an omission includes (unless there is express provision to the contrary) a reference to –

    (a)   a deliberate omission to do something;

    (b)   a refusal to do it;

    (c)   a failure to do it.

(4) A reference (however expressed) to providing or affording access to a benefit, facility or service includes a reference to facilitating access to the benefit, facility or service.

(5) Where this Act disapplies a prohibition on harassment in relation to a specified protected characteristic, the disapplication does not prevent conduct relating to that characteristic from amounting to a detriment for the purposes of discrimination within section 13 because of that characteristic.

(6) A reference to occupation, in relation to premises, is a reference to lawful occupation.

(7) The following are members of the executive –

    (a)   a Minister of the Crown;

    (b)   a government department;

    (c)   the Welsh Ministers, the First Minister for Wales or the Counsel General to the Welsh Assembly Government;

    (d)   any part of the Scottish Administration.

(8) A reference to a breach of an equality clause or rule is a reference to a breach of a term modified by, or included by virtue of, an equality clause or rule.

(9) A reference to a contravention of this Act does not include a reference to a breach of an equality clause or rule, unless there is express provision to the contrary.

(10) "Member", in relation to an occupational pension scheme, means an active member, a deferred member or a pensioner member (within the meaning, in each case, given by section 124 of the Pensions Act 1995).

(11) "Employer", "deferred member", "pension credit member", "pensionable service", "pensioner member" and "trustees or managers" each have, in relation to an occupational pension scheme, the meaning given by section 124 of the Pensions Act 1995.

(12) A reference to the accrual of rights under an occupational pension scheme is to be construed in accordance with that section.

(13) Nothing in section 28, 32, 84, 90, 95 or 100 is to be regarded as an express exception.

213 References to maternity leave, etc.

(1) This section applies for the purposes of this Act.

(2) A reference to a woman on maternity leave is a reference to a woman on –

(a) compulsory maternity leave,
(b) ordinary maternity leave, or
(c) additional maternity leave.

(3) A reference to a woman on compulsory maternity leave is a reference to a woman absent from work because she satisfies the conditions prescribed for the purposes of section 72(1) of the Employment Rights Act 1996.

(4) A reference to a woman on ordinary maternity leave is a reference to a woman absent from work because she is exercising the right to ordinary maternity leave.

(5) A reference to the right to ordinary maternity leave is a reference to the right conferred by section 71(1) of the Employment Rights Act 1996.

(6) A reference to a woman on additional maternity leave is a reference to a woman absent from work because she is exercising the right to additional maternity leave.

(7) A reference to the right to additional maternity leave is a reference to the right conferred by section 73(1) of the Employment Rights Act 1996.

(8) "Additional maternity leave period" has the meaning given in section 73(2) of that Act.

214 Index of defined expressions

Schedule 28 lists the places where expressions used in this Act are defined or otherwise explained.

Final provisions

215 Money

There is to be paid out of money provided by Parliament any increase attributable to this Act in the expenses of a Minister of the Crown.

216 Commencement

(1) The following provisions come into force on the day on which this Act is passed –

(a)   section 186(2) (rail vehicle accessibility: compliance);
(b)   this Part (except sections 202 (civil partnerships on religious premises), 206 (information society services) and 211 (amendments, etc)).

(2) Part 15 (family property) comes into force on such day as the Lord Chancellor may by order appoint.

(3) The other provisions of this Act come into force on such day as a Minister of the Crown may by order appoint.

217 Extent

(1) This Act forms part of the law of England and Wales.

(2) This Act, apart from section 190 (improvements to let dwelling houses) and Part 15 (family property), forms part of the law of Scotland.

(3) Each of the following also forms part of the law of Northern Ireland –

(a)   section 82 (offshore work);
(b)   section 105(3) and (4) (expiry of Sex Discrimination (Election Candidates) Act 2002);
(c)   section 199 (abolition of presumption of advancement).

218 Short title

This Act may be cited as the Equality Act 2010.

Schedules

Schedule 1

Section 6

Disability: supplementary provision

PART 1
DETERMINATION OF DISABILITY

1 Impairment

Regulations may make provision for a condition of a prescribed description to be, or not to be, an impairment.

2 Long-term effects

(1) The effect of an impairment is long-term if –

(a)   it has lasted for at least 12 months,
(b)   it is likely to last for at least 12 months, or
(c)   it is likely to last for the rest of the life of the person affected.

(2) If an impairment ceases to have a substantial adverse effect on a person's ability to carry out normal day-to-day activities, it is to be treated as continuing to have that effect if that effect is likely to recur.

(3) For the purposes of sub-paragraph (2), the likelihood of an effect recurring is to be disregarded in such circumstances as may be prescribed.

(4) Regulations may prescribe circumstances in which, despite sub-paragraph (1), an effect is to be treated as being, or as not being, long-term.

3 Severe disfigurement

(1) An impairment which consists of a severe disfigurement is to be treated as having a substantial adverse effect on the ability of the person concerned to carry out normal day-to-day activities.

(2) Regulations may provide that in prescribed circumstances a severe disfigurement is not to be treated as having that effect.

(3) The regulations may, in particular, make provision in relation to deliberately acquired disfigurement.

4 Substantial adverse effects

Regulations may make provision for an effect of a prescribed description on the ability of a person to carry out normal day-to-day activities to be treated as being, or as not being, a substantial adverse effect.

5 Effect of medical treatment

(1) An impairment is to be treated as having a substantial adverse effect on the ability of the person concerned to carry out normal day-to-day activities if –

    (a)   measures are being taken to treat or correct it, and

    (b)   but for that, it would be likely to have that effect.

(2) "Measures" includes, in particular, medical treatment and the use of a prosthesis or other aid.

(3) Sub-paragraph (1) does not apply –

    (a)   in relation to the impairment of a person's sight, to the extent that the impairment is, in the person's case, correctable by spectacles or contact lenses or in such other ways as may be prescribed;

    (b)   in relation to such other impairments as may be prescribed, in such circumstances as are prescribed.

6 Certain medical conditions

(1) Cancer, HIV infection and multiple sclerosis are each a disability.

(2) HIV infection is infection by a virus capable of causing the Acquired Immune Deficiency Syndrome.

7 Deemed disability

(1) Regulations may provide for persons of prescribed descriptions to be treated as having disabilities.

(2) The regulations may prescribe circumstances in which a person who has a disability is to be treated as no longer having the disability.

(3) This paragraph does not affect the other provisions of this Schedule.

8 Progressive conditions

(1) This paragraph applies to a person (P) if –

    (a)   P has a progressive condition,

    (b)   as a result of that condition P has an impairment which has (or had) an effect on P's ability to carry out normal day-to-day activities, but

    (c)   the effect is not (or was not) a substantial adverse effect.

(2) P is to be taken to have an impairment which has a substantial adverse effect if the condition is likely to result in P having such an impairment.

(3) Regulations may make provision for a condition of a prescribed description to be treated as being, or as not being, progressive.

9 Past disabilities

(1) A question as to whether a person had a disability at a particular time ("the relevant time") is to be determined, for the purposes of section 6, as if the provisions of, or made under, this Act were in force when the act complained of was done had been in force at the relevant time.

(2) The relevant time may be a time before the coming into force of the provision of this Act to which the question relates.

PART 2
GUIDANCE

10 Preliminary

This Part of this Schedule applies in relation to guidance referred to in section 6(5).

11 Examples

The guidance may give examples of –

    (a)   effects which it would, or would not, be reasonable, in relation to particular activities, to regard as substantial adverse effects;

    (b)   substantial adverse effects which it would, or would not, be reasonable to regard as long-term.

12 Adjudicating bodies

(1) In determining whether a person is a disabled person, an adjudicating body must take account of such guidance as it thinks is relevant.

(2) An adjudicating body is –

    (a)   a court;

    (b)   a tribunal;

    (c)   a person (other than a court or tribunal) who may decide a claim relating to a contravention of Part 6 (education).

13 Representations

Before issuing the guidance, the Minister must –

    (a)   publish a draft of it;

(b) consider any representations made to the Minister about the draft;
(c) make such modifications as the Minister thinks appropriate in the light of the representations.

14 Parliamentary procedure

(1) If the Minister decides to proceed with proposed guidance, a draft of it must be laid before Parliament.

(2) If, before the end of the 40-day period, either House resolves not to approve the draft, the Minister must take no further steps in relation to the proposed guidance.

(3) If no such resolution is made before the end of that period, the Minister must issue the guidance in the form of the draft.

(4) Sub-paragraph (2) does not prevent a new draft of proposed guidance being laid before Parliament.

(5) The 40-day period –

(a) begins on the date on which the draft is laid before both Houses (or, if laid before each House on a different date, on the later date);
(b) does not include a period during which Parliament is prorogued or dissolved;
(c) does not include a period during which both Houses are adjourned for more than 4 days.

15 Commencement

The guidance comes into force on the day appointed by order by the Minister.

16 Revision and revocation

(1) The Minister may –

(a) revise the whole or part of guidance and re-issue it;
(b) by order revoke guidance.

(2) A reference to guidance includes a reference to guidance which has been revised and re-issued.

Schedule 2

Section 31

Services and public functions: reasonable adjustments

1 Preliminary

This Schedule applies where a duty to make reasonable adjustments is imposed on A by this Part.

2 The duty

(1) A must comply with the first, second and third requirements.

(2) For the purposes of this paragraph, the reference in section 20(3), (4) or (5) to a disabled person is to disabled persons generally.

(3) Section 20 has effect as if, in subsection (4), for "to avoid the disadvantage" there were substituted –

> "(a)   to avoid the disadvantage, or
> (b)   to adopt a reasonable alternative method of providing the service or exercising the function."

(4) In relation to each requirement, the relevant matter is the provision of the service, or the exercise of the function, by A.

(5) Being placed at a substantial disadvantage in relation to the exercise of a function means –

(a)   if a benefit is or may be conferred in the exercise of the function, being placed at a substantial disadvantage in relation to the conferment of the benefit, or

(b)   if a person is or may be subjected to a detriment in the exercise of the function, suffering an unreasonably adverse experience when being subjected to the detriment.

(6) In relation to the second requirement, a physical feature includes a physical feature brought by or on behalf of A, in the course of providing the service or exercising the function, on to premises other than those that A occupies (as well as including a physical feature in or on premises that A occupies).

(7) If A is a service-provider, nothing in this paragraph requires A to take a step which would fundamentally alter –

(a)   the nature of the service, or
(b)   the nature of A's trade or profession.

(8) If A exercises a public function, nothing in this paragraph requires A to take a step which A has no power to take.

3 Special provision about transport

(1) This paragraph applies where A is concerned with the provision of a service which involves transporting people by land, air or water.

(2) It is never reasonable for A to have to take a step which would –

(a)   involve the alteration or removal of a physical feature of a vehicle used in providing the service;
(b)   affect whether vehicles are provided;
(c)   affect what vehicles are provided;
(d)   affect what happens in the vehicle while someone is travelling in it.

(3) But, for the purpose of complying with the first or third requirement, A may not rely on sub-paragraph (2)(b), (c) or (d) if the vehicle concerned is –

(a)   a hire-vehicle designed and constructed for the carriage of passengers, comprising more than 8 seats in addition to the driver's seat and having a maximum mass not exceeding 5 tonnes,

(b)   a hire-vehicle designed and constructed for the carriage of goods and having a maximum mass not exceeding 3.5 tonnes,

(c)   a vehicle licensed under section 48 of the Local Government (Miscellaneous Provisions) Act 1976 or section 7 of the Private Hire Vehicles (London) Act 1998 (or under a provision of a local Act corresponding to either of those provisions),

(d)   a private hire car (within the meaning of section 23 of the Civic Government (Scotland) Act 1982),

(e)   a public service vehicle (within the meaning given by section 1 of the Public Passenger Vehicles Act 1981),

(f)   a vehicle built or adapted to carry passengers on a railway or tramway (within the meaning, in each case, of the Transport and Works Act 1992),

(g)   a taxi,

(h)   a vehicle deployed to transport the driver and passengers of a vehicle that has broken down or is involved in an accident, or

(i)   a vehicle deployed on a system using a mode of guided transport (within the meaning of the Transport and Works Act 1992).

(4) In so far as the second requirement requires A to adopt a reasonable alternative method of providing the service to disabled persons, A may not, for the purpose of complying with the requirement, rely on sub-paragraph (2)(b), (c) or (d) if the vehicle is within sub-paragraph (3)(h).

(5) A may not, for the purpose of complying with the first, second or third requirement rely on sub-paragraph (2) of this paragraph if A provides the service by way of a hire-vehicle built to carry no more than 8 passengers.

(6) For the purposes of sub-paragraph (5) in its application to the second requirement, a part of a vehicle is to be regarded as a physical feature if it requires alteration in order to facilitate the provision of –

(a)   hand controls to enable a disabled person to operate braking and accelerator systems in the vehicle, or

(b)   facilities for the stowage of a wheelchair.

(7) For the purposes of sub-paragraph (6) (a), fixed seating and in-built electrical systems are not physical features; and for the purposes of sub-paragraph (6)(b), fixed seating is not a physical feature.

(8) In the case of a vehicle within sub-paragraph (3), a relevant device is not an auxiliary aid for the purposes of the third requirement.

(9) A relevant device is a device or structure, or equipment, the installation, operation or maintenance of which would necessitate making a permanent alteration to, or which would have a permanent effect on, the internal or external fabric of the vehicle.

(10) Regulations may amend this paragraph so as to provide for sub-paragraph (2) not to apply, or to apply only so far as is prescribed, in relation to vehicles of a prescribed description.

4 Interpretation

(1) This paragraph applies for the purposes of paragraph 3.

(2) A "hire-vehicle" is a vehicle hired (by way of a trade) under a hiring agreement to which section 66 of the Road Traffic Offenders Act 1988 applies.

(3) A "taxi", in England and Wales, is a vehicle –

(a)   licensed under section 37 of the Town Police Clauses Act 1847,

(b)   licensed under section 6 of the Metropolitan Public Carriage Act 1869, or

(c)   drawn by one or more persons or animals.

(4) A "taxi", in Scotland, is –

(a) a hire car engaged, by arrangements made in a public place between the person to be transported (or a person acting on that person's behalf) and the driver, for a journey starting there and then, or

(b) a vehicle drawn by one or more persons or animals.

Schedule 3

Section 31

Services and public functions: exceptions

PART 1
CONSTITUTIONAL MATTERS

1 Parliament

(1) Section 29 does not apply to the exercise of –

(a) a function of Parliament;

(b) a function exercisable in connection with proceedings in Parliament.

(2) Sub-paragraph (1) does not permit anything to be done to or in relation to an individual unless it is done by or in pursuance of a resolution or other deliberation of either House or of a Committee of either House.

2 Legislation

(1) Section 29 does not apply to preparing, making or considering –

(a) an Act of Parliament;

(b) a Bill for an Act of Parliament;

(c) an Act of the Scottish Parliament;

(d) a Bill for an Act of the Scottish Parliament;

(e) an Act of the National Assembly for Wales;

(f) a Bill for an Act of the National Assembly for Wales.

(2) Section 29 does not apply to preparing, making, approving or considering –

(a) a Measure of the National Assembly for Wales;

(b) a proposed Measure of the National Assembly for Wales.

(3) Section 29 does not apply to preparing, making, confirming, approving or considering an instrument which is made under an enactment by –

(a) a Minister of the Crown;

(b) the Scottish Ministers or a member of the Scottish Executive;

(c) the Welsh Ministers, the First Minister for Wales or the Counsel General to the Welsh Assembly Government.

(4) Section 29 does not apply to preparing, making, confirming, approving or considering an instrument to which paragraph 6(a) of Schedule 2 to the Synodical Government Measure 1969 (1969 No. 2) (Measures, Canons, Acts of Synod, orders, etc.) applies.

(5) Section 29 does not apply to anything done in connection with the preparation, making, consideration, approval or confirmation of an instrument made by –

(a) Her Majesty in Council;

(b)   the Privy Council.

(6) Section 29 does not apply to anything done in connection with the imposition of a requirement or condition which comes within Schedule 22 (statutory provisions).

3 Judicial functions

(1) Section 29 does not apply to –

    (a)   a judicial function;

    (b)   anything done on behalf of, or on the instructions of, a person exercising a judicial function;

    (c)   a decision not to commence or continue criminal proceedings;

    (d)   anything done for the purpose of reaching, or in pursuance of, a decision not to commence or continue criminal proceedings.

(2) A reference in sub-paragraph (1) to a judicial function includes a reference to a judicial function conferred on a person other than a court or tribunal.

4 Armed forces

(1) Section 29(6), so far as relating to relevant discrimination, does not apply to anything done for the purpose of ensuring the combat effectiveness of the armed forces.

(2) "Relevant discrimination" is –

    (a)   age discrimination;

    (b)   disability discrimination;

    (c)   gender reassignment discrimination;

    (d)   sex discrimination.

5 Security services, etc.

Section 29 does not apply to –

    (a)   the Security Service;

    (b)   the Secret Intelligence Service;

    (c)   the Government Communications Headquarters;

    (d)   a part of the armed forces which is, in accordance with a requirement of the Secretary of State, assisting the Government Communications Headquarters.

PART 2
EDUCATION

6

In its application to a local authority in England and Wales, section 29, so far as relating to age discrimination or religious or belief-related discrimination, does not apply to –

    (a)   the exercise of the authority's functions under section 14 of the Education Act 1996 (provision of schools);

    (b)   the exercise of its function under section 13 of that Act in so far as it relates to a function of its under section 14 of that Act.

7

In its application to an education authority, section 29, so far as relating to age discrimination or religious or belief-related discrimination, does not apply to –

(a) the exercise of the authority's functions under section 17 of the Education (Scotland) Act 1980 (provision of schools);

(b) the exercise of its functions under section 1 of that Act, section 2 of the Standards in Scotland's Schools etc. Act 2000 (asp 6) or section 4 or 5 of the Education (Additional Support for Learning) (Scotland) Act 2004 (asp 4) (general responsibility for education) in so far as it relates to a matter specified in paragraph (a);

(c) the exercise of its functions under subsection (1) of section 50 of the Education (Scotland) Act 1980 (education of pupils in exceptional circumstances) in so far as it consists of making arrangements of the description referred to in subsection (2) of that section.

8

(1) In its application to a local authority in England and Wales or an education authority, section 29, so far as relating to sex discrimination, does not apply to the exercise of the authority's functions in relation to the establishment of a school.

(2) But nothing in sub-paragraph (1) is to be taken as disapplying section 29 in relation to the exercise of the authority's functions under section 14 of the Education Act 1996 or section 17 of the Education (Scotland) Act 1982.

9

Section 29, so far as relating to age discrimination, does not apply in relation to anything done in connection with –

(a) the curriculum of a school,

(b) admission to a school,

(c) transport to or from a school, or

(d) the establishment, alteration or closure of schools.

10

(1) Section 29, so far as relating to disability discrimination, does not require a local authority in England or Wales exercising functions under the Education Acts or an education authority exercising relevant functions to remove or alter a physical feature.

(2) Relevant functions are functions under –

(a) the Education (Scotland) Act 1980,

(b) the Education (Scotland) Act 1996,

(c) the Standards in Scotland's Schools etc. Act 2000, or

(d) the Education (Additional Support for Learning) (Scotland) Act 2004.

11

Section 29, so far as relating to religious or belief-related discrimination, does not apply in relation to anything done in connection with –

(a) the curriculum of a school;

(b) admission to a school which has a religious ethos;

(c)   acts of worship or other religious observance organised by or on behalf of a school (whether or not forming part of the curriculum);

(d)   the responsible body of a school which has a religious ethos;

(e)   transport to or from a school;

(f)   the establishment, alteration or closure of schools.

12

This Part of this Schedule is to be construed in accordance with Chapter 1 of Part 6.

PART 3
HEALTH AND CARE

13 Blood services

(1) A person operating a blood service does not contravene section 29 only by refusing to accept a donation of an individual's blood if –

(a)   the refusal is because of an assessment of the risk to the public, or to the individual, based on clinical, epidemiological or other data obtained from a source on which it is reasonable to rely, and

(b)   the refusal is reasonable.

(2) A blood service is a service for the collection and distribution of human blood for the purposes of medical services.

(3) "Blood" includes blood components.

14 Health and safety

(1) A service-provider (A) who refuses to provide the service to a pregnant woman does not discriminate against her in contravention of section 29 because she is pregnant if –

(a)   A reasonably believes that providing her with the service would, because she is pregnant, create a risk to her health or safety,

(b)   A refuses to provide the service to persons with other physical conditions, and

(c)   the reason for that refusal is that A reasonably believes that providing the service to such persons would create a risk to their health or safety.

(2) A service-provider (A) who provides, or offers to provide, the service to a pregnant woman on conditions does not discriminate against her in contravention of section 29 because she is pregnant if –

(a)   the conditions are intended to remove or reduce a risk to her health or safety,

(b)   A reasonably believes that the provision of the service without the conditions would create a risk to her health or safety,

(c)   A imposes conditions on the provision of the service to persons with other physical conditions, and

(d)   the reason for the imposition of those conditions is that A reasonably believes that the provision of the service to such persons without those conditions would create a risk to their health or safety.

15 Care within the family

A person (A) does not contravene section 29 only by participating in arrangements under which (whether or not for reward) A takes into A's home, and treats as members of A's family, persons requiring particular care and attention.

PART 4
IMMIGRATION

16 Disability

(1) This paragraph applies in relation to disability discrimination.

(2) Section 29 does not apply to –

    (a)   a decision within sub-paragraph (3);

    (b)   anything done for the purposes of or in pursuance of a decision within that sub-paragraph.

(3) A decision is within this sub-paragraph if it is a decision (whether or not taken in accordance with immigration rules) to do any of the following on the ground that doing so is necessary for the public good –

    (a)   to refuse entry clearance;

    (b)   to refuse leave to enter or remain in the United Kingdom;

    (c)   to cancel leave to enter or remain in the United Kingdom;

    (d)   to vary leave to enter or remain in the United Kingdom;

    (e)   to refuse an application to vary leave to enter or remain in the United Kingdom.

(4) Section 29 does not apply to –

    (a)   a decision taken, or guidance given, by the Secretary of State in connection with a decision within sub-paragraph (3);

    (b)   a decision taken in accordance with guidance given by the Secretary of State in connection with a decision within that sub-paragraph.

17 Nationality and ethnic or national origins

(1) This paragraph applies in relation to race discrimination so far as relating to –

    (a)   nationality, or

    (b)   ethnic or national origins.

(2) Section 29 does not apply to anything done by a relevant person in the exercise of functions exercisable by virtue of a relevant enactment.

(3) A relevant person is –

    (a)   a Minister of the Crown acting personally, or

    (b)   a person acting in accordance with a relevant authorisation.

(4) A relevant authorisation is a requirement imposed or express authorisation given –

    (a)   with respect to a particular case or class of case, by a Minister of the Crown acting personally;

    (b)   with respect to a particular class of case, by a relevant enactment or by an instrument made under or by virtue of a relevant enactment.

(5) The relevant enactments are –

    (a)   the Immigration Acts,

    (b)   the Special Immigration Appeals Commission Act 1997,

    (c)   a provision made under section 2(2) of the European Communities Act 1972 which relates to immigration or asylum, and

    (d)   a provision of Community law which relates to immigration or asylum.

(6) The reference in sub-paragraph (5)(a) to the Immigration Acts does not include a reference to –

(a) sections 28A to 28K of the Immigration Act 1971 (powers of arrest, entry and search, etc.), or

(b) section 14 of the Asylum and Immigration (Treatment of Claimants, etc.) Act 2004 (power of arrest).

18 Religion or belief

(1) This paragraph applies in relation to religious or belief-related discrimination.

(2) Section 29 does not apply to a decision within sub-paragraph (3) or anything done for the purposes of or in pursuance of a decision within that sub-paragraph.

(3) A decision is within this sub-paragraph if it is a decision taken in accordance with immigration rules –

(a) to refuse entry clearance or leave to enter the United Kingdom, or to cancel leave to enter or remain in the United Kingdom, on the grounds that the exclusion of the person from the United Kingdom is conducive to the public good, or

(b) to vary leave to enter or remain in the United Kingdom, or to refuse an application to vary leave to enter or remain in the United Kingdom, on the grounds that it is undesirable to permit the person to remain in the United Kingdom.

(4) Section 29 does not apply to a decision within sub-paragraph (5), or anything done for the purposes of or in pursuance of a decision within that sub-paragraph, if the decision is taken on grounds mentioned in sub-paragraph (6).

(5) A decision is within this sub-paragraph if it is a decision (whether or not taken in accordance with immigration rules) in connection with an application for entry clearance or for leave to enter or remain in the United Kingdom.

(6) The grounds referred to in sub-paragraph (4) are –

(a) the grounds that a person holds an office or post in connection with a religion or belief or provides a service in connection with a religion or belief,

(b) the grounds that a religion or belief is not to be treated in the same way as certain other religions or beliefs, or

(c) the grounds that the exclusion from the United Kingdom of a person to whom paragraph (a) applies is conducive to the public good.

(7) Section 29 does not apply to –

(a) a decision taken, or guidance given, by the Secretary of State in connection with a decision within sub-paragraph (3) or (5);

(b) a decision taken in accordance with guidance given by the Secretary of State in connection with a decision within either of those sub-paragraphs.

19 Interpretation

A reference to entry clearance, leave to enter or remain or immigration rules is to be construed in accordance with the Immigration Act 1971.

PART 5
INSURANCE, ETC.

20 Services arranged by employer

(1) Section 29 does not apply to the provision of a relevant financial service if the provision is in pursuance of arrangements made by an employer for the service-provider to provide the service to the employer's employees, and other persons, as a consequence of the employment.

(2) "Relevant financial service" means –

(a)　insurance or a related financial service, or

(b)　a service relating to membership of or benefits under a personal pension scheme (within the meaning given by section 1 of the Pension Schemes Act 1993).

21 Disability

(1) It is not a contravention of section 29, so far as relating to disability discrimination, to do anything in connection with insurance business if –

(a)　that thing is done by reference to information that is both relevant to the assessment of the risk to be insured and from a source on which it is reasonable to rely, and

(b)　it is reasonable to do that thing.

(2) "Insurance business" means business which consists of effecting or carrying out contracts of insurance; and that definition is to be read with –

(a)　section 22 of the Financial Services and Markets Act 2000,

(b)　any relevant order under that Act, and

(c)　Schedule 2 to that Act.

22 Sex, gender reassignment, pregnancy and maternity

(1) It is not a contravention of section 29, so far as relating to relevant discrimination, to do anything in relation to an annuity, life insurance policy, accident insurance policy or similar matter involving the assessment of risk if –

(a)　that thing is done by reference to actuarial or other data from a source on which it is reasonable to rely, and

(b)　it is reasonable to do that thing.

(2) In the case of a contract of insurance, or a contract for related financial services, entered into before 6 April 2008, sub-paragraph (1) applies only in relation to differences in premiums and benefits that are applicable to a person under the contract.

(3) In the case of a contract of insurance, or a contract for related financial services, entered into on or after 6 April 2008, sub-paragraph (1) applies only in relation to differences in premiums and benefits if –

(a)　the use of sex as a factor in the assessment of risk is based on relevant and accurate actuarial and statistical data,

(b)　the data are compiled, published (whether in full or in summary form) and regularly updated in accordance with guidance issued by the Treasury,

(c)　the differences are proportionate having regard to the data, and

(d)   the differences do not result from costs related to pregnancy or to a woman's having given birth in the period of 26 weeks ending on the day on which the thing in question is done.

(4) "Relevant discrimination" is –

(a)   gender reassignment discrimination;
(b)   pregnancy and maternity discrimination;
(c)   sex discrimination.

(5) For the purposes of the application of sub-paragraph (3) to gender reassignment discrimination by virtue of section 13, that section has effect as if in subsection (1), after "others" there were inserted "of B's sex".

(6) In the application of sub-paragraph (3) to a contract entered into before 22 December 2008, paragraph (d) is to be ignored.

23 Existing insurance policies

(1) It is not a contravention of section 29, so far as relating to relevant discrimination, to do anything in connection with insurance business in relation to an existing insurance policy.

(2) "Relevant discrimination" is –

(a)   age discrimination;
(b)   disability discrimination;
(c)   gender reassignment discrimination;
(d)   pregnancy and maternity discrimination;
(e)   race discrimination;
(f)   religious or belief-related discrimination;
(g)   sex discrimination;
(h)   sexual orientation discrimination.

(3) An existing insurance policy is a policy of insurance entered into before the date on which this paragraph comes into force.

(4) Sub-paragraph (1) does not apply where an existing insurance policy was renewed, or the terms of such a policy were reviewed, on or after the date on which this paragraph comes into force.

(5) A review of an existing insurance policy which was part of, or incidental to, a general reassessment by the service-provider of the pricing structure for a group of policies is not a review for the purposes of sub-paragraph (4).

(6) "Insurance business" has the meaning given in paragraph 21.

PART 6
MARRIAGE

24 Gender reassignment: England and Wales

(1) A person does not contravene section 29, so far as relating to gender reassignment discrimination, only because of anything done in reliance on section 5B of the Marriage Act 1949 (solemnisation of marriages involving person of acquired gender).

(2) A person (A) whose consent to the solemnisation of the marriage of a person (B) is required under section 44(1) of the Marriage Act 1949 (solemnisation in registered

building) does not contravene section 29, so far as relating to gender reassignment discrimination, by refusing to consent if A reasonably believes that B's gender has become the acquired gender under the Gender Recognition Act 2004.

(3) Sub-paragraph (4) applies to a person (A) who may, in a case that comes within the Marriage Act 1949 (other than the case mentioned in sub-paragraph (1)), solemnise marriages according to a form, rite or ceremony of a body of persons who meet for religious worship.

(4) A does not contravene section 29, so far as relating to gender reassignment discrimination, by refusing to solemnise, in accordance with a form, rite or ceremony as described in sub-paragraph (3), the marriage of a person (B) if A reasonably believes that B's gender has become the acquired gender under the Gender Recognition Act 2004.

25 Gender reassignment: Scotland

(1) An approved celebrant (A) does not contravene section 29, so far as relating to gender reassignment discrimination, only by refusing to solemnise the marriage of a person (B) if A reasonably believes that B's gender has become the acquired gender under the Gender Recognition Act 2004.

(2) In sub-paragraph (1) "approved celebrant" has the meaning given in section 8(2)(a) of the Marriage (Scotland) Act 1977 (persons who may solemnise marriage).

PART 7
SEPARATE AND SINGLE SERVICES

26 Separate services for the sexes

(1) A person does not contravene section 29, so far as relating to sex discrimination, by providing separate services for persons of each sex if –

    (a)   a joint service for persons of both sexes would be less effective, and
    (b)   the limited provision is a proportionate means of achieving a legitimate aim.

(2) A person does not contravene section 29, so far as relating to sex discrimination, by providing separate services differently for persons of each sex if –

    (a)   a joint service for persons of both sexes would be less effective,
    (b)   the extent to which the service is required by one sex makes it not reasonably practicable to provide the service otherwise than as a separate service provided differently for each sex, and
    (c)   the limited provision is a proportionate means of achieving a legitimate aim.

(3) This paragraph applies to a person exercising a public function in relation to the provision of a service as it applies to the person providing the service.

27 Single-sex services

(1) A person does not contravene section 29, so far as relating to sex discrimination, by providing a service only to persons of one sex if –

    (a)   any of the conditions in sub-paragraphs (2) to (7) is satisfied, and
    (b)   the limited provision is a proportionate means of achieving a legitimate aim.

(2) The condition is that only persons of that sex have need of the service.

(3) The condition is that –

(a)   the service is also provided jointly for persons of both sexes, and
(b)   the service would be insufficiently effective were it only to be provided jointly.

(4) The condition is that –

(a)   a joint service for persons of both sexes would be less effective, and
(b)   the extent to which the service is required by persons of each sex makes it not reasonably practicable to provide separate services.

(5) The condition is that the service is provided at a place which is, or is part of –

(a)   a hospital, or
(b)   another establishment for persons requiring special care, supervision or attention.

(6) The condition is that –

(a)   the service is provided for, or is likely to be used by, two or more persons at the same time, and
(b)   the circumstances are such that a person of one sex might reasonably object to the presence of a person of the opposite sex.

(7) The condition is that –

(a)   there is likely to be physical contact between a person (A) to whom the service is provided and another person (B), and
(b)   B might reasonably object if A were not of the same sex as B.

(8) This paragraph applies to a person exercising a public function in relation to the provision of a service as it applies to the person providing the service.

28 Gender reassignment

(1) A person does not contravene section 29, so far as relating to gender reassignment discrimination, only because of anything done in relation to a matter within sub-paragraph (2) if the conduct in question is a proportionate means of achieving a legitimate aim.

(2) The matters are –

(a)   the provision of separate services for persons of each sex;
(b)   the provision of separate services differently for persons of each sex;
(c)   the provision of a service only to persons of one sex.

29 Services relating to religion

(1) A minister does not contravene section 29, so far as relating to sex discrimination, by providing a service only to persons of one sex or separate services for persons of each sex, if –

(a)   the service is provided for the purposes of an organised religion,
(b)   it is provided at a place which is (permanently or for the time being) occupied or used for those purposes, and
(c)   the limited provision of the service is necessary in order to comply with the doctrines of the religion or is for the purpose of avoiding conflict with the strongly held religious convictions of a significant number of the religion's followers.

(2) The reference to a minister is a reference to a minister of religion, or other person, who –

(a)   performs functions in connection with the religion, and

(b)   holds an office or appointment in, or is accredited, approved or recognised for purposes of, a relevant organisation in relation to the religion.

(3) An organisation is a relevant organisation in relation to a religion if its purpose is –

(a)   to practise the religion,

(b)   to advance the religion,

(c)   to teach the practice or principles of the religion,

(d)   to enable persons of the religion to receive benefits, or to engage in activities, within the framework of that religion, or

(e)   to foster or maintain good relations between persons of different religions.

(4) But an organisation is not a relevant organisation in relation to a religion if its sole or main purpose is commercial.

30 Services generally provided only for persons who share a protected characteristic

If a service is generally provided only for persons who share a protected characteristic, a person (A) who normally provides the service for persons who share that characteristic does not contravene section 29(1) or (2) –

(a)   by insisting on providing the service in the way A normally provides it, or

(b)   if A reasonably thinks it is impracticable to provide the service to persons who do not share that characteristic, by refusing to provide the service.

PART 8
TELEVISION, RADIO AND ON-LINE BROADCASTING AND DISTRIBUTION

31

(1) Section 29 does not apply to the provision of a content service (within the meaning given by section 32(7) of the Communications Act 2003).

(2) Sub-paragraph (1) does not apply to the provision of an electronic communications network, electronic communications service or associated facility (each of which has the same meaning as in that Act).

PART 9
TRANSPORT

Application to disability

32

This Part of this Schedule applies in relation to disability discrimination.

Transport by air

33

(1) Section 29 does not apply to –

(a)   transporting people by air;

(b)   a service provided on a vehicle for transporting people by air.

(2) Section 29 does not apply to anything governed by Regulation (EC) No 1107/2006 of the European Parliament and of the Council of 5 July 2006 concerning the rights of disabled persons and persons with reduced mobility when travelling by air.

Transport by land

34

(1) Section 29 does not apply to transporting people by land, unless the vehicle concerned is –

    (a)   a hire-vehicle designed and constructed for the carriage of passengers and comprising no more than 8 seats in addition to the driver's seat,

    (b)   a hire-vehicle designed and constructed for the carriage of passengers, comprising more than 8 seats in addition to the driver's seat and having a maximum mass not exceeding 5 tonnes,

    (c)   a hire-vehicle designed and constructed for the carriage of goods and having a maximum mass not exceeding 3.5 tonnes,

    (d)   a vehicle licensed under section 48 of the Local Government (Miscellaneous Provisions) Act 1976 or section 7 of the Private Hire Vehicles (London) Act 1998 (or under a provision of a local Act corresponding to either of those provisions),

    (e)   a private hire car (within the meaning of section 23 of the Civic Government (Scotland) Act 1982),

    (f)   a public service vehicle (within the meaning given by section 1 of the Public Passenger Vehicles Act 1981),

    (g)   a vehicle built or adapted to carry passengers on a railway or tramway (within the meaning, in each case, of the Transport and Works Act 1992),

    (h)   a taxi,

    (i)   a vehicle deployed to transport the driver and passengers of a vehicle that has broken down or is involved in an accident, or

    (j)   a vehicle deployed on a system using a mode of guided transport (within the meaning of the Transport and Works Act 1992).

(2) Paragraph 4 of Schedule 2 applies for the purposes of this paragraph as it applies for the purposes of paragraph 3 of that Schedule.

PART 10
SUPPLEMENTARY

Power to amend

35

(1) A Minister of the Crown may by order amend this Schedule –

    (a)   so as to add, vary or omit an exception to section 29, so far as relating to disability, religion or belief or sexual orientation;

    (b)   so as to add, vary or omit an exception to section 29(6), so far as relating to gender reassignment, pregnancy and maternity, race or sex.

(2) But provision by virtue of sub-paragraph (1) may not amend this Schedule –

    (a)   so as to omit an exception in paragraph 1, 2 or 3;

    (b)   so as to reduce the extent to which an exception in paragraph 1, 2 or 3 applies.

(3) For the purposes of an order under sub-paragraph (l)(a), so far as relating to disability, which makes provision in relation to transport by air, it does not matter whether the transport is within or outside the United Kingdom.

(4) Before making an order under this paragraph the Minister must consult the Commission.

(5) Nothing in this paragraph affects the application of any other provision of this Act to conduct outside England and Wales or Scotland.

Schedule 4

Section 38

Premises: reasonable adjustments

1 Preliminary

This Schedule applies where a duty to make reasonable adjustments is imposed on A by this Part.

2 The duty in relation to let premises

(1) This paragraph applies where A is a controller of let premises.

(2) A must comply with the first and third requirements.

(3) For the purposes of this paragraph, the reference in section 20(3) to a provision, criterion or practice of A's includes a reference to a term of the letting.

(4) For those purposes, the reference in section 20(3) or (5) to a disabled person is a reference to a disabled person who –

    (a)   is a tenant of the premises, or
    (b)   is otherwise entitled to occupy them.

(5) In relation to each requirement, the relevant matters are –

    (a)   the enjoyment of the premises;
    (b)   the use of a benefit or facility, entitlement to which arises as a result of the letting.

(6) Sub-paragraph (2) applies only if A receives a request from or on behalf of the tenant or a person entitled to occupy the premises to take steps to avoid the disadvantage or provide the auxiliary aid.

(7) If a term of the letting that prohibits the tenant from making alterations puts the disabled person at the disadvantage referred to in the first requirement, A is required to change the term only so far as is necessary to enable the tenant to make alterations to the let premises so as to avoid the disadvantage.

(8) It is never reasonable for A to have to take a step which would involve the removal or alteration of a physical feature.

(9) For the purposes of this paragraph, physical features do not include furniture, furnishings, materials, equipment or other chattels in or on the premises; and none of the following is an alteration of a physical feature –

    (a)   the replacement or provision of a sign or notice;

(b)   the replacement of a tap or door handle;

(c)   the replacement, provision or adaptation of a door bell or door entry system;

(d)   changes to the colour of a wall, door or any other surface.

(10) The terms of a letting include the terms of an agreement relating to it.

3 The duty in relation to premises to let

(1) This paragraph applies where A is a controller of premises to let.

(2) A must comply with the first and third requirements.

(3) For the purposes of this paragraph, the reference in section 20(3) or (5) to a disabled person is a reference to a disabled person who is considering taking a letting of the premises.

(4) In relation to each requirement, the relevant matter is becoming a tenant of the premises.

(5) Sub-paragraph (2) applies only if A receives a request by or on behalf of a disabled person within sub-paragraph (3) for A to take steps to avoid the disadvantage or provide the auxiliary aid.

(6) Nothing in this paragraph requires A to take a step which would involve the removal or alteration of a physical feature.

(7) Sub-paragraph (9) of paragraph 2 applies for the purposes of this paragraph as it applies for the purposes of that paragraph.

4 The duty in relation to commonhold units

(1) This paragraph applies where A is a commonhold association; and the reference to a commonhold association is a reference to the association in its capacity as the person who manages a commonhold unit.

(2) A must comply with the first and third requirements.

(3) For the purposes of this paragraph, the reference in section 20(3) to a provision, criterion or practice of A's includes a reference to –

(a)   a term of the commonhold community statement, or

(b)   any other term applicable by virtue of the transfer of the unit to the unit-holder.

(4) For those purposes, the reference in section 20(3) or (5) to a disabled person is a reference to a disabled person who –

(a)   is the unit-holder, or

(b)   is otherwise entitled to occupy the unit.

(5) In relation to each requirement, the relevant matters are –

(a)   the enjoyment of the unit;

(b)   the use of a benefit or facility, entitlement to which arises as a result of a term within sub-paragraph (3)(a) or (b).

(6) Sub-paragraph (2) applies only if A receives a request from or on behalf of the unit-holder or a person entitled to occupy the unit to take steps to avoid the disadvantage or provide the auxiliary aid.

(7) If a term within sub-paragraph (3)(a) or (b) that prohibits the unit-holder from making alterations puts the disabled person at the disadvantage referred to in the first requirement, A is required to change the term only so far as is necessary to enable the unit-holder to make alterations to the unit so as to avoid the disadvantage.

(8) It is never reasonable for A to have to take a step which would involve the removal or alteration of a physical feature; and sub-paragraph (9) of paragraph 2 applies in relation to a commonhold unit as it applies in relation to let premises.

5 The duty in relation to common parts

(1) This paragraph applies where A is a responsible person in relation to common parts.

(2) A must comply with the second requirement.

(3) For the purposes of this paragraph, the reference in section 20(4) to a physical feature is a reference to a physical feature of the common parts.

(4) For those purposes, the reference in section 20(4) to a disabled person is a reference to a disabled person who –

    (a)   is a tenant of the premises,
    (b)   is a unit-holder, or
    (c)   is otherwise entitled to occupy the premises,

and uses or intends to use the premises as the person's only or main home.

(5) In relation to the second requirement, the relevant matter is the use of the common parts.

(6) Sub-paragraph (2) applies only if –

    (a)   A receives a request by or on behalf of a disabled person within sub-paragraph (4) for A to take steps to avoid the disadvantage, and
    (b)   the steps requested are likely to avoid or reduce the disadvantage.

6 Consultation on adjustments relating to common parts

(1) In deciding whether it is reasonable to take a step for the purposes of paragraph 5, A must consult all persons A thinks would be affected by the step.

(2) The consultation must be carried out within a reasonable period of the request being made.

(3) A is not required to have regard to a view expressed against taking a step in so far as A reasonably believes that the view is expressed because of the disabled person's disability.

(4) Nothing in this paragraph affects anything a commonhold association is required to do pursuant to Part 1 of the Commonhold and Leasehold Reform Act 2002.

7 Agreement on adjustments relating to common parts

(1) If A decides that it is reasonable to take a step for the purposes of paragraph 5, A and the disabled person must agree in writing the rights and responsibilities of each of them in relation to the step.

(2) An agreement under this paragraph must, in particular, make provision as to the responsibilities of the parties in relation to –

(a)   the costs of any work to be undertaken;

(b)   other costs arising from the work;

(c)   the restoration of the common parts to their former condition if the relevant disabled person stops living in the premises.

(3) It is always reasonable before the agreement is made for A to insist that the agreement should require the disabled person to pay –

(a)   the costs referred to in paragraphs (a) and (b) of sub-paragraph (2), and

(b)   the costs of the restoration referred to in paragraph (c) of that sub-paragraph.

(4) If an agreement under this paragraph is made, A's obligations under the agreement become part of A's interest in the common parts and pass on subsequent disposals accordingly.

(5) Regulations may require a party to an agreement under this paragraph to provide, in prescribed circumstances, prescribed information about the agreement to persons of a prescribed description.

(6) The regulations may require the information to be provided in a prescribed form.

(7) Regulations may make provision as to circumstances in which an agreement under this paragraph is to cease to have effect, in so far as the agreement does not itself make provision for termination.

8 Victimisation

(1) This paragraph applies where the relevant disabled person comes within paragraph 2(4)(b), 4(4)(b) or 5(4)(c).

(2) A must not, because of costs incurred in connection with taking steps to comply with a requirement imposed for the purposes of paragraph 2, 4 or 5, subject to a detriment –

(a)   a tenant of the premises, or

(b)   the unit-holder.

9 Regulations

(1) This paragraph applies for the purposes of section 36 and this Schedule.

(2) Regulations may make provision as to –

(a)   circumstances in which premises are to be treated as let, or as not let, to a person;

(b)   circumstances in which premises are to be treated as being, or as not being, to let;

(c)   who is to be treated as being, or as not being, a person entitled to occupy premises otherwise than as tenant or unit-holder;

(d)   who is to be treated as being, or as not being, a person by whom premises are let;

(e)   who is to be treated as having, or as not having, premises to let;

(f)   who is to be treated as being, or as not being, a manager of premises.

(3) Provision made by virtue of this paragraph may amend this Schedule.

Schedule 5

Premises: exceptions

1 Owner-occupier

(1) This paragraph applies to the private disposal of premises by an owner-occupier.

(2) A disposal is a private disposal only if the owner-occupier does not –

- (a)   use the services of an estate agent for the purpose of disposing of the premises, or
- (b)   publish (or cause to be published) an advertisement in connection with their disposal.

(3) Section 33(1) applies only in so far as it relates to race.

(4) Section 34(1) does not apply in so far as it relates to –

- (a)   religion or belief, or
- (b)   sexual orientation.

(5) In this paragraph –

"estate agent" means a person who, by way of profession or trade, provides services for the purpose of –
- (a)   finding premises for persons seeking them, or
- (b)   assisting in the disposal of premises;

"owner-occupier" means a person who –
- (a)   owns an estate or interest in premises, and
- (b)   occupies the whole of them.

2

(1) Section 36(1)(a) does not apply if –

- (a)   the premises are, or have been, the only or main home of a person by whom they are let, and
- (b)   since entering into the letting, neither that person nor any other by whom they are let has used a manager for managing the premises.

(2) A manager is a person who, by profession or trade, manages let premises.

(3) Section 36(1)(b) does not apply if –

- (a)   the premises are, or have been, the only or main home of a person who has them to let, and
- (b)   neither that person nor any other who has the premises to let uses the services of an estate agent for letting the premises.

(4) "Estate agent" has the meaning given in paragraph 1.

3 Small premises

(1) This paragraph applies to anything done by a person in relation to the disposal, occupation or management of part of small premises if –

(a)   the person or a relative of that person resides, and intends to continue to reside, in another part of the premises, and

(b)   the premises include parts (other than storage areas and means of access) shared with residents of the premises who are not members of the same household as the resident mentioned in paragraph (a).

(2) Sections 33(1), 34(1) and 35(1) apply only in so far as they relate to race.

(3) Premises are small if –

(a)   the only other persons occupying the accommodation occupied by the resident mentioned in sub-paragraph (1)(a) are members of the same household,

(b)   the premises also include accommodation for at least one other household,

(c)   the accommodation for each of those other households is let, or available for letting, on a separate tenancy or similar agreement, and

(d)   the premises are not normally sufficient to accommodate more than two other households.

(4) Premises are also small if they are not normally sufficient to provide residential accommodation for more than six persons (in addition to the resident mentioned in sub-paragraph (1)(a) and members of the same household).

(5) In this paragraph, "relative" means –

(a)   spouse or civil partner,

(b)   unmarried partner,

(c)   parent or grandparent,

(d)   child or grandchild (whether or not legitimate),

(e)   the spouse, civil partner or unmarried partner of a child or grandchild,

(f)   brother or sister (whether of full blood or half-blood), or

(g)   a relative within paragraph (c), (d), (e) or (f) whose relationship arises as a result of marriage or civil partnership.

(6) In sub-paragraph (5), a reference to an unmarried partner is a reference to the other member of a couple consisting of –

(a)   a man and a woman who are not married to each other but are living together as husband and wife, or

(b)   two people of the same sex who are not civil partners of each other but are living together as if they were.

4

(1) Section 36(1) does not apply if –

(a)   the premises in question are small premises,

(b)   the relevant person or a relative of that person resides, and intends to continue to reside, in another part of the premises, and

(c)   the premises include parts (other than storage areas and means of access) shared with residents of the premises who are not members of the same household as the resident mentioned in paragraph (b).

(2) The relevant person is the person who, for the purposes of section 36(1), is –

(a)   the controller of the premises, or

(b)   the responsible person in relation to the common parts to which the premises relate.

(3) "Small premises" and "relative" have the same meaning as in paragraph 3.

5

A Minister of the Crown may by order amend paragraph 3 or 4.

Schedule 6

Section 52

Office-holders: excluded offices

1 Work to which other provisions apply

(1) An office or post is not a personal or public office in so far as one or more of the provisions mentioned in sub-paragraph (2) –

    (a)   applies in relation to the office or post, or

    (b)   would apply in relation to the office or post but for the operation of some other provision of this Act.

(2) Those provisions are –

    (a)   section 39 (employment);

    (b)   section 41 (contract work);

    (c)   section 44 (partnerships);

    (d)   section 45 (LLPs);

    (e)   section 47 (barristers);

    (f)   section 48 (advocates);

    (g)   section 55 (employment services) so far as applying to the provision of work experience within section 56(2) (a) or arrangements within section 56(2) (c) for such provision.

2 Political offices

(1) An office or post is not a personal or public office if it is a political office.

(2) A political office is an office or post set out in the second column of the following Table –

Political setting	*Office or post*
Houses of Parliament	An office of the House of Commons held by a member of that House
	An office of the House of Lords held by a member of that House
	A Ministerial office within the meaning of section 2 of the House of Commons Disqualification Act 1975
	The office of the Leader of the Opposition within the meaning of the Ministerial and other Salaries Act 1975
	The office of the Chief Opposition Whip, or of an Assistant Opposition Whip, within the meaning of that Act

Scottish Parliament	An office of the Scottish Parliament held by a member of the Parliament
	The office of a member of the Scottish Executive
	The office of a junior Scottish Minister
National Assembly for Wales	An office of the National Assembly for Wales held by a member of the Assembly
	The office of a member of the Welsh Assembly Government
Local government in England (outside London)	An office of a county council, district council or parish council in England held by a member of the council
	An office of the Council of the Isles of Scilly held by a member of the Council
Local government in London	An office of the Greater London Authority held by the Mayor of London or a member of the London Assembly
	An office of a London borough council held by a member of the council
	An office of the Common Council of the City of London held by a member of the Council
Local government in Wales	An office of a county council, county borough council or community council in Wales held by a member of the council
Local government in Scotland	An office of a council constituted under section 2 of the Local Government etc. (Scotland) Act 1994 held by a member of the council
	An office of a council established under section 51 of the Local Government (Scotland) Act 1973 held by a member of the council
Political parties	An office of a registered political party

(3) The reference to a registered political party is a reference to a party registered in the Great Britain register under Part 2 of the Political Parties, Elections and Referendums Act 2000.

3 Honours etc.

A life peerage (within the meaning of the Life Peerages Act 1958), or any other dignity or honour conferred by the Crown, is not a personal or public office.

Schedule 7

Section 80

Equality of terms: exceptions

PART 1
TERMS OF WORK

1 Compliance with laws regulating employment of women, etc.

Neither a sex equality clause nor a maternity equality clause has effect in relation to terms of work affected by compliance with laws regulating –

(a)   the employment of women;

(b)   the appointment of women to personal or public offices.

2 Pregnancy, etc.

A sex equality clause does not have effect in relation to terms of work affording special treatment to women in connection with pregnancy or childbirth.

PART 2
OCCUPATIONAL PENSION SCHEMES

3 Preliminary

(1) A sex equality rule does not have effect in relation to a difference as between men and women in the effect of a relevant matter if the difference is permitted by or by virtue of this Part of this Schedule.

(2) "Relevant matter" has the meaning given in section 67.

4 State retirement pensions

(1) This paragraph applies where a man and a woman are eligible, in such circumstances as may be prescribed, to receive different amounts by way of pension.

(2) The difference is permitted if, in prescribed circumstances, it is attributable only to differences between men and women in the retirement benefits to which, in prescribed circumstances, the man and woman are or would be entitled.

(3) "Retirement benefits" are benefits under sections 43 to 55 of the Social Security Contributions and Benefits Act 1992 (state retirement pensions).

5 Actuarial factors

(1) A difference as between men and women is permitted if it consists of applying to the calculation of the employer's contributions to an occupational pension scheme actuarial factors which –

(a)   differ for men and women, and

(b)   are of such description as may be prescribed.

(2) A difference as between men and women is permitted if it consists of applying to the determination of benefits of such description as may be prescribed actuarial factors which differ for men and women.

6 Power to amend

(1) Regulations may amend this Part of this Schedule so as to add, vary or omit provision about cases where a difference as between men and women in the effect of a relevant matter is permitted.

(2) The regulations may make provision about pensionable service before the date on which they come into force (but not about pensionable service before 17 May 1990).

Schedule 8

Section 83

Work: reasonable adjustments

PART 1
INTRODUCTORY

1 Preliminary

This Schedule applies where a duty to make reasonable adjustments is imposed on A by this Part of this Act.

2 The duty

(1) A must comply with the first, second and third requirements.

(2) For the purposes of this paragraph –

  (a)   the reference in section 20(3) to a provision, criterion or practice is a reference to a provision, criterion or practice applied by or on behalf of A;

  (b)   the reference in section 20(4) to a physical feature is a reference to a physical feature of premises occupied by A;

  (c)   the reference in section 20(3), (4) or (5) to a disabled person is to an interested disabled person.

(3) In relation to the first and third requirements, a relevant matter is any matter specified in the first column of the applicable table in Part 2 of this Schedule.

(4) In relation to the second requirement, a relevant matter is –

  (a)   a matter specified in the second entry of the first column of the applicable table in Part 2 of this Schedule, or

  (b)   where there is only one entry in a column, a matter specified there.

(5) If two or more persons are subject to a duty to make reasonable adjustments in relation to the same interested disabled person, each of them must comply with the duty so far as it is reasonable for each of them to do so.

3

(1) This paragraph applies if a duty to make reasonable adjustments is imposed on A by section 55 (except where the employment service which A provides is the provision of vocational training within the meaning given by section 56(6)(b)).

(2) The reference in section 20(3), (4) and (5) to a disabled person is a reference to an interested disabled person.

(3) In relation to each requirement, the relevant matter is the employment service which A provides.

(4) Sub-paragraph (5) of paragraph 2 applies for the purposes of this paragraph as it applies for the purposes of that paragraph.

PART 2
INTERESTED DISABLED PERSON

4 Preliminary

An interested disabled person is a disabled person who, in relation to a relevant matter, is of a description specified in the second column of the applicable table in this Part of this Schedule.

5 Employers (see section 39)

(1) This paragraph applies where A is an employer.

Relevant matter	*Description of disabled person*
Deciding to whom to offer employment.	A person who is, or has notified A that the person may be, an applicant for the employment.
Employment by A.	An applicant for employment by A.
	An employee of A's.

(2) Where A is the employer of a disabled contract worker (B), A must comply with the first, second and third requirements on each occasion when B is supplied to a principal to do contract work.

(3) In relation to the first requirement (as it applies for the purposes of sub-paragraph (2)) –

   (a)   the reference in section 20(3) to a provision, criterion or practice is a reference to a provision, criterion or practice applied by or on behalf of all or most of the principals to whom B is or might be supplied,

   (b)   the reference to being put at a substantial disadvantage is a reference to being likely to be put at a substantial disadvantage that is the same or similar in the case of each of the principals referred to in paragraph (a), and

   (c)   the requirement imposed on A is a requirement to take such steps as it would be reasonable for A to have to take if the provision, criterion or practice were applied by or on behalf of A.

(4) In relation to the second requirement (as it applies for the purposes of sub-paragraph (2)) –

   (a)   the reference in section 20(4) to a physical feature is a reference to a physical feature of premises occupied by each of the principals referred to in sub-paragraph (3)(a),

   (b)   the reference to being put at a substantial disadvantage is a reference to being likely to be put at a substantial disadvantage that is the same or similar in the case of each of those principals, and

   (c)   the requirement imposed on A is a requirement to take such steps as it would be reasonable for A to have to take if the premises were occupied by A.

(5) In relation to the third requirement (as it applies for the purposes of sub-paragraph (2)) –

(a) the reference in section 20(5) to being put at a substantial disadvantage is a reference to being likely to be put at a substantial disadvantage that is the same or similar in the case of each of the principals referred to in sub-paragraph (3)(a), and

(b) the requirement imposed on A is a requirement to take such steps as it would be reasonable for A to have to take if A were the person to whom B was supplied.

6 Principals in contract work (see section 41)

(1) This paragraph applies where A is a principal.

Relevant matter	*Description of disabled person*
Contract work that A may make available.	A person who is, or has notified A that the person may be, an applicant to do the work.
Contract work that A makes available.	A person who is supplied to do the work.

(2) A is not required to do anything that a disabled person's employer is required to do by virtue of paragraph 5.

7 Partnerships (see section 44)

(1) This paragraph applies where A is a firm or a proposed firm.

Relevant matter	*Description of disabled person*
Deciding to whom to offer a position as a partner.	A person who is, or has notified A that the person may be, a candidate for the position.
A position as a partner.	A candidate for the position.
	The partner who holds the position.

(2) Where a firm or proposed firm (A) is required by this Schedule to take a step in relation to an interested disabled person (B) –

(a) the cost of taking the step is to be treated as an expense of A;

(b) the extent to which B should (if B is or becomes a partner) bear the cost is not to exceed such amount as is reasonable (having regard in particular to B's entitlement to share in A's profits).

8 LLPs (see section 45)

(1) This paragraph applies where A is an LLP or a proposed LLP.

Relevant matter	*Description of disabled person*
Deciding to whom to offer a position as a member.	A person who is, or has notified A that the person may be, a candidate for the position.

A position as a member.   A candidate for the position.

                                              The member who holds the position.

(2) Where an LLP or proposed LLP (A) is required by this Schedule to take a step in relation to an interested disabled person (B) –

(a)   the cost of taking the step is to be treated as an expense of A;

(b)   the extent to which B should (if B is or becomes a member) bear the cost is not to exceed such amount as is reasonable (having regard in particular to B's entitlement to share in A's profits).

9 Barristers and their clerks (see section 47)

This paragraph applies where A is a barrister or barrister's clerk.

Relevant matter	*Description of disabled person*
Deciding to whom to offer a pupillage or tenancy.	A person who is, or has notified A that the person may be, an applicant for the pupillage or tenancy.
A pupillage or tenancy.	An applicant for the pupillage or tenancy.
	The pupil or tenant.

10 Advocates and their clerks (see section 48)

This paragraph applies where A is an advocate or advocate's clerk.

Relevant matter	*Description of disabled person*
Deciding who to offer to take as a devil or to whom to offer membership of a stable.	A person who applies, or has notified A that the person may apply, to be taken as a devil or to become a member of the stable.
The relationship with a devil or membership of a stable.	An applicant to be taken as a devil or to become a member of the stable.
	The devil or member.

11 Persons making appointments to offices etc. (see sections 49 to 51)

This paragraph applies where A is a person who has the power to make an appointment to a personal or public office.

Relevant matter	*Description of disabled person*
Deciding to whom to offer the appointment.	A person who is, or has notified A that the person may be, seeking the appointment.
	A person who is being considered for the appointment.
Appointment to the office.	A person who is seeking, or being considered for, appointment to the office.

12

This paragraph applies where A is a relevant person in relation to a personal or public office.

Relevant matter	*Description of disabled person*
Appointment to the office.	A person appointed to the office.

13

This paragraph applies where A is a person who has the power to make a recommendation for, or give approval to, an appointment to a public office.

Relevant matter	*Description of disabled person*
Deciding who to recommend or approve for appointment to the office.	A person who is, or has notified A that the person may be, seeking recommendation or approval for appointment to the office.
	A person who is being considered for recommendation or approval for appointment to the office.
An appointment to the office.	A person who is seeking, or being considered for, appointment to the office in question.

14

In relation to the second requirement in a case within paragraph 11, 12 or 13, the reference in paragraph 2(2)(b) to premises occupied by A is to be read as a reference to premises –

    (a)   under the control of A, and

    (b)   at or from which the functions of the office concerned are performed.

15 Qualifications bodies (see section 53)

(1) This paragraph applies where A is a qualifications body.

Relevant matter	*Description of disabled person*
Deciding upon whom to confer a relevant qualification.	A person who is, or has notified A that the person may be, an applicant for the conferment of the qualification.
Conferment by the body of a relevant qualification.	An applicant for the conferment of the qualification.
	A person who holds the qualification.

(2) A provision, criterion or practice does not include the application of a competence standard.

16 Employment service-providers (see section 55)

This paragraph applies where –

(a)   A is an employment service-provider, and
(b)   the employment service which A provides is vocational training within the meaning given by section 56(6)(b).

Relevant matter	*Description of disabled person*
Deciding to whom to offer to provide the service.	A person who is, or has notified A that the person may be, an applicant for the provision of the service.
Provision by A of the service.	A person who applies to A for the provision of the service.
	A person to whom A provides the service.

17 Trade organisations (see section 57)

This paragraph applies where A is a trade organisation.

Relevant matter	*Description of disabled person*
Deciding to whom to offer membership of the organisation.	A person who is, or has notified A that the person may be, an applicant for membership.
Membership of the organisation.	An applicant for membership.
	A member.

18 Local authorities (see section 58)

(1) This paragraph applies where A is a local authority.

Relevant matter	*Description of disabled person*
A member's carrying-out of official business.	The member.

(2) Regulations may, for the purposes of a case within this paragraph, make provision –

(a)   as to circumstances in which a provision, criterion or practice is, or is not, to be taken to put a disabled person at the disadvantage referred to in the first requirement;
(b)   as to circumstances in which a physical feature is, or is not, to be taken to put a disabled person at the disadvantage referred to in the second requirement;
(c)   as to circumstances in which it is, or in which it is not, reasonable for a local authority to be required to take steps of a prescribed description;
(d)   as to steps which it is always, or which it is never, reasonable for a local authority to take.

19 Occupational pensions (see section 61)

This paragraph applies where A is, in relation to an occupational pension scheme, a responsible person within the meaning of section 61.

Relevant matter	Description of disabled person
Carrying out A's functions in relation to the scheme.	A person who is or may be a member of the scheme.

PART 3
LIMITATIONS ON THE DUTY

20 Lack of knowledge of disability, etc.

(1) A is not subject to a duty to make reasonable adjustments if A does not know, and could not reasonably be expected to know –

(a) in the case of an applicant or potential applicant, that an interested disabled person is or may be an applicant for the work in question;

(b) in any other case referred to in this Part of this Schedule, that an interested disabled person has a disability and is likely to be placed at the disadvantage referred to in the first, second or third requirement.

(2) An applicant is, in relation to the description of A specified in the first column of the table, a person of a description specified in the second column (and the reference to a potential applicant is to be construed accordingly).

Description of A	Applicant
An employer	An applicant for employment
A firm or proposed firm	A candidate for a position as a partner
An LLP or proposed LLP	A candidate for a position as a member
A barrister or barrister's clerk	An applicant for a pupillage or tenancy
An advocate or advocate's clerk	An applicant for being taken as an advocate's devil or for becoming a member of a stable
A relevant person in relation to a personal or public office	A person who is seeking appointment to, or recommendation or approval for appointment to, the office
A qualifications body	An applicant for the conferment of a relevant qualification
An employment service-provider	An applicant for the provision of an employment service
A trade organisation	An applicant for membership

(3) If the duty to make reasonable adjustments is imposed on A by section 55, this paragraph applies only in so far as the employment service which A provides is vocational training within the meaning given by section 56(6)(b).

Schedule 9

Section 83

Work: exceptions

PART 1
OCCUPATIONAL REQUIREMENTS

1 General

(1) A person (A) does not contravene a provision mentioned in sub-paragraph (2) by applying in relation to work a requirement to have a particular protected characteristic, if A shows that, having regard to the nature or context of the work –

    (a)   it is an occupational requirement,

    (b)   the application of the requirement is a proportionate means of achieving a legitimate aim, and

    (c)   the person to whom A applies the requirement does not meet it (or A has reasonable grounds for not being satisfied that the person meets it).

(2) The provisions are –

    (a)   section 39(1)(a) or (c) or (2)(b) or (c);

    (b)   section 41(1)(b);

    (c)   section 44(1)(a) or (c) or (2)(b) or (c);

    (d)   section 45(1)(a) or (c) or (2)(b) or (c);

    (e)   section 49(3)(a) or (c) or (6)(b) or (c);

    (f)   section 50(3)(a) or (c) or (6)(b) or (c);

    (g)   section 51(1).

(3) The references in sub-paragraph (1) to a requirement to have a protected characteristic are to be read –

    (a)   in the case of gender reassignment, as references to a requirement not to be a transsexual person (and section 7(3) is accordingly to be ignored);

    (b)   in the case of marriage and civil partnership, as references to a requirement not to be married or a civil partner (and section 8(2) is accordingly to be ignored).

(4) In the case of a requirement to be of a particular sex, sub-paragraph (1) has effect as if in paragraph (c), the words from "(or" to the end were omitted.

2 Religious requirements relating to sex, marriage etc., sexual orientation

(1) A person (A) does not contravene a provision mentioned in sub-paragraph (2) by applying in relation to employment a requirement to which sub-paragraph (4) applies if A shows that –

    (a)   the employment is for the purposes of an organised religion,

    (b)   the application of the requirement engages the compliance or non-conflict principle, and

    (c)   the person to whom A applies the requirement does not meet it (or A has reasonable grounds for not being satisfied that the person meets it).

(2) The provisions are –

    (a)   section 39(1)(a) or (c) or (2)(b) or (c);

(b)   section 49(3)(a) or (c) or (6)(b) or (c);

(c)   section 50(3)(a) or (c) or (6)(b) or (c);

(d)   section 51(1).

(3) A person does not contravene section 53(1) or (2)(a) or (b) by applying in relation to a relevant qualification (within the meaning of that section) a requirement to which sub-paragraph (4) applies if the person shows that –

(a)   the qualification is for the purposes of employment mentioned in sub-paragraph (1)(a), and

(b)   the application of the requirement engages the compliance or non-conflict principle.

(4) This sub-paragraph applies to –

(a)   a requirement to be of a particular sex;

(b)   a requirement not to be a transsexual person;

(c)   a requirement not to be married or a civil partner;

(d)   a requirement not to be married to, or the civil partner of, a person who has a living former spouse or civil partner;

(e)   a requirement relating to circumstances in which a marriage or civil partnership came to an end;

(f)   a requirement related to sexual orientation.

(5) The application of a requirement engages the compliance principle if the requirement is applied so as to comply with the doctrines of the religion.

(6) The application of a requirement engages the non-conflict principle if, because of the nature or context of the employment, the requirement is applied so as to avoid conflicting with the strongly held religious convictions of a significant number of the religion's followers.

(7) A reference to employment includes a reference to an appointment to a personal or public office.

(8) In the case of a requirement within sub-paragraph (4)(a), sub-paragraph (1) has effect as if in paragraph (c) the words from "(or" to the end were omitted.

3 Other requirements relating to religion or belief

A person (A) with an ethos based on religion or belief does not contravene a provision mentioned in paragraph 1(2) by applying in relation to work a requirement to be of a particular religion or belief if A shows that, having regard to that ethos and to the nature or context of the work –

(a)   it is an occupational requirement,

(b)   the application of the requirement is a proportionate means of achieving a legitimate aim, and

(c)   the person to whom A applies the requirement does not meet it (or A has reasonable grounds for not being satisfied that the person meets it).

4 Armed forces

(1) A person does not contravene section 39(1)(a) or (c) or (2)(b) by applying in relation to service in the armed forces a relevant requirement if the person shows that the application is a proportionate means of ensuring the combat effectiveness of the armed forces.

(2) A relevant requirement is –

    (a)   a requirement to be a man;

    (b)   a requirement not to be a transsexual person.

(3) This Part of this Act, so far as relating to age or disability, does not apply to service in the armed forces; and section 55, so far as relating to disability, does not apply to work experience in the armed forces.

5 Employment services

(1) A person (A) does not contravene section 55(1) or (2) if A shows that A's treatment of another person relates only to work the offer of which could be refused to that other person in reliance on paragraph 1, 2, 3 or 4.

(2) A person (A) does not contravene section 55(1) or (2) if A shows that A's treatment of another person relates only to training for work of a description mentioned in sub-paragraph (1).

(3) A person (A) does not contravene section 55(1) or (2) if A shows that –

    (a)   A acted in reliance on a statement made to A by a person with the power to offer the work in question to the effect that, by virtue of sub-paragraph (1) or (2), A's action would be lawful, and

    (b)   it was reasonable for A to rely on the statement.

(4) A person commits an offence by knowingly or recklessly making a statement such as is mentioned in sub-paragraph (3)(a) which in a material respect is false or misleading.

(5) A person guilty of an offence under sub-paragraph (4) is liable on summary conviction to a fine not exceeding level 5 on the standard scale.

6 Interpretation

(1) This paragraph applies for the purposes of this Part of this Schedule.

(2) A reference to contravening a provision of this Act is a reference to contravening that provision by virtue of section 13.

(3) A reference to work is a reference to employment, contract work, a position as a partner or as a member of an LLP, or an appointment to a personal or public office.

(4) A reference to a person includes a reference to an organisation.

(5) A reference to section 39(2)(b), 44(2)(b), 45(2)(b), 49(6)(b) or 50(6)(b) is to be read as a reference to that provision with the omission of the words "or for receiving any other benefit, facility or service".

(6) A reference to section 39(2)(c), 44(2)(c), 45(2)(c), 49(6)(c), 50(6)(c), 53(2)(a) or 55(2)(c) (dismissal, etc.) does not include a reference to that provision so far as relating to sex.

(7) The reference to paragraph (b) of section 41(1), so far as relating to sex, is to be read as if that paragraph read –

    "(b)by not allowing the worker to do the work."

PART 2
EXCEPTIONS RELATING TO AGE

7 Preliminary

For the purposes of this Part of this Schedule, a reference to an age contravention is a reference to a contravention of this Part of this Act, so far as relating to age.

8 Retirement

(1) It is not an age contravention to dismiss a relevant worker at or over the age of 65 if the reason for the dismissal is retirement.

(2) Each of the following is a relevant worker –

(a)   an employee within the meaning of section 230(1) of the Employment Rights Act 1996;
(b)   a person in Crown employment;
(c)   a relevant member of the House of Commons staff;
(d)   a relevant member of the House of Lords staff.

(3) Retirement is a reason for dismissal only if it is a reason for dismissal by virtue of Part 10 of the Employment Rights Act 1996.

9 Applicants at or approaching retirement age

(1) A person does not contravene section 39(1)(a) or (c), so far as relating to age, in a case where the other person –

(a)   has attained the age limit, or would have attained it before the end of six months beginning with the date on which the application for the employment had to be made, and
(b)   would, if recruited for the employment, be a relevant worker within the meaning of paragraph 8.

(2) The age limit is whichever is the greater of –

(a)   the age of 65, and
(b)   the normal retirement age in the case of the employment concerned.

(3) The reference to the normal retirement age is to be construed in accordance with section 98ZH of the Employment Rights Act 1996.

10 Benefits based on length of service

(1) It is not an age contravention for a person (A) to put a person (B) at a disadvantage when compared with another (C), in relation to the provision of a benefit, facility or service in so far as the disadvantage is because B has a shorter period of service than C.

(2) If B's period of service exceeds 5 years, A may rely on sub-paragraph (1) only if A reasonably believes that doing so fulfils a business need.

(3) A person's period of service is whichever of the following A chooses –

(a)   the period for which the person has been working for A at or above a level (assessed by reference to the demands made on the person) that A reasonably regards as appropriate for the purposes of this paragraph, or
(b)   the period for which the person has been working for A at any level.

(4) The period for which a person has been working for A must be based on the number of weeks during the whole or part of which the person has worked for A.

(5) But for that purpose A may, so far as is reasonable, discount –

(a) periods of absence;
(b) periods that A reasonably regards as related to periods of absence.

(6) For the purposes of sub-paragraph (3)(b), a person is to be treated as having worked for A during any period in which the person worked for a person other than A if –

(a) that period counts as a period of employment with A as a result of section 218 of the Employment Rights Act 1996, or
(b) if sub-paragraph (a) does not apply, that period is treated as a period of employment by an enactment pursuant to which the person's employment was transferred to A.

(7) For the purposes of this paragraph, the reference to a benefit, facility or service does not include a reference to a benefit, facility or service which may be provided only by virtue of a person's ceasing to work.

11 The national minimum wage: young workers

(1) It is not an age contravention for a person to pay a young worker (A) at a lower rate than that at which the person pays an older worker (B) if –

(a) the hourly rate for the national minimum wage for a person of A's age is lower than that for a person of B's age, and
(b) the rate at which A is paid is below the single hourly rate.

(2) A young worker is a person who qualifies for the national minimum wage at a lower rate than the single hourly rate; and an older worker is a person who qualifies for the national minimum wage at a higher rate than that at which the young worker qualifies for it.

(3) The single hourly rate is the rate prescribed under section 1(3) of the National Minimum Wage Act 1998.

12 The national minimum wage: apprentices

(1) It is not an age contravention for a person to pay an apprentice who does not qualify for the national minimum wage at a lower rate than the person pays an apprentice who does.

(2) An apprentice is a person who –

(a) is employed under a contract of apprenticeship, or
(b) as a result of provision made by virtue of section 3(2)(a) of the National Minimum Wage Act 1998 (persons not qualifying), is treated as employed under a contract of apprenticeship.

13 Redundancy

(1) It is not an age contravention for a person to give a qualifying employee an enhanced redundancy payment of an amount less than that of an enhanced redundancy payment which the person gives to another qualifying employee, if each amount is calculated on the same basis.

(2) It is not an age contravention to give enhanced redundancy payments only to those who are qualifying employees by virtue of sub-paragraph (3)(a) or (b).

(3) A person is a qualifying employee if the person –

(a) is entitled to a redundancy payment as a result of section 135 of the Employment Rights Act 1996,

(b) agrees to the termination of the employment in circumstances where the person would, if dismissed, have been so entitled,

(c) would have been so entitled but for section 155 of that Act (requirement for two years' continuous employment), or

(d) agrees to the termination of the employment in circumstances where the person would, if dismissed, have been so entitled but for that section.

(4) An enhanced redundancy payment is a payment the amount of which is, subject to sub-paragraphs (5) and (6), calculated in accordance with section 162(1) to (3) of the Employment Rights Act 1996.

(5) A person making a calculation for the purposes of sub-paragraph (4) –

(a) may treat a week's pay as not being subject to a maximum amount;

(b) may treat a week's pay as being subject to a maximum amount above that for the time being specified in section 227(1) of the Employment Rights Act 1996;

(c) may multiply the appropriate amount for each year of employment by a figure of more than one.

(6) Having made a calculation for the purposes of sub-paragraph (4) (whether or not in reliance on sub-paragraph (5)), a person may multiply the amount calculated by a figure of more than one.

(7) In sub-paragraph (5), "the appropriate amount" has the meaning given in section 162 of the Employment Rights Act 1996, and "a week's pay" is to be read with Chapter 2 of Part 14 of that Act.

(8) For the purposes of sub-paragraphs (4) to (6), the reference to "the relevant date" in subsection (1)(a) of section 162 of that Act is, in the case of a person who is a qualifying employee by virtue of sub-paragraph (3)(b) or (d), to be read as reference to the date of the termination of the employment.

14 Life assurance

(1) This paragraph applies if a person (A) takes early retirement because of ill health.

(2) It is not an age contravention to provide A with life assurance cover for the period starting when A retires and ending –

(a) if there is a normal retirement age, when A attains the normal retirement age;

(b) in any other case, when A attains the age of 65.

(3) The normal retirement age in relation to A is the age at which, when A retires, persons holding comparable positions in the same undertaking are normally required to retire.

15 Child care

(1) A person does not contravene a relevant provision, so far as relating to age, only by providing, or making arrangements for or facilitating the provision of, care for children of a particular age group.

(2) The relevant provisions are –

(a)	section 39(2)(b);
(b)	section 41(1)(c);
(c)	section 44(2)(b);
(d)	section 45(2)(b);
(e)	section 47(2)(b);
(f)	section 48(2)(b);
(g)	section 49(6)(b);
(h)	section 50(6)(b);
(i)	section 57(2)(a);
(j)	section 58(3)(a).

(3) Facilitating the provision of care for a child includes –

(a) paying for some or all of the cost of the provision;

(b) helping a parent of the child to find a suitable person to provide care for the child;

(c) enabling a parent of the child to spend more time providing care for the child or otherwise assisting the parent with respect to the care that the parent provides for the child.

(4) A child is a person who has not attained the age of 17.

(5) A reference to care includes a reference to supervision.

16 Contributions to personal pension schemes

(1) A Minister of the Crown may by order provide that it is not an age contravention for an employer to maintain or use, with respect to contributions to personal pension schemes, practices, actions or decisions relating to age which are of a specified description.

(2) An order authorising the use of practices, actions or decisions which are not in use before the order comes into force must not be made unless the Minister consults such persons as the Minister thinks appropriate.

(3) "Personal pension scheme" has the meaning given in section 1 of the Pension Schemes Act 1993; and "employer", in relation to a personal pension scheme, has the meaning given in section 318(1) of the Pensions Act 2004.

PART 3
OTHER EXCEPTIONS

17 Non-contractual payments to women on maternity leave

(1) A person does not contravene section 39(1)(b) or (2), so far as relating to pregnancy and maternity, by depriving a woman who is on maternity leave of any benefit from the terms of her employment relating to pay.

(2) The reference in sub-paragraph (1) to benefit from the terms of a woman's employment relating to pay does not include a reference to –

(a) maternity-related pay (including maternity-related pay that is increase-related),

(b) pay (including increase-related pay) in respect of times when she is not on maternity leave, or

(c)   pay by way of bonus in respect of times when she is on compulsory maternity leave.

(3) For the purposes of sub-paragraph (2), pay is increase-related in so far as it is to be calculated by reference to increases in pay that the woman would have received had she not been on maternity leave.

(4) A reference to terms of her employment is a reference to terms of her employment that are not in her contract of employment, her contract of apprenticeship or her contract to do work personally.

(5) "Pay" means benefits –

(a)   that consist of the payment of money to an employee by way of wages or salary, and
(b)   that are not benefits whose provision is regulated by the contract referred to in sub-paragraph (4).

(6) "Maternity-related pay" means pay to which a woman is entitled –

(a)   as a result of being pregnant, or
(b)   in respect of times when she is on maternity leave.

18 Benefits dependent on marital status, etc.

(1) A person does not contravene this Part of this Act, so far as relating to sexual orientation, by doing anything which prevents or restricts a person who is not married from having access to a benefit, facility or service –

(a)   the right to which accrued before 5 December 2005 (the day on which section 1 of the Civil Partnership Act 2004 came into force), or
(b)   which is payable in respect of periods of service before that date.

(2) A person does not contravene this Part of this Act, so far as relating to sexual orientation, by providing married persons and civil partners (to the exclusion of all other persons) with access to a benefit, facility or service.

19 Provision of services etc. to the public

(1) A does not contravene a provision mentioned in sub-paragraph (2) in relation to the provision of a benefit, facility or service to B if A is concerned with the provision (for payment or not) of a benefit, facility or service of the same description to the public.

(2) The provisions are –

(a)   section 39(2) and (4);
(b)   section 41(1) and (3);
(c)   sections 44(2) and (6) and 45(2) and (6);
(d)   sections 49(6) and (8) and 50(6), (7), (9) and (10).

(3) Sub-paragraph (1) does not apply if –

(a)   the provision by A to the public differs in a material respect from the provision by A to comparable persons,
(b)   the provision to B is regulated by B's terms, or
(c)   the benefit, facility or service relates to training.

(4) "Comparable persons" means –

(a)   in relation to section 39(2) or (4), the other employees;

(b)   in relation to section 41(1) or (3), the other contract workers supplied to the principal;

(c)   in relation to section 44(2) or (6), the other partners of the firm;

(d)   in relation to section 45(2) or (6), the other members of the LLP;

(e)   in relation to section 49(6) or (8) or 50(6), (7), (9) or (10), persons holding offices or posts not materially different from that held by B.

(5) "B's terms" means –

(a)   the terms of B's employment,

(b)   the terms on which the principal allows B to do the contract work,

(c)   the terms on which B has the position as a partner or member, or

(d)   the terms of B's appointment to the office.

(6) A reference to the public includes a reference to a section of the public which includes B.

20 Insurance contracts, etc.

(1) It is not a contravention of this Part of this Act, so far as relating to relevant discrimination, to do anything in relation to an annuity, life insurance policy, accident insurance policy or similar matter involving the assessment of risk if –

(a)   that thing is done by reference to actuarial or other data from a source on which it is reasonable to rely, and

(b)   it is reasonable to do it.

(2) "Relevant discrimination" is –

(a)   gender reassignment discrimination;

(b)   marriage and civil partnership discrimination;

(c)   pregnancy and maternity discrimination;

(d)   sex discrimination.

Schedule 10

Section 88

Accessibility for disabled pupils

1 Accessibility strategies

(1) A local authority in England and Wales must, in relation to schools for which it is the responsible body, prepare –

(a)   an accessibility strategy;

(b)   further such strategies at such times as may be prescribed.

(2) An accessibility strategy is a strategy for, over a prescribed period –

(a)   increasing the extent to which disabled pupils can participate in the schools' curriculums;

(b)   improving the physical environment of the schools for the purpose of increasing the extent to which disabled pupils are able to take advantage of education and benefits, facilities or services provided or offered by the schools;

(c)   improving the delivery to disabled pupils of information which is readily accessible to pupils who are not disabled.

(3) The delivery in sub-paragraph (2)(c) must be –

    (a)   within a reasonable time;

    (b)   in ways which are determined after taking account of the pupils' disabilities and any preferences expressed by them or their parents.

(4) An accessibility strategy must be in writing.

(5) A local authority must keep its accessibility strategy under review during the period to which it relates and, if necessary, revise it.

(6) A local authority must implement its accessibility strategy.

2

(1) In preparing its accessibility strategy, a local authority must have regard to –

    (a)   the need to allocate adequate resources for implementing the strategy;

    (b)   guidance as to the matters mentioned in sub-paragraph (3).

(2) The authority must also have regard to guidance as to compliance with paragraph 1(5).

(3) The matters are –

    (a)   the content of an accessibility strategy;

    (b)   the form in which it is to be produced;

    (c)   persons to be consulted in its preparation.

(4) Guidance maybe issued –

    (a)   for England, by a Minister of the Crown;

    (b)   for Wales, by the Welsh Ministers.

(5) A local authority must, if asked, make a copy of its accessibility strategy available for inspection at such reasonable times as it decides.

(6) A local authority in England must, if asked by a Minister of the Crown, give the Minister a copy of its accessibility strategy.

(7) A local authority in Wales must, if asked by the Welsh Ministers, give them a copy of its accessibility strategy.

3 Accessibility plans

(1) The responsible body of a school in England and Wales must prepare –

    (a)   an accessibility plan;

    (b)   further such plans at such times as may be prescribed.

(2) An accessibility plan is a plan for, over a prescribed period –

    (a)   increasing the extent to which disabled pupils can participate in the school's curriculum,

    (b)   improving the physical environment of the school for the purpose of increasing the extent to which disabled pupils are able to take advantage of education and benefits, facilities or services provided or offered by the school, and

    (c)   improving the delivery to disabled pupils of information which is readily accessible to pupils who are not disabled.

(3) The delivery in sub-paragraph (2)(c) must be –

    (a)   within a reasonable time;

    (b)   in ways which are determined after taking account of the pupils' disabilities and any preferences expressed by them or their parents.

(4) An accessibility plan must be in writing.

(5) The responsible body must keep its accessibility plan under review during the period to which it relates and, if necessary, revise it.

(6) The responsible body must implement its accessibility plan.

(7) A relevant inspection may extend to the performance by the responsible body of its functions in relation to the preparation, publication, review, revision and implementation of its accessibility plan.

(8) A relevant inspection is an inspection under –

    (a)   Part 1 of the Education Act 2005, or

    (b)   Chapter 1 of Part 4 of the Education and Skills Act 2008 (regulation and inspection of independent education provision in England).

4

(1) In preparing an accessibility plan, the responsible body must have regard to the need to allocate adequate resources for implementing the plan.

(2) The proprietor of an independent educational institution (other than an Academy) must, if asked, make a copy of the school's accessibility plan available for inspection at such reasonable times as the proprietor decides.

(3) The proprietor of an independent educational institution in England (other than an Academy) must, if asked by a Minister of the Crown, give the Minister a copy of the school's accessibility plan.

(4) The proprietor of an independent school in Wales (other than an Academy) must, if asked by the Welsh Ministers, give them a copy of the school's accessibility plan.

5 Power of direction

(1) This sub-paragraph applies if the appropriate authority is satisfied (whether or not on a complaint) that a responsible body –

    (a)   has acted or is proposing to act unreasonably in the discharge of a duty under this Schedule, or

    (b)   has failed to discharge such a duty.

(2) This sub-paragraph applies if the appropriate authority is satisfied (whether or not on a complaint) that a responsible body of a school specified in sub-paragraph (3) –

    (a)   has acted or is proposing to act unreasonably in the discharge of a duty the body has in relation to the provision to the authority of copies of the body's accessibility plan or the inspection of that plan, or

    (b)   has failed to discharge the duty.

(3) The schools are –

    (a)   schools approved under section 342 of the Education Act 1996 (non-maintained special schools);

(b)   Academies.

(4) This sub-paragraph applies if a Tribunal has made an order under paragraph 5 of Schedule 17 and the appropriate authority is satisfied (whether or not on a complaint) that the responsible body concerned –

(a)   has acted or is proposing to act unreasonably in complying with the order, or
(b)   has failed to comply with the order.

(5) If sub-paragraph (1), (2) or (4) applies, the appropriate authority may give a responsible body such directions as the authority thinks expedient as to –

(a)   the discharge by the body of the duty, or
(b)   compliance by the body with the order.

(6) A direction may be given in relation to sub-paragraph (1) or (2) even if the performance of the duty is contingent on the opinion of the responsible body.

(7) A direction may not, unless sub-paragraph (8) applies, be given to the responsible body of a school in England in respect of a matter –

(a)   that has been complained about to a Local Commissioner in accordance with Chapter 2 of Part 10 of the Apprenticeships, Skills, Children and Learning Act 2009 (parental complaints against governing bodies etc.), or
(b)   that the appropriate authority thinks could have been so complained about.

(8) This sub-paragraph applies if –

(a)   the Local Commissioner has made a recommendation to the responsible body under section 211(4) of the Apprenticeships, Skills, Children and Learning Act 2009 (statement following investigation) in respect of the matter, and
(b)   the responsible body has not complied with the recommendation.

(9) A direction –

(a)   may be varied or revoked by the appropriate authority;
(b)   may be enforced, on the application of the appropriate authority, by a mandatory order obtained in accordance with section 31 of the Senior Courts Act 1981.

(10) The appropriate authority is –

(a)   in relation to the responsible body of a school in England, the Secretary of State;
(b)   in relation to the responsible body of a school in Wales, the Welsh Ministers.

6 Supplementary

(1) This paragraph applies for the purposes of this Schedule.

(2) Regulations may prescribe services which are, or are not, to be regarded as being –

(a)   education;
(b)   a benefit, facility or service.

(3) The power to make regulations is exercisable by –

(a)   in relation to England, a Minister of the Crown;
(b)   in relation to Wales, the Welsh Ministers.

(4) "Disabled pupil" includes a disabled person who may be admitted to the school as a pupil.

(5) "Responsible body" means –

(a)   in relation to a maintained school or a maintained nursery school, the local authority or governing body;

(b)   in relation to a pupil referral unit, the local authority;

(c)   in relation to an independent educational institution, the proprietor;

(d)   in relation to a special school not maintained by a local authority, the proprietor.

(6) "Governing body", in relation to a maintained school, means the body corporate (constituted in accordance with regulations under section 19 of the Education Act 2002) which the school has as a result of that section.

(7) "Maintained school" has the meaning given in section 20 of the School Standards and Framework Act 1998; and "maintained nursery school" has the meaning given in section 22 of that Act.

Schedule 11

Section 89

Schools: exceptions

PART 1
SEX DISCRIMINATION

1 Admission to single-sex schools

(1) Section 85(1), so far as relating to sex, does not apply in relation to a single-sex school.

(2) A single-sex school is a school which –

(a)   admits pupils of one sex only, or

(b)   on the basis of the assumption in sub-paragraph (3), would be taken to admit pupils of one sex only.

(3) That assumption is that pupils of the opposite sex are to be disregarded if –

(a)   their admission to the school is exceptional, or

(b)   their numbers are comparatively small and their admission is confined to particular courses or classes.

(4) In the case of a school which is a single-sex school by virtue of sub-paragraph (3)(b), section 85(2)(a) to (d), so far as relating to sex, does not prohibit confining pupils of the same sex to particular courses or classes.

2 Single-sex boarding at schools

(1) Section 85(1), so far as relating to sex, does not apply in relation to admission as a boarder to a school to which this paragraph applies.

(2) Section 85(2)(a) to (d), so far as relating to sex, does not apply in relation to boarding facilities at a school to which this paragraph applies.

(3) This paragraph applies to a school (other than a single-sex school) which has some pupils as boarders and others as non-boarders and which –

(a) admits as boarders pupils of one sex only, or

(b) on the basis of the assumption in sub-paragraph (4), would be taken to admit as boarders pupils of one sex only.

(4) That assumption is that pupils of the opposite sex admitted as boarders are to be disregarded if their numbers are small compared to the numbers of other pupils admitted as boarders.

3 Single-sex schools turning co-educational

(1) If the responsible body of a single-sex school decides to alter its admissions arrangements so that the school will cease to be a single-sex school, the body may apply for a transitional exemption order in relation to the school.

(2) If the responsible body of a school to which paragraph 2 applies decides to alter its admissions arrangements so that the school will cease to be one to which that paragraph applies, the body may apply for a transitional exemption order in relation to the school.

(3) A transitional exemption order in relation to a school is an order which, during the period specified in the order as the transitional period, authorises –

(a) sex discrimination by the responsible body of the school in the arrangements it makes for deciding who is offered admission as a pupil;

(b) the responsible body, in the circumstances specified in the order, not to admit a person as a pupil because of the person's sex.

(4) Paragraph 4 applies in relation to the making of transitional exemption orders.

(5) The responsible body of a school does not contravene this Act, so far as relating to sex discrimination, if –

(a) in accordance with a transitional exemption order, or

(b) pending the determination of an application for a transitional exemption order in relation to the school,

it does not admit a person as a pupil because of the person's sex.

4

(1) In the case of a maintained school within the meaning given by section 32 of the Education and Inspections Act 2006, a transitional exemption order may be made in accordance with such provision as is made in regulations under section 21 of that Act (orders made by local authority or adjudicator in relation to schools in England).

(2) In the case of a school in Wales maintained by a local authority, a transitional exemption order may be made in accordance with paragraph 22 of Schedule 6, or paragraph 17 of Schedule 7, to the School Standards and Framework Act 1998 (orders made by Welsh Ministers).

(3) In the case of a school in Scotland managed by an education authority or in respect of which the managers are for the time being receiving grants under section 73(c) or (d) of the Education (Scotland) Act 1980 –

(a) the responsible body may submit to the Scottish Ministers an application for the making of a transitional exemption order, and

(b) the Scottish Ministers may make the order.

(4) Where, under section 113A of the Learning and Skills Act 2000, the Learning and Skills Council for England make proposals to the Secretary of State for an alteration in the admissions arrangements of a single-sex school or a school to which paragraph 2 applies –

(a) the making of the proposals is to be treated as an application to the Secretary of State for the making of a transitional exemption order, and

(b) the Secretary of State may make the order.

(5) Where proposals are made to the Welsh Ministers under section 113A of the Learning and Skills Act 2000 for an alteration in the admissions arrangements of a single-sex school or a school to which paragraph 2 applies –

(a) the making of the proposals is to be treated as an application to the Welsh Ministers for the making of a transitional exemption order, and

(b) the Welsh Ministers may make the order.

(6) In the case of a school in England or Wales not coming within sub-paragraph (1), (2), (4) or (5) or an independent school in Scotland –

(a) the responsible body may submit to the Commission an application for the making of a transitional exemption order, and

(b) the Commission may make the order.

(7) An application under sub-paragraph (6) must specify –

(a) the period proposed by the responsible body as the transitional period to be specified in the order,

(b) the stages within that period by which the body proposes to move to the position where section 85(1)(a) and (c), so far as relating to sex, is complied with, and

(c) any other matters relevant to the terms and operation of the order applied for.

(8) The Commission must not make an order on an application under sub-paragraph (6) unless satisfied that the terms of the application are reasonable, having regard to –

(a) the nature of the school's premises,

(b) the accommodation, equipment and facilities available, and

(c) the responsible body's financial resources.

PART 2
RELIGIOUS OR BELIEF-RELATED DISCRIMINATION

5 School with religious character etc.

Section 85(1) and (2)(a) to (d), so far as relating to religion or belief, does not apply in relation to –

(a) a school designated under section 69(3) of the School Standards and Framework Act 1998 (foundation or voluntary school with religious character);

(b) a school listed in the register of independent schools for England or for Wales, if the school's entry in the register records that the school has a religious ethos;

(c) a school transferred to an education authority under section 16 of the Education (Scotland) Act 1980 (transfer of certain schools to education authorities) which is conducted in the interest of a church or denominational body;

(d)   a school provided by an education authority under section 17(2) of that Act (denominational schools);

(e)   a grant-aided school (within the meaning of that Act) which is conducted in the interest of a church or denominational body;

(f)   a school registered in the register of independent schools for Scotland if the school admits only pupils who belong, or whose parents belong, to one or more particular denominations;

(g)   a school registered in that register if the school is conducted in the interest of a church or denominational body.

6 Curriculum, worship, etc.

Section 85(2)(a) to (d), so far as relating to religion or belief, does not apply in relation to anything done in connection with acts of worship or other religious observance organised by or on behalf of a school (whether or not forming part of the curriculum).

7 Power to amend

(1) A Minister of the Crown may by order amend this Part of this Schedule –

(a)   so as to add, vary or omit an exception to section 85;

(b)   so as to make provision about the construction or application of section 19(2)(d) in relation to section 85.

(2) The power under sub-paragraph (1) is exercisable only in relation to religious or belief-related discrimination.

(3) Before making an order under this paragraph the Minister must consult –

(a)   the Welsh Ministers,

(b)   the Scottish Ministers, and

(c)   such other persons as the Minister thinks appropriate.

PART 3
DISABILITY DISCRIMINATION

8 Permitted form of selection

(1) A person does not contravene section 85(1), so far as relating to disability, only by applying a permitted form of selection.

(2) In relation to England and Wales, a permitted form of selection is –

(a)   in the case of a maintained school which is not designated as a grammar school under section 104 of the School Standards and Framework Act 1998, a form of selection mentioned in section 99(2) or (4) of that Act;

(b)   in the case of a maintained school which is so designated, its selective admission arrangements (within the meaning of section 104 of that Act);

(c)   in the case of an independent educational institution, arrangements which provide for some or all of its pupils to be selected by reference to general or special ability or aptitude, with a view to admitting only pupils of high ability or aptitude.

(3) In relation to Scotland, a permitted form of selection is –

(a)   in the case of a school managed by an education authority, arrangements approved by the Scottish Ministers for the selection of pupils for admission;

(b)   in the case of an independent school, arrangements which provide for some or all of its pupils to be selected by reference to general or special ability or aptitude, with a view to admitting only pupils of high ability or aptitude.

(4) "Maintained school" has the meaning given in section 22 of the School Standards and Framework Act 1998.

Schedule 12

Section 94

Further and higher education exceptions

PART 1
SINGLE-SEX INSTITUTIONS, ETC.

1 Admission to single-sex institutions

(1) Section 91(1), so far as relating to sex, does not apply in relation to a single-sex institution.

(2) A single-sex institution is an institution to which section 91 applies, which –

(a)   admits students of one sex only, or
(b)   on the basis of the assumption in sub-paragraph (3), would be taken to admit students of one sex only.

(3) That assumption is that students of the opposite sex are to be disregarded if –

(a)   their admission to the institution is exceptional, or
(b)   their numbers are comparatively small and their admission is confined to particular courses or classes.

(4) In the case of an institution which is a single-sex institution by virtue of sub-paragraph (3)(b), section 91(2)(a) to (d), so far as relating to sex, does not prohibit confining students of the same sex to particular courses or classes.

2 Single-sex institutions turning co-educational

(1) If the responsible body of a single-sex institution decides to alter its admissions arrangements so that the institution will cease to be a single-sex institution, the body may apply for a transitional exemption order in relation to the institution.

(2) A transitional exemption order relating to an institution is an order which, during the period specified in the order as the transitional period, authorises –

(a)   sex discrimination by the responsible body of the institution in the arrangements it makes for deciding who is offered admission as a student;
(b)   the responsible body, in the circumstances specified in the order, not to admit a person as a student because of the person's sex.

(3) Paragraph 3 applies in relation to the making of a transitional exemption order.

(4) The responsible body of an institution does not contravene this Act, so far as relating to sex discrimination, if –

(a)   in accordance with a transitional exemption order, or

(b) pending the determination of an application for a transitional exemption order in relation to the institution,

it does not admit a person as a student because of the person's sex.

(5) The responsible body of an institution does not contravene this Act, so far as relating to sex discrimination, if –

(a) in accordance with a transitional exemption order, or
(b) pending the determination of an application for a transitional exemption order in relation to the institution,

it discriminates in the arrangements it makes for deciding who is offered admission as a student.

3

(1) In the case of a single-sex institution –

(a) its responsible body may submit to the Commission an application for the making of a transitional exemption order, and
(b) the Commission may make the order.

(2) An application under sub-paragraph (1) must specify –

(a) the period proposed by the responsible body as the transitional period to be specified in the order,
(b) the stages, within that period, by which the body proposes to move to the position where section 91(1)(a) and (c), so far as relating to sex, is complied with, and
(c) any other matters relevant to the terms and operation of the order applied for.

(3) The Commission must not make an order on an application under sub-paragraph (1) unless satisfied that the terms of the application are reasonable, having regard to –

(a) the nature of the institution's premises,
(b) the accommodation, equipment and facilities available, and
(c) the responsible body's financial resources.

PART 2
OTHER EXCEPTIONS

4 Occupational requirements

A person (P) does not contravene section 91(1) or (2) if P shows that P's treatment of another person relates only to training that would help fit that other person for work the offer of which the other person could be refused in reliance on Part 1 of Schedule 9.

5 Institutions with a religious ethos

(1) The responsible body of an institution which is designated for the purposes of this paragraph does not contravene section 91(1), so far as relating to religion or belief, if, in the admission of students to a course at the institution –

(a) it gives preference to persons of a particular religion or belief,
(b) it does so to preserve the institution's religious ethos, and
(c) the course is not a course of vocational training.

(2) A Minister of the Crown may by order designate an institution if satisfied that the institution has a religious ethos.

6 Benefits dependent on marital status, etc.

A person does not contravene section 91, so far as relating to sexual orientation, by providing married persons and civil partners (to the exclusion of all other persons) with access to a benefit, facility or service.

7 Child care

(1) A person does not contravene section 91(2)(b) or (d), so far as relating to age, only by providing, or making arrangements for or facilitating the provision of, care for children of a particular age group.

(2) Facilitating the provision of care for a child includes –

(a)   paying for some or all of the cost of the provision;
(b)   helping a parent of the child to find a suitable person to provide care for the child;
(c)   enabling a parent of the child to spend more time providing care for the child or otherwise assisting the parent with respect to the care that the parent provides for the child.

(3) A child is a person who has not attained the age of 17.

(4) A reference to care includes a reference to supervision.

Schedule 13

Section 98

Education: reasonable adjustments

1 Preliminary

This Schedule applies where a duty to make reasonable adjustments is imposed on A by this Part.

2 The duty for schools

(1) This paragraph applies where A is the responsible body of a school to which section 85 applies.

(2) A must comply with the first and third requirements.

(3) For the purposes of this paragraph –

(a)   the reference in section 20(3) to a provision, criterion or practice is a reference to a provision, criterion or practice applied by or on behalf of A;
(b)   the reference in section 20(3) or (5) to a disabled person is –
    (i)   in relation to a relevant matter within sub-paragraph (4)(a), a reference to disabled persons generally;
    (ii)   in relation to a relevant matter within sub-paragraph (4)(b), a reference to disabled pupils generally.

(4) In relation to each requirement, the relevant matters are –

    (a)   deciding who is offered admission as a pupil;

    (b)   provision of education or access to a benefit, facility or service.

3 The duty for further or higher education institutions

(1) This paragraph applies where A is the responsible body of an institution to which section 91 applies.

(2) A must comply with the first, second and third requirements.

(3) For the purposes of this paragraph –

    (a)   the reference in section 20(3) to a provision, criterion or practice is a reference to a provision, criterion or practice applied by or on behalf of A;

    (b)   the reference in section 20(4) to a physical feature is a reference to a physical feature of premises occupied by A;

    (c)   the reference in section 20(3), (4) or (5) to a disabled person is –

        (i)   in relation to a relevant matter within sub-paragraph (4)(a), a reference to disabled persons generally;

        (ii)   in relation to a relevant matter within sub-paragraph (4)(b) or (c), a reference to disabled students generally;

        (iii)   in relation to a relevant matter within sub-paragraph (4)(d) or (e) below, a reference to an interested disabled person.

(4) In relation to each requirement, the relevant matters are –

    (a)   deciding who is offered admission as a student;

    (b)   provision of education;

    (c)   access to a benefit, facility or service;

    (d)   deciding on whom a qualification is conferred;

    (e)   a qualification that A confers.

4

(1) An interested disabled person is a disabled person who, in relation to a relevant matter specified in the first column of the table, is of a description specified in the second column.

Case	*Description of disabled person*
Deciding upon whom to confer a qualification.	A person who is, or has notified A that the person may be, an applicant for the conferment of the qualification.
A qualification that A confers.	An applicant for the conferment by A of the qualification.
	A person on whom A confers the qualification.

(2) A provision, criterion or practice does not include the application of a competence standard.

(3) A competence standard is an academic, medical or other standard applied for the purpose of determining whether or not a person has a particular level of competence or ability.

5 The duty relating to certain other further or higher education courses

(1) This paragraph applies where A is the responsible body in relation to a course to which section 92 applies.

(2) A must comply with the first, second and third requirements; but if A is the governing body of a maintained school (within the meaning given by that section), A is not required to comply with the second requirement.

(3) For the purposes of this paragraph –

(a)   the reference in section 20(3) to a provision, criterion or practice is a reference to a provision, criterion or practice applied by or on behalf of A;

(b)   the reference in section 20(4) to a physical feature is a reference to a physical feature of premises occupied by A;

(c)   the reference in section 20(3), (4) or (5) to a disabled person is –

(i)   in relation to a relevant matter within sub-paragraph (4)(a), a reference to disabled persons generally;

(ii)   in relation to a relevant matter within sub-paragraph (4)(b), a reference to disabled persons generally who are enrolled on the course.

(4) In relation to each requirement, the relevant matters are –

(a)   arrangements for enrolling persons on a course of further or higher education secured by A;

(b)   services provided by A for persons enrolled on the course.

6 The duty relating to recreational or training facilities

(1) This paragraph applies where A is the responsible body in relation to facilities to which section 93 applies.

(2) A must comply with the first, second and third requirements.

(3) For the purposes of this paragraph –

(a)   the reference in section 20(3) to a provision, criterion or practice is a reference to a provision, criterion or practice applied by or on behalf of A;

(b)   the reference in section 20(4) to a physical feature is a reference to a physical feature of premises occupied by A;

(c)   the reference in section 20(3), (4) or (5) to a disabled person is a reference to disabled persons generally.

(4) In relation to each requirement, the relevant matter is A's arrangements for providing the recreational or training facilities.

7 Code of practice

In deciding whether it is reasonable for A to have to take a step for the purpose of complying with the first, second or third requirement, A must have regard to relevant provisions of a code of practice issued under section 14 of the Equality Act 2006.

8 Confidentiality requests

(1) This paragraph applies if a person has made a confidentiality request of which A is aware.

(2) In deciding whether it is reasonable for A to have to take a step in relation to that person so as to comply with the first, second or third requirement, A must have regard to the extent to which taking the step is consistent with the request.

(3) In a case within paragraph 2, a "confidentiality request" is a request –

   (a)   that the nature or existence of a disabled person's disability be treated as confidential, and
   (b)   which satisfies either of the following conditions.

(4) The first condition is that the request is made by the person's parent.

(5) The second condition is that –

   (a)   it is made by the person, and
   (b)   A reasonably believes that the person has sufficient understanding of the nature and effect of the request.

(6) In a case within paragraph 3, a "confidentiality request" is a request by a disabled person that the nature or existence of the person's disability be treated as confidential.

9 The duty for general qualifications bodies

(1) This paragraph applies where A is a qualifications body for the purposes of section 96.

(2) Paragraphs 3 and 4(1), so far as relating to qualifications, apply to a qualifications body as they apply to a responsible body.

(3) This paragraph is subject to section 96(7).

Schedule 14

Section 99

Educational charities and endowments

1 Educational charities

(1) This paragraph applies to a trust deed or other instrument –

   (a)   which concerns property applicable for or in connection with the provision of education in an establishment in England and Wales to which section 85 or 91 applies, and
   (b)   which in any way restricts the benefits available under the instrument to persons of one sex.

(2) Sub-paragraph (3) applies if, on the application of the trustees or the responsible body (within the meaning of that section), a Minister of the Crown is satisfied that the removal or modification of the restriction would be conducive to the advancement of education without sex discrimination.

(3) The Minister may by order make such modifications of the instrument as appear to the Minister expedient for removing or modifying the restriction.

(4) If the trust was created by a gift or bequest, an order must not be made until the end of the period of 25 years after the date when the gift or bequest took effect.

(5) Sub-paragraph (4) does not apply if the donor or the personal representatives of the donor or testator consent in writing to making the application for the order.

(6) The Minister must require the applicant to publish a notice –

(a)   containing particulars of the proposed order;
(b)   stating that representations may be made to the Minister within a period specified in the notice.

(7) The period must be not less than one month beginning with the day after the date of the notice.

(8) The applicant must publish the notice in the manner specified by the Minister.

(9) The cost of publication may be paid out of the property of the trust.

(10) Before making the order, the Minister must take account of representations made in accordance with the notice.

2 Educational endowments

(1) This paragraph applies to an educational endowment –

(a)   to which section 104 of the Education (Scotland) Act 1980 applies, and
(b)   which in any way restricts the benefit of the endowment to persons of one sex.

(2) Sub-paragraph (3) applies if, on the application of the governing body of an educational endowment, the Scottish Ministers are satisfied that the removal or modification of the provision which restricts the benefit of the endowment to persons of one sex would be conducive to the advancement of education without sex discrimination.

(3) The Scottish Ministers may by order make such provision as they think expedient for removing or modifying the restriction.

(4) If the Scottish Ministers propose to make such an order they must publish a notice in such manner as they think sufficient for giving information to persons they think may be interested in the endowment –

(a)   containing particulars of the proposed order;
(b)   stating that representations may be made with respect to the proposal within such period as is specified in the notice.

(5) The period must be not less than one month beginning with the day after the date of publication of the notice.

(6) The cost of publication is to be paid out of the funds of the endowment to which the notice relates.

(7) Before making an order, the Scottish Ministers –

(a)   must consider representations made in accordance with the notice;
(b)   may cause a local inquiry to be held into the representations under section 67 of the Education (Scotland) Act 1980.

(8) A reference to an educational endowment includes a reference to –

(a)   a scheme made or approved for the endowment under Part 6 of the Education (Scotland) Act 1980;

(b)   in the case of an endowment the governing body of which is entered in the Scottish Charity Register, a scheme approved for the endowment under section 39 or 40 of the Charities and Trustee Investment (Scotland) Act 2005 (asp 10);

(c)   an endowment which is, by virtue of section 108(1) of the Education (Scotland) Act 1980, treated as if it were an educational endowment (or which would, but for the disapplication of that section by section 122(4) of that Act, be so treated);

(d)   a university endowment, the Carnegie Trust, a theological endowment and a new endowment.

(9) Expressions used in this paragraph and in Part 6 of the Education (Scotland) Act 1980 have the same meaning in this paragraph as in that Part.

Schedule 15

Section 107

Associations: reasonable adjustments

1 Preliminary

This Schedule applies where a duty to make reasonable adjustments is imposed on an association (A) by this Part.

2 The duty

(1) A must comply with the first, second and third requirements.

(2) For the purposes of this paragraph, the reference in section 20(3), (4) or (5) to a disabled person is a reference to disabled persons who –

(a)   are, or are seeking to become or might wish to become, members,

(b)   are associates, or

(c)   are, or are likely to become, guests.

(3) Section 20 has effect as if, in subsection (4), for "to avoid the disadvantage" there were substituted –

"(a)   to avoid the disadvantage, or

(b)   to adopt a reasonable alternative method of affording access to the benefit, facility or service or of admitting persons to membership or inviting persons as guests."

(4) In relation to the first and third requirements, the relevant matters are –

(a)   access to a benefit, facility or service;

(b)   members' or associates' retaining their rights as such or avoiding having them varied;

(c)   being admitted to membership or invited as a guest.

(5) In relation to the second requirement, the relevant matters are –

(a)   access to a benefit, facility or service;

(b)   being admitted to membership or invited as a guest.

(6) In relation to the second requirement, a physical feature includes a physical feature brought by or on behalf of A, in the course of or for the purpose of providing a benefit,

facility or service, on to premises other than those that A occupies (as well as including a physical feature in or on premises that A occupies).

(7) Nothing in this paragraph requires A to take a step which would fundamentally alter –

(a)   the nature of the benefit, facility or service concerned, or
(b)   the nature of the association.

(8) Nor does anything in this paragraph require a member or associate in whose house meetings of the association take place to make adjustments to a physical feature of the house.

Schedule 16

Section 107

Associations: exceptions

1 Single characteristic associations

(1) An association does not contravene section 101(1) by restricting membership to persons who share a protected characteristic.

(2) An association that restricts membership to persons who share a protected characteristic does not breach section 101(3) by restricting the access by associates to a benefit, facility or service to such persons as share the characteristic.

(3) An association that restricts membership to persons who share a protected characteristic does not breach section 102(1) by inviting as guests, or by permitting to be invited as guests, only such persons as share the characteristic.

(4) Sub-paragraphs (1) to (3), so far as relating to race, do not apply in relation to colour.

(5) This paragraph does not apply to an association that is a registered political party.

2 Health and safety

(1) An association (A) does not discriminate against a pregnant woman in contravention of section 101(1)(b) because she is pregnant if –

(a)   the terms on which A is prepared to admit her to membership include a term intended to remove or reduce a risk to her health or safety,
(b)   A reasonably believes that admitting her to membership on terms which do not include that term would create a risk to her health or safety,
(c)   the terms on which A is prepared to admit persons with other physical conditions to membership include a term intended to remove or reduce a risk to their health or safety, and
(d)   A reasonably believes that admitting them to membership on terms which do not include that term would create a risk to their health or safety.

(2) Sub-paragraph (1) applies to section 102(1)(b) as it applies to section 101(1)(b); and for that purpose a reference to admitting a person to membership is to be read as a reference to inviting the person as a guest or permitting the person to be invited as a guest.

(3) An association (A) does not discriminate against a pregnant woman in contravention of section 101(2)(a) or (3)(a) or 102(2)(a) because she is pregnant if –

(a)   the way in which A affords her access to a benefit, facility or service is intended to remove or reduce a risk to her health or safety,

(b)   A reasonably believes that affording her access to the benefit, facility or service otherwise than in that way would create a risk to her health or safety,

(c)   A affords persons with other physical conditions access to the benefit, facility or service in a way that is intended to remove or reduce a risk to their health or safety, and

(d)   A reasonably believes that affording them access to the benefit, facility or service otherwise than in that way would create a risk to their health or safety.

(4) An association (A) which does not afford a pregnant woman access to a benefit, facility or service does not discriminate against her in contravention of section 101(2)(a) or (3)(a) or 102(2)(a) because she is pregnant if –

(a)   A reasonably believes that affording her access to the benefit, facility or service would, because she is pregnant, create a risk to her health or safety,

(b)   A does not afford persons with other physical conditions access to the benefit, facility or service, and

(c)   the reason for not doing so is that A reasonably believes that affording them access to the benefit, facility or service would create a risk to their health or safety.

(5) An association (A) does not discriminate against a pregnant woman under section 101(2)(c) or (3)(c) because she is pregnant if –

(a)   the variation of A's terms of membership, or rights as an associate, is intended to remove or reduce a risk to her health or safety,

(b)   A reasonably believes that not making the variation to A's terms or rights would create a risk to her health or safety,

(c)   A varies the terms of membership, or rights as an associate, of persons with other physical conditions,

(d)   the variation of their terms or rights is intended to remove or reduce a risk to their health or safety, and

(e)   A reasonably believes that not making the variation to their terms or rights would create a risk to their health or safety.

Schedule 17

Section 116

Disabled pupils: enforcement

PART 1
INTRODUCTORY

1

In this Schedule –

"the Tribunal" means –
(a)   in relation to a school in England, the First-tier Tribunal;
(b)   in relation to a school in Wales, the Special Educational Needs Tribunal for Wales;

  (c) in relation to a school in Scotland, an Additional Support Needs Tribunal for Scotland;

"the English Tribunal" means the First-tier Tribunal;
"the Welsh Tribunal" means the Special Educational Needs Tribunal for Wales;
"the Scottish Tribunal" means an Additional Support Needs Tribunal for Scotland;
"responsible body" is to be construed in accordance with section 85.

PART 2
TRIBUNALS IN ENGLAND AND WALES

2 Introductory

This Part of this Schedule applies in relation to the English Tribunal and the Welsh Tribunal.

3 Jurisdiction

A claim that a responsible body has contravened Chapter 1 of Part 6 because of a person's disability may be made to the Tribunal by the person's parent.

4 Time for bringing proceedings

(1) Proceedings on a claim may not be brought after the end of the period of 6 months starting with the date when the conduct complained of occurred.

(2) If, in relation to proceedings or prospective proceedings under section 27 of the Equality Act 2006, the dispute is referred for conciliation in pursuance of arrangements under that section before the end of that period, the period is extended by 3 months.

(3) The Tribunal may consider a claim which is out of time.

(4) Sub-paragraph (3) does not apply if the Tribunal has previously decided under that sub-paragraph not to consider a claim.

(5) For the purposes of sub-paragraph (1) –

  (a) if the contravention is attributable to a term in a contract, the conduct is to be treated as extending throughout the duration of the contract;
  (b) conduct extending over a period is to be treated as occurring at the end of the period;
  (c) failure to do something is to be treated as occurring when the person in question decided on it.

(6) In the absence of evidence to the contrary, a person (P) is to be taken to decide on failure to do something –

  (a) when P acts inconsistently with doing it, or
  (b) if P does not act inconsistently, on the expiry of the period in which P might reasonably have been expected to do it.

5 Powers

(1) This paragraph applies if the Tribunal finds that the contravention has occurred.

(2) The Tribunal may make such order as it thinks fit.

(3) The power under sub-paragraph (2) –

(a) may, in particular, be exercised with a view to obviating or reducing the adverse effect on the person of any matter to which the claim relates;

(b) does not include power to order the payment of compensation.

6 Procedure

(1) This paragraph applies in relation to the Welsh Tribunal.

(2) The Welsh Ministers may by regulations make provision as to –

(a) the proceedings on a claim under paragraph 3;

(b) the making of a claim.

(3) The regulations may, in particular, include provision –

(a) as to the manner in which a claim must be made;

(b) for enabling functions relating to preliminary or incidental matters (including in particular a decision under paragraph 4(3) to be performed by the President or by the person occupying the chair);

(c) enabling hearings to be conducted in the absence of a member other than the person occupying the chair;

(d) as to persons who may appear on behalf of the parties;

(e) for granting such rights to disclosure or inspection of documents or to further particulars as may be granted by the county court;

(f) requiring persons to attend to give evidence and produce documents;

(g) for authorising the administration of oaths to witnesses;

(h) for deciding claims without a hearing in prescribed circumstances;

(i) as to the withdrawal of claims;

(j) for enabling the Tribunal to stay proceedings;

(k) for the award of costs or expenses;

(l) for settling costs or expenses (and, in particular, for enabling costs to be assessed in the county court);

(m) for the registration and proof of decisions and orders;

(n) for enabling prescribed decisions to be reviewed, or prescribed orders to be varied or revoked, in such circumstances as may be decided in accordance with the regulations.

(4) Proceedings must be held in private, except in prescribed circumstances.

(5) The Welsh Ministers may pay such allowances for the purpose of or in connection with the attendance of persons at the Tribunal as they may decide.

(6) Part 1 of the Arbitration Act 1996 does not apply to the proceedings, but regulations may make provision in relation to such proceedings that corresponds to a provision of that Part.

(7) The regulations may make provision for a claim to be heard, in prescribed circumstances, with an appeal under Part 4 of the Education Act 1996 (special educational needs).

(8) A person commits an offence by failing to comply with –

(a) a requirement in respect of the disclosure or inspection of documents imposed by virtue of sub-paragraph (3)(e), or

(b) a requirement imposed by virtue of sub-paragraph (3)(f).

(9) A person guilty of the offence is liable on summary conviction to a fine not exceeding level 3 on the standard scale.

PART 3
TRIBUNALS IN SCOTLAND

7 Introductory

This Part of this Schedule applies in relation to the Scottish Tribunal.

8 Jurisdiction

A claim that a responsible body has contravened Chapter 1 of Part 6 because of a person's disability may be made to the Tribunal by –

(a)   the person's parent;
(b)   where the person has capacity to make the claim, the person.

9 Powers

(1) This paragraph applies if the Tribunal finds the contravention has occurred.

(2) The Tribunal may make such order as it thinks fit.

(3) The power under sub-paragraph (2) –

(a)   may, in particular, be exercised with a view to obviating or reducing the adverse effect on the person of any matter to which the claim relates;
(b)   does not include power to order the payment of compensation.

10 Procedure etc.

(1) The Scottish Ministers may make rules as to –

(a)   the proceedings on a claim under paragraph 8;
(b)   the making of a claim.

(2) The rules may, in particular, include provision for or in connection with –

(a)   the form and manner in which a claim must be made;
(b)   the time within which a claim is to be made;
(c)   the withdrawal of claims;
(d)   the recovery and inspection of documents;
(e)   the persons who may appear on behalf of the parties;
(f)   the persons who may be present at proceedings alongside any party or witness to support the party or witness;
(g)   enabling specified persons other than the parties to appear or be represented in specified circumstances;
(h)   requiring specified persons to give notice to other specified persons of specified matters;
(i)   the time within which any such notice must be given;
(j)   enabling Tribunal proceedings to be conducted in the absence of any member of a Tribunal other than the convener;
(k)   enabling any matters that are preliminary or incidental to the determination of proceedings to be determined by the convenor of a Tribunal alone or with such other members of the Tribunal as may be specified;
(l)   enabling Tribunals to be held in private;
(m)   enabling a Tribunal to exclude any person from attending all or part of Tribunal proceedings;

(n) enabling a Tribunal to impose reporting restrictions in relation to all or part of Tribunal proceedings;

(o) enabling a Tribunal to determine specified matters without holding a hearing;

(p) the recording and publication of decisions and orders of a Tribunal;

(q) enabling a Tribunal to commission medical and other reports in specified circumstances;

(r) requiring a Tribunal to take specified actions, or to determine specified proceedings, within specified periods;

(s) enabling a Tribunal to make an award of expenses;

(t) the taxation or assessment of such expenses;

(u) enabling a Tribunal, in specified circumstances, to review, or to vary or revoke, any of its decisions, orders or awards;

(v) enabling a Tribunal, in specified circumstances, to review the decisions, orders or awards of another Tribunal and take such action (including variation and revocation) in respect of those decisions, orders or awards as it thinks fit.

11 Appeals

(1) Either of the persons specified in sub-paragraph (2) may appeal on a point of law to the Court of Session against a decision of a Tribunal relating to a claim under this Schedule.

(2) Those persons are –

(a) the person who made the claim;

(b) the responsible body.

(3) Where the Court of Session allows an appeal under sub-paragraph (1) it may –

(a) remit the reference back to the Tribunal or to a differently constituted Tribunal to be considered again and give the Tribunal such directions about the consideration of the case as the Court thinks fit;

(b) make such ancillary orders as it considers necessary or appropriate.

12 Amendment of Education (Additional Support for Learning) (Scotland) Act 2004

The Education (Additional Support for Learning) (Scotland) Act 2004 (asp 4) is amended as follows –

(a) in section 17(1), omit "to exercise the functions which are conferred on a Tribunal by virtue of this Act";

(b) after section 17(1), insert –

"(1A) Tribunals are to exercise the functions which are conferred on them by virtue of –
    (a)   this Act, and
    (b)   the Equality Act 2010";

(c) in the definition of "Tribunal functions" in paragraph 1 of Schedule 1, after "Act" insert "or the Equality Act 2010".

PART 4
ADMISSIONS AND EXCLUSIONS

13 Admissions

(1) This paragraph applies if appeal arrangements have been made in relation to admissions decisions.

(2) A claim that a responsible body has, because of a person's disability, contravened Chapter 1 of Part 6 in respect of an admissions decision must be made under the appeal arrangements.

(3) The body hearing the claim has the powers it has in relation to an appeal under the appeal arrangements.

(4) Appeal arrangements are arrangements under –

(a)   section 94 of the School Standards and Framework Act 1998, or
(b)   an agreement between the responsible body for an Academy and the Secretary of State under section 482 of the Education Act 1996, enabling an appeal to be made by the person's parent against the decision.

(5) An admissions decision is –

(a)   a decision of a kind mentioned in section 94(1) or (2) of the School Standards and Framework Act 1998;
(b)   a decision as to the admission of a person to an Academy taken by the responsible body or on its behalf.

14 Exclusions

(1) This paragraph applies if appeal arrangements have been made in relation to exclusion decisions.

(2) A claim that a responsible body has, because of a person's disability, contravened Chapter 1 of Part 6 in respect of an exclusion decision must be made under the appeal arrangements.

(3) The body hearing the claim has the powers it has in relation to an appeal under the appeal arrangements.

(4) Appeal arrangements are arrangements under –

(a)   section 52(3) of the Education Act 2002, or
(b)   an agreement between the responsible body for an Academy and the Secretary of State under section 482 of the Education Act 1996,

enabling an appeal to be made by the person's parent against the decision.

(5) An exclusion decision is –

(a)   a decision of a kind mentioned in 52(3) of the Education Act 2002;
(b)   a decision taken by the responsible body or on its behalf not to reinstate a pupil who has been permanently excluded from an Academy by its head teacher.

(6) "Responsible body", in relation to a maintained school, includes the discipline committee of the governing body if that committee is required to be established as a result of regulations made under section 19 of the Education Act 2002.

(7) "Maintained school" has the meaning given in section 20(7) of the School Standards and Framework Act 1998.

Schedule 18

Public sector equality duty: exceptions

1 Children

(1) Section 149, so far as relating to age, does not apply to the exercise of a function relating to –

   (a)   the provision of education to pupils in schools;

   (b)   the provision of benefits, facilities or services to pupils in schools;

   (c)   the provision of accommodation, benefits, facilities or services in community homes pursuant to section 53(1) of the Children Act 1989;

   (d)   the provision of accommodation, benefits, facilities or services pursuant to arrangements under section 82(5) of that Act (arrangements by the Secretary of State relating to the accommodation of children);

   (e)   the provision of accommodation, benefits, facilities or services in residential establishments pursuant to section 26(1)(b) of the Children (Scotland) Act 1995.

(2) "Pupil" and "school" each have the same meaning as in Chapter 1 of Part 6.

2 Immigration

(1) In relation to the exercise of immigration and nationality functions, section 149 has effect as if subsection (1)(b) did not apply to the protected characteristics of age, race or religion or belief; but for that purpose "race" means race so far as relating to –

   (a)   nationality, or

   (b)   ethnic or national origins.

(2) "Immigration and nationality functions" means functions exercisable by virtue of –

   (a)   the Immigration Acts (excluding sections 28A to 28K of the Immigration Act 1971 so far as they relate to criminal offences),

   (b)   the British Nationality Act 1981,

   (c)   the British Nationality (Falkland Islands) Act 1983,

   (d)   the British Nationality (Hong Kong) Act 1990,

   (e)   the Hong Kong (War Wives and Widows) Act 1996,

   (f)   the British Nationality (Hong Kong) Act 1997,

   (g)   the Special Immigration Appeals Commission Act 1997, or

   (h)   a provision made under section 2(2) of the European Communities Act 1972, or of Community law, which relates to the subject matter of an enactment within paragraphs (a) to (g).

3 Judicial functions, etc.

(1) Section 149 does not apply to the exercise of –

   (a)   a judicial function;

   (b)   a function exercised on behalf of, or on the instructions of, a person exercising a judicial function.

(2) The references to a judicial function include a reference to a judicial function conferred on a person other than a court or tribunal.

4 Exceptions that are specific to section 149(2)

(1) Section 149(2) (application of section 149(1) to persons who are not public authorities but by whom public functions are exercisable) does not apply to –

(a)   a person listed in sub-paragraph (2);

(b)   the exercise of a function listed in sub-paragraph (3).

(2) Those persons are –

(a)   the House of Commons;

(b)   the House of Lords;

(c)   the Scottish Parliament;

(d)   the National Assembly for Wales;

(e)   the General Synod of the Church of England;

(f)   the Security Service;

(g)   the Secret Intelligence Service;

(h)   the Government Communications Headquarters;

(i)   a part of the armed forces which is, in accordance with a requirement of the Secretary of State, assisting the Government Communications Headquarters.

(3) Those functions are –

(a)   a function in connection with proceedings in the House of Commons or the House of Lords;

(b)   a function in connection with proceedings in the Scottish Parliament (other than a function of the Scottish Parliamentary Corporate Body);

(c)   a function in connection with proceedings in the National Assembly for Wales (other than a function of the Assembly Commission).

5 Power to amend Schedule

(1) A Minister of the Crown may by order amend this Schedule so as to add, vary or omit an exception to section 149.

(2) But provision by virtue of sub-paragraph (1) may not amend this Schedule –

(a)   so as to omit an exception in paragraph 3;

(b)   so as to omit an exception in paragraph 4(1) so far as applying for the purposes of paragraph 4(2)(a) to (e) or (3);

(c)   so as to reduce the extent to which an exception referred to in paragraph (a) or (b) applies.

Schedule 19

Section 150

Public authorities

PART 1
PUBLIC AUTHORITIES: GENERAL

Ministers of the Crown and government departments

A Minister of the Crown.

A government department other than the Security Service, the Secret Intelligence Service or the Government Communications Headquarters.

Armed forces

Any of the armed forces other than any part of the armed forces which is, in accordance with a requirement of the Secretary of State, assisting the Government Communications Headquarters.

National Health Service

A Strategic Health Authority established under section 13 of the National Health Service Act 2006, or continued in existence by virtue of that section.

A Primary Care Trust established under section 18 of that Act, or continued in existence by virtue of that section.

An NHS trust established under section 25 of that Act.

A Special Health Authority established under section 28 of that Act other than NHS Blood and Transplant and the NHS Business Services Authority.

An NHS foundation trust within the meaning given by section 30 of that Act.

Local government

A county council, district council or parish council in England.

A parish meeting constituted under section 13 of the Local Government Act 1972.

Charter trustees constituted under section 246 of that Act for an area in England.

The Greater London Authority.

A London borough council.

The Common Council of the City of London in its capacity as a local authority or port health authority.

The Sub-Treasurer of the Inner Temple or the Under-Treasurer of the Middle Temple, in that person's capacity as a local authority.

The London Development Agency.

The London Fire and Emergency Planning Authority.

Transport for London.

The Council of the Isles of Scilly.

The Broads Authority established by section 1 of the Norfolk and Suffolk Broads Act 1988.

A regional development agency established by the Regional Development Agencies Act 1998 (other than the London Development Agency).

A fire and rescue authority constituted by a scheme under section 2 of the Fire and Rescue Services Act 2004, or a scheme to which section 4 of that Act applies, for an area in England.

An internal drainage board which is continued in being by virtue of section 1 of the Land Drainage Act 1991 for an area in England.

A National Park authority established by an order under section 63 of the Environment Act 1995 for an area in England.

A Passenger Transport Executive for an integrated transport area in England (within the meaning of Part 2 of the Transport Act 1968).

A port health authority constituted by an order under section 2 of the Public Health (Control of Disease) Act 1984 for an area in England.

A waste disposal authority established by virtue of an order under section 10(1) of the Local Government Act 1985.

A joint authority established under Part 4 of that Act for an area in England (including, by virtue of section 77(9) of the Local Transport Act 2008, an Integrated Transport Authority established under Part 5 of that Act of 2008).

A body corporate established pursuant to an order under section 67 of the Local Government Act 1985.

A joint committee constituted in accordance with section 102(1)(b) of the Local Government Act 1972 for an area in England.

A joint board which is continued in being by virtue of section 263(1) of that Act for an area in England.

Other educational bodies

The governing body of an educational establishment maintained by an English local authority (within the meaning of section 162 of the Education and Inspections Act 2006).

The governing body of an institution in England within the further education sector (within the meaning of section 91(3) of the Further and Higher Education Act 1992).

The governing body of an institution in England within the higher education sector (within the meaning of section 91(5) of that Act).

Police

A police authority established under section 3 of the Police Act 1996.

The Metropolitan Police Authority established under section 5B of that Act.

The Common Council of the City of London in its capacity as a police authority.

PART 2
PUBLIC AUTHORITIES: RELEVANT WELSH AUTHORITIES

Welsh Assembly Government, etc.

The Welsh Ministers.

The First Minister for Wales.

The Counsel General to the Welsh Assembly Government.

A subsidiary of the Welsh Ministers (within the meaning given by section 134(4) of the Government of Wales Act 2006).

National Health Service

A Local Health Board established under section 11 of the National Health Service (Wales) Act 2006.

An NHS trust established under section 18 of that Act.

A Special Health Authority established under section 22 of that Act other than NHS Blood and Transplant and the NHS Business Services Authority.

A Community Health Council in Wales.

Local government

A county council, county borough council or community council in Wales.

Charter trustees constituted under section 246 of the Local Government Act 1972 for an area in Wales.

A fire and rescue authority constituted by a scheme under section 2 of the Fire and Rescue Services Act 2004, or a scheme to which section 4 of that Act applies, for an area in Wales.

An internal drainage board which is continued in being by virtue of section 1 of the Land Drainage Act 1991 for an area in Wales.

A National Park authority established by an order under section 63 of the Environment Act 1995 for an area in Wales.

A port health authority constituted by an order under section 2 of the Public Health (Control of Disease) Act 1984 for an area in Wales.

A joint authority established under Part 4 of the Local Government Act 1985 for an area in Wales.

A joint committee constituted in accordance with section 102(1)(b) of the Local Government Act 1972 for an area in Wales.

A joint board which is continued in being by virtue of section 263(1) of that Act for an area in Wales.

Other educational bodies

The governing body of an educational establishment maintained by a Welsh local authority (within the meaning of section 162 of the Education and Inspections Act 2006).

The governing body of an institution in Wales within the further education sector (within the meaning of section 91(3) of the Further and Higher Education Act 1992).

The governing body of an institution in Wales within the higher education sector (within the meaning of section 91(5) of that Act).

PART 3
PUBLIC AUTHORITIES: RELEVANT SCOTTISH AUTHORITIES

Scottish Administration

An office-holder in the Scottish Administration (within the meaning given by section 126(7)(a) of the Scotland Act 1998).

National Health Service

A Health Board constituted under section 2 of the National Health Service (Scotland) Act 1978.

A Special Health Board constituted under that section.

Local government

A council constituted under section 2 of the Local Government etc. (Scotland) Act 1994.

A community council established under section 51 of the Local Government (Scotland) Act 1973.

A joint board within the meaning of section 235(1) of that Act.

A joint fire and rescue board constituted by a scheme under section 2(1) of the Fire (Scotland) Act 2005.

A licensing board established under section 5 of the Licensing (Scotland) Act 2005, or continued in being by virtue of that section.

A National Park authority established by a designation order made under section 6 of the National Parks (Scotland) Act 2000.

Scottish Enterprise and Highlands and Islands Enterprise, established under the Enterprise and New Towns (Scotland) Act 1990.

Other educational bodies

An education authority in Scotland (within the meaning of section 135(1) of the Education (Scotland) Act 1980).

The managers of a grant-aided school (within the meaning of that section).

The board of management of a college of further education (within the meaning of section 36(1) of the Further and Higher Education (Scotland) Act 1992).

In the case of such a college of further education not under the management of a board of management, the board of governors of the college or any person responsible for the management of the college, whether or not formally constituted as a governing body or board of governors.

The governing body of an institution within the higher education sector (within the meaning of Part 2 of the Further and Higher Education (Scotland) Act 1992).

Police

A police authority established under section 2 of the Police (Scotland) Act 1967.

Schedule 20

Section 186

Rail vehicle accessibility: compliance

1 Rail vehicle accessibility compliance certificates

(1) A regulated rail vehicle which is prescribed, or is of a prescribed class or description, must not be used for carriage unless a compliance certificate is in force for the vehicle.

(2) A "compliance certificate" is a certificate that the Secretary of State is satisfied that the regulated rail vehicle conforms with the provisions of rail vehicle accessibility regulations with which it is required to conform.

(3) A compliance certificate is subject to such conditions as are specified in it.

(4) A compliance certificate may not be issued for a rail vehicle unless the Secretary of State has been provided with a report of a compliance assessment of the vehicle.

(5) A "compliance assessment" is an assessment of a rail vehicle against provisions of rail vehicle accessibility regulations with which the vehicle is required to conform.

(6) If a regulated rail vehicle is used for carriage in contravention of sub-paragraph (1), the Secretary of State may require the operator of the vehicle to pay a penalty.

(7) The Secretary of State must review a decision not to issue a compliance certificate if before the end of the prescribed period the applicant –

(a)   asks the Secretary of State to review the decision, and
(b)   pays any fee fixed under paragraph 4.

(8) For the purposes of the review, the Secretary of State must consider any representations made by the applicant in writing before the end of the prescribed period.

2 Regulations as to compliance certificates

(1) Regulations may make provision as to compliance certificates.

(2) The regulations may (in particular) include provision –

(a)   as to applications for and issue of certificates;
(b)   specifying conditions to which certificates are subject;
(c)   as to the period for which a certificate is in force;

(d)   as to circumstances in which a certificate ceases to be in force;
(e)   dealing with failure to comply with a specified condition;
(f)   for the examination of rail vehicles in respect of which applications have been made;
(g)   with respect to the issue of copies of certificates in place of those which have been lost or destroyed.

3 Regulations as to compliance assessments

(1) Regulations may make provision as to compliance assessments.

(2) The regulations –

(a)   may make provision as to the person who has to have carried out the assessment;
(b)   may (in particular) require that the assessment be one carried out by a person who has been appointed by the Secretary of State to carry out compliance assessments (an "appointed assessor").

(3) For the purposes of any provisions in the regulations made by virtue of sub-paragraph (2)(b), the regulations –

(a)   may make provision about appointments of appointed assessors, including (in particular) –
  (i)   provision for an appointment to be on application or otherwise than on application;
  (ii)   provision as to who may be appointed;
  (iii) provision as to the form of applications for appointment;
  (iv)   provision as to information to be supplied with applications for appointment;
  (v)   provision as to terms and conditions, or the period or termination, of an appointment;
  (vi)   provision for terms and conditions of an appointment, including any as to its period or termination, to be as agreed by the Secretary of State when making the appointment;
(b)   may make provision authorising an appointed assessor to charge fees in connection with, or incidental to, the carrying out of a compliance assessment, including (in particular) –
  (i)   provision restricting the amount of a fee;
  (ii)   provision authorising fees that contain a profit element;
  (iii) provision for advance payment of fees;
(c)   may make provision requiring an appointed assessor to carry out a compliance assessment, and to do so in accordance with any procedures that may be prescribed, if prescribed conditions (which may include conditions as to the payment of fees to the assessor) are satisfied;
(d)   must make provision for the referral to the Secretary of State of disputes between –
  (i)   an appointed assessor carrying out a compliance assessment, and
  (ii)   the person who requested the assessment,
  relating to which provisions of rail vehicle accessibility regulations the vehicle is to be assessed against or to what amounts to conformity with any of those provisions.

(4) For the purposes of sub-paragraph (3)(b) to (d) a compliance assessment includes pre-assessment activities (for example, a consideration of how the outcome of a compliance assessment would be affected by the carrying out of particular proposed work).

4 Fees in respect of compliance certificates

(1) The Secretary of State may charge such fees, payable at such times, as are prescribed in respect of –

(a)   applications for, and the issue of, compliance certificates;
(b)   copies of compliance certificates;
(c)   reviews under paragraph 1(7);
(d)   referrals of disputes under provision made by virtue of paragraph 3(3)(d).

(2) Fees received by the Secretary of State must be paid into the Consolidated Fund.

(3) Regulations under this paragraph may make provision for the repayment of fees, in whole or in part, in such circumstances as are prescribed.

(4) Before making regulations under this paragraph the Secretary of State must consult such representative organisations as the Secretary of State thinks fit.

5 Penalty for using rail vehicle that does not conform with accessibility regulations

(1) If the Secretary of State thinks that a regulated rail vehicle does not conform with a provision of rail vehicle accessibility regulations with which it is required to conform, the Secretary of State may give the operator of the vehicle a notice –

(a)   identifying the vehicle, the provision and how the vehicle fails to conform;
(b)   specifying the improvement deadline.

(2) The improvement deadline may not be earlier than the end of the prescribed period beginning with the day the notice is given.

(3) Sub-paragraph (4) applies if –

(a)   the Secretary of State has given a notice under sub-paragraph (1),
(b)   the improvement deadline specified in the notice has passed, and
(c)   the Secretary of State thinks that the vehicle still does not conform with the provision identified in the notice.

(4) The Secretary of State may give the operator a further notice –

(a)   identifying the vehicle, the provision and how the vehicle fails to conform;
(b)   specifying the final deadline.

(5) The final deadline may not be earlier than the end of the prescribed period beginning with the day the further notice is given.

(6) The Secretary of State may require the operator to pay a penalty if –

(a)   the Secretary of State has given notice under sub-paragraph (4), and
(b)   the vehicle is used for carriage at a time after the final deadline when the vehicle does not conform with the provision identified in the notice.

6 Penalty for using rail vehicle otherwise than in conformity with accessibility regulations

(1) If the Secretary of State thinks that a regulated rail vehicle has been used for carriage otherwise than in conformity with a provision of rail vehicle accessibility regulations with which the use of the vehicle is required to conform, the Secretary of State may give the operator of the vehicle a notice –

    (a)   identifying the provision and how it was breached;
    (b)   identifying each vehicle operated by the operator that is covered by the notice;
    (c)   specifying the improvement deadline.

(2) The improvement deadline may not be earlier than the end of the prescribed period beginning with the day the notice is given.

(3) Sub-paragraph (4) applies if –

    (a)   the Secretary of State has given a notice under sub-paragraph (1),
    (b)   the improvement deadline specified in the notice has passed, and
    (c)   the Secretary of State thinks that a vehicle covered by the notice has after that deadline been used for carriage otherwise than in conformity with the provision identified in the notice.

(4) The Secretary of State may give the operator a further notice –

    (a)   identifying the provision and how it was breached;
    (b)   identifying each vehicle operated by the operator that is covered by the further notice;
    (c)   specifying the final deadline.

(5) The final deadline may not be earlier than the end of the prescribed period beginning with the day the further notice is given.

(6) The Secretary of State may require the operator to pay a penalty if –

    (a)   the Secretary of State has given notice under sub-paragraph (4), and
    (b)   a vehicle covered by the notice is at a time after the final deadline used for carriage otherwise than in conformity with the provision identified in the notice.

7 Inspection of rail vehicles

(1) If the condition in sub-paragraph (2) is satisfied, a person authorised by the Secretary of State (an "inspector") may inspect a regulated rail vehicle for conformity with provisions of the accessibility regulations with which it is required to conform.

(2) The condition is that the Secretary of State –

    (a)   has reasonable grounds for suspecting that the vehicle does not conform with such provisions, or
    (b)   has given a notice under paragraph 5(1) or (4) relating to the vehicle.

(3) For the purpose of exercising the power under sub-paragraph (1) an inspector may –

    (a)   enter premises if the inspector has reasonable grounds for suspecting that the vehicle is at the premises;
    (b)   enter the vehicle;

(c)   require any person to afford such facilities and assistance with respect to matters under the person's control as are necessary to enable the inspector to exercise the power.

(4) An inspector must, if required to do so, produce evidence of the Secretary of State's authorisation.

(5) For the purposes of paragraph 5(1) the Secretary of State may draw such inferences as appear proper from any obstruction of the exercise of the power under sub-paragraph (1).

(6) Sub-paragraphs (7) and (8) apply if the power under sub-paragraph (1) is exercisable by virtue of sub-paragraph (2)(b).

(7) The Secretary of State may treat paragraph 5(3)(c) as satisfied in relation to a vehicle if –

(a)   the inspector takes steps to exercise the power after a notice is given under paragraph 5(1) but before a notice is given under paragraph 5(4), and

(b)   a person obstructs the exercise of the power.

(8) The Secretary of State may require the operator of a vehicle to pay a penalty if –

(a)   the operator, or a person acting on the operator's behalf, intentionally obstructs the exercise of the power, and

(b)   the obstruction occurs after a notice has been given under paragraph 5(4) in respect of the vehicle.

(9) In this paragraph "inspect" includes test.

8 Supplementary powers

(1) For the purposes of paragraph 5 the Secretary of State may give notice to a person requiring the person to supply the Secretary of State by a time specified in the notice with a vehicle number or other identifier for a rail vehicle –

(a)   of which the person is the operator, and

(b)   which is specified in the notice.

(2) The time specified may not be earlier than the end of the period of 14 days beginning with the day the notice is given.

(3) If the person does not comply with the notice, the Secretary of State may require the person to pay a penalty.

(4) If the Secretary of State has given a notice to a person under paragraph 5(1) or 6(1), the Secretary of State may request the person to supply the Secretary of State, by a time specified in the request, with a statement detailing the steps taken in response to the notice.

(5) The time specified may not be earlier than the improvement deadline.

(6) The Secretary of State may treat paragraph 5(3)(c) or (as the case may be) paragraph 6(3)(c) as being satisfied in relation to a vehicle if a request under sub-paragraph (4) is not complied with by the time specified.

9 Penalties: amount, due date and recovery

(1) In this paragraph and paragraphs 10 to 12 "penalty" means a penalty under this Schedule.

(2) The amount of a penalty must not exceed whichever is the lesser of –

    (a)   the maximum prescribed for the purposes of this sub-paragraph;

    (b)   10% of the turnover of the person on whom it is imposed.

(3) Turnover is to be determined by such means as are prescribed.

(4) A penalty must be paid to the Secretary of State before the end of the prescribed period.

(5) A sum payable as a penalty may be recovered as a debt due to the Secretary of State.

(6) In proceedings for recovery of a penalty no question may be raised as to –

    (a)   liability to the penalty;

    (b)   its amount.

(7) Sums paid to the Secretary of State as a penalty must be paid into the Consolidated Fund.

10 Penalties: code of practice

(1) The Secretary of State must issue a code of practice specifying matters to be considered in determining the amount of a penalty.

(2) The Secretary of State may –

    (a)   revise the whole or part of the code;

    (b)   issue the code as revised.

(3) Before issuing the code the Secretary of State must lay a draft of it before Parliament.

(4) After laying the draft before Parliament, the Secretary of State may bring the code into operation by order.

(5) The Secretary of State must have regard to the code and any other relevant matter –

    (a)   when imposing a penalty;

    (b)   when considering an objection under paragraph 11.

(6) In sub-paragraphs (3) to (5) a reference to the code includes a reference to the code as revised.

11 Penalties: procedure

(1) If the Secretary of State decides that a person is liable to a penalty the Secretary of State must notify the person.

(2) The notification must –

    (a)   state the Secretary of State's reasons for the decision;

    (b)   state the amount of the penalty;

    (c)   specify the date by which and manner in which the penalty must be paid;

    (d)   explain how the person may object to the penalty.

(3) The person may give the Secretary of State notice of objection to the penalty on the ground that –

    (a)   the person is not liable to the penalty, or

    (b)   the amount of the penalty is too high.

(4) A notice of objection must –

    (a)   be in writing;

    (b)   give the reasons for the objection;

    (c)   be given before the end of the period prescribed for the purposes of this sub-paragraph.

(5) On considering a notice of objection the Secretary of State may –

    (a)   cancel the penalty;

    (b)   reduce the amount of the penalty;

    (c)   do neither of those things.

(6) The Secretary of State must inform the objector of the decision under sub-paragraph (5) before the end of the period prescribed for the purposes of this sub-paragraph (or such longer period as is agreed with the objector).

12 Penalties: appeals

(1) A person may appeal to the court against a penalty on the ground that –

    (a)   the person is not liable to the penalty;

    (b)   the amount of the penalty is too high.

(2) The court may –

    (a)   allow the appeal and cancel the penalty;

    (b)   allow the appeal and reduce the amount of the penalty;

    (c)   dismiss the appeal.

(3) An appeal under this section is a re-hearing of the Secretary of State's decision and is to be determined having regard to –

    (a)   any code of practice under paragraph 10 which has effect at the time of the appeal;

    (b)   any other matter which the court thinks is relevant (whether or not the Secretary of State was aware of it).

(4) An appeal may be brought under this section whether or not –

    (a)   the person has given notice of objection under paragraph 11(3);

    (b)   the penalty has been reduced under paragraph 11(5).

(5) In this section "the court" is –

    (a)   in England and Wales, a county court;

    (b)   in Scotland, the sheriff.

(6) The sheriff may transfer the proceedings to the Court of Session.

(7) If the sheriff makes a determination under sub-paragraph (2), a party to the proceedings may appeal against the determination on a point of law to –

    (a)   the Sheriff Principal, or

    (b)   the Court of Session.

13 Forgery, etc.

(1) Section 188 has effect –

    (a)   as if a compliance certificate were a "relevant document";

(b)   as if subsection (4) included a reference to a compliance certificate.

(2) A person commits an offence by pretending, with intent to deceive, to be a person authorised to exercise a power under paragraph 7.

(3) A person guilty of an offence under sub-paragraph (2) is liable on summary conviction to a fine not exceeding level 4 on the standard scale.

14 Regulations

A power to make regulations under this Schedule is exercisable by the Secretary of State.

15 Interpretation

(1) In this Schedule –

"compliance assessment" has the meaning given in paragraph 1(5);
"compliance certificate" has the meaning given in paragraph 1(2);
"operator", in relation to a rail vehicle, means the person having the management of the vehicle.

(2) If an exemption order under section 183 authorises the use of a rail vehicle even though the vehicle does not conform with a provision of rail vehicle accessibility regulations, a reference in this Schedule to provisions of rail vehicle accessibility regulations with which the vehicle is required to conform does not, in relation to the vehicle, include a reference to that provision.

Schedule 21

Section 189

Reasonable adjustments: supplementary

1 Preliminary

This Schedule applies for the purposes of Schedules 2, 4, 8, 13 and 15.

2 Binding obligations, etc.

(1) This paragraph applies if –

(a)   a binding obligation requires A to obtain the consent of another person to an alteration of premises which A occupies,

(b)   where A is a controller of let premises, a binding obligation requires A to obtain the consent of another person to a variation of a term of the tenancy, or

(c)   where A is a responsible person in relation to common parts, a binding obligation requires A to obtain the consent of another person to an alteration of the common parts.

(2) For the purpose of discharging a duty to make reasonable adjustments –

(a)   it is always reasonable for A to have to take steps to obtain the consent, but

(b)   it is never reasonable for A to have to make the alteration before the consent is obtained.

(3) In this Schedule, a binding obligation is a legally binding obligation in relation to premises, however arising; but the reference to a binding obligation in sub-paragraph (1)(a) or (c) does not include a reference to an obligation imposed by a tenancy.

(4) The steps referred to in sub-paragraph (2)(a) do not include applying to a court or tribunal.

3 Landlord's consent

(1) This paragraph applies if –

    (a)   A occupies premises under a tenancy,

    (b)   A is proposing to make an alteration to the premises so as to comply with a duty to make reasonable adjustments, and

    (c)   but for this paragraph, A would not be entitled to make the alteration.

(2) This paragraph also applies if –

    (a)   A is a responsible person in relation to common parts,

    (b)   A is proposing to make an alteration to the common parts so as to comply with a duty to make reasonable adjustments,

    (c)   A is the tenant of property which includes the common parts, and

    (d)   but for this paragraph, A would not be entitled to make the alteration.

(3) The tenancy has effect as if it provided –

    (a)   for A to be entitled to make the alteration with the written consent of the landlord,

    (b)   for A to have to make a written application for that consent,

    (c)   for the landlord not to withhold the consent unreasonably, and

    (d)   for the landlord to be able to give the consent subject to reasonable conditions.

(4) If a question arises as to whether A has made the alteration (and, accordingly, complied with a duty to make reasonable adjustments), any constraint attributable to the tenancy must be ignored unless A has applied to the landlord in writing for consent to the alteration.

(5) For the purposes of sub-paragraph (1) or (2), A must be treated as not entitled to make the alteration if the tenancy –

    (a)   imposes conditions which are to apply if A makes an alteration, or

    (b)   entitles the landlord to attach conditions to a consent to the alteration.

4 Proceedings before county court or sheriff

(1) This paragraph applies if, in a case within Part 3, 4, 6 or 7 of this Act –

    (a)   A has applied in writing to the landlord for consent to the alteration, and

    (b)   the landlord has refused to give consent or has given consent subject to a condition.

(2) A (or a disabled person with an interest in the alteration being made) may refer the matter to a county court or, in Scotland, the sheriff.

(3) The county court or sheriff must determine whether the refusal or condition is unreasonable.

(4) If the county court or sheriff finds that the refusal or condition is unreasonable, the county court or sheriff –

(a)   may make such declaration as it thinks appropriate;

(b)   may make an order authorising A to make the alteration specified in the order (and requiring A to comply with such conditions as are so specified).

5 Joining landlord as party to proceedings

(1) This paragraph applies to proceedings relating to a contravention of this Act by virtue of section 20.

(2) A party to the proceedings may request the employment tribunal, county court or sheriff ("the judicial authority") to direct that the landlord is joined or sisted as a party to the proceedings.

(3) The judicial authority –

(a)   must grant the request if it is made before the hearing of the complaint or claim begins;

(b)   may refuse the request if it is made after the hearing begins;

(c)   must refuse the request if it is made after the complaint or claim has been determined.

(4) If the landlord is joined or sisted as a party to the proceedings, the judicial authority may determine whether –

(a)   the landlord has refused to consent to the alteration;

(b)   the landlord has consented subject to a condition;

(c)   the refusal or condition was unreasonable.

(5) If the judicial authority finds that the refusal or condition was unreasonable, it –

(a)   may make such declaration as it thinks appropriate;

(b)   may make an order authorising A to make the alteration specified in the order (and requiring A to comply with such conditions as are so specified);

(c)   may order the landlord to pay compensation to the complainant or claimant.

(6) An employment tribunal may act in reliance on sub-paragraph (5)(c) instead of, or in addition to, acting in reliance on section 124(2); but if it orders the landlord to pay compensation it must not do so in reliance on section 124(2).

(7) If a county court or the sheriff orders the landlord to pay compensation, it may not order A to do so.

6 Regulations

(1) Regulations may make provision as to circumstances in which a landlord is taken for the purposes of this Schedule to have –

(a)   withheld consent;

(b)   withheld consent reasonably;

(c)   withheld consent unreasonably.

(2) Regulations may make provision as to circumstances in which a condition subject to which a landlord gives consent is taken –

(a)   to be reasonable;

(b)   to be unreasonable.

(3) Regulations may make provision supplementing or modifying the preceding paragraphs of this Schedule, or provision made under this paragraph, in relation to a case where A's tenancy is a sub-tenancy.

(4) Provision made by virtue of this paragraph may amend the preceding paragraphs of this Schedule.

7 Interpretation

An expression used in this Schedule and in Schedule 2, 4, 8, 13 or 15 has the same meaning in this Schedule as in that Schedule.

Schedule 22

Section 191

Statutory provisions

1 Statutory authority

(1) A person (P) does not contravene a provision specified in the first column of the table, so far as relating to the protected characteristic specified in the second column in respect of that provision, if P does anything P must do pursuant to a requirement specified in the third column.

Specified provision	Protected characteristic	Requirement
Parts 3 to 7	Age	A requirement of an enactment
Parts 3 to 7 and 12	Disability	A requirement of an enactment
		A relevant requirement or condition imposed by virtue of an enactment
Parts 3 to 7	Religion or belief	A requirement of an enactment
		A relevant requirement or condition imposed by virtue of an enactment
Section 29(6) and Parts 6 and 7	Sex	A requirement of an enactment
Parts 3, 4, 6 and 7	Sexual orientation	A requirement of an enactment
		A relevant requirement or condition imposed by virtue of an enactment

(2) A reference in the table to Part 6 does not include a reference to that Part so far as relating to vocational training.

(3) In this paragraph a reference to an enactment includes a reference to –

    (a)   a Measure of the General Synod of the Church of England;

(b)   an enactment passed or made on or after the date on which this Act is passed.

(4) In the table, a relevant requirement or condition is a requirement or condition imposed (whether before or after the passing of this Act) by –

(a)   a Minister of the Crown;

(b)   a member of the Scottish Executive;

(c)   the National Assembly for Wales (constituted by the Government of Wales Act 1998);

(d)   the Welsh Ministers, the First Minister for Wales or the Counsel General to the Welsh Assembly Government.

2 Protection of women

(1) A person (P) does not contravene a specified provision only by doing in relation to a woman (W) anything P is required to do to comply with –

(a)   a pre-1975 Act enactment concerning the protection of women;

(b)   a relevant statutory provision (within the meaning of Part 1 of the Health and Safety at Work etc. Act 1974) if it is done for the purpose of the protection of W (or a description of women which includes W);

(c)   a requirement of a provision specified in Schedule 1 to the Employment Act 1989 (provisions concerned with protection of women at work).

(2) The references to the protection of women are references to protecting women in relation to –

(a)   pregnancy or maternity, or

(b)   any other circumstances giving rise to risks specifically affecting women.

(3) It does not matter whether the protection is restricted to women.

(4) These are the specified provisions –

(a)   Part 5 (work);

(b)   Part 6 (education), so far as relating to vocational training.

(5) A pre-1975 Act enactment is an enactment contained in –

(a)   an Act passed before the Sex Discrimination Act 1975;

(b)   an instrument approved or made by or under such an Act (including one approved or made after the passing of the 1975 Act).

(6) If an Act repeals and re-enacts (with or without modification) a pre-1975 enactment then the provision re-enacted must be treated as being in a pre-1975 enactment.

(7) For the purposes of sub-paragraph (1)(c), a reference to a provision in Schedule 1 to the Employment Act 1989 includes a reference to a provision for the time being having effect in place of it.

(8) This paragraph applies only to the following protected characteristics –

(a)   pregnancy and maternity;

(b)   sex.

3 Educational appointments, etc: religious belief

(1) A person does not contravene Part 5 (work) only by doing a relevant act in connection with the employment of another in a relevant position.

(2) A relevant position is –

    (a)   the head teacher or principal of an educational establishment;

    (b)   the head, a fellow or other member of the academic staff of a college, or institution in the nature of a college, in a university;

    (c)   a professorship of a university which is a canon professorship or one to which a canonry is annexed.

(3) A relevant act is anything it is necessary to do to comply with –

    (a)   a requirement of an instrument relating to the establishment that the head teacher or principal must be a member of a particular religious order;

    (b)   a requirement of an instrument relating to the college or institution that the holder of the position must be a woman;

    (c)   an Act or instrument in accordance with which the professorship is a canon professorship or one to which a canonry is annexed.

(4) Sub-paragraph (3)(b) does not apply to an instrument taking effect on or after 16 January 1990 (the day on which section 5(3) of the Employment Act 1989 came into force).

(5) A Minister of the Crown may by order provide that anything in sub-paragraphs (1) to (3) does not have effect in relation to –

    (a)   a specified educational establishment or university;

    (b)   a specified description of educational establishments.

(6) An educational establishment is –

    (a)   a school within the meaning of the Education Act 1996 or the Education (Scotland) Act 1980;

    (b)   a college, or institution in the nature of a college, in a university;

    (c)   an institution designated by order made, or having effect as if made, under section 129 of the Education Reform Act 1988;

    (d)   a college of further education within the meaning of section 36 of the Further and Higher Education (Scotland) Act 1992;

    (e)   a university in Scotland;

    (f)   an institution designated by order under section 28 of the Further and Higher Education Act 1992 or section 44 of the Further and Higher Education (Scotland) Act 1992.

(7) This paragraph does not affect paragraph 2 of Schedule 9.

4

A person does not contravene this Act only by doing anything which is permitted for the purposes of –

    (a)   section 58(6) or (7) of the School Standards and Framework Act 1998 (dismissal of teachers because of failure to give religious education efficiently);

    (b)   section 60(4) and (5) of that Act (religious considerations relating to certain appointments);

    (c)   section 124A of that Act (preference for certain teachers at independent schools of a religious character).

5 Crown employment, etc.

(1) A person does not contravene this Act –

(a) by making or continuing in force rules mentioned in sub-paragraph (2);
(b) by publishing, displaying or implementing such rules;
(c) by publishing the gist of such rules.

(2) The rules are rules restricting to persons of particular birth, nationality, descent or residence –

(a) employment in the service of the Crown;
(b) employment by a prescribed public body;
(c) holding a public office (within the meaning of section 50).

(3) The power to make regulations for the purpose of sub-paragraph (2)(b) is exercisable by the Minister for the Civil Service.

(4) In this paragraph "public body" means a body (whether corporate or unincorporated) exercising public functions (within the meaning given by section 31(4)).

Schedule 23

Section 196

General exceptions

1 Acts authorised by statute or the executive

(1) This paragraph applies to anything done –

(a) in pursuance of an enactment;
(b) in pursuance of an instrument made by a member of the executive under an enactment;
(c) to comply with a requirement imposed (whether before or after the passing of this Act) by a member of the executive by virtue of an enactment;
(d) in pursuance of arrangements made (whether before or after the passing of this Act) by or with the approval of, or for the time being approved by, a Minister of the Crown;
(e) to comply with a condition imposed (whether before or after the passing of this Act) by a Minister of the Crown.

(2) A person does not contravene Part 3, 4, 5 or 6 by doing anything to which this paragraph applies which discriminates against another because of the other's nationality.

(3) A person (A) does not contravene Part 3, 4, 5 or 6 if, by doing anything to which this paragraph applies, A discriminates against another (B) by applying to B a provision, criterion or practice which relates to –

(a) B's place of ordinary residence;
(b) the length of time B has been present or resident in or outside the United Kingdom or an area within it.

2 Organisations relating to religion or belief

(1) This paragraph applies to an organisation the purpose of which is –

(a) to practise a religion or belief,
(b) to advance a religion or belief,
(c) to teach the practice or principles of a religion or belief,

(d)   to enable persons of a religion or belief to receive any benefit, or to engage in any activity, within the framework of that religion or belief, or

(e)   to foster or maintain good relations between persons of different religions or beliefs.

(2) This paragraph does not apply to an organisation whose sole or main purpose is commercial.

(3) The organisation does not contravene Part 3, 4 or 7, so far as relating to religion or belief or sexual orientation, only by restricting –

(a)   membership of the organisation;

(b)   participation in activities undertaken by the organisation or on its behalf or under its auspices;

(c)   the provision of goods, facilities or services in the course of activities undertaken by the organisation or on its behalf or under its auspices;

(d)   the use or disposal of premises owned or controlled by the organisation.

(4) A person does not contravene Part 3, 4 or 7, so far as relating to religion or belief or sexual orientation, only by doing anything mentioned in sub-paragraph (3) on behalf of or under the auspices of the organisation.

(5) A minister does not contravene Part 3, 4 or 7, so far as relating to religion or belief or sexual orientation, only by restricting –

(a)   participation in activities carried on in the performance of the minister's functions in connection with or in respect of the organisation;

(b)   the provision of goods, facilities or services in the course of activities carried on in the performance of the minister's functions in connection with or in respect of the organisation.

(6) Sub-paragraphs (3) to (5) permit a restriction relating to religion or belief only if it is imposed –

(a)   because of the purpose of the organisation, or

(b)   to avoid causing offence, on grounds of the religion or belief to which the organisation relates, to persons of that religion or belief.

(7) Sub-paragraphs (3) to (5) permit a restriction relating to sexual orientation only if it is imposed –

(a)   because it is necessary to comply with the doctrine of the organisation, or

(b)   to avoid conflict with strongly held convictions within sub-paragraph (9).

(8) In sub-paragraph (5), the reference to a minister is a reference to a minister of religion, or other person, who –

(a)   performs functions in connection with a religion or belief to which the organisation relates, and

(b)   holds an office or appointment in, or is accredited, approved or recognised for the purposes of the organisation.

(9) The strongly held convictions are –

(a)   in the case of a religion, the strongly held religious convictions of a significant number of the religion's followers;

(b)   in the case of a belief, the strongly held convictions relating to the belief of a significant number of the belief's followers.

(10) This paragraph does not permit anything which is prohibited by section 29, so far as relating to sexual orientation, if it is done –

(a)   on behalf of a public authority, and

(b)   under the terms of a contract between the organisation and the public authority.

(11) In the application of this paragraph in relation to sexual orientation, sub-paragraph (1)(e) must be ignored.

(12) In the application of this paragraph in relation to sexual orientation, in sub-paragraph (3)(d), "disposal" does not include disposal of an interest in premises by way of sale if the interest being disposed of is –

(a)   the entirety of the organisation's interest in the premises, or

(b)   the entirety of the interest in respect of which the organisation has power of disposal.

(13) In this paragraph –

(a)   "disposal" is to be construed in accordance with section 38;

(b)   "public authority" has the meaning given in section 150(1).

3 Communal accommodation

(1) A person does not contravene this Act, so far as relating to sex discrimination or gender reassignment discrimination, only because of anything done in relation to –

(a)   the admission of persons to communal accommodation;

(b)   the provision of a benefit, facility or service linked to the accommodation.

(2) Sub-paragraph (1)(a) does not apply unless the accommodation is managed in a way which is as fair as possible to both men and women.

(3) In applying sub-paragraph (1)(a), account must be taken of –

(a)   whether and how far it is reasonable to expect that the accommodation should be altered or extended or that further accommodation should be provided, and

(b)   the frequency of the demand or need for use of the accommodation by persons of one sex as compared with those of the other.

(4) In applying sub-paragraph (1)(a) in relation to gender reassignment, account must also be taken of whether and how far the conduct in question is a proportionate means of achieving a legitimate aim.

(5) Communal accommodation is residential accommodation which includes dormitories or other shared sleeping accommodation which for reasons of privacy should be used only by persons of the same sex.

(6) Communal accommodation may include –

(a)   shared sleeping accommodation for men and for women;

(b)   ordinary sleeping accommodation;

(c)   residential accommodation all or part of which should be used only by persons of the same sex because of the nature of the sanitary facilities serving the accommodation.

(7) A benefit, facility or service is linked to communal accommodation if –

(a)   it cannot properly and effectively be provided except for those using the accommodation, and

(b)   a person could be refused use of the accommodation in reliance on sub-paragraph (1)(a).

(8) This paragraph does not apply for the purposes of Part 5 (work) unless such arrangements as are reasonably practicable are made to compensate for –

(a)   in a case where sub-paragraph (1)(a) applies, the refusal of use of the accommodation;

(b)   in a case where sub-paragraph (1)(b) applies, the refusal of provision of the benefit, facility or service.

4 Training provided to non-EEA residents, etc.

(1) A person (A) does not contravene this Act, so far as relating to nationality, only by providing a non-resident (B) with training, if A thinks that B does not intend to exercise in Great Britain skills B obtains as a result.

(2) A non-resident is a person who is not ordinarily resident in an EEA state.

(3) The reference to providing B with training is –

(a)   if A employs B in relevant employment, a reference to doing anything in or in connection with the employment;

(b)   if A as a principal allows B to do relevant contract work, a reference to doing anything in or in connection with allowing B to do the work;

(c)   in a case within paragraph (a) or (b) or any other case, a reference to affording B access to facilities for education or training or ancillary benefits.

(4) Employment or contract work is relevant if its sole or main purpose is the provision of training in skills.

(5) In the case of training provided by the armed forces or Secretary of State for purposes relating to defence, sub-paragraph (1) has effect as if –

(a)   the reference in sub-paragraph (2) to an EEA state were a reference to Great Britain, and

(b)   in sub-paragraph (4), for "its sole or main purpose is" there were substituted "it is for purposes including".

(6) "Contract work" and "principal" each have the meaning given in section 41.

Schedule 24

Section 203

Harmonisation: exceptions

Part 1 (public sector duty regarding socio-economic inequalities)

Chapter 2 of Part 5 (occupational pensions)

Section 78 (gender pay gap)

Section 106 (election candidates: diversity information)

Chapters 1 to 3 and 5 of Part 9 (enforcement), except section 136

Sections 142 and 146 (unenforceable terms, declaration in respect of void terms)

Chapter 1 of Part 11 (public sector equality duty)

Part 12 (disabled persons: transport)

Part 13 (disability: miscellaneous)

Section 197 (power to specify age exceptions)

Part 15 (family property)

Part 16 (general and miscellaneous)

Schedule 1 (disability: supplementary provision)

In Schedule 3 (services and public functions: exceptions) –

(a)   in Part 3 (health and care), paragraphs 13 and 14;
(b)   Part 4 (immigration);
(c)   Part 5 (insurance);
(d)   Part 6 (marriage);
(e)   Part 7 (separate and single services), except paragraph 30;
(f)   Part 8 (television, radio and on-line broadcasting and distribution);
(g)   Part 9 (transport);
(h)   Part 10 (supplementary)

Schedule 4 (premises: reasonable adjustments)

Schedule 5 (premises: exceptions), except paragraph 1

Schedule 6 (office-holders: excluded offices), except so far as relating to colour or nationality or marriage and civil partnership

Schedule 8 (work: reasonable adjustments)

In Schedule 9 (work: exceptions) –

(a)   Part 1 (general), except so far as relating to colour or nationality;
(b)   Part 2 (exceptions relating to age);
(c)   Part 3 (other exceptions), except paragraph 19 so far as relating to colour or nationality

Schedule 10 (education: accessibility for disabled pupils)

Schedule 13 (education: reasonable adjustments), except paragraphs 2, 5, 6 and 9

Schedule 17 (education: disabled pupils: enforcement)

Schedule 18 (public sector equality duty: exceptions)

Schedule 19 (list of public authorities)

Schedule 20 (rail vehicle accessibility: compliance)

Schedule 21 (reasonable adjustments: supplementary)

In Schedule 22 (exceptions: statutory provisions), paragraphs 2 and 5

Schedule 23 (general exceptions), except paragraph 2

Schedule 25 (information society services)

Schedule 25

Section 206

Information society services

1 Service providers

(1) This paragraph applies where a person concerned with the provision of an information society service (an "information society service provider") is established in Great Britain.

(2) This Act applies to anything done by the person in an EEA state (other than the United Kingdom) in providing the service as this Act would apply if the act in question were done by the person in Great Britain.

2

(1) This paragraph applies where an information society service provider is established in an EEA state (other than the United Kingdom).

(2) This Act does not apply to anything done by the person in providing the service.

3 Exceptions for mere conduits

(1) An information society service provider does not contravene this Act only by providing so much of an information society service as consists in –

    (a)   the provision of access to a communication network, or
    (b)   the transmission in a communication network of information provided by the recipient of the service.

(2) But sub-paragraph (1) applies only if the service provider does not –

    (a)   initiate the transmission,
    (b)   select the recipient of the transmission, or
    (c)   select or modify the information contained in the transmission.

(3) For the purposes of sub-paragraph (1), the provision of access to a communication network, and the transmission of information in a communication network, includes the automatic, intermediate and transient storage of the information transmitted so far as the storage is solely for the purpose of carrying out the transmission in the network.

(4) Sub-paragraph (3) does not apply if the information is stored for longer than is reasonably necessary for the transmission.

4 Exception for caching

(1) This paragraph applies where an information society service consists in the transmission in a communication network of information provided by a recipient of the service.

(2) The information society service provider does not contravene this Act only by doing anything in connection with the automatic, intermediate and temporary storage of information so provided if –

(a)   the storage of the information is solely for the purpose of making more efficient the onward transmission of the information to other recipients of the service at their request, and

(b)   the condition in sub-paragraph (3) is satisfied.

(3) The condition is that the service-provider –

(a)   does not modify the information,

(b)   complies with such conditions as are attached to having access to the information, and

(c)   (where sub-paragraph (4) applies) expeditiously removes the information or disables access to it.

(4) This sub-paragraph applies if the service-provider obtains actual knowledge that –

(a)   the information at the initial source of the transmission has been removed from the network,

(b)   access to it has been disabled, or

(c)   a court or administrative authority has required the removal from the network of, or the disablement of access to, the information.

5 Exception for hosting

(1) An information society service provider does not contravene this Act only by doing anything in providing so much of an information society service as consists in the storage of information provided by a recipient of the service, if –

(a)   the service provider had no actual knowledge when the information was provided that its provision amounted to a contravention of this Act, or

(b)   on obtaining actual knowledge that the provision of the information amounted to a contravention of that section, the service provider expeditiously removed the information or disabled access to it.

(2) Sub-paragraph (1) does not apply if the recipient of the service is acting under the authority of the control of the service provider.

6 Monitoring obligations

An injunction or interdict under Part 1 of the Equality Act 2006 may not impose on a person concerned with the provision of a service of a description given in paragraph 3(1), 4(1) or 5(1) –

(a)   a liability the imposition of which would contravene Article 12, 13 or 14 of the E-Commerce Directive;

(b)   a general obligation of the description given in Article 15 of that Directive.

7 Interpretation

(1) This paragraph applies for the purposes of this Schedule.

(2) "Information society service" –

(a)   has the meaning given in Article 2(a) of the E-Commerce Directive (which refers to Article 1(2) of Directive 98/34/EC of the European Parliament and of the Council of 22 June 1998 laying down a procedure for the provision of information in the field of technical standards and regulations), and

(b)   is summarised in recital 17 of the E-Commerce Directive as covering "any service normally provided for remuneration, at a distance, by means of electronic equipment for the processing (including digital compression) and storage of data, and at the individual request of a recipient of a service".

(3) "The E-Commerce Directive" means Directive 2000/31/EC of the European Parliament and of the Council of 8 June 2000 on certain legal aspects of information society services, in particular electronic commerce, in the Internal Market (Directive on electronic commerce).

(4) "Recipient" means a person who (whether for professional purposes or not) uses an information society service, in particular for seeking information or making it accessible.

(5) An information society service-provider is "established" in a country or territory if the service-provider –

(a) effectively pursues an economic activity using a fixed establishment in that country or territory for an indefinite period, and
(b) is a national of an EEA state or a body mentioned in Article 48 of the EEC treaty.

(6) The presence or use in a particular place of equipment or other technical means of providing an information society service is not itself sufficient to constitute the establishment of a service-provider.

(7) Where it cannot be decided from which of a number of establishments an information society service is provided, the service is to be regarded as provided from the establishment at the centre of the information society service provider's activities relating to that service.

(8) Section 212(4) does not apply to references to providing a service.

Schedule 26

Section 211

Amendments

1 Local Government Act 1988

Part 2 of the Local Government Act 1988 (public supply or works contracts) is amended as follows.

2

In section 17 (local and other public authority contracts: exclusion of non-commercial considerations) –

(a) omit subsection (9), and
(b) after that subsection insert –

"(10) This section does not prevent a public authority to which it applies from exercising any function regulated by this section with reference to a non-commercial matter to the extent that the authority considers it necessary or expedient to do so to enable or facilitate compliance with –

(a) the duty imposed on it by section 149 of the Equality Act 2010 (public sector equality duty), or
(b) any duty imposed on it by regulations under section 153 or 154 of that Act (powers to impose specific duties)."

3

Omit section 18 (exceptions to section 17 relating to race relations matters).

4

In section 19 (provisions supplementary to or consequential on section 17) omit subsection (10).

5 Employment Act 1989

(1) Section 12 of the Employment Act 1989 (Sikhs: requirements as to safety helmets) is amended as follows.

(2) In subsection (1), for "requirement or condition", in the first three places, substitute "provision, criterion or practice".

(3) In that subsection, for the words from "section 1(1)(b)" to the end substitute "section 19 of the Equality Act 2010 (indirect discrimination), the provision, criterion or practice is to be taken as one in relation to which the condition in subsection (2)(d) of that section (proportionate means of achieving a legitimate aim) is satisfied".

(4) In subsection (2), for the words from "the Race Relations Act" to the end substitute "section 13 of the Equality Act 2010 as giving rise to discrimination against any other person".

6 Equality Act 2006

The Equality Act 2006 is amended as follows.

7

(1) Section 8 (equality and diversity) is amended as follows.

(2) In subsection (1) –

   (a)   in paragraph (d) for "equality enactments" substitute "Equality Act 2010", and

   (b)   in paragraph (e) for "the equality enactments" substitute "that Act".

(3) In subsection (4) for "Disability Discrimination Act 1995 (c. 50)" substitute "Equality Act 2010".

8

In section 10(2) (meaning of group) for paragraph (d) substitute –

      "(d)   gender reassignment (within the meaning of section 7 of the Equality Act 2010),".

9

For section 11(3)(c) (interpretation) substitute –

      "(c)   a reference to the equality and human rights enactments is a reference to the Human Rights Act 1998, this Act and the Equality Act 2010."

10

(1) Section 14 (codes of practice) is amended as follows.

(2) For subsection (1) substitute –

"(1) The Commission may issue a code of practice in connection with any matter addressed by the Equality Act 2010."

(3) In subsection (2)(a) for "a provision or enactment listed in subsection (1)" substitute "the Equality Act 2010 or an enactment made under that Act".

(4) In subsection (3) –

(a)   in paragraph (a) for "section 49G(7) of the Disability Discrimination Act 1995 (c. 50)" substitute "section 190(7) of the Equality Act 2010", and

(b)   for paragraph (c)(iv) substitute –
        "(iv)   section 190 of the Equality Act 2010."

(5) In subsection (5)(a) for "listed in subsection (1)" substitute "a matter addressed by the Equality Act 2010".

(6) In subsection (9) for "section 76A" to "duties)" substitute "section 149, 153 or 154 of the Equality Act 2010 (public sector equality duty)".

11

In section 16(4) (inquiries: matters which the Commission may consider and report on) for "equality enactments" substitute "Equality Act 2010".

12

In section 21(2)(b) (unlawful act notice: specification of legislative provision) for "equality enactments" substitute "Equality Act 2010".

13

After section 24 insert –

"24A Enforcement powers: supplemental

(1) This section has effect in relation to –
        (a)   an act which is unlawful because, by virtue of any of sections 13 to 18 of the Equality Act 2010, it amounts to a contravention of any of Parts 3, 4, 5, 6 or 7 of that Act,
        (b)   an act which is unlawful because it amounts to a contravention of section 60(1) of that Act (or to a contravention of section 111 or 112 of that Act that relates to a contravention of section 60(1) of that Act) (enquiries about disability and health),
        (c)   an act which is unlawful because it amounts to a contravention of section 106 of that Act (information about diversity in range of election candidates etc.),
        (d)   an act which is unlawful because, by virtue of section 108(1) of that Act, it amounts to a contravention of any of Parts 3, 4, 5, 6 or 7 of that Act, or
        (e)   the application of a provision, criterion or practice which, by virtue of section 19 of that Act, amounts to a contravention of that Act.

(2) For the purposes of sections 20 to 24 of this Act, it is immaterial whether the Commission knows or suspects that a person has been or may be affected by the unlawful act or application.

(3) For those purposes, an unlawful act includes making arrangements to act in a particular way which would, if applied to an individual, amount to a contravention mentioned in subsection (l)(a).

(4) Nothing in this Act affects the entitlement of a person to bring proceedings under the Equality Act 2010 in respect of a contravention mentioned in subsection (1)."

14

Omit section 25 (restraint of unlawful advertising etc.).

15

Omit section 26 (supplemental).

16

(1) Section 27 (conciliation) is amended as follows.

(2) For subsection (1) (disputes in relation to which the Commission may make arrangements for the provision of conciliation services) substitute –

"(1) The Commission may make arrangements for the provision of conciliation services for disputes in respect of which proceedings have been or could be determined by virtue of section 114 of the Equality Act 2010."

17

(1) Section 28 (legal assistance) is amended as follows.

(2) In subsection (1) –

(a) in paragraph (a) for "equality enactments" substitute "Equality Act 2010", and
(b) in paragraph (b) for "the equality enactments" substitute "that Act".

(3) In subsection (5) for "Part V of the Disability Discrimination Act 1995 (c. 50) (public" substitute "Part 12 of the Equality Act 2010 (disabled persons:".

(4) In subsection (6) –

(a) for "the equality enactments", on the first occasion it appears, substitute "the Equality Act 2010", and
(b) for "the equality enactments", on each other occasion it appears, substitute "that Act".

(5) In subsection (7) –

(a) in paragraph (a) for "equality enactments" substitute "Equality Act 2010", and
(b) in paragraph (b) for "the equality enactments" substitute "that Act".

(6) In subsection (8) for "Part V of the Disability Discrimination Act 1995 (c. 50)" substitute "Part 12 of the Equality Act 2010".

(7) In subsection (9) for "equality enactments" substitute "Equality Act 2010".

(8) In subsection (12) –

(a) for "A reference in" to "includes a reference" substitute "This section applies", and

(b)   after paragraph (b) add "as it applies to the Equality Act 2010."

18

For section 31(1) (duties in respect of which Commission may assess compliance) substitute –

> "(1) The Commission may assess the extent to which or the manner in which a person has complied with a duty under or by virtue of section 149, 153 or 154 of the Equality Act 2010 (public sector equality duty)."

19

(1) Section 32 (public sector duties: compliance notice) is amended as follows.

(2) For subsection (1) substitute –

> "(1) This section applies where the Commission thinks that a person has failed to comply with a duty under or by virtue of section 149, 153 or 154 of the Equality Act 2010 (public sector equality duty)."

(3) In subsection (4) for "section 76A" to "Disability Discrimination Act 1995" substitute "section 149 of the Equality Act 2010".

(4) In subsection (9)(a) for "section 76 A" to "Disability Discrimination Act 1995 (c. 50)" substitute "section 149 of the Equality Act 2010".

(5) In subsection (9)(b) for "in any other case" substitute "where the notice related to a duty by virtue of section 153 or 154 of that Act".

(6) In subsection (11) for "section 76B" to "Disability Discrimination Act 1995" substitute "section 153 or 154 of the Equality Act 2010".

20

Omit section 33 (equality and human rights enactments).

21

(1) Section 34 (meaning of unlawful) is amended as follows.

(2) In subsection (1) for "equality enactments" substitute "Equality Act 2010".

(3) In subsection (2) –

(a)   after "virtue of" insert "any of the following provisions of the Equality Act 2010", and

(b)   for paragraphs (a) to (c) substitute –
> "(a)   section 1 (public sector duty regarding socio-economic inequalities),
> (b)   section 149, 153 or 154 (public sector equality duty),
> (c)   Part 12 (disabled persons: transport), or
> (d)   section 190 (disability: improvements to let dwelling houses)."

22

(1) Section 35 (general: definitions) is amended as follows.

(2) In the definition of "religion or belief", for "Part 2 (as defined by section 44)" substitute "section 10 of the Equality Act 2010".

(3) For the definition of "sexual orientation" substitute –

" "sexual orientation" has the same meaning as in section 12 of the Equality Act 2010."

23

In section 39(4) (orders subject to affirmative resolution procedure) for ", 27(10) or 33(3)" substitute "or 27(10)".

24

Omit section 43 (transitional: rented housing in Scotland).

25

Omit Part 2 (discrimination on grounds of religion or belief).

26

Omit section 81 (regulations).

27

Omit Part 4 (public functions).

28

In section 94(3) (extent: Northern Ireland) –

    (a)   omit "and 41 to 56", and

    (b)   omit "and the Disability Discrimination Act 1995 (c. 50)".

29

(1) Schedule 1 (the Commission: constitution, etc.) is amended as follows.

(2) In paragraph 52(3)(a) for "Parts 1, 3, 4, 5 and 5B of the Disability Discrimination Act 1995 (c. 50)" substitute "Parts 2, 3, 4, 6, 7, 12 and 13 of the Equality Act 2010, in so far as they relate to disability".

(3) In paragraph 53 for "Part 2 of the Disability Discrimination Act 1995 (c. 50)" substitute "Part 5 of the Equality Act 2010".

(4) In paragraph 54 for "Part 2 of the Disability Discrimination Act 1995" substitute "Part 5 of the Equality Act 2010".

30

In Schedule 3 (consequential amendments), omit paragraphs 6 to 35 and 41 to 56.

Schedule 27

Section 211

Repeals and revocations

PART 1
REPEALS

Short title	Extent of repeal
Equal Pay Act 1970	The whole Act.
Sex Discrimination Act 1975	The whole Act.
Race Relations Act 1976	The whole Act.
Sex Discrimination Act 1986	The whole Act.
Local Government Act 1988	Section 17(9).
	Section 18.
	Section 19(10).
Employment Act 1989	Sections 1 to 7.
	Section 9.
Social Security Act 1989	In Schedule 5, paragraph 5.
Disability Discrimination Act 1995	The whole Act.
Pensions Act 1995	Sections 62 to 65.
Greater London Authority Act 1999	Section 404.
Sex Discrimination (Election Candidates) Act 2002	Section 1.
Civil Partnership Act 2004	Section 6(l)(b) and (2).
Education (Additional Support for Learning) (Scotland) Act 2004	In section 17(1) "to exercise the functions which are conferred on a Tribunal by virtue of this Act".
Equality Act 2006	Section 25.
	Section 26.
	Section 33.
	Section 43.
	Part 2.
	Section 81.
	Part 4.

In section 94(3) "and 41 to 56" and "and the Disability Discrimination Act 1995 (c. 50)".

In Schedule 3 –

(a) paragraphs 6 to 35;

(b) paragraphs 41 to 56.

PART 2
REVOCATIONS

Title	Extent of revocation
Occupational Pension Schemes (Equal Treatment) Regulations 1995 (S.I. 1995/3183)	The whole Regulations.
Employment Equality (Religion or Belief) Regulations 2003 (S.I. 2003/1660)	The whole Regulations.
Employment Equality (Sexual Orientation) Regulations 2003 (S.I. 2003/1661)	The whole Regulations.
Disability Discrimination Act 1995 (Pensions) Regulations 2003 (S.I. 2003/2770)	The whole Regulations.
Occupational Pension Schemes (Equal Treatment) (Amendment) Regulations 2005 (S.I. 2005/1923)	The whole Regulations.
Employment Equality (Age) Regulations 2006 (S.I. 2006/1031)	The whole Regulations (other than Schedules 6 and 8).
Equality Act (Sexual Orientation) Regulations 2007 (S.I. 2007/1263)	The whole Regulations.
Sex Discrimination (Amendment of Legislation) Regulations 2008 (S.I. 2008/963)	The whole Regulations.

Schedule 28

Section 214

Index of defined expressions

Expression	Provision
Accrual of rights, in relation to an occupational pension scheme	Section 212(12)
Additional maternity leave	Section 213(6) and (7)
Additional maternity leave period	Section 213(8)
Age discrimination	Section 25(1)
Age group	Section 5(2)

Armed forces	Section 212(1)
Association	Section 107(2)
Auxiliary aid	Section 20(11)
Belief	Section 10(2)
Breach of an equality clause or rule	Section 212(8)
The Commission	Section 212(1)
Commonhold	Section 38(7)
Compulsory maternity leave	Section 213(3)
Contract work	Section 41(6)
Contract worker	Section 41(7)
Contravention of this Act	Section 212(9)
Crown employment	Section 83(9)
Detriment	Section 212(1) and (5)
Disability	Section 6(1)
Disability discrimination	Section 25(2)
Disabled person	Section 6(2) and (4)
Discrimination	Sections 13 to 19, 21 and 108
Disposal, in relation to premises	Section 38(3) to (5)
Education Acts	Section 212(1)
Employer, in relation to an occupational pension scheme	Section 212(11)
Employment	Section 212(1)
Enactment	Section 212(1)
Equality clause	Section 212(1)
Equality rule	Section 212(1)
Firm	Section 46(2)
Gender reassignment	Section 7(1)
Gender reassignment discrimination	Section 25(3)
Harassment	Section 26(1)
Independent educational institution	Section 89(7)
LLP	Section 46(4)
Man	Section 212(1)
Marriage and civil partnership	Section 8
Marriage and civil partnership discrimination	Section 25(4)
Maternity equality clause	Section 212(1)
Maternity equality rule	Section 212(1)
Maternity leave	Section 213(2)

Responsible body, in relation to a further or higher education institution	Section 91(12)
Responsible body, in relation to a school	Section 85(9)
School	Section 89(5) and (6)
Service-provider	Section 29(1)
Sex	Section 11
Sex discrimination	Section 25(8)
Sex equality clause	Section 212(1)
Sex equality rule	Section 212(1)
Sexual orientation	Section 12(1)
Sexual orientation discrimination	Section 25(9)
Student	Section 94(3)
Subordinate legislation	Section 212(1)
Substantial	Section 212(1)
Taxi, for the purposes of Part 3 (services and public functions)	Schedule 2, paragraph 4
Taxi, for the purposes of Chapter 1 of Part 12 (disabled persons: transport)	Section 173(1)
Tenancy	Section 38(6)
Trade	Section 212(1)
Transsexual person	Section 7(2)
Trustees or managers, in relation to an occupational pension scheme	Section 212(11)
University	Section 94(4)
Victimisation	Section 27(1)
Vocational training	Section 56(6)
Woman	Section 212(1)

INDEX

References are to paragraph numbers.